# GOD is LOVE

Collected Writings of
## BISHOP K. H. TING

Cook Communications Ministries International,
Colorado Springs, CO 80918
Cook Communications, Paris, Ontario
Kingsway Communications, Eastbourne, England

First printing 2004
Printed in the United States of America
1 2 3 4 5 6 7 8 9 10 Printing/Year 08 07 06 05 04

# CONTENTS

A Note from the Publisher .......................... 7
Introducing Bishop K. H. Ting ...................... 11

**Preface**
    The Emerging Church in China .................... 17
    Letter to a Believer ............................ 20

**Section One: God's Love**
    The Word Became Flesh ......................... 27
    Creation and Redemption ........................ 30
    My View of God ............................... 36
    Believing in What Kind of God? ................... 47
    The Church Universal ........................... 53
    Love is for Those with Ears to Hear ............... 56
    Love and Optimism ............................ 61
    Love Sees the Big Picture ....................... 74
    A Christian's Approach to the Bible ............... 78
    On Christian Theism ........................... 91
    The Cosmic Christ ............................. 108
    Resurrection Hope ............................. 119
    Theology and Context .......................... 122
    Foreword to *Theological Writings from*
        *Nanjing Seminary* ........................... 129
    The Message of Christmas ....................... 135

**Section Two: God's Love Extends to All People**
    The Gospel of Christ is for All ................... 141
    Understanding the Heart of God .................. 151
    God's Love Revealed in Scripture ................. 155
    God's Love Transcends Our Sin ................... 160
    Christ Cares for All Our Needs ................... 164
    God's Love Extends to the Atheist ................ 171
    The Three-Self's Contribution to
        Christianity in China ......................... 178
    Women in the Church ........................... 195
    God's Love Compels Sinners to Accept Christ ....... 198

## Section Three: God's Love Teaches Us to Know and Serve

GOD CALLS US TO SERVE . . . . . . . . . . . . . . . . . . . . . . . . . . 207

LOVE SPEAKS THE TRUTH. . . . . . . . . . . . . . . . . . . . . . . . . . 213

THE MAN WHO WRESTLED WITH GOD. . . . . . . . . . . . . . . . 215

WHY MUST THERE BE PREACHERS? . . . . . . . . . . . . . . . . . . . 223

ON BEING A GOOD PASTOR . . . . . . . . . . . . . . . . . . . . . . . . 238

THE CHURCH AFTER THE CULTURAL REVOLUTION . . . . . . . . 242

BUILDING UP THE BODY OF CHRIST . . . . . . . . . . . . . . . . . . 260

LOOKING TO THE FUTURE . . . . . . . . . . . . . . . . . . . . . . . . . 266

RECONCILIATION IN A CLASSLESS SOCIETY. . . . . . . . . . . . . . 277

LIFE SHOULD HAVE A MISSION . . . . . . . . . . . . . . . . . . . . . . 282

MODERN THEOLOGIES . . . . . . . . . . . . . . . . . . . . . . . . . . . 287

GOD IS LOVE . . . . . . . . . . . . . . . . . . . . . . . . . . . . . . . . . . . 315

A PERSONAL RESPONSE TO PASTORAL CONCERNS . . . . . . . . . 319

FAITH WITHOUT WORKS DOESN'T DEMONSTRATE
    GOD'S LOVE . . . . . . . . . . . . . . . . . . . . . . . . . . . . . . . . . 324

RESPONSIBILITIES OF HIGHER CHRISTIAN EDUCATION . . . . . . 328

FINDING GOD'S IMAGE IN MAN. . . . . . . . . . . . . . . . . . . . . . 331

CARING FOR GOD'S CREATION. . . . . . . . . . . . . . . . . . . . . . . 339

MY VIEW OF THESE FIFTY YEARS . . . . . . . . . . . . . . . . . . . . . 342

DEVELOPMENT AND ENRICHMENT OF THE TSPM . . . . . . . . 345

## Section Four: Our Responses to God's Love

LOVE NEVER ENDS . . . . . . . . . . . . . . . . . . . . . . . . . . . . . . . 353

THE BREADTH AND DEPTH OF THE LOVE OF GOD. . . . . . . . . 358

THE FRAGRANCE OF THE GOSPEL . . . . . . . . . . . . . . . . . . . . 360

JESUS BRINGS GOOD NEWS . . . . . . . . . . . . . . . . . . . . . . . . . 367

HOW IS THE CHURCH TO LOVE CHRIST? . . . . . . . . . . . . . . . 372

STRETCHING OUT OUR ARMS IN LOVE . . . . . . . . . . . . . . . . 376

BUILDING UP THE CHURCH. . . . . . . . . . . . . . . . . . . . . . . . . 381

OUR PILGRIMAGE . . . . . . . . . . . . . . . . . . . . . . . . . . . . . . . . 386

WHAT THE SPIRIT IS SAYING TO THE CHURCH IN CHINA . . . . 390

WHY THE THREE-SELF MOVEMENT? . . . . . . . . . . . . . . . . . . 397

RUNNING THE CHURCH WELL . . . . . . . . . . . . . . . . . . . . . . 410

BUILDING THE CHURCH FOR THE FUTURE . . . . . . . . . . . . . . 415

THOUGHTS OF THE FUTURE UPON RETIREMENT . . . . . . . . . . 423

QUESTIONS AND ANSWERS ON THE PRESENT-DAY CHURCH . . 428

ON SCHOOLS OF THEOLOGY . . . . . . . . . . . . . . . . . . . . . . . . 434

UNCHANGING FAITH, EVOLVING THEOLOGY . . . . . . . . . . . . . . 448
THEOLOGY ADAPTING TO A CHANGING CULTURE . . . . . . . . . . 451
MAN: AN INCOMPLETE CREATION . . . . . . . . . . . . . . . . . . . . 456
THE BIBLE: A SOURCE OF TRUTH FOR CHRISTIAN
   AND NON-CHRISTIAN . . . . . . . . . . . . . . . . . . . . . . . . . . 461
THE TRUTH REPRESENTED BY THE RESURRECTION . . . . . . . . 463

**Section Five: Christianity in a Socialist China**
A WIDE DOOR FOR EFFECTIVE WORK HAS OPENED,
   AND THERE ARE MANY ADVERSARIES . . . . . . . . . . . . . . . . 469
DEVELOPMENT OF CHURCH STRUCTURE . . . . . . . . . . . . . . . . 476
MR. Y. T. WU: A LASTING INFLUENCE FOR MARXISM AND
   CHRISTIANITY, PART 1 . . . . . . . . . . . . . . . . . . . . . . . . . . 485
MR. Y. T. WU, PART 2 . . . . . . . . . . . . . . . . . . . . . . . . . . . 491
MR. Y. T. WU, PART 3 . . . . . . . . . . . . . . . . . . . . . . . . . . . 505
IS RELIGION AN OPIATE? . . . . . . . . . . . . . . . . . . . . . . . . . 515
RELIGION AND SOCIALISM: CAN THEY CO-EXIST? . . . . . . . . . . 526
THE CHURCH AND CHINA'S NEW CONSTITUTION . . . . . . . . . 544
THE STRENGTH OF DEMOCRATIC SOCIALISM . . . . . . . . . . . . 547
RELIGIOIUS LIBERTY IN CHINA: MY PERSPECTIVE . . . . . . . . . 550
THE CHURCH AND STATE . . . . . . . . . . . . . . . . . . . . . . . . . 562
DARING TO LOVE THE CHURCH AND COUNTRY . . . . . . . . . . . 576
LET US WORK FOR THE REUNIFICATION OF CHINA . . . . . . . . 578
THE INFLUENCE OF JAPANESE AGGRESSION ON
   CHURCH AND STATE . . . . . . . . . . . . . . . . . . . . . . . . . . 580

**Appendix:**
OPENING ADDRESS . . . . . . . . . . . . . . . . . . . . . . . . . . . . . . 587
SPEECH AT THE MEMORIAL SERVICE FOR MS. WU YIFANG . . . . 589
THE TREE OF LIFE IS EVER GREEN . . . . . . . . . . . . . . . . . . . 593
IN MEMORY OF THE REV. EDWARD HEWLETT JOHNSON . . . . . 597
A FRIEND REMEMBERED . . . . . . . . . . . . . . . . . . . . . . . . . . 601
PREFACE TO THE DICTIONARY OF BIBLICAL LITERATURE . . . . . 603
A REVIEW OF *RELIGION UNDER SOCIALISM IN CHINA* . . . . . . . 605
FAREWELL REMARKS ON A VISIT TO INDIA . . . . . . . . . . . . . . 614

**Epilogue**
TWELVE QUESTIONS FOR BISHOP TING . . . . . . . . . . . . . . . . 619

# A Note from the Publisher

ॐ

This book is published to give Western Christians, interested in the emerging Chinese Church, an opportunity to examine for themselves the theological thinking of the Chairman of the Three-Self Patriotic Movement (TSPM) and President of the China Christian Council (CCC) Bishop K. H. Ting, now retired. It is our hope that this book will encourage greater dialogue and openness to find biblical truth and mutual support of all Christians in China and America.

China first received the gospel in 635 A.D. when the Nestorians traveled the Silk Road and established a Chinese church near the present-day city of Xian. Mateo Ricci, a Jesuit, went to China in 1589 and the first Chinese Bishop, Luo Wenzao, was consecrated in 1685. The late 1700s saw many European and North American mission societies serving in China. While many worked to establish an indigenous church in China, the church was linked inexorably to the outside world.

Then came 1949 and political upheaval. Foreign missionaries were expelled and Chinese believers assumed full responsibility and leadership of the church. Henry Venn of the Church Missionary Society served in Africa during the 1850s. He believed that if the African church were to be successful it would be as a "native church, under native pastors, and a native Episcopate" just as it developed in Germany and England in previous centuries. Venn was the first to promote the Three-Self Movement: self-governing, self-supporting, self-propagating. The last fifty years have demonstrated the wisdom of those words as they relate to the church of China.

During the very difficult 1950s many Christians stepped forward both at the local and national level. One such young man was Ding Guang Xun (K. H. Ting). His path was different from many Chinese church leaders because he worked with the new government. This book is the collected writings of Bishop K. H. Ting. They were not written as a systematic theology but they do represent Bishop Ting's theological thinking from 1940 until the present day. In many cases these writings are transcriptions of sermons and speeches given on special occasions. The dates and occasions are given after each section. Eight articles are made available for the first time. Of special interest are Bishop Ting's responses to twelve questions ranging from issues of Christian orthodoxy to church and state. These questions and answers are found in the epilogue.

Like all theological thinking, Bishop Ting's theology has been shaped by Scripture, earlier theologians, training and contemporaries. His ideas are sometimes new, evocative and disturbing. They seem to contradict our understanding of historic biblical Christianity. Some have charged Bishop Ting with heretical teaching, specifically teaching salvation through love. Yet in his own words, Tings says, "Justification by love is a poor and misleading imitation of justification by faith. I have never approved of its usage ... I do affirm my faith, with all Christians, as formulated in the Apostles' Creed and Nicean Creed, although I admit my inadequacy to explain the creeds well."

Bishop Ting's political views are likewise unsettling and problematic to those of us convinced of a multi-party democratic government. Freedom of religion and separation of church and state are the reasons our forefathers came to these shores. We believe the church may influence government; government may not regulate or influence the church. Yet we ourselves admit that racism is in our not too distant past and there are heartbreakingly poor people in the wealthiest nation in the world. What would our Puritan forefathers say of Christianity in America today or, for that matter, Luther, Calvin, Wesley, or Wilberforce?

There are issues that seperate us, but we should recognize that a dialogue is beginning and that there is an openness that has not been possible for many years. We must also identify that Bishop Ting has spoken out in support of diversity in the Chinese church, which includes

Lutherans, Methodists, Baptists, Anglicans, Charismatics, and others of various historic Christian traditions. There is more opportunity to express this diversity than in the past.

The church throughout China has demonstrated a work of the Holy Spirit in lives of believers under extreme circumstances. Based on government statistics, the church has grown from under 1 million in the 1950s to over 17 million believers today. Many in the West consider the total of believers to be much larger, perhaps 50–70 million. Now, by God's grace and the faithfulness of millions of Chinese believers, the church in China again faces a new day.

As China and the Chinese church move into the 21st Century there is reason to hope for a better relationship between our great nations and a mutual sharing and support of believers for Christ and His Kingdom. May a new generation of Christian leadership in China continue to build and disciple the church to the glory of God!

### 1 Corinthians 13:12 (NIV)

"Now we see but a poor reflection as in a mirror; then we shall see face to face. Now I know in part; then I shall know fully, even as I am fully known."

### 1 John 4:1 (NIV)

"Dear friends, do not believe every spirit, but test the spirits to see whether they are from God..."

### John 14:6 (NIV)

"Jesus answered, 'I am the way and the truth and the life. No one comes to the Father except through me.'"

*May we all: Seek Truth, Embrace Truth, Love Truth*

# Introducing
# Bishop K. H. Ting

## ɞ

**B**ishop K. H. Ting was born in Shanghai in 1915. His parents were both Christians. His maternal grandfather was an Anglican priest. Ting attended St. John's University in Shanghai run by the American Episcopal Church where he learned English and studied theology. Many of St. John's alumni became leaders in the Chinese church. In 1937 Ting received his B.A. from St. John's and in 1942 his B.D. in Theology at which time he was ordained an Anglican priest. He was married that same year to Kuo Siu May. For the next several years, Ting served as a pastor in the Shanghai Community Church (International) before leaving China for five years in 1946.

Ting grew up in a politically unstable period for China. In 1908, Dowager Empress Tzu Hsi died. In 1911, after more than a decade of trying, Sun Yat-sen finally led a successful revolt against the Qing dynasty. Sun Yat-sen set up a democratic republic but was never able to consolidate the government into a stable rule of China. Strong regional warlords caused continued turmoil across China. Ting was ten when Sun Yat-sen died in 1925 and sixteen when the Japanese invaded China in 1931.

When the Japanese occupied China, China's Christians were angry at the occupation of their country. At the YMCA in Shanghai, Ting led Bible studies that included discussion of social and political issues. To this day, social and political issues remain a part of Ting's theological thinking.

During those early years, Ting was greatly impressed by Wu Yaozong. Mr. Wu taught transformation of social order as a precursor to

personal spiritual transformation. Several sections of this book reference Mr. Wu who became a lifelong friend.

In 1946, after the war with Japan was concluded, Ting moved to
Canada for one year to serve in the Student Christian Movement. He
then moved to New York in 1947 where he studied for his Master's
degree at Union Theological Seminary. After completing his degree,
Ting took a position as the Secretary of the World's Student Christian
Federation of the World Council of Churches in Geneva, Switzerland.

In 1951, Bishop Ting, his wife and young son, returned to China,
and in 1952 a second son was born. This tumultuous period for
Christians in China was the period of consolidation of power by Mao
Tse-Tung. China and the United States were on opposite sides of the
Korean War. Missionaries were expelled. Contacts and ties to the outside church were cut. Throughout this period, Ting supported many of
the positions of the Chinese government.

In 1953, the Three-Self Patriotic Movement (TSPM) closed most of
the Protestant theological schools and combined their faculty and students into the Jinling Theological Seminary in Nanjing. Ting was
appointed its Principal by the TSPM. In 1955 he was consecrated as
Bishop of the Anglican Church though the time of denominationalism
was fast coming to a close in China.

During this period, Mao launched the "Hundred Flowers" campaign
when Chinese were encouraged to express new ideas and suggest
improvements. This openness was short lived. During this period,
Bishop Ting spoke against the government's negative views toward the
church and Christianity.

As a leader of the TSPM, Bishop Ting became a worldwide
spokesperson for the Chinese revolution and the church's response to
it. Bishop Ting believed that Christianity and socialism should work
together to improve Chinese society. In 1958, all Protestant denominations combined under the TSPM. Many churches were closed and
believers practiced their Christian faith the only way they could, with
their families at home. By the 1960s only a handful of students studied
at Jinling as the storm clouds gathered for Christians throughout China.

Then came the Cultural Revolution from 1966-76. All churches
were closed. Jinling Seminary closed and became the headquarters for

the Red Guard. Bibles and Christian books were destroyed whenever they were found. Christian leaders were imprisoned and sent for re-education. Bishop Ting lost all his positions in the church. He and others from the seminary were sent to work in the gardens with local farmers. When the political tides reversed a few years later many pastors and TSPM leaders had disappeared.

A new period began in 1978 with the rise of Deng Xiao Ping. From the ashes of the Cultural Revolution, the church emerged alive and with a greater vitality than before. At the national level, in 1980, Bishop Ting became the leader of both the reinstated TSPM and the newly formed China Christian Council (CCC), which was responsible for the internal activities of the church.

Nanjing Union Seminary (Jinling) was reopened and Bishop Ting was reinstated as Principal. In 1985 Amity Foundation was created and Bishop Ting was named President. With the help of the United Bible Society and other friends of the church in China, nearly 40,000,000 Bibles and hymnals have been printed and distributed as of 2004 by Amity Printing Press.

Although all churches were closed until the mid to late 1970s, today there are approximately 50,000 registered churches or meeting points throughout China. In addition to Jingling Seminary, over twenty other seminaries and Bible schools have reopened. Most have increased their student enrollment and built new campuses with housing for students. Elders and lay leaders ranging from sixteen to eighty-six years are coming for short-term training during summer and holiday breaks. They are taught in thirty- and ninety-day courses and are able to return home to more effectively lead their churches.

University students and their professors, in numbers never before experienced, have a desire to study and understand Christianity. Many believe the success in the West is linked to Christianity.

In 1998 Bishop Ting presented his controversial idea of "theological reconstruction." Ting says the goal of "theological reconstruction" is to make theology in China indigenous while remaining in accord with the Bible and historical Christian doctrine. The intent is to encourage Chinese Christians to wholeheartedly become involved with issues of modern Chinese society. Some Christians are concerned that this path undermines justification by faith, the centrality of Christ to the Gospel, and the authority of the Scriptures. In the Epilogue, Bishop Ting responds to those criticisms by affirming those same doctrines central to historical Christianity.

While there is much uncertainty and change in China as to the role of the Church, over the past several decades it is apparent that God has placed a protective covering over believers in China so that the Chinese church today is more alive and vital than it was 50 years ago. There is a yearning and a heart's desire from nearly every village and city for the Christian gospel. The Lord knows what is in store for his church in China and we in the West should thank God for the faithfulness of our Christian brothers and sisters in China.

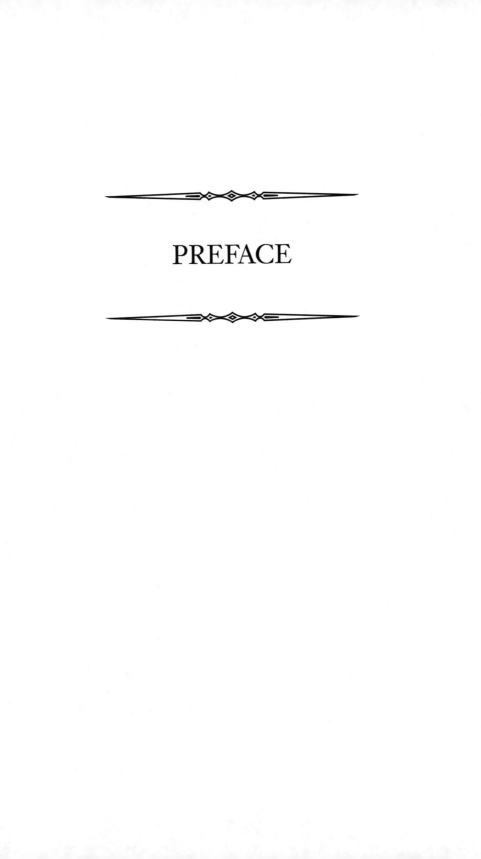

# PREFACE

# The Emerging
# Church in China

I am very pleased to be asked to write the preface to this first issue of the *Chinese Theological Review*.

Chinese is now so extensively used in the Chinese churches that friends outside not well versed in the language find it frustrating trying to know some of the thinking that is going on among Chinese Christians. The *Review* is truly something that has come for such a time as this, and we hope it can appear regularly on a year-to-year basis.

There are persons abroad who try to make out that the Chinese Church and its Three-Self Movement (for self-government, self-support and self-propagation) are opportunist, serving political purposes and preaching a biased message not fully Christian. Just a casual reading of the articles presented here will show how little ground this accusation has. This accusation is actually based on a very condescending view of church members. The fact is that, in our structurally postdenominational church, our Bible-loving, Bible-honoring and Bible-studying Christians are not theologically so blind and indiscriminating as to fall victim to false teachings thrust upon them by preachers.

On the other hand, I wish to give my personal reaction to the alarm and disappointment voiced by some friends abroad upon their failure to find in China anything approaching liberation theology, and that after over thirty years since Liberation! To them Chinese Christianity is still "pre-liberation" and "colonial," and Chinese Christians, theologically conservative and politically pro-socialist, are compartmentalized and dwell in two realms. Even granting that the church services they attend and the sermons they hear are not representative of the whole of China, their impression is not altogether wrong. In fact the articles collected here may to a certain extent confirm their impression. While

I do not mean to justify this state of affairs, I do feel that, in this connection, a Chinese angle of approach may be worth mentioning.

The separation of spirituality from society and the viewing of things as belonging to two realms have had a long history within the church with quite strong theological undergirding. It represents one important tradition in the 19th and 20th century missionary heritage and still has strong staying power in China today. What has come to be a motto in the Three-Self Movement, *ai guo ai jiao* (love the church and love the motherland), at least permits this dichotomy. After all, compartmentalism has not proved itself in our post-Liberation period to be such a harmful thing as it sometimes has been in the past. Our observations over the last thirty years do not bear out the judgment that such a stance necessarily leads Christians to be apolitical. Certainly these Christians are no less participatory than other Christians or other citizens. Furthermore, they change theologically too, although the changes are not so spectacular as some of our friends would like them to be.

The Three-Self Movement and the more recently organized China Christian Council aim at uniting all men and women of Protestant faith. We want to avoid the reproduction of the pattern in some other countries in which Protestants are grouped into "ecumenicals" and "evangelicals." Faith, hope, love and experience combine to tell us that, in the concrete situation of China in which we find ourselves, it is possible to avoid that pattern. Hence we want to ensure the growth of this unity and do nothing to jeopardize it. The last thing we want is a split in the fellowship. For the sake of this unity, in matters of faith, worship and theology, our policy is generally one of equality and mutual respect, not one of offending or inciting people's religious feelings. To convert certain Christians from their compartmentalism to theologies with articulate social and political content, or vice versa, is not our priority. Our priority is to work together on such things as printing Bibles, reopening churches, publication of Christian literature, strengthening theological training centers, working both in political and theoretical fields for the better implementation of the policy of religious freedom, improving the work of Christian nurture in churches as well as in groups meeting in homes, and so on. These are the very things which unite us and help us discover and learn from each other.

Ours is a unity worth paying the price. We have not found that this unity results in stagnation. Three-Self is a newborn thing since Liberation and independence. It is neither "pre-liberation" nor "colonial." It is a mass movement in which very many Christians move forward together, although perhaps at a slower pace than expected by some.

With all the importance given these days to contextualization, it may not be in fashion to say that in our view theology must be in conversation not only with the social and cultural context within which the church finds its being, but also within the minds and hearts of the masses of the Christians within the fold of the church. A "contextualized theology" appreciated only by socially conscientized intellectuals abroad but foreign to its own church constituency right at home is an anomaly. We are supported spiritually by our own Christians in China. To them is our first attachment. To be truly their own native sons and daughters is the glory of our theologians. We write first of all for domestic consumption, that is, for Chinese Christians' nourishment and edification. We meet them where they are in ways they can accept. We do not impose on them anything they are not ready for. Theological changes are definitely taking place, but these changes, instead of attuning themselves to elitist tastes elsewhere, must reflect and push forward changes—slow as these may seem—in the spirituality and intellectuality of the masses of Chinese Christians. Theologians and rank-and-file Christians need to be in a dialogical give-and-take relationship of mutual learning and nurturing. Dialogues with culture, with natural and social sciences, with philosophy and with theologians' international community are valuable insofar as they can be channeled to serve the needs of rank-and-file Christians. We value the work of those theologians who can part with their individualistic heroism, humbly and not condescendingly orient themselves to the fellow Christians at their gate, listen earnestly to them, learn from them and summarize their insights. Chinese Christians are supporting all the positive changes in our society brought about by socialism. The religious commitment and spirituality of these Christians—no matter of what sort theologically—cannot really remain untouched by their social and political stand, although in many cases the changes are just "touches" and are nothing drastic. It is for theologians to be sensitive to these touches and to reflect them honestly and reverently in their work.

It is this new, unprecedented width in the range of Christian one-ness, brought to reality as "ecumenicals" became more evangelical and "evangelicals" became more ecumenical in the last thirty years, that I think is the growing edge of Chinese theological renewal and deserves more attention and thanksgiving.

If all of this is a defense, it is one not of compartmentalism, but of the right of Christians of all sorts to be equally regarded, of our respon-sibility to keep Christians of all sorts in the common bond of fellowship, and of the importance of staying close to and reflecting and molding the constituency given to us.

I sincerely believe the publication of this *Review* will help greatly in presenting the thought content of present-day Chinese Protestantism in international interchurch exchanges across language barriers. I am sure I represent the authors of all the articles and Chinese Christians in gen-eral in saying that we are grateful to the readers for their interest, con-cern and prayers, and that we would appreciate their reflections on the phenomena herein made manifest as something of what Protestantism is in present-day China.

—Preface to the *Chinese Theological Review*, 1985

## LETTER TO A BELIEVER

I received your letter of June 16 some time ago, but because I have been out of Nanjing and have only just come back, I am late in reply-ing and I hope you'll forgive me.

I agree with your view that many problems remain in the imple-mentation of the policy of religious freedom, and these are good neither for the church nor for the country. And I agree with you when you say that many believers are unhappy over some of the "regulations" which have been put on them.

But when you say that "The central authorities pay virtually no attention to this," or "and there is no one in the upper echelons of the church who dares to argue strongly on just grounds, mainly because they are afraid to lose their rice bowls and their official posts," then I cannot agree with you.

If the central authorities pay no attention to implementation of the religious policy, then how has it happened that in the last decade over 4,000 Christian churches have been opened and three million Bibles published? Of course, we cannot say that every government department stresses implementation of the policy, but it is my feeling that the departments in charge, that is the United Front Department and the Religious Affairs Bureau, pay a great deal of attention to it. Otherwise, the situation today would be vastly different.

Of course there are those in the church who fear losing their rice bowl or official post, but to say that there is no one who reflects the situation to the government and demands the implementation of the policy, is not based on fact. Recently the national CCC and TSPM wrote a letter to the Chinese Customs with a copy to the Standing Committee of the National People's Congress arguing strongly and justifiably about inventory and confiscation of imported religious books.

My estimation of our current situation is that there are all sorts of difficulties with the implementation of the religious policy, but that implementation is going on and developing. Ground is not being lost.

When we have a government like this, should we be talking about opposition and fighting, or contact and dialogue? This is a very important question. Some anti-China Christian publications from Hong Kong give the impression that Christians who oppose and struggle against the government are the only true Christians. I hope you and Brother Y do not feel this way. As long as there is room for us to dialogue and have contact with government, we should not act rashly. As for the fact that those in the government do not believe in God, this does not constitute a reason for opposing the government either.

It is precisely because many people from religious circles nationwide regularly exert themselves to reflect problems to the government and strive for the implementation of the religious policy, and the fact that the government proceeds from uniting with the mass of the people and is willing to consider our views, that we have the religious freedoms we have today. No matter how opposed some Christians may be to the CCC and TSPM at all levels, they too enjoy these religious freedoms and this is undeniably due to the efforts of all levels of the TSPM and CCC. When these Christians quote the articles in the Constitution related to religious freedom, they may not realize how much effort the CCC and TSPM have expended in the formation of those very articles.

It can be said that there have been many difficulties with the implementation of the clauses on religious freedom in the Constitution, or that implementation has been too slow, or that some cadres in some places refuse to implement it, but as a member of the NPC Commission on Constitutional Revision, I know how this clause was drafted. It is unjust to say, "The aim of this clause is to cheat our people and international opinion."

To sum up, as long as we can set out the facts, be reasonable, and have the possibility for things to change for the better, it is my opinion that Chinese Christians are by no means at a pass where they will be smashed to pieces. I do not believe God would be pleased with these rash "evangelists" who claim that this is the situation. This touches on the question of a Christian's view of his or her own nation.

Brother Y, whom you mentioned, seems to love the church, but much of what he writes is not in accord with facts, though it is very much in accord with the views of certain anti-China persons in Hong Kong. The fact that certain Hong Kong publications treasure and exaggerate his letters and manuscripts is not surprising.

I would welcome you to write an essay on liberation theology. Liberation theology originated with a Peruvian Catholic priest, Gustavo Gutierrez. It accepts those things in Marxism that Christians are able to accept, but what he writes is theology, not Marxism. As far as I know, liberation theology is not related to the Soviet Union. I have never seen liberation theology that praises or belittles the Soviet Union. I feel it is worthwhile to introduce liberation theology to Chinese academic circles, but not to propose it for China. First, because the eternal theme of

theology is reconciliation—with God and with others—and not liberation and second, because there is no need to speak of liberation where
the people are holding power. What we should talk about is unity and
stability and reconstruction. I wonder if you agree?

—Letter to a Believer,
1988, Brother X

# Section One:
# GOD'S LOVE

# The Word Became Flesh

*This meditation was written in December 1940 during the war with Japan when K. H.Ting was a young priest in Shanghai.*

No one can deny that this world is full of suffering, sorrow, oppression, and violence against people. All that is rational is destroyed by its own rationality, while the irrational flourishes and extends its control. From our human perspective, it appears that the world is bent on its own destruction.

But this is not God's way of seeing things. God has never despaired of humankind. God feels that we can be saved and has therefore come into our midst for our salvation.

Today, darkness does indeed cover the earth. We cannot see the light. Yet Christians, believing in the Incarnation, are profoundly aware that God has not abandoned us. God is not far away but has entered our world and lives among us.

We should maintain a positive outlook. We should view the world optimistically and with hope. We should be prophets in the darkness, facing the light which is about to dawn.

"Who, though he was in the form of God, did not regard equality with God as something to be exploited, but emptied himself, taking the form of a slave ... to the point of death—even death on a cross" (Phil. 2:6).

From this we can see four thing: 1) our Lord Jesus originally occupied a high position; 2) but this high position meant nothing to him; 3) he sacrificed this position to come among us, to become like a slave and to share our sufferings and needs; 4) as a result, he suffered death, even death upon the cross.

If we celebrate the birth of our Lord Jesus at Christmas only because of the first point, then there is not much meaning to our celebration.

The greatness of Jesus does not lie in his original position, which he gained through no effort of his own. His greatness lies in what the other three points tell us about him, his sense of righteousness and his effort to achieve it.

Suffering can temper us, but it can also make us tremble. It can make us remember and yearn for past heights and make us wonder whether all our efforts were worthwhile. Suffering can shake our present faith and make us long to recover earlier days when we did not suffer.

There is no clear way before us yet, and we still must taste deeper suffering. It is precisely at this time that Christians learn from our Lord.

"[They] wrapped him in bands of cloth, and laid him in a manger, because there was no place for them in the inn" (Luke 2:7).

The world was crowded in those days. Two thousand years later we are still in the same situation. We can understand the difficulties that Mary faced as a mother.

Christmas is a busy season. Everyone's mind is full of his or her own plans. They leave the baby Jesus to his cold manger.

Factory bosses and shopkeepers take advantage of the Christmas season to produce and sell all sorts of novelties. They are busy getting rich. Lovers make use of the Christmas season to compete with each other in gift-giving. They become preoccupied with the objects of their affections. Soldiers in Europe look forward to a forty-eight hour ceasefire, a temporary halt to the killing, when at least they can enjoy a bit of fresh air (or has this now been vetoed?). And the poor? They hope Santa Claus might bring them a bit of ease and comfort once a year.

Christmas is a splendid holiday. We all bring our own desires to our celebrations. Our lives are crowded with all sorts of illusions, grand designs and selfish hopes. But the mission of our Lord Jesus, the true spirit of Jesus, has been left in the manger where no one will see it, because there is no room anywhere else!

"Do not be afraid; for see—I am bringing you good news of great joy for all the people" (Luke 2:10).

Fear is the most common phenomenon of this earth, Millions of people live in fear all the time because of some event or another, Fear is like the giant hand of the devil hovering above us, ready to seize hold of our lives.

What people basically fear is simply insecurity. People need to have a sense of security, If a person feels insecure, if he or she feels that there is nothing they can depend on, that their food, clothing or shelter are threatened, then that person is afraid. Millions of people today fear that tomorrow they will be jobless and that wives and children will starve to death.

Fear and anxiety cause people to shrink back and become passive. Only active struggle can root our fear.

"Do not be afraid." This is the gospel the shepherds heard. "Therefore I tell you, do not worry about your life, what you will eat or ... what you will wear" (Matt. 6:25). Yes! What is the use of being anxious? "And can any of you by worrying add a single hour to your span of life?" (Matt. 6:27). "But strive first for the kingdom of God and his righteousness, and all these things will be given to you as well" (Matt. 6:33).

Yes, only by participating in the great work of "building up the kingdom of God on earth" can we overcome fear. Great love drives out fear. Haven't we seen mother love expressed in a life which never flinches from difficulties or dangers? Only when we begin to see the people through the eyes of fervent love, only when we deliberately sacrifice our own interests for their sakes (which is also for our own sakes) in order to establish the kingdom of heaven on earth, only then will we be truly able to overcome fear and hold back the devil's hand. In that kingdom, the people will no longer fear insecurity of any kind.

This is the good news of great joy for all the people.

*–Published in a Church magazine,*
Xiaoxi, *Shanghai, 1940*

# CREATION AND REDEMPTION

Recently, a Christian whom I do not know has written me a number of letters, raising his contention that the phrase "All people are born of God," which appears in the Catechism, is wrong, and that it should say "All people have been created by God." I understand his meaning to be: God has divided people into two categories and most people have simply been created by God, while only those who are saved because of faith, were born of God.

I am not so well versed in biblical terminology. My feeling is simply that, when we speak of humankind, whether we say created by, or born of, is not of great issue. In speaking of Christ the Bible explains that he is the only Son born of the Father, that he is the first-born, and was not created. In the Nicene Creed we also find the phrase "born, not created." But when it comes to people, naturally the more common term is "created," as "God created humankind," but "born of" is also found, as in Acts 17:29: "Since we are God's offspring," (at the time, Paul was speaking to the Athenians, who worshipped the unknown god, in the Areopagus), and also in 1 John 2:29: "everyone who does right has been born of him."

I am saying that as far as Christ is concerned, it is necessary to say that he is the only Son of God, born and not created; for humans, however, it seems unnecessary to say that Christians are the offspring of God while non-Christians may only be said to have been created by God. There is no clear evidence in the Bible, either, for distinguishing between "born of" and "created." To emphasize the distinction creates theological problems. These days, people generally say that all people are God's children, and I do not feel that one has to take issue with this. It is not necessary to say, no, *you* are not God's children, only *we* are God's children. This is not helpful in bringing people to Christ, and it leads to a problem: if God has made only believers his children and given them eternal life, then, is the God who has created the great majority of humanity only to finally become children of hell, a God to be believed in and loved?

If we consider the problem in theological terms, then I think the issue is how to bring creation and redemption together. My Christian correspondent has divided the world into two parts: one which has been created by God—the mineral, plant and animal worlds, such as the grasses and trees, birds and animals, natural human beings—all these were created by God and it seems that God has little feeling for them; created today, gone tomorrow, and the human beings among them will even suffer eternal punishment. The other part is born of God. It is a cut above the created part, it has been chosen. In addition to being created, it has been *redeemed*. In the eyes of this Christian, born of and created by cannot be discussed in the same breath. Obviously, he makes a very clear distinction between creation and redemption. I suspect that he sees it this way: God is the Lord of all creation, Christ is the Lord of Salvation and each minds his own store.

This is classic theological thinking. Carried to its logical development, it evolves into the following attitude: true, the world has been created by God, but creation is finished; the world has been possessed by Satan and is his dominion. When Christ came into the world, it is as if he slipped behind enemy lines to save those who could be saved. It may be that quite a number of Christians hold such a worldview.

Setting creation and redemption in opposition to one another and separating the Lord of Creation from the Lord of Redemption, emphasizes redemption at the expense of creation. God the Father and God the Son are split and each tends to his own. This view, which tears apart the Trinity, appeared early in the history of the Church. Some heresies go to the extreme of making the Lord of Creation and the Lord of Redemption into two opposing gods. My Christian correspondent in his treatise on "created" and "born of" has not gone this far.

Christ is Lord of both creation and redemption, as Colossians 1:15–20 says quite clearly. On the one hand it says that Christ is head of the entire body of the church and that redemption was realized through the blood of his cross. On the other hand it says that all creation depends on him, that he was before all things and all things were created through him. Ephesians 1:22–23 is similar: Christ is both head over all things, the fullness of creation, and all things in heaven and on earth find their fullness in him. It also says that he is the fullness of the church and that the church is his body. Christ's relationship to creation is described very clearly in the Gospel of John: all things came into being through him, and without him not one thing came into being. Hebrews says that all things are sustained by Christ's powerful word. The creation undertaken by God through Christ is proceeding even now. Creation has not failed, it has not lost out to Satan. Though John said, "All creation is sleeping beneath the hand of the Evil One," this is simply to point out the savagery of sin, to make the reader draw a clear line between him or herself and sin; it is not describing the Christian worldview. In 1 Tim. 4:4, Paul says, "For everything created by God is good, and nothing is to be rejected, provided it is received with thanksgiving." The New Testament recognizes Christ's creation; it also recognizes his redemption. This is one and the same Christ, and creation and redemption are a unity, not an opposition. There are not two Gods, each tending to his own.

Today, we are sending off a group of seminary graduates who are leaving our alma mater to work in the church. Other classmates will be going out to work in the church after another year or two. When we go to another country, we need to know something about the situation there; the same is true when we go out into the church. Let me introduce one aspect of the situation in the church—I hope you can all agree, or at least, that you will not be too quick to disagree. Theological thinking in the Chinese Church tends in one direction, that is, one doctrine is lifted up and that doctrine is the issue of being saved by faith, the question of salvation. We tend to pass over or ignore completely the issue of creation. Literary and art circles once had their "one-book-ism" which meant that once an author had written one book and made a name, that author wrote nothing else. The Chinese Christian Church sometimes seems to have one doctrine, that of personal salvation, personal grace. Out of all the riches of Christianity, only this is left.

Several centuries ago, Thomas Aquinas said that grace in no way negates or abolishes nature but is a fulfillment of it. This may be the most famous of Aquinas' sayings. The question of the relationship between nature and grace is that of the relationship between creation and redemption. This is a problem that the Chinese Church has not done very well at solving. The most obvious sign of this is that many people who join the church believe that by simply believing in Jesus they will be saved, blessed and given grace.

The eighth chapter of Romans tells us that the whole creation has been groaning until now. This is to say that creation is not yet finished. The world and the people in it are all products at various stages of completion who have appeared in the process of God's creation. A few individuals are not the only objects of redemption. The whole creation, the whole world is the object of Christ's work of redemption. We are half-finished products, and our duty is to assist God in the project of creation and at the same time, transform ourselves from half-finished, to finished, products. Creation contains redemption; the purpose of redemption is to fulfill God's creation.

Recently a letter was sent to our church magazine *Tian Feng* asking: Are Christians allowed to smoke? The meaning was, if Christians smoke could this eventually have an effect on whether they were saved? Could they go to hell? But many questions which touch on how one should treat creation seldom suggest themselves to us: Why should so much farmland be used for growing tobacco? It is like growing opium. Is it really a good use of nature? Is it in line with God's original meaning for creation? To take this further, in the United States the number of smokers is decreasing, yet the cultivation of tobacco is not and cigarettes are exported to the Third World, to countries such as China where today many people smoke American cigarettes. Don't Christians care about this? Do they condone it? Oppose it? Such questions far surpass those of personal salvation and blessing. They are related to the well-being of millions of people. They are moral issues, ones Christians should be concerned with. To enlarge the scope of Christians' concerns, to guide them, with Christianity as their starting point, in considering moral issues which transcend the personal—this to me is the principle by which to raise the quality of our Chinese Christian Church.

The creation that God undertook through Christ is in the process of being spoiled and desecrated by humankind. Wars plunge thousands, millions of people into misery, their homes are destroyed and families broken up, people are made destitute and homeless. The earth produces enough food for everyone, yet because of human selfishness and greed, many die of hunger each year. We have all seen pictures of adults and children in parts of Africa who are simply skin and bones, on the brink of death. People have done a poor job of watching over and safeguarding God's world; rather they fell forests, burn timber and oil. All this destroys the ecological balance. The Third World has suffered the most. This damage to the globe for their own self-interest by a minority of people, this theft of the right of the majority to sustain existence and enjoy a good life, takes many forms. To take an example closer to home, in Chinese society today, corruption—the use of public resources for personal profit—is rife. A Christianity which turns a blind eye to all this, one which thinks all this bears no relation to the gospel, which believes the gospel is concerned only with personal salvation, is not a two-legged Christianity, but a lame one.

Most Chinese Christianity speaks only of personal blessings and salvation; it has no moral message for the world, yet the Bible has a great number of passages concerned precisely with what relations between people should be. How the Old Testament prophets lifted up social righteousness and social justice. We seldom hear sermons preached today on the Old Testament prophets or on Christ's Sermon on the Mount. Christianity has become an immoral, amoral religion. There are so many events taking place in the world today which are counter to God's plan for the world he created in Christ, and to all of this Christianity says, it's nothing to do with me. Christianity even limits the scope of God's dominion, preaching a God who cares only about the individual believer's soul, who cares only about the church and not about the world and all that is in it. Is this not a worldview and a view of God in which God, having created the world, has now stood aside for Satan?

I hope that graduates of Nanjing Seminary and those of the other seminaries in China will take with them when they go into the church to work a holistic Christian view of God, Christology and worldview, and in appropriate situations, use language appropriate to the situation, follow the teachings of the Bible and spread them, thus raising the quality of our churches.

This is looking at the significance of our work from a long-term perspective. I certainly do not think that our graduates should go to a place and ignore everything except for preaching the salvation of Christ, styling themselves as local prophets and publishing their views on the problems they encounter there in and outside the church. We have all sorts of limits and this is not something I am asking of our graduates. We must first do well in the work of uniting all those around us and in setting ourselves on a firm footing. A few days ago we received a long-distance call from an alumnus who graduated from Nanjing Seminary a few years ago. He said that the Three-Self Patriotic Movement of Protestant Churches in China and the China Christian Council where he was were holding elections and that someone whom everyone knew was a disreputable person would be serving as deputy chair. He was livid and asked me what to do, whether to struggle against this. I told him that it was good that he was infuriated by these goings on, but that this person certainly must have support and it was unwise to beat his head against a stone, the losses would outweigh the gains. My purpose in saying this is to tell you that I am not suggesting that you go out and enter randomly into the fray, striking out all around and laying yourselves open to trouble. That would not help.

The important thing is that we be clear in our minds that the gospel of Christ is not merely one of personal blessing. In fact it is not that at all. Personal blessing is no more than the fulfillment of selfish personal desires. The gospel of Christ includes the renewal of this world, bringing it into line with the beautiful plan of the God who created it through Christ. This requires the church to announce a moral message, a message of service to people. The Lord Jesus himself said: "The Son of Man has come not to be served, but to serve, and to lay down his life for the salvation of many." Please note the "and" here. This means that laying down one's life for redemption and serving people are not opposites, but are one. Laying down one's life for the salvation of many is joined to serving people, is included in that service. Let us go forth to serve the people with minds to help God realize his creation, and in our service make manifest the great event of the saving Lord laying down his life for humanity.

No matter where you go, may the Lord be with you, may he help you to manifest before people the truth, goodness, beauty and all riches found in Christ, that by your excellent witness you may bring people to know Christ.

—Creation and Redemption, 1995

℘

# My
# View of God

First of all I want to thank Union Theological Seminary in the Philippines and the President of the Seminary for the honor you give the church in China and to me personally. I trust that what you do today will result in a closer relationship between our two peoples and our two churches. We in China have a high evaluation of the witness of the Christians in the Philippines to Jesus Christ, calling people's attention to human worth as children of God and to democracy as the mandate of history in accordance to the will of God. We, the church in China, have much to learn from our fellow Christians in the Philippines. Thank you also for the invitation to address this distinguished group of church leaders, professors and students. This is a good opportunity for me to bring the warm greetings of your fellow Christians in China. Let me also thank the President for the kind exaggerations in his citation.

I would like to speak to you on how more and more Chinese Christians, and I as one of them, have come to think of God as Love, as the only possible way to think of God at all. Perhaps I do not need to say that what I have to tell you is not so much for the instruction of Philippine Christians as a report to you on how we in China are trying to help our constituencies to grow into a more mature spirituality with a vision of God intellectually honest, spiritually edifying and morally challenging.

Let me begin by telling you something about myself. I was born into a family in which the grandfather on my mother's side was an Anglican priest. I received the larger part of my formal education in China. My career in the church can be simply divided into two periods. The first period was in working among students through the Student Christian Movement, first in China, then in Canada and then on the international scene. The second period has been with theological education and religious studies in China, centering in Nanjing Theological Seminary and Nanjing University. Both of these periods are important to me in my theological formation and reorientation.

I would like to help you to see right away where I stand on your theological map. After the great social and political turmoil called the Cultural Revolution, which cut off my theological and intellectual communication with the outside world for over ten years, I found upon resuming my international contacts three Western schools of thought most consonant with the fumblings and gropings of Chinese Christian intellectuals: liberation theology, writings in one way or another influenced by process philosophy, and the thinking of Teilhard de Chardin. This you will find understandable given not only the theme of change passed down from influential ancient Chinese classics, but also the motif of liberation and all the dynamism and zigzags of change and reform China has been going through.

My early training made me think of God largely in terms of his omnipotence, his power, his might, his self-sufficiency, his self-containment, and his changelessness. Yes, in terms of his love too, but love was not God's supreme attribute and was often overshadowed by his righteousness, his severity, his anger, his judgment and his arbitrariness.

The vicissitudes of all these years have moved me to a spirituality that affirms Christ's place in God's whole creative process and sees the kind of love embodied in Jesus in the four Gospels as the nature of God. Love is at the back of God's whole creative process. Today, when I say Jesus Christ is the revelation of God, I mainly think of him as the revealer of God's love. From struggling with the question of Jesus' divinity and Godlikeness I have moved to the Christ likeness of God. Love becomes for me God's number one attribute.

I am fascinated by what Alfred North Whitehead says toward the end of his *Process and Reality* about what he calls the "Galilean vision" in which God is perceived as a being loving, creating, educating, persuading and expecting human responses. When the Western world accepted Christianity, he says, Caesar conquered. Let me quote:

> The brief Galilean vision of humility flickered throughout the ages, uncertainly. But the deeper idolatry of

fashioning God in the image of the Egyptian, Persian
and Roman rulers was retained. The church gave unto
God the attributes that belonged exclusively to Caesar.

Whitehead laments over the fact that, in so much of Christianity,
God is conceived in terms of "the ruling Caesar, or the ruthless moralist, or the unmoved mover." China, of course, has no lack of our own
autocratic rulers in whose image various Chinese religions have fash-
ioned their God. But it is the all-encompassing love at the heart of reality, sharing the joys and the suffering of the created order, and moving
the world toward greater coherence and greater love, that Christ
reveals.

Let me help you locate me in your socio-political map too. My conviction in God as love and my conviction in socialism as the path China
is to take strengthen each other. Socialism is love organized for the
masses of the people. The collapse of the Soviet Union and Eastern
European state power has had its effect on me, but has not shattered my
conviction that, for China, neither feudalism, nor colonialism, nor capitalism is acceptable as an alternative to the social system we call socialism with Chinese characteristics which, in forty years, has enabled
twelve hundred million human beings to live more decently and gives
us ground to hope that they can live still more decently in the next century. A longer view of history tells us that socialism is not an accident
or a mishap that can now be erased. Socialism has only had a very short
history. It has no charted course and no model to copy. While I am quite
upset by many of the things done in the name of socialism, I still think
socialism is a good name to describe the road for Chinese society that
avoids the pitfalls of feudalism, colonialism, and capitalism, all of which
China has experienced and found disappointing. It is a road that liber-
ates and develops the country's productive power to an unprecedented
extent, thus improving the people's material livelihood, cultural level
and self-respect.

We attach our hope to socialism, not so much because we know
exactly in detail what the socialist way is, but because we are fed up by
all the other choices open to us. What is common in these other choices
is the large scale of private ownership of the means of production and
the unfair distribution of wealth, requiring the masses of the people to

bear the cost by enduring endless suffering. People in that state cannot easily recognize God as love. We look for a corrective to all social systems that believe that the nastiest of men and women with the nastiest self-interest will work for the benefit of the masses of the people. What is called for is a brake to the unbridled search for private profit. The failure of the Soviet Union, which was just one experiment in social planning, has done nothing to improve the attractiveness of feudalism, colonialism and capitalism. It is quite unthinkable that China is now to switch itself away from its socialist path and return to the old ways. I do believe that, with the gradual rise in economic and educational level, we can expect an increase of democracy in this socialism with Chinese characteristics.

Does the advocacy of atheism affect my support of socialism? No, it does not. I look at both atheists and ourselves as half-completed products in God's creative process and that we are all becoming. There are atheists who are sincerely devoted to efforts to fashion a more humane society. Their cry against God is really a cry in favor of humanity. Their atheism is worthy of our sympathy in so far as it is a rejection of the false notions of God we religious people propagate. Who is the God they have in mind when they deny his existence? It is the tyrannical Jupiter who chains Prometheus to a cliff because he does good for humanity, or the ruthless underworld King Yen in Chinese popular religion who sends out emissaries to fetch people to be thrown into everlasting hell fire as punishment for their misdeeds. Atheistic humanism is actually one form of human seeking after God without being aware of it, and can be our ally, as it can help greatly to salvage authentic faith. We can join forces with humanitarians of many sorts to oppose the idolatry in those views of God that diminish human dignity and block human liberation. Some of my friends abroad are surprised that I sometimes speak as highly as I do of certain atheists and communists. There is a part of me as a Christian which utters a hearty "Amen" to what they advocate, a part of me that refuses to rebuke them, but rather warms to them and wants to work with them against forces we both want to combat, even though we get our orders in doing certain things together from different chains of command.

The New Testament is the source of our knowledge about Jesus

Christ and through him about God. The record is fragmentary and does not give us as complete a picture of the person as we would like to have. But two portraits are unmistakable:

## (1) JESUS THE GREAT LOVER OF MEN AND WOMEN

He tells us about the father who believes in the prodigal son and waits for his return, about the shepherd who has his ninety-nine sheep in the fold and yet cannot bear to lose one that is missing. We see a Jesus who weeps with those who suffer and rejoices with those who rejoice, a Jesus who refuses to condemn a person who has gone astray but protects her, a Jesus who has loved his friends and loves them to the end, one who tells his friends, "Do not let your hearts be troubled, believe in God, believe also in me." This Jesus introduces a new scale of things in which Sabbath rules are subordinate to human needs. The picture we get of him in the New Testament touches the chord in all that is best in human nature: the lonely man, homeless and self-forgetful, with his outpouring of love and sympathy, his suffering and agony, his tender words on the cross, and the final victory over ruthless power. He lived and died as one who loves, a true lover.

## (2) JESUS THE COSMIC CHRIST

He is not just the crucified one on the cross, the only image that has meaning to many Christians. He is the one who sustains the universe by his word of power. His is the primacy over all creation. He exists before all things, and all things are held together in him. He is the image of the invisible God, the first born of all creation. In him all things were created, things visible and invisible, whether thrones or dominions or rulers or powers. It is not that God carried on his work of creation for six days and then stopped and ceded its control to the successful rebellion of Satan, and then the redeemer came into the world to rescue some individuals out of it to be returned to God, leaving all others to eternal damnation. As creativity is inexhaustible and creation a long, ongoing process, Christ has been and is with God, in all the creative work in the universe to this day. He has to do with creation just as much as he has to do with redemption. Redemption is a part of God's ongoing work of making a world of his design. The New

Testament does not allow us to think that God is the creator and not the redeemer, and Christ is the redeemer and not the creator.

Now the essence of Christianity is the appeal to the person of Christ as the revelation of the nature of God. When these two portraits of Jesus, Jesus the lover of men and women and Jesus the Christ in whom all things are created, are put together, we come to know God whom Christ reveals as the Cosmic Lover, or Creator-Lover.

It is unfortunate that this is not the God many Christians in China, and I suppose, elsewhere, know to be God.

The most commonly recognized attributes of God are his almightiness, his omnipresence, his omniscience, his severity, and his unrelenting judgment of nonbelievers. We talk of love as an attribute of God, too, but his love seems to be very arbitrary and enjoyed only by a few who are specially selected, or who please God in special ways. To the others, God is essentially a punisher-rewarder, a being hard to please. Hence, fear of God's displeasure is the mark of much that goes under the name of Christianity.

I was brought up in a Christianity very much like that. We went to church every Sunday to curry God's favor. If there was illness within in family, it was God's punishment for some hidden sin. When I went to be a theological student to prepare myself for the ministry of the church, the common notion in the family and in church circles was that such an act of dedication would win God's pleasure and bring health and well being to my family and myself.

Today, as I move about the Chinese Church at its grassroots, I find that this is still the level of spirituality many are at. In some villages as many as half of the Christians became Christians when there was illness on the part of some family member who supposedly got healed when Christians came to pray and drive out the evil spirits. Many Christians at the grassroots enjoy "testimony meetings" in which anybody can speak. At such meetings a common pattern emerges: Some misfortune happens to a person; he or she searches for his or her sin or sins; after identifying the sin or sins and confessing to God and much praying, God moves away the misfortune. On the other hand, misfortune lingers and intensifies for those who are hardhearted and do not repent, culminating in unending suffering and death in the family.

Holding on to this image of God is accompanied by a spirituality of acquisition and utilitarianism. We give God praises and honor and get, in return, health, wealth, protection from catastrophe in this life, and eternal bliss in heaven. It is highly ironic that, while Christ was laughed at for his ability to save others but not himself, so many of his followers are only eager to save themselves by getting into the church as if it were Noah's Ark, without a faith that concerns itself with the welfare of the people outside.

The image of God we find here is essentially what Whitehead calls that of the "Ruling Caesar" with all his power over human fate. It is so far from the Christ we have come to know, to love and to adore as we read the four Gospels, with all his tenderness and rejection of power and coercion over men and women.

To say that God is love is to affirm God as the Cosmic Lover and to see love as the force directing God's ever-continuing work of creation, redemption and sanctification. Love is the supreme attribute of God, above all other attributes and subordinating them all. Christians are to make Christ like love the definition of God, the motivation in all God's work of creation in nature and history. It is first of all in the ongoing process of creation that we are to see the supreme expression of God's love. It is not a mark of higher religion to discern God's love in terms of personal fortunes and misfortunes. God looks forward to and is working toward the emergence of a commonwealth of human beings who, out of their free will, choose to be co-creators with him of goodness, truth and beauty and of all things of value to God and to humanity. God's love does not coerce. It works through education, persuasion, transfiguration and sanctification. In God's creative process the world and all of us are thus far half-made products. Through this process men and women are being transformed from obedience to arbitrary commands to willing acceptance of the invitation of love, i.e., transferred from the realm of necessity to the realm of freedom.

We have been trained to think of God largely in terms of superior power that can either crush us or make us powerful. This is often a projection and legitimization of our power-hungry, exploitative, monopolistic social structures and attitudes. But, in the New Testament, God's power comes out of weakness and he exercises sovereignty through crosses, not through conquests. We must not fashion God in the image of Egyptian, Persian, Roman and Chinese potentates, thereby giving to God the attributes that belong exclusively to Pharaoh, Caesar and their like. We need to relegate to the side all those attributes such as his absolute power, his absolute knowledge. His absolute changelessness, his absolute dominion, his arbitrariness and intolerance, imposed on God as a reflection of an absolutization of human beings' own cravings, especially those of male human beings. These attributes need to be de-absolutized and subordinated to God's supreme attribute of love.

God is no cosmic tyrant who forces obedience. He lures, invites and waits for free responses and does not resort to scolding and reprimanding. That is why we in China find the Gospels' analogy of transformation of seeds and the growth of plants and trees in air, rain and sun more appealing than the image of the sheep that are constantly treated with rod and staff. God is the will-to-fellowship, not the will-to-power. We want to depart from a severe and intimidating God, a bulldozer God, who is not the Christ like God the four Gospels lure us to want to believe in. We like the image of God in Hosea 11:4, of one who secures us with reins, leads us with bonds of love, lifts us like a little child to the parent's cheek, and bends down to feed us. When I was a theological student, I wrestled with the problem of Christ's two natures, ending up with his divinity. Today, it seems to me that to confess that Christ is Godlike is not half so important as to affirm that God is Christ like and that Christ like love is the way God runs the cosmos.

You have seen that, in affirming love as the supreme attribute of God, I have relegated his omnipotence and omniscience to the second place. We cannot think of God in his self-contained existence, in abstraction from the world, but in terms of his creative activity in the world. He works in his creation tirelessly and inexhaustibly to bring about the realization of the potentialities which he has implanted there. God in his love craves for the emergence in the universe of persons whom he can have fellowship with. Fellowship implies freedom. Human enjoyment of this freedom implies God's respect for human choices and therefore the curtailment of his own omnipotence. Insofar as human beings have the right to make choices, including wrong choices, and insofar as God respects this right, God does not have a pre-knowledge of how a person will exercise his or her free-dom or right to make choices. Thus, God's omniscience is also rela-tivized. By permitting freedom to his creatures and accepting their misuse of it, God can bring about better results than in any other way. The possibility of disobedience is the price of liberty, and liberty is the condition of selfhood and selfhood the preliminary to fellowship.

There is a popular Chinese movie condemning feudalism in which a young woman's fiancé has died but she is still compelled to marry into the family as daughter-in-law. After the tearful wedding she enters the bridal chamber, only to find a five-foot long tree trunk on the bed. She is expected to live the rest of her life with that log as her husband. How can she have fellowship and communion with such a non-person?

God being love, more and more of us are seeing that the father fig-ure is not necessarily the only or the best analogy for characterizing him. For centuries and to this day, in China anyway, what is taken for granted in the father is his severity, and in the mother her loving kind-ness. In fact, the proper Chinese way to refer to one's own father in polite conversation is the "severe one in my family," while "the loving one in my family" is reserved for the mother. We all know of fathers of whom love is hardly an attribute. There are biblical passages that show no hesitation in using the image of the mother to indicate how God loves. In Isaiah 66 and 49, God says: "As a mother comforts her son, so shall I myself comfort you," and "Can a woman forget the infant of her breast, or a mother the child of her womb? But should even these for-get, I shall never forget you." And in Psalm 131, the psalmist says, "I am calm and quiet like a weaned child clinging to its mother." Thus, to say that God has the attributes of the father is not to say he does not have the attributes of the mother.

To assert the cosmic dimension of Christ's role and to ascertain God as the Cosmic Lover does not mean that everything that happens in nature and history is God's work and design. Many things are happen-ing that contradict God's loving kindness and are harmful to the welfare of the world. Creation is a long process yet incomplete and, as Paul insists, imperfect and subject to frustration, especially as it involves the making of free human beings who are not slaves but children of God. A world still in the making must be one in which ugliness and devilry have their place. Events all over the world are telling us how tortuous the way is toward the perfect community of free, loving children of God, and how dear a price in suffering God and human beings have to pay for every inch of progress toward that goal.

That God is the great lover working out his purpose for the world brings in its train an understanding of all reality not as being so much as becoming. It gives us hope for history and beyond. We have no idea as to how the end of history as we know it will come about, but can be sure it will be the triumph of love and grace.

We receive great consolation in reading Romans 5:15–17 where a comparison is made between the effect upon the world of Christ's grace and Adam's fall. There Paul speaks of the infinitely greater impact of Christ on humanity than that of Adam, using such expressions as "much more," "vastly exceeding," "in far greater measure," and "out of all proportion." We are elated and get a sense of liberation upon reading this. The Incarnation profoundly affects human and cosmic life in all its aspects. It is inconceivable that any area of human endeavor should be permanently affected by Adam's fall and unaffected by grace. Too often, Christians make the effect of Adam's fall universal while limiting Christ's grace only to the few who profess a belief in him. It really amounts to saying that the Incarnation of the Son of God has made less of an impact on humanity than the fall of Adam. But this a not a view that can go along with the vision of a God whose name is love and whose concern is to bring about through redemption, education and sanctification a humanity that will reach perfection as free, intelligent and voluntary creators with God.

The way from alpha to omega is not always a straight line, but love accompanies the pilgrims. "The Love that moves the Sun and the other stars," in Dante's great words, becomes a love which brings meaning to human existence and hence redeems men and women from triviality, frustration, cheapness and lovelessness. We do have to go through tortuous ways, but we remember Christ's words: "A woman in labor is in pain because her time has come; but when her baby is born she forgets her anguish in her joy that a child has been born in the world." We see the darkness that appears before dawn as well as the dawn that will surely arrive after darkness. As is so well said in Psalm 30: "Tears may linger at nightfall, but rejoicing comes in the morning." This view of nature, history and ourselves as becoming instills life with meaning and direction. This is essentially a long-ranged and forward-looking world-view. Teilhard de Chardin makes a moving prophecy when he says, "Someday, after we have mastered the wind, the waves, the tide and gravity, we shall harness for God the energies of love: and then for the second time in the history of the world, humanity will have discovered fire." I also like the cosmology and view of history Lu Xun, the greatest modern Chinese writer, presents so beautifully:

> Myriads of beautiful people and beautiful deeds weave
> a heavenly tapestry, moving like tens of thousands of
> flying stars, spreading far and wide, even to infinity—
>
> Things and their reflections dissolve, flicker, expand,
> melt into each other, but then draw back, approaching
> a semblance of their original selves. Their edges are
> variable as those of summer clouds, shot through with
> sunlight, emitting flames the color of mercury.
>
> All things without exception mesh and interweave into
> a fabric, ever lively, ever unfolding.

Christians as a little flock are heartened by the vision of Christ leading the whole creation toward the goal of unity in God. In this saving work of his, all human movements of progress, liberation, democracy, humanization and love are joined. The church is important as a place where Christ is explicitly known, confessed, adored and preached. The world needs the church's gospel of forgiveness and reconciliation and peace. But God's saving work is not coterminous with the boundary of the church. It has the whole cosmos as its arena. As Vatican II says, "Many elements of sanctification and truth are found outside the visible structure of the church and so the helps necessary for salvation are always and everywhere available to all who are obedient to the dictates of conscience." I like to think that, if these elements are arcs of a circle, Christ is the perfect round in whom they will all be completed, fulfilled and united.

In spite of the darkness human beings in many parts of the world find themselves in, there have always been courageous souls with their firm belief in the final triumph of God's grace. I would like to close with a few inspiring lines left us by Victor Hugo:

> Will the future ever arrive?—Should we continue to look upwards? Is the light we can see in the sky one of those which will presently be extinguished?

> The ideal is terrifying to behold, lost as it is in the depths, small, isolated, a pinpoint, brilliant but threatened on all sides by the dark forces that surround it; nevertheless, no more in danger than a star in the jaws of the clouds.

Human beings are fumbling and groping for a faith in God as revealed in Jesus Christ. We all see in a mirror, dimly. This address tells you where I am, and where many of my fellow Christians in China are, that is, the sort of spirituality the Holy Spirit is guiding us to in our pilgrimage. I will want to be open to any help that enables further growth in understanding.

—My View of God, Manila, 1993

# BELIEVING IN WHAT KIND OF GOD?

*A speech made by Bishop K. H. Ting to students at*
*Nanjing Union Theological Seminary at the beginning of the floods*
*in China this summer. It comes in response to claims by some members*
*within the Chinese church that the floods and other calamities are*
*"signs" of God's judgment and the end of the world.*

We Christians are very concerned about whether or not people believe in God and Christ. If someone believes in God and Christ, we acknowledge him or her as "one of us," otherwise that person is simply "not one of our own." As to the kind of God and the kind of Christ that the person may believe in, we don't delve too closely into that. However, we need only take a closer look at the Bible to know that it contains many Scriptures that seek to help us establish a correct view of God and Christ.

I should draw on several biblical passages here to explain this point: First of all, let us take a look at Jonah the preacher. God called him to go to Nineveh, so he went there and told Nineveh that it faced destruction. This caused him to feel very pleased with himself. But later, when God didn't destroy Nineveh, Jonah felt very annoyed. God says to Jonah in Jonah 4:10–11, "You are sorry about the gourd, though you did not have the trouble of growing it, a plant which came up one night and died the next. And should not I be sorry about the great city of Nineveh, with its hundred and twenty thousand people, who cannot tell their right from their left, as well as cattle without number?" These words show us that it is definitely not God's intention to destroy humankind. One who takes delight in preaching destruction is a kind of preacher like Jonah.

Genesis 18:20–32 gives us the same message: Abraham first asks God "Will you really sweep away the innocent and wicked together? Suppose there are fifty innocent in the city (Sodom); will you really sweep it away and not pardon the place because of the fifty innocent there?" God replied, "If I find in Sodom fifty innocent, I shall pardon the whole place for their sake." When Abraham continues to ask, "What if the number of righteous are only 45, or 40, or 30, or 20, or 10?" God's reply is always, "I will also not destroy this city." Thus, this portion of Scripture also fully demonstrates God's overwhelming kindness. God certainly does not look upon human beings with hatred and certainly does not take delight in attacking and wiping them out. God's heart is filled with love, and he cherishes and treasures all His people.

Once we have this view of God, we need to get rid of all the deceptive talk from both inside and outside the church that seeks to vilify the image of God and present God as one who is hostile toward humankind, unbearably cruel and brutal. This also includes descriptions that play up the "gospel" of the destruction of the world and the planet, with some even misusing the name of science in order to back up their views.

The God who is clearly revealed and demonstrated to us by Jesus is a God of love. In the person of Christ himself we see that God is love:

In the parable of the prodigal son the father's love is so profound and so unwavering. This love causes him to believe deep down that his son will indeed return. He eagerly awaits his son's return. It is this same love that melts the son's heart of stone and causes him to return home, this same love that leads his father to accept him once again as his true son (Luke 15).

When the shepherd of one hundred sheep loses one of them, how he loves that confused and straying sheep. He doesn't just wait for the sheep to return; he goes and looks for it until he finds the place where the little sheep is. Then he carries it home and rejoices with his friends (Luke 15).

Jesus loved his friends so much that when he saw his friends upset about a death within their family, he himself could not help weeping (John 11:3–35).

When Jesus saw a young man with his heart set on heaven, he loved him and directed him as to what he still lacked (John 3:1–13).

His love caused him to weep for Jerusalem (Luke 19:41).

Jesus deeply loves the hungry people of the world—the homeless, the naked without any clothes to wear, the sick, the suffering and the imprisoned. He points out that, regardless of whether they believe or not, whatever we do for them we do for him (Matt. 25).

The woman who had five husbands and was looked down upon by others (John 4:7–20), the woman who had committed adultery and was declared sinful by those who believed themselves righteous (John 8:3–11), the one who, because of her repentance for her sins, could not but use her own tears and hair to wipe Jesus' feet (Luke 7:37–46), Jesus loved them all.

The person who saw Jesus coming and climbed a tree to see him, who expressed a desire to repent and who gave back several-fold that which he had cheated from others (Luke 19:1–10), Jesus loved him.

The robber who was crucified with the Lord Jesus and who still had a conscience, Jesus also loved him and told him that they would enter Paradise together (Luke 23:42).

When his dearest friends scattered in the face of adversity, some even denying him, he was grieved but he still loved them.

When he was hung high on the cross but while his heart was still beating, we can imagine that he thought of his good friends Peter, John, James, Mary Magdalene, Lazarus, Martha, and Mary ... he loved them all.

And then there is this verse: "There is no greater love in the world than this, that one should lay down his life for his friends" (John 15:13).

It is this kind of Christ who causes us to believe that love is the greatest of God's attributes and that this is the most important truth in the universe. Saying that hatred and destruction is the true meaning behind the universe is irreconcilable with the belief that God is love. It is this love that compels God to propel the whole creation unceasingly toward perfection. The Bible calls on us not to be too troubled about what the end of time will be like, and Jesus himself didn't give us any clear predictions about this. The Bible does tell us that God is love, and that is enough. According to the belief that God is love, we cannot possibly hold that, in the final analysis, both good and evil will perish together, that the positive will perish together with the negative, that innocent babes will perish alongside murderous despots. We can be certain that the end of history cannot possibly result in total destruction but can only result in the fulfillment and victory of love and grace, the realization of the whole universe becoming truly perfect and believing in love.

Yet aren't there a certain number of sayings in the Bible that hint at the destruction of heaven and earth in the end? This touches upon the question of our approach to the Bible.

The Bible is a book that, through the movement of the Holy Spirit in certain holy people in ancient times, progressively reveals God's inherent character to humankind. It also records how people's understanding of God has improved over time. The holy people of ancient times were human, not gods, and the process of being touched and then spreading the information they received was more or less influenced by the fact of their humanity coupled with the limitations of their particular historical period. As Martin Luther said when talking of the Bible:

When the baby Jesus was sleeping in the manger, the manger contained not only the baby Jesus but it also contained straw.

The Bible has many parts where faith, spirituality, morals and ethics, theology, literature, etc. reach their loftiest heights, but we cannot say that this is true for every part of the Bible, that all parts reach the same heights.

For thousands of years now, human understanding of culture and science has been changing with each passing day. Some people believe that since there is material in the Bible that does not correspond to current scientific findings, this means that the Bible is of no worth. This is a superficial way of looking at things. The Bible's worth is not to be found through science but through faith, spirituality, morals and ethics, theology, literature. We never require of any other ancient writings that they match up to the scientific views of the 20th century. If our interest is in science, there are several hundred, several thousand different modern scientific works in the bookstore, that we can browse and use for study and reference.

Some Christians think that since some church pastors often stress how the Bible is "God's word," that means that each chapter, each verse, each phrase, even each word, each punctuation mark and each stroke of each character must all be completely without error. The reality is not like this. To give an example: Any high school student knows that the circumference of any circle is equal to 3.14159... times its diameter. This is the well-known mathematical value pi. Perhaps not many high school students know how this value pi is calculated. But, if you go and look at the Bible, you can find a place that says that the diameter of a circle is one third of its circumference (2 Chron. 4:2). Obviously, this is not accurate enough for scientific purposes. But we cannot, for this reason, deny the Bible's worth, for the Bible is not meant to be a mathematical textbook.

Even if some internal discrepancies do exist within the Bible in the areas of faith, spirituality, morals and ethics, and theology, we can still attribute these to the phenomenon of understanding that develops and advances gradually. Within the space of 1,000 years, the things that God revealed and taught to the tribe of Israel in the areas of faith, spirituality, morals and ethics, and theology developed and increased gradually.

In this way, people's understanding of God increased at a steady but uneven pace.

The leap in understanding from Psalm 137:9, which speaks of seizing infants and dashing them against rocks, to the knowledge that God is love (1 John 4:16) is an extremely great one. From the viewpoint of God, this represents the pinnacle of God's gradual self-revelation; from the viewpoint of humankind, it is also the pinnacle of their understanding of God.

If we just latch on to isolated words or phrases in the Bible, holding them up as God's Word while totally ignoring other words in the Bible, then what ridiculous stuff we can make out of it all! For doesn't the Bible also contain the words of the devil (Job 1:9; Matt. 4:3)? So, we must grasp biblical truth in its entirety. We cannot just "help ourselves" to the bits we like or seize on certain fragments and present them as the whole truth—the result of this brings harm to others and ourselves. When we read the Bible we need to accept theological guidance, seeing through the whole Bible how God increases human understanding of him.

Recently, some people, both inside and outside of the church, have been putting it about that the last days are imminent, deceiving heaven knows how many people in the process. They couch their claims in biblical and scientific terms, saying that the appearance and spread of AIDS is God's punishment and a sign of the last days and the coming end of the world. Well, there are many innocent children who don't yet even know their left hand from their right but who have also been infected with AIDS. Where is God's justice in that? These people say that the Arab-Israeli conflicts, various dark deeds committed within the church, wars, earthquakes and pestilences are all "signs" of the last days and Jesus' Second Coming. Yet all these things go against the fact that God is love, and these people are thus deceiving and duping the masses. Actually, these so-called "signs" have occurred time and time again throughout the whole of human history. This kind of exaggeration can lead to all kinds of negative results, such as presenting the protection and building up of the Motherland as mere futile labor without any meaning. Likewise, patriotism is portrayed as useless, the Three-Self principles as useless, running the church well as meaningless—all becomes nonsense according to this way of thinking. We thus have no choice but to attach great importance to all this, not letting any person try, whatever their motives, to replace the Gospel of Christ with a "Gospel of Doom."

—February 11, 1998

&

# THE CHURCH UNIVERSAL

*Luke 2:34, "Behold, this child is set for the fall and rising of many in Israel, and for a sign that is spoken against (and a sword will pierce through your own soul also), that thoughts out of many hearts may be revealed."*

We as Christians look forward with anticipation to the bringing of the whole universe, all in heaven and on earth, into unity in Christ when the time becomes ripe. However, the Christ who is ultimately the unifier is first of all a divider, as Simeon's prophecy declares. The taking on of human flesh by the Son of God was the occasion for the laying bare of what was in the hearts of men and women. In the New Testament we see that human beings, in confronting him, reveal themselves to be roughly speaking in one or the other of three categories. First, there were Christ's despisers, rejecters, haters, and enemies, such as the Herods, the Caiaphases, the Pilates, the Pharisees and the Sadducees. Then there were the Gamaliels and perhaps the Nicodemuses, liberals in various degrees who chose to be noncommittal and to refrain from making a judgment. Then, there were those who, in spite of the human finite form of the Christ they saw, could recognize in him the Son God had made heir to the whole universe, through whom he had created all orders of existence, the effulgence of God's splendor and the stamp of God's very being, sustaining the universe by his word of power. In this Christ they got a vision of an order of things as God would want to order them, and to this Christ they could not but commit themselves in praise, adoration and action.

The polarization of men and women into these groups—despisers, liberals and friends—happens not only when we are faced with the fact of Incarnation. It happens whenever there are newborn things in history. Herbert Butterfield put it aptly when he said, "It is curious how we unconditionally endorse the revolution of the past, yet have no understanding of the contemporary revolution we are experiencing." Hence the despisers and those who hold back.

The division of people into those who are for and those who are against and those who are noncommittal and their changes from one category to another happen also when there are newborn things in church. This has been the case almost all through history. Movements that represent the cutting edge of the church in the world have almost without exception faced the fate of receiving ill-treatment from forces of the status quo, and have too often become captured by them later, and tamed into something just docile, conventional and harmless.

Now newborn things, like newborn babies, are often not comely and beautiful right from the beginning. In the words of W.H. Auden, they

> Ruffle the perfect manners of the frozen heart,
> And compel it to be awkward and alive.

In so doing there is bound to be no scarcity of awkwardness, haphazardness, faults and mistakes, which give some the pretexts for opposition and some grounds for hesitation. But we know, in making a judgment, we need to grasp the essence of the matter under consideration, not its aberrations. It is the essence of the matter that counts because of its relative stability and permanence. If virtue lies just in avoiding mistakes, the one who does nothing about anything would be the most virtuous person. Then learning would be entirely irrelevant and out of place.

Today, we two Chinese Christians have come to Geneva to do two things:

First, our coming is an acting out for Christians in China and perhaps in the world to see the oneness of the Body of Christ and the relatedness of the church in China to the Church Universal. We are not relaxing our efforts to make the church in China Chinese. This is a question of "to be or not to be" for the Church of Jesus Christ in China today. It is evident that, as long as our Chinese people think of Christianity as something Western, there is no way to show that at its center there is the universal and absolute claim upon all men and women of Jesus Christ as Lord. At the same time, if we do not cherish our identity and selfhood, we will have nothing to give to the Church Universal. But, important as the fostering of a Chineseness certainly is at a particular stage of our church, it bears an inescapable provisionality about it because it concerns only the form of our selfhood, whereas the substance and the justification for the existence of this selfhood is necessarily its being the Church of Jesus Christ. And this substance we share and affirm with the churches of the whole world. We need to protect the growth of the Chinese particularity of our church, but this particularity will be void of spiritual content if it is cut away from the universality of Jesus Christ, of his gospel and of his church. We hope our visit can be a sort of actualization of this truth, first of all to our fellow Christians in China.

Second, with a hope to find Geneva continuing to be the spearhead of the Church's new adventures, defender of the Church's new experiments of engagement in the world and incubator for a child born perhaps a little ahead of its time, we have come to plea for a serious evaluation which Three-Self as a newborn thing in the church deserves and, as much as possible, to change our negators in some parts of the world into Gamaliels, and our Gamaliels into friends. It is sheer superficiality, irresponsibility and complacency to dismiss it as a manufacture of a political party, or as the unprincipled yielding to political pressure on the part of not so faithful Christians seeking survival. We think Three-Self, with all the laicization and the post-denominationalism and the kind of theological reorientation that have come in its train, is an ecclesiological necessity, a pre-requisite for evangelistic communication in such a country as China to be possible as already being borne out by facts. It is a process through which the church in China ceases to be a dot on the missionary map of other churches but comes to be itself. The Church Universal needs us to be true to our identity as Chinese Christians in order to add to the richness and breath of its understanding and worship of Christ. So might not Three-Self really be a child born in the household of God and destined to be a sign for something beyond itself? Could it be really one of the important breakthroughs in history that has a significance and message for Christians elsewhere too? We hope our visit here can mark the beginning of a process of give and take within the family of God that will bring about better and deeper understanding. We hope this understanding will enable us Chinese Christians to improve our self-understanding through viewing our aims and undertakings from new angles that you can provide. We do stand in need of the correctives which can come to us through closer relatedness to Christians elsewhere. And the result of all of this is that we in our witness everywhere will be supported and strengthened by the enhanced spiritual richness and by the intensified thanksgiving and prayers of the whole worldwide church.

—Address at Worship, Ecumenical Center, Geneva, 1983

## LOVE IS FOR THOSE WITH EARS TO HEAR

We are not three wise men from the East, but eleven not so wise men and women from the North, from China, seven men and four women, ranging in age from around thirty to around seventy. Four of us are from Shanghai, three from Nanjing, one each from Guangzhou, Chengdu, Fuzhou and Beijing. In making this visit we feel we are encircled by the loving care of God in every step, supported by the prayers of our fellow Christians in China and warmly received by the Christians of Australia. For all this love, this prayer and this welcome, our hearts are full of thanksgiving to God who is the source of all good things.

In Chapters 2 and 3 of Revelation, there are seven messages that the Risen Christ gives through John to the seven churches of Ephesus, Smyrna, Pergamum, Thyatira, Sardis, Philadelphia and Laodicea. The messages are all different because all seven churches are different in the cultural milieus in which they are situated, different in the problems they each face, different in their strengths and weaknesses. The messages do not try at all to impose the same pattern on all the seven churches. Yet, all seven messages end up in the same way: "He who has an ear, let him hear what the Spirit says to the churches." Each of the messages is for all Christians everywhere to hear.

This probably explains the reason for a delegation from the Australian Council of Churches to go to China in 1986, and for the eleven of us to be here now.

The principle of particularity, or individuality, or locality, or nationality belongs very much to the New Testament conception of the church. The Church Universal only exists in the particular churches in all their forms across the world and the ages. There are historical moments for a church to discover its own people and aspire not to remain a replica of churches elsewhere. We need to be ourselves. Only by acquiring a Chinese selfhood, a Chinese identity, can the Church of Jesus Christ in China live down its colonial past history and its image as something Western, earn its right to be heard by the Chinese people and not be edged out of the world. And it is only as our church ceases to be a dot on the missionary map of other churches, but becomes truly Chinese, that we can bring our spiritual insights to the Church Universal, to the enhancement of its worship and understanding of Christ. So, in personnel, in organization, in material resources, in ways of appropriating and expressing the Christian faith, we are not relaxing our efforts to make the church in China Chinese, that is, as Chinese as the church in Australia is Australian.

The Archbishop of Canterbury said in Hong Kong two years ago that, when Christians in England ended the tutelage of Rome and formed themselves into an independent church, it was a Three-Self Movement too. Since we came to Australia we have learned that the Church of England in Australia has recently changed its name into the Anglican Church of Australia. So you are moving in the same direction and we feel supported.

We thank God and the Australian churches for all the good things that missionaries from this land did in China. Their deeds of love will remain and continue to bear fruits acceptable to God. And we know that good missionaries even in those days wanted to work hard in order to make themselves dispensable. So we would like them to think that the emergence and the growth of a self-governing, self-supporting and self-propagating church in China is in a real sense their success and their glory, not in any sense their loss or failure.

But, at the same time, there is an inevitable provisionality in our whole aspiration for a national selfhood. Any selfhood for a church must have as its content the absolute and universal claim of Jesus Christ as Lord, and this we share with Christians everywhere in the world and in history. We must not only be rooted in the Chinese soil, but must also be related to the Church Universal as one of its parts. We cannot afford not to listen to what the Holy Spirit speaks to other churches. When we say Three-Self, self-isolation must not be one of them, nor self-sufficiency. So, we have come here to check our watches, as it were, or to compare notes, and this is desirable from time to time.

Ours is a small church in a big country. For the first time in history, a part of the Third World hitherto semi-feudal and semi-colonial with all its backwardness and the burden of outdated traditions has moved into the stage of building up a new socialist life largely on its own shoestring. It is within such a country that we Christians, a very small fraction of its population, have been called to build up the church as the Body of Christ. We are faced with many formidable problems. We look for a Christology and a spirituality which is faithful to the historic confession of Christ as the universal mediator of salvation, does justice to the essential unity of the Godhead in his work of creation, redemption and sanctification, and yet makes room for all that is true, and good, and beautiful in nature, in history and in humanity and is adverse to their opposites. We would like to enlarge our understanding of this Christ through contacts with Christians in Australia. Ours is a church not slow in bearing witness to Jesus Christ and hence is a growing church. But we don't know well enough how evangelism is happening through us. We need to summarize our experiences theologically so that our Christians can be better guided in carrying on evangelism, and we look for any experience elsewhere that can be a message to us. In ecclesiology, we have found ourselves in a post-denominational stage of history, but we are not clear or agreed as to the next step. The China Christian Council is to be a transitional body. It is to be located somewhere beyond a National Council of Churches but yet a long way from the united Church of China. We want to protect the unity we have entered into thus far, but we also need to protect and indeed encourage the variety and the many-colored splendor of the Church of Jesus Christ without which unity is barrenness. We look for successful experiences as well as experiences of failure in this area. The Uniting Church of Australia is such an inspiring newborn thing in church history that we are excited by the great opportunity to learn about both the path it has traversed and its way ahead.

As to what we have heard of God's message, if any, that may be of importance to other churches, it is perhaps this: God's strength is found in our weakness. Ours is a weak church. Like the Christians in Corinth not many of us are wise according to worldly standards, not many are powerful, not many are of noble birth. The years of the so-called Cultural Revolution were times of nationwide suffering under political ultra-leftism. The policy of religious freedom was trampled upon by the power of lawlessness, and all our churches were closed down for over ten years. Christians could only meet in homes if we could meet at all. That was all the Christianity we had to start with when the Cultural Revolution came to nothing and the policy of religious freedom could be in operation again. Yet, we have seen with our own eyes how true Paul's words are when he says: "But God chose what is foolish in the world to shame the wise, God chose what is weak in the world to shame the strong, God chose what is low and despised in the world, even things that are not, to bring to nothing things that are." Many Chinese Christians, in the spirit of the message to the church in Laodicea have indeed bought some gold refined in fire, some white clothes to clothe themselves, and ointment for their eyes so that they see how the weakness of God is stronger than men. Through all the thick and thin of those years, Christians seemed to hear more distinctly the echo of the very assuring words "It is the Lord," and to have their faith in the Risen Lord strengthened. Protestant churches are being opened or reopened in the last few years at the rate of one each day. Evangelism, Christian nurture, religious publication and theological training are extending, especially locally and regionally. An old Chinese poem seems to express aptly our situation:

> With mountains and waters all around,
> we wondered whether there was a way out,
> Yet, in the dark shades of willows,
> flowers brightened us up
> and we soon found ourselves reaching another village.

And we came to realize more surely than ever that between alpha and omega there is not a straight line, but many curves and zigzags. Catastrophes and sufferings are but the mother's birth pangs. They bring forth one after another newborn lives, "for the end is not yet."

"When a woman is in travail she has sorrow, because her hour has come; but when she is delivered of her child, she no longer remembers the anguish, for joy that a child is born into the world." This, to us, is history. We know God is not a taskmaster. As Hosea tells us, he leads us with cords of compassion and bands of love; he becomes to us as one who eases the yoke on our jaws, who bends down to us and feeds us. The root attribute of God is not his omnipotence or his omniscience, or his omnipresence, or his self-existence, but his love. Love is not just an attribute of God, but is of God, for God is love. He is the Lover at the heart of reality. The disclosure that God is one who loves with the kind of love as enacted in Jesus Christ, crowns and corrects whatever else that may be said about God. Love is creative and seeks the very best. Everything that is truly good will not be lost but will be preserved and transformed for that Kingdom to come in which Love will be supreme. That is essentially what we mean when we say God is sovereign.

The self-governing, self-supporting and self-propagating church of China still has many baffling problems, some of which I have already mentioned but, under God, she is not weaker but stronger, the number of Christians not smaller but bigger, the light of their witness not dimmer but brighter, and the range of their unity is wider than ever in its history. Our prayer—and we know you will want to make this your prayer too—is that that part of the Body of Christ which is in China may in a true sense and in all situations accept Christ's love for her, and his consecration and cleansing, so that Christ might present her to himself all glorious, with no stain or wrinkle, holy and without blemish (Eph. 5:26–27).

Our visit to Australia is an important landmark in the history of Christianity in China. We have before us a period of mutual sharing of God's messages to you and to us. We look forward to a most enriching two-week-long spiritual banquet ahead of us. We thank God because we are sure that, through this visit, Chinese Christians will be stronger Christians, owing to the life and witness and prayer of our fellow Christians of Australia.

—Sermon in Sydney Cathedral, March 18, 1984

# LOVE AND OPTIMISM

1949 was a special year for China. From one standpoint the United States "lost" China in that year and, from another, in that same year the Chinese people won our liberation. For us Chinese Christians that liberation marks the beginning of a process in our church known as the Three-Self Movement. I will have other chances to go into that movement. For the present I will try to describe to you how Chinese Christians have striven to find our own path in the theological undergirding of our faith.

There were two things that greatly jolted us Chinese Christians upon liberation. First, through direct contacts with revolutionaries, we found them on the whole very different from Chiang Kai-shek's KMT officials, and far from the caricature made by some missionaries and Chinese church leaders. They were certainly not the monsters and rascals they were said to be, but quite normal human beings with idealism, serious theoretical interests and high ethical commitment. For the liberation of their compatriots, many of them sacrificed their all. To serve the people was not only a slogan but also their life-purpose. They have taken over from ancient Chinese Christian sages the teaching that they were to be "severe in making demands on themselves" and "sad before the whole people are sad and happy only after the whole people are happy." Many practiced mutual criticism and relentless self-criticism in order to make themselves useful to the revolutionary cause. And, although they had no high regard for religion at all, they did not attempt to persecute or liquidate religion either. Here I am of course talking about the true revolutionaries, neither the pseudo-revolutionary ultra-leftists of a later decade, nor the disappointing party members whom the rectification movement today aims to reform. In discovering these true revolutionaries the Chinese were both happy for seeing in them the hope for the future of China, and fearful before the haunting question whether there was still any ground for the existence of Christianity. Indeed, at that time, a number of Christians, in joining revolutionary ranks, did move away from the church and from faith.

Second, there were some in the church who refused so stubbornly to be impressed by the new arrivals on the scene that they began to advance theological, but highly political, arguments to negate Liberation and new China. The world is the realm of Satan, they said, condemned to imminent destruction. The Christian is not to love the world and whatever is in it, even that which is lovable. Those who accept Christ and those who do not constitute an absolute contradiction, with no common language between the two. Human beings are evil and a person who does not confess faith in Christ can do nothing good, and the better his or her conduct, the more truly he or she is Satan masquerading as an angel. The animal with two horns and the red horse referred to in Revelation are actually representations of the Communist Party. On the basis of these hermeneutics new China will be short-lived. The church is holy and without blemish and, therefore, needs no change and should reject all criticism and self-criticism. The right-wrong question or the good-bad dichotomy is not God's concern. What God is concerned with is not any ethical distinction between good and evil, right and wrong, justice and injustice, because God is opposed not only to human evil but also to human good. The doctrine of the security of the believer ensures those elected by Christ the freedom to do anything, while others are condemned no matter how good their work is. This provided the assurance of God's acceptance of a Christian even if he or she should commit all sorts of crimes against the new life the people had only recently entered into. That is antinomianism and, in the early fifties, was the main theological weapon used by those in church circles who were determined not to be reconciled to the fact of new China. It won some Christians for a time, but was disgusting to many more Christians, and drove some of them away from the church for good.

These two facts set Chinese Christians thinking. On the one hand, while being truly impressed by the conduct and deeds of the revolutionaries, many of us found it impossible to take leave of Christ but chose to say with Peter, "You, Lord, have the words of eternal life. To whom can we go?" On the other hand, antinomian reactionism actually wanted us to stand and work against the people's liberation movement with all its goodness and beauty, and that was certainly an ethically indefensible alternative. Caught in between, Chinese Christians all over the country started to do theological reflection on their own. It was a mass movement seeking theological reorientation, entirely spontaneous, involving tens of thousands of Christians in re-studying the Bible in relation to social changes around us and in discussion, oral as well as written. I do not know if there was any phenomenon in church history that was comparable. Perhaps because history has traditionally been written as the feats of individual leaders and geniuses, any mass movement, least of all a theological one, would seldom have been given importance. But, in China in the early '50s, theology came out of the theologian's study and became a tool in the hands of laymen and women struggling to keep their faith vital and yet enabling them to relate themselves positively to the new reality as they found it. This was a mass movement for self-enlightenment, not incomparable to the Enlightenment in Europe, if we remember Immanuel Kant's characterization of the Enlightenment as "man's release from his self-incurred tutelage." And tutelage is "man's inability to make use of his understanding without direction from another." Kant says, "Have courage to use your own reason! That is the motto of the Enlightenment!"

Participants in this movement of theological rethinking were at first mostly rank-and-file Christians and clergy at the grassroots. Those theologically trained tended to keep themselves a little aloof from the discussion that they perhaps regarded as something not quite sophisticated enough. This is understandable; they were situated in the rear and hence not quite sensitive to the poignancy of the new problems, and rather critical of theological propositions crudely put, while lay Christians were situated at the boundary between the church and the world, and could not but feel the pressure of these problems and be driven to formulate questions, think them through and attempt to answer them. Their main recourse had to be to the Bible which, when re-read, gave them "new lights" or "new insights," as so commonly referred to in China since then.

A mass movement is not like doing embroidery and cannot be expected to show neatness and precision. There is no lack of over-statements. But two lines of W.H. Auden's poetry give a good description of the contribution the theological mass movement made to the Chinese Church:

> Ruffle the perfect manners of the frozen heart,
> And compel it once again to be awkward and alive.

Much of the discussion at the early stage had to do with questions about the world and about human beings. The world is certainly no paradise, but is it hell? Human beings are of course no angels, but are they, as a result of Adam's sin, so depraved that they are completely insulated from truth, goodness and beauty, each of them, in the words of Calvin, just "a worm five feet tall"?

To our revolutionary humanist friends, we like to point out that between the actual moral state of humanity as it is and the vision of the highest state humanity aspires to attain, there is distance which humanity by its own ability certainly cannot bridge. Many a conscientious revolutionary, in all their seriousness in self-examination, would readily feel at home in Paul's predicament about his failure to do what he knew he ought to do, and his inclination to do the very thing that he hated (Rom. 7:15). In other words, human beings are not in the state that God means them to be in. The factor in human nature which makes this so is appropriately called by Christians sin. Human beings cannot depend on themselves but have to depend on God's deliverance in order to rise from that state. True, as far as China is concerned, the change from feudalism-capitalism to socialism is all-important for the restoration of human dignity, but the change has not done away with this state of human spiritual poverty. "Lord, you have made us for yourself so that we can find no rest until we find it in you." Many human beings living within the socialist social system can echo this utterance of Augustine's from the depths of their hearts. So, in China today whether religion still has its place to exist in spite of the improvement in the material, cultural and moral life is no longer a question for Christians. The fact that the number of Christians in China has increased and not decreased in the last thirty-five years also partially answers the question. We only hope and pray that things will change in church and society in such a way that the day will soon come for the present more or less frozen state of mutual respect between Christians and revolutionaries in matters of basic convictions to be supplemented by a kind of conversation between them that will strengthen and not impair mutual understanding and national unity.

On the other hand, it is important for any understanding of the Chinese Christians' mind to know that for thousands of years in the teaching and writings of sages and scholars there has been no idea of an inborn perversity in human nature. Rather than seeing any need for trying to explain this perversity by resorting to some theory of a fall on the part of the first human beings, ancient Chinese folklore simply accepts the natural goodness and strength of human beings. The first ancestors of humanity were Fu Xi and Nü Wo who supposedly lived at the time the universe was first opened up. "Nü Wo tempered multi-coloured stones to mend the heaven with, and chopped off the feet of sea turtles with which to support heaven at its four corners." (Lie Tzu: *Emperor Tang's Queries*; also Huai Nan Tzu: *Lessons from Surveying Cosmic Mysteries*.) So, it was a human being who mended the broken heaven and set up pillars to support it when it got slanted. The human person is the supreme hero on whom even the universe depends for support. This conception of the relation between the celestial and the human is vastly different from much of Western philosophical anthropology.

Mao Zedong the poet was very much an inheritor of this tradition when he wrote:

Mountains!
Piercing the blue of heaven, your barbs
unblunted!
The skies would fall
But for your strength supporting. (1934 or 1935)

Mencius, widely regarded in China as second only to Confucius himself, taught that human nature is essentially good. It was he who said, "All human beings are compassionate in heart," and referred to that universal compassion as "the beginning of benevolence." This compassion and humility, discrimination between right and wrong and sense of shame are all-innate and are "the beginnings of goodness." Since the Song dynasty this has been the prevailing view on human nature among Chinese intellectuals. Down to the 1920s any Chinese pupil in learning the first Chinese characters would study the "Three-Character Rhyme," which opens with the sentence "At birth, a person is good by nature."

Because of the age-long education in this spirit, Chinese, in spite of all the suffering they have borne, are at the bottom of their hearts optimistic. They are likely to affirm that even in war what is disclosed of men and women is not just their brutality and evil, but also their fortitude and comradeship. Then, in the course of the Chinese revolution and reconstruction also, there have emerged countless men and women of courage, ingenuity and self-sacrifice.

From this background it is easy to see why Christians who do recognize the fact of sin and human finiteness find it impossible to go so far as to ignore the latent image of God in man and the indwelling of the Holy Spirit in the world by lightly resorting to the formula of "utter depravity," or seeing with Nietzsche, humanity as "only a disease on the skin of the earth."

We do not want to negate all cultures outside of the influence of the church. There are certainly initiatives approaching in various degrees the Christian understanding of God in these cultures that we cannot afford to sweep aside as valueless. We find, for instance, that 3,000 years ago the *Classic of Poetry*, in a section named *Da ya*, had this to say:

Abundant sacrifice to Heaven stood.
Burnt-oblation ascending,
Divine favor descending,
Simple fragrance arriving timely,
God's blessing bestowed kindly.
After her son's selfless offering,
Eternal afflictions cease coming.

And Lao Tzu is supposed to have said over 2,500 years ago:

There is already begotten before
Heaven and Earth came into being:
serenely silent,
peacefully alone,
eternally faithful,
the Immovable Mover, like
the caring Mother of all things.
I do not know its name
And describe it as Tao.

Can we fairly say that these are worthless or worse than worthless just because they have emerged outside the Christian tradition? Toward non-Christian spirituality we certainly should avoid the arrogance of the elder brother in our Lord's parable, or that of Jonah in his attitude to the Ninevites. We should welcome any and every move Godward on the part of men and women, no matter how slight.

Human sin has affected creation but the created world after all is still under God and it is not the devil's occupied territory. Otherwise in what sense can we honestly say "God so loved the world that he gave his only begotten son to the world," or that God became flesh in Jesus Christ? Commenting on Romans 1:20 Luther says, "For all the things that God made were 'very good' (Gen. 1:31) and are still good." For his proofs Luther went on to quote from 1 Timothy 4:4: "Everything created by God is good," and from Titus 1:15: "To the pure all things are pure." Luther affirms that "all creation is the most beautiful book or Bible; in it God has described and portrayed Himself."

In the 1950s, Chinese Christian journals published hundreds of articles dealing with the question of the world and of humanity. What I have given you is only a description of the general ideas advanced in those years.

From debating on the level of God's creation and the indwelling of the Holy Spirit not only in the church but also in the world and in history, Chinese Christians moved forward and grounded our thinking on a more solid Christological foundation. Many Chinese Christian intellectuals from a social gospel background found, as if for the first time, the Christ of St. John's Gospel and Ephesians and Colossians and claimed him as their own. He is the pre-existent Logos, the crown or the fulfillment of all creation, the revealer in all fullness of its nature and meaning. His Incarnation is not an intrusion into an alien world, but a divine yes to creation and God's means for human redemption and renewal. They listen with joy to Paul's words of adoration of the Christ as "the image of the invisible God, the first-born of all creation; for in him all things were created, in heaven and on earth, visible and invisible, whether thrones or dominions or principalities or authorities—all things were created through him and for him. He is before all things, and in him all things hold together" (Col. 1:15–17). Christians in new China re-read this passage with thanksgiving because we find it liberating. The ascended Christ is like sunshine filling the universe, both its mountain and its valleys, and bringing out every spark of color latent everywhere. Reality is one gigantic process, one in which matter and simple organisms attain higher and higher forms of existence, with the loving community as the ultimate attainment of the image of God on the part of men and women, just as the triune God Himself is a community of love. It deepens our understanding of the Christ and puts the people's historical movements with all their shortcomings and flaws in the perspective of cosmic evolvement. T. S. Eliot describes aptly this experience of the discovery of the greater Christ:

> "The end of all our exploring
> Will be to arrive where we started
> And know the place for the first time."

Romans 5:15 becomes full of meaning to us as we read it again in the new light: "If by the offence of the one man all died, much more the grace of God and the gracious gift of the one man, Jesus Christ, abound for all." The words "much more" take upon themselves a meaning previously untapped. We are led to see Christ as stronger than Adam, his gift stronger than disobedience, and grace stronger than sin.

It is inconceivable that the incarnation of the Son of God should have made less of an impact on humanity than the fall of Adam. Too often we make sin universal while narrowing down divine grace and redemption to a limited few, as if Adam has left a deeper imprint on humanity than has Christ. The verse assures us that our human solidarity with Christ is more universal, more decisive and more efficacious than is our solidarity with Adam. The greatest word in the New Testament is not sin, it is Grace.

Justin Martyr spoke of *Logos Spermatikos*, the presence of seeds of the Logos in all human beings. This view has been received warmly by many Chinese thinking Christians in recent decades.

We also appreciate the words of Thomas Aquinas to the effect that grace does not supplant nature, but perfects it. Indeed the New Testament sees all creation as embodying Christ from the very beginning. Grace is not so much added on to nature, as in Luther's simile of snow falling on a dunghill, but is the ground for nature.

Christ spoke of the joy of the mother for having given birth to a child into the world. Here we are led to see that Christ harbors no antagonistic attitude to the world, to humanity and to nature.

Thus, as we shift away from the belief-unbelief antithesis as the sole question Christianity asks of humanity, to a greater appreciation of the unity of God's creative, redemptive and sanctifying work in the universe and in history, many contemporary thoughts and movements begin to be seen not in contrast with the divine revelation or destructive of it, but are rather aids in illuminating it, partial as they indeed are. They are not adversaries but glimpses of the way of Christ. In looking at realities this way, we think we are not diminishing the significance of the unique divine Christ, but are magnifying his glory and confirming his claims.

God being love, the final fate of happenings and undertakings in nature and history cannot be their total destruction. They will be sifted, some surely to be destroyed but others to be transfigured and sublimated in Christ and by Christ, to be received by God at the final consummation. They will be safe and secure in God's hand. Hence not only the historic but also the ultimate importance and value of what one does with nature and in the world, and what one makes of oneself.

China makes so much of 1949 as the year of the people's liberation that Christians elsewhere have wondered what Chinese Christians since 1949 think of liberation theology.

We think very highly of liberation theology as a theology permitting and mobilizing Christians in Latin America to join with the masses of people around them in their struggle for independence, democracy and a more humane socio-economic system. We also appreciate liberation theology for its emphasis on context and praxis. The resultant biblical hermeneutics is fresh, eye opening, morally compelling and politically conscientizing. We consider liberation theologians to be our friends and inspiring fellow-pilgrims.

Our reservation is that, much as we do see the urgency of the taking over of political power by the peoples in the Third World from the hands of foreign intruders and despotic rulers, we in our situation do not see fit to absolutize liberation and to make it the theme or content of Christian theology. We are ready to see context and praxis as a test-ground for truth, but hesitate to go further and take them as a source for salvific knowledge. Inductive knowledge basing its material on the experience of historical existence will need the depth and mystery of deductive knowledge with its basis in revelation. Messages we collect through both channels collaborate to lighten our darkness about human nature and to lead us to see that the theme of the Christian gospel and of Christian theology must of necessity be the reconciliation of God and humanity in Jesus Christ.

From our revolutionary history we do realize that the poor, by virtue of their disadvantageous position in society and their lack of vested interests, on the whole suffer less from attachment to the status quo, as they have nothing or little to lose in a revolutionary change, except the fetters of poverty and degradation. As a result, insofar as social questions are concerned, other things being equal, there is some epistemological advantage on their part that the privileged are not likely to possess to the same degree or with the same ease.

However, we, especially in our post-Liberation state, would hesitate to think that the poor, just because they are poor, are necessarily the bearers of truth and that the mandate of history is necessarily in the hands of the poor in their struggle against the rich. To be poor is miserable. The poor deserve justice. But poverty is no virtue, unless voluntary, and does not always bring with it wisdom. To make a messiah of the poor just because they are poor and to pit the poor against the rich without the guidance provided by correct theory is neither Marxist nor Christian. We saw its harm all the more clearly during the Cultural Revolution that turned out to be very anti-cultural and not in any sense a revolution either.

In post-Liberation China, especially after the problem of private ownership of the means of production had been solved, we entered the historical period of national consolidation and reconstruction. The advocates of "perpetual revolution," however, still saw class struggle as the key for this stage of history, as much as it was during the previous stage when the forces of reaction were still in power. In order to make revolution perpetual, they decided that the revolutionary camp was to be composed of all the poorer people and the counter-revolutionary camp was to be composed of the richer persons, especially the intellectuals and the veteran revolutionaries who were now the power-holders. We saw the havoc this view of history caused to the unity and the reconstruction of the country. These ultra-leftist dogmatists in the name of revolution created a tremendous amount of chaos and anarchy that hurt so many innocent people. They did many of the things that the enemies of China would like to have done but were unable to do.

Negative praxis in China teaches us a lot about the danger of absolutizing the revolutionary justice of the poor just by virtue of their poverty. We need a saner understanding of human nature, including the human nature of the poor, so as to work for a social system in which the power of human egoism can be effectively curtailed and in which human nature finds the best environment possible for its flowering into something of beauty.

Thus, while traditional Western theology dialogues with Western philosophy and explains sin in terms of the history of the doctrine of sin, and liberation theology dialogues with present-day Third World realities and aims at overcoming the forces of sin through social struggle, we in China want our church and theology to take root in the Chinese soil, and guard the concept of sin both from its simplistic denial by humanist optimism and its unwarranted universalization in the name of orthodoxy. If much of European theology helps believers live with the reality of world hunger and liberation theology moves them to share in the struggle for overcoming hunger, we in new China are concerning ourselves with the evangelistic task of showing our fellow-citizens, to whom hunger is no longer the number one problem, that we do not live by bread alone, but by the word of God's mouth.

Ours is a big but in many ways still backward country. Our church is a small one, still having the task to live down completely the stigma of being a Western import. In the last thirty-five years our experiences as a nation, as a church, and as individual Christians go a long way to tell us that strength is found in weakness and life in death. Resurrection from the dead to us in not just something that happened to Christ, but a principle or law that governs nature and history. An old Chinese poem seems to express aptly our experiences.

> With mountains and waters all around
> We wondered whether there was a way out.
> Flowers brightened us up in the dark shades of willows,
> And we soon found ourselves reaching another village.

And we came to know the Risen Christ all the more intimately. We realize more surely than ever that between alpha and omega there is not a straight line, but many zigzags and curves. Catastrophes and sufferings, of which we had plenty during the so-called Cultural Revolution are but the mother's birth pangs. They bring forth one after another newborn things, "for the end is not yet." "When a woman is in travail she has sorrow, because her hour has not yet come; but when she is delivered of her child, she no longer remembers the anguish, for joy that a child is born into the world" (John 16:21). This, to us, is history. Creation is a process as yet incomplete and subject to frustration. Birth pangs are antecedent to the emergence of creatures who will eventually respond to their Creator and cooperate among themselves lovingly, intelligently and voluntarily. They will then be truly sons and daughters, not slaves. A world still in this process must inevitably be one in which ugliness and devilry have their place. We may well recall the inspiring words of Teilhard de Chardin: "Someday, after we have mastered the wind, the waves, the tide and gravity, we shall harness for

God the energies of love; and then for the second time in the history of the world man will have discovered fire."

Our Christology is not one that lingers at the divinity and Godlikeness of Christ, but is one that tells of the Christlikeness of God. In Christ we know God is no severe taskmaster. As Hosea tells us, he leads us with cords of compassion and bands of love; he becomes to us one who eases the yoke on our jaws, who bends down to us and feeds us. The root attribute of God is not his omnipotence, or his omniscience, or his omnipresence, or his self-existence, or his majesty and glory, but his love. Love is not just an attribute of God, but is Godlike, for God is Love. He is the Lover at the heart of reality. The disclosure that God is one who loves with the kind of love as embodied in Jesus Christ, crowns and corrects whatever else may be said about God. Love is creative and seeks the very best. God is not only the source of cosmic order and the first cause of all happenings in the world. In a more important sense, God is the Lover to whom every chain of cause and effect returns in the end. Everything that is of some good is not going to be lost but is safe in God, that is, will be preserved and transformed for that Kingdom to come in which Love will be supreme. That is essentially what is meant when we say God is sovereign.

With this theological orientation we seem to approach the vicissitudes of world affairs with a calm detachment and passionate involvement. It is a longer view of history than any humanly possible, and yet makes sharing in the day-to-day burden and struggle for the renewal of the people's life worthwhile. It makes the role of Christians at once participatory and critical.

After all these years we still have different theological tendencies. But they coexist in mutual respect within the fellowship of Christians holding to the content of the historic creeds. A Christology true to the New Testament and to the tradition of the church, evolved in a mass movement, and shared by most Christians, is providing the theological ground for the unprecedented wide-ranging postdenominational unity that the China Christian Council embodies.

What has been said above is merely one Chinese Christian's assessment of the theological fermentation in China in the wake of her political liberation.

The seven churches in Asia Minor were situated in different milieus and faced with different problems and consequently received different messages from the Holy Spirit. But, at the end of all seven messages, the same exhortation appears: "He who has an ear, let him hear what the Spirit says to the churches." This explains the desire on the part of Japanese as well as Chinese Christians to get acquainted with each other's spiritual histories and dramas. Our present visit in Japan and this presentation have been made with the faith that, through hearing the Spirit's messages to each other, Christians in Japan and in China can strengthen each other and together enter into the wisdom of God more deeply.

—Doshisha University, 1984

# LOVE SEES THE BIG PICTURE

Doctors and medical students generally assume: "As long as I am curing diseases I must be all right." The world's problems are indeed complicated but, for a doctor, the question is simple. He cannot be far from right, as long as he is busy curing diseases.

But do they have the right to think that their duty is "simple"? Can the clinic be an ivory tower? In this "one world" can anybody rightly undertake a merely technical job without thinking of its implications and repercussions on other people's lives?

In a novel called, *The Cross and the Arrow,* we are told of a house owned by a group of Nazi army officials in which they put twelve charming-looking girls. A doctor was kept in the house to keep the girls free from diseases and infection, so as to protect the Nazi officials. The doctor did his job wonderfully well. None of the twelve suffered from V. D. The Nazis could use them in any way they chose. But, at the end of a short period, the girls could not bear any more of it. They all became insane.

Was that doctor's job simple, then? "As long as I am curing diseases I am all right." Does one have the right to take that for granted? Can one really cure diseases without taking into consideration men and women as total personalities? Is a doctor's job just the "simple" and "technical" one of fighting against germs in human bodies, or is it really a job of repairing personalities? In the case of that particular doctor in the story, was he in any way responsible for driving the girls to insanity? Was he treating the girls as things to be used or as persons? In the middle of the night, when he examines himself, can he have a quiet conscience and consider himself a "good doctor"?

There is another story, "The Soldier Who Has Not Yet Died," written by a Japanese novelist who was put in jail because of the publication of that story during the war years. He was talking about his own mental struggle. As a medical student in Tokyo he had to study so hard to know anatomy, surgery, etc., in order to cure diseases. But he found it was so easy for people to be killed—through the massacres on the battlefields and through the slower process of factory life, child labor, undernourishment, unsanitary housing, etc. "We are restoring individuals to health, one by one, through a very careful and slow process. But look at the mass production of deaths and of maimed bodies by war and social injustice. The social system we are living in is nullifying our hard efforts." This terrible feeling of frustration every sincere and thinking medical student must have!

The dilemma, of course, is felt not only by doctors and medical students, but also by people in all specialized fields. There is the social worker who follows up one case day and night, but the world is producing more cases in one day than all the social workers can possibly handle in a year. There is the engineer who thinks that his job is to construct bridges and highways and residences for the benefit of his fellow men, but these things can all be destroyed overnight in a war, and even he himself is enlisted to do his bit in defending "my country, right or wrong." There is the minister who considers his job to preach the gospel of peace and love, but there are so many other forces, political, economic and military, undoing on a much larger scale the very things he tries to do. The clinic, the church, the laboratory, the workshop, the farm, etc., are all not good ivory towers in which we may disregard what others are making the world to be.

Especially after the invention and use of the atomic bomb, more and more conscientious scientists have come to wonder whether there can really be such a thing as the "amorality" of science, whether the scientist has the right to limit himself to "pure science." In fact he has come to realize that science can no longer be "pure" or "neutral" in the present-day world. It has to serve some cause. The question is what cause or whose cause we should make it serve.

In the past, we could have told ourselves: "Our job is pure research. We are not interested in other affairs. We are concerned only to discover facts and processes. How our discoveries may be used by others is no concern of ours." But, today, scientists are realizing the selfishness and danger of that attitude. They are beginning to say: "We cannot be content to sell our skill and knowledge to the highest bidder. We have to ask to what purpose our work is to be put. Will it serve to enrich a few individuals and endanger the welfare and peace of the whole world or will it be for the benefit of mankind in general? We dare not face the tribunal of our conscience if in our absorption in 'technical science' we are unwittingly contributing to making the world more miserable." The scientist is coming out of his laboratory and wants to find out what is happening in the world.

In the January 1947 issue of the *Atlantic Monthly* under the title, "A Scientist Rebel," Professor Norbert Weiner, a mathematical authority whose ideas played a significant part in the development of the theories of guided missiles during the war, expressed his great indignation at being requested by another technician to supply certain information that would perfect the atomic bomb, less than two years after victory over Germany and Japan. He said in part, "In the past the comity of scholars has made it a custom to furnish scientific information to any person seriously seeking it. However ... (Now) to provide scientific information is not necessarily an innocent act, and may entail the gravest consequences ... The experience of the scientists who have worked on the atomic bomb has indicated that in any investigation of this kind the scientist ends by putting unlimited powers in the hands of the people whom he is least inclined to trust with their use ... I do not expect to publish any future work of mine which may do damage in the hands of irresponsible militarists...."

Technical knowledge is important. But it is more important that the right person is going to use the knowledge. In other words, we have to ask ourselves in receiving technical training: What are we going to use it for? I am interested to know whether a knife is sharp or not, but I am much more anxious to know in whose hand that knife is put, especially if it is sharp. Our technical skill is just comparable to the sharpness of a knife. If an education merely imparts or transmits certain information and data and skills, it is like merely sharpening a knife without seeing to the sanity of the one holding it, or like training ourselves to shoot arrows without pointing them to any target.

That leads us to the question of the purpose of receiving a university education. Is it a good university education if it just imparts technical competence in a particular field? Should it also help students answer aright the question: What are you going to do with it?

In moments of crisis and decision, it is not your technical knowledge that counts. It is what you are that counts. The heroic deed of Dr. Slotin clearly shows the point. He was a young Canadian scientist from Winnipeg who took part in the atomic research in New Mexico. One day, while experimenting in the laboratory, he detected an explosion. If he did not step forward to do something about it quickly, the whole group in the room would be destroyed. At the split of a second, he had no hesitation to let himself be killed in order to save the lives of the other scientists.

Was it his science or technical knowledge that made him do so? No, it was something else. What was that something else and could the universities he attended claim the credit for having given him that something? What was in his mind when he took that step? Did he expect the surviving scientists to continue to work on the atomic research to help destroy the world? Or did he die in order to help bring life and prosperity and happiness to men and women of the world?

There are universities in our world today where the reason for their being maintained does not seem to be the education of persons but the production of technical workers. Through technicalization and departmentalization, they are no longer "universities" in the true sense of the word ... They are places for the acquisition of nuggets of knowledge and certain skills. A graduate in engineering in such an institution is hypothetically a good engineer. But I question how good an engineer he can really be, if he has not been primarily educated as a person, whose technical development is not achieved at the expense of other values but is rather achieved in unity and harmony with the maturation of other interests and abilities, especially those enabling him to enjoy, appropriate and develop creatively the rich, universal, cultural heritage of human history. But, unfortunately, as he is, there are reasons to classify him in the category, not of socialized and individualized personalities, but of sliding rules, T-squares, thumb tacks and reinforced concrete with which he can feel very much more at home. Of course, this kind of narrowing down of life does not necessarily happen to engineers, but can happen to any university student. For instance, one writer has somewhere asked the embarrassing question of, "How many students first became anti-Semitic or anti-Black and assumed a false sense of racial snobbishness during their college days?"

A university is true to its highest calling only as it moves its students to seek a more abundant life by relating their life-purpose to the whole of mankind as a world community. It is here that the Student Christian Movement is both a witness and a help. The Canadian Student Christian Movement is a fellowship of university students who want to make the most of their university life as Christians and in fellowship with other Christians. It helps the universities do a total job.

—From *The Canadian Student*, 1947

# A CHRISTIAN'S APPROACH
# TO THE BIBLE

I feel it is a great honor as well as a heavy responsibility to address this assembly of biblical scholars. Talking to you about the Bible is like bringing coals to Newcastle. But my excuse is a recent report that people in

Newcastle are no longer digging coal there. They have found importing coal from China to be actually less expensive, and prefer to keep the coal there for possible future emergency.

I am to say something about the Chinese Christians' approach to the Bible. Though my remarks are based on Chinese Protestantism, I hope the scholars of Judaism and Islam present will gain something of the flavor of Chinese religion.

Let me begin by saying that most Chinese Protestants are Bible-loving, Bible-possessing and Bible-reading Christians. The Bible occupies an especially important place in Chinese Christians' thinking and life. It is a living reality or "real presence." This is especially so since their Bibles were mostly taken away from them by the Red Guards during the Cultural Revolution, and it is only recently that they have been able to possess Bibles again.

I think there is a need to mention certain historical and theological facts that have conditioned greatly the Chinese Christians' approach to the Bible.

(1) China is the homeland of Confucius. The humanist, ethical cultural tradition of China of 2,500 years' standing tolerates religion, but religion is no big thing. This has been intensified in the last forty years by an official ideology which has even less appreciation of religion.

(2) China was a mission field. The Western missionary work put its emphasis mainly on extension and not so much on the building up of the church as the Body of Christ. Evangelistic missionaries were mostly inclined toward fundamentalism, hence the preponderance in China today of evangelicalism and fundamentalism.

(3) In recent years there has not been communication with churches in other lands. The resultant isolation is hard to overcome even now.

(4) Non-Roman Catholic Christianity has entered the period of post-denominational unity. This unity, as is embodied in the China Christian Council, is of very wide range. We are thankful for this unity. However, it curtails to some extent theological creativity and ecclesiological pioneering out of a fear for upsetting that unity.

(5) Since the Cultural Revolution, there has been nationwide criticism of a dogmatic approach to Marxism. Among scholars in the social

sciences, proceeding from a word or phrase of Karl Marx is no longer in vogue as a methodology. It has been replaced by investigation into religion as it exists in our society. A simplistic equating of religion with opium—a word with unpleasant historical associations for Chinese people—is now considered superficial. More and more scholars feel that the term opiate is an inadequate definition of religion and that Chinese religion can, to some extent, be adapted to socialism.

These facts do mean that we are encumbered by heavy burdens past and present, but do not mean that Chinese Christians' biblical understanding has remained changeless. The freeing of the Chinese Church from its tutelage under Western missions and its need to take into account somehow the Chinese context make certain theological affirmations and accommodations unavoidable, and that has had quite significant effects on the way the Bible is approached.

I spoke of the strong fundamentalist presence within Chinese Protestantism but, if we take the last forty years as a whole, we must say that the Chinese fundamentalists have changed a lot too. A most marked sign of their change is the recognition that the Bible is an open book that permits and asks Christians to constantly reap from it new insights. They like to talk about the "new light" and the "manna" which is fresh every new day but becomes stale the next day. One of my fundamentalist colleagues uses the description of the opening of the sealed scroll by the Lamb with the marks of sacrifice as given in Revelation 5, to show that the Bible is not a sealed book and that the Lamb with the marks of sacrifice is continuing to open it for the Chinese Christians. They admit there is a reservoir of meaning in biblical texts for posterity to explore and appropriate. They should be able to agree somehow with Paul Ricoeur who says. "The text's career escapes the finite horizon lived by its author. What the text means now matters more than what the author meant when he wrote it," and "To make one's own what was previously foreign remains the ultimate aim of all hermeneutics." This approach to the Bible readies Chinese Christians to accept new ideas as long as there is no direct violation of their view of biblical authority and inspiration. It allows a good amount of give and take among Christians of varying theological shades. It is an implicit rejection of the monopoly of subjective individualistic interpretation and an actual affirmation of a more inclusive understanding of the Christian community, and that makes for a broader spectrum of unity.

No matter how greatly the Bible is honored from cover to cover, the actual working Bible for Christian individuals and groups is bound to be only selections of certain parts of the whole Bible, and the contents of these working Bibles change slightly or radically with the inner growth of the readers and changes in the social context. The way I choose to deal with my subject is to identify certain groups or clusters of biblical passages which have become often cited, memorized and preached upon by Chinese Christians in the last forty years, especially in the last ten years or so. In order to avoid too much arbitrariness, I am basing my choices mainly on a study of the articles that have appeared in the *Nanjing Theological Review* and *Tian Feng Monthly*.

In the first place, there are those biblical passages that have to do with thanksgiving for deliverance and with finding of strength in weakness. This is not hard to understand if we remember the suffering the Chinese Christians went through personally and as a church under ultra-leftism which was dogmatist, extreme and sometimes even brutal. It culminated in the ten years of the so-called Cultural Revolution when religious leaders were grouped together with intellectuals and higher political figures as persons who took the capitalist road. They had to go through criticism sessions and were treated as undesirable elements in society. All churches were closed down and put to other uses. The most Christians could do was to meet quietly in small groups of five or ten in homes. They could not understand why God allowed all of this to happen, and wondered in great anguish if this would not be the end of Christianity in China once more. Yet, they found strength in recalling, for instance, Christ's own words in the Beatitudes: "Blessed are you when men revile you and persecute you and utter all kinds of evil against you falsely on my account. Rejoice and be glad for your reward is great in heaven, for so men persecuted the prophets who were before you" (Matt. 5:11–12).

But the Cultural Revolution came to an end. We were ushered into a period of implementing the principle of religious freedom. Coming out of that period of suffering and bewilderment was in a real sense deliverance and liberation. Christians find Psalm 23 expresses most appropriately their experiences and feelings. At the end of the Cultural Revolution, those Protestant leaders on the national level who were still living and able to attend a meeting came together. They wasted no time on commiserating with each other or trumpeting about having borne suffering. Instead they drafted and sent out a pastoral letter which elaborated on Psalm 23, especially the verse "Even though I walk through the valley of the shadow of death, I fear no evil, for thou art with me, thy rod and staff, they comfort me." This verse has been resounding ever since. Such verses are played up neither for wallowing in one's personal suffering, nor in hostility to the world. They rather express the Christians' faith and thanksgiving for God's continuing presence and care. They are often quoted alongside other passages which speak of the ultimate triumph of God's justice, for instance, Isaiah 42:3: "A bruised reed he will not break, and a dimly burning wick he will not quench, he will faithfully bring forth justice," and 2 Corinthians 4:8–11: "We are hard pressed, but never cornered, bewildered, but never at our wit's end, hunted, but never abandoned to our fate, struck down, but never killed. Wherever we go, we carry with us in our body the death that Jesus died, so that in this body also the life that Jesus lived may be revealed. For Jesus' sake we are all our life being handed over to death, so that the life of Jesus may be revealed in this mortal body of ours."

In a devotional piece on Romans 9:21 ("Surely the potter can do what he likes with the clay"), my colleague Wang Weifan treats God's reshaping of ourselves in this way:

"God is the potter, we are clay. As the potter molds the vessel so we are shaped by the potter's hand. We may have been rejected as useless by the world, but God's profound grace will never abandon us. God will turn the potter's wheel and form us anew ... Though I be shattered, I will not complain, for God will gather up the pieces, and when they have been ground to dust and mixed back into the clay, God will work them anew and shape me to his use, in order to realize his beautiful plan."

Lao Tzu, a sage as ancient and as influential in China as Confucius, made a very good commentary on the biblical messages on the power of powerlessness when he said of water: "What is of all things most yielding can overwhelm that which is most hard. Being substanceless, it can enter in even where there is no crevice. That is how I know the value of action which is actionless."

As we look back, we are thankful for having suffered in our powerlessness with the rest of the Chinese people during the Cultural Revolution because that has become a token of our identity and credibility as a part of the people and increases our rapport with them. To suffer with the people is to relinquish any protection by foreign and domestic powers and thus to present Christianity as something Chinese with a right to be heard. In the 19th century Chinese Christians did not experience powerlessness because many were protected by unequal treaties and extra-territoriality. The unprecedented influx of new Christians in large numbers into the church today testifies to the power of powerlessness. In this way, unlike Job, we seem to have been enabled to see more clearly the value and tangible result of our suffering.

A second group of biblical passages that have taken on importance in the course of the last forty years has to do with our understanding of the person of Christ.

There have always existed side by side within Chinese Protestantism two theological lines which both stood in need of correction by a more biblical Christology. On the one hand, there were those whose concern was only soteriological and to whom Christ was only important as the great personal redeemer and savior from a world that was nothing but the occupied territory of Satan.

On the other hand, quite a large contingent of Chinese Protestant intellectuals embraced Christian faith largely owing to their fascination with Jesus the Teacher and by the Sermon on the Mount. Y. T. Wu, the founder of the Three-Self Movement, started off as a Christian through the impact of the Sermon on the Mount, although a much fuller Christian faith developed in him in subsequent years. Here is a description of his conversion experience from one of his own writings, dated 1947:

> "One spring night thirty years ago"—that was around the year 1917—"I was in the home of an American friend. I read the Sermon on the Mount in Matthew's Gospel for the first time. Like lightning, those three

chapters woke me up from my slumbers. I opened my eyes and saw a vision. I saw a great, noble personality, awesome and gentle, deep and penetrating—He took hold of my soul. He almost stopped me from breathing. When I returned home, I cried out for joy. I was moved to tears. I could not help confessing to this vision, 'Lord, you are my Savior.'"

That faith inspired Y. T. Wu and many others to devote themselves to the cause of national salvation in struggling against Japanese fascist aggression and that of liberation and people's democracy against the dictatorship of Chiang Kai-shek.

With the success of the people's revolutionary movement, the Communist Party, the People's Liberation Army, the people's government and the democratic parties all emerged before the people. They showed great moral caliber and had a high appeal to Christian intellectuals. These Christians felt that the New Being whom Paul talked about was there already, not in Christ but without him. Many of these Christians who were so attracted chose to join movements and organizations thought to be more effective. That was a time our church lost membership and some of our best intellects. Those who remained did not necessarily take a light view of the selflessness of many revolutionaries and the transformations in society. Many affirmed them as the work of God's hand and signs of his grace. But they did not want to quit the church. They somehow felt that, beyond the Sermon on the Mount, there was something which Christianity offered that made them want to say with Peter, "Lord, to whom shall we go? Your words are words of eternal life."

They still valued the Sermon on the Mount and Jesus as Teacher, but the times they were in demanded of them a faith more adequate, one that enabled them to affirm a uniqueness about Christ's teaching and give them a stronger buttressing of their faith in him. They began to study the New Testament anew. They were impressed, as never before, by the Christ as extolled in St. John's Gospel and some of the epistles, notably Colossians and Ephesians, the one through whom and for whom all things in heaven and on earth, visible and invisible, whether thrones or sovereignties or authorities or powers were created, and in whom all things hold together as Paul says in Colossians 1:13–20. There is Hebrews 1:3 where Christ is said to be the radiance of God's glory, the stamp of God's very being, one who sustains the universe by his word of power. Christ as Logos of St. John's Gospel comes to them in a new, powerful way. A new vista is opened when reading that Christ is the true light that gives light to everyone who comes into the world (John 1:9). All these passages help Chinese Christian intellectuals get a more solid grounding for their faith in Jesus Christ. They tell the Christians of something cosmic in the nature of Christ in whom all the truth, goodness and beauty they find in nature and human history abide and find their fulfillment and coronation. That discovery means a transition both from the Christ who is a moralist and from the Christ who unites himself only with believers to the Christ who fills all things. The Incarnation is not a remedy concocted to clean up the mess made by Adam's sin. Christ did not come into a world that is alien territory. The New Testament sees all creation as embodying Christ from the very beginning. Colossians 1:15 says that his is the primacy over all creation. This discovery of the fuller and greater Christ forbids us from depriving human activities outside the space of Christian faith of positive value.

Christ is the Christ of creation, but also the Christ of resurrection. If there is one New Testament word that has become so much more full of meaning to Chinese Christians, that word is resurrection. And if there is one name of Jesus that is more personal, more precious than any other name, and occupies the highest place in the faith of the Chinese Church, that name is the name of the Risen Christ. Resurrection and rising from the dead is no longer something just said of Christ. It is an experience and a truth of Chinese Christians ourselves. This is a personal Christ still, but with a transformed self-understanding of the relationship with Christ. It has been described by one Chinese evangelical as an experience similar to that of the Shulammite maiden in the Song of Solomon, the change from one who says, "my beloved is mine," (2:16) to "I am my beloved's" (7:10). Christ is no longer seen as a religious possession, but as the source of faith and the ground of one's being. In the same vein, Wang Weifan writes in his essay, "Changes in Theological Thinking in the Church in China":

"Thirty odd years ago, Jesus was for many Christians little more

than something to make up for human deficiency, a source of consolation in times of pain, someone to fill the void or compensate the loss …
Now Christ is rather the Leader to whom they are subject. They are
ready to follow Jesus to Gethsemane, no longer using 'Father give this
and that to me … but, instead, praying: 'Not my will but thy will be
done.'"

The discovery of the cosmic nature of Christ enlarges the
Christology of Chinese Christians of both kinds. It is a unifying experience that provides the theological groundwork for the wide range of
unity represented by the China Christian Council.

This experience of the Chinese Christians is aptly described by T.S.
Eliot when he wrote: "The end of all our exploring/Will be to arrive
where we started/And to know the place for the first time." It is good
to know the Greater Christ as if for the first time.

A third group of biblical passages that have drawn the Chinese
Christians' special attention includes those that speak of God's love and
lead us to think of this love as God's supreme attribute. There are passages that directly speak of God's great love such as "God so loved the
world that he gave his only Son. That everyone who has faith in him
may not perish but have eternal life" (John 3:16) and "God is love, he
who dwells in love is dwelling in God, and God in him" (1 John 4:16).
There are passages in which Jesus himself speaks of God's care for all
creation, including the lilies of the field and the birds in the sky (Matt.
6:26–30). There are Jesus' parables, such as those in Luke 15, using
human situations to show with what intensity God loves his lost children. When Jesus makes love his commandment, he is not imposing
any moral imperative arbitrarily, or a principle for peaceful interpersonal relationships. He is revealing something in the very nature of God
and the very structure of creation.

For a long time the church taught in actuality about a God whose
supreme attribute is not his love but his almightiness and terrifying rule.
Justification by faith as a doctrine is so exaggerated that this God, in his
righteousness and anger, judges men and women and condemns them
to eternal fire on the grounds of their disbelief. There is opposition and
enmity between God and the work of human hands, even all human
good work. He bestows his love only on the believers. The world is a

realm God has given up. Everything beautiful and attractive to the eyes and ears is the work of Satan in the garb of the angel of light. Believers are those rescued from this world. One consequence of this teaching is Christian's enmity toward those outside the fold of the church, somewhat like Jonah's toward the Ninevites.

Chinese Christians are coming out of this worldview and like to say with St. Paul: "The earth is the Lord's and all that is in it" (1 Cor. 10:26) and "Everything that God has created is good, and nothing is to be rejected provided it is accepted with thanksgiving" (1 Tim. 4:4). James says, "Every good and generous action and every perfect gift come from above, from the Father who created the lights of heaven" (1:18). The Old Testament appeals to "the starry heavens above and the moral law within" (Ps. 19) as declaring the glory and nature of God. Jesus explicitly bases his gospel of God's Kingdom upon evidence and similitudes from the natural order. We feel it is only this affirmation of the world that makes it possible to speak of Christians' joy in God's creation and of faith and celebration in God's doings.

Chinese Christians are not ridding themselves of the notion of sin. We know how human beings bring our ambiguous condition to every enterprise we undertake. Our seemingly disinterested acts frequently conceal interested motives. So many good human causes turn to their opposites in the course of their development. I have met several conscientious non-Christian revolutionaries who put a high demand on themselves who say they agree with Paul when he says, "I do not understand my own actions. For I do not do what I want, but I do the very thing I hate," in Romans 7:15. These clashes within the soul and the ambivalent character of whatever good one may do show how human beings are constantly in need of forgiveness, correction, healing, and spiritual support.

But the question remains as regards the degree of human fallenness and the justice of condemning the whole human race to utter depravity. We like to look upon redemption in continuity with God's creation and refuse to make the two antithetical. In China where, for hundreds of years, the first six Chinese characters a pupil was given to learn on the first day of schooling said that human nature was good. There is an understandable revolt to Nietzsche's treatment of human beings as "only a disease on the skin of the earth," or Calvin's reference to "a worm five feet high." In spite of the fall, a human being is still the image of God, and the mirror of his glory, as St. Paul says in 1 Corinthians 11:7.

Chinese Christians receive great consolation from Romans 5 where it is said, "God's act of grace is out of all proportion to Adam's wrongdoing. For if the wrongdoing of that one man brought death upon so many, its effect is vastly exceeded by the grace of God and the gift that came to so many by the grace of the one man, Jesus Christ ... If, by the wrongdoing of one man, death established its reign through that one man, much more shall those who in far greater measure receive grace and the gift of righteousness live and reign through the one man Jesus Christ." Here, St. Paul is making a comparison between the effect of Adam's sin and that of Christ's grace. We like to note especially how Paul uses expressions such as "out of all proportion," "is vastly exceeded," "much more," and "in far greater measure." Chinese Christians are elated and get a sense of liberation in reading this. Too often, we have made original sin universal while limiting grace and redemption only to the few who profess a belief in Christ. It really means that the Incarnation of the Son of God has made less of an impact on humanity than the fall of Adam. This is not a view that can go along with the vision of God whose name is love and whose concern is to create, that is, to redeem, educate and sanctify humanity toward perfection as free and intelligent co-creators.

To know God as love is to say that the supreme attribute of God is not his power and might, nor his omniscience, nor his deity, nor his majesty and dominion and righteousness. Transcendence signifies the inexhaustibility of the cosmic love and immanence, the unfailing presence of that love in the whole creation. Whitehead's caricature in *Process and Theology* of much of the prevailing theological notions of God of his day either as "the ruling Caesar, or the ruthless moralist, or the unmoved mover" has strong appeal to us, because these notions went to mission fields sometimes in even more aggravated forms. We yearn for a different God, a God who first of all loves as the Cosmic Lover, one whose love is exemplified in Jesus Christ. Chinese Christians want to depart from a rather severe and intimidating God, a cosmic tyrant, who is not the Christ like God the four Gospels make us want to believe in. Chinese Christians like the symbolism in Prophet Hosea (11:4) in referring to God intimately as the one who secures us with reins, leads us with bonds of love, lifts us like a little child to the parent's own cheek and bends down to feed us.

God's justice is not denied but it is a dimension of his love. This God hates and is angry too. But his anger and indignation are only the reverse side of his love. They are directed at that which hinders love. Only a God of love can "let justice roll down like the waters, and righteousness like an over-flowing stream" (Amos 5:24).

This emphasis on God as the great lover working out his purpose for the world brings in its train an understanding of reality as becoming. It gives us hope for and beyond history. We cannot fathom the actual time and the actual way the end of history as we know it will come about, but we can be sure that it will be the ultimate triumph of love and grace. Love accompanies the pilgrim but the way from alpha to omega is never a straight line. We have to go through much adversity but on the way we encourage each other, as we did during the years of the Cultural Revolution, by recalling Christ's own words: "A woman in labor is in pain because her time has come; but when her baby is born she forgets her anguish in her joy that a child has been born in the world." The church is the watcher on a watch-tower who sees the darkness that appears before dawn as well as the dawn that will surely arrive after darkness, and knows the anguish of birth in history as well as well as the joy, after birth pangs, of the coming of the newborn baby. As is so well said in Psalm 30:5: "Tears may linger at nightfall, but rejoicing comes in the morning."

A fourth group of biblical passages that have stood out these years have to do with the unity of Christians. I am thinking of such passages as the Psalmist's song on how good and pleasant it is to live together as brothers in unity, Christ's prayer for the oneness of his disciples in John 17 and Paul's polemic against division among Christians in 1 Corinthians Chapter 1 and his exhortation in Ephesians on one body, one Spirit, one hope, one Lord, one faith, one baptism and one God and Father of all. Passages like these have become important for two reasons: (1) to affirm the postdenominational unity Protestant Christians

in China have entered into, and to thank and praise God for that, and
(2) to argue against divisiveness and the tendency to return to old ways
so as to protect the post-denominational unity which is still in some
ways fragile.

We in China did reproduce many of the denominations in Western
countries. But, after all, denominational history was short in China;
denominationalism remained largely alien and Chinese Christians'
denominational loyalty was weak. Thus, we could leave denominations
behind without too much difficulty, especially under circumstances not
favorable to the proliferation of organizations that were not too different to begin with. But there have been three groups of Christians who,
owing to their particular ways of articulating their faith and of viewing
ecclesiology, do not quite feel at home in the postdenominational existence they have nevertheless entered, namely, the Seventh-Day
Adventists, the adherents of the Little Flock and those of the True Jesus
Church. In order to ensure our unity, we have the policy of mutual
respect in matters of faith and worship. However, experience tells us
that it is almost too hard to expect Christians in the majority to honor
to the full the special characteristics of those in the minority. And the
exaggeration of the unique points in the theological position of these
minority groups made by some of their leaders in some parts of China
makes the maintenance of unity still harder. We want to avoid the
restoration of any of those denominations. Many of our church leaders
return to the Bible for resources for the consolidation of our unity.

At this point I would like to add that we are only post-denominational. Our China Christian Council, which is the only Chinese national
Protestant body that has some ecclesial nature, is not the Church of
Christ in China, not yet anyway. It is more than a national council of
denominational churches but less than a national church. That is the
degree of unity we are able to reach so far and want to protect from retrogression.

We find the Bible with its central message of reconciliation and
covenanting a source book for inspiring Christian people's unity. There
are some people who seem to be anxious to bring about splits. In order
to justify themselves they also go to the Bible, but can only resort to
passages about those not within the Christian fold, such as "Can Christ

agree with Belial, or a believer join with an unbeliever?" This lack of fairness to fellow Christians is not anything rank-and-file Christians are likely to endorse.

By this time you will probably have got the impression that Chinese theologians have not ventured to take heroic, not to say sensational, steps to make headlines in their theological pursuits. It is our conviction that we should stay where our constituencies are and wrestle with their problems in ways helpful and acceptable to them. Each doing his or her own thing without regard to the need of the church in its present state, or to its acceptability by Christians, or to the harm it does to Christians' unity, is not something highly regarded or encouraged. Hence the importance given to Chinese evangelicalism and fundamentalism in our theological work.

In a time when there is much talk of political theology, the four groups of biblical passages that I have chosen as representative of the theological landscape in the church in China may sound odd to politically-minded Christians in the West, as they are all traditional inner-church themes. What I need to say is that it is exactly the orientation to the historic heritage of the church that enables the church I come from, a minority of less than one percent of the population, to keep its unity and survive, and to have something unique and at the same time appealing to present before our fellow Chinese.

—Speech at the Joint Meeting of the American Academy of Religion and the Society of Biblical Literature, 1990

જી

# ON CHRISTIAN THEISM

Our Christian belief in God is, generally speaking, not so much the result of reasoning or persuasion as of spiritual insight. This is not surprising. We know our mother not because we have been persuaded by some argument or demonstration but because from childhood on we have felt her love. Many carpenters who have never heard the pi equals 3.1416 still know that the circumference of a circle is a little more than three times its diameter and this is enough for the practical needs of their work.

But for the theological student or church worker today, just to believe in God and not to know how to give a reasoned explanation of this belief is not enough. Theological understanding is too important to be neglected. We do not subscribe to the various atheistic theories but we must also know where they are wrong and, even more, what the right view is. We must think deeper so that when we go out to preach the truth of the gospel our words may carry weight because of their reasonableness. In 1 Peter 3:15 we read, "Always be ready to make your defense to anyone who demands from you an accounting for the hope that is in you; yet do it with gentleness and reverence."

## CHRISTIANITY AND THE IDEALISM-MATERIALISM QUESTION

Is Christianity idealist or materialist? Many people both within and outside the church are interested in this question. Some Christians are trying to deny that Christianity is idealist because to be idealist, they think, is to be politically backward. Some are trying to prove that Christianity is materialist because to be materialist is assumed to be politically progressive.

Some people think that materialists are of necessity progressive and idealists are backward or even reactionary, but the situation is not as simple as that. The early Taoists and Lao Tzu and Chuang Tzu did not believe in God or in spirits and explained everything by the heavenly Tao resident in all nature. They had therefore a strong tendency toward atheistic and materialistic thought. But at the same time they had a strong aristocratic spirit and represented aristocratic interests. Wang Yangming's doctrine of an instinctive conscience would seem to be idealist but it encouraged a spirit of individual initiative, a recognition of right and wrong and a questioning of tradition, which both in his time and since has had a forward-looking influence too important to be neglected.

It is not natural to Christian understanding to divide all thinking into the two categories of materialist and idealist, with a deep gulf between then. People ask if Christianity is materialist or idealist. The question itself does not correspond with reality. Other people may ask the question if they like but we are not obliged to accept the dichotomy and answer it simplistically. To answer that question simplistically is to adopt a scheme or framework imposed on us from outside our Christian understanding.

There are many ways of dividing mankind. Some are universally recognized and others are questionable. No one questions the validity of dividing all mankind into the two categories of men and women, or of dividing the present generation into those born in either the 19th or the 20th century, for a 21st century birth is still to come and those born in the 18th century are now probably all dead.

But there are other doubtful classifications because they do not include all individuals. For example, some people in the West, in order to vilify socialist communities, would classify all socialists as either Stalinist or anti-Stalinist. But this classification is not a fair one and is, in fact, only intended to confuse the mind and break up socialist unity. Again, the Jews considered circumcision important and divided all men into the two categories of the circumcised and the uncircumcised. Paul said, "For neither circumcision nor uncircumcision is anything; but a new creature is everything." As a Christian, the question was whether a person had or had not become a new creature.

We do not think it is satisfactory classification to group all shades of thought under either materialist or idealist. It is a simplification of facts. Would it not be truer to say that there has never been a 100 percent materialist or a 100 percent idealist? Idealism and materialism not only stand opposed to each other, they also interpenetrate each other, for they are not only mutually exclusive, but mutually influential as well. They have points of disagreement as well as agreement. There is some idealism in a materialist and some materialism in an idealist. Someone has said, "Tao Xingzhi was once an idealist and his name then was Tao Zhixing. Afterwards he became a materialist and changed his name to Tao Xingzhi." But I cannot think of Mr. Tao as simply as that. Man is the most complex of animals and his thinking is very complex. In all thinking there is development. A man may change his name overnight but intellectual development cannot get away from the fact of a certain continuity in the process. The *Soviet Philosophical Dictionary* describes Pavlov in these words: "Great Russian physiologist and thinker, inheritor of 19th-century Russian materialistic philosophy and the progressive traditions of a naturalistic science ... his theories dealt a death blow to idealistic psychology and laid the foundation for a true materialist psychology." And yet we know that Pavlov was at least a devout member of the Orthodox church. Evidently the coexistence of materialism and idealism is as common as their mutual opposition.

It is even more difficult to classify Christianity as either idealist or materialist, because, although it is in form a product of history, it is essence not an ideology and not a structure built upon an economic base. Its true substance is revelation, the incarnation, and therefore it transcends all human lines of division. Some Christians accept the line between idealism and materialism and say, "We are not idealist," or even say, "We are materialist." This is all unnecessary because we do not need to accept the dichotomy itself.

Christianity, in its organization, its expression in thought and its ceremonies has of course been deeply influenced by human history but in essence it is not a fruit of history. The gospel comes from the free revelation of God. This gospel is Christ himself, through whom all things were made. A theologian of Western Europe has said, "The greatest danger facing Western theology today is that of reducing Christianity to an ideology and thus placing it in opposition to another ideology—communism." This is true. What we preach is the gospel. It is Christ and that is something entirely different from an ideology. It is something that moves in a different orbit from any system of thought. If we always remember that we will have a clear understanding from which to perceive that all talk of comparison of Christianity with communism, of similarities or differences, is beside the point and superfluous.

## IS CHRISTIANITY AN OPIATE?

"Religion is the opiate of the people." This caricature of Christianity is forceful and cutting.

But regardless of how applicable it is to Christianity, let us note first of all that the point of criticism is valid only as it is directed against the religion of certain time or of certain persons and not against religion itself at its highest.

To analyze the effect which religious belief can have on some individuals is permissible, but the question whether God exists or not is an entirely different thing. Let us grant, for argument's sake, that you have discovered that the religion of certain individuals has had a narcotic effect upon them. This discovery does not at all prove that the universe is without a creator. The mental state of some believers may be so chaotic that they seek for an anesthetic and use religion as an opiate. Some preachers may even take pride in presenting religion in this light and of course this is not good. But what does this prove regarding the existence of God? The thinking of some religious believers is backward and needs help, but the fact that these backward believers use religion as an opiate has no bearing on the question of the being of God, Similarly, if they do not resort to an opiate that would not prove either that God exists or does not exist. The existence of God is a different and independent question.

There are many things in the world that can be used as opiates, not just religion. Literature, art and science can all become means of intoxication and escape from reality. The other day we had a meeting with some students from the University of Nanjing, some of them students of astronomy. This is the point I tried to make: Let us imagine a man who because of some great grief has become very pessimistic about the world, his country and his family and so he seeks for an escape from reality in order to numb his mind. Is it not possible that such a man would choose astronomy as his opiate? Day and night he might sit at his telescope drawing calmness of mind from the great emptiness of space. But the fact that he was using astronomy as an opiate would not mean that the sun, the moon and the stars that he saw through his telescope did not really exist. On the contrary, it is possible that his observations might make a great contribution to the advance of astronomy. His subjective psychological state is one thing while the objective existence of the universe is quite another.

If anyone discovers that certain religious believers in certain periods of history have used religion as an opiate and should therefore draw the conclusion that God does not exist, we must say to them, "Your logic is not good. You have no right to draw this conclusion."

Certainly it is a painful fact, which we cannot deny, that religion as preached by some preachers and received by some believers is an opiate. The forceful statement "religion is the opiate of the people" was made not only by Marx but also by the English clergyman Charles Kingsley, a man who had great sympathy for the downtrodden working classes. At that time the destructive features of capitalism had appeared, the life and security of workers was without protection and even six-year-old children had to work in factories under inhuman conditions. In the fact of such conditions a large part of the church of those days did nothing but urge people to control themselves and accepting deprivation, saying that after this life they would enjoy happiness in heaven. That was why Kingsley made this stinging statement. But the use of Christianity as an opiate is an accident and does not belong to the essence of Christianity. In Matthew 27:34 we read that when our Lord was hanging upon the cross a well-meaning individual, wishing to relieve the pains of Christ's death, offered him a drink of some opiate, but when he had tasted it he would not drink. Did he not have the right to drink it? Why did he refuse? Our Lord, at the end of his human life, at the most important moment when he was bearing the sins of all mankind upon the cross, wanted to keep a clear mind to the very end. He was not willing to use a drugged and benumbed mind to complete the work which his Father had given him to do. See how, without hesitation, he refused the opiate. Consider, if he had consented to drink the drug, he might have escaped the pain, but then he would no longer have known what was going on around him. The seven great words from the cross would have been left unsaid and the meaning of the cross itself would have remained dark and unclear to posterity.

What Christ gives is forgiveness, consolation and strength—not a benumbed spirit. We pray, "Your will be done on earth as it is in heaven." Where is there any opiate in prayer? This is the highest religion, the religion of revelation that is Christianity. St. Ambrose (340–397) once said:

> "You rich men, when will your greed end? Will it continue until there is nothing left on earth but yourselves?

How do you dare to take all nature as your own? The world was made for all men—how can you claim it as your private property? Nature does not recognize the rich—it produces the common man. The products of nature are for the use of all and God wants the world and all it contains to be for the use of all." (Ambrose, *De Nabuthe Jezraelita*, [1 PL 14:732])

The saint who said this certainly was not a man who had been benumbed by some opiate. In the national museum of literature in Prague there is a statue John Hus, under which is carved this memorable saying of his, "Woe unto me if I remain silent. For it would be better for me to die than to not take a stand against great wickedness, as this would make me an accomplice to sin and hell." Who dares to say that a man who talks like this had been drugged with opiate? People do not take primitive conditions of early communist society as a reason for distrusting the future of the communist cause; they do not, because of the absurdities of alchemy, look down upon modern chemistry nor, because of the superstitions of old-time astrology, despise modern astronomy. In the same way we must not judge the gospel of Christ by narcotic religion

We should study religion concretely, and not proceed from *a priori* definitions; otherwise we will fall into the error of dogmatism. Feudalistic barons said they were acting for heaven and then proceeded to oppress the people. The Taiping leaders also said they had been appointed by heaven to liberate the people and they fought for them. Both used the word "heaven" but with what different meanings. If we say that religion is, by its very nature, reactionary so that its progressive manifestations are, for that reason, more dangerous than its reactionary manifestations, then what can we say of the Chinese Christian church today whose members have shown themselves able to support new China and uphold socialism?

## THE EXISTENCE OF GOD

The Bible does not discuss the question of God. The first book in the Bible does not begin with an argument in favor of the existence of God but with the declaration, "In the beginning God created the heavens and the earth."

Why did not God manifest himself to us in such a way that his existence could not be doubted? We know that God is invisible, infinite, indefinable. To lay down a definition implies limitation. But God is infinite and anything man can define is not God. Everything in the world is subject to definition—God alone defies every definition that man makes. St. Anselm said, "God is that, than which nothing greater can be imagined" (Anselm, *Proslogion*, ch. 4). Clement of Alexandria said, "We cannot know what God is but we can know a little of what he is not." If the existence of God were as plain to us as the existence of a table, what place would there be for faith? Faith is higher than scientific demonstration. Faith is the only thing in the world that will call people to great achievements and great sacrifices. Someone said, "Religion is betting your life on the existence of God." Yes, religion is exploration, fellowship, love, and deep calling unto deep. Science may one day discover the existence on Mars of intelligent beings like humans but that scientific demonstration will not give us fellowship with them. Fellowship can be established upon the basis of mutual trust.

Take the parable of the Prodigal Son. The elder brother was living a tasteless life without faith, hope and love. Although he daily saw the face of his father, his father's existence meant nothing to him, much less was there any real fellowship. But when the younger brother found himself in serious trouble his one thought was to return to the bosom of his merciful father. You may call it adventure or the great decision. Certainly it was a venture of faith. And so he returned. What he found was the love of a father and not the cold sentence of an impartial law. He truly became the son of his father. And after this experience his knowledge of his father and his relation with his father was something different from what it had been before. The father's love has now transcended scientific reasoning and become the experience of faith, This relation and this experience was not understood even by the older brother and outsiders would know still less what is this deep calling unto deep.

How far can we go in understanding God on the basis of our own reason and our observation and analysis of nature?

From observation of nature we may perceive a certain order and conclude that behind nature there is a mind of intelligence. The Roman emperor and philosopher Marcus Aurelius, who was not a Christian, said, "This world is either a haphazard miscellany or an ordered unity. If it is the former, what is there for me to consider except how I myself will ultimately return to dust? But if it is the latter then I am in the presence of the mind that created that order. I am filled with awe and have a ground on which to stand" (Marcus Aurelius, *Meditations*, Book 6, No. 10). If you are walking through a trackless desert and come upon a wristwatch lying on the ground, you would at once conclude that someone had been there before you for the sands of the desert, no matter how they evolved, would never of themselves produce a wristwatch. The wristwatch in itself is an indication of a mind, an intelligence, a purpose. The universe is much more complicated than a wristwatch and its workings much more exact. How could it possibly be the result of an accidental concurrence of phenomena without a mind or intelligence behind it? We cannot deny that behind the manifestations of nature there must be a mind, an intelligence, a purpose. Of course, to make this affirmation does not solve every problem but to fail to make this affirmation leaves still greater problems unsolved.

Anyone who views the universe thoughtfully ought to reach this conclusion. But if one views the universe only in the light of reason one will not be able to proceed further. One will not be able to perceive from nature more than this about God who transcends nature.

You will have seen that I am pessimistic about the ability to find and recognize a personal God in nature by reason alone. What I maintain is that all that nature can give us is a certain sense of something immeasurable and mysterious, beyond our power to interpret.

Paul told the Athenians to "search for God and perhaps grope for him and find him—though indeed he is not far from each one of us. For 'in him we live and move and have our being'" (Acts 17:27–28). Again, "he has not left himself without a witness in doing good—giving you rains from heaven and fruitful seasons. And filling you with food and your hearts with joy" (Acts 14:17). Again, "Ever since the creation of the world his eternal power and divine nature, invisible though they are, have been understood and seen through the things he has made. So they are without excuse" (Rom. 1:20). But on the basis of human reason, how much can we know of this God? We can know something of his creative activity but how much can we know of his purity, his righteousness, his love and his redemptive purpose? Who would not have a pessimistic answer to this question? We recall the Old Testament words, "Can you find out the deep things of God? Can you find out the limits of the Almighty?" (Job 11:7). So it is not surprising that Paul also presents another side to the picture: "For since, in the wisdom of God, the world did not know God through wisdom God decided, through the foolishness of our proclamation, to save those who believe" (1 Cor. 1:21).

The foolishness of preaching is no less than the revealed truth of God. The mystery of nature can only be unfolded by some revelation. Only when we have accepted the revelation and come to know the Lord of revelation can we understand the mystery of nature. But from that moment on we can see in every part of nature the handiwork of God.

Let us take an illustration. Some of you are graduating this year. You think to yourself, I have been away from home for a long time. I must go home and see my mother before reporting for work. When you get there, she is not at home. But you know her and love her and as you go in and look around, everything in the house reminds you of her. Now, supposing you had one of your classmates with you, someone who did not know your mother. As he looks around the room it will not remind him of anything—to him it is just a room.

It is like this for us with nature. Unless you have come to know God through revelation and faith, nature itself will only be space and mystery and not much else. But if after receiving the revelation you again look at nature, all is now new. You perceive that all the truth, goodness and beauty of the world proclaim the glory and working of God.

In short, we Christians on the one hand recognize that the witness of nature is not enough. We cannot expect to know God from it and therefore we are not disturbed when someone says they cannot find God in nature. On the other hand, we do not look upon nature with suspicion or denigrate it because it is, after all, the handiwork of God. Thomas Aquinas sums it up very well: "Grace does not negate nature but fulfills it."

Finally, the knowledge of God comes only through revelation. John

1:18 tells us, "No one has ever seen God. It is God the only Son, who is close to the Father's heart who has made him known." Jesus himself says, "I am the way, and the truth, and the life. No one comes to the Father except through me" (John 14:6). The truth of these two passages is borne out by the experience of countless Christians.

## ENVIRONMENT AND SIN

Modern thinking has a tendency to attribute all the ills of society to a bad social system, as though there could be no other source for them, such as man himself.

For Christians this tendency is an important corrective. In the past we thought little about the social order. Our bias was simply to attribute all evil to one's sinful nature. We said, the question of sin is the only question and once it is solved any social system will be good. If it is not solved, no social system will be good. Today, we must acknowledge our mistake. It is true that the question of sin is fundamental. But we cannot expect everybody to repent at once and thus solve the problem of sin. It is still necessary to live together before all have repented and been regenerated. What kind of society will be best for our common life? That is an important question. The difference between socialism and capitalism is very great. Out studies during the past few years have shown us the superiority of socialism. We certainly cannot think of the two systems as of equal value for China.

But can we deny the existence of sin? Certainly not. In New China the level of morality has been greatly raised. Does that mean that the question of sin has been solved? Decidedly not.

The fact that we must come into a good environment (New China) in order to manifest a better standard of behavior does not mean that we are without sin, rather it is a demonstration that we are carrying a heavy load of sin, so that we are not free from the influence of environment. Consider your old grandfather or grandmother, crippled with rheumatism so that they cannot move around much in winter. Then spring and summer come and they become livelier. Does that mean they are now well? No. It only proves the weakness of their bodies.

Not long ago I went to visit some country churches and on the bus

I sat by the driver watching him as he alertly turned the steering wheel, now this way and now that. I wondered: If the road were perfectly straight and perfectly level, would it be possible for the driver to be less alert? Could he, after setting the direction, take his hands from the wheel and sit there reading a book? I answered my own question: no. Even if the road were as straight as a ruler and as level as a pane of glass there is bound to be a certain amount of play in the setting of the wheels. And if there were any play at all, even if it is too small to be noticeable, the result would be that without the steering of the driver the car sooner or later would go into the ditch. As a saying in one of the old classics has it: "A mistake of a thousandth of an inch can put one wrong by a thousand miles." Of course, the straighter and smoother the road, the better. But the most up-to-date factory cannot produce a car which will obviate this weakness inherent in the nature of the car. Our life in the world is like this. We must work for an improved social order and environment but human sin is not thereby cancelled. We still need a Master to come and hold the steering wheel of our life.

In a school where I once studied we had in the gymnasium a ball about the size of a basketball but much heavier, with an off-center weight in it. The result was that no matter how you tried you could not roll it straight. It was very exasperating. Is not one's life like that? In the presence of God, yesterday, today and tomorrow we still can be described in the words of Isaiah, "All we like sheep have gone astray; we have all turned to our own way" (Isa. 53:6).

In today's society the level of moral behavior has been raised and this is a fact that we Christians should welcome. We should not go around looking for flaws as if the only way to vindicate our faith is to discover that things in the world are as bad as ever. We should welcome a social system that is able to raise the level of moral life. Although the change of a social system can only limit the effectiveness of sin, it cannot solve the problem of sin. Sin can only be healed by love, forgiveness, salvation and grace. It is not a matter of social progress.

Perhaps someone will accuse me of having too pessimistic a view of man. But what pessimism is there in this view? It is instead great optimism. When the Prodigal Son came to understand his own situation, our Lord said of him, "He came to himself" (Luke 15:17). Evidently in his sin he was not himself but when he repented, his true self showed itself. From this we see that Jesus had a very high view of man, one that certainly cannot be called pessimistic.

## THE REASON FOR UNBELIEF

Some people are always analyzing Christians, trying to explain why we believe in God and saying that we are looking for an opiate. But why is it that from the beginning of the world there have been people who would not believe in God? There are two reasons, the first a general or universal one, the second one that has become much more real since the 19th century.

### Moral and spiritual reason

To believe in God or to believe that there are living beings on Mars may seem both to be acts of believing, but they are vastly different. If you believe there is life on Mars you just believe it and, if you don't, it makes no difference in your moral or spiritual life. It makes no demands upon you whether you believe or do not believe. Your life, your thinking and your actions will be the same.

Belief in God is a different thing. If you don't believe, that is all there is to it, but if you do believe, the consequences are great. Adam sinned and then when God drew near he hid himself in the trees because he did not dare to look upon the face of God. We can imagine how happy he would have been there, if there had not been any such person as this God. If he had remained hidden for a long time would not he and his children have come to believe that God after all did not exist?

Peter knelt at Jesus' feet saying, "Go away from me, Lord, for I am a sinful man" (Luke 5:8). Since he knew Jesus to be Lord, and himself to be a sinner, should he not instead have repented? Why would he ask Jesus to depart? Yes, we have all had this experience of both wanting Christ and not wanting him. Christ is what we want, but yet he demands that we repent. If we are not willing to repent, if we are unwilling to pay the moral and spiritual price we can only ask this Christ to leave us, and even wish that he did not exist.

Belief in God sometimes becomes an opiate, that is true. But consider how often refusal to believe in God becomes an opiate.

How many people there have been since the beginning of history who have drugged themselves by a denial of God's existence so that they could continue to sin, avoid responsibility, and stifle the reproaches of their conscience! Sometimes we meet people like this in our churches. They are morally reprobate but refuse to repent and the result is that having departed from God they gradually come to deny his existence. The only way they can recover their faith is first to repent of their sin.

### The church's failure to manifest God

A second reason for the world refusing to believe in God is the failure, the darkness and the sin of the churches. Jesus said, "Let your light shine before others, so that they may see your good works and give glory to your Father in heaven" (Matt. 5:16), but we do not do this. People are not able to see Christ's Father, full of love, justice and purity in the life, the thinking and the work of Christians. Instead, what people can see in the church is a God whom their own sense of morality and justice does not allow them to believe in. This is an important reason why people today do not believe in God.

The French Catholic writer Jacques Maritain, in his *True Humanism*, says: "What is the source of communist atheism? It is that the Christian world is not true to its own principles, thus arousing the hostility of communists who then go on from hating the Christian world to hating Christianity itself."

Nikolai Berdyaev, a Russian theologian, in his book *The Origins of Russian Communism*, writes:

> Christians who condemn the communists for their godlessness and anti-religious persecutions cannot lay the whole blame upon these godless communists. They must assign part of the blame to themselves and that a considerable part. They must be not only accusers and judges; they must also be penitents. Have Christians done very much for the realization of Christian justice in social life? Have they striven to realize the brotherhood of man without the hatred and violence of which they accuse

the communists? The sins of Christians and the sins of the historical churches have been very great, and these sins bring with them their punishment.

The Armenian Christian Tiran Nersoyan, in his book *A Christian View of Communism* says:

From a practical point of view, atheism is the result of the necessity felt by the founders of Marxism and communism to free the proletariat from the influence of priests and reactionaries in order to secure their complete allegiance to themselves. It is also probable that atheism may have had the additional attraction for them of being the most drastic way of eliminating the causes of disunion among the peoples of different religions and sects from which their ranks have been recruited.

We need not agree entirely with these writers. But because of the sins of the church and especially because the church in the field of politics was often on the side of the enemies of the people, the church lost its ability to show forth God. This point is one that we in the Chinese church especially can appreciate. The Three-Self Patriotic Movement is calling the whole church out of bondage to imperialism and reaction of all sorts and this makes it a movement of great significance to the future of Christian witness in China.

In their criticism of religion people have mainly centered their attention on some of the evil results of religion in personal and social life, such as its inhibiting influence on human development, its harmful effect on health, its upholding of private ownership of the means of production, but have not touched upon the substance of our faith. Some of the things criticized are foreign, or now a thing of the past, while others are Chinese in origin and are still problems. These should rouse us to greater vigilance and self-examination, amending what is wrong and strengthening what is right.

Today we should enter fully into the Three-Self Patriotic Movement, purifying and rectifying the church lest it come under evil influences and justly suffer rebuke from the world. Only by doing this can we make possible the conditions for witnessing to the substance of our faith—the truth of the gospel.

## FAITH AND FELLOWSHIP

Atheism has for a long time existed alongside the church—it is not something that the church has just met in China in the last few years. We must not be alarmed. We should recognize the right of all shades of atheism and agnosticism to exist and become accustomed to living with them, learn how to profit from their criticism of religion, and learn how to present to gospel to people who have been influenced by these theologies. Theism and atheism are matters of personal faith and worldview, not matters of the state or government. A state or a government cannot hold to either theism or atheism. But there are some in the West who try to use this question as an instrument in the cold war and this we do not approve of. We know that neither cold war nor hot war will change an atheist into a theist. The West has published many books on the subject of Christianity and communism but they are not of much value to us because their authors have been too much influenced by the anti-Soviet, anti-communist spirit of an apostle but with the self-righteousness of the elder brother. We know that only as the church rectifies itself and becomes truly the church can the gospel radiate the liberating strength of its own truth and bring people to a knowledge of sin, repentance, and confession of Christ as Lord. To use the question of atheism and theism to foment division and disorder would do not good but a great deal of harm.

A nation or government cannot be either theistic or atheistic. These are questions of faith and faith is personal. It does not pertain to a nation or a government. Note the characters for faith (*xinyang*) both have a "man" character on the left-hand side. An individual person can believe or not believe in God but a nation or a government is not a single individual. It can neither believe in God nor not believe in God. We Christians need not take it seriously when some nation calls itself a Christian nation. We see that their government leaders assume the title of religion and appear to be very devout but their purpose could be just to advance their own political ends and get support for their actions. They call their nation a Christian nation and their government a Christian government. But Christ has said that his kingdom is not of this world so how can a nation or government dare call itself by the name of Christian? The true purpose of such boasting is simply to use the name of Christian to advance their own ends, to get glory in the eyes of the world, but the result is only to drag down the name of Christian until it is viewed with suspicion and even hatred by the world. We know from history that those who make a pretense of religion can appear very devout. Even Herod who wanted to kill the Christ child pretended that he wanted to worship him. And we know well how Herod's successors have cleverly used religion to advance their dreams of world hegemony. Jesus said, "Not all who call me Lord, Lord, shall enter into the kingdom of heaven." This we must never forget.

We Christians must be wary and not be taken in by any nation or government just because it assumes the name of Christian. The question we should ask is not whether a nation constantly uses the name of God, but whether its principles and policies are good and whether it really fulfills the responsibilities that God demands of a nation. Only by weighing a nation by this rule can we avoid being deceived. Only in this way can we judge factually and fairly. In regard to the political leadership of any nation, what we should ask is not who the leader is, or what he believes, but what the practical content of the leadership is. Instead of asking about the religious faith of any leader, we should ask whether we approve of the constitutional principles of this government and how the leading party and people join together to carry out those principles. Communists are atheists. But differences in worldview do not prevent political unity. We do not approve of their atheism, but we welcome their political leadership and we welcome their frank attitude regarding questions of belief, too. They tell the world openly what they think about religion and so there is less danger of them trying to use religion. Everything is straightforward and open and clear, unlike the so-called Christian countries where religion is used by pretenders so that questions become confused and the issues of right and wrong are not clear.

The building of the church in a socialist country is a task that has never been faced by the church in all the first nineteen centuries of church history. In self-government, self-support and self-propagation we face a difficult responsibility. Why does God give this responsibility to us and not to someone else? Is it because we are better? No. God has his own purpose and it is one that we cannot fathom. But at least we know, just because our Chinese church is a weak minority group, that we can demonstrate how the church of God in weakness can show strength and we can show the workings of God's might and give glory to God. God has indeed chosen the foolish things of the world put to shame those that are wise and the weak things to put shame those that are strong. This shows that the strength is from God and not from ourselves.

—Delivered at Nanjing Seminary, 1957

# THE COSMIC CHRIST

To some Christians, to talk of the Cosmic Christ sounds like removing Christ to some celestial outer space. But this is actually not so.

In order to appreciate any proposition, it is important to know the particular circumstances under which it has come up and the particular problems it addresses. So let me describe to you the struggle in China in the course of which the notion of the Cosmic Christ has come to the fore on the part of more and more Christians. You will see that the notion is the result of the impact of historical changes upon inherited faith. That impact drives Christians to go back to the New Testament and meet there familiar words glistening with splendor and meaning as if for the first time. I am referring to passages on the person of Christ in, for instance, Colossians, Ephesians, Hebrews and St. John's Gospel.

The historical changes were those since the coming into being of the People's Republic of China in 1949, which marked the beginning of a period of direct encounter between Christians and communist revolutionaries. In this direct encounter people, including Christians, were greatly impressed by the moral goodness which the new acquaintances, the revolutionaries, manifested and the goodness they could inspire in others. Their frugality, their self-sacrifice, their honesty in self-analysis, their relentlessness in dealing with corruption within their ranks, their program for nation-building and their humility made them the incarnation of all that Confucius and other sages taught about the virtuous life. For instance, I knew of one Communist Party member who endorsed Paul's description of human nature as so often not doing what ought to be done, and doing exactly what ought not to be done. I understand some Western Christians, equally impressed, went so far as to say that the new person spoken of by Paul has arrived, not in Christ but outside of Christ. Anyway, these revolutionaries were the opposite of the caricatures of them meted out for popular consumption by the press under the previous regime. As a result, the writings of Marx, Engels, Lenin, Stalin and Chairman Mao easily became bestsellers.

Human nature being what it is, historical movements with high aims have a tendency to relapse and even to develop into their opposites unless there is constant, thoroughgoing criticism and self-criticism. With the gradual passing away of revolutionaries of the earlier generations, there is a decline in revolutionary spirit and over all moral standards. Bureaucracy and corruption have crept in, as you have heard. But let us not easily write off the spirit of dedication on the part of the revolutionaries so many of whom are hardworking and self-giving even today. It is not a phenomenon of no consequence but one that makes Christians in China stop and think. It challenges us to a good understanding and explanation from the point of view of our faith.

All along, Christian evangelism has capitalized on human depravity and lack of virtue as the entering point for preaching about sin and on Christ as Savior. How are Christians to account for the new phenomenon that seems to make Christians' faith pale and superfluous?

The most catastrophic blow was on those Christians who knew and admired Jesus only as a great moral teacher, a social reformer and the leader of what some of them liked to refer to as the Christian Movement owing to their dislike of the word "church." They considered the Sermon on the Mount the epitome of Christian faith. Their faith in their cause was greatly shattered when they found that the Christians' program for changing China was almost nothing to compare with the large-scale and very impressive performance the revolution has brought forth. For instance, opium-smoking and prostitution, which Christians had spoken against for a century, were done away with in a matter of months. In the mind of many Christians there lurked the notion that Christians only talked a lot, but the communists put their words into practice. That notion was demoralizing to the Christians. Thus, the '50s were years when many Chinese Christians were greatly bewildered. As Chinese, they welcomed the liberation and reforms it made possible but, as Christians, how were they to think of the raison d'etre of Christian faith? Quite a number left the church to join organizations considered to be more effective, among whom were many of Y. T. Wu's students and some of his close friends.

But not all Christians were bewildered. There were hardliners who engaged themselves in the building up of a Great Wall against the inroads of new realities and new thinking. Their way of keeping themselves unmoved in their faith was to refuse to see any good outside Christian faith. They thought nothing of the difference between justice and injustice, or between good and evil. The only divide they could see was the one between belief and unbelief. It was an even more negative version of Tertullian's "What has Athens to do with Jerusalem?" They found their proof text in 2 Corinthians 6:14–17 where it is said, "Do not team up with unbelievers ... What agreement has the temple of God with idols?... Come away and leave them, separate yourselves, touch nothing unclean." To them, God has lost the world he created to Satan. The world has become Satan's occupied territory. Their proof text is 1 John 5:19 which says, "The whole world lies in the power of the evil one." They used 2 Corinthians 11:14–15 to negate the beauty and goodness they saw around them: "No wonder, Satan himself masquerades as angel of light, so it is easy enough for his agents to masquerade as agents of good." Thus, as one preacher of that school wrote, "God hates good even more than he does evil, because the good is far more deceptive."

The practical implication of all of this was to shun anything of beauty in art and in nature, to write off any good human hands did and, meanwhile, to win the lost and wait for deliverance. With this worldview, these Christians got comfort and the strengthening of their faith by looking for signs of the worsening of the human situation in the world. Some looked to the imminent return of Chiang Kai-shek's forces from Taiwan and the outbreak of the Third World War by which a vengeful God would in his anger bring about the annihilation of the world and the punishment of all unbelievers.

Many Chinese Christians found this kind of teaching unacceptable and politically dangerous. That teaching actually drove a good number of Christians to quit the church "to join the revolution," as the saying went in those days. By the way, we have found that this kind of teaching dies hard. Today, forty-two years after 1949, it still has a fluctuating market in China.

Many of those other Christians who remained with the church seemed to hear the question Christ asked of the Twelve (John 6:67), "Do you also want to leave?" They chose to answer like Peter, "To whom shall we go? Your words are words of eternal life." They began to bring the situation they were in to a renewed study of the Bible, fully conscious that 1949 marked a great shift in nation and perhaps in spirituality for Christians. Former understandings of reality and of truth might need to be de-absolutized so as to open a way for new insights and a new spirituality.

For Chinese Christians the significance of knowing Christ as having a cosmic nature lies essentially in ascertaining two things: (1) the universal extent of Christ's domain, concern and care, and (2) the kind of love which we get a taste of in Jesus Christ as we read the Gospels being the first and supreme attribute of God and basic to the structure and dynamic of the universe, in the light of which we get an insight as to how things go in the world. I will not try to take you into the world of Chinese classics, but will only say that what it teaches about the unity of the universe and the benevolence with which it is governed does prepare the Chinese mind to treat favorably the proposition of cosmic Christ.

First, the universal extent of Christ's work, concern and care. Christ is not so small as to concern himself only with religious or spiritual or ecclesiastical things, or only with believers, or only with making converts of those who do not yet consciously believe in him. He is the one who sustains the universe by his word of power (Heb. 1:3). His is the primacy over all creation. He exists before all things, and all things are held together in him (Col. 1:15, 17). It is not that God created the world but ceded its control to the successful rebellion of Satan, and Christ came to rescue certain individuals out of it to be returned to God. As creativity is inexhaustible and creation a long process, Christ has everything to do with Creation thus far and with Creation as it goes on now. His concern is to bring Creation to its fruition when love, justice and peace become the rule. Redemption, like education and sanctification, does not stand against Creation but is one process with Creation. Not only communities of Christians here and there, but humankind as a whole and, indeed, the whole cosmos are within the realm of Christ's redemptive work. The Holy Spirit, in the same way, is not only the giver of gifts to the Christians or to the church, but also inspires all created beings with great goodness and beauty.

The question as to how Christians are to think of non-church values, that is, values on the part of those who profess no faith in Christ is, of course, not unique to mid-20th-century Chinese Christians. The 1st-century Christians faced it as soon as the gospel reached the non-Jewish world. Right at that point began the church's process of discrimination, adaptation and assimilation. Insofar as China is concerned, the early Nestorian church had no hesitation in incorporating Chinese national culture, as shown by the fact that the 2,000-character inscription on the Nestorian Tablet uses the classical *Book of Changes* and the *Odes* nearly thirty times each, and the *Spring and Autumn Annals* nearly twenty times. Matteo Ricci also pioneered in bridge building between Christianity and non-church values. James Legge was a sort of Protestant Matteo Ricci. It was most unfortunate that the constructive missionary approach of both was invalidated in a fit of self-mutilating doctrinaire orthodoxy. The intransigent approach that ensued caused Christianity to mean alienation. The missionary approach in old China went largely the way of divorcing the converts from their heritage and from the people's socio-political movements and protecting them with Western colonial military and economic power. That led it to the verge of a disastrous collapse with the success of the communist revolution in 1949.

My guess is that more or less the same story of alienation was repeated in other Third World countries. It seems that the depreciation of national cultures was particularly a vice of colonialism in its effort to justify itself. It was chauvinism and colonialism that was served when syncretism was thrown around as an alarmist label. But nearness of human beings of different cultures to each other, brought about by modern technology and by the passing of colonialism, made the holding of nihilistic attitudes toward non-church goodness untenable. What is unique about Chinese Christians' experience in 1949 is only that the breakthrough happened in a traumatic way, and that it was brought about by the challenge of a revolutionary movement under communist leadership.

We receive great consolation in reading Romans 5:15–17 where a comparison is made between the effect of Christ's grace and that of Adam's fall. There Paul speaks of the infinitely greater impact of Christ on humanity than that of Adam by using such expressions as "much more," "vastly exceeded," "in far greater measure," and "out of all proportion." We are elated and get a sense of liberation upon reading this. The Incarnation profoundly affects human and cosmic life in all its aspects. It is inconceivable that any area of human endeavor should be unaffected by grace. But too often, we make sin universal while limiting grace only to the few who profess a belief in Christ. It really amounts to saying that the Incarnation of the Son of God has made less of an impact on humanity than the fall of Adam. But this is not a view that can go along with the vision of a God whose name is love and whose concern is to create, that is, to redeem, educate and sanctify a humanity that will reach perfection as free and intelligent agents or co-creators with him.

Can we square the existence of atheism with the cosmic role of Christ? I think we can, as much as we can square the existence of many other things in the world with his cosmic role. In the first place, we have good reason to be grateful if we realize how much any denial of God, just the use of the term atheism, helps to bring up the question of God, and that is an evangelistic service in any society which has little to suggest the idea of God. Then, atheists are not all of a piece. Some atheists do give consideration only to what they can gain by assuming such a posture. There are rice atheists at least as much as there were rice Christians in the earlier days of Christianity in China. But there are other atheists whose cry against God is really a cry in favor of humanity. They are sincerely devoted to efforts to fashion a more humane society. Their atheism is not superficial but worthy of our sympathy. It is the rejection of false notions of God we religious people have put forward. The atheists' judgments can only be made on the basis of the ideas of God they come across, which usually are such distorted representations of the reality of God that atheists can hardly be expected to take that reality seriously. Who is the God they have in mind when they deny his existence? It is the tyrannical Jupiter who chains Prometheus to a cliff because he does good for humanity, or the ruthless underworld King of Yen in Chinese popular religion who sends out emissaries to fetch people to be thrown into everlasting hell fire as punishment for their demerits on earth. Atheistic humanism can be our ally as it can help greatly to salvage authentic faith. We can join forces with these humanitarians to oppose the idolatry in those views of God that diminish human dignity and block human liberation. From our point of view, in the human pilgrimage toward the Kingdom of God, we need not absolutize the opposition between theists and atheists. We both "see in a mirror, dimly" (1 Cor. 13:12), while undergoing transformation into new persons in Christ.

Some of my friends are surprised that I sometimes speak as highly as I do of certain atheists and communists. What I want to say is that there is a part of me which utters a hearty "Amen" to what they do and say, a part of me that refuses to rebuke them, but rather warms to them and wants to work together with them against forces we both want to combat, even though they and I have our different objects of ultimate loyalty and get our orders in doing certain things together from different chains of command. It is the conviction of many of my colleagues that, as long as there is space for Christian witness to be borne and for dialogue on issues to be carried on, we must for the good of the church refrain from adopting confrontation and martyrdom as church policy.

To assert the cosmic dimension of Christ's role does not mean that everything that happens in nature and in history is Christ's work and design. Many things are happening that contradict God's loving kindness and are harmful to the welfare of the world. Creation is a long process yet incomplete and, as Paul insists, imperfect and subject to frustration, especially as it involves the making of free human beings who are not slaves but children of God. A world still in making must be one in which ugliness and devilry have their place. Events all over the world are telling us how tortuous the way is toward the perfect community of free, loving children of God, and how dear a price in suffering God and human beings have to pay for every inch of progress toward that goal.

In the 19th century the picture that inspired many Western Christians was that of the church going into the world and gathering all nations unto its fold. Today, what catches all Christians' vision is the picture of Christ leading the whole Creation toward the goal of unity in God. In this saving work of his, all human movements of progress, liberation, democracy and humanization are joined. The church is important as the place where Christ is explicitly known, confessed, adored and preached. The world needs the church's gospel of forgiveness and reconciliation and peace. But God's saving work is not coterminous with the boundary of the church. It has the whole cosmos as its limit. As Vatican II says, "Many elements of sanctification and truth are found outside the visible structure of the church and so the helps necessary for salvation are always and everywhere available to all who are obedient to the dictates of conscience." I like to think that, if these elements are arcs of a circle, Christ is the perfect round in whom they will all be completed, fulfilled and united.

That the whole of reality is God's concern and Christ's domain seems to be a proposition already commonly accepted in Western churches but, in China, we are still in the process of winning more Christians to see that this is true. We in China are bringing out of the Bible how Abraham received blessing from Melchizedek, the pagan king of Salem, how Cyrus, King of Persia, a Gentile, carried out God's purpose and made possible the rebuilding of the holy city and the holy temple, how Nebuchadnezzer of Babylon also worked for God who thereby bestowed on him a recompense, and how, in Isaiah 19, God calls Egypt "my people" and Assyria "the work of my hands," alongside Israel "my possession." Because we have seen and experienced goodness, truth and holiness among followers of other paths and ways than that of the church, we cannot resist a vision of the universal creative and redemptive activity of God for all humankind, aside from the particular redemptive activity of God in the history of Israel and in the person and work of Jesus Christ. This is implied when we say Christ is cosmic.

The other implication of discovering the cosmic dimension or nature of Christ is to ascertain love, the kind of love we get a glimpse of in Jesus' earthly life, as the supreme attribute of God and the principle by which the cosmos is run.

That God is love has become pretty much a platitude. We need to make Christlike love the definition of God, the all-commanding part of the revelation of the nature of God himself. We have been trained to think of God mostly in terms of superior power that can either crush us or make us powerful. This is often a projection and legitimization of our power hungry, exploitative, monopolistic social structures and attitudes. But in the New Testament God's power is made perfect in weakness and he exercises sovereignty through crosses, not through conquests. We must stop fashioning God in the image of Egyptian, Persian, Roman and Chinese rulers, thereby giving to God the attributes which belong exclusively to Pharaoh, Caesar and their like. We need to relegate to the side all those attributes such as his absolute power, his absolute knowledge, his absolute changelessness, his absolute dominion and majesty, his arbitrariness and intolerance, imposed on God but reflecting largely an absolutization of human beings', especially male human beings', own cravings. These attributes need to be de-absolutized and subordinated to God's supreme attribute of love.

That Christ is cosmic gives us assurance that God is the cosmic lover, not any cosmic tyrant or punisher. He works by education and persuasion rather than coercion and forced obedience. He lures and invites and waits for free response and does not resort to scolding and reprimanding. That is why many of us in China find the Gospels' analogy of the transformation of seeds and the growth of plants in air, rain and sun more appealing than that of beating and controlling the sheep with rod and staff. God's is the will-to-fellowship, not the will-to-power. For Chinese Christians, to discard the image of a vengeful, frightening God, God the omnipotent in dealing with humans, and to come to adore God the Lover, the Sympathizer, the fellow-sufferer who comes to us, is a shift that is truly liberating.

During the so-called Cultural Revolution which turned out to be not only anti-cultural but also abusive of revolution as an honored word, when injustice, hatred, thirst for power and arbitrary condemnation of the innocent ran riot, the image of God the Lover was seen to be such a shining contrast and source of comfort and hope that many were drawn to this God. He spoke lovingly to the heavy-laden and gave the unacceptable in the world an acceptability and rest they could not find elsewhere.

We like Alfred North Whitehead's caricature in his *Process and Reality* of much of the prevailing theological notions of God of his days as "the ruling Caesar, or the ruthless moralist, or the unmoved mover," because these notions went to mission fields sometimes in even more aggravated forms. We yearn for a different God, a God who first of all loves as the Cosmic Lover with a love exemplified in Jesus Christ. We want to depart from a severe and intimidating God who is not the Christ like God the four gospels lure us to want to believe in. We like the image of God in Hosea (11:4) of one who secures us with reins, leads us with bonds of love, lifts us like a little child to the parent's cheek and bends down to feed us. To confess that Christ is Godlike is now seen to be not so important as to affirm that God is Christ like and that Christ like love is the way God intends for the running of the cosmos.

God being love, more and more of us are seeing that the father figure is not necessarily the only or the best analogy for understanding him. For centuries and to this day, in China anyway, what is taken for granted in the father is his severity, and in the mother her loving-kindness. In fact, the proper Chinese way to refer to one's father in conversation is "the severe one in my family," while "the loving one in my family" is reserved for the mother. I assume that we all know of fathers of whom love is hardly an attribute. There are biblical passages that show no hesitation in using the image of the mother to indicate how God loves. In Isaiah 66:13, it is God who says, "As a mother comforts her son, so shall I myself comfort you." Again, in Isaiah 49:15, "Can a woman forget the infant at her breast, or a mother the child of her womb? But should even these forget, I shall never forget you." And in

Psalm 131:2, the Psalmist says, "I am calm and quiet like a weaned child clinging to its mother."

This emphasis on God as the great Lover working out his purpose for the world brings in its train an understanding of reality as becoming. It gives us hope for and beyond history. We cannot fathom the actual time and manner the end of history as we know it will come about, but are sure it will be the triumph of love and grace. The way from alpha to omega is never a straight line, but love accompanies the pilgrims. We have to go through tortuous ways, but we know how Christ says to us: "A woman in labor is in pain because her time has come; but when her baby is born she forgets her anguish in her joy that a child has been born in the world." We see the darkness that appears before dawn as well as the dawn that will surely arrive after darkness. As is so well said in Psalm 30:5: "Tears may linger at nightfall, but rejoicing comes in the morning."

These two points about Christ—the cosmic extent of his role and the Christ like love with which God runs the universe—are not entirely foreign to Chinese culture. A passage in Lao Tze's *Tao Te Ching* says:

> The supreme Tao, How it floods in every direction!
> This way and that, there is no place where it does not go.
> All things look to it for life, and it refuses none of them:
> Yet when its work is accomplished it possesses nothing.
> Clothing and nourishing all things, it does not lord it over them.
> Since it asks for nothing from them,
> It may be classed among things of low estate;
> But since all things obey it without coercion.
> It may be named supreme.
> It does not arrogate greatness to itself,
> And so fulfills its greatness.

This passage prepares the Chinese soil for receiving a Christ whose dimensions are cosmic.

The Cosmic Christ is a rich concept. It says something of Christ the meaning of which is quite beyond human understanding. We are only groping. It is a notion that has come to Christians who are no longer satisfied with the classical two-nature debate and want to make a shift. What I have tried to do is to present before you what we in China have in mind when we say fumblingly and clumsily that Christ is cosmic. For now we see through a glass, darkly, but then face to face.

—Talk to the Friends of the Church in China,
England, 1991

# RESURRECTION HOPE

Our hearts are deeply thankful to God who has made all circumstances to work together so that we are able to meet here face to face.

When I was considering what to say on this occasion, many things crowded into my mind. Should I talk on Chinese socialism, or on religious freedom as we find it in China? Or about the Three-Self Movement and the attempt to make Christianity in China Chinese? Or about our post-denominational existence, or the theological fermentation and reorientation at the grassroots in the last thirty years? Or our deprivation during the years of the Cultural Revolution and our present difficulties and problems, of which we have many? No, what I ought to dwell upon at this moment must be the thing that has become the most real and most precious to us Chinese Christians after these last thirty years. It is the faith in the Risen Christ.

I do not mean we in China have got some new circumstantial evidence for the Empty Tomb. I simply mean to say that, when we try to review and summarize what China as a nation has gone through or what Chinese Christians as a Church have gone through, resurrection comes up as the word most descriptive of our experiences. To have had some experience of dying and rising up again in our individual life, in our national life and in the life of our Church conditions many of us to see that resurrection from the dead is actually the law by which God carries on his work of the world's creation, redemption and sanctification, the principle by which the whole universe is sustained and gov-

erned. It helps many of us to give away somehow some of our foolishness and slowness of heart in seeing the necessity and naturalness that
Christ should suffer before entering his glory. Thus we have been
enabled to appropriate for ourselves something of the mystery of the
Risen Lord, and to realize his presence and nearness more surely and
more intimately.

How strongly many Chinese Christians feared at the time of the
Liberation in 1949 that we were losing so many things dear to us, only
to find later they were mostly just excess baggage. But it was during the
Cultural Revolution, which turned out to be quite anti-cultural and not
much of a revolution either, that the Chinese people suffered so much
and we Christians suffered so much with them. We felt the gospel to be
something precious, but the Red Guards and the so-called rebels
thought of it as nothing but poisonous weed. We had no means of communicating it or of answering the attacks in the big-character posters.
Not a single church remained open. There was left no government
organ to protect us from lawlessness. We had no rebel group of our own
to support us, nor any bandwagon to ride on. It would have been fortunate if we could just worship in a small group in a home. We were
very weak indeed, a little flock. By all human reckoning Christianity,
perhaps for the fourth time in Chinese history, was again breathing its
last breath.

What we were blind to was that when we were weak and dying life
was in the offing. As Shelley wrote, "If winter comes, can spring be far
behind?" Strength is found in weakness, as life in dying. As Paul put it,
"What you sow does not come to life unless it dies. What is sown is per-
ishable, what is raised is imperishable; it is sown in dishonor, it is raised
in glory; it is sown in weakness, it is raised in power."

After having lost so much, we find there are more Christians in
China than ever before, and they are more dedicated too. After every
church having been closed, we find that for three years now one or
two churches are being opened or reopened every two or three days,
and with much greater enthusiasm and vigor. And because we have
been a part of the suffering fate of the Chinese people, we today are
no longer so dissociated from them, but are in much better conversa-
tional relations with them than in the past.

Thus, we seem to understand Paul when he said, "We are afflicted in every way, but not crushed; perplexed, but not driven to despair; persecuted, but not forsaken; struck down, but not destroyed; always carrying in the body the death of Jesus, so that the life of Jesus may also be manifested in our bodies," and all this by the grace of God. A grain of wheat remains a grain if it does not get into the soil and die there; but if it does, it will bear many seeds. This is reassuring and seems to have been proven.

We Christians have tried so often to wrap up the remains of Jesus Christ with the cloth we have brought. Others have tried so often to seal Jesus Christ up in his tomb with big, heavy stones. But the living Christ himself cannot be bound or enclosed. He broke out of any man-made tomb.

The resurrection truth tells us that the meek are to inherit the earth. This always reminds me of the philosophy of Lao Tzu who spoke of water when he said,

"What is of all things most yielding can overwhelm that which is most hard.
Being substanceless, it can enter in even where there is no crevice. That is how I know the value of action which is actionless.
But that there can be teaching without words,
Value in action which is
actionless, Few indeed can understand."

I think here Lao Tzu was feeling after something the Christian resurrection truth represents.

The resurrection truth tells us that it is through loss, poverty, suffering and death that life is attained, in nation as well as in Church. It tells us life does not depend on power, wealth or property but on the Risen Christ, the Lord of life, who is also the Ascended Christ, sitting at the right hand of God and upholding the universe by his word of power.

That a person who has died is to come to life again is in all common sense an absurd claim. Yet, almost a fourth of humankind is more or less committed to the resurrection story of Jesus. This is so because this message of hope has touched the chord in the hearts of so many in the world who simply refuse to accept defeat, humiliation, suffering, darkness and death as having the ultimate say and who see, in the midst of all vicissitudes, this message as the key to comprehend history and reality. It gives them comfort and confidence and strength by restoring their faith in the value of truth, goodness and beauty.

I have not got anything new or unexpected to report to you. The resurrection truth is an old truth. Your T. S. Eliot says aptly in one of his poems: "The end of all our exploring will be to arrive where we started, and know the place for the first time." Knowing the Risen Christ as if for the first time, that we feel enlarges our faith and builds up our faith. And we are heirs to this message and its witnesses. Our visit here is a great occasion for us to share our knowledge of this Christ to our mutual enrichment, so that our steadfastness in him may be strengthened and our thanksgiving enhanced. May the God of peace who brought again from the dead our Lord Jesus equip us with everything good so that we may do his will, through Jesus Christ.

—Lambeth Palace Chapel,
October 1, 1982

# THEOLOGY AND CONTEXT

What is theological reconstruction and why is it important? There are still those persons in the church who do not have a very clear understanding of the issue, and some who misunderstand it. Others think that it is an attack upon our basic faith and therefore will have no part of it.

Basic Christian faith is not the same thing as theological thinking, and we should make a distinction between them. Our basic Christian faith comes as revelation from God; it is not a matter of somebody making some pronouncement which then becomes faith. Faith is from God, not something thought up by humans. The Trinity, the Incarnation, the resurrection of Christ: these are basic creeds of Christian faith and do not change. We live amid changes and as times change all sorts of questions arise; these new questions tend to present difficulties for believers. Theologians and teachers of theology put forth theological views based on their studies to assist believers to be able to understand and continue to maintain their faith in a new era, to help them continue to be loyal to their basic faith. Thus, theological viewpoints can change; in fact they must.

Many theological views receive a lot of emphasis for a certain period of time, but when circumstances change, their importance diminishes and new theological views take prominence. Prior to the American Civil War, for example, it was the view (a theological view) that black people had no souls and that there was nothing wrong in working them like animals on the land. Lincoln freed the slaves by the war, and this theological view gradually lost ground. Thus theological viewpoints can be played down and even disappear. There are many other examples as well. In the Bible the mother of the sons of Zebedee implores Jesus that one day her sons will sit, one at his right side and one at his left. This is her prayer. But Jesus rebukes her—this will not come about because of her prayer, though we should pray. It is the content of her prayer that is the problem and Jesus helps her adjust the theological view reflected in her prayer. There are very many theological views in the church; for example, those regarding the Lord's Supper. Theological views can differ greatly: Some say real wine should be used for communion, others want grape juice; some worship on Saturday, others on Sunday. These are the result of different theological views and are not a part of basic faith.

Theological reconstruction or adaptation can help us to better maintain our basic faith unchanged. I believe it is crucial to separate basic faith from theological thinking.

In fact, our thinking requires frequent adjustments on all fronts. Communist thinking is also being continually adjusted. For the past few months, I have noticed in the newspapers the phrase "the three represents," though I didn't know who was being represented. Later

I saw an article that explained this did not refer to three persons, but was a request that Party members represent three important things: the advanced forces of production; advanced cultural direction; and the greatest benefit for the great masses of the people. The Chinese People's Political Consultative Conference journal, CPPCC, noted that the "three represents" summarized scientifically and in three aspects the aim, nature and duty of the Communist Party. They were formulated to answer the question of what sort of Party should be established for a new historical era. As Chinese Christians, we should care about these "three represents." Once I understood them, I felt greatly comforted, because the "three represents" do not say that the Chinese Communist Party represents anti-religious forces. Today the conflict between theism and atheism has been diminished. Prior to the Cultural Revolution, if a newspaper or periodical carried an article on religion, it would almost certainly lump it together with the idea of religion as opium. In those days, if one did not call religion opium, one would be suspected of not being a genuine Marxist. Today, we have no more articles like this, the "opium theory" has been vastly played down and we can see from this that Communist thinking is constantly changing too. My confidence in the Chinese Communist Party's policy of freedom of religion was increased by learning about the "three represents." Thinking in natural science is always being adjusted as well. Thus, if some adjustment takes place in Christian theological thinking, it is nothing remarkable. Playing down some theological views today is permissible, and in fact, necessary.

Recently, in Qingdao we held a symposium on approaches to the Bible. One's view of the Bible is extremely important; it is the "master switch." If we have an incorrect view of the Bible, we will be incorrect in many things, and in our thinking. On the final day of the symposium, I said in my remarks that perhaps Chinese Christianity could play down the idea of "justification by faith." I said this because it is overemphasized in China, as if it is the all in all of Christian faith. The idea is that anyone who believes will go to heaven after death, and those who do not believe will go to hell. This is an idea that denies morality. By extension, Hitler and Mussolini, as Christians, would be in heaven, while Confucius, Laozi, Mozi and Zhou Enlai, non-believers, would be in hell. This is the only logical conclusion according to this idea. Such a Christianity may appeal to some, but can we really imagine that most Chinese would be willing to accept it over the long run? Some people say, I really love my parents, but as non-believers they will be in hell while I, as a believer, will enjoy heaven. I really cannot bear such thinking. I have received letters from a few pastors who say they can no longer stand in the pulpit and preach such things. They are pastors of conscience and so they welcome theological reconstruction and put their hopes in it.

At the Qingdao conference on approaches to the Bible, there were dozens of people present when I raised the idea of playing down justification by faith and I asked those who did not agree, as well as those who did, to speak with me afterwards. A number of people felt that playing down this idea would allow a better understanding of God, enable people to know God as a God of love. If God were to send people to hell because of their unbelief, this would create problems in our idea of God—how then could God be a God of love?

The word "justification" in the Greek New Testament has no equivalent in Chinese, which creates problems in interpretation. We should note the way Today's Chinese version deals with this. Today's Chinese Bible was published in 1979, 60 years after the Mandarin Union Version. Today's Chinese Bible does not use the Chinese term *chengyi* for justification as the Union Version does. In most cases where the Union Version has *chengyi*, Today's version translates as "in an appropriate relationship with God" (Rom. 1:17; 3:28, 30; 4:5, 25; Gal. 2:16, 21; 3:8, 11, 21, 24; 5:4–5). This is both in line with what most theologians in the world today understand by "justification or righteousness" and is extremely helpful in correcting the mistaken view of "justification by faith" found in grassroots churches.

When we speak of playing down the doctrine of "justification by faith" then, we mean first of all a superficial and doctrinaire understanding, which, with the mention of "justification by faith" makes a simplistic connection with heaven and hell as if this were the whole meaning of "justification by faith." Actually, in the Bible Paul's use of "justification by faith" is always closely linked to the important ideas of grace, reconciliation, being made new in Christ, tearing down barriers, etc. In Paul's letters, the word "hell" does not occur. Paul said, "For I could wish that I myself were accursed and cut off from Christ for the sake of my own people, my kindred according to the flesh" (Rom. 9:3). What feeling is this? In our discussions of "justification by faith," this is something to keep in mind.

The uplifting of justification by faith by Paul in the 1st century and Martin Luther in the 16th, was not a matter of dealing with the question of individual salvation only, but a desire that those already in the church would oppose Jewish legalism and papal hegemony. Some people think that without justification by faith, Christianity has nothing to offer. There are no grounds for such a worry. Paul's writings contain many messages which should be loudly and uniquely proclaimed, and which are more easily accepted than justification by faith, for example, "faith, hope and love, these three; and the greatest of these is love." In fact, if we are not willing to play down justification by faith, but insist on emphasizing it, we will create a host of theological difficulties for ourselves (for example, whether or not truth, goodness and beauty exist outside the church).

To play down does not mean to eradicate. Playing down simply means not making this the all in all of Christianity, but manifesting *all* the riches of Christian faith. We live in a socialist society, and Chairman Jiang Zemin hopes that religions can adapt to this socialist society. Socialist society is at present the most advanced society known to humanity. There are still many bad things left from the old society, such as drugs, corruption and waste, and we do not want to adapt to these things, but to those things which are the essence of socialism, especially in terms of adapting our thinking, and not only general thinking, but theological thinking.

At the same time, Christianity must adapt to our ever-progressing society, and narrow the gap with Chinese intellectual circles. We Christians cannot be content to stay at a lower level, but must dialogue with intellectuals to ensure our future. Otherwise, we will begin to resemble Falun gong or some other cult. If that happens we will not have a future. Thus, theological reconstruction is not only for adaptation to socialist society, but to raise our level to that of our culture and intellectual circles. If we do not do this, intellectuals will look down on us and pay no attention to us. We will be left behind.

The level of theological studies in the West is in many respects higher than our own and many westerners with theological education are not that willing to have anything to do with us. In the 1950s, they were interested in understanding how we would implement Three-Self Chinese Christianity under socialism, but they are not so interested in what we are doing now. Some say our colleagues have only two phrases they trot out for foreign guests: "Thank the Lord" and "Praise the Lord." These are fine, but not conducive to discussion. They feel there is no theology in the Chinese Church or that our theology is very primitive. When we send delegations overseas, or invite people here, what sort of theological thinking shall we have for discussions? In four years of seminary, few of our students are able to achieve a high level of theology. People from churches overseas do not simply want to hear "Praise the Lord"; they want to have a theological discussion. Even at the seminary, they feel that China has no theology. Theological reconstruction aims to raise the level of theological thinking in the Chinese Church, so that we have a theology to discuss.

We have had some concrete results in theological reconstruction over the past two years. I have seen a letter from an instructor in the philosophy department at People's University, and another from an instructor at the Party School in Anhui, both expressing how pleased they were that we are undertaking theological reconstruction and that they had great hopes for it. They are intellectuals but not Christians, and they did not want to see Christianity go the way of Falun gong, but rather wanted to see it improving. I have received even more such letters from colleagues within the church. These letters made me very happy and made me feel even more the need for theological reconstruction. We must not disappoint our friends inside and outside the church.

We in the TSPM and three self organizations at all levels, provincial and municipal have been promoting theological reconstruction for nearly two years, but there are some colleagues within three-self organization who are still not very committed to it. Why is this? One reason may be that they are not very sensitive to theology or to what theology is. Another reason may be that for decades TSPM has stressed broadening unity and this has become its paramount focus. We must continue to emphasize unity, but sometimes this has meant that people are afraid to deal with theology in case it affects their basic faith. This has caused stagnation in theology. Another reason may be that they do not understand the changes that have taken place in theology worldwide. Today in Martin Luther's Germany the opposition to the pope has been played down to the extent that they speak of signing a pact of friendship with the Vatican, announcing the cessation of their disagreements over "justification by faith." I hope Chinese pastors will not simply follow the methods of 19th century foreign missionaries and some church leaders for the sake of church growth and pushing faith only, but rather emphasize Jesus' morality and ethics. This is in keeping with theological trends in the world today.

Some say you are liberals, modernists while we are traditionalists, evangelicals: we cannot adjust our theological thinking. But this doesn't really appear to be so. Several months ago, we had as our guest the Anglican Archbishop of Sydney, Australia, a prominent evangelical. When we introduced Chinese theological reconstruction, he thought this was an excellent thing for the Chinese church to do. He quoted Jesus' teaching from the Bible: "You have heard it said ...but I tell you ..." Isn't Jesus telling us to adjust our theological thinking here? Though he is an evangelical, the archbishop upheld the adjustment and reconstruction of theological thinking, and held up Jesus as a model for us.

I hope that our clergy, theological teachers and students will lead the way and show our Christians that they are participating in theological reconstruction. When the TSPM and CCC send delegations overseas for meetings and visits, the first criterion is politics, then language; theology should also be a consideration. We don't pay much attention to people's level of theological training when putting delegations together at present and most of those we send are not really able to have a theological discussion, which leads to foreigners thinking that we have no theology. I recently met a friend who had gone overseas to attend a meeting and asked him a few questions about it, but he couldn't answer them, saying merely, "I just went along to familiarize myself with the situation." This is not good enough. In future I hope we will consider people's theological abilities in choosing those to send overseas.

I hope what I have said here will help you in considering the value of theological reconstruction, and enable it to continue to develop, so that there may be a new day in Chinese Christianity, pleasing to our friends in and outside the church here at home and garnering respect in the church ecumenical.

—Speech on the 50th Anniversary of the Three-Self Patriotic Movement of the Protestant Church in China K. H. Ting

# FOREWORD TO *THEOLOGICAL WRITINGS FROM NANJING SEMINARY*

The publication of *Theological Writings from Nanjing Seminary* is a joyous event.

If theology is the church in the act of thinking, then I feel that *Theological Writings from Nanjing Seminary* does indicate to a fairly large extent what the Chinese Protestant Church has been reflecting on over these years, as well as how that process has taken place. Our theological work is naturally conditioned by the historical and ecumenical church, but it is not imitation work. It is rather based on reflection by Chinese Christians ourselves as we face up to the problems of the Chinese Church. We naturally welcome and are grateful for the listening in and advice of theologians from overseas, but they are no longer the arbiters of right and wrong. The rank-and-file Chinese Christians are not only those whose quality of faith is to be enhanced through our theological work, but also are turning more and more from being just listeners and passive receivers to being active participants in dialogue.

These forty-some essays do not touch on every issue of theological reflection in the Chinese Church but, even so, one can see from them that in these years the field and scope for theological reflection has been rather limited. Certain hot issues in international theological circles, such as those related to church order, views on biblical authority, history, peace and justice, women's liberation and sexuality issues in today's society, issues concerning the family and the environment, the ethics of ecology, and so on, have received little attention here. In fact, these issues are almost a blank page. The theological reflection of any church at any time has its limits and lacunae and China is no exception. This in turn tells us how essential is the opportunity for mutual exchange, complementarity and enrichment offered by the Church Universal.

As far as China is concerned, I think that, in addition to the usual limitations affecting theological reflection, there are other conditions which impinge on the situation: Chinese Christian unity, from the national to all levels of organization, is a good deal broader than that which comes under the aegis of councils of churches or other church bodies in other countries and regions. The range of its unity is unprecedented. To maintain such a broadly based unity, we adhere to the principle of mutual respect in matters of faith and worship. There are quite a number of Chinese Christians who disdain or even disavow the value of theological thinking; they too are part of our unity. For the sake of unity, the individual theologian does tend to exercise a certain amount of restraint in expressing his or her views. This shapes a situation in which there is more of tolerance and making allowances and less of innovation. We might say that this is the price we pay for unity, but improperly handled, it could lead to theological stagnation. The poet-essayist Su Dongpo once praised the painter Wu Daozhi by saying that he "brought forth something new from within the norm." It has been our experience that for the sake of uniting and keeping things tranquil, the church frequently emphasizes the "norm," and that, therefore, the "new" comes forth infrequently. If I am not mistaken, it seems that other churches also find themselves in this situation: Theological creativity is in inverse ratio to the degree of unity a church maintains.

This much is fact, but I would not like to overstate the case inappropriately. Those engaged in theological work in China are well aware that vis à vis the mass of Christians in China their role is educative and that they have a responsibility to improve the quality of people's faith. For this reason, they have never been willing to pursue their own interests without regard for the effectiveness of their theology. They do not see their overseas counterparts as their audience. They humble themselves, identify with Chinese Christians, establish lines of communication with them, take the people's issues as their own, and take pleasure in being able to help them, without undue pressure, to improve. They prefer not to say anything startling which transcends the "norm" and is thus far removed from the mass of Christians.

From a larger point of view, Chinese Christians have, for over one hundred years, always been a very small minority, surrounded on all sides by non-Christian and even anti-Christian thinking and influence. Even today the number of Christians in China is lower than one percent of the population. From time to time those who regard themselves as radicals and are hostile to religion appear here and there in China, making use of current movements and slogans to lend them momentum, manufacturing opinions that would incriminate religion. In such circumstances, there is an unevenness in the implementation of China's policy of religious freedom, and having such a policy is a very different matter from not having such a policy. This policy is of great benefit for the very existence and functioning of Christianity in China. At the very least it has given Christianity time to make self-government, self-support and self-propagation a reality and to strive to make the church well-governed, well-supported and one in which propagation is done well, so as to be able to meet our fellow Chinese on a more advantageous footing.

This is why we believe that, as long as the church can have the space to carry on the worship of God and to witness to Christ to men and women in the world and to enter into dialogue as regards the implementation of the policy of religious freedom and other policies, we should enjoy and make use of these opportunities with thankful hearts. Some people overseas seem to assume that our correct course should be one of confrontation and martyrdom. But I think that, in the Chinese context, this would be an abrogation of responsibility toward God's

Church and its members. Such behavior would also be heedless of the nation's safety and opposed by the mass of Christians. However, given the situation of the church in our country, it is understandable that a fairly large portion of Christians tend, consciously or not, to make personal salvation in Christ the sole message of the church, to the neglect of all other concerns.

After so many years, has a Chinese systematic theology taken shape in the Chinese Church? I can only say, not yet. It is not that there have not been individuals who have been inspired to try, but how representative their finished works have been is a very big question. What I am about to say now may be "self-justification": Paul, faced with flourishing churches on every hand, was busy making visits and writing letters, using theology to solve the pressing questions of the time and place. As for his systematic theology, it was up to those who came after him to put it in order.

But this is not to say that after forty years, theology is in disarray, or that a general theological direction has not emerged in Chinese Christianity. I believe that a central concept in Chinese Christian theological reflection is in the process of taking shape. A central feature for growing numbers of Christian intellectuals, especially the younger and middle-aged among them, is the Cosmic Christ. This Christ is the co-creator working with God in the process of creation, the revealer of God's love, the Risen Lord who sustains all things by his word of power.

The reason we say that Christ is the revealer of God's love is that in reading the four gospels we are so deeply moved by his kind of love for men and women to the end that no lesser description can be sufficient. In him humankind receives an insight into the way the highest reality in the universe exists by loving. The first attribute of this highest existence is not so much his coercive power and might, his omnipotence, his omniscience, his omnipresence, his deity, or his majesty, sovereignty and arbitrariness, but his love to the end. Love is the first factor in the universe, the mover in the work of creation. Ours is a universe of love in the process of being formed. We are still uncompleted products of the process, but at the same time, co-creators with God. From what we know of the love on the part of the father and the mother and of the person in love, Christ helps us to grope and fumble after the reality of the highest existence in the universe and to learn to call him Father.

Increasingly, we cast off the pedantry over the human and divine natures of Christ. Beyond Christ's human/divine issue, our theological thinking is liberated and deepened and finds greater cohesion in terms of Christ's cosmic nature. The cosmic nature of Christ is the Christology to be found in the New Testament books of Colossians, Ephesians and the Gospel of John. It is a conception which contains great riches, able to break boldly through the barriers of the traditional thinking and enrich Christians' worship and spiritual life, which can further challenge denominational biases, and lead to the trust and unity many envision, I am not trying to suggest that the phrase "Cosmic Christ" has already entered into the common vocabulary of the mass of theological workers, but it can be said that increasing numbers of Christians are encountering this Christ by various paths, and, in their own ways, are bringing people to know and adore this Christ. Inspired and stirred by Christ's sublime love which impels him to serve and not to be served, to the extent of giving his life as a ransom for others, his disciples have chosen to engage themselves in the world as salt and light bringing benefits to humankind. In this way our personal life gains meaning by becoming harmonious with the principle by which the universe is run.

Many of us share the feeling that intellectual circles in China may be today more well-disposed toward and sympathetic to Christianity than at any time since Christianity was introduced to China. The Nanjing Theological Seminary Library has over a hundred volumes of works of research and appreciation of Christianity and of translations of Western theological works—all done by scholars outside the church. I expect that the publication of the present volume will gain the attention and interest of intellectuals outside the church.

I would like to raise a point here for their consideration. Friends outside the church frequently express their opinion that Christians and non-Christians are all patriotic Chinese and supporters of socialism, and that the only difference is that Christians just add to this a faith in life in paradise after death. Their reason for saying this is simply to express their feeling that there is not a great distance separating

Christians from the mass of the Chinese people, and thus to affirm that Christians are part of the United Front in China and to uphold the policy of religious freedom and oppose discrimination against religion. We are of course grateful for this. At the same time, we also agree that there are Christians who look after the cultivation of their souls for the sake of gaining paradise after death. However, the majority of Christians care far more about life after birth than they do about life after death. Like ordinary people, they must live, work, study, and establish families; they have ideas, they seek truth, goodness, beauty, and such being the case, they do care about the things of this world. I think the readers of Theological Writings from Nanjing Seminary will find that the essays presented here do not treat Christian faith as a ticket to paradise. Using a vocabulary that is old and that seems hard to change, Christian faith presents a worldview and a spiritual culture. It is a guide on how to view life, how to be involved in reality and moreover how, through the common body of the church, to gain for oneself and for all humankind what Christ called "abundant life." These essays demonstrate the Christian goal of helping people to live and to live well. Without the emphasis on living a good life, how can we find our places within the United Front? A few years ago one of the social science publications carried an essay which held that religious believers think only of going to heaven, and "muddle through" while on earth, "not daring to look upon the colors of this world or hear its myriad sounds," "not daring to think of anything not found in the scripture," and viewing "reasonable calls for improving material life as the source of sin." That the writer characterizes religion in this way is probably due to the fact that he or she has never made friends with a religious believer.

This volume has been edited by Reverends Chen Zemin, Wang Weifan and Zhang Xianyong of Nanjing Theological Seminary. We are most grateful for all their hard work. We hope the publication of this volume will be helpful in the exchange of ideas and will further the flourishing of Chinese theology.

—Foreword to *Theological Writings From Nanjing Seminary,* 1992

# THE MESSAGE OF CHRISTMAS

**W**ith the recent establishment of the Amity Printing Press, I asked Ms. He Huibin to do a painting for a Christmas card of a mother and child against a sky filled with doves of peace. Inside was printed this verse from Luke 1: "Here am I, the servant of the Lord; let it be with me according to your word" (v. 38).

God is the Lord of Creation and his work of creation continues today. The goal of this creation is a world of harmony that will embrace both the present world and the world to come. In this new heaven and new earth, there will be no more darkness, no more of people cheating and destroying each other. People will treat one another as brothers and sisters. In that world, everyone will obey God. This obedience will not be coerced. It does not come about against one's will or because good will be returned for good and evil for evil, but is happily given and done out of love, out of the knowledge that God's will is perfect and beautiful. It is a kind of conscious free choice, an identification of will with God.

In that world of harmony I suspect traffic lights and traffic police will still be needed, but there will be no war, murder, seizure, imprisonment, or execution by firing squad. It will not be a place of monotonous sameness; differences will still exist, and they will be much greater than they are now. In this way, life and thought will be greatly enriched, for without differences, life and thought would be too bland. But conflicts and life-and-death struggles between people of the sort we have seen in the past will no longer exist.

With this goal in mind, and after a long period of revelation, discipline, education and inspiration, God nurtured a small group among all humanity—that rebellious, barbaric, clamorous and disobedient humanity who showed no consideration for the will of the Father— who knew and loved the Lord, who waited upon the Lord, served the

Lord and dedicated themselves to him. Day and night they expected God to show strength with his arm, scatter the proud in the thoughts of their hearts, bring down the powerful from their thrones and lift up the lowly, fill the hungry with good things and send the rich away empty. This band of people would constitute the groundwork for the Incarnation on earth. And in the person of Mary we see the pinnacle and the crystallization of this process of preparing the ground. In her person, God could at last anticipate the appearance of a sufficient spirit of dedication to serve as the carrier of the Incarnation. God himself and the whole cosmos could be said to be holding their breath, awaiting her reply. Her reply concerned the whole people. She had complete freedom and right to say, no, I am just a girl, I cannot allow it to be with me as you said. But her upbringing made her reverence for God as great; her soul rejoiced in God her savior. She did not feel this was a disaster; she felt she had been blessed. She had seen God show strength with his arm, scatter the proud, cast down the high and raise up the lowly, fill the hungry and send the rich away empty. It made her happy to be able to be part of such a work of creation. This is to say that she had her own sense of values and she used her freedom correctly. She consented to offer her cooperation for the Incarnation, allowing herself to become mother to the Incarnation.

It is a person's values, formed through a long period of training, that dictate how that person will choose at a crucial moment. A person who follows a path ahead of her time because of her values, who does something on behalf of history and humankind that will not be immediately understood, will suffer, but will also feel she has won some victory because of it.

I recently read a poem by the Guatemalan poet Otto Rene Castillo (1936–1967) which can serve as a depiction of Mary's suffering and her joy. The poem is called "Tomorrow in the Heavenly Scales."

> On that day, when we
> Tell the enthusiasms of our generation
> To those not yet born,
> But who will live with kindness on their faces,
> Those of us who have suffered most
> Will be the victors.

Walking ahead of the times
Requires bearing a greater burden of sorrow,
Yet,
To be able to love the world
Through the eyes of those yet to be born—
How great and beautiful a thing that is.
And, while all around is still cold and dark
To know that you are the victor,
That too is a wonderful thing.

The angel's conversation with Mary begins Mary's life of suffering, but she was steadfast, because she knew that God would not be defeated in the end. As she endured her suffering, she had already won.

We cannot speak with any great clarity about why the Incarnation is essential to God's work of creation, nor what role Christ and Christ crucified plays in the event of our reconciliation with God. However, our own personal experience and that of the greater portion of humanity over the last 2,000 years tell us that Jesus is our Redeemer. Through his revelation, inspiration, example, teaching and touch, we have repented, we have been saved and we have gained new lives. This has not come about through inference or hearsay, but through reliance on the eyes of the spirit. Like Mary Magdalene, we have seen the Lord and recognized him as truly the Rabboni (Master) who died and has risen.

In the actualization of the Incarnation, Mary's assent played a decisive role. God wants to continue his work of creation, but God is not a steamroller. God does not use force or make people act against their will. God can only strive for people's consent. Through God's work, 2,000 years ago, the created world finally reached the level represented by Mary, a co-worker with God. We can imagine Mary's place in salvation history. For 2,000 years, she has been the example of cooperation with God and has received her due reverence.

Karl Barth said: "I am not opposed in principle to statues of Mary, as long as they are not placed upon the altar, but rather set among the congregation, *facing* the altar." Yes, Mary is first of all a representative of the best in humankind. She stands in our midst and with her love, her dedication, her cooperation, brings our Lord Jesus Christ among us.

We often speak of witnessing to the Lord, of spreading the Lord's word. This means that we, like Mary, sacrifice ourselves in order to actualize our commitment, to be carriers of Christ and bring Christ into the world.

Many people today have forgotten where we came from and how we struggled in the beginning. They want to enjoy material things, they have a desire for this or that, and they want to live a life of luxury. Everything revolves around themselves and their own benefit. Sacrificing oneself for some lofty goal is seen as stupid. Though life-and-death struggles are rare, tension builds easily in interpersonal relationships and a spirit of reconciliation is lacking. The church should not go with the times. We should hold high Christ and emulate Mary. The most important message of Christmas is not eating a big meal or having a grand old time, but the emulation of Mary and all those of her day who, like her, waited for Christ to come into the world. It is to know Christ more profoundly, to introduce Christ more effectively, and to enable the love of Christ among us to spread throughout the world.

—Nanjing Seminary, Christmas, 1987

# Section Two:
# God's Love Extends to All People

# The Gospel of Christ
## is for All

The gospel of Christ is not just for the Jews; it is for all humankind. What an important message this is. In Acts 10, we see how difficult it was for this message to be affirmed in the churches of the apostles' day. Peter initially saw the Lord's saving grace as a gift exclusively for the Jews. But through Cornelius, the Lord led them little by little to see that the grace of salvation was actually prepared by the Lord for all humankind. This was a bitter lesson for Peter, but he learned it.

That the Gentiles were to share in Christ's salvation is a profound mystery. Paul said, "In former generations this mystery was not made known to humankind, as it has now been revealed to his holy apostles and prophets by the Spirit, that is, the Gentiles have become fellow heirs, members of the same body, and sharers in the promise in Christ Jesus through the gospel" (Eph. 3:5–6). Without the revelation of this mystery, Christianity would have remained a religion of the Jews; even we would have had no way of believing. From this we can see the tremendous significance of what is recorded in the tenth chapter of Acts: It was not only an important event for Peter himself and for the history of the Church—it also assumed a place of importance in God's plan of salvation.

Today, let us first set aside this question of how the Gentiles received salvation and ask God to show us how the Holy Spirit leads human beings step by step, ridding them of their pride and arrogance, opening up their ignorance so that they come to see the light.

Paul called the Holy Spirit "a spirit of wisdom and revelation" (Eph. 1:17), who was able to enlighten "the eyes of your heart" (Eph. 1:18). Let us take our Bibles and see together how this Spirit leads us, how we thirst for the Spirit to give us wisdom and revelation. Then let

the Lord tell us through the Spirit, what the rules of the Spirit's leading are.

## THE SPIRIT PREPARES AND ORDAINS

It appears that sometimes God's will is not shown by direct revelation,
rather, through the arrangement of various circumstances, he opens
up our ignorance and stubbornness.

By reading Acts 9:36 to 10:8, we see that there was in Joppa a
nucleus of disciples who believed in the Lord. Peter came to Joppa
because Dorcas fell ill. And Simon, the tanner, had a house there. At
Caesarea was Cornelius, a Gentile who was friendly to the Jews. Each
of these facts seen on its own is mere circumstance, coincidence, but
putting them together, we cannot help but see the action of God himself. They are all part of God's excellent plan.

Long before the death of Jesus, God placed Gentiles who were in
sympathy with the Jews around them as they worshipped in their
synagogues and went about their daily lives. God did this in order
that the gospel might be owned by all humanity. At the time no one
foresaw what role these people would play. But when the Lord's suitable day came, they became the bridges by which the gospel flowed
from the Jews to the world. Cornelius was such a man. A Gentile, he
was "a devout man who feared God with all his household; he gave
alms generously to the people, and prayed constantly to God" (Acts
10:2).

The Spirit's arrangements far surpass human understanding. We
see only the little that is in front of us, a speck, an event, a thing, but
the Spirit sees the whole.

Let us each think back: How did we get to where we are today? Was
it through plans we made years ago? Wasn't it rather by the convergence of all sorts of coincidences coming one after another, shattering
our well-laid schemes? When things around us were out of our control,
we complained, didn't we? We struggled; we tried to run away. And
yet, looking back from today's vantage point, we have come to see
God's hand at work and are left with no alternative but to praise God
and admit the excellence of God's plans over our own.

When Paul tried to preach the gospel in Asia, he seemed to meet blank walls everywhere. By rights he should have been bitterly frustrated. He had committed no offense, and he was able to discern that he was "forbidden by the Holy Spirit," and that "the spirit of Jesus did not allow" it (Acts 16:7). But he was an apostle and could see God's hand at work in this. How could Paul have known that door closed in Asia in order for the Lord to arrange things so that the gospel could enter Europe? Today we recognize this as something tremendously important historically, but at the time even Paul could not see its significance. Thus we can see that we are "nearsighted and blind" (2 Pet. 1:9) to the work of the Holy Spirit which proceeds according to long-range plans and what would be best for the whole situation.

The Lord has told us through the prophet Isaiah (55:9) that his thoughts are higher than our thoughts. But we frequently forget this and cause ourselves much suffering. Paul said: "All things work together for good for those who love God" (Rom. 8:28). Unfortunately, we love ourselves too well and do not love God enough. And so we often do not see how everything is working together for good. Instead we become impatient and start to complain. This is because we are too concerned for ourselves, too focused on how things affect us for good or for ill, and forget to be concerned for God's greater—hundreds and thousands of times greater—will.

But stupid human conceit cannot block the Holy Spirit. The Spirit's work does not need to wait for human understanding of its purpose in order to be accomplished; if it did, how long would it have to wait? It provides the conditions necessary of its own accord, so that God's plan may be realized.

We should be aware that ours is a very narrow view. Like the frog at the bottom of the well, we see only a part of the sky. What we consider important is not necessarily important from God's point of view. Thus, we should not persist in our shortsightedness when looking at what God has done. We should recognize that "our knowledge is imperfect"... we "thought like a child, reasoned like a child ... For now we see in a mirror dimly" [the original has it "in riddles"] (1 Cor. 13:9–12).

This being the case, we should surrender, and in the completeness of God's love and mercy, do our small part with joy.

## WE MUST OPEN THE GATE TO THE HOLY SPIRIT

The gospel belongs to all; this is the will of God. Why did the Lord not tell Peter straight out, so he would know? Why go to all the bother of arranging so many things? The reason lay in Peter's spiritual pride.

The Lord did not tell the disciples directly that this gospel was for all the peoples of the world. When he sent them out, the Lord said: "Go therefore and make disciples of all nations" (Matt. 28:19). Prior to his ascension, he further commanded the disciples to be his witnesses not only in Jerusalem and all Judea and Samaria, but "to the ends of the earth" (Acts 1:8). But because of the spiritual pride of the disciples these words did not seem to have much effect. They were God's chosen! They were the descendents of Abraham, possessing the highest and most perfect truth. They were above all others! They knew what was clean and what was unclean. The Gentiles were nothing to them.

Such a one was Peter. Peter believed in the Lord, but his heart was troubled. Many things were hidden there which had nothing to do with Jesus, some were even hostile to him. His spiritual pride caused him, without quite realizing it, to turn a deaf ear to some of the things Jesus said.

As he was praying on the rooftop, three times in a vision God bade him to eat foods that Jews never touched. Each time, Peter refused saying, "These things are unclean" and "I have never eaten such things." The Holy Spirit said, "What God has cleansed you must not call profane." But Peter slammed the door on the Holy Spirit.

Never eating what has not been eaten before; never thinking what has not been thought before; never doing what has not been done before—thus Peter clung to his own one-sided standards of cleanness before God, and by so doing, placed limits on the Holy Spirit. He allowed the Spirit to move only within the habitual, the familiar, the known.

The Spirit, however, is an active Spirit. "The wind blows where it chooses, and you hear the sound of it, but you do not know where it comes from or where it goes. So it is with everyone who is born of the Spirit" (John 3:8). How could the activity of the Spirit be confined or circumscribed by human appetites, human habits and human prejudices?

The Lord himself tells us: "But the Advocate, the Holy Spirit, whom the Father will send in my name, will teach you everything, and remind you of all that I have said to you" (John 14:26). "When the Spirit of truth comes, he will guide you into all the truth" (John 16:13). Now the Spirit had come. When the Spirit wanted to guide Peter into a new truth, Peter was unwilling to follow, saying, "I have never eaten these things." And thus Peter shut the door and shut it tight. Peter, who would deny the Lord three times, on this occasion resisted the leading of the Holy Spirit three times as well. He shrunk his life into a hard shell, preferring a life without air or light, as long as he felt clean.

Today, too, the Spirit is eager that Christians should be willing for the Spirit to lead them into ever greater truth. The Spirit wants us to eat many things we have never eaten before, think many thoughts we have never thought before, and do many things we have never done before. And we? May we obey, open the door, and in hope and faith, allow the Lord to lead us forward and to grant us wisdom and revelation.

## FROM THE "HOUSETOP" TO THE "GROUND"

In his vision, God called Peter three times to eat those things he had always considered unclean. Peter did not obey. But it was enough to raise a doubt in him and cause him to think.

"Now while Peter was greatly puzzled about what to make of the vision that he had seen, behold, suddenly the men sent by Cornelius appeared. They were asking for Simon's house and were standing by the gate" (Acts 10:17). Things happen so quickly, just like this. How often, when we meet with difficulty, have we not known where to begin, but longed to put things off for a while so we could wait longer upon the housetop for the Lord to make the problem clear? But things develop in a way that does not permit us to remain on the housetop enjoying our ease; the problem is already at the gate, knocking at the door. Life demands that we make prompt and daring decisions.

But we need not be afraid. This is all the Holy Spirit's doing. The Spirit said to Peter: "Now get up, go down, and go with them without hesitation, for *I have sent them*" (Acts 10:20).

The Holy Spirit leads us to the housetop to pray; the Holy Spirit also leads us down to the door to face the problems that we do not know how to face. Both on the housetop above and on the ground below the Holy Spirit is with us—helping us as we kneel to pray, accompanying us as we encounter other kinds of people through the Spirit's leading. The Spirit speaks to us through visions and unfolding circumstances, speaks to us from beginning to end, speaks to us until we understand.

The Spirit had no choice but to interrupt Peter's prayers on the housetop. We should understand that because of our shortcomings, our sin and our pride, what God can get through to us on the housetop is very limited. God sends us downstairs for a lesson. To be sent downstairs is not to be made to leave God, but to obey God. If we insist on remaining on the housetop, we will be hindering the Holy Spirit.

Some people feel that we must first get everything clear, clear up all mysteries and completely understand God's plan of salvation, before we can follow God. But this is ridiculous; perhaps it is simply an excuse for not following God. Only when we follow the single ray of light God has given us, will we begin to understand. God has said: "Anyone who resolves to do the will of God will know whether the teaching" (John 7:17). When the Lord called his disciples saying: "Follow me," how could the apostles possibly know all that "following the Lord" might entail? But they resolutely left all behind and followed him. And the more they followed the better they understood. When the Wise Men from the East saw the star, did they fully realize the meaning of the birth of Christ? Yet they did not hesitate, and in following the star, they finally found Christ.

The Lord's plan is like this: Some truths we cannot enter into on the housetop. He wants us to "get up and go down, go with them, do not hesitate, for I have sent them." We must follow the single ray of light the Lord has given us—because of our shortcomings and our weakness, it can only be a single ray—putting our hand in the Lord's hand and following the path laid before us. We cannot wait to set out until everything is clear to us. Only by taking that first step will we understand more as we go along. This is the life of faith.

One of Newman's hymns says: "I do not ask to see the distant scene; One glimpse enough for me." This is not a song of small faith or lack of spiritual formation. This is truly a prayer of one of great faith and great spiritual depth.

We preachers must spend a great deal of time praying on the housetop, praying about all that God has entrusted to us, one by one with thanksgiving. This is a matter of course, absolutely essential. However, we should not expect that we would receive full illumination on the housetop about each person and thing. We can entrust everything fully to the Lord and then by faith, allow the Holy Spirit to lead us downstairs and into the world. We can go down with light hearts, because this is what the Lord wants of us and because we go with the Holy Spirit continuing to lead us. The Spirit will open up our ignorance, give us wisdom and revelation and open the eyes of our hearts without fail.

> Arise, my love, my fair one,
> and come away; for now the winter is past,
> the rain is over and gone.
> The flowers appear on the earth;
> the time of singing has come,
> and the voice of the turtledove
> is heard in our land.
> The fig tree puts forth its figs,
> and the vines are in blossom;
> they give forth fragrance.
> Arise, my love, my fair one,
> and come away. (Song 2:10–13)

What a tender, loving appeal God is making to us! This day God would have us go forth with joy and eagerness, like young people in love, to receive all the good things that have been prepared for us. He waits patiently outside the door: "O my dove, in the clefts of the rock, in the covert of the cliff" (Song 2:14). "A garden is locked my sister, my bride, a garden locked, a fountain sealed" (Song 4:12). Why do we lock ourselves in, seal ourselves off from the Holy Spirit's leading? Why do we hesitate, making the Spirit wait outside our door, disappointing the Spirit?

## THE SPIRIT UNITES

The Spirit is a Spirit that unites. That Spirit led Peter to the all-important discovery that Cornelius was human, like Peter himself. "Stand
up; I am only a mortal" (Acts 10:26). Very commonplace, isn't it? And
yet Peter learned this lesson at great cost to himself. He lowered himself from the housetop; he came to see that a Gentile, one whom he
had always looked upon as too "unclean" to associate with, could
actually be acceptable to God. In this way the Holy Spirit bridges the
chasm between one person and another.

And this is not all. Peter soon learned another new lesson.
Cornelius shared with Peter the same salvation by the same Lord and
received the same grace from the same Spirit. A long-standing separation was finally healed, for the Holy Spirit not only unites person to
person, but believer to believer.

We can imagine that there were people at the time who objected
to Peter's easy acceptance of Cornelius, people who were afraid that
Gentiles like Cornelius would harm the church and dilute the gospel.

Cornelius made a great contribution to the church. The Holy Spirit
used him not only to break through Peter's ignorance, not only to
build a bridge between the gospel and the Gentiles, but also to greatly
enrich the life of the church. Could Jewish Christians alone have fulfilled God's hopes and demands for the world? Would homogeneity
have been the church's hallmark? Certainly not. The inestimable
length, breadth, height and depth of Christ's love demand the acceptance and witness of innumerable disciples from around the world. All
the mysteries of the gospel, all the truth, goodness and beauty of life,
must be explored and shared by Corneliuses of countless eras, regions
and cultures. The growth of the life of the Church until it is filled with
the true light of glory, until Christians come to know the depths and
breadth of all the wisdom of the gospel, still lies in the future. In the
past generations of saints have made beautiful witness and enriched
the spiritual treasury of later generations in the church. Yet, "since
God had provided something better so that they would not, apart
from us, be made perfect" (Heb. 11:40).

But we should feel greatly ashamed. For so many years, we have
hardly tolerated each other, let alone acted out of mutual respect or

to enrich one another. We have dealt in suspicion, ostracism, discord—sometimes even to the point of splitting hairs on a question as fine as hair. Since Liberation, things have improved considerably. Within the church, the different denominations with different theologies, different church orders and different liturgies, have been able to work together as the right hand works with the left. In this way the church can truly be the church, just as Paul says: "Maintain the unity of the Spirit in the bond of peace ... (When) each part is working properly, (this) promotes the body's growth in building itself up in love."

## WE ARE CO-WORKERS WITH THE SPIRIT

"While Peter was still speaking, the Holy Spirit fell on all who heard the word" (Acts. 10:44). The Holy Spirit had been working behind the scenes all along, but now the Spirit began its work directly, interrupting Peter. "And as I began to speak, the Holy Spirit fell upon them" (Acts 11:15).

Before Peter could finish what he was saying, he was cut off. But this did not upset him. He had not after all told the Spirit to wait till he finished talking before coming down. He stepped aside at once so that he would not get in the way of the Holy Spirit.

This shows us an important truth—a truth about how we should work together with the Holy Spirit. The work we do is extremely important because we are working with the Spirit. The Spirit works through us to do some pioneering preparatory work. When everything is ready, God himself begins to work. Then we should retreat to a place where we will not obstruct the work of the Spirit.

We should maintain that what we do is of almost no importance (because it is the Lord working), to forestall our own arrogance. But we should also emphasize that what we do is of the utmost importance (because the Lord has entrusted it to us), to avoid self-disparagement. Our work is important and we should take responsibility for it. But our work is also unimportant and we have no room for conceit. This is the Lord's work; no one is worthy of it. But precisely because this is the Lord's work, whether we are worthy or not is unimportant.

## WHO WAS I THAT I COULD HINDER GOD?
## (ACTS 11:17)

To begin with, Peter's spirit was blocked, "I have never eaten these things"—this is representative of his whole frame of mind. But the experiences of these two or three days wrought a great transformation in Peter. He saw that Gentiles too were truly recipients of the grace of the Holy Spirit. He could not help asking, "Who was I that I could obstruct God?"

When Peter saw the Holy Spirit working in the person of a Gentile, he was not at all jealous and bore not the slightest bit of malice toward the Gentiles when he discovered that Jews had no monopoly over the Holy Spirit. He simply humbly admitted the facts and thanked God.

Today our spiritual arrogance causes us not to recognize the truth the Spirit wants to lead us into. Where do we base this pride? The most precious thing we have—salvation—comes from the Lord himself, and not from any goodness in us.

Peter said: "I truly understand that God shows no partiality." He saw this truth only after an experience of spiritual suffering. May we too truly be able to see this truth.

"If you know that he (God) is righteous, you may be sure that every one who does right has been born of him" (1 John 2:29). Since this is so, we should be humble and thank God.

The Spirit is most marvelous, working where we least expect. What then should we do? Let us not say: "I have never eaten these things," thereby denying the Spirit. Let us rather say with humble and grateful hearts: "What was I that I could hinder the Lord?"

In this way we receive the wisdom and revelation given us by the Spirit and enter a step further into the truth.

—The Spirit of Wisdom and Revelation, 1954

# UNDERSTANDING
# THE HEART OF GOD

I never thought I would be in Hollywood meeting so many movie stars and people engaged in the film industry. Thank you for this opportunity.

There are three people in the story of the Prodigal Son: the father, the younger son and the elder son. I want to say something about all three, but especially about the father.

First of all, the father helps us to see the heart of God. What we see of God in Jesus' life and teachings is for the most part not his omnipotence, might or severity, not his power to compel humans to submit, not his desire for revenge, not his merciless punishment of humankind, but his love, sympathy, respect for humans and his patient waiting for human awakening. When the younger son decided to leave home, the father was very unhappy, but he did not impose his will upon his son. God can seem excessively tolerant, almost powerless, for God will not force his son or use high-handed methods against him. He does not long for human obedience under pressure, but for fellowship that comes from the heart. If fellowship is not freely willed and given, then it is not fellowship. If there is only one path that can be taken and all others are blocked, if one is not allowed to choose wrongly, then there is no free will involved. Thus we see that in order to respect humanity, God limits his power. In his dealings with humans, he would rather wait patiently as we act out of our own volition. His methods are reconciliation, creation, redemption, sanctification, education and persuasion.

There is an anti-feudal story in China about a young woman whose fiancé died. The feudal custom required her to be married into his family anyway and serve them as a daughter-in-law. When she entered her bridal chamber after the tear-filled wedding ceremony, she saw a five-foot long plank lying on the bed. This was to be her husband for life. The story ends with her struggle to throw off the fetters of feudalism and join the Red Detachment of Women in the war against Japan. Imagine: What kind of fellowship could she have with a piece of wood? How could she have loved it? In the same way, the true emotion God is waiting for is fellowship. God's nature does not permit him to treat the prodigal son as a robot that takes orders. It is fellowship God is seeking; he is not a conqueror, not a tyrant who compels submission. The apex of God's creation will be the appearance of a new type of human in the universe, one that will willingly and joyfully be a co-creator with God. All creation and ourselves have been, until now, beings and creatures in process, unfinished products. During this change, every man and woman among us is undergoing a transformation, from persons who can only follow orders mechanically to persons who can respond joyfully to God's invitation, new persons who can take an active part in the process of creation.

Because of the pastoral background of the Jewish people, the Bible contains many references to the shepherd and the sheep: "The Lord is my shepherd, I shall not want." "We are his people, the sheep of his pasture." We know that the pastoral relationship requires no more than obedience of the sheep; they need only follow. The shepherd is constantly giving orders and scolding and when the sheep go astray; the shepherd controls them with his rod and staff, forcing them to obey. But when humans obey because they have been scolded, this is not the highest virtue they can aspire to.

We Chinese have been an agrarian people for thousands of years, and one of the Bible's other analogies for the divine-human relationship is more amenable to our culture; that is, the relationship between the gardener or farmer and plants and crops. "A sower went out to sow"; "unless a grain of wheat falls into the earth and dies, it remains alone; but if it dies, it bears much fruit." When we read these and similar passages, we think of the gardener or farmer who, without the use of rod or staff, without orders to compel obedience, plants the seed, fertilizes it and allows the plant to grow in sunshine and rain, and protects it until it grows to fullness. When everything has been done that needs to be done, there is a period of waiting, waiting for nature to take its course. During that time the farmer's most effective form of aid is to do nothing but wait.

Lao Tzu's influence on Chinese culture is not inferior to that of

Confucius himself. He teaches us not to act rashly when doing nothing is called for. This is not an admonition to do nothing, but rather teaches us not to act unthinkingly before the time is ripe. The story of the return of the prodigal son shows us a God who cultivates through his eternal love, who grows, who watches, who patiently waits for us to grow in Christ. There is nothing he cannot do, but he prefers to restrain this power because he is unwilling to force us to his will.

God moves the universe through his great love. He warmly, movingly, without a hint of annoyance and without limit sustains his relationship with people. Moreover, with their cooperation, he brings all possible goodness into the world. To affirm God as the Lover of the universe is to see love as the agent of God's never-ending, ongoing creation. Love is God's highest attribute, which surpasses all his other attributes and relegates them to second place.

I do not say that God's highest attribute is his justice. If justice were higher than love, if we left God's love behind in order to emphasize God's justice, this would inevitably lead to a warped religion. Such a religion would see God as a Master who rewards and punishes. If a person met with misfortune it would be because that person had offended God somehow, inflamed God's anger. When things were going well for this person, it would be because he or she had somehow pleased God. Such a Christianity, concerned with avoiding trouble and benefiting oneself, would be a utilitarian faith and would have lost what separates it from cruder forms of religion.

Let us talk about the younger son. In him we see the condition of so many men and women in this world. Looking at the younger son, we see that people are not effortlessly good. People can either sink very low or rise to the heights proper to sons and daughters of God. Humanity finds itself in the shadow of sin, but at the same time it can never shake off the father's merciful love. There is a power within us which compels us to do the things we do not want to do and to avoid doing what we should. The correct term for this power is sin. As Paul said, "I do not understand my own actions, for I do not do what I want, but I do the very thing I hate" (Rom. 7:15). He goes on to say that it is the sin that dwells within us that makes us this way. Luke, chapter 15, tells us that when we leave God's path, we are no longer where God wanted us to be when he created us. But this need not become a reason to destroy ourselves. When the prodigal son fed the pigs for his master, he was still his father's son. Jesus had a great deal of faith in the prodigal son. He said that the prodigal "came to himself." The father never lost hope in his return; he was waiting for it. We should not see human life as unchanging. We are all changing. We are not immobile like a dead, stiff butterfly pinned to a piece of cardboard. We are subjects who come from the past, live in the present and hope for the future. The prodigal and we ourselves are all in the process of changing. We are all beings in process in God's hand and this gives the prodigal and every one of us hope.

Let us turn now to the elder brother. In the elder brother we can see many people in our churches who lack loving hearts. The elder brother stayed with the father and his situation seems quite good. But he is not happy about the new life his younger brother is about to begin. When he speaks to his father, he does not say "my brother," but "this son of yours." It is the father who says "this brother of yours."

An important truth about people is that we were created to have loving hearts in the end. We are lovers-in-the-making, we are still being created. St. John of the Cross said: "When our days come to their end, we will be judged according to the love in our hearts." In Matthew, chapter 25, Jesus himself tells us that it will not be those who think they are close to God but do not have love who enter the kingdom of heaven, but rather the brothers and sisters who have love in their hearts. This elder brother reminds us of Jonah, an evangelist who had no love in his heart for his hearers. He feared that they might repent and turn to God. In past years when we in China talked about how to treat our compatriots, we said we must overcome the "Jonah attitude" or the "elder brother syndrome." If we have no love in our hearts for others, there is no way we can truly hope for them to accept Christ. Perhaps you have heard of the great growth in the number of new Christians in China. If it were not for the fact that most Christians act with great love and care in their work, this would not have happened. When people see their deeds of love, they are bound to ask what Christianity is and they are willing to listen to the message Christianity has for them.

Since God is the Lover in the universe, he prefers to act through teaching and waiting rather than by coercion. Though not a few Christians lack loving hearts, since humankind is changing, they too, are changing. A world in transformation is bound to have its dark and ugly side. Our comfort lies in the faith that says that no matter how dark things are, the world and we ourselves are changing and that change is taking place within God's creative process, as we evolve from half-finished products to better ones.

The line from alpha to omega is not straight. But love and grace go with us wherever we go. We must follow a tortuous and winding path, but the words of Christ comfort us: "When a woman is in labor she has pain because her hour has come. But when her child is born, she no longer remembers the anguish because of the joy of having brought a human being into the world" (John 16:21).

All reality and all people are evolving—this is the Christian point of view. This comforts us and fills us with gratitude.

—All Saints Church, Hollywood
September 1993

# GOD'S LOVE
## REVEALED IN SCRIPTURE

My title is rather long but not at all complicated. Because God reveals things to us in the Bible gradually, revelations are not single events over and done with. In the same way, human understanding of God's revelation does not come all at once either but unfolds and increases gradually.

From its earliest section to the most recent, the biblical text records over 1,000 years of history. Over this long period, God has many times and in many ways corrected people's misperceptions of God and led them step by step to understand God better. As it says in

Hebrews 1:1, "Long ago God spoke to our ancestors in many and various ways by the prophets."

Jesus' own words in John 16:12–13 express the same idea. "I still have many things to say to you, but you cannot bear them now. When the Spirit of truth comes, he will guide you into all truth."

Why should this be so? Why doesn't God tell us everything he has to tell us all at once? Why spend over 1,000 years of Bible history telling us? Because we would not understand all at once and, if we could, we could not bear it. Apart from our sinfulness and weakness, each one of us absorbs so much in terms of culture and tradition that has been shaped by those who came before us. Our ideas and viewpoints, the way we think, all this comes from our families, our parents, teachers, neighbors, friends, classmates and colleagues. And much more comes to us from novels, movies and television. Once they have taken shape, these ideas, viewpoints and ways of thinking become ingrained and are very hard to change.

We know that God's love extends beyond the Israelites to many other peoples. God made this explicit to people in many and various ways in the Old Testament. He announced it in Amos 9:7. "Are you not like the Ethiopians to me, O people of Israel? Says the Lord. Did I not bring Israel up from the land of Egypt, and the Philistines from Caphtor and the Arameans from Kir?" Again in Isaiah 19:25: "Whom the Lord of hosts has blessed, saying, 'Blessed be Egypt my people, and Assyria the work of my hands, and Israel my heritage'." However, by New Testament times, many people still had not taken in what they had heard, maintaining that God was only the God of Israel and God loved only the Israelites. This being the case, it would naturally take a very long time for God to correct the Israelites' misperception of him.

When God used Peter to enable the gospel of Christ to break through the bonds of Jewish ethnicity and spread to all the peoples of the world, the first thing required was that Peter receive the gentile Cornelius. Peter's resistance to this was great (Acts 10). It had been ingrained in Peter that he should not come into contact with "unclean things" and this was an obstacle to God's wonderful will. God had to use other means gradually to turn Peter's thinking around. Later his thinking did change a little but he was still rather stubborn. In the church too, there were some who still clung to tradition and did not change a bit.

## God's love extends to all peoples

There was a very long period when, in the eyes of the Israelites, God was the God of Israel, the one who led them into Canaan. The Israelites believed that God wanted them to slaughter the original inhabitants of Canaan. Today we see this as a barbaric and inhumane act, something that could not be the will of God. But, at the time, Joshua and others felt that this was God's righteousness. Many such views of God can be found preserved in the Old Testament books of Deuteronomy and Joshua.

Consider two passages:

> But as for the towns of these peoples that the Lord your God is giving you as an inheritance, you must not let anything that breathes remain alive. You shall annihilate them—the Hittites and the Amorites, the Canaanites and the Perizzites, the Hivites and the Jebusites—just as the Lord your God has commanded. (Deut. 20:16–17)

> So Joshua defeated the whole land, the hill country and the Negeb and the lowland and the slopes, and all their kings; he left no one remaining, but utterly destroyed all that breathed, as the Lord God of Israel commanded." (Josh. 10:40)

Such views persisted for a long time, right up until the exile. Psalm 137:9 still calls for the Babylonian infants' heads to be dashed against the stones. Jonah is another example. Coming from a narrow ethnic background he was only too anxious that the people of Nineveh not repent so that he could call down the wrath of God to destroy the city. But God is a merciful God. God told Jonah, "Should I not be concerned about Nineveh, that great city, in which there are more than a hundred and twenty thousand persons who do not know their right hand from their left?" (2:11). We see from this that the Israelites' misperceptions of God died hard.

However, through a long period of revelation and teaching from

God, the view that God's love extends to all peoples is becoming more widely accepted. Finally, in 1 John 4:16 we read, "God is love." We might consider this as the height of biblical revelation about the nature of God. It can also be considered the pinnacle of human under-stand of God. It is many years from Deuteronomy and Joshua to 1 John. God felt that humanity had progressed to such an extent that some people, at least, could embrace this revelation that God is love and so he spoke this simple and clear truth. In other words, only after a long passage of time would there be some people able to under-stand, accept and take up this simple truth that God is love.

And so some say that there is internal development in the Bible. I would say that we have no reason to oppose such a view.

"God is love." Love is not a sometime attribute of God. Love is not merely on attribute of God among others. Love is the foremost attrib-ute of all God's attributes. This *is* the gospel. John 3:16 begins, "For God so loved the world" and only then says that God sent his only son into the world to complete his plan for redemption through the incar-nation, giving eternal life to those that believe in him. Without love on God's part, God could be seen simply as a deity absorbed in his own perfection, unconcerned for human being. If we speak only of God's righteousness and do not speak of God's love, the image we give of God is that of a punisher. Christian faith becomes a religion of fear and dread brought down the level of common primitive folk religion. In fact, righteousness is derived from love. Only with love as the prereq-uisite can there be talk of righteousness.

## THE JUST NATURE OF LOVE

There are four children in my family, including me. Once my parents had to be away from home for some time and my father knew that we would quarrel over food, so he made a rule. One of us must cut what-ever we ate, be it cake or fruit, into four pieces (in each) and let the other three choose first, taking the last piece for him or herself. This made it much fairer and we didn't quarrel. I have always remembered this and have always thought my father the wisest and fairest of fathers. He loved us four children and his love never changed. His fair-mindedness and righteousness were expressions of his love.

When love reaches many people, the just nature of love will be made manifest.

During the Second World War Hitler put all the Jews in Germany into concentration camps and sent them to places specially constructed to kill them. They were stripped of their gold teach, their hair, their clothing and locked into windowless rooms where they were gassed. Over five million died. This cruel and barbaric act is called the Holocaust. Some supports of Hitler claimed that the Jews were guilty of murdering Jesus and should be punished for their crime. They quoted the Old Testament, using as evidence the Israelites' attack on Canaan and their holy war against weaker peoples, saying the massacres were God's command. They negated the love of God in the name of God's righteousness, thereby extinguishing God's love and portraying God as a hater of humankind and a brutal punisher. We must shout at those who hold such a view of God that God is not Satan, nor is God a fascist! The Holocaust is condemned by all who speak of righteousness in this world. When we speak of God's righteousness, we must not for moment forget that it must be founded primarily on God's merciful love.

When China was invaded by the Japanese military empire, forty million soldiers and civilians lost their lives. There were people in our church then who said that this was God's punishment of China. But many people in the church also asked why God would punish the Chinese victims and not the Japanese invaders. God is love, God is righteous, but this righteousness must be under the rule of God's love.

God is the cosmic lover. With a heart of merciful love he is constantly creating and redeeming. This teaching has been the decisive revelation for my own spiritual journey. It has deepened my faith, my hope and my love.

This view of revelation has helped me to attain a more complete and consistent approach to the Bible. I would like you to ponder the following: Is there development taking place in the view of God and other concepts in the Bible? Can this understanding help us better to discover the treasures hidden in the Bible?

The God described in the book of Joshua and the God of 1 John do not seem to be the same God, but there cannot be two gods in the one Bible. I can only say that due to human obtuseness, God's revelation must progress gradually. It must develop, moving from low to high. The understanding of God expressed by people in the Bible also evolves gradually until it reaches perfection. If we deny that the view of God in the Bible changes and develops, what other means have we to reconcile the supposed contradictions in the Bible? Let us humbly await wisdom from God, and may the Chinese church gain a view of God and the Bible that will be pleasing in God's sight.

—Address to the Sixth National Christian Conference, 1998

છ૭

# God's Love Transcends Our Sin

In the biological world, the higher animals are able to express joy and sorrow using their vocal chords. Humanity is more advanced and uses language to express thoughts and feelings. This is a great step forward. Using language to communicate elevates people's thoughts and feelings and makes them more precise. Soon people discover that there are many thoughts and feelings that cannot be expressed in language. We often hear people say things like, "I just don't know how to put my gratitude into words." Kant said that beauty is something that cannot be put into words. He also felt that imprecise concepts were richer in expressiveness than clear ones. This is why humanity has pushed beyond language to find means of expression. Poetry is one of these. Poetry can often express things difficult to put into our usual language. Some means of expression, such as art, dispense with language completely. Poetry and painting are more ambiguous and obscure, and it is this very vagueness that makes them more expressive and allows human beings space for imagination and creativity. This is what we call providing food for thought. Music is another language beyond words with an obscurity about it that speaks to our hearts in so many words of joy, of sorrow and pain, of regret, of thanksgiving. Certain eternal ideas in human hearts, ideas philosophers and theologians have no way to address clearly, can come out in music.

There is another type of language important in human culture and that is the language of verisimilitude, of symbol. We announce a message through an event in order to illustrate a truth. The prophet Hosea spoke of taking a fallen woman as a wife to symbolize God's great love. Jesus spoke through the washing of feet, the breaking of the bread, the cross, and so many other forms of unspoken language, so that generations of believers might, through imagination, prayer, meditation and waiting, enter more deeply into experience. Such forms of expression provide a channel for us to enter into the inner world of Christ.

The early church gathered around the Incarnation of Christ countless of the best and most beautiful proclamations, stories and poetry. And the church through the ages continued even more in this way. People brought the best and most beautiful art, music, dance, poetry, plays and carvings to be presented to Christ, to worship Christ. Symbols for the season of Christ's coming into the world are most numerous by far. Angels in heaven, flocks of sheep on the earth, poor shepherds, the star in the East, the humble manger, the beautiful Holy Mother freely working with God—these increasingly rich symbols— speak in people's hearts so much that cannot be expressed in words. These things, sifted through history, have come down to us as things of eternal value that have an eternal message.

How is it that Christ is so great that over 2,000 years a growing number of people have come to revere and worship him? I will approach this question from just one of many possible angles.

We often say that the word Incarnation (John 1:14) is extremely rich in meaning. Incarnation first of all confirms that God is a God who transcends nature, world and history. Without this transcendence, we could not speak of Incarnation. It is this all-transcending God entering in among us that draws us to himself and allows us to gain revelation. People's concept of God often determines their view of human life. Knowledge of the all-transcendent God leads us inevitably to accept the concept of transcendence and give it meaning for human life. It then becomes a voice at our ear ceaselessly urging us on, urging us not to be content with our surroundings, demanding that human beings transcend the given, transcend the present, ourselves, all evil and darkness, transcend our achievements and even our fate.

In certain circumstances, for some people, Christian faith does indeed have a narcotic effect. Some say religion is an opiate and we cannot completely deny this. However, an even more important effect of Christianity is transcendence. Christianity leads people to transcend, to advance, to break out of the status quo and never to lose heart. As the prophet Jeremiah said: "My anguish, my anguish! I writhe in pain! Oh, the walls of my heart! My heart is beating wildly; I cannot keep silent." We can say this is a transcendent movement of the seed of the Christian concept of God in the field of our hearts.

Morality has suffered in our society recently. Some say they will do anything in order to get money or power. It seems as if the notion of "devil take the hindmost," out of favor for so many years, is okay now and even justified. Laughter sometimes greets the suggestion to learn from Lei Feng. There is a lot of anxiety about this. A number of people have said to me lately that it seems there is something to this original sin we Christians talk about.

Accepting the idea of original sin does not make someone a Christian. Original sin in itself is a counsel of pessimism. If a person accepts the idea of original sin and pushes it to its logical extreme, he or she will either be completely self-indulgent or suicidal. Original sin is not the Christian gospel. Christianity allows people to know a God of salvation, a God who destroys the power of sin, a transcendent God. It is this God who, in a time of moral decline, enables many to resist, to turn back, be rescued and find new strength.

That a person can have a consciousness of sin and recognize him or herself as a sinner does not imply weakness. Only because we see God's highness do we become conscious of our lowliness. This lowliness then becomes the threshold of transcendence; it shows that we have heard the call of transcendence and have accepted its challenge.

To become conscious of sin is to become conscious that all is not well, to have a consciousness of suffering, a concern for the world. Only if this is our starting point can we speak of reform and improvement. This is to say that when we feel emptiness within and an awareness of the reality of sin, when we fear that life is in vain and long to cast off this feeling of emptiness and meaninglessness, all this is not necessarily negativity and decadence. It is actually a transcendence of the status quo, the prerequisite for the liberation and actualization of life.

A student from Nanjing Normal University went to Xiangshui County in northern Jiangsu to do research. There were 8,831 Christians there and most got along well with their friends and families, and were law-abiding. One Christian told him: "Before I became a Christian, I stole, got into fights, cursed at people, gambled—the whole lot. But after I became a Christian, I stopped all that." In one rural collective things constantly went missing, but after the people became Christians, this too stopped. In the first six months of 1987, a court heard 238 civil disputes, 58 criminal cases, and 60 economic cases. In none of these was a believer at fault. The head of a rural police station said: "I've been in the job nine years and have never had a Christian brought in for a crime." Cremation is promoted in that area; 53 percent of non-believers cooperate, but 100 percent of Christians. These Christians may never even have heard of such things as the transcendence of God, but having believed in God, they enthusiastically live and work according to teachings such as "do unto others"; "it is more blessed to give than to receive"; "you should be as your Heavenly Father in all things." In reality transcendence becomes their motive force. Will this not attract even more people to the Lord?

Discontentment with things as they are, gaining the impetus of transcendence—this explains why the Christian concept of God touches people and illustrates the greatness of Christ. This is also why Christ's advent and Incarnation charms people.

Christianity is a religion that makes use of a great many symbols to preserve the thoughts, sayings and ways of acting which generations of Christians have held to be precious. It does not ask us to go back 2,000 years and use those thought patterns. It wants us to transcend the surface, to explore the deeper and more numerous meanings hidden within the symbol and not to be constrained by the appearance. It desires us to "be transformed," and in old symbols "discern what is the will of God—what is good and acceptable and perfect" (Rom. 12:2).

I am very happy that there are more intellectuals today taking a new look at the Christian message. Some have a friendly approach to Christianity and appreciate the good actions of the Christians among their neighbors and in society; some appreciate the concept of God in Christianity that lifts up the transcendence of God; some have dedicated themselves to this God by becoming Christians, while others are more willing to be unbaptized converts to the culture and theology of Christ. We welcome them all. The voices that rejoiced in Christ's coming into the world originally were not uniform, but were of many kinds and colors.

Martin Luther said that Christ came to the manger, but the manger contained straw as well as Christ. Let us put these words to work in the church today. People want to see Christ in the church. Let us clean out the straw and make Christ manifest, so that the church may truly be the church. This is the common goal that binds us together.

—Talk at Nanjing Seminary, 1988

ॐ

# CHRIST CARES
# FOR ALL OUR NEEDS

I am most grateful to be able to worship with you this evening. It gives me special pleasure to learn that this is the church which sent Jim Endicott to be a missionary in China. He did so much to give Christianity an image which China could somehow appreciate. Today, in China, we have a revolution to which Christianity is not any longer a stranger, and a Christianity to which revolution is not any longer a stranger either. And we are grateful for this missionary who contributed much to the evolvement of both.

We have just read the wonderful story of the feeding of the five thousand. There are a few things that I wish to call your attention to.

First, the disciples thought that Christ's work just consisted of *talking* about the Kingdom. As to the question of feeding the multitude, it was none of his business and, therefore, none of their business either. They said, send the crowd away, let them all go their own ways and get whatever food they can. But Christ said, "give ye them to eat." Now, what the disciples were advocating was actually the principle of each looking after oneself, that is, each doing his or her own thing. If this is put into practice, as indeed it has been in China and elsewhere, the result is inevitably for the strong and mighty to dominate and for the common people to be their victims. It all ends up in a full-fledged capitalism which is defined by world-renowned economist John Maynard Keynes as "the extraordinary belief that the nastiest of men for the nastiest of motives will somehow work for the benefit of us all," and we know it has not worked out that way.

Second, in order to feed the people, Christ instructed the disciples that the multitude be divided into groups of roughly fifty people each and that they all be seated in groups rather than walking about in disorder. Since it was Christ that said that, I suppose people would be kind enough not to call that regimentation or curtailment of individual freedom. Let us say it is some necessary discouragement of individualism, a certain amount of program, planning and organization. And we know from our experience in China that this is necessary.

Third, let us note that Christ looked up to heaven, blessed the food, broke the bread and gave the food to the disciples to set before the multitude. My guess is that there were all sorts of views and opinions in the multitude as regards the person of Jesus Christ. But Christ respected them all. His care was for the whole multitude, indeed the whole humanity, not just those in the crowd who knew him personally. Let us realize God is so great that it would not be true to his nature for his love and care to be reserved only to those who consciously profess his name. I do not think he minds terribly much that there are those who for some reason or other cannot acknowledge but have to deny his name.

Fourth, although it was far from being a banquet, there was no shortage. Everybody could be full. Nobody needed to suffer from starvation. What relief that must be for parents to know their children will not need to go to bed that night in hunger. And that is an important part of the meaning of the word liberation. When I say China is a liberated country, I do have in mind the fact that, through some planning and organization, we are able to feed almost one-fourth of humanity with the food produced on only one-seventh of the arable land of the earth. It is not a miracle as Christ's was, but it is an achievement of some sort we want to thank God for.

Fifth, let us note that there were twelve baskets full of food left over but nothing is said of what happened to them. Where did they go? Thrown away and gone to the garbage? Just left there to be devoured by animals which came by night? Sold to someone who could pay a good price and who hoarded it up until there was a shortage of grain and the market price went up, and then sold so that the rich got still richer and the poor still poorer? So the biblical silence on the disposal of the left-over food sets us thinking. Now, usually, the Christian message comes to us by what the Bible says but, sometimes, it also comes to us by what the Bible refrains from saying. Is it thinkable that the silence of St. Luke's Gospel on this very point is meant for the Holy Spirit to set us thinking and to lead us into seeing that the problem was not really solved by feeding five thousand people once? What can twelve basketfuls of food do to relieve the fifty thousand, and the five hundred thousand and the five and even fifty million poor people of the world of their hunger? So this Biblical silence has become for us a symbol of the unfinished responsibility, a symbol of the unhelpfulness of mere philanthropy in a world which is producing poverty and hunger much faster than our kind-hearted philanthropist can catch up with. Traditional ethics looks only at the actors, the hungry men and women on the street, the beggars, the thieves and the robbers, but the mystery of the twelve basketfuls urges us to examine the social order which mass-produced them.

Our good earth cannot produce enough for everybody's greed.

How are we to distribute wealth and opportunities more justly and fairly? That is the question the gospel story has raised for us.

When I was a primary school boy I lived in Shanghai. I knew something of how the wealthy lived in those days. But some miles away there was Yangchow, an area which was so poor that, whenever there was a drought, and that was often, men and women there would come to Shanghai, barefooted and in rags, in groups big and small, to seek work. They were so bony and lifeless that their very look was frightening to me. They didn't really expect any wages. Just food for survival and they would work. And many could find neither work nor food. They became beggars. Some of them died on the street because of hunger and cold. Girls were sold as prostitutes. For boys, to be able to be accepted as an apprentice in a barber shop and eventually become a barber would be considered the best of luck. These were the downtrodden, and they constituted the majority of our people.

Now some two years ago I was able to visit that area. There are no landlords to extort exorbitant rentals from the peasants any more. There is hydraulic irrigation now. People are living in brick houses, not in mud ones any longer. Men and women are studying, from kindergarten to university, or are working in factories or the farm. Many women factory workers are wearing leather shoes and there are watches on their wrists. Some of them wear woolen trousers and dacron shirts, with a pen or two in the pocket. And they are on bikes, too. These things may not mean much to you but to them it is such a tremendous change. When I heard their laughter, I was almost in tears, because I was thinking of the plight of their forebears. How I wished to tell the young people there of what I had seen, so that they wouldn't forget the past.

There are defects, mistakes, excesses. China is not a paradise. But our society today is one which expects from its citizens an increased scope in the exercise of the will and of reason. There is now certainly a much more equitable distribution of wealth and opportunities. And landlords have now become working people too. In China, all of this has been brought about through a great social upheaval, i.e., the ownership of the means of production having been changed from a small section of our population to the masses of the people themselves. We call that liberation. It is liberation in the true sense of the word because our people have gained freedom, not lost it, and are now able to work through organized efforts for greater freedom for themselves and for future generations.

I do think Christians have good reasons to be concerned with the question of material distribution. After Christ's resurrection, he walked with two of his disciples on their way to Emmaus. Do you remember that it was not when he was expounding the scriptures to them or when their hearts got very warm that they came to know who he was? And it was not when he sat down to eat with them either. It was only when he took bread and blessed it and gave the bread to them that their eyes were opened and they knew him to be the Christ. So, could we not say that the distribution of the bread to humanity really has something of the sacrament in it? The way wealth and opportunities are distributed, i.e., the way society is organized, does have a lot to do with the manifestation of Jesus Christ to men and women.

We know that the God Jesus Christ came to reveal to us is a God who is at the same time loving and almighty. Now, if people do take their conception of God seriously, this sort of a God is really not so easy to visualize. From people's experiences of injustice and deprivation and suffering, people for whom nothing in life is cheerful and gay, it is much easier to visualize a God who is loving but not almighty, or a God who is almighty but not loving, or a God who is neither loving nor almighty. And yet we insist God is both loving and almighty in spite of the evils and suffering around us. That is demanding a lot. So people find it hard to hold to this Christian conception of God. They feel the attraction of the death-of-God hypothesis. The death of God as a theological fad was short-lived but the death of God as a working philosophy of life is spreading. A Jewish rabbi had this to say to us: "When I say we live in the time of the death of God, I mean that the thread uniting God and humanity, heaven and earth, has been broken. We stand in a cold, silent, unfeeling cosmos, unaided by any purposeful power beyond our own resources. After Auschwitz, what else can a Jew say about God?"

So here, in a naked way, we see how social and economic and political injustice eats away at man's faith in a God who is at once almighty and loving. It is only the achievement of a healthier social system and a fairer distribution of the world's goods to men and women, with all the prosperity and peace and joy and progress it entails, that will enable men and women to see some reasonableness in our Christian conception of God, the God who is the *Father Almighty*, and to find causes for thanksgiving to that God.

Thus the question of distribution certainly has a very important evangelistic dimension to it which we must not lose sight of. The water which runs through the hydraulic irrigation system in Yangchow is of course cold, but I like to think of the warmth it brings to human life, the warmth in the hearts of parents who today can give full rice bowls to their healthy children, the warmth of the assurance that their adolescent girls don't need to do out of hunger anything unworthy of self-respect. Thus we see that matter is not necessarily such an evil, it can be made into a channel for transmitting in some way some grace of God. This is *Sacrament* in the rudimentary sense of the word, for this matter now represents and conveys something of God's love and care to men and women.

Let us be serious when we say this is God's world. It means this world is not Satan's. It means the thread uniting God and humanity, heaven and earth, has not been broken and we do not stand in a cold, silent, unfeeling cosmos. It means God the Father Almighty, the all-loving and all-powerful God, God the Creator, is today carrying on his work of Creation to its final completion. It means what we human beings do with our hands and minds is meaningful, is of value, is not to be destroyed or thrown to the garbage at the end of history, but to be received by Christ, to be transfigured, to be perfected and made acceptable to God. We appreciate Thomas Aquinas when he said that grace does not supplant nature, but perfects nature. For the Incarnation of the Son of God to have happened at all means that there is not a total disparity between God and the world, between grace and nature. To say that man is fallen is to say that he is not at present in his proper state, the state where he belongs, the state for which he is made. It certainly does not mean that all his work is to go to nothing. The incarnation of the Son of God has surely made more of an impact on humanity than the Fall of Adam. Human solidarity with Christ is more universal, more powerful, than human solidarity with Adam through sin. We believe in a universality of divine grace. We look at the world in the splendor of the Ascended Christ. What human beings do to promote community, to make love more possible and more available to the masses of our people, is in consonance with God's work of creation and redemption and sanctification, because God himself, the Father, the Son and the Holy Spirit, has the image of the loving community and humanity that was created in that image, and is moving in the direction of recovering that image. The creation itself will be set free from its bondage and obtain its glorious liberty of the children of God. This is how we look at the world and at history, and at human aspirations and movements and struggles. And this is a source of our optimism and thanksgiving.

Now the feeding of the five thousand takes us to a world which is a community of sharing, a world in which life is so organized that men and women can be brothers and sisters to each other. As we live our daily life may the vision of this coming world sustain us in the fellowship of faith and hope and love.

O Lord Jesus Christ who taught us to pray, give us this day our daily bread, help us to see that while for us, this is just something to say, for millions and millions of thy children today, for no fault of their own, this is a desperate cry. Help us, O Christ, to pray earnestly, thy Kingdom come, thy will be done on earth as it is in heaven. We yearn to see that Kingdom come, and make us worthy instruments of its arrival.

—Timothy Eaton Memorial Church
Toronto, Canada,
November 4, 1979

# GOD'S LOVE
## EXTENDS TO THE ATHEIST

It may be odd for a preacher to tell a group of Christians at worship that there are positive things to be said of those who see no value in worship and, indeed, deny the very existence of God, the object of our worship. But this is exactly what I will try to do because of the spiritual dimension the whole question opens up.

I find it impossible to put all atheists in the same class. For our present purposes, atheists may be grouped into at least three categories.

First, there are atheists who are moral bankrupts. Their life is so selfish, so mean, so irresponsible and so chaotic that they simply cannot afford to believe in God because they fear that God, if there be one, certainly cannot approve of them and would interfere with their way of life. Their atheism is really a sort of opium to benumb themselves, even if only temporarily.

What complicates matters a bit is that these atheists are sometimes unscrupulous and cynical enough to want to appear to be patronizers of religion. All through history, and in our present-day world too, politicians in large numbers put on the garb of religiosity in order to make use of religion to further their unspeakable selfish ends. We remember, for instance, King Herod, who pretended to want to worship the newborn Christ, although his real intention was to find the child and kill him.

Let us call this first group the unscrupulous atheists. Dostoyevsky surely only had atheists of this type in mind when he said, "If there is no God everything is permitted."

Second, there are honest atheists who take the concept of God seriously and honestly find it impossible but to be nihilists and agnostics.

We Christians insist that God is father, and that God is almighty too. Have you ever realized that in a world of tremendous suffering and deprivation and alienation, that is demanding a lot? Either God is neither able nor willing to eliminate evil, or he is able but not willing, or he is not able though willing, or he is both able and willing. Now only the last is worthy of deity but, to many in misery and desperation, the last does not seem to be the case. With human injustice, alienation and evil all around, it is really hard to believe that God is the Almighty Father. It is so much easier to feel that we are standing in a cold, silent, unfeeling cosmos, unaided by any purposeful power beyond our own resources. So there are atheists who have tried hard to take the question of God seriously and whose honest doubts and unbelief deserve our sympathetic understanding.

Third, there is the humanitarian atheism of the reformers and revolutionaries. They have to reject God because the God they have been told about is nothing better than a maintainer of the status quo, an opponent of any change in structures and in values, a protector of any social order which is moribund and has no justice in it, a God who gets himself involved in the injustices of the oppressive society. He has taken the side of the oppressor/exploiter class and the exploited and oppressed must reject him.

Why did Chinese reformist and revolutionary intellectuals reject the God of the Christians? Because Christians the world over seemed to stand on the side of Chiang Kai-shek, the enemy of the Chinese people. Because, in 1949, when the People's Liberation Army was about to cross the Yangtze River in its pursuit of the forces of Chiang Kai-shek, some Christians were praying that God would perform a miracle so that the soldiers of the People's Liberation Army would drown in the river. That was certainly a very political, reactionary and brutal sort of prayer to offer. We had in China the leader of a certain Christian sect who, soon after the liberation of Shanghai in 1949, gave signals from the ground to bombers sent by Chiang Kai-shek to bomb the city. He was defended on the ground that he, being a regenerated man, could not sin, even when committing acts that in themselves were evil, because he was no longer under law. In other words, an elect person, being predestined to salvation, is absolved from the moral law. Justification by faith becomes lawlessness. If you profess faith in Christ, everything is permitted. This is antinomianism. It presents a God who permits Christians and the "Christian nations" to do anything.

Now, if our God is so reactionary in political matters, what right do we have to expect our humanitarians and revolutionaries not to be atheists? So it is often the theists who provoke people to atheism by the unworthiness of our conceptions of God. Here we see how a wrong notion of God is actually a worse thing than atheism. What those atheists deny is not so much the reality of God as the adequacy of the ideas of God that are presented to them by the believers. Their inadequacy makes these atheists completely oblivious of the question of the reality of God.

Atheism of this kind is not something entirely negative. It has positive contents. It is the discovery and the emphasis of the human factor. It is a cry in favor of humanity. It inspires men and women to take their destiny in their own hands. It protests against fatalism and defeatism. This protest is exactly what is needed in a society that has been stagnant for thousands of years. In their very denial of God we hear the human cry for liberation and dignity. They reject false notions of God in order to liberate the people.

There is something sublime in this sort of atheism. That a person is destined by nature to engage in creative work, that alienation of humanity from each other is not natural to human life but is imposed by a social order at odds with itself, that people's lives are destined to be free and can be realized and expressed in creative labor, that labor in the new social order will express the laborers' care for the people and will assume an honorable, humane character, all these profound convictions of our humanitarian and revolutionary friends are based on anthropological and social premises that are ultimately theological.

We are fascinated by the story of Prometheus as narrated by Aeschylus. He is the legendary monument of resistance and defiance. He stole fire from heaven to help humankind in its struggle against nature. He angered Zeus, who chained him to a rock and sent a vulture to prey on his liver. If he submitted to his oppressor his miserable torment would end. But he preferred to serve his vulture and his rock rather than be Zeus's "faithful boy." This is what he said,

> Be sure of this. I would not change my state of evil fortune for your servitude. Better to be the servant of this rock than to be faithful boy to Father Zeus.

Now the humanitarians and revolutionaries whom we meet in large numbers in the world are the Prometheuses of history. The defenders of Zeus are understandably not listened to and their deity rejected.

Dostoyevsky equated atheism with moral nihilism when he said, "If there is no God everything is permitted." Maybe it was his fear of God that was preventing him from doing all sorts of things he would like to do. Blaise Pascal also thought that without faith in God people would turn into monsters and the order of nature into chaos. But I think their judgments were too sweeping. They never met those atheists who would not permit themselves to do a lot of things. They have so disciplined themselves that they cannot bring themselves to do anything harmful to the cause of the people's liberation.

They are lovers of humanity, ready to sacrifice everything for the welfare of their fellow men and women. They are not seekers of self-interest or a good, easy life for themselves. They practice comradely love and care among the people. The most important mark of the revolutionaries is not hatred, but love. The true revolutionaries are guided by strong feelings of love. In a revolutionary situation there is indeed a lot of hatred, but the revolutionaries hate because they love. Their love for humankind makes them hate the forces that alienate men and women and make society inhumane. Their passion for justice results in their impatience with injustice. I think there is much truth in the remark made by Archbishop Temple several decades ago: "The atheist who is moved by love is moved by the Spirit of God: an atheist who lives by love is saved by his faith in the God whose existence (under that name) he denies."

These humanitarians and revolutionaries are human beings and can also make mistakes. But they know how their personal mistakes bring harm to the cause of revolution and, thus, are most strict in self-discipline and self-criticism. They take their mistakes and the task of personal remolding seriously so as to ensure that they transcend low and selfish interests. It is really quite unkind to call that "brainwashing." It is something altogether conscious and conscientious.

Can we not try to get inside the mind of the revolutionary humanist, recognize the honesty of his search, appreciate the justice of his reservation and fear about the social consequences of much of our preaching about God, tell him that we too are almost as atheistic as he is when it comes to the kind of God that he has to reject, and join with him in the quest for a social system in which love would be made available to the masses of the people? In so doing, we shall not be losing our faith in God but equipping ourselves as evangelists to the revolutionaries and making progress in our own spiritual pilgrimage.

Unfortunately, there are Christians today who need to resort to elaborating on other people's moral failings and spiritual vacuum in order to strengthen their own religious faith and to prop up their missionary enterprise. Christians have no right to boost ourselves by finding fault with the revolutionaries. We should rather be moved and humbled by their dedication. They present before us a nonreligious spirituality that we Christians cannot afford to ignore. It is important that we see God at work through those conscientious souls who, because for them the word God fails to convey any meaning, deny that he exists. I cannot honestly think there is nothing spiritual in them for me to embrace, and indeed, for Christianity to appropriate.

It is under the leadership of many of these truly consecrated revolutionaries that the Chinese people have been liberated and their material and cultural life greatly elevated. Today, almost a quarter of the human population is being fed on one-seventh of the arable land of the earth. The people's food is not good but nobody needs to starve and eat the bark of trees anymore. One-fourth of our whole population is in school receiving their education. Thanks to the leadership of these revolutionaries we now have a much more just society in China and the way has been prepared for the Christian conception of God, the God who is at once all loving and all powerful, to be visualized more easily.

The question has been raised as to whether we Christians can be "fellow travelers" with these atheists. My answer is affirmative. All through history, Christians have been fellow-traveling with non-Christians and atheists of all sorts in all sorts of undertakings. Why make an exception now?

Jesus Christ is much greater than our conventional conception of him. In the New Testament we meet the Christ we are yet to know in full. In St. John's Gospel, in Ephesians, in Colossians, we encounter the Cosmic Christ, the crown and fulfillment of the whole creation, the clue to the meaning of God's creative work. This Christ is the Logos who teaches all humankind. He is the light that lighteth every one. At the end of history, he will receive from humanity, both from believers and from nonbelievers, from theists and atheists, our work, not to be destroyed and thrown into the garbage, but to be transfigured, to be perfected, to be offered to God the Father of us all. The Christian gospel does not discard other insights. It makes room for the multiple manifestation of truth.

We have no reason to be afraid of truth that comes from sources other than Christianity. There is no truth but truth. God lets different people achieve their several provisional unities of truths. We will not know how to synthesize them into one body of truth until the last day. We can only have faith that the world will become intelligible and our knowledge will become one harmonious whole when the divine purpose for history is achieved. Provisional unities of truths we can observe with joy and thanksgiving because they illuminate us and point toward the ultimate unity in Christ which is the promise of his revelation.

I believe there is something unique, something revelatory in Christ that speaks even to the Chinese revolutionary. The revolutionary also stands in need of revelation, of the guidance of the Holy Spirit into further and deeper truth. I would like to say to the revolutionary: "Carry on your valuable work but gain a fuller sense of its meaning and importance by relating it to the ongoing creative, redemptive and sanctifying movement in the universe under what we call God, so that all your undertakings in industry, in agriculture, in science and technology, in art and music, get an even deeper grounding. Religious faith will not dampen your revolutionary spirit, but will purify it, make it more sublime, more acceptable to God." In other words, we do have an evangelistic task there. But that is only half of the picture. The other half is the purifying effect the revolutionary could bring to our church in all its oldness, its institutionalism and its immobility. I visualize a day when the two halves will meet and merge. Then it will be a new world and a new Christianity. What can be said about China is only that today, revolution and Christianity are discovering each other. They are no longer such strangers. But this is still very far from real meeting. I see evangelism as pouring out the divine life in which Christ has called us to share, entering into all that is good in human spirituality and, thus, discovering together the highest and the deepest truth of the gospel. Evangelism is not just for us to bring Christ to men and women, but also to bring Christ out of them for the deification of ourselves and of the whole humankind.

So the revolutionary atheists are not necessarily the enemies of authentic Christianity. In our churches too often contrasts are overdrawn, false simplifications are made of complex problems. The Christian community has become a prey to arrogance in its relations with those it should be seeking to understand. We might well ask ourselves: Is the church not cutting itself off from valuable allies against idolatry by ill-defined, ill-considered attacks upon them? Or, is the church really too indistinguishable from the world for us to expect it not to be so? An atheist that denies false gods who dehumanize people and give their blessing to bondage and injustice—is that not a good partner in a united front for the church on its pilgrimage? Out experience in China tells me that, for the sake of political unity, i.e., for the sake of uniting themselves with as many Chinese citizens as possible in the common task of building up new China, the revolutionaries in large numbers are not at all eager to impose their atheism on others and are taking seriously the implementation of the policy of religious freedom. You have heard that, since the downfall of the Gang of Four, more and more churches, temples and mosques are being re-opened for worship. Is it really good for us Christians to assume a posture of cynicism, and not one of friendship and goodwill?

This chat is really a plea for humility, humility before a God who does wonderful things in wonderful ways. God works in mysterious ways, ways far surpassing our set ways of thinking. If we can get a glimpse of this about God, I will be glad.

—Vancouver,
November 1979

# THE THREE-SELF'S CONTRIBUTION TO CHRISTIANITY IN CHINA

Can Three-Self be dispensed with, or is it necessary? Chinese Christians attach great importance to this question.

From the middle of the 19th century on there were people in the church who spoke of Three-Self. They realized that if the church was to thrive in any country, it could not be dependent on foreign countries for long; it was necessary for local Christians to support the church themselves. Some were dissatisfied with racial injustices existing in the church. Others, out of a sense of national awakening, were averse to missionaries and national preachers who taught Christians not to love their motherland. These experiences were all valuable. However there were also those who, mouthing Three-Self slogans, used indigenization as a facade, or advertised that they already practiced Three-Self, in order to cover up the foreign religion which they in fact represented. At that time few people discussed the importance of Three-Self from the perspective of the nature of the church. It was also hard to find people who spoke of the necessity of Three-Self from the standpoint of defending the motherland.

On the eve of China's liberation, questions about Three-Self subsided in our church. At that time, the most outstanding question was: Will there be freedom of religion in China under the leadership of the Communist Party? Will it be possible for the church to continue to exist? Many Christians prepared themselves to go to jail or to undergo all kinds of persecution. But for Christians in China the answer to this question became clear, for the most part, by the early 1950s. Beginning then, Chinese Christians more and more realized that this was not the biggest problem.

This is not to say that the policy of religious freedom has been well implemented in each and every part of the country since the early

1950s. We know that after 1957 there were ultra-leftist tendencies and that excessive relapses occurred, especially during the Cultural Revolution. Since the downfall of the Gang of Four, the government at all levels has been doing tremendous work to carry out the policy of religious freedom. However, even today problems still exist in many places. Three-Self organizations and Christian councils must continue to work with the government at all levels to solve these problems. So long as there is resistance to and transgression of the policy of religious freedom, hindrance of normal religious activities and violation of people's rights, we are obliged to work with concerned parties to seek proper solutions. At the same time, we will oppose all unlawful activities within the church, as well as infiltration from abroad.

But we realize that the attitude toward religious freedom of all bodies in China which determine policy, make laws or are involved with administration (the National People's Congress, the Chinese People's Political Consultative Conference, the Central Committee of the Party, the Central People's Government and the Religious Affairs Bureau of the State Council) is very clear. What remains are only problems of implementation on the local level, and these problems are receiving more and more attention as time goes on. The Bureau of Religious Affairs clearly expressed support for our proposal regarding the revision of the article on religion in the national Constitution. This gives us great encouragement. During the past three years, Protestant churches have been opening and re-opening at the rate of one or two churches every two or three days. This is also an indication of the situation with regard to religious freedom in China.

Not long after Liberation, Chinese Christians began to realize that if there was to be a bright future for the church, it was not enough to depend only on the state's policy of religious freedom. It is true that people are free to believe in Christianity, but do they want to exercise this freedom? In the early '50s did not some people exercise their religious freedom by leaving the church?

The Holy Spirit acting through history made the church in China ask itself a question far more important than that of religious freedom. This was the first time that Chinese Christians all over China formulated and tried to answer our own question. It was a question about the nature of the Chinese Church: how was the church to break away from a place it was unwilling to be in and enter a new life? How was the church to repent, to change, to re-direct and renew itself, to establish itself as the Body of Christ, to make the church not only a church in people's minds, but primarily a church according to the mind of Christ?

Chinese Christianity was not without an answer to this question. A common and concise answer, which all the Christians of the country could accept and support was: Follow the Three-Self road.

Usually participants in any great movement in history cannot completely comprehend its full meaning right from the beginning. It is only after the passing of a few years, several decades, or even several hundred years that the full meaning becomes clearer and clearer to posterity.

In the beginning, Christianity was merely a sect of Judaism. Because it had not yet broken out of its Jewish narrowmindedness, Christianity required people to accept Jewish laws such as circumcision in addition to accepting Jesus as Lord. Paul introduced the idea of justification by faith over against justification by law, which enabled Christianity to break out of its Jewish framework. This provided the necessary conditions for Christianity to become the common religious faith of the people of every race on the shores of the Mediterranean Sea. It also provided the necessary conditions for Christianity to become a Western religion, and finally, a world religion. This was the first barrier in history which Christianity broke through, and it was perhaps the most important barrier. The incidents recorded in chapters 10 and 15 of the book of Acts had much to do with the future course of church history, and even of world history, but Paul and Peter had no means of foreseeing this.

However, Christianity is still basically a Western world religion or a world Western religion. Men and women today are yearning for a new breakthrough. On the horizon of history, besides Christianity in its Western form, we will see it in Eastern and Southern and Northern forms, and forms which embody the special cultural characteristics of each people. Then, the multicolored picture of Christianity will really appeal to people's hearts and move their inner beings. During the last several years, farsighted men and women in churches of every country have come forth and promoted a Christianity that takes root in their own countries. We value such work and accomplishments very highly, despite its fragmentary and limited nature.

The church in China is very small. But in two respects the Chinese Christian Three-Self Movement is significant for world church history as a sort of breakthrough.

(1) Located in the eastern part of the world and in such a country as China, Christianity is now making itself indigenous on a large scale, at a comparatively rapid pace and at a deep level. Many Christians throughout the whole world (including missionaries) had this dream, but it is now being fulfilled.

(2) Historically, since the appearance of this new thing called socialism, in a society with a history of several thousand years of feudalism and over one hundred years of semi-colonialism; at a time when several hundred million people, having gone through a long serious trial so that even today they are carrying its wounds, are anxious to bring about more changes and are using both hands to construct a new life under socialism; at a time when industrial and agricultural production, cultural thinking, morality and the spiritual life are all undergoing changes and present China with a rich, colorful and very lively new prospect; in an environment where many new things are so inspiring even as there are old things which still cause people to sigh; Christians, numbering very few in the whole population, are consciously trying to root Christianity in the soil of their land, so that new qualities will spring forth. This has never happened before in history. This is the unique characteristic of the mission of our Chinese Christians. Our success will strengthen the faith many people in China and in the world have in Christ and in the Church. Our failure would be their loss.

Thus, colleagues and fellow Christians, when Three-Self is promoted, it is not due to anybody's ambition to reach for something beyond our grasp, wanting to astonish people by performing something unnecessary. The reconstruction of the motherland requires that Chinese Christians act in this way; the mission of witnessing to the

gospel requires that Chinese Christians follow this path; the self-realization of the catholicity or universal nature of the Christian Church
requires that Chinese Christians do this. We will speak below of these
three aspects.

### (1) THE RECONSTRUCTION OF THE MOTHERLAND OBLIGES US TO ACT IN THIS WAY

After the Opium War, China was considered the sick man of East Asia,
and suffered all kinds of humiliation at the hands of foreign aggressors. Foreign warships and troops could go anywhere they pleased,
and foreign goods occupied our markets. National industry could not
compete and survive. The people suffered poverty and sickness, and
beggars filled the streets. Today, this situation is long past. Chinese
Christians are happy and thankful because of this. It is only reasonable that we develop an ardent love for China.

The incarnation of God not only shows us God's great love by
entering the world, experiencing human misery, and completing his
work of salvation by dying on the cross, but at the same time, it tells
us something of how we should regard the flesh and material things.
Because they are channels by which God enters into the world, flesh
and material things are not to be despised. They are worthy, and can
become, indeed ought to become, vessels conveying holy love. We
believe that God's love and concern for man is all-embracing. Bodily
and material life, intellectual development, the socio-political sphere,
ethics and morality are all included within the realm of God's love and
concern. He wants us to escape from suffering, and enjoy peace and
prosperity in a more reasonable social system. Such an environment
will be more helpful for seeking and discovering truth, and for knowing and submitting to God's revelation.

We know that Christ, the Word incarnate, was a citizen of a particular country, not a man without a country. He did not adopt a
nihilistic attitude toward his own people. He studied his national culture and religious traditions. He announced that he came not to abolish these traditions, but to fulfill them. His people were under the
political domination of Rome, and because of this, when he looked on
the capital city, he wept. This was patriotism in that situation.

In the Bible, patriotic feelings often showed themselves in the grief and indignation the people harbored when their motherland was in peril. Psalm 137 is quite typical:

> "By the waters of Babylon there we sat down and wept, when we remembered Zion. On the willows there we hung up our lyres. For there our captors required of us songs, and our tormentors, mirth, saying, 'Sing us one of the songs of Zion!' If I forget you, O Jerusalem, let my right hand wither! Let my tongue cleave to the roof of my mouth if I do not remember you, if I do not set Jerusalem above my highest joy!"

However, the Bible also portrays a patriotism filled with exaltation at the renewal and reconstruction of the motherland. Psalm 126 is an example:

> "When the Lord restored the fortunes of Zion, We were like those who dream. Then our mouth was filled with laughter, and our tongue with shouts of joy; Then they said among the nations, 'The Lord has done great things for them.' The Lord has done great things for us: We are glad. Restore our fortunes, O Lord, Like the watercourses in the Negeb! May those who sow in tears reap with shouts of joy!"

During the disaster-ridden days experienced by the Chinese people, many of us did not cry with our suffering compatriots. This guilt is very hard for us to wipe out. Since the Chinese people have overthrown the three big mountains of feudalism, imperialism and bureaucratic capitalism, great changes have taken place. Today, on one-seventh of the world's arable land, we can feed one-fourth of the world's people. This is a great accomplishment. Now our country is putting more and more energy into the four modernizations. We Christians should be filled with gladness at the reconstruction of the motherland and rejoice with those who rejoice.

However, the work of liberation is of long duration. China is still far from ideal, and there are vast areas of underdevelopment and darkness. People are now working hard in every field to expand the bright side and to overcome the dark side. They are making progress in the conquest of underdevelopment. Naturally, Chinese Christians do not stand aloof from all this activity. In the life of the nation, the church should make a clear distinction between right and wrong. She ought to protect, learn from and promote the good, and bring about the accomplishment of the good quickly. At the same time, the church ought to criticize and oppose evil things and hasten their demise. This is real patriotism in today's situation.

As for the Christian Church itself, we should naturally make certain adaptations so as to suit the conditions of the motherland. When Christianity entered China, it was associated with Western colonialism. This had serious consequences for both China and the Christian Church. It was necessary for Chinese Christians to open a new page in the history of Christianity. Today, our country is independent and autonomous. If the Christian Church as an organization does not seek independence and autonomy but continues to rely on others, would not this make the church a foreign enclave within the People's Republic of China? If foreign enemies are allowed to use our religion to carry out their objective of invading and destroying the rights and interests of the motherland and reversing the new life of the people, would not this make our Christian Church the partner of these enemies in China?

Patriotism, whether it comes from grief and indignation over danger to the motherland, or from exaltation at her progress, arises from a sense of right and wrong, a sense of justice, and a sense of national belonging. It has led people to unstintingly perform all kinds of work and make all kinds of sacrifices to advance the motherland's welfare. It is something praiseworthy. Our Christian Church ought to nourish this spirit, and certainly not despise it. During these years, Christians in our country have produced great results along the path of Three-Self and have sprung up on many fronts making contributions to the welfare of the people. Some have even made outstanding contributions. They have not failed the teachings and aspirations of both the motherland and the church. These stirring examples of love of country and of one's church are the pride of the Chinese people and of the Chinese Church. They are worthy of our emulation.

There is a line of thought overseas which is critical of the patriotism of Chinese Christians. It says that a good Christian cannot but hold a different political view and be a member of the opposition, and that he or she should necessarily oppose whoever is in authority. This is the mission of the prophet, they say. We seem to have heard something similar during the Cultural Revolution. It called for people to rise up and make revolution against the revolutionaries. We cannot agree with this dose of poison in the garb of revolution. The Chinese people paid a great price before acquiring state power. We are just beginning to change our old society and create a new life for ourselves. Why should this state now become the object of revolution? Is this not a call to destroy our own cause? Patriotism impels us to support the new social system won by the people, to defend it, to eliminate the remaining bad parts, and to correct and improve it. The theory which opposes itself to any and every authority is not in accord with patriotism but with anarchy, subversion and counter-revolution. We wonder why those people who want us to accept this theory do not seem to carry it out themselves in their own countries?

## (2) IN ORDER TO BEAR EFFECTIVE WITNESS TO THE GOSPEL, CHINESE CHRISTIANS MUST PROMOTE THREE-SELF.

Buddhism and Islam also came to China from abroad, but today everyone considers them Chinese religions. Christianity is different, for until a short time ago people considered it a foreign religion. This was because it had not become Sinicized in personnel, finance and thought. Sometimes, politically, it even stood on the side of the invader. This was the major reason why the Chinese people resisted Christianity for many years.

In the 1950s, Y. T. Wu and other Christian leaders began to promote Three-Self. Although even the *People's Daily* wrote an editorial in support of it, old habits die hard, and many continued to regard Christianity as a foreign religion. At that time, the survival of Christianity depended mainly on the state's policy of religious freedom. Only survival was possible; bearing witness was out of the question.

Because Three-Self conforms to the essence of the church and is in accord with the tide of history, it soon received the support of

Christians throughout the country and the sympathy of the great mass of the people, once it was launched. This change in the people's view of Christianity is irreversible. Today, in the decade of the '80s, in spite of shortcomings in our work, more and more people in China have come to recognize that they should no longer look upon Christianity as a foreign religion.

This change has tremendous significance for our work of bearing witness to the gospel. It enables us to have more opportunities to associate with our fellow citizens, and to have more of a common language with them. We have freed ourselves from a situation of separation from the masses. Christians are active in many fields: politics, culture, industrial and agricultural production, health and technology. It is possible for us to make many friends and exchange opinions with others. We can learn many things from our fellow citizens and others are also interested in listening to the message of Christianity from us.

In the last thirty years Christians have not become fewer, but have increased to the highest point in Chinese Christian history. In analyzing the numerous reasons for this, it cannot be denied that the basic one behind all the others is that Chinese Christianity has opted for the Three-Self road. With the disappearance of foreign oil, foreign matches and foreign cloth from the vocabulary of the Chinese people, is it thinkable that a foreign religion would remain? Indeed, should it be possible for this foreign religion to remain for some time, how would it fare? Would people be willing to associate themselves with it? Would they have good feelings toward such a religion? Would they take the step to accept Christ as Lord? If so, what would it mean?

In 2,000 years of Christian mission history and in the more than one hundred years of missionary history in China, there are numerous examples, both positive and negative, which help us to discover this extremely important law: the rejection of a transplanted foreign organ is not only a biological and surgical phenomenon, but also a big question in mission history, and becomes especially acute in the wake of national consciousness when the situation can even burst into an intense conflict. From this we learn that, if the church is to be firm, it cannot rely upon the support of political power inside or outside the country. The only way to gain its right to be heard is for the church to practice the Three-Self principle and to become the church of its own country.

Everybody who has tried to lead others to Christ knows that to lead someone to accept the gospel of Christ is entirely different from leading someone to visit a park. Nor is it as simple as sending somebody a copy of the Bible. This is because the gospel of Christ demands that human beings in the first place recognize the problem of sin. The concept of sin, especially the concept of oneself as sinner, is considered to be something stupid and is not taken to heart by ordinary people. This is a stumbling block inherent in the gospel. To all people, the gospel itself has the nature of being foreign. This foreignness often makes us resist and reject the gospel. But we simply cannot eliminate this element in order to make the gospel easier for people to accept. Without it, the question of salvation becomes pointless. What is left would be but an ordinary set of teachings exhorting people to be good. Although this is good too, it is no longer the gospel. That is to say, because the gospel is gospel, it is no light matter for people to commit themselves to it, as if there were no resistance. The gospel carried in itself this cause for resistance to accepting it. For this reason, the preacher must take special care to safeguard the channel through which the gospel comes into the human heart. He or she should not allow any additional foreignness to stand in the way, lest further resistance and difficulties be caused. In this way, if there are people who refuse to accept the gospel, it will only be due to its inherent stumbling block, but not to foreign materials external to the gospel put there by the messenger.

There are some people overseas who ignore the lessons of history, trampling on our Three-Self principle of the past thirty years. In the name of evangelizing China they are recreating in the minds of the Chinese people the image of Christianity as a foreign religion. They rely on nothing but a certain economic superiority, shielded by certain anti-China political forces in places like Hong Kong, and protected by the foreign passports which they possess. Relying on these things they think that they are a cut above other people, that they may occupy a commanding position, and that they can defy our principled stand. Considering the size of the world, we can see that this kind of position, which consciously takes an attitude of animosity toward our Three-Self stand, may for some time attract a few blind followers, but it certainly offends the broad masses of the Chinese people who have stood up, and it will arouse their strong aversion and disgust. If this approach to evangelism is allowed to be carried through, only shame will be brought to Christ and the door to the gospel will be closed. Precisely because there are such people, we cannot but pose the question of jurisdiction over the work of evangelism and church-building inside China. Several years ago, a pastor of an overseas Chinese church came back to China to visit his relatives. After having come into contact with many Christians, he came finally to the conclusion that preachers who have left China for over twenty years are no longer qualified to preach in China. Christians abroad are no longer able to feel the pulse of the Chinese people or to understand "the limits God has apportioned us" (2 Cor. 10:13), and who "boast beyond limit, in other men's labors" (15), leaving behind the fields which they know well and insisting on coming to China to do something not in their own line of duty, should listen to this overseas Chinese pastor.

## (3) FOR THE CHRISTIAN CHURCH
### TO FINALLY AND FULLY REALIZE ITS CATHOLICITY,
### CHRISTIANS IN CHINA SHOULD PROCEED IN OUR OWN WAY

Paul said that in the coming ages God would show forth the immeasurable riches of his grace toward us in Christ Jesus. The unfathomable riches of Christ are like a treasure which is waiting to be opened up by Christians of different cultures and upbringings, and then to be integrated into the common treasury of the whole church. It is in this process that the church achieves its catholicity. The cultures of nations need the grace of Christ's gospel for their sublimation, and the church of Christ can prosper only by absorbing from the cultures of all nations.

Today, Christianity is a world religion. It is no longer the religion of a certain people or a few peoples, but has spread to many countries in all continents. Its worldwide scope is to a great extent connected with the colonial expansion of capitalism, and thus it has congenital deficiencies and weaknesses. The catholicity of the church includes, to be sure, the extensiveness of the church in geographical terms. But this is, after all, only a question of expanse and does not exhaust the meaning of catholicity. Catholicity in all its fullness should include the question of depth, which is the more essential, i.e., how the church takes root in all cultures, so that the radiance of the gospel, shining through the prisms of the various particular cultures, gives off a brilliance which stirs the hearts of men and thereby greatly enriches the treasury of the universal church. Only in this way will worship before the throne of God be like a hundred flowers blossoming and like multiple colors showing forth, enhancing the joy shared by God and men alike.

Measured by this demand, the church in the world today is still far from the full realization of its catholicity. As far as the church in China is concerned, we have taken a few important steps on the road of Three-Self politically, personnel-wise, organizationally and financially. This is precious and fundamental but we still cannot say that our church is already well-governed, well-supported, and one in which propagating is done well. We are still lagging very far behind, especially with regard to correctly understanding and assimilating our contemporary Chinese culture and historical heritage, so as to integrate it with Christianity to the highest level permitted by our Christian faith, and relinquishing all those things from Western tradition which are not integral to the church.

A year or two ago, an Asian church leader wrote that the church in his country was as yet only a dot on the missionary map of Western churches. This remark is deeply poignant. When the New Jerusalem comes down from heaven, with its twelve gates in the east, west, north and south, inviting the multitudes of every nation and tribe and tongue and people to pass through, will the Chinese Church have its own contingent? Or will it simply be a dot on the map in the offering plate of other contingents?

Paul told us that it pleases God for all the fullness to dwell in Christ. The fullness which is inherent in Christ, his manifold wisdom, has yet to be absorbed, digested and exchanged by people of various particular cultural backgrounds, so that it can be shared by all in the church. In this way the church marches toward the goal of actualizing its catholicity. According to the teaching of Paul, the breadth and length and height and depth of Christ's love are only to be comprehended by all the saints. The Book of Hebrews also tells us that God "has foreseen something better" for the church, that all those throughout history who have been tested for their faith "should not be made perfect apart from us."

It is therefore clear that individuality and catholicity, particularity and universality, are not contradictory, or mutually exclusive, but are complementary to each other. The fuller a church in a particular country actualizes its particularity, the richer the diversity of the whole church and the more substantial its universality. If the church in a particular country cannot even attain its independence, then talk about interdependence with other churches is largely empty words.

Here let us consider the movements of theological reorientation at the grassroots which took place in Chinese Christianity during the '50s. This movement was spontaneous, not organized by anybody. But it had a very strong mass character and was extensive. Having entered the historical stage of new China, thousands upon thousands of grassroots Christians, though aroused by patriotism, did not want to give up their Christian faith lightly. But they were unable to keep intact a lot of the theological viewpoints instilled in them in the past. At a time when they were establishing their new political standpoint, they had to do some hard theological thinking themselves, so that they could not only face up to the political reality but find a viable theological position as well. This was a movement from the bottom up. At first, not too many clergymen were involved. Far more numerous were those who found themselves on the border between church and society, those who were drawn into the current of the times, such as Christian workers, peasants, teachers and other intellectuals, and some of the pastors at the grassroots who were close to these people, among whom we especially cherish the memory of Rev. Huang Peiyong.

Is the world in the hand of the devil? What is the status of the world in the mind of God? How should Christians look at history? Should Christians only be concerned with questions of belief and unbelief and of life after death? Should Christians be concerned with issues of right and wrong? Should they differentiate good from evil? What is meant by being spiritual? Should Christianity negate and deny reason? What is the scope of God's care and love and of the work of the Holy Spirit? How does one assess the true, the good, and the beautiful outside the realm of the church? How should Christians think of the nation? Of patriotism? What is the place of the Bible in divine revelation? How should one look at the holiness of the Church in the face of the many evil deeds being exposed there? How can we recognize anew the holy love of God, his intentions in carrying out the ongoing work of creation, redemption and sanctification? In this providence of God, how should the role of Christ as revealed in Colossians and Ephesians be understood? These and other problems have impelled us Chinese Christians to reflect and to explore. Thousands of articles were written, a small portion of which appeared in publications such as *Tian Feng, En Yan,* and *Theological Review.* They helped form the vigorous upsurge in theological thinking among the mass of church-goers, showing forth the flowers of a mass movement in theology.

What is most precious is that these problems which cropped up in history were raised and discussed by Chinese Christians themselves. This was a Christian mass movement of self-enlightenment. Some of the opinions expressed might be extreme, but what was extreme could be corrected. We should not negate the essential aspect of the movement simply because there were some extreme opinions in it. What is fascinating is that the creative activity of theology shifted from theological professionals to grassroots believers. I do not know whether there were similar theological mass movements during the period of the Reformation in Europe or during the Peasant War in Germany. Anyway, this must be a rare phenomenon in church history. Today we must proceed on the basis of this theological reorientation movement; we must not retreat. We should encourage that spirit of daring to think, daring to blaze new trails, daring to enable theological thinking to open its doors to the reality of the world. We should identify ourselves with what we can and reserve differences where we must. In this way we not only usher Chinese Christianity into the possibility of dialogue with others, but also strengthen its theological foundation, develop its own characteristics and substantially enrich the catholicity of the church.

There are people who as soon as they talk about the catholicity, universality, ecumenicity or internationality of the church, ignore and forget all-important differences. They show a kind of excessive tender-heartedness marked by not distinguishing between right and wrong. It seems as if "fellowship in Christ" were something which neglects principle, standpoint or vigilance, a situation in which everyone is just kind and nice to everyone else. This is a vulgarization of the church's catholicity, making of it an extremely shallow cosmopolitanism which encourages people to pay no attention to the weal and woe of their motherland. Genuine catholicity is a process of development. The firmer a national church roots itself among its people, the stronger its individuality and the more it contributes to the catholicity of the universal church. Because of this, though we affirm the universality of the church and are consequently developing certain international contacts, we do not place this above everything else. Old China lost a lot because our customs were in the hands of foreign powers and we could not levy tariffs to protect the development of our national industry. Today, in order to protect the growth of the Chinese church and to keep it free from an excessive pounding from abroad (even if this is a "pounding of love"), our international contacts cannot but be limited and selective. We are not keeping this as a secret. The international contacts which the Chinese Church entertains must be in accord with our Three-Self principle, or at least not detrimental to it.

Chinese Christians ardently love Christ, the Bible and the Church; they also ardently love their motherland. Whither do we lead this enthusiasm of the believers is something for which we must be held answerable before God and the Chinese people. It is often said that we should satisfy the spiritual needs of our fellow Christians. This is right in principle. But we must examine first of all whether those needs are consonant with God's nature and will, whether they are consonant with his revelation and guidance to the Chinese Church today. To be spiritual is good, but when the teaching of the Bible is put into the context of present-day Christian life in China, what is it to be spiritual? Today, in the church in China, whether it be in pastoral work, in education for Christian nurture, in worship, preaching, prayer, church life or the formation of sound spirituality, there is a new lifestyle and witness which is suitable to Christians in China. Viewpoints, thoughts and methods which match the spirit of the Three-Self principle are breaking through old conventions to emerge and grow to maturity. These newborn things in the church will be loved and welcomed by the broad mass of Christians. We should love them, want them to grow and to be successful that they might soon blossom and bear fruit; we have no reason to despise them. Nor have we any reason to hold fast to the old things we learned in the past that are already without vitality today.

In certain places there are bad elements who neither belong to the church nor know anything about Christianity. Yet they are carrying out misdeeds and cheating honest people in the name of Christ, using the practice of reactionary superstitious societies. Some of them even resort to beating, smashing and looting in true Cultural Revolution style, committing crimes and doing all manner of evil. These things go beyond what we call religious questions. Be these elements in the church, the home or any other place, we must not be misled by their religious garb, but must oppose them in no uncertain terms, and support the authorities concerned to restrain them by law, so that our Christianity will not be discredited.

Today, the reality of the Chinese Church is still far from the Church in the mind of Christ. In many places, the pastoral work of the church has been neglected and the situation has still not improved much. In some places there is a lack of content in worship services and Christian meetings about which our members have their complaints, but for a long time we have made no improvement. In other places emphasis is put only on church growth, without knowing that nurture should be more important in the present situation, for otherwise our faith would become one-sided and even heretical. In some places people lack mutual respect in matters of belief, with the result that fellow Christians are hurt and alienated. Some of our faithful have not yet heard of activities through which many things that are non-Christian have been brought into Christianity. In addition, there has been interference and temptation from outside which tries to pull us backward and destroy us. All these things tell us that the task of the Three-Self Committee and the China Christian Council is both tremendous and glorious. We are glad to point out that, though our problems are many, and though we are not all very wise, but are simply the small "five loaves and two fishes," yet God's work takes great strides forward, overcoming all obstacles, exceeding all we have ever dared to imagine. It is a test for faith, it is also a calling for us to be of one heart and one mind. May we say that all those who are in consonance with the teaching of the Bible and who believe in Jesus Christ as Lord wherever they are, are members of the Church, and it is they who are to be served, to be united and to be strengthened by the Three-Self Committee and the China Christian Council. In matters of faith we must uphold the principle of mutual respect, not opposing or slighting one another. We need especially to heed Paul's reminder: "Speaking the truth in love, we are to grow up in every way into him who is the head, into Christ, from whom the whole body, joined and knit together by every joint with which it is supplied, when each part is working properly, makes bodily growth and upbuilds itself in love."

The Three-Self Committee and the China Christian Council are but temporary vessels, the scaffold of the building in the construction process. We, too, each one of us, are but the numerous bamboo poles or steel tubes which form the closely grouped scaffolding. As soon as this building of the body of Christ is completed, standing uniquely on the horizon, the scaffold will disappear. Yet, today, the Three-Self Committee and China Christian Council still have much to do. We must do our best. Let us be the many ordinary bamboo poles tied together by the rope of love and be humble; let no one of us protrude, but rather form as a whole a strong scaffold; let us find our tiny, individual task and meaning in the building up of this work of Christ—the Chinese Church.

—The Three-Self's Contribution to Chinese Christianity, 1982

## 🕉

# WOMEN IN THE CHURCH

Whehen Christ teaches us to pray to "Our Father who art in heaven," he certainly does not mean that God is like any human father. He has in mind the father who helps the child to walk "with cords of compassion" and "with the bands of love," or the father who gives his child good things to eat when the child is hungry, or the father who looks expectantly for the return of his prodigal son.

In our human world, very many fathers are not like these. Human fatherhood presents a very complex image. Many men and women have never experienced any father love in their life. According to the traditional Chinese view, severity is the necessary mark of the father. The proper way to refer to one's own father in high class conversation is "the severe one in my family." Too many fathers are not only severe but also ill-tempered. When they are unjustly treated in places where they work, they often give vent to their pent-up feelings on the child at home. Often it is the father who beats a child. So, in the experience of many, the father image is one of unreason. Very likely he is rude to his wife, too. In rural areas there are still cases of the man blaming his wife for the birth of a girl, and even drowning the infant. Because for centuries our society has been deformed by patriarchalism, human fatherhood has also been deformed. It is often not something of beauty that can serve the purpose of showing forth the character of God.

With the rise of the women's movement, there has arisen in the church the beginnings of a new public opinion: Our knowledge of God is not to be circumscribed by what we know of human maleness. Our understanding of God's love needs to be broadened and deepened by looking at human womanhood and motherhood too. We have come to see that, when Jesus calls God Father, what he means is not that God has a sex and is male and not female, but that God is love and not brute power, and that the world is a family with this God as its loving Father. All the love in the human world that is beautiful and unselfish, including mother-love, can help us understand God better. The Incarnation tells us that God has become a part of humanity and that is its message. As to the fact that Jesus was a man, that was as accidental as his height and the color of his eyes. I see no theological necessity for Immanuel to have to happen in the form of a male only.

Today, more and more Christians and biblical scholars are discovering that the Bible, in spite of the patriarchal ethos in which its writers lived, still contains some passages that talk of God's love in terms of motherhood. Women Christians are often especially sensitive to such passages because they, being women, have suffered discrimination and oppression in our patriarchal society and patriarchal church. We know those who are underprivileged often enjoy an epistemological advantage in grasping some truth first and more easily. So, in knowing God as Father, they are less prone to equate God with male domination. Our church has suffered from male-centeredness for too long, resulting in a bias in our view of God which awakened women Christians must help us overcome today.

For instance, women Christians have especially been struck by Isaiah 49, where God is said to be like a mother breast-feeding her child. There God says of himself: "Can a woman forget her sucking child, that she should have no compassion on the son of her womb?" (v. 15)

In Isaiah 46 God says: "Hearken to me, O house of Jacob, all the remnant of the house of Israel, who have been borne by me from your birth, carried from the womb; even to your old age I am he, and to gray hairs I will carry you. I have made, and I will bear; I will carry and will save" (v. 3–4).

Psalm 131:2 describes the psalmist's feeling of restfulness in God: "I have calmed and quieted my soul, like a child quieted at its mother's breast."

These passages show no hesitation in using the image of the mother in referring to the loving care of God.

Jesus himself compared his love and care for the people to that of a hen for her chickens. Facing Jerusalem, he laments: "How often would I have gathered your children together as a hen gathers her brood under her wings, and you would not!"

In Luke 15, right before the story of a loving father in his dealings with his two sons, Jesus used the story of a woman's joy when she finds the one lost piece of silver to put across to us the joy of the father in heaven in the return of a penitent sinner.

In Genesis 1 we read of the creation of human beings in God's own image—"male and female created he them." So the image of God is not male only but female also. Her goodness, her tenderness, her kindness, her softness, her caring, her long-suffering and the quietness of her work of love and self-sacrifice—all exist in great fullness in God.

There is a Hebrew word used to connote the love of God which has the root idea of the womb. It seems to suggest that this love not only enwraps, protects and nourishes the embryo, but also refuses to possess it, rather helping its growth and, when the time is ripe, allowing it to begin its independent existence in the outside world.

In the latter part of the 2nd century, Clement of Alexandria said certain things that are enlightening: "God is Love, /God can only be perceived in Love, /Father in his inexpressible being, /Mother in her compassionate pity for us." It was also Clement who said, "To the child, Logos is everything. Logos is Father and also Mother, is Teacher and also Nurse. ... It is the Father's milk which feeds the child. Only Logos feeds us children with the milk of love. Those who suck this breast can enjoy true bliss. So to seek is to suck. The Father feeds all those children who seek his Logos with the milk of love from his breast." The church soon turned patriarchal and we heard no sayings of this kind until quite recently.

Aside from the rise of feminism, the changed general theological atmosphere is another factor to account for the present emergence of women's points of view in regard to God. The age-old view that God is changeless, unmoved and impassable, that is, incapable of suffering, is no longer tenable. Alfred North Whitehead in his *Process and Reality* points out that the Christian theological tradition has for long mistakenly conceived of God either as the ruling Caesar, or the ruthless moralist, or the unmoved mover. He calls us to recover the "Galilean vision" in which God is shown to be Christ-like love. The highest attribute of God is not his omnipresence, or his omnipresence, or his omniscience, or his honor and majesty, but his love. He is the Cosmic Lover, "the fellow-sufferer who understands." Nothing which is truly good is lost in that reign where love is supreme. It is in this climate that mother-like love sheds its light on our search for a fuller understanding of the nature of God.

We often forget about God's righteousness when we talk of his love but, more often, we forget God's love when we talk of his righteousness. Righteousness is also love. When love is extended to the whole humanity or a large group of humanity, it becomes righteousness, or justice, or fairness. Parents who have several children in their family find this easy to understand.

Our knowledge of God's love is far from adequate. We need to continue to fathom and enter into this love with the help of all manifestations of human love of the best quality, as shown not only by men, but also by women. We count on our women theological students to give their unique contributions to our exploration.

—Commencement Address
Nanjing Seminary
July 8, 1986

$\infty$

# GOD'S LOVE COMPELS SINNERS TO ACCEPT CHRIST

Two or three years ago I spent some time in a convalescent hospital in the suburbs of Nanjing near the Sun Yat-sen Mausoleum. Many people there were aware that I believed in Christ and at mealtime religion was often the topic of discussion. There were a few boors who would make jokes about Christian belief in the resurrection and the like. I remember one, a particularly objectionable type, who said; "You say there is a God—bring him out and show him to me and I'll believe."

To non-Christians looking at us from the outside, Christianity is just a bunch of doctrines. They would find it easier to believe without these doctrines. With the doctrines, it is just not worth it to them. Yet there are some highly educated people who do believe and find nothing ridiculous about Christianity. The anti-Christians cannot understand such people; they have no way to explain it. When they mention such people in their writings, they simply pass over their religious faith without a word—Sun Yat-sen for example, or Einstein, the writer Lao She, Dr. Lin Qiaoru, Xu Guangqi or Pavlov. Writers of essays and biographies do not mention their religion. They are presented as if they were all atheists, which seems rather dishonest.

Actually, almost without exception, the reason Christians became Christian was not because a bunch of doctrines convinced them to turn to Christ. All of us were first touched by love, compelled by love. We first felt the kind of love with which Christ loves us and, touched by the highest, most beautiful, best love there is in this world, we came to the realization that we fell short, that we were sinners. And because of this we willingly gave up everything to accept Christ. We did not first work out each doctrine intellectually. First, we were touched in our deepest feelings, in the depths of our souls, attracted and melted by Christ's love. And because of this we prostrated ourselves and submitted to Christ.

Doctrines are of course important. Their specialized language safeguards a message, a gospel—the gospel of God's love for humankind. God is love, love made manifest in Christ. This is a universe of love. The basic principle and foundation of the universe is love. We are all objects of God's love. God did not hesitate to pay a heavy price for us. Christianity moves and compels people, not by its doctrines, but by the love made manifest, love held high and spread abroad, love waiting eagerly for the final coming of a world of love. This love draws countless men and women who give their all to enlarge love's realm.

Doctrine is more concerned with matters of orthodoxy. It inevitably tends toward the rejection of any thought or faith alien to itself. Overemphasis on orthodox doctrine always leads easily to monotony, oppressiveness and a lack of vitality. But love is lively and unrestrained, rich and varied, full of creativity. Love is the richest and most colorful spirit on earth. It is infectious, inestimable, unpredictable and incalculable.

Some people insist that love cannot be devoid of self-interest, that love always has a secret motive. When we see the love of Christ, we must proclaim that there is love without strings, altruistic love. Christ represents this kind of love. We find this kind of love in the person of many faithful Christians as well.

If those friends at the convalescent hospital could approach the four gospels with humble hearts, they would surely get a taste of this kind of genuine love.

How deep, how unchanging was the father's love in the parable of the Prodigal Son. His love tells him that the son will surely return. He eagerly anticipates it. It is this love which melts the son's heart of stone and allows the father to take him back anew as his true son. How the shepherd loved that one sheep that was lost out of the hundred. He did not wait for the sheep to come back, but went to look for it. Finding it, he carried it home.

Jesus so loved his friends that when he saw them suffering over a death in the family, he could not help crying.

When he saw an ambitious youth, he loved him and pointed out to him what it was that he still lacked.

His love made him weep over Jerusalem.

His love for the hungry, the homeless, the naked, the sick, and those in prison was so deep that he said, whatever you do for these people, you have done for me.

The woman despised by the world because she had five husbands, the woman accused of adultery by those who called themselves righteous, the woman who wept over her sins, washed Jesus' feet with her tears and dried them with her hair—Jesus loved them all.

The man who saw Jesus coming and climbed a tree so as to see him better, who expressed his willingness to repent and return to those he had cheated nine times their due—Jesus loved him.

His closest friends fled during his passion and some denied him. He was deeply wounded, yet he still loved them.

One sentence says it all: "Having loved his own who were in the world, he loved them to the end" (John 13:1).

There is no greater love on earth than one who would lay down his life for his friends. This is the love of Christ.

This is the Christ in whom we are bold to believe. Love is the true essence of human life. Love is the greatest truth. Love is the most fundamental attribute of God. Love is the intrinsic attribute of the universe. Natural disasters—storms, earthquakes, volcanoes erupting—happen in our universe. We do not understand why, but even so, we do not believe that the true essence of the universe is hatred or destruction. No, we believe that the true essence of the universe is love and wholeness, the love manifest in Christ. With this love in our universe, we are held firm, we can be at peace, we can live with strength and meaning, we can give thanks and praise.

This is a world lacking in love, a world that needs love. If people can have love, they can feel secure. So many people long for love, but cannot get it.

The transition from semi-feudalism and semi-colonialism to socialism was a long process. Change was a way of life and there were setbacks. In the past the Chinese people lived an agricultural life more or less in harmony with nature: "Work by day, rest at night; what has the emperor to do with me?" But such a life is no longer an option. In the course of all the changes and setbacks, social relationships were easily strained. Things happened that harmed all sides. Add to this some political movements we could have done without, and the suffering grew. So many people were driven to distraction and experienced the inconstancy of human relationships. They felt they had no love, and they longed for it. Christ's gospel of love can satisfy this longing.

Those who "take class struggle as the key link" cannot hear the gospel of love. To speak of love seems like speaking out of tune to them, harmful to the struggle, a failure to distinguish right from wrong, friend from foe. It is capitulationism. China today is no longer in the historical stage of taking class struggle as the key link. Today everyone wants peace and stability. The gospel of love, the gospel of reconciliation, is more to the point. If you look around, you will see that the numbers of those who believe in Christ are increasing, not decreasing.

Some years ago, the well-known writer Ba Jin went to Japan. At one of the places he visited, his host was bald. Later the man told him his story. During the Cultural Revolution, he was swayed by the propaganda of China's extreme left and became an ultra-leftist, attacking and harming many people in Japan. Later he was struck with a deep sense of guilt. He felt he had to do something to apologize, but there was no way to make compensation, so he decided to shave his head from then on.

When I read Ba Jin's essay, I was shaken. The "take class struggle as the key link" line, the leftist line, the line of hate, appeared in China from the late 1950s on, and there were echoes of it in the church. On some issues, this line influenced me, too. I do not need to resort to the Japanese man's counsel of despair in seeking to express my repentance. On the basis of what I know today, I am doing what I can to oppose leftism. In the Seminary, in the Church, in society, I use whatever strength I have to keep "leftism" from continuing to harm people. I ask God to accept this way of showing my repentance. Leftism attacks people politically, extending the scope of attack and shrinking the scope of unity. From a faith point of view, leftism tramples love underfoot; it is a negation of the gospel. We oppose leftism today and raise up love, spreading the spirit of mutual love in the world, to let love, the love of Christ, awaken the many frozen hearts.

For students at this Seminary, the situation is different. No matter what the state of your spiritual life when you came here, your first task is to enter into and go deeper into the four gospels, to enter more deeply into the Bible and there see this Christ, know this Christ, grow familiar with this Christ, be moved by his love, sit beside him and receive his teachings, welcome him among us, and become more and more like him. In this way, before we know it, we will become vessels God can use. We can go out and take Christ's love into the world so that it may enter into the depths of many more hearts. As this semester begins, let us being our pilgrimage anew.

—Lecture, Nanjing Seminary
March 2, 1988

## SECTION THREE:
# GOD'S LOVE TEACHES US TO KNOW AND SERVE

# God Calls Us to Serve

## Is there a missionary call?

Yes, to every Christian. It is most natural for Christians to want to tell others of Christ. My friend Chuan Wen is a typical example. How, surprisingly soon after his conversion, he began to go about, not only selling insurance policies, which was his occupation, but trying to convert people to his new convictions and new life. To be sure, he committed many blunders. We felt it was dangerously quick. We doubted whether he was not doing more harm than good to himself, to others and to the church. Perhaps, from the standpoint of commonsense. It was we who had to learn anew for ourselves and to give a greater allowance to the movement of the Spirit which escapes our inclination to "patternize" things.

Converts like Chuan Wen may be said to be naturally missionary right from the moment the seed of the gospel takes root in their hearts. We do not need to make them missionary-minded by invoking all the clever devices of missionary education to convince them that they have got something worth passing on the others. You rather think of Christ saying: If these should hold their peace, the stones would immediately cry out.

If this is true of individual converts, this is also true of the "younger churches" as churches. The one thing they discover for themselves very quickly is that evangelism is the life-blood of the church. It is only in reaching the gospel out into the world that the church can keep it vital for itself. Nothing can really kill the church until the church is induced to forget its missionary task.

Let us not be too sure that we have any right to say that we and our church are too weak to be missionary. Let us rather say that we and our church are not missionary enough to be strong. Indeed, I do not see why God needs to give us strength, even though we say we want it in our prayers, unless it is used by us to proclaim the lordship of Christ to the millions and millions of people around us who have not yet heard it proclaimed.

The truth actually amounts to this: If Christ has become anything to you, he must be everything to you. And if he indeed is everything to you, how anxious you must be that he should be made to mean everything to all people everywhere. That anxiety in you corresponds in a small way to the eternal hunger in the heart of God himself, his eternal longing for the whole of humankind to return to him. The missionary vocation is thus not anything about which we have to be argumentative, as if the force of our arguments were necessary to prop it up. God being what he is, the conquest of the world with love can have no alternative. If happily we realize this and let ourselves be used in this, ours is really the most glorious vocation—the nearest humanly possible vocation to that of the incarnation itself. It is through this vocation that something of God is made knowable to us in terms of our contemporary, everyday, flesh-and-blood realities.

## IS CHRIST WANTED BY INDIA, CHINA, AND AFRICA?

First of all, let us realize that no matter whether India, China and Africa want Christ or not, Christ wants India, China and Africa. The seats for these nations must not be vacant when peoples shall come from the east and the west, from the south and the north, to make their places in the feast of the kingdom.

As to India, China and Africa themselves, as well as all other countries, they both want Christ and do not want him. In their sensitivity, they cannot easily want him because he is uncomfortably challenging and demanding. But they, also in their sensitivity, know that it is Christ and nothing less that they need in order to obtain the grace of God and the deliverance from sin to the full status and liberty of the children of God. Thus to Christ, human beings offer violent resistance just as they also give themselves up in utter humility and gratitude. To Christ, we not only say, "Depart from me, for I am a sinner," we are also driven back to confess, "Lord, to whom shall we go? You have the words of eternal life" (John 6:68).

But why do we need to be so concerned with the question of whether Christ is wanted by men and women? Do we have any right to expect people to want him? Should we not rather assume that he will have to be unwanted and rejected? For, if otherwise, where lies the hardship, the challenge and, indeed, the necessity of missionary work? We are like the man who asked Christ, "Will those who are saved be few?" (Luke 13:23) and he might answer, "What is that to you, follow me."

Whenever the church is not quite confident of its own belief, it starts to look eagerly for external factors to justify its existence. If people do not seem to want Christ, we think that the principles of tolerance should forbid us to impose our religion upon others. But tolerance is sometimes very doubtful as a Christian virtue and is a very convenient cover-up for spiritual exhaustion. Everybody seems happy but issues are blurred. When someone is drowning the help called for is not so much for your tolerance of their ideas but a life-belt that you know to be a life-belt.

## ARE MISSIONARIES WANTED?

It is unmistakable that missionaries are wanted by the younger churches. They are needed for many reasons and these reasons will mostly hold good even when the younger churches have grown much stronger. They bring to us the experiences and heritages of the older and stronger churches; they link us with the church universal and through them we get a glimpse of the reality and the richness of the whole body of Christ. They bring us tried methods and techniques that can be made useful in our lands. By their life and deeds and by their being what they are, they can gain access to many sorts of people who otherwise can hardly be reached. As fellow-students in Christ, they learn and teach and train the youth so that, before too long, we can be ready to tackle the big untackled areas. They watch and are inspired by non-Christians who come to accept Christ for the first time and they see the New Testament having tremendous impact on the life and mind of the new converts and communities. This, all its simplicity and straightforwardness, should be very enriching to the total spiritual heritage of the world church if the missionary can interpret it aright. Last but not least, missionaries are important to their mother churches as live wires keeping the missionary torch burning and church life vigorous.

Part of the reason for Christians in the West to ask whether the younger churches still want missionaries is the amount of romantic discussion about the wonders of the younger churches and about how Western missionaries are to work under "native leadership." This discussion has helped Christians in the West to see once again that their job is to let the church grow and achieve maturity and not to keep mission stations going permanently. It has also reminded Christians of the East of our own responsibilities. But I wish that it had not created a broad the notion that the younger churches are really mature enough today to dispense with Western personnel help. Such idealization of the younger churches is harmful and may undermine much of the missionary interest which would otherwise become manifest.

## WHAT ABOUT PRIORITIES?

It is obvious that all countries have an equal claim. China does not need Christ any more or any less badly than the United States or India. But the line of demarcation today is not national. We Christians are looking at the entire non-Christian world as the area to be won for Christ. There, a total strategy is called for. We need to spread out our resources more evenly.

Missionary work among other peoples will enable us to gain a fuller understanding of the gospel itself. It is only in evangelizing that you really start to evangelize yourself. In the gospel of Christ there is such a deep, unplumbed and hidden treasure that it cannot be fully explored by anything less than the whole human race. We shall not know the eminence of the gospel, and our worship is bound to be incomplete, until it comes to include all for whom it was meant. It will take the whole of humanity to embody the Christ that is yet to be and to bring to full expression the unsearchable riches of Christ. We might very well remind ourselves that the New Testament, which is so essential to our faith, has come to be written only as a result of the missionary work of the apostolic church.

Think of the oppression and injustice that has been done and is still being done by the big powers to the peoples of the countries which are today at the receiving end of missions. In great humility and penitence Christians must attempt, at least partially, to undo the wrong that has been done. Other forces from your countries are there to give a negative testimony to Christianity and it is up to Christian forces to give positive testimony to counteract this.

## HOW MUCH DO I HAVE TO SACRIFICE?

For every pleasure you have to give up something. In this the missionary merely shares the common situation of all human beings. We Christians of the East have much to thank the missionaries for but it is perilous for you to think of your task in terms of sacrifice.

We are hesitant to greet a missionary who is obsessed with the idea of self-sacrifice. He reminds us of Jonah. Poor Jonah survived not only his three days in the stomach of a whale but also the centuries since then and is still occasionally incarnating himself in his more refined form in the duty-bound, unhappy and self-pitying missionary!

An unwilling missionary like Jonah can do some good but can also cause a lot of trouble. He works out a sense of duty. His response to the call of God is merely intellectual and is not a response of the whole person. He has no joy and no deep love and he cannot hide the fact very long. By virtue of his sacrifice he feels that he ought to be ministered to rather than to minister and he almost feels that his sacrifice puts him in a good bargaining position with God. He forgets that a Christian's vocation is really the highest fulfillment of himself as God sees him. He is finding life and not losing it. There need be no passive, unwilling obedience or the crushing of our own will. We should make a living, willing, joyful and grateful offering of ourselves and of our will to God.

The most powerful illustration of this humility and willingness in taking up a God-given vocation I can think of is that of Mary when the angel of God broke to her God's call to the unexpected task of giving birth to Christ. It was a task of glory, to be sure, but it was also one of unthinkable humiliation. All now owe her eternal gratitude for her ready consent to become instrumental in the most tremendous event in human history, the even of the incarnation of God and the redemption

of man. May we ponder anew the joy, the gratitude and the eager coop-
erativeness in her simple answer "Behold, I am the handmaid of the
Lord; let it be unto me according to your word" (Luke 1:38).

## WHO IS QUALIFIED?

Our Christian vocation is so glorious that nobody is worthy of it. But
at the same time, it is so glorious that your worthiness and your
unworthiness do not count at all.

Perhaps as a result of much discussion as to what a missionary
should be like or should not be like, some missionaries have been led
to take themselves too seriously. They become self-conscious, tense
and stiff instead of just being themselves, natural and at ease.

We must take our vocation seriously so that God may use us. Yet,
in another sense, we need not take it so seriously that we do not leave
room for the Holy Spirit to operate in us. What we do is extremely
important because it is God's work. But, at the same time, what we do
is also extremely unimportant exactly for the same reason. Just as a
physician of the body only establishes certain conditions in the patient
and in the environment under which God, who is the God of health
and wholesomeness, restores the physical well-being in the patient, so
a missionary merely establishes certain conditions under which the
Holy Spirit can work to restore the health in the souls of men and
women. I am quite prepared to question whether much of the fruit of
the missionary work has not been reaped in spite of the missionaries
rather than through them. Even Jonah, the unwilling missionary,
could be instrumental in bringing about repentance on the part of the
people of Nineveh, but we feel sorry for Jonah himself.

It is very important for missionaries and all Christians to realize
their own unimportance, as this is the only way our importance can be
viewed in its true perspective. And this perspective can probably help
missionaries to strike a happy balance between seriousness and relax-
ation about their job.

And do not let us forget the life-transforming power of the vocation. The power which works through us works also in us and, in spite
of our unworthiness, transforms our own lives and makes us new in
ways as significant as the transformation of the lives of the people to

whom we are sent. We are called not because we are good but because we have heard the gospel. And as we respond to that one-sided call of God, we are upheld and made into God's fellow-workers.

—Article in *Student World*, 1948

## LOVE SPEAKS THE TRUTH

As history moves forward from 1982 to 1983, let us remember that in using AD to indicate the year, we humans, consciously or not, put the birth of Jesus Christ at the center of things. This is a recognition of sorts that Christ's birth is of decisive significance for us, for history and for the world.

People's growing recognition of the whole significance of Christ has developed over 2,000 years. In "The Warrior and the Fly," Lu Xun quotes Schopenhauer, who felt that our estimation of a person's physique seems to shrink with distance, while our estimation of his spirit grows greater with our distance from him. When Christ was in the world, his words and actions did not always amaze people or cause them to suddenly see the light. At the time people paid little attention to many of Christ's words and actions or did not understand them, and some were misunderstood. Few people heard him say what is recorded in John 18, verses 19–24, for example, though it is familiar to us, and even fewer understood it.

The scene is a trial, with many people crowded into a large court-yard, some shouting, others cursing—all sorts of people watching what was going on. Those who had placed their hopes on Jesus were disappointed. They did not know what to think of him now. Jesus' followers, those who sympathized with him, were silent and some sought to distance themselves from him. Some still hoped that at the last moment God would send an army of angels to save this Jesus. The authorities, Herod, Annas, Caiaphas and Pilate could not have cared less about Jesus' fate. But having a criminal like Jesus was actually an opportunity for them to even up the contradictions that had built up among them. It was a dark, forbidding courtyard, a place where right and wrong were reversed, where there was no possibility of arguing. No one wanted to hear what was right and what was wrong, what was true or what was false. They would not have listened. It was a trial where the death sentence was a foregone conclusion.

What Jesus said there was an affront to the authorities and an officer struck him. Jesus did not strike back, but he did answer. Jesus answered his enemies solemnly and with dignity; his words were an accusation and a protest: "If I have spoken wrongly, testify to the wrong. But if I have spoken rightly, why do you strike me?" His answer was neither obsequious nor haughty.

Jesus' natural and easy speech reflected an unshakable faith deep in his soul—God is ruler of the universe, God has jurisdiction over it and holds it. This God is all-powerful and all-loving; this God is the highest truth. Equivocation is not the grounding principle of the universe. Right is right and wrong is wrong and history is the process of right overcoming wrong. Right and wrong may be temporarily unclear or muddled, but ultimately right and wrong will be clear.

There in Annas' courtyard, Jesus' voice was weak, but it is a conscienticizing voice. All through the ages the echoes of the question Jesus asked there and then have resounded in every corner of the universe. Annas, Caiaphas and Pontius Pilate could work hand in glove to have Jesus suppressed, but all the Annases and Caiaphases and Pontius Pilates in history have failed to suppress the growing resonance of Jesus' protest and the response of those who heard it, and followed him.

Jesus' words imply his great belief in human beings' ability to distinguish right from wrong. He believes that humans have the intelligence to judge rightly. Hitler said that a lie told thousands of times becomes the truth. Jesus did not deceive people. He said when you speak, call right right and wrong wrong. Truth and justice, not lies, will win out.

Please note one thing: Christ did not say that people should follow him without question because he is the Son of God. He did not say that he, being the Son of God, cannot err and therefore must be obeyed. He says "if," "if I have spoken wrongly," and "if I have spoken rightly." He admits he may be wrong and encourages people to make a judgment about him for themselves. He does not even want to assert that to strike is necessarily wrong. He just invites people not to strike in haste, but to consider whether what he has said is right or not. He says, "if I have spoken rightly, why do you strike me?"

As this year begins, let us think anew of the fact that the power of words depends not on how loudly they are uttered but on their correspondence to the ultimate principle by which the whole universe is governed. Often truth, when first spoken, sounds very weak, but because it is the truth, it must dislodge and overtake falsehood at last. The voice of truth, the voice of reason, of justice, might at times sound weak, but it is never really weak. Our faith in the Risen and Ascended Christ, in the Risen Lord who sits at the right hand of the Father and sustains the universe by his word of power, includes such an optimistic faith. Paul said, "the weakness of God is stronger than men." History is not made by proud people in rebellion against God. History is in the hand of God whose name is Love. Before this God all human fury is to subside and give way to willing obedience and humble adoration. To him be honor and glory forever.

—Jesus' Protest, Nanjing, 1983

# THE MAN WHO WRESTLED WITH GOD

Jacob was a descendent of Abraham. God chose Abraham from among all humankind. God dealt graciously with him and his descendents, especially watching over and guiding them through special testing and blessings, because according to God's wonderful plan, the Savior Christ was to be born of Abraham's descendents, the horn of salvation, the light of dawn, the King of glory, and incarnate Lord himself.

His mother's favorite from boyhood, Jacob was a person who thought only of himself. Of the many things he did that hurt others, three spring most readily to mind: (1) When his older brother Esau returned tired from the fields, Jacob seized his chance and by means of a simple bowl of lentil soup, took Esau's place as the eldest son. (2) Their father was old and his eyesight poor and Jacob, disguised as Esau, tricked his father into giving him the blessing, which should have been for the eldest son. (3) Jacob's father-in-law, too, was a man who looked out for himself, but Jacob, by a cleverer ruse than his, increased the number and fatness of his own goats while his father-in-law's became thinner and fewer.

Jacob was truly a selfish man, good at turning things to his own advantage and making his way up in the world, while causing others to come to grief—a very slick operator.

For twenty years, Jacob, depending on his wits and wiles, seemed to get along very well, working out his own problems. Though he did suffer at times, in general, he always landed on his feet. In his own eyes, the twenty years he spent away from home were a success. As he put it, "for with only my staff I crossed this Jordan; and now I have become two companies" (Gen. 32:10).

We recall that when God called Abraham, God told him, "In you all the families of the earth shall be blessed" (Gen. 12:3). Clearly, God was not calling him so that he as an individual or a people could be blessed. God called him to be the bridge of blessing, to become the vessel of blessing, so that all humankind might gain God's blessing through him. Jacob had to be aware of this, because when his grandfather Abraham died, Jacob was already fifteen. What's more, his father Isaac had received the same charge from God (Gen. 26:4). And Jacob himself received this charge once again (Gen. 28:14), so there was even less reason for him not to have known about it. But when this charge came down to Jacob, he spared no thought for anyone else, he thought only of grabbing the advantage for himself. Even after God showed him the ladder to heaven in his dream at Bethel, and made him the best promise, he placed conditions on God's promise, making it center around him: "If God will be with me, and will keep me in this way that I go, and will give me bread to eat and clothing to wear, so that I come again to my father's house in peace, then the Lord shall be my God, and this stone, which I have set up for a pillar, shall be God's house; and of all that you give me I will surely give one-tenth to you" (Gen. 28:20–22). This was his vow, no better than a business transaction.

The meaning of "Jacob" in the original language is "grasp"—a perfect description of Jacob's personality. He was born grasping the heel of his older twin brother Esau. "Grasp" sums up Jacob's outlook on life. It was his principle for dealing with people and things.

We have such people in the world today—people whose outlook on life is to grasp for all they are worth. They may be a little cleverer than Jacob, the opportunities presented to them may be better or worse, but their purpose is the same—to grasp fame, favor, position, power and whatever else comes their way. Some of them go a step further than Jacob. Their motto is "everyone for himself and the devil take the hindmost." Some people even carry this outlook into the church, where, be it in spiritual formation or in the ministry of the church, they persist in getting whatever they can. How sad and pathetic this is.

Jacob had been away for twenty years and now was going to return. He'd see his brother Esau the next day. How would Esau act? Would he treat him as a brother? Jacob had no way of knowing; he only knew that Esau was coming to meet him with four hundred men. And Jacob? He was still the old, shrewd Jacob. In order to be prepared for anything, he divided his people, flocks, herds and camels into two groups. That way, if Esau came and killed one group, the other might still escape. Jacob prepared an advance party bearing gifts besides, to make a good impression on Esau. From all this, we see that Jacob gave a lot of thought to the matter. And in addition, Jacob prayed: "Deliver me, please, from the hand of my brother, from the hand of Esau, for I am afraid of him; he may come and kill us all" (Gen. 32:11). He expressed no regrets for all his offenses against God and against his brother twenty years before.

Jacob spent twenty years plotting and intriguing. Even his brother did not know whether to consider him a brother or an enemy. Was this the life God wanted him to lead? Was this the condition one of God's chosen should be in? What pleases God, what God bestows, is goodness. Where was the good in Jacob?

Jacob spent all his humanity; all he had left was himself. This was fine for him, he was not afraid to face God. But it was then that he had the most peculiar experience. The description we are given in the Bible is very simple, but its implications are profound. We cannot entirely draw them all out. On this first day of the term, I would like to call your attention to three:

## (1) THE SEQUENCE OF PENIEL AND BETHEL

Twenty years before, when Jacob had not been away from home long, he had an experience of Bethel. He dreamed there was a ladder there, with its top reaching to Heaven and angels of God going up and down (Gen. 28:10–17).

Bethel represents the sweetest spiritual communion with the Lord, an unobstructed intimacy with God. Spiritual experience seems to reach its zenith there. This place is "the house of God and the gate of Heaven." Yes, Bethel is warm; it is burning hot.

Yet twenty years later, Jacob experienced Peniel. He did not find a sweet and favorable response from God there. Rather he clashed with God, struggled and wrestled with God.

First Bethel, then Peniel—what is the pattern here? Doesn't it make more sense for us, before the Lord, to deal with the sin of Peniel first and then later to cross the Jordan and Bethel, there to enjoy forever the presence and love of God? Common sense would tell us that God should first send suffering and then sweetness, wouldn't it? Why does the sweet come first and the bitter after in this case?

I hope our students will not try so much to substitute your own feelings for God's law of what is sweet and what bitter. Yes, Bethel was a good experience, but Jacob still had many hidden sins, which he had not confessed or dealt with there. God did not require him to clear these things up right then, but that did not mean he was off the hook forever. Sin is still sin and does not disappear of its own accord simply because we do not for a time recognize it as sin. After twenty years, two hundred years or even 2,000 years have passed, things seem clearer, and people realize that some things which seemed perfectly justified at the time, God has always viewed as sin, and in truth, as great sin, which must be dealt with. This is not a question of the sweet and the bitter, it is one that partakes much more of the divine nature, and is much closer to what is in God's heart and mind (1 Sam. 2:35).

Many of our Christians like Bethel and do not like Peniel. They want a God who praises us, not one who comes to wrestle with us. They do not want to allow God to wound our self-assurance or conceit. The result is that the definition of what is good and what evil, what is false and what true, in the end all depended on Jacob's inveterate nature, and this was extremely dangerous.

Our Bible tells us how Paul went to Arabia where he spent a period of quiet time, but it also tells us how the Lord wrestled with his beloved Peter on the housetop in Joppa (Acts 10). And as for the Lord Jesus himself, he was transfigured on the mountaintop, but he also prayed a sorrowful and troubled prayer in the garden of Gesthemane and sweated drops of blood.

Bethel is good, of course. But we see that it did not change Jacob much, while in fact Peniel did change him greatly. Thus, he was no longer called Jacob, but Israel, one who had wrestled with God.

Let us make this seminary our Bethel. May you see here the ladder leading to Heaven, with God's angels ascending and descending, bringing down food for you from above. But we do not want to escape Peniel either. Whatever happens, when we wrestle our opponent is not another person, but the Lord himself and he will not harm us. We could, during your four years of study here, shut the gate and lock it, cutting you off from the world outside, while you single-mindedly pursued that sweet "life on the mountaintop." We probably could, if we really wanted to. But if we did this, it would not take a whole four years for our students to become useless to the church. True Christians today cannot spend their lives with their heads stuck in the sand. All mature Christians, who love the truth, must not fear the inevitable mental and spiritual wrestling they will meet with. Only through such wrestling can we come to know the Lord and ourselves better. We will come to know the truth better and understand better the interconnectedness of Christian love of God and of others, and love for the country and for the church, and have a better knowledge of the future of the church. Without Peniel, we will still be Jacob and we cannot truly know Bethel.

## (2) PRAYER IS WRESTLING WITH GOD

Prayer is one of our goals in coming to seminary. Prayer brings you to the Word. I hope that while you are here, much of your time will be spent in prayer.

The nature of true prayer is indeed like wrestling with God. Sadly, too much of our prayer is simply heaped-up worn-out phrases which have lost the character prayer should have.

True prayer is: (1) knowing that what we pray for is in accord with the nature of God; (2) based on the right we enjoy in Christ to pray; (3) boldly, almost rudely, to grasp God and, without letting go, to pray to God.

Job said: "Oh, that I knew where I might find him, that I might come even to his dwelling! I would lay my case before him, and fill my mouth with arguments ... Would he contend with me in the greatness of his power? No, but he would give heed to me. There an upright person could reason with him, and I should be acquitted forever by my judge" (Job 23:3–7).

Abraham prayed thus for Sodom: "Will you indeed sweep away the righteous with the wicked?... Far be it from you to do such a thing, to slay the righteous with the wicked, so that the righteous fare as the wicked! Far be it from you! Shall not the Judge of all the earth do what is just?" (Gen. 18:22–24). He held onto Yahweh's nature, that Yahweh must act justly and return good for evil and would not just let go, but prayed. This is a prayer of faith.

The Canaanite woman also prayed to God in this way. The Lord had already refused her, but she said: "Yes, Lord, yet even the dogs eat the crumbs that fall from their master's table" (Matt. 15:21–28). She did not let go, did not easily give up her chance to wrestle. She held tight to the Lord's nature to have pity and compassion and was even bold enough to argue with him. This is the prayer of faith.

As long as what we pray for is in accord with the nature of God, we

Christians do not fear that our prayers will go amiss and we can pray boldly and with confidence. The Holy Spirit will come to help us pray in this way, enabling us to gain blessings from God's hand. God will be sure to answer such a prayer, so that we are emboldened to thank him even before He does, as when the Lord Jesus lifted his eyes to heaven before Lazarus had moved within his tomb and said, "Father, I thank you for having heard me" (John 11:41).

The important thing is that we must know that what we pray for is in accord with God's nature. And to ensure this, we must "become participants of the divine nature" (2 Pet. 1:4).

We often see another kind of prayer, very pious perhaps, but issuing not from the nature of God, but from our own natures. Didn't the mother of James and John pray the Lord Jesus to allow her sons to sit one at his right hand and one at his left? This prayer was for herself; it was a "grasping" prayer, the prayer of Jacob pre-Peniel, like the vow he made at Bethel.

It may be asked, since God is omnipotent, why did he not overcome Jacob and defeat him? Why did the Bible go so far as to say that God saw that he did not prevail against Jacob?

Yes, God is omnipotent. Speaking of power, ten Jacobs would be powerless before the omnipotence of God. But God was only wrestling with Jacob—in those twenty years, God restrained his power all along, set aside his omnipotence for a time—in order that Jacob might come to know this omnipotence and learn well to be humble and obey.

God is omnipotent, yet willingly allows that omnipotence to be overcome by our faith and prayers. This is entirely due to God's profound love.

The crux is: God must touch the hollow of your thigh, but this is a healing touch. God will not hit us harder than he feels is necessary, and he will not crush us, or break us more than we need. But we must after all accept from God some beatings, within limits, some scrapes and bruises, so that we better bear on our bodies God's power and our own weakness. Paul carried on his body the mark of Jesus, a thorn in the flesh, that he might "boast all the more gladly of my weaknesses, so that the power of Christ may dwell in me" (2 Cor. 12:9).

Notice that what Jacob experienced in Bethel came after sundown: "He came to a certain place, and stayed there for the night, because the sun had set. Taking one of the stones of the place, he put it under his head and lay down in that place" (Gen. 28:11). When he had finished wrestling with God, it was morning: "The sun rose upon him as he passed Penuel, limping because of his hip" (Gen. 32:31). Peniel does not represent suffering, nor darkness, what it leads into is the brightness of the face of God and the joy of dawn.

### (3) THE IMPORTANT THING IS WHETHER GOD BLESSED (HIM)
In the course of wrestling with God, Jacob made two requests: He asked his opponent to bless him, and he asked his opponent to tell him his name. The first request God agreed to and blessed him. The second God did not accede to, saying: "Why is it that you ask my name?"

If God had told Jacob one of his names, whether the name was Yahweh or Elohim, or something else, it would be nothing more than a formula to a human ear. If people took an excessive interest in the name of God, the spiritual experience of wrestling with God would be dimmed and the blessing gained from God forgotten. It would even lead to factional strife among disciples. Isn't this a reversal of the trivial and the important?

Our Lord is a God who bestows blessings—this is the important thing. As an address—*Shen*, Lord, God, Yahweh, *Shangdi*—any of these will do, because my God is your God and he is the same Lord we all serve. It is a fact that in Christianity we have churches with different denominational traditions. But the important thing is that we have only one Lord who blesses and he has blessed the church with everything. We need not ask: Does this one belong to Paul? This one to Cephas or that one to Apollo? All we need ask is: Has God himself blessed this person? That is the important thing.

In this seminary, though we make the Bible the foundation of our unity, though our basic faith is one, we do reserve some differences—in certain of our views, in liturgy and in terms for God. But we do not see anything bad in this. We believe this bears witness to how richly the Lord has blessed the churches. These differences, after all, are secondary. What is truly important is that this is your Bethel, the house of God. This is also Peniel, the place where you can look upon the face of God. What is truly important is this: that this is a place God himself has blessed.

And for us, this is good enough.

—Address at the Opening Convocation Nanjing Seminary,
Fall Semester, 1955

# WHY MUST THERE BE PREACHERS?

On a visit to Beijing in the autumn of 1951, I got together with half a dozen of my old classmates. The conversation turned to how we had gone our separate ways in the years since we had parted—it was a replay of our many enthusiastic dinner-table discussions of student days. One classmate suddenly asked me, "The church is a dark place. Why would you still want to be a preacher nowadays?" I briefly gave him my reasons and was met with an unexpected silence that lasted for some time. It was only when we were called to eat that things grew lively again.

In those moments of silence I was overcome by a feeling of extreme isolation and loneliness. In our student days my predilection for church work would definitely have provoked an argument, but we were none of us so young anymore. They politely changed the subject, and I was struck by the realization that people saw the church as so unclean, so mired in its own sinfulness, that they wanted nothing to do with it. The church's prospects are far from bright if people meet us with an embarrassed silence.

In that silence, gloom swept over my heart like a black cloud. I have a great love for the church but my friends did not find the church loveable. They were wrong, but how could my tongue right such an error? Should I have glossed over all the ways in which the church has been used for over a hundred years to insult the Lord's name? I don't have the skill for it, or the stomach.

I could not help feeling depressed, because the church I loved and believed in, the church I had dedicated myself to, had been exploited to such an extent that my old classmates could not comprehend why I would be involved in it. Why would anyone still want to be a preacher nowadays? They simply couldn't understand it. Can we even comprehend it ourselves? Once I had felt the loving arm of God around my shoulders urging me to "feed my sheep," I gladly obeyed, going to work in the church. Only now did I see that this church was unworthy of the name. Had I really followed the wrong path?

It has been two or three years since that reunion in Beijing. Why would one want to be a preacher nowadays? No preacher with a conscience can avoid the question. Who would want to be the perfunctory sort of preacher who, being a monk, goes on ringing the bell? We all want to retain the sense of dedication, the clarity, liveliness and sharpness we had at ordination, or when we made the decision to dedicate our lives to the work of preaching. In these last two or three years our nation has continued to progress rapidly. It is heartwarming to see that the church, too, had made great strides towards new life. And as the nation and the church advance, we see more clearly the meaning and pleasure of the work we have chosen.

Why must we still be preachers? Both to strengthen my own faith and to provide a point of reference for others, I would like to share my experience with my co-workers in the church.

## WE PREACH THE TRUTH

Preachers must take the lead because we have received a commission and what we preach is the truth. The gospel is the truth, a priceless treasure. It alone can fill the void in people's hearts. Nothing can take its place. People of all times and places need the gospel. Yesterday, today and tomorrow, it is the truth. Its truth will shine out if we can rid it of all the non-gospel elements that have crept in and sullied it over the last hundred years or more.

### Deep calling to deep

The gospel is truth, but it is not the scientific sort of truth that can be measured in a laboratory. Like the love between two persons, the truth of the gospel is real, but there is no way to quantify it.

"As a deer longs for flowing streams, so my soul longs for you, O God" (Ps. 42:1). The soul's thirst cannot be quantified, classified or explained. But we know that the truth of God's gospel can satisfy our spiritual hunger, just as the stream quenches the deer's thirst.

St. Augustine prayed, "Lord, you have put a restless heart in me; I can never find rest until I rest in you." We know from our hearts that this is precisely the state of things. "Come to me, all you that are weary and are carrying heavy burdens, and I will give you rest" (Matt. 11:28). Weary and carrying heavy burdens—wasn't this just how I felt? "Come to me." Wasn't this the invitation I so anxiously awaited in the depths of my soul? "I will give you rest." Wasn't this the sweetness I found when I accepted the Lord?

"You will know the truth, and the truth will set you free" (John 6:68). "Go away from me, Lord, for I am a sinful man!" (Luke 5:8). This was Peter's dilemma before the Lord, and it is ours as well. We desire God and are not willing to depart from God for we know God alone is our Lord of grace. But at the same time, we do not dare desire God and we are glad when God departs from us, at least temporarily, because we are not yet truly willing to cut ourselves off from sin.

The truth of the Bible should not be compared with ordinary truth. It speaks to us in the very depths of our souls. Its dialogue with us is truly "deep calling to deep" (Ps. 42:7). St. Bernard said that only a loving heart can comprehend the loving heart of Jesus. The Holy Spirit speaks to us in the very depths of our lives of the existence, omnipotence, wisdom, glory, majesty, sanctity, compassion and justice of God. It also speaks of our sinfulness and rebelliousness, of God's care and patience, of the mystery of the incarnation, of the beauty of Christ's birth, the salvation through the precious cross, the glory of the resurrection, of the Holy Spirit, the church, and the blessing of the sacraments and holy orders, of the mission to preach the gospel and build up the Lord's body, of the hope of God's kingdom to come, of our Christian task to reconcile with others in this world and need to serve others. This is food necessary to people in all times and places. Science is not much help to us in understanding all this. But this is a truth people know in the depths of their souls, because it is in keeping with all they hope for.

### Truth does not reject truth

We say that Christianity is truth. But this is not to imply that everything outside Christian doctrine is false. Christians have no monopoly on truth, nor do they reject it. Many things have appeared in human history that conform to the truth. Christians should not look askance at scientific achievements. Many of the persons, events and people's movements that have emerged in the world today are very close to the truth and we should welcome them with grateful hearts, learn from and support them, and pray for them, because there is only one God from who comes all truth, goodness and beauty in the universe. "Every generous act of giving, with every perfect gift is from above, coming down from the Father of lights" (James 1:17).

The gospel of Christ is truth. It is good and most worthy to be preached. But we must acknowledge that not everything outside the gospel is bad or opposed to the truth.

We know that some Christians, seeing the good done by people outside the church today, are not at all grateful to the Lord but have taken a very wrong road. They make every effort to find faults and weaknesses in unbelievers, as if only then can Christians take comfort and believe that the gospel still has merit! Why must we take an attitude so lacking in conscience and charity? Is our faith to be built on the wrongs, faults and weaknesses of others? It is a fact that humans are sinners, with faults and weaknesses. But this is not the foundation of our faith; this is not the gospel. The gospel begins from the love of God: "God so loved the world that he gave his only Son" (John 3:16). From this we see that our faith is built upon the merciful love of God. With God there is love, there is the gospel—what shall we fear? Amidst the struggles and battles of the universe, the genuinely determinative factors are not sin, unrighteousness and Satan, but God, the people pleasing to God, God's justice and God's truth.

The road some have taken is an unfortunate one. We should be firm in our conviction that the gospel is truth, the truest truth, the most important truth concerning God's love for humans and God's redemption of them. We do not, however, necessarily think that everything else is bad or false. There is only "one God and Father of all, who is above all and through all and in all" (Eph. 4:6). "From him and through him and to him are all things" (Rom. 11:36). In God there is no contradiction, only harmony, for in him there was not "Yes and No" but in him it is always "Yes" (2 Cor. 1:19). What we know today is limited and we cannot see our way out of some things because we find them contradictory. We should accept these as lessons from God in humble waiting and learn from Paul how to understand them: "O the depth of the riches and wisdom and knowledge of God! How unsearchable are his judgments and how inscrutable his ways!" (Rom. 11:33). But this does not stand in the way of our fulfilling the responsibility God has so clearly shown to us today. When that day comes, we will see the truth in all its fullness, just as Paul said: "For we know only in part ... but when the complete comes, the partial will come to an end. When I was a child, I spoke like a child, I thought like a child, I reasoned like a child; when I became an adult, I put an end to childish ways. For now we see in a mirror, dimly, but then we will see fact to face. Now I know only in part; then I will know fully, even as I have been fully known" (1 Cor. 13: 9–12).

### Make the truth of the gospel known

In the Louvre there is a famous painting of Adam and Eve leaving the Garden of Eden. In the background of the painting we see in the distance cherubim with a flaming sword barring the gates of Eden so that they cannot return. But against all expectation, the eyes of Adam and Eve are not turned back towards the gates. In the dark sky, dim but not recognizable, there is a shining cross. This is what Adam and Eve are gazing at. This painting illumines for us the central conviction of the gospel: to restore a right relationship with God. To reconcile with God, as at the beginning, humans must rely on the cross. It was at the very moment of human sin that God entered into the suffering of the cross with the aim of destroying sin. The cross is not simply the wooden instrument upon which Christ suffered for three hours 2,000 years ago

on Golgotha. The crucified Christ is that "lamb slain from the foundation of the world" (Rev. 13:8). Leading people to gaze upon and to
know the cross and calling to them, "Here is the Lamb of God, who
takes away the sin of the world" (John 1:29) is the work we preachers
do. Only such a savior can satisfy the hunger and thirst of our souls,
for not only is he a great historical figure, he is the Lord of history, the
Savior of sinners, the Doctor of souls, Friend of the lonely, the
Comforter of the afflicted, the Way, the Truth and the Life. He is a high
priest to speak for us at the right hand of God. This is the Lord we must
preach and it is the truth of this Lord that we must manifest. This is the
truth our congregations are seeking. We must satisfy their hunger and
thirst. Otherwise their seeking will lead them astray. They will be led
into mistaken understandings of the Bible and we will be responsible.

The gospel is the truth, the eternal truth of God. The commission
we have received to preach the gospel is no small matter. How can we
not tremble as we share and explain the sacred words of God? Does
long service in the church really bring us to the point of feeling it
doesn't matter? Were we not worthy after all? "But we have this treasure in clay jars, so that it may be made clear that this extraordinary
power belongs to God and does not come from us" (2 Cor. 4:7). We do
not preach the gospel because we are good and other people are bad
but because we have heard the truth, we have been moved by this
truth, thawed by the great love of God and because the Lord has chosen and called us by laying hands on us. Let us one day be worthy to
say with Paul, "I was not disobedient to the heavenly vision" (Acts
26:19). "Therefore, since it is by God's mercy that we are engaged in
this ministry, we do not lose heart. We have renounced the shameful
things that one hides; we refuse to practice cunning or to falsify God's
word; but by the open statement of the truth we comment ourselves
to the conscience of everyone in the sight of God" (2 Cor. 4:1–2).

Each week, believers are willing to accept God's own truth from
our hands. What great faith this shows in us! How can we give ourselves up as hopeless and hold our own ministry as of little account?
How can we not keep our eyes on God, strive to praise and study, do
our utmost to rid ourselves of the old poisons, so that the sacred words
of God may not be diminished by passing through our lips? When

Jesus prayed he said of his disciples, "I have been sanctified for them." How can we not even more sanctify ourselves for the sheep? Christ also said, "Sanctify them in the truth; your word is truth" (John 17:17). May what we believe and what we preach be God's word, that is, the truth of God that makes people turn from evil and be sanctified. There is no more joyful thing on earth than to preach this truth.

## NEW LIGHT, NEW FINDINGS

It is a joyful thing to be a minister in new China, not simply because we preach God's eternal truth but because God has been especially good to us, lifting our ignorance, giving us much new light, allowing us to see more deeply how broad and deep Christ's love is, how wonderful and unparalleled is the gospel. How sweet and abundant the treasures of scripture.

God's truth is unchanging. It does not change with history and it does not increase or decrease because of the times. But our comprehension of the truth becomes daily more abundant as the times progress and viewpoints change. The Bible has always contained much truth but we did not see it for what it was. We listened but did not hear. Today the Holy Spirit is at work in our hearts and this truth has suddenly shown forth. Only now do we know how clouded our vision was, how dull the faith in our hearts.

"The unfolding of your words gives light." Today the Lord's words have been opened up on a grand scale. The Bible is spreading its light in the hearts of believers who love God and love the truth. This is the time when we can be preachers. What a wonderful opportunity this should be.

### Blind, but now we see ...

We can truly respond to much in God's truth saying, "I was blind, but now I see." Let us look at the place of love for country and love for church in the Bible.

In the past we thought that Christians, being spiritual, should not be concerned about national affairs. In this way many patriotic exemplars in the Bible became "a garden locked, a fountain sealed" (Song 4:12). Indeed, the Bible does not directly mention the term patriotism.

But the sentiment of love for one's native land is everywhere apparent. The strange thing is that we were blind to it in the past.

The Jewish people are unsurpassed in spiritual dedication and zealous patriotism. They are the most country-loving as well as the most religion-loving people in the world. There is no contradiction between these two types of love, just as a child loves both its mother and its father. The two loves are in complete harmony. For the Israelites, Jerusalem is the place both best loved and most long for, where both the temple and the throne of Dave—the center of religious and national life—could be found. All the Old Testament prophets had a fervent concern for the fate of the nation. Centuries before Christ, the prophet Isaiah compared Israel to a mother's warm embrace:

> Rejoice with Jerusalem, and be glad for her,
> all you who love her;
> rejoice with her in joy,
> all you who mourn over her—
> that you may nurse and be satisfied
> from her consoling breast;
> that you may drink deeply with delight
> from her glorious bosom. (Isa. 66:10–11)

The Songs of Ascents in the book of Psalms (120–34) were chanted on the road to Jerusalem to keep the holy days. As they approached Jerusalem from afar and glimpsed the gates of the city and the heights of the temple, they could not help bursting into song:

> Our feet are standing within your gates, O Jerusalem.
> Jerusalem—built as a city that is bound firmly together.
> To it the tribes go up, the tribes of the Lord,
> as was decreed for Israel, to give thanks to the name of the Lord.
> For there the thrones for judgment were set up,
> the thrones of the house of David.
> Pray for the peace of Jerusalem:
> "May they prosper who love you.
> Peace be within your walls, and security within your towers."
> For the sake of my relatives and friends,
> I will say, "Peace be within you."
> For the sake of the house of the Lord our God,
> I will see your good." (Ps. 122:2–9)

Here also we see how concerned the people were for the peace and prosperity of Jerusalem. We see the most heartfelt love for country and wholehearted gratitude to Yahweh.

> When the Lord restored the fortunes of Zion, we were like
>     those who dream.
> Then our mouth was filled with laughter, and our tongue
> with
>     shouts of joy;
> then it was said among the nations, "The Lord has done great
>     things for them"
> The Lord has done great things for us, and we rejoiced.
> Restore our fortunes, O Lord, like the watercourses in the
>     Negeb.
> May those who sow in tears reap with shouts of joy.
> Those who go out weeping, bearing the seed for sowing,
> shall come home with shouts of joy, carrying their sheaves.
> (Ps. 126:1–6)

> "If I forget you, O Jerusalem, let my right hand wither!
> Let my tongue cling to the roof of my mouth, if I do not
> remember you, if I do not set Jerusalem above my high-
> est joy" (Ps. 137:5–6).

How many Christians in China today would speak this way of our own country?

> How very good and pleasant it is
> when kindred live together in unity!
> It is like the precious oil on the head,
> running down upon the beard,
> on the beard of Aaron,
> running down over the collar of his robes.
> It is like the dew of Hermon,
> which falls on the mountains of Zion.
> For there the Lord ordained his blessing,
> life forever more. (Ps. 133)

Here we see not only the psalmist's concern for harmony among all the branches of the kindred of Israel, we also see his love for the beauty of his land. We can compare it to the Chinese poem: "Vast is the sky, boundless the wilds; the wind blows through the grass, revealing sheep and cows." Such imagery comes only with a deep and true patriotism.

When the nation is in distress, the common people face murder, pillage and foreign occupation—truly unspeakable suffering. Jeremiah felt such grief; he wrote a lament:

> My eyes are spent with weeping; my stomach churns;
> my bile is poured out on the ground
> because of the destruction of my people,
> because infants and babies faint
> in the streets of the city. (Lam. 2:11)

He recalls days of peace and prosperity, likening them to gold, pure gold:

> How the gold has grown dim, how the pure gold is
>     changed!
> The sacred stones lie scattered at the head of every
>     street.
> The precious children of Zion, worth their weight in
>     fine gold—
> How they are reckoned as earthen pots, the work of a
>     potter's hands! (Lam. 4:12)

The nation in ruins, the people humiliated. The prophet Jeremiah is not indifferent. His words are moving:

> Women are raped in Zion, virgins in the towns of
>     Judah.
> Princes are hung up by their hands; no respect is
>     shown to the elders ...
> The joy of our hearts has ceased; our dancing has
>     turned to mourning. (Lam. 5:11–12, 15)

The Lord Jesus loves all humanity and gave up his life for all humanity. But this did not lessen his fervent love for his own nation. "When Jesus saw Nathanael coming towards him, he said of him, 'Here is truly an Israelite in whom there is no deceit'" (John 1:47). Here, Jesus reveals his feelings for his own people, the Israelites. It is as if we were to say today that the Chinese working people are the most loyal and true, most hardworking, most honest and reliable.

Two events are recorded in Luke 19:41–45. Jesus drew near Jerusalem and the sight of it caused him to weep because he knew enemies were coming who would plunge the people into misery. Then, entering the temple, he drove out the sinners and evil-doers.

The juxtaposition of these two events tell us that for Jesus, love for nation and people and love for God and church are entirely harmonious.

The apostle Paul was called to preach to the Gentiles, yet his care for his own people of Israel was undiminished. For their sake, he said:

> I am speaking the truth in Christ—I am not lying; my conscience confirms it by the Holy Spirit—I have great sorrow and unceasing anguish in my heart. For I could wish that I myself were accursed and cut off from Christ for the sake of my own people, my kindred according to the flesh. (Rom. 9:1–3)

Only those with such deep love for their own people are capable of being preachers.

From these passages, it is evident that the Bible has never asked believers not to love their own country. What the Bible says is clear enough but we were blind to it in the past. Today the Lord has made it clear to us.

### The Lord wants us to see

We are using the issue of patriotism simply as an example. The Lord's light shines upon many other truths in the Bible that reflect God's truth.

"Your word is a lamp to my feet and light to my path" (Ps. 119:105). But this light can only shine when God's word has been unfolded or opened up to us. God can unfold God's word at the appropriate time. We can only pray, "Open my eyes, so that I may behold wondrous things out of your law" (Ps. 119:18). Now is the time deemed appropriate by the Lord.

Jesus said to his disciples, "You do not know now what I am doing, but later you will understand" (John 13:7). He also said, "I still have many things to say to you, but you cannot bear them now. When the Spirit of truth comes, he will guide you into all the truth" (John 16:12–13). "But the advocate, the Holy Spirit, whom the Father will send in my name, will teach you everything, and remind you of all that I have said to you" (John 14:26). God knows that the vessels we have received are too small. They can hold only a little at a time. And so God nourishes us gradually, day by day, age by age, according to our needs.

It cannot be denied that the Holy Spirit is today leading the Chinese church into the truth the Spirit has for us, bringing to mind much the Bible long ago told us, though our stubbornness and arrogance kept us from seeing it.

### Build a holy temple worthy of our country

It is a wonderful thing to be a preacher today because, in addition to the two reasons given above, there is another highly important one. Today China is progressing rapidly on every front and people in all sectors of society have glorious missions. Preachers too have a glorious mission which is to make the church a good church, one that becomes the dwelling place of God, one that gains the people's love, and one that can match the progress being made in all fields by the Chinese people.

Must the church follow a path opposed to our nation? Did the Lord say that we must hate what the people like, and like what the people hate? Is it a sin for the church to see eye to eye on some matters with the people? Can the church only glorify God by placing itself in opposition to the nation and its people? Absolutely not.

Paul said he did not simply want to please people (Gal. 1:10). But which people was he referring to? From the context we see that Paul was speaking of some false apostles in the church who were confusing the believers' faith and these false prophets should "be accursed." "We did not submit to them even for a moment" (2:5). With reference to the common people, Paul wants us to "abound in love" (1 Thess. 3:12) and "always seek to do good to one another and to all" (1 Thess. 5:15). Peter said, "We must obey God rather than any human authority" (Acts 5:29), though the context tells us this refers to the priests and not to the ordinary people. Even more pleasing to the church of the apostles was this image of the church:

> Day by day, as they spent much time together in the temple, they broke bread at home and ate their food with glad and generous hearts, praising God and having the goodwill of all the people. And day-by-day the Lord added to their number those who were being saved. (Acts 2:46–47)

If we genuinely love the church, then we will certainly want to return to its true features of holiness and beauty so that it may find favor with all the people. A Christian who truly love the Lord and loves the church, seeing a lack of holiness and progress in the church, will say, "It is zeal for your house that has consumed me" (Ps. 69:9). They will be determined to dispel the darkness in the church and cleanse it of all that people find objectionable, making it pure as snow, so that it will be able to glorify God and lead people to God. This is what "worthy of new China" means. Today, as China advances, what reason can there be for the church to take a path opposed to that of the country? God will be glorified if the church can renew its spirit and forge ahead courageously, keeping pace with the country in construction on all fronts. At the same time, won't this bring glory to the church in the eyes of the country?

In order to preach the gospel everywhere, we should act quickly to put life within the church to rights so that it is worthy of new China. Think about it. Because of the darkness within the church and the bad conduct of many Christians, many of our compatriots are suspicious of, or reject, religious faith. Yes, we are justified by faith and our good conduct will not save us. However, our bad conduct will certainly harm others! Our conduct, good or bad, is closely connected to whether others will be able to be justified by faith before the Lord. This is a very serious matter. Imagine how many people would be added to those who believe in the Lord if our preachers were all holy and righteous in their actions, clearly distinguishing right from wrong. So let us hasten to become new persons with right conduct in this wonderful age. Let the light of the church shine before people, calling them to see our good actions so that glory returns to our father in heaven.

In ancient times, David did not allow religion to fall behind the nation's life. With everything going smoothly in the country, David turned his thoughts to the building of the temple:

> Now when the king was settled in his house, and the Lord had given him rest from all his enemies around him, the king said to the prophet Nathan, "See now, I am living in a house of cedar, but the ark of God stays in a tent." (2 Sam. 7:1–2)

> O Lord, remember in David's favour all the hardships
>   he endured;
> How he swore to the Lord and vowed to the might one
>   of Jacob,
> "I will not enter my house or get into my bed;
> I will not give sleep to my eyes or slumber to my eye
>   lids,
> Until I find a place for the Lord, a dwelling place for
>   the Mighty One of Jacob." (Ps. 132:1–5)

When God's people had returned and were in the midst of a great building up, God's word came to the ears of the prophet Haggai:

> Is it a time for you yourselves to live in your paneled houses, while this house lies in ruins? ...Thus says the Lord of hosts: Consider how you have fared. Go up to the hills and bring wood and build the house, so that I may take pleasure in and be honoured, says the Lord. (Hag. 1:4, 7–8)

Clearly, the Lord wants our church to progress and develop along with the life of the nation and its people. For one hundred or so years, under the control, manipulation and corruption of imperialism, the Chinese church was most unworthy of its name. It followed along behind Western churches, modeling itself on them, not knowing what it believed, hoped for or loved. Its situation was truly painfully bleak, broken and foul. But we need not be downhearted. "A bruised reed he will not break, and a dimly burning wick he will not quench" (Isa. 42:3). God wants us to work with him, building up the church anew, making it pure and bright, beautiful and attractive and strong, as are so many other new structures in new China.

Building up the nation is an all-round task. A good nation must be good in all aspects. Our religious and spiritual life is an aspect that cannot be overlooked. A chain is only as strong as its weakest link because all the links are important. If all our nation's links are strong, except for the church, the whole chain of the nation will be weak. No matter how many children a mother has, she hopes they will all grown to be good and beautiful. If one of them is physically weak, or does not strive to progress, this is unlucky for the whole family—how she suffers. Isn't this true of our country too? The nation does not want anyone to lag behind.

Since liberation, the church has not lagged behind the progress of the life of the nation as a whole. The goal of self-government, self-support and self-propagation has clarified the direction for the church. Looking at the church in Nanjing we can see the new atmosphere. An unprecedented spirit of fellowship, equality and friendship between men and women preachers has appeared. Two neighboring seminaries, which had held fruitless discussions on union for the past fifteen years, have, on a voluntary basis, not only come together but have united with ten other seminaries in east China. Coordination and cooperation among the denominations has developed to a point where they share each other's burdens and supply each other's needs. Half the repair costs for a church in the city came through voluntary aid from other Nanjing churches. This would have been unimaginable in the past. But the glory should not go to ourselves, rather we should praise our Lord who loves the church, who has not only brought the church back to himself, but has washed, healed, settled, and nourished it, truly showing us: "The latter splendour of this house shall be greater than the former" (Hag. 2:9).

Today, as the nation embarks on the construction, the Lord wants us to "consider how you have fared" and make the Lord pleased and honored. The road before us is still long! The mission that has fallen on our shoulders is to make the Chinese church truly become a holy temple according to the Lord's heart. This is glorious, joyful and proud, is it not?

## CONCLUSION

The gospel is truth—this is reason enough to consider preaching a worthy calling. With this and the two considerations discussed above, how can we not dedicate our prayers to the Lord for wisdom, work hard and strive to be worthy workers?

A pastor is a sculptor of the life of the soul who must meticulously shape that life to completeness, just as the heavenly Father is complete. What dedication this is. Can we take up the title of pastor—this sacred title—a pastor who is true and just, discerns right from wrong, and feeds the sheep?

A preacher is worthy, but we have no right to be proud. Much is required of us in these times. If we are slack in our own spiritual life, political study, knowledge in ministry and moral formation we may fall out of the running—the worst fate for a preacher. We should ask God to give us a humble heart, not a false and pharisaic humility, but a genuine humility arising from a sense of honor about our holy orders. Only in this way, with a cautions and conscientious heart, can we purse progress and allow God to lessen our unworthiness.

To know that our work is considered useful by God, the people, the church and the nation is the greatest reward. May the work we do be this kind of work. Then one day we will hear the voice of the Holy Spirit: "They will rest from their labours, for their deeds follow them" (Rev. 14:13).

—Article in *Nanjing Theological Review*, 1954.

# ON BEING A GOOD PASTOR

The Bible contains many analogies of the relationship between humankind and God; the most frequent is also that with which we are most familiar—the sheep and the shepherd. Beside this, there is the relationship between servant and master, child and parent, the clay and the potter. The chick and the hen, trees and grasses and the farmer—analogies such as these abound in the Bible.

The Jews were a pastoral people, so the relationship between the sheep and the shepherd is most often alluded to. "The Lord is my shepherd, I shall not want" (Ps. 23). "We are his people, the sheep of his pasture" (Ps. 95). Jesus told of a man who had a hundred sheep; losing one, he searched until he found it and carried it home across his shoulders, rejoicing with his friends and neighbors.

What the shepherd requires of the sheep is obedience, that they follow instructions and obey. As he herds the sheep, the shepherd is constantly admonishing them, keeping them in line with the rod and the staff he carries, so that not even one will stray. Sheep do not have much sense of self, they will go wherever you want. Such obedience in a sheep is what makes a good sheep. But in people obedience does not necessarily lead to the heights of moral integrity. A person who can only obey orders might perhaps be considered a good slave, but not a person of high moral integrity.

For thousands of years, the culture of China has been based upon agriculture. As a Chinese who has been raised in this culture, I am fond of the analogies in the Bible which compare the relationship between God and humankind to that between the farmer and plants. Grasses and trees, wheat and other crops flourish in the care of the farmer, are nourished by the sun and the rain, and grow. This process of growth is where plants differ from sheep. In the four gospels we read the analogies to Jesus sowing the seed, to the fruit tree, the lilies, the mustard seed, the grape arbor, the fig tree. The germination and growth of these plants is not due to admonitions from the farmer, nor to beating from the farmer's rod and staff. The farmer must loosen the soil, plant the seed, fertilize, eliminate pests, pull up the weeds. After all this patient work, he does not pull up the young shoots to make them grow. After doing everything he can do, he must wait patiently, he must allow the sunshine and the rain to play their parts, allow nature to complete its cycle of growth, and finally he will reap a good harvest, and the fruits of his labor will be "a hundred-fold, sixty-fold and thirty-fold." The old saying, "Ten years to grow a tree, a hundred years to raise a person," tells us that growth is a process, a process of renewal and change.

All this is simply to illustrate what sort of preachers and pastoral workers in China, and especially you who graduate today and enter the church, should be. We are pastors, giving pastoral care to people in the name of God. We are not caring for lambs, but for people. Jesus said, "How much more valuable is a human being than a sheep." We must not go after people with rod and staff. People must not be beaten.

The good shepherd should be like a good farmer, helping Christians grow with the same will which spends ten years growing a tree and one hundred years raising a person. In this sense the shepherd is an educator, an artist, a sculptor who works with great precision. This growth process is our work of co-creation with God, our Creator Lord, the process by which humans are raised from that primitive half-finished state to a state of wholeness and completion. An artist or sculptor does not add what is not needed, but allows the natural beauty of the artwork to shine forth, and safeguards it. Every person God gives into our care is one of God's works-in-progress, or a work which has not yet been brought to perfection. They all partake of the sacred, and this does not brook disrespect or thoughtless treatment on our part.

China is a nation in which cultural education is not sufficiently widespread. As educated people, we do not have the right to do just as we please; we must respect our fellow Christians and co-workers. Our churches and meeting points must become schools for democracy, places where we all experience the democratic lifestyle. If whatever the pastor says goes, if the pastor becomes the "boss" of a church or meeting point, this is unhealthy. The pastor should encourage believers to be involved in decisions about church affairs, to become "masters" of the church. We need to learn how to be good leaders, that is, leading as well as practicing democracy, especially since in our context, the temptation to dictatorial action is great and we can easily find ourselves behaving in this way.

For a long time China was a feudal society. Feudal societies revere age and that is a good thing. But feudal societies also practice patriarchy, where everything goes according to the word of one person—economic authority, authority over personnel, etc., are all controlled by a single person. This is tyranny, and tyranny is not a characteristic of Christianity.

A big problem for our Chinese Christianity today is the fact that in many places authority rests in the hands of a single individual. The national church organizations receive many letters every day reflecting this problem. In many grassroots churches the finances have not been made public for many years, no reports have been made, personnel have remained unchanged, and all is decided by the pastor. Some pastors practice virtual tyranny. In places where this is the case, all wisdom seems to rest with the pastor, the pastor knows all and the congregation knows nothing. The Church of Christ cannot be run in this fashion. In the Church of Christ, as in the case of taking ten years to grow a tree and one hundred years to raise a person, everyone must be allowed to grow. Christians must grow and pastors too. All who enter into Christ enjoy Christ's fullness.

We must pay special attention to the growth of women Christians, nurturing their confidence. There is much male-female inequality in the church today and there is bias against women believers. They are excluded, even though they may not feel so themselves. We must protect women believers and allow them to have a greater say in the church and to take part in the leadership.

In places where there is tyranny, Christians feel oppressed. Though they may not speak out, this is only a surface calm. Many people feel the unfairness of it all and it will come to the surface eventually.

A healthy person does not need a doctor. I think the church can be compared to a special kind of hospital. In this hospital that is the church, pastor and lay people are all caught up in God's creative process, they are all works-in-progress in God's work of creation. Everyone is, to a greater or lesser degree, a patient, and, in the same way, everyone is a doctor.

Democracy does not mean simply that the minority follows the majority during elections. Democracy is a way of interacting with others, a style of doing things.

Recently the Chinese People's Political Consultative Conference passed "Regulations on Political Consultation, Democratic Oversight and Political Participation." These three items have to do with socialist democracy: the first says that solving problems must be done through consultation; the second that administrative power must be supervised; and the third stipulates mass participation. I think the whole society, including the Church should do as follows: (1) everything must be done in consultation, one or two people must not have the power to decide things; (2) there must be oversight; where there is power there should be supervision; (3) people should have a voice in the discussion of important issues. Then the pastor will not be seen as a superman and the people as morons. This is the path toward growth for everyone.

It is my hope that as each class of seminarians from Nanjing Union Theological Seminary and the other seminaries in China enter into the church, they will take with them the democratic way of doing things, to make the church a church of equality, unity and love. Your alma mater cannot give you much in the way of material assistance, but I hope that in thinking, in spirit, you will not lose touch with us, but maintain a relationship with us in the Lord. Wherever your work takes you, unite the believers, love the country and love the church, and go forward together.

We hope that as the Chinese Church receives into its band of coworkers each new generation, it will continue to grow and mature and become the Church beloved of the Lord.

—Commencement Address,
Nanjing Seminary, 1995

# THE CHURCH AFTER THE CULTURAL REVOLUTION

Delegates, Colleagues and Fellow Christians:

The Chinese National Christian Conference has not met for quite some time. That we are able to gather together today is the result of several factors: the smashing of the Gang of Four by the Chinese people under the leadership of the Communist Party; the end of disturbances and the realization of unity and stability over the last four years; the efforts over the last thirty years of Chinese Christians, who cherish both our church and our motherland, to uphold the principle of self-government, self-support and self-propagation for our church; Christ's protection of our colleagues and fellow Christians during the ten years of turmoil, enabling us to hold fast to our faith and maintain our Christian fellowship. Above all else, our gathering here today is due to the leading, the blessing and the grace of our heavenly Father and eternal loving God. With grateful hearts, we have come to take part in this conference.

In the four years since the smashing of the Gang of Four, and

especially during the recent months of preparations for this conference, a great many pastoral workers and lay people around the
nation have been looking to the future and pondering the question:
What should the Chinese Church be doing in the days to come? The
Standing Committee of the National Three-Self Movement (TSPM)
discussed this question in our week-long enlarged meeting held at
the end of February. Since the distribution of "An Open Letter to
Brothers and Sisters in Christ Throughout China" by that meeting on
March 1 of this year, Christians from around the nation have been
more concerned about this question, and they have put forward a
great number of opinions and suggestions.

We have come to the realization that now it is no longer as it was
before Liberation: What the Chinese Church should be doing has
become our own question, and it will be decided by ourselves, rather
than by others for us. We are controlling our own affairs and our discussions have been most enthusiastic. The independence of the church
has actually been achieved. We are inspired and rejoice over this, in
our belief that the TSPM is very precious, and the outlook for Chinese
Christianity is very hopeful.

It is especially worthwhile to point out that although we have been
separated by great distances and have not seen one another for a long
time, although we have had many different experiences over the past
years, and despite the fact that outside anti-China forces have never
ceased in sowing dissension, we are surprisingly united in our views on
so many important matters. It can truly be said that we are "of the
same mind, having the same love, in full accord and of one mind."
How would we be able to explain this unity of heart and mind had not
the Holy Spirit been at work, allowing us to communicate with one
another in Christ?

I would now like to draw our opinions together in order to facilitate our further discussions over the next several days.

I think that what I have to say may be summarized in three sen-
tences:

(1) The accomplishments of the TSPM have been great;

(2) The mission of the TSPM is not over;

(3) The church must not only be self-run but well-run.

## (1) THE ACCOMPLISHMENTS OF THE TSPM HAVE BEEN GREAT

Although a small number of missionaries and church leaders proposed that the church implement the principle of self-government, self-support and self-propagation even before 1949, it could be truly realized on a nationwide scale only after Liberation. The Chinese people were oppressed by feudalism over a long period of time, and since the 19th century they were oppressed by colonialism and imperialism as well. The Chinese people have an anti-imperialist, anti-feudal revolutionary tradition, but Christianity entered China under the protection of the Western powers during the period of Western colonial expansion into China. Our people have a hatred of the unequal treaties which were forced upon China, but the foreigners' right to do missionary work depended on these very same treaties. Thus, ever since the entry of Christianity into China, it was difficult for the Chinese people to accept this religion because, although originally good, it had become an appendage to the machine of Western aggression, having a thousand and one links with colonialism and imperialism. Feudalism, imperialism and bureaucratic capitalism long weighed like three mountains on the backs of the Chinese people. Although there were missionaries and Chinese church leaders who sympathized with and supported the people's efforts for liberation, in general, Christianity most often stood on the side of the reactionaries rather than with the Chinese people. As far as quite a large number of us are concerned, as a result of our affiliation with that kind of Christianity, our national consciousness certainly became weak; we were not of one mind with our own people and seemed to have become semi-Western. It was because of this that some of our Chinese people had the distressing saying: "One more Christian means one less Chinese." This saying was not without its measure of truth. At that time Christianity was generally regarded as a foreign religion about which they harbored deeply negative feelings. The clamor within the church against the Communist Party and the people was especially loud around the time of Liberation. How could the Christian gospel be effectively preached under such conditions when Chinese Christians and the people of the motherland lacked a common language? At that time, China was the country in which the Western missionary societies spent the most money and the field to which they sent the most missionaries. But the number of Christians was never large, and of that number quite a few were "rice" Christians.

Such a Christianity backed by foreign power lost its source of support after Liberation. As it became isolated within China, Christianity faced a difficult situation. It was then that Chinese Christians discovered that God would not quench the dimly burning wick of Chinese Christianity, but would enable it to begin to shine forth. In God's providence two things came to our aid: The first was the policy of religious freedom of the People's Republic of China, formulated by Chairman Mao and Premier Zhou; the second was the TSPM launched by Chinese Christians ourselves. It may be said without reservation that these two are signs which show that God has not abandoned us, but has prepared for us a new opportunity and a new beginning.

Communists being atheists, how can they also advocate the freedom of religion? There was a time when many of us raised this question, but after many years of observations and learning through experience, we do not feel that it is such a difficult thing to understand.

Communists are forthright. They do not cover up their view of religion but bring it out in the open for all to see. There are parties and politicians in the world who make use of religion for their own ends while making a big show of their respect for the church and their assistance to the faith. Because the Communist Party does not wish to make any use of religion, it can forthrightly express its view of religion in no uncertain terms. We are completely free not to accept the Communist Party's religious outlook, but this should not suggest that we oppose all Communist Party points of view. For example, it would make no sense for us to oppose the Communist Party's proposal for the United Front.

The Chinese Communist Party attaches tremendous importance to the United Front. Communists know better than anyone else that building up new China is not only the work of one party, but of all the people. They are uniting all who can be united for the common struggle. Like all other citizens, those who believe in Jesus Christ ardently desire a strong and prosperous motherland and look forward to the early realization of the four modernizations; it is only natural that Christians are part of the United Front. There is freedom to maintain any religious faith and outlook and any worldview, and any view of the Bible under the principle of mutual respect. It is in this way that unity and stability, the formation of the United Front and the realization of the four modernizations are made possible. In the West there are those who persist in saying that the Communist Party wants to make uniform everyone's worldview and does not permit people to believe in religion. This view is utterly incorrect and reveals a real ignorance on the part of those who would think that the communists are so foolish.

The Gang of Four and the Communist Party are completely different. The Gang of Four wanted neither the four modernizations nor unity and stability. They had no use for veteran cadres, intellectuals, religious believers or the United Front. Because they wanted to eradicate religion, they had no regard for the policy of religious freedom. They disbanded all the Religious Affairs Bureaus, whose duty it was to act on behalf of the government in implementing the policy of religious freedom on all levels. The Gang of Four is not the Communist Party and the Communist Party is not the Gang of Four. The two should not be confused.

It was precisely because the Chinese Communist Party had this policy of religious freedom that we Christians were protected by the state after Liberation, even though we were not very popular with the people. Thus, Christianity was given the opportunity for a continued existence.

But this was not all. God also moved leaders with advanced thinking within the church to launch the TSPM.

For Christianity to continue to exist in China and to serve as a witness to Jesus Christ, it would not have been enough to rely only on the national policy of religious freedom. It was also necessary to develop much more of a common language with the Chinese people, so that a foreign religion could be transformed into one which was China's own. Three-Self is a patriotic movement of Chinese Christians. It encourages Chinese Christians to develop a sense of national self-respect, to love our motherland, and to dedicate ourselves to the goal of national prosperity, walking and thinking together with our compatriots. With regard to the church, it stands for self-government, self-support and self-propagation, advocating an independent Chinese Church run by Chinese Christians ourselves.

The TSPM has accomplished at least the following three things over the last thirty years.

First, making Chinese Christians patriotic Christians. The TSPM helps us to differentiate major issues of principle in politics, so that we come to see that it is right to love the motherland. In 1949, many Christians did not quite understand the people's liberation movement and objected to it so much that some of us, in complying with the wishes of certain individuals, prayed that God would drown the Liberation Army in the Yangtze River which it was about to cross to liberate the whole country. Today, no matter where we Chinese Christians meet, the overwhelming majority supports the people's liberation movement heartily. We give thanks to God in our prayers for the achievements of socialist new China. We are all willing to make our contributions toward the four modernizations of our country. That Christians should love our country has been taken for granted. This is the first time that a whole generation of Christians has emerged in this land of China who are patriotic and who have a common language with our compatriots since Christianity was introduced into China in the 19th century.

"Patriotism" is a good word. Moses, Daniel and many other prophets in the Bible were patriotic. In Western countries, however, abuse of this word has caused many righteous people to loathe it so that, as soon as they hear the word "patriotism," they think of national chauvinists who bully weak nations, of those die-hards who wave banners for reactionary governments, crying: "This is my country, right or wrong." As for us, we would see first of all what a country has wrought for its broad masses before we make any evaluation of it. New China is the people's China. It exists for the broad masses of the people. It has brought liberation, benefits and happiness to its people. It is revolutionary and progressive. We love this country, of course. Needless to say, new China still has bad things left over from the old society and the people themselves have shortcomings. But the people have also been trying hard to overcome these shortcomings and bad things, in order to make the cause proceed from victory to victory. We feel therefore in the right and fully justified to love such a motherland.

Patriotism is the profound feeling of the people toward their motherland. This feeling reflects the self-respect and self-confidence of the nation. It embodies the heroic commitment and struggle of its people to make their motherland independent, prosperous and strong. A patriot works actively to overcome the backwardness of the country, but without the inferiority complex which unduly humbles him or herself. Nor will he or she do anything which hurts the national dignity or falls short of national prestige.

We Christians see more clearly today than before that the Christian faith does not demand from us that we negate or look down on our nationality, but rather that we acknowledge it in good faith. The Book of Revelation tells us Jerusalem will descend from heaven one day. At that time there will be no temple, and many things which we have in today's world will be no more, including nationality. All these things will become one in Christ and Christ will become all in all. But today is not yet that day. Today, in consonance with divine providence, people belong to this or that nation and country. When the son of God became flesh, even he did not become a stateless nihilist. Jesus and many of his disciples were Jews. The gospel took form by uniting itself with Jewish life and culture. Paul also had strong national feelings, he called his compatriots "my brethren, my kinsmen by race." We are born Chinese not by our choice, nor our parents,' it is God who so ordains. In this world, we cannot be good internationalists in the world family unless we first are patriots and stand with the Chinese people.

Secondly, changing the countenance of Christianity in China. Christianity in China has by and large rid itself of the control and exploitation of imperialism, bureaucratic capitalism and feudalism. It has become a religious community of self-government, self-support and self-propagation. It is no longer a dependent of foreign missionary societies, but is organized by a part of the Chinese citizenry out of our faith in and love of Christ. It is more and more a Christianity with Chinese characteristics. This Christianity does not take European and American Christianity as the norm, but it is also not anti-foreign. While affirming the universality of Christianity, we understand that

Chinese Christianity cannot talk of making contributions to world Christianity unless it rids itself of its colonial nature, ceases to be a replica of foreign Christianity, does not antagonize or dissociate or alienate itself from the cause of the Chinese people, but joins them in that cause, plants its roots in Chinese culture, forms a Chinese self, and becomes a Chinese entity.

Chinese Christianity cannot change or cover up its history. Rather, we have to fully accept the historical lessons and write new pages for our history. The TSPM has changed the countenance of the Christianity of the semi-colonial, semi-feudalistic old China to bring it into consonance with the face of socialist new China. It has cleansed the church and enabled the light of the gospel to shine forth.

These two accomplishments of the TSPM lead inevitably to a third one, that is the TSPM has helped persons in various circles of our society to gradually change their impressions of Chinese Christians and Chinese Christianity.

When Chinese Christian leaders put forward the principle of Three-Self it was affirmed by Premier Zhou, and soon afterward was supported and encouraged by the *People's Daily*. During all these years, Chinese Christianity has implemented the principle of self-government, self-support and self-propagation, and Christians throughout the country have been doing many patriotic deeds. In the eyes of an increasing number of our compatriots, Christianity is no longer a foreign religion and Christians are no longer looked upon as foreign-worshipping or mere rice Christians. More and more people have recognized that Christians too are Chinese citizens who have the same national self-respect as they do and that Christianity is a religion which Chinese citizens are fully entitled to believe and uphold by their own choice. That there is such a change in public opinion means there will be fewer obstacles on the way to implementing the policy of religious freedom in the country. At present, the Three-Self organizations are helping in many ways to implement the policy of religious freedom in various parts of the country. In our work we come across many cadres and people who understand that Christianity is no obstacle to the four modernizations. They have good will toward us, respect our faith and firmly adhere to the policy in dealing with us. In the past thirty years, quite a lot of people have accepted the gospel of Christ and joined the church. The number of Christians throughout the country has increased to a certain extent. Anyway there is no sign of decrease. Now how could this be possible without the efforts of the TSPM to create the necessary conditions and to set up a new image of Chinese Christianity? Many things point to the fact that, because we have carried out the TSPM, Christians and Christianity have undergone changes, and more and more people have a new understanding of, and a new relation with, Christians and Christianity. We deem it an honor that our Christianity was not tolerated by the Gang of Four. The maltreatment meted out to churches and Christians by the Gang of Four was unpopular precisely because Christians had carried out the TSPM after Liberation. The broad masses of the people knew that this treatment was not in keeping with the policy of the state. We had the people's sympathy, and that is very precious.

We Christians have the mission to witness to Christ in our motherland but, owing to the historical fact that the introduction of Christianity into China was connected with the imperialist invasion of China, the doors of China have long been closed to the gospel. In view of our long-term mission to witness for Christ, it is obvious that our three accomplishments have tremendous historical significance. Looking back now, we can say that opposition to the TSPM not only showed a lack of patriotism, but in a sense also negated the cause of the gospel and therefore was harmful to the cause of Christianity. We can also now say that the anti-Three-Self road was politically unjust and religiously self-destructive for Christianity. Without the TSPM, Chinese Christianity could not have a present to speak of, nor would it have a future. This has become very clear among us Chinese Christians.

### (2) THE MISSION OF THE TSPM IS NOT YET FINISHED

The accomplishments of the TSPM are great, but its mission is still far from finished.

The pioneering stage of the TSPM is past, but its results must be consolidated, defended, enlarged and developed. This requires us to carry on the TSPM.

For a long time, the TSPM has held high the banner of patriotism, helped us to distinguish wrong from right, to cherish the country and the church, to become good Christians and at the same time good citizens. The TSPM must continue to hold high the banner of patriotism, helping our fellow Christians in our political study and in making our contributions, together with the people of the whole nation, to the task of safe-guarding our national stability and unity, of realizing the four modernizations, of bringing about the return of Taiwan to the motherland and of opposing hegemonism and aggression and safeguarding peace.

There are many new Christians who, besides lacking spiritual edification, know little of the TSPM. Christians are eager to receive education and re-education on the movement. We should therefore explain to them the principles of self-government, self-support and self-propagation as well as the compatibility of loving one's country and one's church. With the help of the TSPM we must teach fellow Christians of the whole nation, especially the younger ones, to care deeply for our motherland and the socialist cause, and be proud of the history and progress of our country. We must help them to observe the teachings of Christ, to increase the demands they make of themselves, to study and work hard, to oppose the corrosion of unhealthy thinking coming both from inside and outside of China so that, no matter whether it be in the family, in the neighborhood, in production or at their work posts, they are all good witnesses who bear beautiful fruit, thus shining forth for the Lord and their motherland.

Today, whether we Christians go to church to attend religious activities, or meet in homes for worship, we are all glorifying God and benefiting our fellow men so long as we praise and serve God, exhort each other, and edify each other. However, there are anti-China organizations abroad which wantonly proclaim an "underground evangelism" and raise money for their own designs. They claim to establish in China their so-called "underground churches." Let it be asked, if they indeed have no ulterior motives and are not doing some illegal business, why must they go underground? Some leaders of these organizations live very corrupt lives; their actions are not worthy of the word "evangelism." For the sake of protecting our church from impurity and of safeguarding our national security, we must heighten our vigilance over their use of religion to make money, to launch anti-China propaganda and to carry out their subversive plots against us. We church workers and Christians are resolved to observe the laws as loyal citizens. We are resolved to protect the name of the church, disapproving of anybody inside or outside China who humiliates the church by conducting in the name of Christianity illegal activities detrimental to the physical and mental well-being of our fellow Christians and to public order.

To defend and uphold religious freedom is an integral part of the Chinese people's efforts to uphold socialist democracy and the legal system. The efforts we religious people make from the standpoint of patriotism have been regarded by the central leadership in a speech at the recently held National People's Congress as "precious efforts." This gives us great encouragement. Today, the policy of religious freedom is being implemented in various parts of the country and remarkable strides have been made as far as Christianity is concerned. This is something Christians throughout the nation feel happy and heartened about. But for various reasons, the implementation of the policy of religious freedom still meets with difficulties in many places. That means we still have a lot to do. The Three-Self organizations must therefore continue to do their best to assist the government and the groups concerned to perform this aspect of their work well.

The above-mentioned are all tasks which the TSPM still has to do. It is for this reason that we say its mission is not yet finished.

## (3) FROM A SELF-RUN TO A WELL-RUN CHURCH

With respect to the church, the main question which the TSPM asks is: Who should run the Chinese Church? The answer is quite clear: it must be self-run; Chinese Christians ourselves have to take over its management. Once this question has been settled, we are faced with a second: How can we make it a well-run church, that is, how shall we build up the body of Christ? The emphasis in self-governing, self-supporting and self-propagating is on the "self"; this means ourselves. Now we must go one step further. The church must be well-governed, well-supported, and do the work of propagation well.

The TSPM has never worked for Three-Self for its own sake. From its beginning, the movement envisioned a well-governed, well-supported well-propagating Church of Christ growing up on Chinese soil. The Lord has shown us that, in order for Christians to build up the body of Christ in China, we must model ourselves after the church of the apostolic age. We must obey the God who reveals himself through the Bible. We must absorb the fine traditions and the solemn lessons of church history. And we must allow the Holy Spirit to show us a path which others have not walked before but which is appropriate for China. We must dare to leave behind the insights and symbolic representations of faith gained by other nations, other ages and other Christians to allow our own spiritual experience to blossom forth, so that the wisdom and stature of the Chinese Church can grow together with the love of God, men, and women for it. However, the policy of religious freedom, along with many other correct policies of the Communist Party, was destroyed during the years of turmoil owing to the obstructive and destructive ultra-leftist line represented by the Gang of Four. Jesus' instruction to us to accomplish the building up of the church was also obstructed in this way.

We are sorry to note that, even though our brothers and sisters are so enthusiastic, the church has not done well in ministering to them during these years. If church members do not live in consonance with the Bible in matters of faith and spirituality, they will gain nothing good. If the church does not act in consonance with the Bible, it will tend to be sidetracked, giving rise to disorder. This does not benefit Christians, the church, or society in the least.

We know that we should be humble and cautious in explaining the Word of God. In dispensing Christ's truth we must be comprehensive and genuine. We must not go according to any human meaning because it is not ourselves we are propagating, but Jesus Christ as Lord. Christian gatherings and church life do not depend on surroundings but, as Paul reminds us, "All things should be done decently and in order." In this way, we will be fit to serve the Lord, so as to more easily give shape to the Body of Christ and witness to those outside the church. There are places now where it is not like this. Christ's truth is falsely spoken, it is not comprehensive and loses its wholeness. When

people gather, the leader follows his or her own will. There are even
those who do not hesitate to say whatever some people would like to
hear in order to better their own position. Serving Christ becomes the
path to riches and the church is made very impure as a result. These
circumstances are easily exploited by evil persons. Christians today
hunger and thirst for the gospel. We must do well our work of carefully watching over them, guiding them and training them. Then the
evil ones will be deprived of their opportunities and the church many
develop in good health.

Pastoral workers and lay people in the church have been moved by
one and the same Holy Spirit to share in common the conviction that,
today, as we continue to carry out the work of the TSPM, the work of
tending the Lord's flock by a well-run church has already been placed
on the agenda for Chinese Christianity.

After the turmoil brought on by the Gang of Four, we Chinese
Christians are urgently in need of Bibles. In order to offer pastoral care,
the Chinese Christian Church must publish the Bible. At present, we
want to continue to publish the edition now in common use, both in
order to meet the urgent needs and to supply our members with what
they are accustomed to.

Over the last decades, there have been developments in our
Chinese language and written characters. Ancient biblical manuscripts
have also been newly discovered. Therefore, it is necessary to carry out
revisions of the Chinese translation of the Bible in order that it better
expresses the original meaning. This, however, is a solemn, holy work
and it must be carried out with care. It is impossible to estimate now
when a new translation can be published and supplied for members'
trial use. In any event, it will be a number of years hence.

We would all like to see periodicals published which would be
helpful in introducing basic Christian doctrine, in studying the Bible,
in cultivating the life of the Spirit, and in raising the standard of our
colleagues' work.

Furthermore, we all feel that regular teaching at Nanjing Union
Seminary should be promptly resumed in order to carry out theological education appropriate to our situation in China and to prepare servants for the Lord's use.

Christians are gathering together in meetings throughout the country, enjoying fellowship in Christ, mutually helping and encouraging one another. But, we are still relatively scattered. We lack ties with other members of the Body of Christ. We don't get the supplies, the interchange, the assistance that we should have. Because of this, we may sometimes be off the mark. We have all felt that we should find ways to enable Christians in any place who wish to benefit from mutual ties to do so.

The proposal to form a Christian organization to carry out certain kinds of church work including those enumerated here and to serve the church and its members according to the principles of self-government, self-support and self-propagation has met with approval throughout the country. It can be seen that this is indeed a universal desire of our Christians.

After study and discussion by all concerned, we can see more clearly now that the TSPM and the national church affairs organization both have as their subjects Christians in China. One is a people's organization made up of Chinese Christians as Chinese, the other is a Christian organization made up of Chinese Christians as Christians. If the TSPM is a patriotic movement on the part of Chinese Christians, then the church affairs organization will represent a Three-Self Patriotic Chinese Church Movement on the part of Christians who uphold patriotism and the Three-Self principle. Both organizations cherish the church and the motherland.

In all matters touching on faith, our principle is one of mutual respect, neither meddling with each other's faith nor making it uniform.

The following question has been raised: Why not put the handling of church affairs under the TSPM as one of its subsidiary departments, as a church affairs subcommittee, for example; why do we need another structure?

We know that in the situation where we have not had an organ for handling church affairs, the TSPM could not help but take on some of the church's own work. For example, rather than awaiting the formation of a church affairs organ, it did much of the work toward publishing the Bible. We also know, however, that it is the patriotic movement of Christians in the entire country. The objective of the TSPM Committee is to unite all Christians in China so as to take an active part in socialist reconstruction and in patriotic movements, to adhere to law of the land, to assist the government in implementing the policy of religious freedom, to work for the complete realization of self-government, self-support and self-propagation by the Chinese Christian Church, to eliminate imperialist influences, to oppose aggression and to defend peace. It was on this basis that the TSPM Committee was formed. How can an organization with such a purpose regularly and permanently take on the duty of developing the work that is the church's own? We can envisage a great deal of work and church affairs. If we gave this work to the TSPM the latter would have to expend a great deal of effort on it. In reality, this would change the original nature and purpose of the TSPM, and its Three-Self principle would be diluted.

In the same way, the idea of making the TSPM subordinate to the church affairs organization is also inappropriate.

For this reason, and taking the actual and historical situation of Christianity in our country as a point of departure, we believe that it is most suitable to set up two different organizations at the national level, even though there may be some duplication of personnel. The national church affairs organization and the TSPM will be on an equal footing, each with its own particular emphasis. The two are comparable to the two hands of a body, joined in a relationship of intimate cooperation. It is not a case of one leading the other. With these two organizations, the scope of our unity is even broader.

As for whether each locality is to set up its own church affairs organization, or how such an organization should be set up, these are matters for each locality to consider for itself.

At the enlarged meeting of the Standing Committee of the TSPM, we sought the guidance of God and had deliberations on the question of forming the new national organization, and decided to carry out the necessary preparations. As we hold this national meeting, we hope we would continue to seek God's guidance on this matter and to exchange ideas fully.

During this national meeting, let us look toward the future and deliberate about how Chinese Christianity should be hereafter. This is certainly not to exclude discussion of the past or present, nor to exclude local problems. If we exclude these, we would not do a good job of discussing the future either. I hope we can, as the saying goes, "Say all we know without reserve." Especially on the subject of making the church well-governed, well-supported and one in which propagation is done well, we have valuable experiences which are worth sharing.

With respect to organization, we are to revise the constitution of the Committee of the TSPM and elect a new committee. Then we are to deliberate on the question of the church affairs organization. If conditions are ripe, we can take advantage of this conference and form the organization on the foundation which has already been prepared.

Colleagues and fellow Christians, before I close, I would like to speak for a moment about our international relationships. We are all happy to note that new China has friends all over the world. There are also a good number of individuals and groups, in churches outside the country, including some former missionaries to China, who have shown friendship toward both new China and Christianity within new China. They are happy to see China's progress on all fronts and they have no intention of interfering in the internal affairs of either our nation or our church. They support and help us through prayer and other means. We do not speak of them in the same breath as overseas anti-China forces. Rather, we welcome their friendly attitudes and are grateful for their prayers and assistance. Chinese Christianity cherishes its own special path, but this does not exclude beneficial international contacts, which we prize. We are willing, insofar as it is within our ability, to develop mutual friendship and give-and-take relationships as within the Body of Christ with foreign churches and Christians that treat us as equals and respect our principled stand of independence and self-determination.

Although we have a good many friends in foreign religious circles, there are also some who are fanning the flames of anti-Chinaism. They exploit our ten years of turmoil in order to deceive Christians. They depend on political and economic power and unscrupulously spread rumors to slander new China, attacking the patriotic thinking, speeches and activities of Chinese Christians. They flatly deny the lessons of past foreign evangelistic activities in China. They ignore the Chinese Christians' independence and self-determination in the work of the gospel and the justice, reasonableness and necessity of self-government, self-support and self-propagation. They look upon Three-Self as a thorn in the flesh and pretend to be ignorant of it, vainly attempting to return Chinese Christianity to its colonial past. Chinese Christianity is now more unified than ever before but they are extremely dissatisfied with this fact and are striving to divide us. To deal with this kind of outside meddling and infiltration, all Christians in our country must, in the spirit of patriotism, increase our vigilance, guard the fruits of the past thirty years and defend the Three-Self path of our church. Christians in our People's Republic of China would use the words of Paul in confronting those who vainly hope to induce us to abandon our Three-Self path: "For I would rather die than have anyone deprive me of my ground for boasting."

We want to declare before the whole world: Church and evangelistic work inside China is the right and responsibility of our Chinese Church; no people outside China, regardless of the color of their skin, should carry on any activity of a missionary nature inside China or directed at China, without the expressed consent of Chinese Church authorities. If such people were indeed motivated by nothing but their faith, then they would at least stop to consider Paul's statement: "My ambition is to preach the Gospel, not where Christ has already been named, lest I build on another man's foundation" (Rom. 15:20). Once Corinth had a church, Paul said to the Corinthians that he wanted "to preach the Gospel in lands beyond" them, in order to avoid boasting of work already done by others, for he did not want to preach the Gospel "in another's field" (2 Cor. 10:16). Now, outside of China there are those who are trying to mobilize Christians to leave their own places where their preaching is most suitable, and send them into our field, thus destroying the foundation of our thirty years of Three-Self. We cannot help asking, why would they want to do this?

We want to bring Christians in other countries to see our Chinese

Christian aspirations for independence. We want to help them to distinguish right from wrong on this matter, so that they may be friends of new China and friends of the Christian Church in new China. We are opposed to the anti-China plotting and the propaganda, infiltration and meddling on the part of anti-China elements in religious circles overseas.

Colleagues and fellow Christians, the TSPM is just, it is reasonable and it is necessary. It has an important political significance as well as an important theological and spiritual significance. Today, this movement must continue to develop toward the future. At the same time, all of us see clearly that tending the Lord's flock, the task which Christ entrusted to Peter after his resurrection, is also the task which has been entrusted to us by our Risen Lord. Our Christians urgently need the church to guide them along a path in which the church and the motherland can both be cherished. They are like the five thousand who came to hear Jesus Christ. We cannot send them out running and searching hither and yon, lest they be cheated. According to the Lord's own instructions, we should instead let all sit around him in an orderly manner. We should take out the five loaves and two fishes to present to Jesus, so that he might take them, bless them and distribute them to all. In this way everyone will have enough to eat, and the church will be able to develop in good health along the correct path. This will be good for Christians, for the church and for the motherland. Although our own strength is limited, we believe that, with the grace and blessing of our Lord Jesus Christ, a self-governing, self-supporting and self-propagating Chinese Church, in consonance with the realities of our motherland, can grow up and become strong on our soil and in our people's midst. With this church we can make a great contribution to our motherland and to the world.

—Opening Address
Third National Chinese Christian Conference, 1980

# BUILDING UP
# THE BODY OF CHRIST

Today as our conference draws to a close, let us consider together the letter which the Holy Spirit inspired John to write to the church in Ephesus found in Revelation 2:1–7, and see how it may help us in our work.

The letter praises the church in Ephesus for its strong point—the ability to recognize false apostles for what they are. The church draws a clear line between itself and the Nicolaitans and does not tolerate such false teachers. It is a church capable of distinguishing between right and wrong and of struggling against what is wrong, thus bearing witness to Christ through perseverance. But the Spirit also points out that the problem with the church in Ephesus was that it had departed from the love it possessed at first.

Please note that the letter does not blame the church in Ephesus for drawing a line or for its struggles, but rather praises it. Under certain circumstances it is necessary to purify the church for the sake of its witness. But the letter reminds its readers that it is not quite enough simply to hate evil. The church is the community of those who love God and of the children of God who love each other. In his letter to the Ephesians, Paul also talks about the church building up itself in love and about speaking the truth in love within the church and forbearing with each other in love. Struggles, no matter how necessary, are likely to injure the body of the church and its principle of love. Thus, at the appropriate time, the Spirit asks the church to repent and calls on it to recover the love it has lost so as to build itself up in love.

The passage in Revelation says: "He who has an ear, let him hear what the Spirit says to the churches." Thus we see that this letter has not been sent only to the church in Ephesus, but to all churches, and this certainly includes our church in China today.

We are meeting as representatives of Chinese Christianity and of Christians all over the country. I believe that this passage has an important message for us.

Since the very beginning, the Three-Self Movement (TSPM) has aimed at improving the life and witness of the church. In order to achieve this there was a period of time when we could not but devote much of our attention to struggles, many of which had to do with the purification of the church. They were necessary and condoned by the Spirit. It would be hard to imagine the state of our church today without them and we are thankful to those of our co-workers who contributed much in those struggles. But there is also a time to remind ourselves of the task of building up the church in love. This is the prayer and demand of our Christian people. The more the TSPM turns to this task, the greater the believers' support for Three-Self.

I am not saying that our leaders have neglected this task in the past, nor am I saying that we are now to do away with all struggles and to love all sorts of disorders in the church. We are certainly not to approve of all the anti-China and anti-Three-Self offensives on the part of some who use Hong Kong as their base. No, this is not at all what I am saying. Rather with respect to our overall situation nationally, today, breaking down must give way to building up, destruction must give way to construction, struggle must give way to reconciliation. Three-Self must be upheld, but it must also be implemented. We want to implement Three-Self by building up the Body of Christ and by running the church well, thus propagating Three-Self and demonstrating its rightness and necessity. Today Christians in some places harbor certain misgivings toward Three-Self, not so much because they are opposed to the Three-Self principle, as because they somehow feel that certain things done in the name of Three-Self seem to be harming the church rather than building it up. The TSPM need only take the building up of the church as its task and Christians will support it wholeheartedly and the justness of its cause will be taken for granted. If bad persons perpetrate outrages within the church, Christians will gladly stand with the TSPM and China Christian Council (CCC) to oppose them.

Our TSPM has been building up the church in love for a long time. The Standing Committee of the TSPM called for the strengthening of the life and witness of the church in 1956. The formation of the CCC six years ago was another landmark in the same direction. I am not saying that we made no efforts to run the church well in the 1950s and '60s, but greater progress has been made over the last six years. We thank God for the contributions made by his many faithful servants in the past, among whom we remember especially Bishop Zheng, who cannot be with us today.

Criticism of empty political sloganeering often tells us that good politics should vindicate itself in good practice and high political consciousness in excellence in specialized fields. Similarly, our call for church autonomy and independence must bear its fruit in the building up of the church, just as the worth of our work for self-government, self-support and self-propagation must be proven by governing ourselves well, supporting ourselves well, and doing the work of propagation well. Since the re-implementation of the policy of religious freedom in 1979, a great many churches and other centers for worship and meetings have emerged. There are countless problems that must be considered in order to build them up. All of us who are leaders at various levels of the TSPM, ordained or not, must build ourselves up through study and spiritual formation, so that with hearts filled with Christ's love and our feet firmly on the ground, we may become true specialists in the building up of Christian communities. Our TSPM and CCC at all levels must rid themselves of any remaining traces of old ways of thought, attitudes and habits accumulated in the days of struggle. Our working style should be that of the church and of the pastor. We must have great sympathy for pastoral colleagues in daily contact with grassroots Christians, do all we can to serve them, not evading, but solving the problems they encounter in that work. To build up the church and elevate the quality of the church, enable our church to find favor in the sight of God, of the Chinese people and especially of Christians—this is the central task of the TSPM and CCC.

In China, a scientist who is devoted to scientific research, raises the level of his or her specialization and produces scientific results that uplift the welfare of humanity, is considered a politically good scientist; likewise a teacher devoted to the work of education, who raises his or her teaching ability and produces well-trained citizens for the nation, is considered a politically good teacher. The same is true of doctors, shop assistants, sales clerks, workers, peasants and artists. In the same way, a person faithful to God's trust, who raises her or his theological and spiritual level and does a good job of pastoral work, shepherding the flock to spiritual fulfillment and enabling them to play an active role in building the four modernizations, ought to be considered a pastor who truly loves country and church.

It is both the will of God and the wish of Christians to run things well. It is also the call of the nation. All enterprises and groups in China are like the children of a family. The family is good only if the children grow up well. Our church is one of those enterprises in the eyes of our country. Our country expects us to do a good job. Thus for us to work for the building up of the church is both to love the church and to love the country.

We must especially cherish our co-workers who uphold Three-Self, who do their pastoral work well and who are able to meet the spiritual needs of believers. If we want to broaden unity, we must respect them, rely on them and value their opinions, for their opinions represent the views of the larger Christian community.

We must have a correct approach to the relationship between the TSPM and the church. The church is the body of Christ, the dwelling place of the Risen Christ and the fellowship of the saints throughout the ages; the church is not subordinate to Three-Self. The church is the main body, while the TSPM and CCC are products of certain concrete historical conditions. They are the servants of the church.

We must also have a correct approach to the relationship between the TSPM and the CCC. Three-Self is a patriotic and church-loving association of Chinese Christians; the CCC is a church affairs organization of Christians who are patriotic and church-loving. The relationship between the two is as close as that between the left and right hands of a body. They cannot work, much less live, apart. Without the TSPM, the CCC would easily fall into leading believers along a way which ignored the issue of Three-Self, reverting to old ways and causing division. Three-Self would exist in name only and the church would forfeit its "favor in the eyes of the Chinese people," and the witness it should bring would lack for hearers. Without the CCC, the TSPM would be distanced from the community of believers, talk grandly of politics, get caught up in formulism and make itself into a mere figurehead and its base of unity would shrink until it could hardly struggle against false apostles and Nicolaitans. Clearly, those who oppose us, at home or overseas, would welcome a split between the TSPM and CCC. Three-Self must serve the building up of the Chinese Church. This was the intention of the elder generation who initiated the Movement and the reason why so many co-workers and fellow Christians became involved in it. This is the only way the TSPM and the CCC can broaden unity and become the engine leading believers forward together.

Three-Self and the CCC are bodies belonging to the whole of Chinese Christianity. Wherever Chinese Christians may be within China, as long as they honor Jesus Christ as Lord and are not anti-revolutionary or involved in anything that is illegal, that is where we should do our work of Three-Self, our work of unity, our educational work, our work to alleviate hardship.

Our church, in building itself up in love, allows for diversity and does not aim at uniformity in matters of faith and worship. In 1 Corinthians 12:3, Paul tells us that no one can say "Jesus is Lord" except by the Holy Spirit. Thus we have no right to dismiss others out of hand. Those who know Jesus Christ as Lord are all moved by the Spirit. In matters of faith and worship, we must not force the minority to follow the majority; we urge the majority to care for the minority. But we also hope that any minority will not fail to recognize, with thankful hearts, that Christians of other backgrounds have also been redeemed by Christ, that our faith is basically the same, and that we have all received this common faith from Jesus Christ himself. It is the revelation and blessing of Christ. To ignore this commonality which unites us and to dwell only on differences—magnifying minor things to overshadow what unites us—is a denial of the action of Christ, a departure from Paul's teaching and a return to the old path of division. Paul teaches us that it is not up to the eye to tell the hand that it has no use for the hand, or up to the head to say it has no use for the foot. We belong together to the one body of Christ. This is the truth of Christ's body, a mystery of the Kingdom, Christ's own prayer to the Father, and his own message to the disciples before he left the world.

It is only as we love each other that others will know that we are Christ's disciples.

Jesus has told us that the church may be compared to crops growing in a field—the good wheat and the bad weeds, sown by Satan while humankind slept. The seven churches mentioned in Revelation all have serious faults, but they still stand as golden lampstands and he who holds the seven stars in his right hand walks among them. Jesus does not ask us to spend all our time trying to pull the weeds from among the wheat, nor to transplant the wheat from this field to another. He says, "Let both grow together until the harvest." In other words, he will separate them then. In our church today, it is our task to grow, to enable the wheat to surpass the weeds and to prevent the weeds from taking over. Those who consider themselves good seeds should be planted in the field, where they may grow; not placing themselves outside, accusing this one and that one of being weeds. Our job is not to blame or pull out, but to enter into the field and grow, so that our church may be run even better.

Long ago in Palestine, there were two brothers living at opposite ends of a piece of land inherited from their father. The elder brother had a family, but the younger had not yet married. One night after harvest, the elder brother thought, "I have a family and more hands, while my brother is single. It must be hard for him to cultivate the land. Let me take him some food." Just then the younger brother, too, was thinking, "I am single and it is easy for me to manage, while my elder brother must find it difficult to maintain a family. I'll take them some food." Laden with crops, they each set out and bumped into each other in the darkness. Crops scattered to the ground as they embraced. Does this not remind us of the words: "Behold, how good it is for brothers to dwell in unity?" As the story goes, it was on that very spot that Jerusalem and the Temple were built many years later. This is the church building itself up in love.

As we meet here in Beijing, let us recall the meeting in Jerusalem found in Acts 15. That was not a "regularly-scheduled meeting," but one that took place under the guidance of the Holy Spirit, liberating thinking and building up the church in love. We pray that the Holy Spirit will also guide us, so that a church will emerge in the East, in the spirit of Three-Self, suited to the image of new China, building up the body of Christ in love and leading many men and women to Christ. May God strengthen the work of our hands. The work of our hands may God strengthen.

—Closing Speech, Fourth National Chinese Christian Conference,
Beijing, 1986

℘

# LOOKING TO THE FUTURE

I have been asked to speak to you about the Protestant Church in China. I will try to go about it by dealing with a number of questions.

First, what do we mean when we say we are postdenominational?

Denominational structures have not existed for over thirty years. The overwhelming majority of our Christians have never been members of any denomination. Denominational habits still linger among older church members. We hold to the principle of mutual respect in matters of faith and worship. But we are not just preserving diversity for the sake of older church members. We want to encourage diversity for realizing the richness of Jesus Christ in his church. We would like to see a Chinese Church with creative diversity in which differences are not merely tolerated but appreciated. We still have a long way to go to achieve this broadness.

The China Christian Council is the organizational and ecclesial expression of our postdenominational unit. It is different from any national council of churches in that we do not any more have denominational churches to form such a council. Yet, it is not the United Church of Christ in China because there are Christians of certain backgrounds who are not ready to go that far. The Little Flock, for instance, interprets the priesthood of all believers in such a way as not to see any significance in the laying on of hands to set apart certain Christians to be ministers. It also interprets the localness of the church in such a way that a church, in order to be a church, must be local and local only. This makes it impossible for them to enter a body which is organized as the church regionally and nationally. A few years ago we had to decide either to go ahead and form the United Church of Christ in China without the Little Flock and one or two similar church groups, or not to go ahead and remain at the lower level of postdemoninational unity by keeping these church groups within the fold of the China Christian Council. The second course was what we decided to take, to the satisfaction of most Protestant groups.

We are glad of the unity we can enjoy. It is closer to Christ's own prayer that we be one. But some thirty years' experience of such a wide range of unity as to include Protestants of all shades tells us also that it inhibits theological creativity and ecclesiological experimentation, owing to the fear of offending certain Christians' sensitivity and breaking up the still fragile unity. It seems to show something of the dilemma human beings are in: there is no choice that is without its encumbrances.

In the past we had in China at least five or six dozen denominations. We were able to enter into the present postdenominational stage of history largely because our denominational history was short and our denominational loyalty weak. Sociologically, the very strong emphasis in China after Liberation on people's unity did have some impact on what Christians chose to do.

Our postdenominational unity is being tested these years when China has adopted a policy of opening itself up to the outside world where denominationalism is the rule. There is at least one group abroad which is trying to restore an old denomination in China. We are glad that so far our unity is strong enough to withstand the pulls from abroad.

Second, how do we look at Three-Self today?

Ours is a church occupied for a number of years with the task of the development and preservation of its Chinese Christian selfhood. We were not satisfied with its status as a dot, albeit a big one, on the missionary map of Western churches. The church in China must not be a replica of something Western, but have a Chinese selfhood in order to gain its right to be heard by our fellow Chinese. Hence our

Three-Self Movement, a movement to achieve self-government, self-support and self-propagation. After working at it for three decades, we are now in a preliminary way self-governing, self-supporting and doing the work of propagating the Christian faith ourselves. In other words, without foreign missionaries and no longer being a mission field of other churches, we are running the church ourselves. That gives it a Chinese image which is all-important, especially in post-Liberation China.

All through church history, the church has always wanted to identify itself in some degree with local and national situations. When the Christian gospel was first presented to the non-Jewish world, the question arose as to whether the evangelists were to take with them Jewish customs and Jewish practices and were to make converts into Jews of sorts. De-Judaization was the decision of the conference specially called for that matter in Jerusalem. Then, when the gospel reached Europe, people with foresight took risks in theology, spirituality and art so as to make it a religion that could speak to the minds and hearts of Europe. When any cultural conditioning has become a constriction to a church in a new area or a new epoch, changes are called for.

Let me say in this connection that the Three-Self Movement is not an anti-missionary movement. We are not opposed to missionaries. They brought the Christian gospel to our land. For all the good work missionaries did, we are grateful to them and thankful to God. But there is a time for missionaries to come and also a time for them not to remain. All good missionaries worked hard to make themselves dispensable as early as possible. We would like the former China missionaries to see the Chinese Church as it is now, not as a denial of their foundation work, but as the fruition of their labor. We do make a distinction between the missionaries and Western colonialism and imperialism.

Early in the '50s, there was in China an accusation movement which was anti-Western and anti-foreign. It was a deviation under the influence of ultra-leftism. Ultra-leftism was a political disease in the body of a revolutionary movement. Leaving aside the question of the motive of the ultra-leftists, they were at least over zealous revolutionaries who did not care about the people's readiness to accept their slogans, but depended on the people's fears or emotions to win their hysterical support. They could not really rally a big following. A lot of intimidation was used to force obedience. To condemn all missionaries as imperialists is a good example of ultra-leftism. For years now I have not met Christians who hold to that view of missionaries. I want to apologize to former China missionaries and their families on behalf of Chinese Christians for all the suffering wrongly imposed on them forty years ago. I will be glad if you take my presence here as a token of healing and reconciliation in Christ after the wrong you have suffered. I assure you we do make a difference between colonialism and imperialism which exploited the missionary movement on the one hand, and the missionaries themselves who were inspired by Christian faith and sacrificed themselves for their love of the Chinese people on the other hand.

The Three-Self Movement is all-important, but has been found to be wanting in two respects:

(1) While we want to be self-governing, self-supporting and self-propagating, we want also to govern ourselves well, support ourselves well and do the work of Christian propagation ourselves well. We have not done well in all these three respects, hence all the present emphasis on doing a good job in church-building, i.e., running the church well. The China Christian Council is the organizational expression of the Christians' common desire that the church be well run. We have today special committees for theological education, publication of Bibles and Christian literature, women's work, rural work, hymnology and so on.

(2) It is not enough and not good for a church to be preoccupied constantly and narrowly with its selfhood. The selfhood of any one church is bound to be impoverished if it does not originate in and is not related to the universal church which gives particular churches their spiritual nourishment. Universality and particularity—those two dwell in each other and enrich each other, to the end that the church throughout the world and throughout history enters into the full richness of Jesus Christ. Thus, today, we are not closed to but welcome international and ecumenical contacts, dialogues and sharing. The China Christian

Council is now a member of the World Council of Churches.
Church visitors are received from all over the world. We participate in international church and religious seminars both abroad
and in China. Theologians and foreign language teachers are
lecturing in our seminaries and universities and colleges. The
Amity Printing Press, which will this year catapult the production of Chinese Bibles in China in ten years to ten million
copies, is a gift of Christians all over the world through the
United Bible Societies.

Third, can we say Chinese Protestantism is entirely united?

The large majority of Chinese Protestants are members of churches
and meeting points under the aegis of the Three-Self Movement and
the China Christian Council. There are at least some 8,000 churches
and tens of thousands of meeting points.

There are meeting points which are not related or not closely
related to the Three-Self Movement and the Christian councils, owing
very often to geographical distances and sometimes to dissatisfaction
for one reason or another with local church leadership. These groups
are nevertheless self-governing, self-supporting and self-propagating
and should not be considered as opposed to the Three-Self Principle
and the China Christian Council.

Then, there exist a small number of leaders of meeting points who
adopt a hostile attitude toward Three-Self organizations and Christian
councils. The so-called China Ministries in Hong Kong and abroad
boast of providing them secret financial backing. They are doing their
utmost to foster the spirit of division among Chinese Protestants.

The policy of the China Christian Council and Three-Self
Movement is to broaden Christian unity through our undiscriminating
services to all Christian groups and through our search for reconciliation and fellowship wherever that is called for.

Fourth, how has the Cultural-Revolution affected the church?

Ours is a post-Cultural Revolution church. We suffered for our
faith for long years from ultra-leftism in the political life of the country. Ultra-leftism disregards actual circumstances and the people's
readiness to participate, and tries to enforce radical changes through
instilling fear. In China ultra-leftism culminated in the Cultural

Revolution which turned out to be neither cultural nor revolutionary. During the Cultural Revolution, all our churches were closed down and many put to other uses. For the Christians to be deprived of church buildings only enabled us to realize that the Church of Jesus Christ does not survive on buildings. Many ministers and Christians suffered persecution in all sorts of ways. We were, to use an expression in King James' version of Hebrews, made a grazing-stock both by reproaches and afflictions. But it was a great period for Christians and the church in all our powerlessness to win the quiet sympathy and good will of the people around. The church in China is weak and powerless, but the gospel itself is strong and full of power. Powerlessness only helps Christians to reveal the powerfulness of Christ himself in bringing people to see the good quality of Christian life and to judge the Christians fairly and to come to faith through their silent witness under duress.

The Cultural Revolution was a great period for Christians to understand that when we are weak and dying life is in the offing, and to learn that strength is found in weakness, and life in dying. Christ's own resurrection tells us that the meek are to inherit the earth. The Chinese philosopher Lao Tzu gives, in speaking about water, a good description of the nature of the church under repression when he says,

> "What of all things most yielding
> Can overwhelm that which is most hard,
> Being substanceless, it can enter in
> even where there is no crevice.
> That there can be teaching
> without words,
> Value in action which is
> actionless,
> Few indeed can understand."

Since the end of the Cultural Revolution and with the overall criticism of ultra-leftism, there has been a return to the principle of religious freedom. Protestant churches are reopening or newly built at the rate of three every two days for the last fourteen years. In addition, there are tens of thousands of groups of Christians meeting in homes. But this does not mean that ultra-leftism has completely disappeared.

In certain parts of China, local government officials are not eager to implement the principle of religious freedom and are trying to disband home groups in violation of that principle. The Three-Self Movement and the China Christian Council are receiving complaints from the grassroots in these areas and referring such cases to the proper government authorities for rectification.

One consequence of ultra-leftism was our inability to carry on adequate theological education for some twenty-four years and, hence, the scarcity and agedness of our church leaders today. For a church of several million members, there are only some 1,200 ordained ministers, most of whom joined the ranks of the clergy in the 1940s. This proportion is probably unheard of in any other part of the world. It is only in recent years that we have been able to strengthen the numbers of our colleagues with theological graduates from our thirteen theological schools.

When you find a church in some such situation as this, it is easily understandable how it is a church in which lay leadership is utterly indispensable. A large proportion of our churches and meeting points are led by lay Christians. And it also becomes understandable why lay training is given priority in the work of provincial and local Christian councils, in view of the ease with which heretical and unbiblical teachings arise, especially in rural areas. Because of the overwhelmingly lay nature of the leadership, it is to be regretted that the sacramental aspects of corporate church life, for example, Eucharist and Baptism and Ordination, cannot be given prominence as they should be, and present a degree of irregularity.

Fifth, how do we look at atheism and at the state under the leadership of a Party which is avowedly atheistic?

The Marxist Chinese Communist Party stands for atheism and has not got any love for religion, but is different from the party in the former Soviet Union in that it puts a strong emphasis on the United Front. The prosperity of the country rather than the propagation of an ideology is given first place in its program. The Party understands that it needs to depend upon and unite with all elements in the population that aspire for national prosperity. This includes the Christians. In order for this unity to be possible, ideological differences must be relegated and minority characteristics such as religious faiths must be respected. That is the very practical basis for the Party leadership's readiness to give allowances to religious freedom, as long as the freedom is not used to subvert the state.

Unlike the former Soviet Union, there has not existed in China an anti-God movement or any anti-religious periodical. The only organization that has to do with atheism is for the academic study of the history of atheism in China. Its existence in China is hardly noticed except in scholarly circles.

I am not terribly upset by the atheists' advocacy of atheism in China because the fact that God was, is and will be forever, cannot be changed by any human denial of his existence. In our overwhelmingly secular society, the very attempt to deny God at least raises before the people the question of God, and that at least leads some people to find the option of God worth pursuing. In 19th-century Europe, Nietzsche, in putting forward the thesis on the death of God, actually enlivened people's interest in the question of God, perhaps for decades.

After all, who are the gods whose existence the atheists deny? They are often the tyrannical Jupiter who chains Prometheus to a cliff because he does good for humanity, and the ruthless underworld King Yen in Chinese popular religion who sends out emissaries to fetch people to be thrown into everlasting hell fire as punishment for their demerits on earth. Atheistic humanism is sometimes actually one form of human seeking after God without using the name God, and can be our ally as it can help salvage authentic faith. We can join forces with humanitarians of many sorts to oppose the idolatry in those views of God that diminish human dignity and block human liberation. Some of my friends are surprised that I sometimes speak as highly as I do of certain atheists and communists. There is a part of me as a Christian which utters a hearty "Amen" to what they advocate and exemplify, a part of me that refuses to rebuke them, but rather warms to them and wants to work with them against forces we both want to combat, even though we get our orders in doing certain things together from different chains of command.

Some Christians in the West condemn the Chinese Christians for our not being anti-communists and for the lack of a spirit of combat in dealing with the communists. Their assumption is that, since communists are atheists and are bound to want to persecute and destroy religion, the mandate for Christians is therefore inevitably one of confrontation and martyrdom. We have not taken their advice to easily call for martyrdom without caring for the welfare of the church and of the nation. As long as there is common ground between communists and Christians as Chinese citizens, as long as there is space for us to maintain Christian worship and witness and church life, and as long as ways are open within the United Front for dialogue and consultation on the implementation of the principle of religious freedom with noticeable results, we see no justification for thinking that atheists are our enemies and that confrontation is called for.

Sixth, are Chinese intellectuals, who have always played a leading role in society, assuming a hostile attitude toward Christianity?

Intellectuals are today more open and friendly to Christianity than at almost any time in past history since the first arrival of Christianity in China in the 7th century in the Nestorian form.

Chinese intellectuals in early years took an attitude of suspicion and superiority toward the missionaries who, for the sake of survival, had to try their best to show that Christianity was not too different from Buddhism and Confucianism. Missionaries tried to justify their presence by helping Chinese emperors with astronomy, geometry, mathematics and science. They also took over from Buddhism and Chinese classics and their terminologies and from Chinese scholars their dress and manners. Missionaries' contributions in education and medicine accounted for the rise of goodwill for them on the part of Chinese people, but did not result in many conversions. After the formation of the People's Republic of China in 1949, with the vogue of the materialist view of the world and of history and especially with the ascendancy of ultra-leftism, the rejection of Christianity has been marked by equating it to the opiate. That was considered the only correct Marxist definition of religion, ignoring all else that Marx and Engels said about religion. Marx, for instance, did not simply dismiss religion as an opiate, but saw its importance as "the general theory of this world and its all-inclusive principle," adding that "to understand human beings requires an understanding of this world, and to understand this world requires an understanding of its general theory and all-inclusive principle," which is religion. Thus, the opiate does not at all exhaust the Marxist understanding of religion.

As a result of the nationwide criticism of ultra-leftism after the downfall of the Gang of Four who controlled the Cultural Revolution, the intellectual climate for Christianity has entered a new stage. There has arisen an unprecedented appreciation for Christianity and the Bible. Before and during the Cultural Revolution, we could hardly find a single article on religion written by academics which did not relate it to the opiate. But, in the last fourteen years or so, many scholars have turned to saying that the opiate is not a good enough definition of religion because, under certain circumstances, such as those described by Frederick Engels in his *Peasant War in Germany,* religion plays a progressive and even revolutionary role. At the same time, many of them have given up the equating of religion to superstition, but affirm religion as a part of human culture and as contributory to human culture. These conclusions may not be exciting to Christians and theologians in the West, but they are epoch-making in People's China after all its devaluation of religion.

After hearing so much about religion as opiate and about the reactionary and deceptive nature of religion, it is refreshing to hear from the highest leading circles of the Communist Party of China about the "five natures of religion in China," namely, its rootedness in the masses of the people, its affinity to ethnic minority races, its international connections, the long life it has before it and its complicatedness. It is clear that all of these five natures offer important support for a fair treatment of religion and a liberal implementation of the principle of religious freedom. Today, it is generally accepted that religion and socialism are compatible in their practical programs.

We of Nanjing Theological Seminary are especially aware of the changed intellectual atmosphere around us. In the fifties our seminary was an isolated dot on the map of Nanjing, a center of religious superstition not worth paying attention to and, hence, deserted by the teachers and students of Nanjing University. Today we are the Center for Religious Studies of Nanjing University where our teachers share in its educational program. *Religion,* a semi-annual publication of the Center, goes to many universities, colleges, social science institutes, religious affairs bureaus of the government and United Front work departments of the Communist Party, and is a good means of communication with the non-Christian world in China.

The church in China sees the intellectual community, especially parts of it that draw near to the church, as an important field of its ministry. They have translated a good number of Western theologians' works into Chinese and have written books on Christianity in a friendly way. I especially like to refer to the "culture Christians" who are the opposite of the "cultured despisers of Christianity" of Europe. Our "culture Christians" have come so near to faith as to have embraced it except that they do not believe in baptism and in going to church. They are bridges or half-way houses between the church and the intellectual world and, therefore, our important allies.

From what I have said, you can see that the role of the church in China has two aspects: one, within the church and, two, toward the outside world. Within the church, we emphasize the seeking of a Chinese Christian selfhood, the guarding of our postdenominational unity through mutual respect in matters of faith and worship, the doing of a good job in building up the spirituality and corporate life of the church, the education of ourselves on the universality of the church, the training of the laity and the broadening of our unity through service and through reconciliation so as to embrace all in China who honor Jesus Christ as Lord. Toward the outside world, we try our best to guard against ultra-leftism in our political life, to elevate the image of Christianity as a Chinese religion, to witness to Christ, especially in response to the openness of the intellectual community today, and to carry on the ongoing discussion with the state with a view to safeguarding the principle of religious freedom. This summarizes the role or ministry of the church in Chinese society as I see it.

It would not help to draw a rosy picture of the church in China. It is important to take a sober look at our situation. But if we recall that, all through the Church's history, it has ever been plagued by problems, weaknesses and mistakes of all sorts, but has witnessed to Christ and has grown in spite of them all and through them all, we take courage in saying with the whole Church of Christ on earth:

Though with a scornful wonder
the world sees us sore oppressed
by schisms rent asunder,
by heresies distressed.
Yet saints their watch are keeping,
their cry goes up, "How long?"
And soon the night of weeping
shall be the morn of song.

—Address at a Retreat for the Baptist World Alliance Nanjing, 1994

# RECONCILIATION IN A CLASSLESS SOCIETY

Today, we have a group of students who, after several years of study, will be leaving our school to take up their posts in the church. Our assessment of your studies over the past few years is quite high; we feel you *are ready* to go to work in the church. Moreover, the church is in urgent need of you. Study and work can shape themselves into a rhythm; in studying, do not forget work and in work do not forget study. This is the best course.

The students we farewell today do not of course have a very definite idea of their future path. And so in the midst of their anticipation, they cannot help feeling a bit uncertain. At such a time, we should ponder once more the original intention we had in dedicating ourselves to the service of the gospel. I am not speaking here of what you may do in your future positions. We must stand back and take a long view in order to understand this enterprise of the gospel in which we are involved.

What makes the gospel of Christ a gospel and indeed *the* gospel does not lie in its recognition of the existence of God, nor in its affirmation of the next world, nor in its pointing out that humans are sinful and helpless. This is not yet Christianity, not yet the gospel. What makes the Christian gospel *the* gospel lies in its proclamation that this God is love, that this God reconciles humanity to himself and human persons to each other. To this end, God became flesh, and opened the door of reconciliation through the cross. This Risen, Ascended Christ is the Lord of Creation. He upholds the universe by his word of power and all the riches of creation have their place in him. He is the fountainhead of reconciliation. He scatters the seeds of reconciliation over the whole earth. He desires humanity to be reconciled to himself and human persons to be reconciled to each other. This is what makes the gospel the gospel.

Humanity's being reconciled to God is of course more fundamental than human persons being reconciled to each other. When a person has been reconciled with God, that person is motivated to work at reconciling with others. Matthew 25:31–46 contains Jesus' teaching about judgment day. Here we find that even work for human reconciliation done by those who do not know him is acceptable to God. This is because objectively this work is done to the body of Christ and is much stronger than the failure to undertake the work of reconciliation by one who says he or she knows Christ. Of course, the more normal thing would be to be reconciled with God through Christ first and then through the love of God, to engage oneself in the work of reconciling with and loving others, and through this work, to deepen one's knowledge of Christ.

When you go to your jobs, you may have to do everything, from preaching, visitation, chairing meetings and teaching classes, to answering the telephone, mopping the floor, cutting stencils and tidying the office. Who knows, maybe you'll even have to buy groceries, cook and wash up. As long as what we are doing, no matter what it is, helps the church to spread this gospel of reconciliation, enabling people to be reconciled with God and with each other, then our work has value. If we must put up with a bit more ourselves, it's really nothing.

The church has been preaching this gospel of reconciliation for nearly 2,000 years. This gospel has the cross, a symbol of humiliation, for its standard. It asks people to admit their guilt and to confess their sins. So for 2,000 years people have not really welcomed this gospel;

some have even opposed it, or concocted ways to dilute it, or to rid it of those parts they do not like. This we must not do. The aim of Three-Self is to make a Western religion into a Chinese religion, so that Chinese people can accept Christ more easily. By no means does it want to preach another Christ, a Christ without power to reconcile humankind to God and to each other.

Over the 2,000 years during which the gospel has been spread, the environment has been more conducive to its success at some times and less so at others. In terms of humanity's historical evolution, we in China left behind the period of class struggle a bit earlier than many other countries and have entered a new period in which the capitalist and landlord classes no longer exist as classes and as the enemy. So taking class struggle as the key link is a thing of the past. Today we are primarily concerned with unity and stability and with reconstruction. This is not only an important turn in human history; it also offers an entirely new, more favorable environment for people to accept the reconciling gospel of Christ.

Ever since humankind left behind the classless society of primitive communism, the social periods through which it has passed—slave, feudal, capitalist—were all filled with class struggle, including ethnic struggle. No matter whether we liked it or not, the struggle never ended. Where there is oppression, there will be revolt. In a society like that, reconciliation seems to be at loggerheads with the prevailing atmosphere. "He who is for me will prosper, he who is against me will be destroyed." "Every man (sic) for himself and devil take the hindmost." These are the declarations of such a world. In such a world, when the strong speak of reconciliation above the table, they are kicking you under it. When the weak speak of reconciliation, if they are not careful they slip into that morass of equivocation where class reconciliation eliminates struggle. During the war against Japan, for example, it was difficult to speak of reconciliation. To speak of reconciliation then was often a traitor's counsel, favorable to betrayal of one's people.

In the days of fierce class antagonism, not only did struggle with our enemies go on without ceasing, but it was difficult to avoid the outbreak of necessary and even unnecessary struggle among the people, many of whom were harmed in error. That reconciliation could not take place where it was most needed is a most unfortunate thing. In these days when we can basically throw off class struggle and political movements and work hard for stability and unity, how should we regard the scars left from those days?

Struggle still exists in China today, but it has already been proclaimed that class struggle is not the key link, that we must strive for stability and unity, and begin to make the transition to a society where friendship exists between people. In a stable and unified society, people can more easily understand the reconciliation bestowed by Christ. The reconciling gospel of Christ is better able to make a contribution to stability and unity in such a society. If the reconciling gospel of Christ sounds like a round peg in a square hole in a society of class struggle, then it will have much more resonance in an environment that places importance on stability and unity.

China has a long history of class struggle and struggle among national groupings. Figuring from the agricultural revolt of the Taipings, there have been over a hundred and fifty years of struggle between oppression and liberation. The "Great Proletarian Cultural Revolution" pushed the philosophy of struggle to its limit—upper vs. lower, spouse vs. spouse, parent vs. child, old vs. young. Rather than friendship between persons, there could only be harm. How we need the gospel of love today, if we are to turn human relationships toward friendship and unity; how we need the gospel of love, the healing power of love, in order to build intimacy and love between persons, to be able to stand in another's shoes, to build forgiveness and tolerance, banishing the mentality of suspicion and habits of unbridled criticism of others. Let us banish the threats so prevalent during the Cultural Revolution, so that anyone who says them will be considered an uncivilized cur. If our gospel of love and reconciliation can achieve this, what a great contribution it will be. Today the demand is for stability and unity. In this atmosphere people will not feel that the reconciling gospel of Christ is empty words; they will feel its substance.

In recent years, the number of Christians has increased. Of course there are many reasons for this, but from what I can see, one of the important reasons is that people are weary of struggle, they yearn for reconciliation. People feel that much of the struggle they have been through was a waste and they are much more willing to seek unity. The Lord Jesus said, "Come to me, all you that are weary and are carrying heavy burdens, and I will give you rest" (Matt. 11:28). Isaiah 30:15 says "In returning and rest you shall be saved; in quietness and in trust shall be your strength." How moving these words are for us today. Notice especially the words people are longing to hear: "return" and "rest" and "coming." Why does the word "return" fall so sweetly on the ear? Because if people have a place to live, they do not wander about lost. We have within us this feeling of "homelessness," and want a place to return to.

"Reconciliation" is something we are seeking.

During the Cultural Revolution, many Christians were willing to be despised and beaten, rather than give false witness, and did not casually sign their names to the big character posters attacking others. In the villages, there is harmony in Christian homes, mothers- and daughters-in-law get along well, as do parents and children, brothers and sisters. They work hard; they do not cheat each other. This has made a deep impression on other people. Many ask, what is this Christianity? How can it produce people like these? Some say they want to believe because Christians are all so friendly. In the cities, many Christian women are involved in the work of residential committees and when quarrels break out, they go to spread reconciliation. Divorces have been avoided because these women visit couples at risk once, twice, five and even ten times to counsel them. And relations between the older and younger generations have been made harmonious because of their counsel. The family, the underpinning for people involved in working for the four modernizations, is thus on solid ground. What worthwhile work this is.

Foreign friends tend to think that the difficulties we face in our work are very great. The greatest difficulty is said to be the unrelenting propagation of atheism. In fact, we know that all work has its difficulties. There is some propagation of atheism but Christians do not fear it, because whatever we think of atheism, the propagation of atheism at least brings the question of God to people's attention and this is not a bad thing. Today, we need to see the favorable conditions before us. Looking at the big picture, China's history has entered a stage without class opposition, one in which stability and unity have become the emphasis. In such circumstances, the message that God and humanity are one in Christ, that people are one, pleases the ear and will be welcomed by more people.

Since this is so, should we not also expect a springtime of Chinese Christian theology? Such a theology would not repeat what has been said by foreign theologians, but would reflect how, in an age no longer dominated by class struggle, Chinese Christians spread the reconciling gospel of Christ to their people; it would reflect how this reconciling gospel transforms the people of China; and it would reflect how the people of China go on to enrich the church's knowledge of this gospel.

You graduates have read a great many books. Now you will now engage yourselves in the reality of the church. I hope you will have a contribution to make in the opening up of a theology with Chinese characteristics.

Let me say that we care about each graduate. No matter where you will be after today, I invite you, like all the graduates that have gone before you, to see yourselves as belonging to the seminary. Please keep up contact with your alma mater and become one of those who pray for it unceasingly and care about its work. We will await with welcome every letter you send us about the quality and reputation of Nanjing Seminary.

—Our Human Longing for Reconciliation, 1986

# LIFE SHOULD HAVE A MISSION

Another semester is here. We welcome back those students who have spent the summer at home; even more do we welcome back those students who have been away doing field study in local churches. And we especially welcome our more than sixty new students.

Take a moment to consider that here in Nanjing, we have gathered over 200 co-workers, classmates and others who busy themselves endlessly providing food, shelter, maintenance and health services, going to class and worship, constructing new buildings, plus all sorts of other activities—what are we doing, after all? What is it we have dedicated ourselves to? We say that we are responding to God's call, but what is it God is doing? Why has God called us? Why is responding to this call worthwhile? I think that the story of the angel appearing to Mary found in Luke 1:26–38 has something to tell us.

Goethe said: "Dear friends, the tree of life is ever green, but theory is gray." The story of the angel appearing to Mary is vivid and moving, full of poetry, as evergreen as the tree of life, while what I am saying is gray theory. But I believe that in saying what he did, Goethe's intention was not to diminish the importance of theory. Rather, with theory as its foil, analysis, synthesis and guide, the tree of life will appear even greener, more attractive, more understandable, and will moreover produce even more trees of life. We in seminary must both foster the spiritual life as if it were the tree of life, so that it may grow greener, and study theory, to know and water this tree, so that it can grow and mature.

Theory helps us to take a broad view of history. This means we temporarily set aside all the minor matters and look first at the overall sweep of history, understanding incidents as part of the whole. Viewed in this way, the conversation between Mary and the angel in the first chapter of Luke's Gospel becomes a sign in the whole history of God's creation, redemption and sanctification.

Our starting point is the love of God, or the God of love. Behind all creation is love. Love is the key to all the mysteries of existence. God's love moved God to create, to teach, to forgive, to save and to sanctify, so that more and more people may find the source of energy of this love. God's ultimate goal is to create a universe of love, a world of love, in which a human community lives by the principle of voluntary mutual love. God is not a steamroller or a bulldozer, crushing or clearing away people's will and freedom. God's will is a will-to-fellowship. God created humanity in God's own image. The very Trinity tells us that God Himself is a community of love.

The visitation of the angel to Mary can be thought of as a sign that as the human-divine relationship develops through the whole unfolding process of God's creation, redemption and sanctification of the world, an important minority has already appeared. God can anticipate that this minority will work with him as intentional co-workers. If God's expectations do not go unfulfilled, but receive a positive response, then the conditions are present among humanity for the Incarnation to happen; that is, human cooperation can be counted on and there is no need to wait.

We know that the angel revealed God's plan to Mary: In order to continue his process of creation, redemption and sanctification, God himself was preparing to become human, to come into the world. Mary was overcome with excitement. This was exactly what Mary, her family and quite a number of her friends among the Israelites had waited for so long. Yet, for a young unmarried woman like her, the sacrifice asked was very great indeed.

The Incarnation is an event of cosmic significance. The question was, would humanity offer its collaboration and cooperation in so great an event, so that it could become a reality? Or would it be indifferent, even resistant, and thus delay God's creation history? While Mary was pondering the problem brought her by the angel, not only were God and the angel awaiting her free choice, but her whole cosmos, all of nature and the whole world seemed to be waiting with bated breath, nervously anticipating her agreement, because the whole creation was still waiting to be released in order to enter into the glory of the freedom of God's children. Could anticipation become reality? Let us look at Mary's response.

We know what she said: "Here am I, the servant of the Lord; let it be with me according to your word." Through her response, she became the vessel of the Incarnation, its carrier, and the history of God's creation, redemption and sanctification entered a new stage.

I like Tu Fu's praise of Li Bai: "Your pen startles the winds and rain; your poems make the gods cry." Mary was a simple young woman, no poet, perhaps she couldn't even write, but her answer could startle the winds and rain and bring tears to the gods more than any line of verse.

We often speak of Christ's obedience. But behind it we see the commitment of the Holy Mother. Her offering was freely made, not coerced; it was responsible, not willful or impulsive. This is a thoroughly self-sacrificing love, a thoroughly self-sacrificing commitment. God would like to see a greater abundance of this love appearing among humanity by means of his creation.

I once quoted the stirring words of Teilhard de Chardin in this hall: "Someday, after we have mastered the wind, the waves, the tide and gravity, we shall harness for God the energies of love; and then for the second time in the history of the world man will have discovered fire." Mary's heedless-of-all-else love for and commitment to God was a new departure, emboldening Teilhard to express his vision.

The whole cosmos has every reason to cherish feelings of thanksgiving and reverence for Mary. And not only the whole cosmos, but the angels and God himself, too, are happy and moved because of her loving heart, her offering, her cooperation, her resolute will and her sacrifice.

We can understand from this why, in the hearts of many Christians for many years now, in their theology and in their spirituality, Mary has such a special place. Even the Protestant theologian Karl Barth said that he was not against having a statue of Mary in church, as long as it was not placed too highly. He thought it should be set not on the altar but among the congregation.

Let us think of it this way: Mary's offering was not her own isolated response as an individual; it was the long-awaited fruit of God's work of creation. It represents the will-to-love for God among humankind, that most understanding, most inclined to do good, intentional and willingly cooperative, incisive minority. The familiar saying, "The traditions of our dead forefathers entangle the minds of the living like a nightmare," does not describe this minority.

The church's mission on earth is to be the carrier of the Incarnation, to bring this "Word in the beginning" among the people. Yes, we must eat, we must have shelter, we must do many things, but behind all this we seek to make ourselves like Mary. In order for the Word to become flesh and show forth among people, we are willing to let it be done to us according to God's word, without counting any cost.

I don't want you to think our seminary such a wonderful place, or think that it is the destination and goal of all your seeking. No, each of us is still receiving God's creation, redemption and sanctification. We are all unfinished products. We all have our weaknesses. Our actions are at variance with our words. We are disappointing. This is no more than a school, a school for learning the lessons of love. We are all students here and we are all teachers. We grow together, and together know God's holiness and goodness. We are all studying how to do these things. This is a more appropriate view of the seminary.

In the worship life of the seminary, in its spiritual life and in theological discussion, you may meet things you are not familiar with. This situation always requires that you learn to respect others, that you learn to value others as yourselves, that you see what you can learn from others. You know the famous passage from Marx: "You praise the constant changes in nature and the infinity of all its pleasing diversity and rich resources. You do not ask of roses and violets that they send forth the same fragrance. Then why do you demand that the most precious thing—the spirit—have only one kind of existence?" In 1 Corinthians 12:3, Paul says that no one can say "Jesus is Lord," except by the Holy Spirit. Clearly, all who recognize Jesus as Lord are moved by the Holy Spirit. So let us learn the lesson of respecting others to enrich our spirits, our spiritual cultivation and our theology. We, each one of us, need only make Mary's response—I am the servant of the Lord, let it be with me according to your word—our daily prayer and offering and we will be able to become a community of love, a community in which we all practice mutual respect, mutual learning, mutual support, and mutual advancement.

—Speech at the Opening Convocation, Nanjing Seminary,
September 9, 1984

# MODERN THEOLOGIES

I would like to introduce to you several schools of theology current abroad which may be of some value for us.

In order to enable you to understand a school of theology, I have to bring it into an encounter with the current state of Chinese theological thinking, point out some of its special features and simplify it as far as possible. In doing this it is difficult to avoid a certain measure of one-sidedness and over-simplification, which is not entirely fair to a school of theology. You need to be aware of this from the outset.

A second reminder is this: in studying theology we need to guard against labeling other people, saying this one is "spiritual" or "of the spirit" while that one is not; this one is "orthodox" and that one "unorthodox." It is easy to set oneself up as judge, but this is of no benefit to the formation, enrichment or progress of one's own theological thinking. This is the attitude of one who is not open to self-improvement. When you hear something you do not quite understand, do not immediately condemn. You should make an effort to understand why this person raises this argument. What problem does he or she hope to resolve by so doing? Do you have an answer to this question yourself? What is it? That is to say, do not be quick to judge. You must be a listener, you must engage in dialogue. We cannot demand perfection of a new idea. We must be sympathetic, enter into the other's system and see the good intentions behind that system's efforts to answer questions. Of course it is quite all right to disagree with an argument, but we must first understand it well, know what it is saying and what it is not saying. We should not twist or exaggerate it. To begin in this way or to frame an argument in a ridiculous way in order to attack it, are methods unworthy of any theologian or scholar.

Liberation theology began in Latin America, primarily in Roman Catholic circles. It has been influential in both North America and Asia and has even had a marked influence among evangelicals. China seems to be one of the few places on the entire globe where Latin American liberation theology has had the least influence.

Liberation theology emphasizes the exodus in the Bible. The exodus is an extremely important event by which God acts in the history of the Hebrews. He hears the cries of the Hebrew people in the midst of their suffering and enables them, after a struggle, to escape Egypt and gain liberation. So many books of the Old Testament tell us that throughout all the years following the exodus, the Israelis, the Jews, always returned to this event. "God has done a great thing for us." The great thing of this phrase almost always refers to the exodus. The exodus event left a very deep imprint on the Hebrew nation.

Besides the emphasis on the exodus, another biblical passage which liberation theology makes particular use of is the Magnificat of Mary beginning in Luke 1:46: "My soul magnifies the Lord, and my spirit rejoices in God my Savior ... He has shown strength with his arm, he has scattered the proud in the imagination of their hearts. He has put down the mighty from their thrones, and exalted those of low degree; he has filled the hungry with good things, and the rich he has sent empty away." Another passage frequently quoted is Jesus' words in the synagogue in Nazareth found in Luke 4: "preach good news to the poor, ... proclaim release to the captives and recovering of sight to the blind, to set at liberty those who are oppressed, to proclaim the acceptable year of the Lord." Still another is Matthew 25:31–46, which speaks of the final judgment based on our treatment of the lowliest of humanity.

An especially important idea of liberation theology is its belief that God is not "unbiased" or "impartial." The partiality of God is directed to the poor: God sides with the poor. The most representative of the liberation theologians is the Peruvian priest Gustavo Gutierrez who wrote the book titled simply *Liberation Theology*, making him the first to raise the banner of liberation theology. He noted that traditional theology focuses its attention on non-believers, while ignoring non-persons. Traditional theology is insensitive to these people. He asks what significance it can have to say to one who leads the life of a non-person, "you are a child of God." This theologian is concerned about the poor of this world, the cast-offs, the alienated, those trodden underfoot by others; these are people who lead a less than human life. He feels that theology should be concerned about these people and not focus its attention exclusively upon non-believers. Gutierrez believes that the exodus expresses God's partiality for the poor of this earth.

Some of the terminology of liberation theology is now current in international theological circles. One of these terms is praxis. At times this refers to the general practice of the people, sometimes it refers to the Christian's practice under the guidance of theology. Liberation theology has no high esteem for the greater part of systematic theology. It proposes that one may gain more of the stuff of which theological thinking is formed through practice.

Liberation theology emphasizes that it is a theology of the world; it advocates entering into the world. Gutierrez says that the central theological problem is not life after death, but life after birth. Whether one goes to heaven or hell after death is not the central theological question. The central theological problem should be the human world, how to enable people to live a life of human dignity once they are in the world.

Many liberation theologians oppose developmentalism. Some people speak continually of the development of the nations of the Third World, or their opening up, but these people do not speak of liberation. Liberation theology believes that the problems of Latin America and the rest of the Third World are not primarily those of opening up to outside interests or of development, but of a fundamental transformation of the social system. The more these countries open themselves to foreign capital investment, the greater becomes their dependency on foreign countries. The Brazilian Archbishop Helder Camara has said, "A man can give aid to an individual and be called a saint, but let him appeal for justice and he may be called a subversive." They feel that in this 20th century the greatest love lies in creating a just society. They say that the real question is not development but independence. Lack of independence carries with it oppression and every type of suffering, so the point of departure for the people must be the search for liberation and not the increase in the average annual per capita income.

There are many schools within liberation theology, and at least a portion of those would say explicitly that the use of violence cannot be avoided at times, because the oppressors make use of a great deal of violence to maintain their control, and this means that those opposed to that control are forced to use violence in overthowing the system. Several dozen priests at least, proponents of liberation theology, have been violently murdered by the reactionary forces in Latin America, or have been assassinated in the social struggle. These events have forced the people to consider the question of using violence to repay violence.

Liberation theologians do their utmost to maintain normal relations with church authorities and the upper strata of the Catholic Church hierarchy. They have established many basic Christian communities not necessarily inside church buildings. In such small gatherings, the priest comes to celebrate the mass, to pray and to read the Bible together with everyone else. At times each one takes a turn to speak, to say what insight he or she gained from reading the Bible. I have read three books in which these ordinary fishermen, workers and peasants have spoken one by one after taking part in the mass and reading the Bible lesson. This is a form of group organization produced by liberation theology.

Liberation theology represents a type of biblical hermenuetic and method. When we study the Bible, we all like to know what the historical background of a book or passage is. We realize that the more we know about the historical background, the more we are able to understand the text. Liberation theology is not at all opposed to researching the background, but says that this is not always very productive. We have no way to rediscover the background of many things in the Bible. What is important for liberation theology is to understand what light has accumulated as this passage passed from generation to generation, from one group of Christians to another. For example, when we study the Book of Exodus, we must know not only the historical background, but how Hebrews and Christians have understood it, how they have received it throughout the many years through which it has come down to us. Such knowledge is precious. That is to say, that when we read a passage in the Bible today, we must be aware that this passage has gained its significance as a property of the Catholic Church. Much light which has come down through history is stored up there, and we must add it to our own knowledge.

When we read the Bible today, we also bring new light to it. Even the communal discoveries of little-educated fishermen and farmers within their basic Christian communities are precious. As I understand it, liberation theologians lay a great deal of stress upon reading the Bible with a democratic spirit. And this is a point which we also stress.

With regard to propagating the gospel, they believe that the mission of the church is not simply to bring Christ to the people. Christ was sent by the Father and continually comes into the world and works through the Holy Spirit at times and in places he himself chooses. Therefore, the mission of the church is not to bring Christ into a Christ-less world but to recognize Christ where he is at work and then bring this recognized Christ and his actions to the poor as the good news. The mission of the church is primarily to proclaim to the people the acceptable year of the Lord. Due to the subordination of all things to the Incarnate, Risen Christ, Christ is already in the world. The church, relying on the illumination of the Holy Spirit, recognizes Christ, and then, like the disciple whom Jesus loved, points out: "It is the Lord." The church's duty to bear witness lies in pointing out the actions of the Lord. This being the case, propagation of the gospel is not only bringing Christ to the poor, but discovering Christ in the poor. It is not only bringing Christ to people, but bringing Christ out of people, because there is already a bit of Christ in the people of this world. Bringing Christ out of them is also propagating the gospel.

There are those among liberation theologians who do not set a high value on the ecumenical movement. One of them puts it this way, "It would be necessary for the myth of the Christian community to disappear, for it prevents the recognition of the division of society into classes and the recognition of class struggle." Gutierrez calls the ecumenical movement "a marriage between senior citizens." He, of course, is being humorous. He further says that the church cannot be united until humanity is united. This view is one we Chinese Christians can somehow appreciate. We believe that the sign of the church should first be holiness, and next "oneness," or "catholicity." To raise "oneness" to an inappropriately high level, and make every thing serve "oneness" often confuses right and wrong.

The influence of liberation theology has reached to many places throughout the world, and has produced some radical schools of theology, black theology in the U.S. for example, which is an expression of liberation theology in North America. Women in capitalist society feel that they are oppressed and feminist theology, which holds that women have a particular sensitivity to the truth of Christianity, has been inspired by liberation theology. Women have been repressed for thousands of years and now demand liberation. Following liberation, they will be able to make a unique contribution to the richness of Christ. They are opposed to paternalism and some oppose calling God Father but not Mother, and similar forms of theological language.

Liberation theology says little about international political problems, so I cannot speak of its position on the Soviet Union or on China. They are very sympathetic to Cuba because they feel that Cuba represents liberation, and they have expressed some friendliness toward China. Gutierrez has given a talk in which he was very affirmative of China. When books on liberation theology mention those nations which have already achieved liberation, China is sometimes mentioned in addition to Cuba. I have not seen any mention of the Soviet Union. Liberation theology does not seem to oppose the Soviet Union, but neither does it endorse it. Its critiques of the U.S. and of Western capitalism are many.

When liberation theology appeared in the 1960s, people saw it as simply one school among many. When the Latin American Bishops' Conference met at Medallin in 1968, liberation theologians were invited as consultants and the resolutions which emerged from the conference used a great deal of liberation theology terminology. This was not due to any endorsement of liberation theology on the part of many bishops, but because the bishops relied on a group of theologians to draft their statements. The Medallin Conference documents are a concentrated expression of liberation theology views. The materials were distributed around the globe and many theologians endorsed them; an even greater number opposed them. Ten years later the Latin American Bishops' Conference met again in Puebla. Pope John Paul II personally attended this meeting. He did not dare express his opposition to liberation theology because it was already quite prevalent among the people. But neither, it seems, was he willing to

allow liberation theology to continue to enlarge the scope of its influence, so his comments were equivocal. Let me quote two of the Pope's
comments. The first is "Priests are not social workers." The meaning of
this remark is quite clearly unfavorable to liberation theology. The
other is "Class struggle is not a path to social order." It is the present
"social order" he wishes to maintain.

Many liberation theology priests took part in the uprising in which
Nicaragua overthrew its fascist overlords and established a democratic
regime. Today, three state ministers of Nicaragua are priests; one is foreign minister, another is minister of culture. The head of the National
Campaign to Eliminate Illiteracy Committee is also a priest. The Pope
wanted them to resign, saying that priests could not participate in government. After a priest serving as an American congressman obeyed
orders to resign, the Pope could deal more easily with the priests in
Nicaragua. But according to reports, the Nicaraguan priests have
refused to resign. They say that in principle, it is undoubtedly correct
that priests should not participate in government, but that in special
circumstances there should be exceptions. One priest said that in normal circumstances a priest should not go to work as a driver, but when
the revolutionary movement required it, he did drive a truck.

Foreign friends frequently ask: "What is the attitude of Chinese
Christians toward liberation theology?" We support liberation, we also
value theology. We feel that theology should be liberated from old traditions, from the fetters imposed upon it by capitalist society. This we
advocate wholeheartedly. Liberation theology marshals a great deal of
evidence to expose the darknesses of society—colonialism, imperialism, etc.—and it plays a great enlightening role. We Chinese Christians
appreciate the Latin American liberation theologians' desire to transform the social system. They advocate that theology be more in dialogue with social science and less in conversation with philosophy and
we also find this very good. As for the partiality of God, that God certainly does discriminate between rich and poor, it was enlightening for
us Chinese Christians in our reading of the Bible that liberation theology pointed this out. Liberation theology is such a good thing that it
hurts us not to be able to endorse it in its entirety. But in the final
analysis, many Chinese Christians believe that the eternal theme for

Christianity and its theology should not be political liberation, as this is a duty limited to a certain period, but should rather be reconciliation of humanity with God. If we do not have this reconciliation between God and humanity but only liberation as our theme, this is not good enough. Even though we in China have already been liberated for over thirty years, many Christians feel it would be very difficult to make this turn in our faith. Reconciliation between God and humanity is the eternal theme of Christian theology. Under this theme there will certainly be discussion of social and political liberation. The latter cannot be easily denied, but they are not the main theme. China has experienced political liberation, but the question of reconciliation between God and humanity still exists. Some liberation theologians give a broad meaning to "liberation," and this is fine in our view, but some do not. One professor puts it thus in one of his essays: "I still contend that the gospel is identical with the liberation of poor people from socio-political oppression." He says it is "identical," he does not say "supports." If he had said "supports," we could agree; if he had said "includes," that would also be good; "requires" would also be fine. But he says "identical," identifying the gospel with social and political liberation. We have reservations about this.

Since Liberation in our country, there have been significant changes and improvements in people's lives. There have also been great changes and improvements in people's spirits. We all welcome these things very much. But the changes we see in China cannot be equated with becoming the new being in Christ of which Paul speaks in his letters. Liberation is extremely important, but liberation does not engage, let alone solve, the question of reconciliation with God. Augustine once said that God has put into our hearts a restlessness, so we cannot find rest until we find it in God. Under any social system, there are many who yearn for this type of rest. We must not lump this kind of rest together with political liberation.

Liberation theology speaks of God's partiality for the poor. There is enlightenment here. But the poor are not the messiahs of the world, as if it were only necessary to liberate the poor and they could then liberate the world. We Chinese Christians do not see it this way. It is right that we should sympathize with and support the poor. The poor are more disposed to accept the truth of revolution. This is true. But the difficulties in social transformation and the ending of poverty are not to be overlooked. We must not idealize or absolutize the poor. We Chinese people want to improve our living standards but we are not egalitarians. Rigid insistence that everyone's material conditions improve simultaneously and all equally—if the per capita income for the entire population is 500 *yuan*, then each one must receive 500 *yuan* and no individual should receive 1000 *yuan*—this kind of egalitarianism does not work. We do want to grow richer, but there will always be some who grow richer first, some later. If the poor are liberators because of their poverty, then the landlords of the past, once their land had been appropriated and they had become poor, might also become a force for revolution. Those who had been poor to begin with and had now benefited through their labor and become rich first, would then become targets of revolution. Is this not the same old doctrine of "perpetual revolution under the dictatorship of the proletariat"? We had a taste of this during the years of the Cultural Revolution. Society was thrown into chaos. In pre-liberation society, as a general rule, the poor were often the oppressed, the rich often the oppressors. It has been this way for the most part, but we cannot define revolution as the poor opposing the rich. The laws by which societies develop are not so simple, particularly since once the people have stood up and gained liberation and live under a people's government, to call once more for the poor to oppose the rich leads to social chaos. This is to damage the very cause of the people themselves. After the problems of imperialist aggression, land reform and the ownership of the means of industrial production have been solved, we need stability and unity in order to raise the standard of living, that is, to allow the people to make the transition from poverty to wealth, though not uniformly.

We need to remind ourselves that in spite of their poverty, the poor may have accepted quite a lot of the ideology of the ruling classes. They are not necessarily the most conscientized section of the population. We should not idolize the poor. More often than not, it is not the poor themselves who produce the correct theory. It is often only those comparatively better-off intellectuals who live in more stable conditions who are able to develop revolutionary theory.

Although Chinese Christians, situated politically in a post-liberation situation, have these reservations about liberation theology, we yet believe that liberation theology is a great and new thing in the history of Christianity. It is without peer, surpassing many traditional systematic theologies. I treasure it greatly, and have little sympathy for certain people who oppose it.

Is liberation theology a ploy or a plot on the part of the ruling classes to lure people from Marxism to religion? No. In Latin America for the most part, Marxism has not yet arrived. For Protestants and Catholics in the Third World, Marxism does not have a great deal of drawing power. Liberation theology leads religious believers from an endurance of suffering to reality, to consciousness and to struggle. Its twenty-odd years of history are evidence that it is not leading the masses from struggle to compliance.

Those who like to equate religion with opium in dealing with any religious phenomenon feel rather awkward faced with liberation theology. To say that religion is opium is truly an over simplification. A person under the soporific influence of opium would not advocate liberation, initiate struggle or sacrifice his or her life in the revolutionary cause. If liberation theology were nothing more than opium, it would not have been necessary for the Pope to go to Latin America to put a damper on it, nor would the reactionary South African government need to oppose black theology on such a grand scale, nor confiscate its publications. I think a more scientific attitude would be to undertake a careful analysis of all the various types of religious phenomena, and to recognize that some religious phenomena are better than others, rather than viewing them as a monolith.

ക

Teilhard de Chardin was a French archaeologist and a Jesuit priest. He spent many years in China doing archaeological work, taking part in the discovery of Peking Man. He stayed in the Chinese interior all during the Sino-Japanese War and died in the U.S. during the 1950s.

If liberation theology has something like Chairman Mao's "Report on the Peasant Movement in Hunan," then I feel that Teilhard's theology somewhat resembles Mao's poetry. For example, like that of Mao's

"Northland Scenes," his language is spare but his vision broad, painting for us a magnificent picture.

His theological vision, like that of liberation theology, is not limited to the question of belief and unbelief. Some theologies revolve back and forth around the belief/unbelief axis. Like that of Teilhard, liberation theology certainly does not deny the distinction between the two, but their field of theological vision is much broader, surpassing this question.

As I understand it, Teilhard wants us to see the grand purpose behind God's creation, along with the whole process of that undertaking. This is what he wants us to set our sights on. Some may ask, what is left of our Christianity if we do not circle round the question of belief and unbelief or of salvation? Teilhard says, the riches of Christian faith are many. It does not merely deal with that one question.

In Teilhard's view, human history is not the whole of history. History begins with the first moment of creation and continues till its end. For the greater part of historical time, there was no humanity. Humans are but animals which have appeared within the "last few moments" of this long history. According to Teilhard, all of history or the whole of time is the history of God working to realize his goal.

Let us set humanity and the issue of belief and unbelief aside for the moment and turn our attention to God.

What is God's purpose? It is to bring creation to the emergence of a partner. This partner whom God yearns to create would put off all baseness, would be a person in the image of God. What then is the image of God? God is a community, a trinity. The concept of trinity tells us that God is a group, a collective. Thus, God's creation must lead to a human community in the universe, or a communal people. God wants to enlarge his community. The community of the Father, Son and Holy Spirit is not enough. It must be enlarged, to enable all humanity to enter. In Teilhard's words, "God is not will-to power but will-to-fellowship." We must first focus our attention on God, only then will we be able to understand Teilhard.

People say, God is omnipotent. If then he desires humanity to be united to him, a humanity wholeheartedly willing to maintain this unity with God to appear on the earth, then God has only to say the word and it will be done. Why then has it been so difficult for such a humanity to be realized? The answer is that consciousness and free will are extremely important. If humanity wants to attain the enjoyment of this unity with God, it must first have consciousness and free will. If these are not present, if humanity is passive, then how can we speak of unity? For example, in the film "The Red Detachment of Women," a young woman was urged to marry a piece of wood representing her deceased fiancé, to put it in the bed and say it was her husband. Could those two be said to be united in any way? Could they become any kind of community? Of course not. The most God could gain by command would be a piece of wood, a machine or a robot. There could be no mutual love between God and robot, no community could be established. Therefore, creation cannot be other than a very, very long historical process. Teilhard could not agree with the view that God undertook creation within six days and then rested forever. Such a viewpoint is completely out of tune with his own. His view is that God creates continually and that he will continue to do so. The process of creation is a very, very long one, with the eventual appearance of a new humanity as its goal. The appearance of this new humanity coincides with the completion of the new being in Christ which Paul spoke of in his letters. What a vast process it is.

We are humans, not gods. When we speak of the whole process of creation it is not easy for us to describe in detail. We speak in generalities. Teilhard has not spoken in great detail either. In his poems, Chairman Mao can evoke the founders of dynasties, or a Genghis Khan, representing ancient Chinese history with a few strokes. He does not need to describe Cao Cao or the Qianlong Emperor in detail. Chairman Mao at least does not do this—a sketchy reference is enough to evoke the response. Teilhard's theology is this kind of poetry, sweeping through history, vast and daring, not an exercise in the detailed brushwork of some traditional Chinese painting.

One very prominent point in Teilhard's thinking is that creation is not only a process of creation, it is also a process of redemption, a process of sanctification and a process of education. Creation, redemption, sanctification and education are joined together as one.

Some Christians tend to make a sharp distinction among the three persons of the trinity. God the Father is the Creator; the Son is the Savior; the Holy Spirit the Sanctifier. There is even a view, which began with the Montanist heresy, which simply divides history into three periods: the first period is that of the creation by God the Father, then comes the period of redemption by the Son, while the present is the era of the Holy Spirit. Teilhard does not play up these distinctions. He emphasizes the unity of creation, redemption and sanctification. The separation of the three persons sometimes easily leads to setting the Lord of Salvation in opposition to the Creator. This can lead to a renewal of the Arian heresy of the early church which had to be dealt with in a series of Councils. Historically, the church has not emphasized the three persons as separate, rather the emphasis has been that, although there are three persons, there is one God. Creation, redemption and sanctification are three aspects of the ongoing work of the one God.

To separate nature from revelation or to deny natural revelation both lead to the same bad result, that is, to debase creation, to form an opposition between the first and second persons of the Trinity, and at the same time to weaken the role of the third.

When the Nicaean Creed mentions the Holy Spirit, it says "through the word of the prophets." The purpose of this is to indicate the pre-existence of the Holy Spirit. Christianity emphasizes the pre-existence of Christ and that of the Holy Spirit. Christ did not first pass from nothingness to existence on Christmas eve, nor did the Holy Spirit first pass from nothingness into existence after Christ's ascension. Christ and the Holy Spirit had been at work long before. Right from the beginning, Father, Son and Holy Spirit were working together. It is in order to safeguard the inseparability of creation, redemption and sanctification that mention is made of the pre-existence of Christ and the Holy Spirit.

We know that the gospel represented by Teilhard and liberation theology is not that of the usual so-called social gospel. Formerly the social gospel in the West was quite simple and its Christology was particularly simple: Christ was a great man, a great teacher. We should learn from him and use him as our model. It did not have a New Testament Christology, while Teilhard has a very highly developed one. He does not only speak of Jesus the Nazarene, he often speaks of the

Cosmic Christ. This Cosmic Christ is mentioned in numerous places in the New Testament. "In the beginning was the Word, and the Word was with God, and the Word was God. He was in the beginning with God; all things were made through him, and without him was not anything made that was made" (John 1:1–3). Jesus Christ is not only a teacher, nor is he only a savior, he participated in creation. And without him, is not anything made. This is the Cosmic Christ. This idea is also found in John 8:58 and 17:24, in 1 Corinthians 8:6, Ephesians 3:9–11, etc. All these you can look up yourselves. Colossians 1:15–20 is particularly worthy of attention: "He (the beloved Son) is the image of the invisible God, the first-born of all creation; for in him all things were created, in heaven and on earth, visible and invisible, whether thrones or dominions or principalities or authorities—all things were created through him and for him. He is before all things, and in him all things hold together. He is the head of the body, the church; he is the beginning, the first-born from the dead, that in everything he might be preeminent." When I was a student, our professors never told us to memorize passages in the Bible, but there were two verses which one theology professor hoped we would memorize; this was one. The other was Hebrews 1:1–3 "(A Son) whom he appointed the heir of all things, through whom also he created the world. He reflects the glory of God and bears the very stamp of his nature, upholding the universe by his word of power." Teilhard wants us to become reacquainted with such a Cosmic Christ, the pre-existent Christ.

What then is history in the palm of God, the creator, savior and sanctifier? In general, it is divided into the following three periods: first is the stage preparatory to the appearance of organic life. At the start of history, there were no organisms at all. This first stage was a very long one. God was preparing the way for organisms. Because Teilhard was an archaeologist, he was particularly interested in this and he wrote much on this period which I do not understand very well. The second period lasted from the appearance of organisms until the advent of humankind. It was again a long process. Organisms gradually divided, subdivided and grew more complex until humanity appeared. In the beginning organisms were extremely simple. Through division, subdivision and increasing complexity, the human being was finally produced of these organisms. Teilhard felt that humanity's appearance was an especially significant point in history. The third phase will be the achievement of human community. Humanity has appeared but the community is not yet accomplished. Contradictions still erupt among people. What will bring this stage to an end? The realization of community. This is the sanctifying work of the Holy Spirit, the saving work of Jesus Christ and the creative work of God.

God is the Father, but his unlimited power is constrained by love. God's omnipotence is great, but his love binds the use of that omnipotence. The human being God awaits is of a genre unique among all creation, of a superior standard. The relationship between God and the human being is not that of architect to building, as when an architect draws up a plan and later a building is made. We cannot look at the relationship between God and humanity in these terms. Likewise, we cannot say that the human being is a clock whose designer or maker is God. It is not thus. The relationship between God and humanity is that of parent to child, one of education and growth. God wants to foster a self in the midst of the universe, one which will be capable of correctly practicing freedom of choice. As a self, naturally it should have freedom and be able to choose freely, because without this freedom, we could not speak of a self. However because this self already knows God's love it would not be willing to choose wrongly. Only the conscious and voluntary use of freedom to make the correct choice is the mark of a humanity desirable in God's eyes, the new being. Up to the present, according to Teilhard, we are a half-finished product of past creation or evolution, an object needing further transformation, or further humanization. We already have this consciousness to some extent, we are in some degree willing to establish a community with God. And so in this sense, we are half-finished products. In spite of this, God wants to use us to advance history, evolution and creation. This is the process by which half-finished products are tempered.

In Romans 5:15 we find the idea that the free gift surpasses the trespass. We acknowledge that the human being is a sinner. We hope that the human being will be able to know himself or herself as a sinner and through this receive the saving power of Christ. But we do not speak of sin as something terribly overwhelming, blowing it out of all proportion, as if there were nothing in the world but sin. According to this passage from Paul, the free gift in the grace of Jesus Christ far surpasses the sin in Adam. He puts it this way, "But the free gift is not like the trespass. For if many died through one man's trespass, much more have the grace of God and the free gift in the grace of that one man Jesus Christ abounded for many." Yes, Adam's sin affected the whole of humanity, but the grace of Christ for all humanity was victorious over the effect of Adam's sin. Yes, the sin of the one man Adam implicated all of us, but the grace of the one Christ played an even greater role. Let us pay attention to this word "abounded." This means that the decisive factor is the grace of Jesus Christ, not the tarnished legacy of Adam. When some Christians evangelize or write essays today, they speak of the brand of Adam on humankind as if it were extremely profound indeed, more so than the mark of the grace of Christ. Our whole humanity is in solidarity with Christ and this far surpasses our oneness with Adam. The benefit Christ brings to humanity far surpasses the harm of Adam. Grace is greater than sin. The grace of the new Adam is stronger than the sin of the old Adam. Because of this, the message of the gospel is God's love, Christ's grace. Original sin is not the gospel. Original sin has already bowed down under Christ's original grace.

When we read Teilhard's theological works, we feel he wants us to become involved in a process, that is, to pass from a relatively small Christ who is united only to members of the church, to a much greater Christ imbued with all creation. Christ is not united only to the church. He is not merely Lord of the Church. Christ brims with all creation. Teilhard wants us to make the transition to such a recognition. This is also to make the transition from a theology which revolves around belief and unbelief, which is limited to the idea of salvation—a narrower kind of theology—to a recognition of the greatness, glory, holiness and grace of the triune God and see God's work of creation, redemption and sanctification in the universe.

The so-called eschaton is the culmination of this third phase. This unique breed of humanity formed of unique qualities is one which both enjoys freedom and chooses correctly, one able to unite with both God and others. When this humanity emerges, the miracle of God's creation is realized and God is satisfied. When this phase draws to a close, the new Jerusalem is at hand. This is an eschatological view which people can more readily understand. And this eschaton is also the beginning of another new phase, though we have no way to conjecture what that phase will be like. Teilhard put it this way: "Someday, after we have mastered the wind, the waves, the tide and gravity, we shall harness for God the energies of love; and then for the second time in the history of the world man will have discovered fire." We know what an important role the first discovery of fire played in the advance of human civilization. This ability greatly enriched our human culture. The second discovery of fire means that we humans will be able to direct this resource of love, giving it free reign. This means autonomy and the ability to care for each other. The point at which this goal is reached Teilhard calls omega. Omega is the final letter of the Greek alphabet. Jesus Christ is the alpha and the omega, the origin and the culmination. This is Teilhard's eschatology.

Teilhard's thought does not revolve within a small circle but is very broad. He has perceived that Christ is the Lord of the cosmos, the master of history. Thus as a person, Teilhard himself is extremely composed. He sees all truth, goodness and beauty and affirms that they are of Christ, and are of God. Once someone took him to the Jade Buddha Temple in Shanghai and he was so taken by the Jade Buddha, even though he was a Christian, that he said, "I love the Buddha of Jade because it tells me of something that Christianity must annex. I feel more and more strongly the need to free our religion from everything that is specifically Mediterranean." What I understand here is that the Jade Buddha is a thing of beauty which has accumulated within it the sweat and blood of countless people seeking after goodness and truth, and nothing of beauty is outside Christ. Therefore, Christianity ought to annex it. The Vatican is located in the Mediterranean area and Teilhard felt that true human religion should cast off such a narrow character. It could then assimilate much more of the things of truth, goodness and beauty. No wonder the Vatican did not like Teilhard, and for several dozen years did not permit publication of his books.

Teilhard's good English friend, the natural scientist Joseph Needham, specialized in the history of science in China and held views close to those of Teilhard. He extended these to modern world history.

In an essay on China, after speaking highly of new China, he said, "We have no reason to suppose that our present condition of civilization is the last masterpiece of universal organization, the highest form of order of which Nature is capable. I believe there are many grounds for seeing in collectivism of the kind which we can approve, a form of organization as much above the outlook of middle-class nations as their form of order is superior to that of primitive tribes. I think it would not be going too far to say that the transition from economic individualism to the common ownership of the world's productive resources by humanity will be a step similar in nature to the transition from lifeless proteins to living cell, and from primitive savagery to the first community, so clear is the continuity between inorganic, biological and social order. By this point of view the future state of social justice is seen as not at all a fantastic utopia, not as a desperate hope, but a form of organization having the full force of the authority of evolution behind it." This is true, good Teilhardism. Teilhard believed that although those who know Jesus in the world today are few in number, we should view this world in the light of the ascended Christ. This is to say that the status of this world has already undergone a change. The incarnation of Christ and his resurrection and ascension have brought about a qualitative change in the world. Christ is not only the forebear, priest and king of Christians; but more, he is the first-born and eternal Logos, the Son of God and the one who upholds all things.

The Holy Spirit does not work only in the church; he works first in the world of which the church is but a part. The church is a standard for the world, reminding people that there exists a spiritual dimension, a divine dimension. Teilhard says, "I believe the world will not be converted to the hopes of Christianity, until Christianity is converted to the hopes of the world to make them divine." Liberation theologians and Teilhard all believe that the church can only be a small organization which has a role to play in the world. The Lord Jesus said, you are the salt of the earth; he did not say you must make this whole world into a large block of salt. He said you are the yeast of the world and this yeast must work within the world to make it into bread; he certainly did not say that the whole world must become a large cake of yeast. Thus the whole church will always be a rather small organization.

Belief/unbelief is still an issue and we cannot ignore it. All people in the world were created by the Heavenly Father, but not everyone is a friend of Jesus Christ. Jesus Christ yearns for friendship, but those who can be counted as friends are the minority. Christians know God, we know Christ; we should have a deeper comprehension of God's intentions than other people to enable God to better enjoy unity with us. But we cannot simply say that those who do not believe in God are not then his sons and daughters, even less can we say that they are all his enemies. God is extremely great and in the case of China, for example, his love is not confined to the several million Christians. God's tolerance is so great, even to the point that in spite of the fact that so many people today do not recognize his existence nor thank him, God is not small-minded; he feels only pity for them. He earnestly hopes that they will come to know him. God is not like us human beings who can only write essays on the question of belief and unbelief.

You may have noticed that I have some appreciation for Teilhard de Chardin's theological viewpoint. Where he disappoints me is that he is after all a product of French culture and French higher education. He has his class and cultural limitations which are mostly expressed in his euro-centrism. His main interest in the world outside the West is archaeological. He feels that the Orient has little of value to offer to the whole of humankind. His Orient is "in a state of inertia." Our resistance to Japan was a great event, and Teilhard was resident in China at the time, but he watched our people's struggle without recognizing its historical significance. He only expressed sorrow at the suffering caused by the war. Also, he seems to underestimate the obstruction to historical progress caused by the rampant forces of evil.

This represents my understanding of Teilhard. I have only read a few of his books and some books and essays about him by others, so this introduction is subjective and may contain things which Teilhard himself would feel misrepresent his views. I can do nothing about that, but hope that you can correct them when you read him for yourselves.

ॐ

Upon entering the 20<sup>th</sup> century, the Western worldview underwent a momentous change. Originally, under the influence of Euclid, Galileo and Newton, people saw the world as a stable, static, solid body. Einstein's theory of relativity and the theories which followed it pointed out that the macrocosm and the microcosm were in a constant state of movement and change. From Plato on, philosophy was concerned with being and saw this being as static. Today, people recognize that everything—including the smallest unit of matter—is changing and "becoming," and even a God who is not in the slightest influenced by the world, who does not even undergo the most minimal change, is hard to imagine. The essentials of dialectics, especially quantitative change, metamorphosis and integration/polarization are increasingly accepted by more and more intellectuals. In such an intellectual atmosphere, Alfred North Whitehead put forward the concept of process philosophy. Its influence on theology led to the appearance of process theology. "Process" implies change, development, the new superseding the old, affirming that the fundamental state of reality and of objects is not static.

Process theology affirms, indeed gives prominence to, God as love. It might be said that this is commonplace in every school of theology. How can it be the main feature of one school? We must make a fine distinction here.

In *Process and Reality*, Whitehead points out that in substance, traditional Christianity easily tends toward three types of error in its view of God: seeing God as "the ruling Caesar, or as the ruthless moralist, or as the unmoved mover." He believes that what traditional theology overlooks is that "Galilean vision," which is to see God as love. The God who is usually highly praised by the churches is the one to whom it "gives the attributes which belong exclusively to Caesar." It sees him "in the image of an imperial ruler," or "in the image of a personification of moral energy," or "in the image of an ultimate philosophical principle," some sort of "being itself," the first cause of everything outside himself, but absolutely unaffected by anything whatever outside himself.

When process theology speaks of those things which belong to the nature of God, the first one affirmed is his love. His omnipotence, omnipresence, omniscience, eternity, transcendence, absolute righteousness and so on, are all placed in subservience to this.

"God is the Cosmic Lover, both causative and affected." Norman Pittenger and Schubert Ogden say that God is "the first cause and the final effect." God is intimately connected to the world. He is not only the creator, he also receives the responses the world makes to him, and makes to these his own response. This does not negate God's divinity, because God's divinity does not imply a distance from the world nor being unaffected by it.

Divinity implies inexhaustibility, eternal devotion and the ability to withstand the provocations of evil, absorb it and turn it to the service and increase of the good. Whitehead said, "Things matter to him and they have their consequences in him." Divinity first and foremost signifies the inexhaustibility of true love in the universe and immanence points to the coexistence of this true love with the entire created world. God's divinity in no way implies indifference.

Process theologians use the term "panentheism," a term first used by the German philosopher K. C. Klaus (1781–1832). Its implications are that God includes and permeates the entire universe; every component part of the universe has its existence in him. What distinguishes this from pantheism is that God's existence surpasses the universe and may by no means be exhausted by it.

If the God of religion is not also the God of the universe or the God of the world, if God cannot convey to humankind a vision as regards the world, but is only concerned with religion, then he cannot be the most high. He may be no more than the object of worship for certain people.

This passage from Pittenger illustrates the point well.

"As I read the writings of some of the greatest theologians in Christian history—often Origen, certainly St. Augustine, St. Thomas Aquinas, Martin Luther, and John Calvin—I am meeting in each of them two different personalities. On the one hand there is the man with a deep faith in God, often a vigorous insistence on his loving care and his gracious concern with creation, and with a feeling of personal relationship which is enjoyed between a prevenient Lover and a creaturely lover-in-the-making who seeks to respond to that prevenience. This is prominent and deeply moving. On the other hand, there is a theological position which seems quite different, with is insistence on absoluteness, unrelatedness, unchangeableness, and impassibility or inability to share in the world's anguish."

Originally, a systematic theology should have enabled us to consciously seek a unified, harmonious whole in theological thought, but in reality a person's theological knowledge can quite unconsciously maintain a number of internal contradictions.

What is "God's glory"? Pittenger puts it this way: "All is for God's 'greater glory.' And that glory is no majestic enthronement as almighty ruler and self-exalted monarch, but is the sheer love-in-act which generously gives, graciously receives and gladly employs whatever of worth or value has been accomplished in a world where God is faithfully active to create more occasions for more good at more times and in more places."

The "Epistle to Diognetus," from early church times contains the following passage which process theologians admire:

> "Did God send for him, as a human mind might assume, to rule by tyranny, fear or terror? Far from it! He sent him out of kindness and gentleness ... He willed to save men by persuasion, not by compulsion, for compulsion is not God's way of working ... He sent him in love, not in judgment ... For God showed himself to be a true friend of man. O, the overflowing kindness of God toward men! God did not hate us, nor drive us away, nor bear us ill-will."

Charles Hartshorne's *The Divine Relativity* was aimed at the singular emphasis on the absoluteness of God of traditional theology. "In each moment of God's life there are new unforseen happenings in the world which only then have become knowable. Hence, God's concrete knowledge is dependent upon the developments in worldly actualities. God's knowledge is always relativized by, in the sense of internally related to, the world."

Not every event in the human world has been decided by God. Due to the fact that God respects human freedom, events undecided by him are many. The God manifest in Christ cannot but be such a God. God is love and only union can satisfy love. And only those beings possessing freedom can aspire to union. Only beings which can choose either well or wrongly have true freedom. These are the constraints accepted by God's omnipotence and omniscience. A fine painting has no prior existence whether in heaven or in the mind of God before the artist paints it. In spite of the fact that color, form and the painter's innate capabilities are all created and given by God, this painting is a creation of the painter in his or her freedom. No matter whether he or she believes in God or not, God is constant in his respect for the freedom which belongs to the painter.

To facilitate understanding of this, Whitehead hypothesizes the primordial nature and the consequent nature of God. The former exists prior to and outside of creation, there are no constraints upon it; it is immutable. It is eternal, absolute and independent of the world. The latter is geared to the world, in relationship with it, affected by it and changes continually. It is within the realm of this latter that God receives our responses and participates in the joys and anguish of the created order.

On the basis of the above, I think everyone would agree that the affirmation of God as love by Whitehead and other process theologians has its own special features.

Perhaps it is in terms of its Christology that some Chinese Christians would raise questions with process theology. But we will discover that cosmic love can accommodate rather than exclude a cosmic Christ, and that it can also accommodate ideas about Christ as Savior.

Process theology recognizes that Christ reveals God, and it emphasizes that this revelation does not negate other truths, but rather gives them depth.

Pittenger says, "God's doing is defined by but not confined to the event we name Jesus Christ." He opposes anyone within Christianity calling the Incarnation and entry of Jesus Christ into the world a divine "rescue operation," which makes it appear that except for Christ's Incarnation, God has not been in the world and is tantamount to saying that his sudden arrival brought God to a place where he had not been before. He further says, "For myself I believe that the finality of Christ is nothing other than his decisive disclosure that God is suffering, saving and ecstatic love. Surely you cannot get anything more final than that. But there may be many approaches to this, many different intimations, adumbrations and preparations."

He says, "Christology is not something exclusive. There is no Christocentrism in the Whiteheadian vision of God when that word is used to make the event of Jesus Christ the only clue to deity and therefore to see him as an anomaly in the God-world relationship. Jesus must be taken as a classical instance, the defining moment if you will, in that wider relationship, not as the absolutely unique and unparalleled moment, without prior intimations and therefore appearing as a bolt from the blue, unrelated to what has gone on before him and what has happened after him."

As for the way people see, explore and know what is prior to the Incarnation and outside it, and their response to God's action and existence, the Incarnation is not a negation of all this, but, to use William Temple's words, offers a "correction and coronation." It is only Christ who can correct and complete the relationship between God and the rest of revealed existence and bring it to its pinnacle.

Whitehead believed that the human mission, or a man's or woman's "true destiny," lay in being a "co-creator in the universe," "partakers in the creative process."

People are all "lovers-in-the-making," "created and hence limited and finite and certainly defective, yet on the way (if we are willing to have it so) toward sharing in the cosmic loving which is nothing other than God himself—whose 'nature and name' (as Wesley's great hymn says) is Love." (Pittenger)

Heidegger felt that the solitariness of every person was his or her ultimate reality, that solitariness was the one and only way he or she could attain self-realization. Whitehead did not agree with this view, believing that our primary existence is within the human collectivity, and that it is there that we attain a relative independence. Participation and individuality are not mutual opposites but are complementary. The more we participate together with others in the life of the collectivity, the more our individuality or personality develops, the more we can enrich the collectivity.

As co-creators with God, the work of our hands is not without significance. The following passage from Pittenger is worthy of consideration:

All our labor for human liberation and all that these efforts and that labor may achieve, are surely safe in God. The divine reality who is the primal creative agency is also the final receptive reality. God treasures the good that is done in the world; he can and does use it for further implementation of good, as he continues the ceaseless divine striving to bring out of the sometimes almost intractable material of a created order, a harmony in which significant and necessary contrast need not bring about senseless and destructive conflict. To serve toward that end, and not to ask for any recompense 'save the knowledge that we do God's will' (as Ignatius Loyola phrased it) is enough for any truly dedicated Christian disciple.

He believes that evil lies in obstructing progress and rejecting cooperation in the social cosmos. It is an egocentrism which accepts the status quo, a deliberate resistance to the choice of the good. Whitehead said, "The conservative is fighting against the essence of the universe."

Whitehead, in speaking of primitive religion, pointed out, "one studies the will of God in order to preserve oneself," while in a highly developed religion, "one studies his goodness in order to be like him."

Pittenger: "Human memory is very partial. It is accompanied by a forgetfulness in which much that was valued is lost ... But God's memory is everlasting and unfailing. The divine knowledge is inclusive of all actuality which has been achieved in the creation. Nothing is forgotten, nothing is cast as rubbish to the void—save evil, which is not so much cast aside as transmuted into potentiality for some other achievement of good." He quotes a poem from Richard Hovey, an early twentieth century American poet:

God has said, Ye shall fail and perish:
But the thrill you have felt tonight
I shall keep in my heart and cherish
When the worlds have passed out of sight.

Pittenger further states, "All that has been good, noble and of value in our lives is taken after death by God into his eternal present—he 'remembers' us."

Whitehead spoke of human beings as "partakers of the creative process" who can find their "true destiny" only in seeing themselves as "co-creators in the universe."

The above has been an elementary introduction to process theology, from which I hope you can make out the contours and some characteristic features.

☙

Let me say again that to rely on one's own already-held ideas to critique others, saying how far they have strayed from orthodoxy, is not the primary goal of our theological study. What we should ask is: what questions are they seeking to answer? Have I ever considered these questions? How do the views I hold deal with these same questions? Could I deal with these questions better by considering a greater variety of factors?

There are many theological schools in the world and a number of them are incompatible with our situation. If we study them, it is simply to increase our knowledge; they may not be worth adopting. I feel there are elements in liberation theology, Teilhard de Chardin and process theology which are worthy of consideration. As theological students in China today and as those involved in the work of theological construction, we must be able to distinguish among them, be capable of critical judgment and be able to absorb new things in order to serve the principle of self-propagation.

Some theologies recognize that the material world is in a process of change and they see this change as linked to the sacred love and creation of God. And this gives these schools of theology a common language with those people in the world awaiting or promoting transformation. China is a nation in which change has been extremely fast and extremely great and one in which a great many things are yet awaiting transformation. The people place their hopes on transformation or reform. Undertaking theological construction in such an environment, it will do us good to keep abreast of process theology, liberation theology and the theologies of those such as Teilhard de Chardin. We can gain a great deal of insight from them.

It is a long process from today until the final realization of the human collectivity as it exists in the will of God, and there are many stages in the process. As for the mid-segments, as far as I know, Teilhard and the process theologians have said nothing. In their systems of thought, these are blanks. They are rebels against capitalism and they have seen the coming of the transformation, but as to how change would happen and what would take the place of the present state of affairs, they offer no answer. Thus, on the one hand, though they emphasize change and were not welcomed by the vested interests who strive to maintain the status quo, on the other hand, they could not avoid disappointing those demanding transformation. As far as I know, Teilhard stayed at that stage until he died. Some process theologians are already aware of this dilemma. John Cobb's book, *Process Theology and Political Theology*, is a breakthrough work in this area.

Liberation theology lays a great deal of stress on praxis. The search for liberation is the present praxis, its specific content is opposition to imperialism and despotism and the bringing about of people's political power. Some of it's advocates are clearly opposed to capitalism and look toward socialism.

We have people who feel that being a Christian means one should not be against anything, which is tantamount to saying that Christians should have no sense of right and wrong, no love and hate. But Paul Tillich once said, "It is a strange work of love to destroy that which is against love."

Speaking of China, we are sympathetic to the three theological schools described above in the quest for transformation, but as far as anti-imperialism, anti-feudalism, anti-bureaucrat-capitalism and the mission of liberation to end oppression goes, we are in the post-liberation stage, that is, in the next stage of historical development. In this historical stage we cannot and should not take class struggle as the key link any longer.

In this stage of history, we are constructing socialism. For China, socialism is much more capable, as a social system, of embodying love than is capitalism.

Capitalism safeguards individual ownership of the means of production, safeguards oppression, places the fate of the broad working masses into the hands of the capitalists. In Third World countries, except for China and a minority of others, it places the people's fate in the hands of the multinationals or their political representatives. To compete with other capitalist groups and preserve themselves, even well-intentioned capitalists move beyond the control of their conscience. As time passes, their conscience becomes numb.

Due to the burden of history and pressure and obstruction from all sides, socialist construction is an arduous process, but it casts off oppression and moves toward realization of a new principle of distribution, "from each according to his ability; to each according to his work." It enables humankind to achieve a level of equality never seen before. The universalization of love is the goal of socialism. Socialism is love on a large scale, organized love, love which has taken shape as a social system.

Fairness, equality and justice—these are not the antithesis of love; they are its necessary content. We do not practice love only within a tiny area. When we are able to practice love within a much broader area, when we distribute love to the masses in a rational way, then love takes on the form of fairness, equality and justice.

Today, China has not as yet implemented love in a very good, complete way. This is a vast undertaking, but socialism as a social system offers a guarantee for its realization.

This undertaking is worthy of Christians' efforts. Love is not something just to be enjoyed by two persons, you and me. Love means we have the same orientation, look toward the future together and step forward together. It is this kind of love which is adequate to enable people to be mutually encouraged, mutually spurred on, mutually supportive, and together become co-partakers in God's creative process.

—Inspiration from Theology,
Nanjing Seminary, 1985

# GOD IS LOVE

This evening, as so many brothers and sisters in Christ gather together from all the denominations in Budapest to welcome the four of us in the Chinese Christian delegation and to worship together, I am moved with gratitude from the bottom of my heart, grateful for God's grace and for each one of you here. I feel especially honored because below this august pulpit is a secret room where Jews were hidden from the Nazis during World War II. To me, this says that Hungarian Christians are not simply preachers and hearers of the Word, they brave dangers to be doers of the Word and bear a beautiful witness to Christ. On my return to China, I will not be able to keep this to myself, but will share it with Chinese Christians.

Let us reflect together this evening on Luke, chapter 9, verses 12 to 17, where one of Jesus' miracles in Galilee is recorded. He did five things: 1) he took the five loaves and two fish from the people's hands, though it was far too little; 2) he told the people to sit down in groups of fifty; 3) he took the food into his hands, looked up to heaven and blessed it; 4) he broke the food; and 5) he distributed it among five thousand people. Though the food the people brought forward was insufficient and not very good, he did not reject it, or throw it away or curse it, but took it, raised it up and increased it, sanctified it and made of it a blessing to the people.

Our God, shown forth in Christ, is not a Destroyer, but a Provider.

My mother died several months ago. For decades, she was the one in all the world who prayed most, and most earnestly, for me. My being a pastor has much to do with her prayers. Not long after the home worship service to celebrate her hundredth birthday, she began to suffer from senile degenerative brain disease, sleeping longer and longer each day, until she did not wake the whole day and finally died.

My mother loved me so much. Her love for Christ, for the Church and for me was the same love; it could not be separated. Of course I was somewhat prepared for her death, but it was the most momentous event in my life. During these several months, I have often thought of her and I have often thought of death. Sometimes I feel she is still very close to me, but at other times, I am overcome by the feeling that she has already turned into nothingness, that only her ashes remain.

Some people claim that all illness can be cured through faith and prayer. I am not one of these. If this were so there would be a population explosion and the ecology would be thrown out of balance.

God being love, I have always believed that a life filled with love and care for others, or a life filled with prayer and praise, cannot end in death and obliteration. Christ's resurrection from the dead assures us that annihilation is not the end of life. Annihilation does not await a life lived in Christ. Christ will take this small and weak life into his hands, bless it, enlarge it and make it useful to humankind. God being love, we cannot imagine good and evil, truth and falsehood, beauty and ugliness alike returning to nothingness.

Our God is not a steamroller. He loves all souls worthy of love. The billows of his love do not stop at those who stand in awe of him, or at those places where the church has spread. All goodness, all truth, all beauty lies within the boundaries of his love.

When Hungarian pastors preach, I imagine they like to tell stories, too. Let me tell you one then, to illustrate that birth and death are both no more than a transition to a new stage of human life. Sometimes at a sickbed, I tell this story to calm a person in the face of death.

Once there was a woman pregnant with twins. As time passed, the twins grew within the mother and developed minds and sensation and later consciousness. They discovered their environment, discovered that they were a pair and discovered their egos. They lived happily within the mother saying, "How lucky we are to live in such a good world. What a good mother we have; she loves us and shares herself with us." A few months later, they became aware of the fact that they could not stay where they were much longer, that they would have to leave. They became afraid. They were afraid that everything was ending and they awaited their destruction with fear. One said, "May this life continue after this." The other, in tears, said, "We're done for. Don't let your imagination run away with you." He saw nothing to look forward to and said, "Our conception and growth led to death in the end, life is completely absurd; there's no meaning in it!" He even went so far as to infer that the mother did not exist, but was just something they had thought up in response to some need. They were both afraid. One was completely hopeless and pessimistic, waiting to be destroyed. The other maintained his faith in the mother, without knowing exactly what it meant to be born.

When the time came, they came crying into the light of the world. When they discovered that they had indeed been born, the first thing they saw upon opening their eyes was that they were in the warm and loving embrace of their mother. The wonder and beauty of this was something they could not have foreseen or understood.

What this story tells us is that in God's hands, life and death are two aspects of the same thing. In the long stream of an individual's life and in the history of humanity, death to one stage of life is birth to another stage.

What is the most important and most fundamental attribute of God? It is God's love, the love shown in Christ, the love which does not hesitate before suffering or the cross, the love which made him give up his life for his friends. The justice of God is also God's love. If love spreads throughout humankind, it becomes justice. This is love entering into the world. Love does not come to destroy, but to sustain, heal, teach, redeem and give life. "When a woman is in labor, she has pain, because her hour has come. But when her child is born, she no longer remembers the anguish because of the joy of having brought a human being into the world" (John 16:21). In these words of Jesus we hear how his heart is drawn to the people of this world. This is how God is. The prophet Hosea tells us that God leads us with bonds of love. He eases the bit in our mouths, he bends down to feed us. God is love. God is the Lover in the cosmos, the Lover at the center of all reality. The revelation of Jesus Christ transcends and corrects all that we as humans are able to say of God. Love seeks the highest good for us. Nothing good will be lost; it will be fulfilled and lifted up, even to that heavenly kingdom which shall be, a kingdom founded in love. When we call God Master, this is what we mean.

Death is simply the end of one stage of life, but it is not the final end of life itself. Death is the development of life into another stage, a stage closer to God, one in which we are better able to bathe in the grace and light of God, one in which our knowledge and love of God will better grow day by day.

To return to my mother—she died, but then again she is not dead. She is still progressing, still praying for me. I can still say as before that she is the one person in the world who prays most fervently for me. There where she is there are also many other saints who love us and who even now sustain us with their prayers. All this is because God is love, because Jesus Christ died for us, because Christ conquered death, because he is the Risen Christ, who sustains creation with his word of power.

This rule—that out of death comes life, that in the midst of death we attain life, that in weakness we gain strength—applies to the life of nations and churches as well as for individuals. We need only rehearse the history of our own nations of Hungary and China as well as that of our churches to see this. My co-worker, Rev. Shen Yifan, will be reporting to you on the situation in China and in the Chinese Church. You will, I am sure, agree that the major tone in our two countries and in our two churches is not one of discouragement, hopelessness or dejection, but one of hope and joy, of thanksgiving and faith.

God is love. This is the greatest fact of all the facts of the cosmos. God being love, we can be at peace, even death will not be difficult for us. We need not be anxious about anything. We can actively participate in movements of social change and play the role we should play in the progress of history, because the love of God is ever at our side.

We have come here to bring you greeting from Chinese Christians, to share the good news we have both received in Christ, to return more and greater glory to the God we both serve, for only God is worthy of all glory.

—Speech while on a visit to the Hungarian Church,
October 5, 1986

# A PERSONAL RESPONSE TO
# PASTORAL CONCERNS

**I** have been deeply moved by the many letters from alumni/ae all over the country expressing their affection and congratulations, both to their alma mater and to me personally. Hands are few and we have not been able to respond individually, for which I hope you will forgive us. I am writing this circular to all of you to speak about things that concern us all.

If you return to campus after many years away, you will still find the East Building, but the West Building has been torn down, and in its place we have built a multi-purpose building. The ground floor houses a kitchen and the students' dining room; on the second floor are large and small reception rooms and a small dining room. On the third floor are ten guest rooms; while on the fourth floor there is a large hall. Our address, Number 13, Da Jian Yin Lane has become Number 17. In addition to the basic theology program, we now have a graduate program, a Bible correspondence course, the *Correspondence* editorial office, and the *Nanjing Theological Review* offices. The main campus also houses the offices of The Amity Foundation, the Nanjing Office of the National TSPM and CCC, the office of the Jiangsu Provincial Three-Self Association and Christian Council, the Nanjing University Religious Studies Institute and the editorial offices of its journal, *Religion*.

I can report to you that the younger generation is gradually succeeding the older one at Nanjing Seminary and that the process is going smoothly. Smoothly and gradually indicates that we are in the midst of change, but there will not be any big ups and downs. We would like to thank you all for your prayers in this respect.

There are some people in our church who scorn theology and see the seminary only as a place for the training of preachers. There are others who also scorn theology and who just want the seminary to be a place for improving the politics of the clergy. The seminary should train its students' preaching ability and graduates in theology should also be outstanding in politics, but if we want to run the church well, we cannot do without the guidance of theological thinking. Theology comes from the intensive study of the Bible, from delving into the church experience and theological exploration of earlier generations and from the broadening vision which flows from the exchange between the church here in China and the Church Ecumenical, all of which we draw on to guide the church's practice. The Chinese Church is so very much in need of theology, so how can some say we don't need it? The Christian Bible is a monumental work of theology so how can we use the phrase "there is no theology in the Bible" as an excuse to deny the value of theology? The Bible, through its language, its poetry and the sense of beauty it bestows, provides us with a great deal of material for theology.

Nanjing Union Theological Seminary has been sending students overseas for study in recent years, in order to increase international theological exchange and to advance Chinese theological construction. This work has met with warm support and cooperation from councils of churches in the United States, Canada, and the United Kingdom.

We have received your many letters raising the various problems facing our church.

Regarding the church as a whole, the recent meeting of the Joint Standing Committees of the CCC and TSPM addressed the current situation by maintaining support for independence and running the grassroots church well. We cannot say that because the issue of independence was raised in the 1950s, that raising it again in the 1990s is a "retrogression." It must be pointed out as often as necessary that China is an independent nation and our Chinese Church is an independent church. We have said this in the past, and we should continue to say it. As for the church at the grassroots, it is very painful for Christians in many places that a minority or even one or two people are in control, finances are not handled openly and the church does not resemble the church of Jesus Christ. We must strongly call upon believers to participate in and supervise the way the church is run so that grassroots churches can become schools of democratic management. This has always been a special characteristic of Protestant Christianity, for the laity have always held a certain degree of authority in the church whether in its Presbyterian, Congregational or Episcopal expressions.

I should report to you alumni that our TSPM and CCC do not take a hostile attitude to the masses of believers and their leaders outside our organizations who confess Jesus Christ as Lord. Our approach to them is that we are members of the same body in the Lord, which they are all our brothers and sisters, including those who are critical of or have complaints about the Three-Self Patriotic Movement. We must consider their criticisms with a sense of humility. We should share whatever advantages we have with them, or assist them by virtue of our more favorable situation. Those who identify with anti-China forces overseas can be found in and outside the church, but these are a minority.

The government registration of religious venues has been a particularly frequent topic in your recent letters.

The first thing which must be clarified on this issue is that the purpose of registration is to allow "underground" meeting points to come out into the open. It is never good in any country if there are some religious believers who must hold their religion in secret or meet clandestinely, and it is never a sign of religious freedom. After registration, underground groups in China can come aboveground and meet openly in the broad daylight. The people and the government authorities in their area can relax, and the believers can feel secure. As long as our religious activities are normal, we need not hide them from anyone, and we can welcome the non-Christians around us to watch, listen and monitor our activities. It appears from the regulations for registration promulgated by the Religious Affairs Bureau of the State Council that a church or meeting point need only comply with six simple and easily achieved demands in order to register. This shows that it is not the intention of the government to cut down the number of churches and meeting points or to use registration as an excuse to harass them, but rather to allow all religious activities to come into the open. The more of these that can move from underground or semi-underground status to aboveground the better.

Frankly, the division of religious activities into sanctioned and unsanctioned, or underground and aboveground is the method used in

the former Soviet Union, not that of socialism with Chinese characteristics. If we can achieve success in the task of registration of religious
venues, if we can ensure that all normal religious activities attain open
and legal status, that will be good enough. Then we can say that this is
a style of religious work which is part of socialism with Chinese characteristics. And I am very hopeful that we will be able to do this.

Mr. Luo Guanzong (Secretary General of the TSPM) and I met with
a leading comrade from the Legal Department of the State Council on
this issue of registration. He told us that registration was simply registration, and separate from their regular work. The provisions of the
regulations for registration, he said, do not specify particular actions,
and this is good, for nothing should be added to complicate their content. The spirit of what he told us is worth careful reflection.

Some people in the TSPM and CCC would like to take the opportunity afforded by registration to undertake a review of the qualifications of all Christian leaders whose groups register. This is
unacceptable. First of all, it is adding to what the regulations require,
and thus makes the work of registration more difficult. Second, it is an
extremely broad subject and the two bodies do not have the resources
to screen so many new people. Third, we have not yet succeeded in
broadening our own unity, so how can we so blithely set ourselves up
as arbiters of others' qualifications? This would broaden the base for
continuing quarrels, not unity. In the process of government registration, the task of the two national Christian bodies lies in encouraging
and assisting churches and meeting points with registration, in
promptly reflecting to the government problems and criticisms from
the church and in clearing the channel for an exchange of views. I
think this is an area where alumni/ae can also assume some responsibility.

I hadn't imagined that even today there would be those who
oppose registration on the grounds that "we are citizens of heaven and
we listen only to God, not to man." They did not raise objections on
this score during the national census, not resist by claiming that they
should not be counted as part of the population of China. They do not
want to have any contact with the government and so I wonder if they
even collect their I.D. cards. The church is certainly a spiritual body,

but on this earth it is also a people's organization. Recently someone showed me a letter from the United States that contained an essay calling for Chinese Christians to resist registration. If we follow isolationism in this work of registration, piling difficulty upon difficulty in the process, it is as if we are cooperating with anti-China groups from overseas!

It is common knowledge that the ruling party of China is an atheist party. Some people overseas seize upon this to paint the Communist Party and government as enemies out to destroy religion. Such people have a poor grasp of the facts. Taking only Christianity as an example, over the past ten years, since the restoration of order following the Cultural Revolution era, an average of three churches have opened every two days, and this does not include the tens of thousands of meeting points which have opened in this time. We have distributed over ten million Bibles, and opened thirteen centers of theological education with several hundred students. Though we are not completely satisfied with the implementation of the policy of religious freedom, can all this be considered typical of a country where religion is seen as the enemy or where religion is being destroyed?

We should not be satisfied with mere statistics of success. Chinese Christianity is facing many problems that our Nanjing Union Theological Seminary alumni/ae should give their attention to and reflect upon. Let me mention just one:

In the last decade or so, Chinese intellectuals have had a more open attitude toward Chinese Christianity than ever in the past. But we Chinese Christians are greatly lacking in the ability to respond and carry on a dialogue with them. We very much need a group of Christian intellectuals with expertise in a variety of fields that would command respect. Such Christian intellectuals should not only worship in our churches, but should take part in church leadership at all levels. They should also enter all sorts of specialized groups where they could meet others in their field, share their faith, contribute to these disciplines and play a role on the international scene. These specialized disciplines include the creative arts and drama, as well as the study of religion as part of the social sciences. We need to form a strong corps of theologically oriented intellectuals with original ideas they can convey in a reasoned and convincing way, intellectuals who can also propound their ideas as Christians from a socialist society with Chinese characteristics in international theological circles.

Since I have not written to you in some time, as soon as I begin I find there is a great deal to say, but I will stop here. I would like to thank my colleague, Zhao Zhi'en (Lecturer in New Testament at Nanjing Seminary), of the alumni/ae working group, who keeps in touch with so many of you. To all of you alumni/ae who give their all for China and the Chinese Church, my best wishes for your physical, mental and spiritual health and well being.

—February 12, 1995

# FAITH WITHOUT WORKS DOESN'T DEMONSTRATE GOD'S LOVE

As a Bishop, who is also President of the China Christian Council and Chairperson of the Three-Self Movement, I frequently receive letters from people in churches all around the country. Some of my correspondents write that they are worried by the idea that believers will go to heaven while non-believers will go to hell. They are upset over this way of understanding God's justice, yet they do not dare to bring it out into the open.

Justice is an ethical concept. From childhood I knew that justice should be done in our world. But those hypocritical Pharisees in Judaism (Jesus often called them hypocrites) defined "justice" in ways ordinary people can hardly fathom. For example, the commandment to keep the Sabbath was originally imbued with the spirit of humanitarianism, giving people one day in seven as a day of rest, as well as a day when they could remember God. But the Pharisees came up with all sorts of strict observances to trip people up: all activities must cease on that day, even how long a distance one might walk was regulated (one faction said you could only walk as far as you could throw a stone). Harvesting wheat was also forbidden and if one of your sheep fell into a well you were forbidden to save it. It is said that some of the Pharisee sects had several thousand of these regulations. Those who observed them were said to be just, otherwise one offended against God's commandment on the Sabbath. Jesus was against the Pharisees. He said they "tie up heavy burdens hard to bear, and lay them on the shoulders of others," and "do not practice what they teach." Paul was loyal to Jesus. His mention of justification by faith in Romans and Galatians was meant to free people from these fetters, to liberate human nature. Paul wrote of the principle of justification by faith in order to allow people to throw off the Pharisees' inhumane strictures on circumcision, keeping the Sabbath, and so on. Only in this way could Christianity break out of the Jewish restrictions and spread to the non-Jewish peoples of the Mediterranean. Only in this way could Christianity evolve from a small Jewish sect into a world religion.

European Catholicism of the Middle Ages also fettered people. It imposed a strict hierarchy on the people and introduced the sale of indulgences. When there was a death in the family and people were grieving, the church announced that indulgences could be bought for a fee. The time of suffering the dead person's soul would have to endure in purgatory was reduced by the amount of indulgences bought. More indulgences meant less suffering. To attack this system oppressing the people, Martin Luther once again lifted high the banner of justification by faith. The church he founded is still known in Chinese as the "church of justification by faith."

Therefore, historically, when advanced religious people like Paul and Martin Luther put forward justification by faith, it was to extend justice, oppose the dark forces of authority, cleanse and simplify religion and seize freedom for the people. The original meaning of justification by faith was progressive. It was a banner of human liberation. Its goal was never to consign people to hell.

Many foreign missionaries came to China in the 19th and 20th centuries and many of them were anxious to attract people to Christianity. They joined justification by faith to the concept of paradise and hell.

And many Chinese, anxious to enter heaven, accepted this. The message of justification by faith was thereby changed: God did not care if your actions were just. God would not ask if you had been selfish or if you had sacrificed for others. God cared only if you believed or not. If you had been a believer in your life, then no matter how selfish or cruel you might have been, you would go to heaven when you died and enjoy eternal blessings. But if you had been an unbeliever, no matter how much you had done for others or for society, after death you would go to hell, where the flames burn for eternity. These people advocated antinomianism, saying God cared nothing for people's good deeds. In this way they were denying the ethical content of the Bible and making God into a selfish (those who believe in me are good; those who do not are evil) God that makes no distinction between truth and falsehood, good and evil. This, of course, is not the view of God we find in the Bible.

There is a growing number of Chinese Christians today who find it hard to accept this idea of faith without works. As one pastor told me in his letter: "My conscience will not permit me to continue to say that non-believers will go to hell." The reason is simple. Looking at the many people like Zhang Side, Lei Feng and others who did not accept Christianity, yet sacrificed their lives for others, he has seen that they are of noble character. How can we tolerate the idea that they are now in hell? My attitude to all those co-workers and fellow Christians who have written to me, unafraid to tell me openly about the doubts they have hidden deep in their hearts of faith, is one of sympathy and understanding. I do not condemn them.

I believe that the God shown forth in Christ is a God of love. This attribute of love comes before and above all other attributes of God. This view of God does not allow me to make God so cruel and brutal that God could send millions of people to the eternal flames of hell. Imagine how many new lives are brought into this world each day at any single maternity hospital in any of our cities and the indescribable joy of their parents. God certainly knows that many of these will not be believers, yet every moment he creates more new lives. If what awaits most of them some decades along the road is eternal hellfire, then God is not a God of love. This is a God more like the King of Hell feared by so many in Chinese folk religion. Have we Christians been influenced by such beliefs, that we think of our God in this way?

Einstein pointed out that the development from a religion of fear to one of ethics is an important step forward in the evolutionary history of religion.

The four gospels tell the life of Jesus. From them we know that though Jesus sometimes spoke of paradise and of hell, he never made belief/unbelief the standard for whether a person went to heaven or hell. Read chapter 25 of Matthew's gospel beginning at verse 31. Here we see that when the Son of Man comes in his glory, he will ask what we have done for others; for in visiting those who are sick or in prison, in feeding the hungry and giving drink to the thirsty, in clothing the naked, in welcoming the stranger, we are doing these things to him.

In the last judgment described here, God does not ask whether we were believers or non-believers. He asks what we did for the impoverished. This is to say that God cares about ethics. The heart of our God is so broad, so filled with love that he could not send some people to hell simply because they did not believe in him.

This is an important passage of Scripture. There are still Christians in China who do not value this passage, who pass over it without pause. For over forty years, countless people in our country have been working in great projects to alleviate poverty, to help the people out of poverty, to achieve a comfortable standard of living and move on to being prosperous. Is this not one with what we find in this biblical passage? It is only right that we Christians also strive for this.

Throughout the Bible, Old and New Testaments, there are innumerable passages that lift up ethics. Six of the Ten Commandments are concerned with ethics. All of the proverbs "exhort people to do good." Jesus said, "For the Son of Man came not to be served but to serve, and to give his life as a ransom for many." Jesus does not set redemption and service at odds with each other here. He says "and" not "but," meaning that giving oneself for many is also to serve. We should not use redemption to cancel out serving, nor should we use serving to deny redemption. In our pulpits and theological seminaries, we should preach the whole gospel, according to the Bible.

There are many other doctrines in Christianity besides justification by faith: God is love, the continuing process of God's creation, the Incarnation, the renewal of creation which comes with Christ's resurrection, the indwelling of the Holy Spirit that brings wisdom, the Sermon on the Mount, the greatest commandments of love for God and loving one's neighbor as oneself, of doing unto others as you would have them do unto you, of serving rather than being served. Paul said that there are faith, hope and love, these three, but the greatest of these is love. The virtue of love is higher than the virtue of faith. How can we ignore this? The biblical message is so very rich for us. If we highlight one doctrine and ignore its historical context, thus playing up the contradiction between belief and unbelief, this will surely damage the unity of our people and lead to endless divisions. What kind of witness will we be able to make then?

It is in lifting high morality that the excellence of Christianity and other religions lies. China is an ancient civilization, a nation of morality and ritual. For Chinese intellectuals especially, a discussion of ethics will be more appreciated than a discussion of paradise and will be more likely to make the religious message heard.

—Speech at an All Religions Meeting, 1996

# RESPONSIBILITIES OF HIGHER CHRISTIAN EDUCATION

Now that students have returned to the seminary to resume their student life after the summer vacation, it seems to be an appropriate time for me to ask the question "What is a seminary?" "What does a seminary do and not do?" Both in China and overseas, there are seminary students who are not clear about this, even up to the time they graduate. This results in difficulties for themselves and for others.

There is an unhealthy phenomenon in the church, which to some extent has become a tradition: the middle character *xue* in the word seminary, which means to study, is not taken seriously or is even opposed. There are those who dislike study or learning, are against knowledge, against research, against thinking, believing that these are matters that use the mind. They are opposed to using the mind. They think that using the mind is something that is unspiritual, something that gives way to satan. They are against thinking and learning. They prefer to receive the Lord's message through the interpretation of dreams or other practices associated with grassroots religion. This is deceiving oneself and others.

At Jinling Theological Seminary, we look at things differently. Those who are in a seminary or school ought to look at things differently. We think that the mind, like other parts of the body, has been created and given to us by God. Mark, Chapter 12 verse 33, tells us to love God with all our hearts, all our mind, and with all our strength. In the English version of the Bible, "with all your mind" when translated into plain Chinese, means "to use your brains." For the holistic development of seminary students we need the following: spirit, compassion, knowledge, experience and community. In the midst of this is knowledge. Therefore, the seminary is not a monastery even if we do not hesitate to set aside time for devotions. We are not against preaching but we are not a preaching institution. We do not encourage faculty and students to go forth to preach and heal. This is not a hospital and we do not perform faith healing. Our seminary is a place for researching into and understanding our faith and church doctrines. And this is where we should put all our focus and energy.

Christ came into the world 2,000 years ago. In these 2,000 years, the church's fundamental beliefs have remained unchanged. The Trinity, the incarnation of Christ, His death on the cross to save the world, His resurrection from the dead on the third day—these remain unchanged. But the world itself is changing, society is changing, people's perspectives are changing. Theological exposition of our basic faith needs to be adapted. The world is changing, the era is in change, students of theology cannot just sit back and relax. They must continually find new ways of interpreting our unchanging faith.

Let me give an example: There are those who pay much attention to propagating the gospel. What they preach is that Christ died on the cross for the forgiveness of sins, so that human beings may be reconciled with God; they ask that others may be reconciled, ask others to accept salvation. However, what is the relationship between the crucifixion and the reconciliation between God and human beings? These evangelists probably will not be able to explain it clearly. This is a theological question. We should first examine the basis for our claim. We often use the word "redemption." In the Bible, it is said "to be the ransom (redemption) of many" so that many will be saved. What is the meaning of this "ransom"? Who is the giver and to whom is it given? Some say it is given to the Lord. Some say it is given to the devil. Should not the evangelist be clear about this? Theology precisely deals with these kinds of questions.

To give another example: Today, we are all concerned about the status of women in society and there is growing consciousness about equality between men and women. How then do we explain Paul's epistles in which he says that women are not allowed to preach in assemblies and are to obey their husbands? This is a question of biblical authoritativeness. Our students and faculty should have an appropriate explanation and should not be vague and ambiguous when preaching the gospel.

There are many issues which the seminary needs to help our fellow students address. If we blindly evade them and do not provide fair and reasonable explanations, then we will simply be relying on our enthusiasm in evangelizing and in running the church. Inevitably, we will be leading believers astray. Those who would be willing to come and listen and believe would be those who are ignorant and foolish and this would bring about a steady decline in the Chinese church. Those who are educated would not bother with the church at all. There is no way we can justify this before God. The only feasible way is for the church to strive at raising its theological and cultural standards, so that it will gain the respect of people from all walks of life, so that believers will come from all levels of society. This is a responsibility we cannot shirk.

Today, the Chinese church is undertaking theological reconstruction. Seminary faculty and students should not lag behind but should catch up. We need to reconstruct our theology, renew it and shed new light to illuminate the church's unchanging faith.

Let us offer before God, the future of the Chinese church, that we may receive the guidance of the Holy Spirit.

> Where there is corruption in the church, Lord, we ask
> that it be cleansed
> Where there is ignorance and obstinacy, Lord, we ask
> for redress
> Where there are deficiencies, Lord help us to fill the
> gaps
> Where there is division, Lord grant us forgiveness and
> love.
> Where we have failed to bear witness to the Lord, we
> ask your help
> Where there is pride, conceit and selfishness, Lord we
> seek your guidance.
> Where there is humility, compassion, unity and love,
> we ask for God's blessings and strength
> We ask all these in the name of Jesus Christ our Lord.
> Amen.

**℘**

# FINDING GOD'S IMAGE IN MAN

We Christians should carry out theological reflection often, if not constantly. We do not reflect on things within some kind of void but rather we ponder over things in the light of our encounters with real-life situations. Our theological viewpoints are constantly challenged by what we meet in real-life, thereby undergoing constant revision, enhancement and renewal.

A theological seminary is not a "Land of Peach Blossoms" (that is, a haven of peace) where we are allowed to cast aside all the different contradictions that exist in the world. When we come to a theological seminary we do not seek to avoid reality. We must have dealings with the real world, have contact, have encounters. Yesterday, Student Union leaders came to my home to have a chat over a cup of tea. The talk turned to one female student who had planned to give 10 *yuan* toward flood-relief efforts. She prayed about it and, during her prayers, the hymn "My Neighbor Is Beside Me" kept playing inside her head. In the depths of her soul, there seemed to be a voice tugging at her, "These people in the disaster areas are my neighbors." Having such thoughts, she said to herself, "I shouldn't just give 10 *yuan*, I should give 50 *yuan*, give of my compassion to the people in the disaster areas." I am not saying this in order to get everyone to increase their giving. In fact, students don't actually have a lot of money to spare, so if they can give one, three or even five *yuan*, then it is already a very good thing and expresses their involvement and a certain disposition to want to help. I mention this case merely because this student's faith does not exist within a void, rather, it has found a point of contact with the real world. I don't know this student's name, but I am pleased that we have such a student, and we certainly have many others like her.

You all know of Martin Luther. Martin Luther once wrote 95 theses for the reform of the Church and stuck them on the door of a church building. Did he conjure up these 95 theses out of thin air? No. They were a product of the process of his struggle with the papal system. Martin Luther constantly rubbed up against the real-life situations around him and was molded by them. This enriched his theological thinking and only then did he produce his famous 95 theses.

When Jesus went to the garden of Gethsemane, it was not with the aim of casting off the cares of the world. He took with Him the problems of the time and went there to pray, to seek His heavenly Father's will. After praying there, Jesus lifted His head and went directly toward Golgotha, where He shed His own blood on the cross for the salvation of all the people of the world. He thus went to Gethsemane first of all to "recharge his batteries" or "set his watch." Perhaps you don't know what "set his watch" means? In the past, watches relied on the movements of clockwork springs and were therefore not terribly accurate. Every day these watches could lose or gain a little. So, when people met, they often "set their watches" by each other.

In seminary we have a course called Systematic Theology. Theology needs a system. The different branches of theology need coordination, need to be brought into line with each other, need to be unified as a whole. We need to make sure there are no contradictions between them. An individual person's theological thinking needs to become a harmonized whole. One's theological viewpoints need to hang together. We don't want to talk about one thing one moment and then suddenly find ourselves maintaining the opposite or the negative of that viewpoint the next moment. When an evangelist starts going on about how the floods are the punishment of God against human beings, what has happened to the biblical revelation that "God is love"? This is an example of inconsistent theological thinking. Such thinking has not been systematized and does not take into account the whole Bible in order to confirm the knowledge we have about and attribute to God.

In the Old Testament we find a person called Jonah. God sent him to go to the city of Nineveh and preach a message of repentance. But Jonah was very eager for the people of Nineveh to receive God's punishment because they did not repent. So, he preached to the people of Nineveh that, after 40 days, God would destroy the city of Nineveh. Jonah's theological thinking contradicted itself, was fragmented and incomplete. Because "God is love," God's inherent loving nature causes Him to love all the sons and daughters that He has created, including those sinners in the city of Nineveh. God has unlimited compassion, and He longed for the people of Nineveh to repent. God hoped His love would move the people of Nineveh to repent, and He was not going to punish them or cause them to be wiped out. The destruction of the city of Nineveh was not at all what God had in mind. Within Nineveh, there were some 12,000 small children who hadn't yet learned to distinguish their left hand from their right. How could God be so hardhearted as to destroy them? In the end, the people of Nineveh did indeed repent and God was delighted. However, Jonah brooded over all this and took it to heart.

*ᔥ*

The topic I want to discuss with everyone here is "My Theological Reflections These Days." I want to talk about two things. The first is:

given today's circumstances, how are we to view God? The second is: given today's circumstances, how are we to view human beings? When the flood peaks came, every second of every minute saw torrential waters rushing in over tens of thousands of square meters of land. People were unable just to stand still and stay put where they were, as they would certainly be swept away by the swift currents of the flood-waters. After the Yangtze River's eight flood peaks, which lasted for a period of two months, the resultant disaster was such as has not been seen for many years. The floodwater which wreaked havoc swallowed up tens of thousands of lives, to say nothing of the many homes which were wiped out in an instant. Now that this huge disaster has befallen us, we are compelled to ponder on how we are to understand the God we believe in. Could it be that God is not love? Does God create here and destroy there? These questions are ones that we Christians especially need to reflect on clearly.

During World War II, Hitler, through his brutal nature, was responsible for over five million Jews being herded into chambers without any windows within concentration camps. Their gold fillings were extracted for later use and then, while the prisoners were still alive, gas was let into the chambers and they were poisoned to death. At that time, within the German church, there were some church leaders close to Hitler who said that the sin of the Jews was so great that it was only right that they were receiving the just punishment of God.

Judaism and Christianity both hold that God is an all-powerful Father. After the Holocaust, one Jewish Rabbi named Rubenstein wrote a book in which he said that there could only be four possibilities concerning God: 1) that He is all powerful but not loving; 2) that He is loving but not all-powerful; 3) that He is neither all-powerful nor loving, 4) that He is both all-powerful and loving. Rubenstein said that his religious faith allows him to believe in the fourth possibility only. The fact of the five million or more Jews subjected to murder, however, caused him to be unable to sustain a faith in an all-powerful Father. He announced that he was renouncing his faith in an all-powerful Father.

We Chinese Christians, especially now, also need to raise this question: With what meaning can we still say that God is an all-powerful

Father? Let us reflect on this a little. God's act of creation is an extremely long process. God is Lord of all creation. He is the same yesterday, today and tomorrow. Why do we need to have such a long period of creation? Because God's inherent loving nature causes Him to be unwilling to use the method of ordering people and compelling them to obey Him in order to complete His will. He is not willing to create countless robots that only know how to obey Him. What He longs for is fellowship. He cannot have fellowship with robots, He wants to create within the universe countless numbers of beings who, through teaching, nurturing, training, salvation, and sanctification, can fully co-operate and join in His work of their own accord. A new kind of humanity, which can share a common goal with Him and can enjoy fellowship with Him and with each other—this is what God understands to be the pinnacle of creation. These new people are to be the joy of God. They can comprehend the heart of God, can become partners with God, can carry out creation together with Him. As for the current time, however, the earth and the people on the earth are all "half-finished products" within God's ongoing process of creation. Regarding the earth, it has its beautiful aspects and also its destructive elements. Regarding human beings, they have wisdom and are able to glorify God, but they also have their destructive, evil and sinful, and weak sides. So, calling us "half-finished products" is not a bad description.

During the floods that recently occurred in China, thousands of heroes emerged who struggled to fight the floodwaters and sacrificed themselves to save others. And yet even they are still not the full realization of God's ultimate hope for complete and perfect people. They are still "half-finished products," because they still carry human weaknesses within themselves. They still have all the defects, all the flaws of half-finished products.

God is the Lord of creation. In the end, a world will emerge from His creation. In it, the people will all be like Mary, the mother of Jesus. They will, completely and of their own accord, accept God's will and not consider their own gains or losses. At that time, we will thus say that this world is complete. But, for now, the vast majority of people are still only half-complete. The whole material and natural world is only half-complete, still a very long way off from the distant image in God's mind of a complete, perfect and beautiful world. Thus, in today's world, natural disasters and human suffering still occur. But these are by no means God's will. The five million Jews gassed to death was not God's will, nor was it God's punishment. The ones God desires to see punished are the kind of people like Hitler. In the struggle against the floodwaters this year, we saw many people give of their precious lives, among them many People's Liberation Army (PLA) soldiers. This is also not God's will or God's punishment. It is a consequence and a product of the forces within nature upon a human society that does not correspond to God's will. Because our world today is still only half-complete, we have not yet attained a fully complete and perfect environment.

God is still an all-powerful Father, but His aims for creation and His image of that creation compel Him to create a new humanity, through salvation and sanctification (including teaching, guiding, nurturing, training), a humanity which has wisdom and which can voluntarily and of its own accord join Him in carrying out His creative process.

છ

The second question is: given today's circumstances, how are we to view human beings?

We are too often used to looking at the darker side of people. Through this year's floods, we need to see that there are also brilliant and great aspects to human nature, see that there is also a kind-hearted side to human beings. During the floods, many people forgot about themselves and sacrificed themselves for the sake of others and in order to save some of the country's resources. We should not turn a blind eye to this. After all we have seen and heard these days, we Christians should ask ourselves whether all this reveals a new aspect and a new challenge to our traditional view of humanity?

Recently, there was a very moving news report which was broadcast several times on television and which made a deep impression on me. In the report we saw a young child of primary school age who was wearing clothes on the top half of her body but whose clothes on the bottom half had already been ripped away in the torrent of the floodwaters. Her two little arms were firmly holding on to a tree trunk. Underneath her body the floodwaters extended as far as the eye could see. Several PLA soldiers in a small boat came up beside her and extended their arms to pluck her from the tree. They put her in the small boat and also took off their own clothes in order to cover her. In the end, the child was saved. This news item deeply moved the hundreds of thousands of viewers who witnessed it on their TV screens because it transmitted a message of deep love and noble humanity. We do not need to ask whether these PLA soldiers believe in Jesus or not, nor do we need to ask whether that little child believes in Jesus. The PLA soldiers did not have the heart to let that little child's life end, they wanted to save her. This is love. This is also love between neighbors in practice.

Not long ago, I also read in a Xi'an newspaper about one young person who had fallen into the water and couldn't swim. A PLA soldier who could swim went to rescue him, risking his life in the deep water in order to pull the young man to shore. After a period of time, the soldier found his energy was just about used up and he realized that it would be impossible to get both of them on to the shore alive. So, after the soldier had done all he could to drag the young man close to the shoreline, he suddenly used up the last of his strength to push the man on to the shore. The young man who couldn't swim was saved, but the PLA soldier, who could swim and who thus should be the one still alive, didn't resurface from the water. In order to save a person whom he didn't even know, he gave his own life. Is this not selfless love? At a meeting where he told of his experience of being saved, the young man shed tears. Jesus said that there is no greater love than when one gives up one's life for one's friends. But these two people could not even be called friends. The PLA soldier had gone as far as being able to exchange his own life for that of another—this is great love!

We see many such incidents on the TV and in the papers. This is love between people, loving one's neighbor. Christians have often said in the past that humans are creatures who are sinners and do evil, that there is no evil that humans wouldn't do, that they possess not a single redeeming feature. According to Calvin, human beings are nothing more than "five foot long worms." According to Nietzche, human beings are like festering sores on the body's skin. Do we not think that such descriptions are degrading toward human beings today? We cannot maintain that love only exists within Christianity or that only the love of Christians has any worth. We have now already seen that there are many expressions of love outside of Christianity. We Christians thus cannot avoid the responsibility of engaging in theological reflection to explain such phenomena.

This year's flood disaster has mobilized the whole country out of a sense of duty and, at same time, brought forth a wave of love. Uncountable numbers of many nameless ordinary people have shown that they possess selflessness and courage. Therefore, how can we join in saying that such people are merely "festering boils on the skin" or "five foot long worms"? We need to adjust our way of viewing people.

Sin exists within human beings and people by themselves have no way of casting off this sinful nature, they need the saving grace of Christ. This is a basic belief that we Christians hold. However, we would be ill-advised to simply dismiss people's goodness and say that people have no redeeming features at all, so that we can better propagate the saving grace of Christ. The tiny bit of goodness that people do possess also stems from God's creation and God's love, the same love that prompted Him to let His only son Jesus Christ go to death on a cross. As far as we theological students are concerned, this year's floods present a challenge. They stir our thinking, inspire us to reflect anew on many questions, and dare us to bid goodbye to many old ways of thinking and speaking. I appreciate Shakespeare's description in one of his plays, where he says how human beings are such fantastic works, so nobly ideal, with strength inexhaustible and actions like angels. He describes us as being the "cream of the universe," and the soul of all things created on earth. Shakespeare uses these words in order to sing the praises of human beings. We do not want to go back to a theological viewpoint that blindly enjoys scoffing at people and belittling people's worth. Our religion should not be a religion that takes great pains to belittle the worth of human beings. I am hoping to see the thriving and flourishing of a religion that affirms people's worth. Although human beings are still only "half-complete products" and still have their sins and flaws, they also still have the soul of the One who created heaven and earth. I hope there will be more and more seminarians who will go out and respond to what these times are trying to tell us.

Today we have talked about people's many, many expressions of excellence. Most of these are the good actions of people outside of the faith. When some Christians hear this they feel uncomfortable inside. They think recognizing that people outside of the faith can also do good deeds somehow reduces the meaning of Christ's atonement. Actually, this reveals a certain narrow-minded theological viewpoint. These people may be outside of the church, but they are not outside of God. 1 John says, "You know that God is righteous; then recognize that everyone who does what is right is His child." (1 John 2:29). We should welcome anything that is excellent among any people. This one theological thought alone is worthy of everyone's reflection.

Our understanding of God and of people is increased through our encounters with the real world. This process allows Chinese Christianity to be able to improve and renew its theology, and this is the aim of my sharing with everyone today. I do not, however, want to force my reflections on you. My goal is rather to encourage you to do a lot more reflection of your own, to go to God to "recharge your batteries," to go to Him to "set your watches," that your love may grow ever richer in knowledge and insight of every kind, enabling you to learn by experience what things really matter (Phil. 1:9–10).

## $\wp$

# CARING FOR GOD'S CREATION

I am a religious believer from China. Among China's one billion people, there are Buddhists, Muslims, Taoists and Christians, both Catholic and Protestant. Our religious beliefs are all different, but when it comes to the environment, we all feel this is an important question tied to the continued existence on this planet of our common humanity.

We Christians affirm the universe and all it contains as God's creation. This affirmation means that the created world is good and holy. The world is not under the occupation of any evildoer. The work of creation is ongoing; in the end it will overcome primitive chaos and the sinful harm humankind has done to the creation and bring both natural and human history to a condition where love, justice and reason are universal. The Christian concepts of the Incarnation and of redemption are sufficient to reflect the value of humanity. Perhaps we can look at the duty of religion in this way: to transform humanity from despoilers of creation into co-creators with God. The heroine of an ancient Chinese legend is called Nü Wo. When she discovered that a corner of the sky was about to fall, she repaired it with multi-colored stones.

But this is not the world we see today. People are doing so many things that lay waste to and despoil nature. Statistics show that every year over two million seven hundred thousand acres of forest are destroyed; if this continues for thirty years, the total area destroyed would be the size of India. Every year one million four hundred thousand acres of good cropland turns into desert. Carbon dioxide in the atmosphere is increasing because of human burning of charcoal, diesel oil and gasoline. The temperature of the earth is rising and if this "greenhouse" effect continues unchecked, in the 21st century there will be a great displacement of land suitable for cultivation. The melting of the northern and southern polar ice caps will raise the water level of the oceans and inundate certain cities. The damage done by industrial gases to the protective ozone layer around the earth will increase and the resultant strengthening of the sun's infrared rays will lead to a greater incidence of cancer in humans and animals.

None of this is incurable. Modern science can deal with these problems. What humanity needs today is the vision to see the earth's environment whole.

All of us religious believers should make an appeal for saving nature and saving the planet, for saving our air and our water. God's creation must be beautified, not despoiled.

To safeguard our earth, we need to unite with others who have the same goal. Anywhere you look, there are religious believers and non-believers, or those who believe differently from ourselves. But in matters of faith we can have mutual respect. Toward all those who are involved in improving the environment and developing the economy, we should be welcoming, grateful, supportive and cooperative. We express this idea in one short phrase in Chinese: "Seek the common ground while reserving differences." Forty years of experience have taught us that whenever we do things in this way, our efforts are crowned with success.

I want to make a special appeal to developing nations: In the mid-20th century, humankind can for the first time gaze upon the earth from space. What we see from this vantage point is the whole earth. The work of healing the planet has grown beyond the work of a single factory, region or nation. We can only approach it from a global standpoint. There is a very unjust state of affairs in the world today—the majority of pollution comes from the industrialized developed countries and many developing countries reap a great deal of harm from this. Take China for example. Only in recent decades have conditions been suitable for us to develop in agriculture, industry and culture; only recently have we been able to satisfy our people's needs. However, China has diverted a large amount of its limited resources to protecting and cleaning up the environment. No doubt many other Third World countries face the same dilemma in choosing between development and the economy. I have heard that some Latin American countries, oppressed by their debts to Western countries, have had to use natural resources which might have contributed to their development to pay off their debts. The annual per capita income of many developing countries has not increased, but decreased over the past decade. It is my hope that as developing countries face this global crisis, they proceed from both a sense of moral responsibility and self-interest in considering how to fulfill their responsibility.

As far as I know, all religions have those adherents who feel they only need to be concerned about the things of heaven. For them, concern for the sufferings of people on earth means lack of love for the transcendent or the spiritual. This is a bad thing. How I wish they could understand that it is equally correct for religion to be concerned about life after birth as it is for it to be concerned about life after death. Cutting down the forests, polluting the air, contributing to the rise in the earth's temperature are also forms of murder, though not as obvious as shooting someone. Ignoring the ecological balance is destruction of God's creation; it leads imperceptibly to the deaths of countless innocent people. The natural world is suffering and cries out to us. I believe that people's concern with the ecology today is God's way of showing his care for and response to this concern. Let us join together in hoping and praying for the coming of a world of love, harmony and beauty.

—Speech, Moscow, 1990

# My View of These Fifty Years

The Three-Self Patriotic Movement (TSPM) of the Protestant churches in China is fifty years old this year—fifty years in which it has felt its way forward. Fifty years is a long time. As we look back on these years with grateful hearts we naturally tend to divide them into several stages in order to see the whole movement more clearly. I am sure that everyone would have their own method for determining the divisions and each method would have its strong points.

In the earlier years, leftist political forces grew stronger in China and with the coming of the Cultural Revolution a perfectly good Three-Self Movement and all of Chinese Christianity were attacked together as anti-revolutionary poisonous weeds. Their treatment was unjust in the extreme and Christians, like all their compatriots, entered upon a long period of suffering. I believe this period was a disaster for *all* Chinese and not just for Chinese Christians.

Following the first period, Chinese Christianity should have been self-governing, self-supporting and self-propagating. This is a point on which the majority of Chinese Christians can understand, agree with and support. But they were not content with this. They were anxious that the Chinese church, in addition to being self-run, should be run well. With things returning to normal after the Cultural Revolution, one voice within the church sounded clearer and clearer. Self-governed must mean well-governed, self-supported must mean well-supported, and self-propagated must mean doing propagation work well. This became known as "running the church well" and this hope was expressed by Christians all over the country. Y. T. Wu's intention in initiating the Three-Self movement was to run the Chinese church well. But this demand that the church be well-run went beyond the mission the Three-Self Patriotic Movement had delineated for itself. When we established the China Christian Council outside the Three-Self organization in 1980, our purpose was to set up an organization that would complement the TSPM and guide our efforts in running the church.

My second period begins in 1980. Since then, the Three-Self Movement has entered upon a new period of running the church well. This is not meant to imply that all the tasks of the first period have been completed and can be set aside. This second period is the continuation of the first. It is an extension and enrichment. Only a Three-Self that runs the church well can satisfy believers and bring more of them to understand and endorse Three-Self.

Running the church well is a rich concept whose meaning includes recovery of church property, restoration of worship, opening new churches, running seminaries, printing and distribution of the Bible, publishing hymnals and church periodicals, ordination of new ministers, drafting all sorts of regulations for ordination, the management of the church and so on.

In the process of striving to run the church well, co-workers and fellow Christians will necessarily begin to ask themselves, privately or publicly: What does "running the church well" mean? Does it mean restoring everything to the way it was before liberation or before the Cultural Revolution? Does it mean modeling our church on a church in some other country?

## THE NEED FOR THEOLOGICAL RENEWAL

We are beginning to realize that theological renewal is a necessary and fundamental issue for running the church well, a crucial issue among many weighty issues facing the church. Many rather nice new buildings are going up at the various seminaries these days but the more important question is, with what sort of theology do we equip our theological students? We live in a socialist society. This being the case, how will our students adapt if we keep to the status quo of the 19th and 20th centuries, mechanically copying all the traditional ways received from the Western missionary movement?

To address this situation, we have identified that the crucial task for running the church well is theological renewal of reconstruction. Our Three-Self Movement has entered upon the highest and most important stage of its fifty years, the third period, the period of theological renewal.

President Jiang Zemin has said that we should actively guide religion to adapt to socialism. Adapting to socialism is a call to all sectors of society, politics, education, literature, art, and so on. It is not designed specifically to inconvenience those of us in religious circles and it is not simply a matter of words because thinking must be adapted as well. We Christians must further adapt in terms of theological thinking. This is especially important for TSM and CCC, for pastoral workers and for theological faculty and students.

We will never change our determination to uphold patriotism, to oppose imperialism, to sustain independence, self-government, self-support, and self-propagation. Nor will we change our purpose of running the church well through opening enough churches and seminaries and printing enough Bibles. The third period is in no way a negation of the first and second periods. It is a deepening of the first two and a theological enriching of them. The experience and wealth amassed in the first two periods will not be lost.

It is worth noting that we are not speaking of three unrelated movements but rather of three interconnected periods of one single movement, each period leading naturally into the next. Throughout the process of the TSM we must uphold independence, love of country and love of church, increased unity and the implementation of the three "wells."

Our future vision of the Chinese church is one that is rich in a theology that respects reason and is more suited to Chinese socialist society. It will be one that can help believers to establish a more harmonious and reasonable faith and witness. Such a theology will gain the attention and ear of our people, especially in intellectual circles and in the Christian community worldwide. Christians overseas will be happy to engage in equal dialogue and exchanges with us. They will no longer take us lightly or say that China has no theology. I deeply believe that more and more Christians will recognize the urgency of theological renewal and be willing to dedicate themselves to this vision.

—*Tian Feng Monthly*, July 2000

ℰ

# DEVELOPMENT AND ENRICHMENT OF THE TSPM

This is the 50th anniversary of the Three-Self Patriotic Movement. Our view of those fifty years is closely related to how we will see the movement fifty years from now, and to how well TSPM/CCC run the church. I would like to share with you my own view of these past fifty years.

As I see it, there have been four high points in these fifty years. By high point I mean developments and clarifications in the organization's self-knowledge and guiding thought which had an all-round impact on its work, and which raised it to new levels.

1) Exposure of the relationship between Western missions and Western imperialism in China, raising the anti-imperialist consciousness of believers and advocating the three-self line of self-government, self-support and self-propagation. This was the beginning of Three-Self. We know that the reputation of missionaries is very high in

Christianity worldwide, and the courage and boldness our church dis-
played in daring to attack them, show that they served imperialism,
and announce our independence amazed Christian circles around the
globe, engendering both anger and criticism as well as praise and com-
mendation.

2) Since Three-Self was something new, well- and ill-intentioned
questions were raised both at home and abroad; enemies, in China
and overseas, sought to attack it; and in China itself, a mass movement in theology and biblical interpretation arose very naturally.
Many articles in which ordinary Christians discussed these issues
appeared in the church monthly *Tian Feng*. Some articles found evidence of Three-Self and patriotism in the Bible and in church history.
There were many responses here and abroad, and overseas there were
critiques of the missionary movement and calls for independence on
the part of churches in Asia, Africa and Latin America. All this confirmed the reasonableness of Three-Self and patriotism for our colleagues here. At the same time, a new discipline appeared in the West:
a "new missiology" which was a critique of traditional missionary
organizations and thinking, reflection on approaches and advocacy of
churches not being run by missionaries, but by Christians in Asia,
Africa and Latin America themselves. There was interest in learning
about the Chinese Three-Self Movement and some adopted a friendly
attitude toward it. Canadian Christians led the way in this transformation, which is still ongoing. This new missiological thinking continues
to have a great impact and has shaped an attack on the original "mission boards."

3) Running the church well. The aim of TSPM; that is, to enable
Christianity in China to be independent and to achieve self-government, self-support and self-propagation, is endorsed by the majority
of our co-workers and fellow-Christians. They also support running
the church well; that is, making it well-run, well-supported and a
church in which self-propagation is done well. Under the rubric of
running the church well, the China Christian Council was established
as a separate entity. But because of the long experience of ultra-leftism, many government cadres and co-workers in the church harbored
lingering fears that the slogan "run the church well" represented a

church standpoint separate from the standpoint and interests of the Chinese people. We knew that the Communist Party is atheist, opposed to religion, and we had heard them say that the church should gradually disappear; in that case why speak of running it well? I recall that Li Zuomin, assistant secretary general of the Central United Front Department held a long discussion with several dozen church co-workers one evening, in order to dispel our anxiety on this score, so that we might set our fears aside and go about running the church well. I also remember the deputy head of the Religious Affairs Bureau under the State Council, Wan Yaobin speaking at what must have been a meeting of the joint standing committee of the TSPM/CCC. He also told us that the government supported us in running the church well. We were delighted to hear it, and our experience in these years tells us that the Party also supports it. In fact the TSPM was founded in order to create conditions for running the church well, and the CCC was founded to serve as the body to run the church well.

4) Advocating theological reconstruction. There are very many aspects to running the church well and the solid construction of theological thinking in the Chinese Church is the most fundamental, most crucial step in running the church well.

At present, many Christians emphasize preaching the gospel and conversion. But if the message we preach is done up in outmoded theological thinking, can it attract modern people whose thinking has already undergone a great renewal? When the incarnate Jesus came into the world, he brought a new message, which we call the New Testament. The New Testament developed out of the Old Testament. Jesus often said, "You have heard that it was said to the ancients ...but I tell you ..." Our theological thinking also need to be renewed before it can persuade, before it can attract people's attention to the message of Christ.

Some of our co-workers have long been exposed to missionaries or theology teachers whose thinking is extremely conservative, and they like to say that they pay no attention to whether something is theology or not, but speak only of Life and faith. They say, if we have the Bible, faith and Life, that's all we need. We don't need to worry about right and wrong. I think they are mistaken. We are human beings, we can think, and these brains we think with were also given by God. If we use our brains, our thoughts will turn to issues and problems. As Christians, when we read the Bible, we cannot help but think of the issues raised by the Bible and by faith, we cannot help but be led to think of the challenges and attacks on faith occasioned by the real world. Human beings cannot exist without thinking and a church cannot exist without thinking theologically; there are no Christians without some sort of theological thinking. Whenever you say a few words about a passage in the Bible, whenever you pray, your view of God and your view of the Bible are apparent in your words, and this is theology.

Party Chairman Jiang Zemin calls upon religion to adapt to socialist society. I do not think we need to see this as prejudice against religion or some sort of harassment of religion. It is not only religion that needs to do this sort of adapting. The need also arises in education, literature and the arts, the social sciences and ethics.

Recently, among some co-workers, the idea arose that Three-Self was enough and that theological reconstruction was something they could take or leave, as they wished. It is also said that others concern themselves only with theological reconstruction, thinking that it has replaced Three-Self. If such tendencies exist, I think both are superficial. Chairman Jiang spoke of actively promoting the adaptation of religion to socialist society. We know that mere mouthing of slogans is a very low form of adaptation. Genuine adaptation must take place in thinking. For religious circles, this must be theological adaptation. Theological reconstruction is not simply making theology adapt to socialist society, it also removes theological obstacles to patriotism and socialism, providing an intellectual foundation for support of patriotism and socialism. And this was the original goal of the Three-Self Patriotic Movement. Theological reconstruction is one with the work of the TSPM; we should not place them in opposition to each other.

To enliven theological thinking, we advocate the diversification of theology in the church; it would be inappropriate to defer to a single authority. Theology in any church should be pluralistic. The Bible lifts up one Christ, one faith, but theological viewpoints should be many; we should not require that they be unified. We should not label someone an "unbeliever" simply because his or her theology is not our own. This makes the church into a "police state" where we are cut off from pastors and co-workers with views different from our own. At the least, this is unethical and unloving. To say someone belongs to "the unbelievers' clique" is to accuse them of being a false Christian, someone who should be ejected from the church. Who gives us the authority to judge?

It is not only on the church level that theological reconstruction is needed; every clergy and co-worker in our church needs individual theological reconstruction. In worldwide Christianity today, especially in the mainstream churches, there is a view that our clergy is lacking in theological thinking and have little of interest to say in dialogue. Cannot we as individuals do something to address this situation by improving our own theological awareness, step by step?

These are what I see as the four high points of the fifty years' of the TSPM. It was not my intention to see these as chronological; they are all part of the development and enrichment of the Three-Self Patriotic Movement of Protestant Churches in China.

# Section Four:
# OUR RESPONSES TO GOD'S LOVE

# LOVE NEVER ENDS

In Western literature—as well as in everyday speech—the names David and Jonathan symbolize friendship. People describe two persons who are very close as being just like David and Jonathan.

The story of David and Jonathan's friendship is recorded in the Book of Samuel in the Old Testament. Saul was King of Israel then and Jonathan was his son and heir. David served Saul. David was young and handsome and very talented in music. He was a fearless fighter against the enemy and had rendered a great service to the people of his land. The people loved him and this made Saul jealous. Saul was suffering from a mental illness, but David served him loyally. Saul both depended on David and wanted to destroy him. He threw his spear at David a number of times, thinking to kill him. Though David had many opportunities to get his revenge and kill Saul, the thought never entered his head. He protected Saul all along because he knew that Israel needed a leader like Saul to fight its enemies.

And what of Jonathan? He watched and saw his father's prestige wane day by day, while David's rose. If this kept up, David would win the people's support and replace Jonathan as King of Israel. If he had been selfish enough, he could have manipulated his father to have David eliminated. But there was no selfishness in him. He was not at all envious. He delighted in David and felt that for David to be king would be better for the nation than if he himself succeeded his father, so he used every means he could to keep him from danger. He argued David's case before Saul; he reported Saul's moods and movements to David, so that David could hide himself in time. The story of David and Jonathan's friendship has been told far and wide by later generations. Both Saul and Jonathan later died in fighting the Philistines. If David had been selfish enough, he might have found reason to be happy about this, but he was not like that. It brought him no joy. Instead, he was distraught at the loss of his dear friend.

The inclusion of this story in the Bible tells us that selfless friendship is wonderful and that love and intimacy between persons is precious and worthy of praise.

Many people today, all over the world, think they have seen through it all. Ideals, friendship, love, morality—all a lie. Only the self striving for its own benefit, is real. Jesus, who said, "No greater love does man have than to lay down his life for his friend," practiced what he preached. But these cynics say, what friend, what sacrifice? This is all crazy talk—devil take the hindmost, that's truth. They feel that the only possible relationship between persons is one of self-interest. One must be ruthless and try to outwit the others. Anything else is false.

I do not think a young person as cynical as this would come to seminary to study theology. However, we may have some students who have been influenced to some extent by such an outlook on life, who might sometimes wonder how much value there is in friendship, moral character, love, or even in Jesus' gospel of love? In coming to Christ and knowing him as Lord? If you have these doubts, let me say to you that such doubts can be answered. But let me also plead with you not to take the path of cynicism. At least give yourself another chance to see if your faith in love can be rekindled, and made to burn brightly.

We hope many more people will discover love and its preciousness, not only human love, but more, the love of God in the body of Christ. We hope they then go on to discover that love is in fact the ultimate and highest motive power behind this whole cosmos, this whole reality and all that exists, its ultimate, highest principle, the ultimate energy behind all energy. The highest attribute of the God revealed in Christ is not God's omnipotence, not God's omnipresence, not God's omniscience, not God's eternity, not God's overarching majesty, but God's love. This attribute surpasses the scope of humanity's perception and imagination. The human mind has no way to comprehend this attribute. Human speech has no words adequate to express it. Only through revelation can we discover that it somewhat resembles the best to be found in human parents. Exhausting the possibilities of language, we call God our Heavenly Father. Only by discovering this love, knowing it and being gripped by it, surrendering to it, can we make a clean break with cynicism.

We want many more people to discover love. If we have the love of Christ, many more things in this world will become worthy of love. Truth, scientific truth, the truth of salvation—are these not worthy of love? Goodness, goodness of heart, of action, of speech, like the innate goodness we see in Christ—are these not worthy of love? Beauty, physical beauty, beauty of mind and spirit and soul, the beauty of literature, sound and color, natural beauty, the beauty of worship—are these not worthy of love? A lofty faith, a constant faith and the hope born of this faith—are these not worthy of love? The gospel of Christ's sacrifice by which the world is saved—is this not worthy of love? In the footprints of goodness and beauty, we announce the gospel, spread the good news, so that all may hear it. Is this undertaking not worthy of love? If, faced with these lovable and precious things, a person still despises him or herself, still only pursues his or her own pleasure, how insignificant their actions are.

There are those who believe that though Christianity speaks of love, we cannot speak of hate and therefore cannot distinguish between true and false and cannot even oppose darkness, evil and error. This is, of course, wrong. Paul said: "(love) does not rejoice in wrongdoing, but rejoices in the truth" (1 Cor. 13:6). Love and hate are a pair of opposites. Without hate there can be no love. Where there is love, there is certainly hate. To rejoice in truth is surely to oppose falsehood; to oppose injustice is surely to uphold justice. It is worth repeating Diderot's words to artists: "It should be the intention of every upright man who plies a pen, a paintbrush or a sculptor's knife to make love more loveable, evil more despicable, and the bizarre more noticeable." I think that all of us who witness to the Lord with Bible in hand should also be included among their ranks.

What beautiful language Paul used to praise love in his letter to the Corinthians. Please note especially the words: "Love never ends" (13:8). Jonathan and David are no longer with us, nor is Paul, but love has not ended. Thousands of years of history have not erased it. Love's attraction grows and grows. Wherever we find a common ideal to sacrifice for it, there is love and there is friendship. Because God is love and God is an eternal God, love never ends. Thus we do not lose hope, even for the extremely selfish, even for the cynical. We hope they will finally be drawn by love, surrender to it, repent and come to the Lord. G. K. Chesterton said of the rose: "If a seed sown in the black soil can turn into such a beautiful rose as this, why cannot men's hearts, over the course of their long journeyings, also change and turn toward the source of all light?" I believe that within a fellowship of love, the little bit of love in each of our hearts can receive sunlight, moisture and nurture and open into beautiful flower.

Before you new students came to the seminary, you probably received a letter from me, did you not? In that letter I urged you not to see the seminary as some lovely garden, a haven set apart from the world, like the poet's hermitage in Tao Yuan's famous lines. We are part of the world, too. I cannot guarantee that all your experiences here will be good ones. But I think you should view the seminary this way: as a community in the Lord, a big family, a place where students and faculty are both learning how to accept the Lord's love. We are all learning, everyone is unfinished, no one is perfect and whole. The lesson of love—this is the most important lesson we Christians have to learn. Our big family here is not as complicated as that of the extended Jia family from the classic novel *Dream of Red Mansions*, but neither is it at all the case that everyone knows exactly what to do for the best in everything. My purpose in introducing David and Jonathan is not to tell you to make friends two by two. My feeling is that our relationships with each other should be like that of David and Jonathan, so that Christ's love continues to be the mainstream of the seminary, enabling each of us not only to hope that others will treat us with love, but more often, to ask ourselves how we can better love—love Christ, love the Church, love the country, love the school, love our teachers, love all our students. I remember a line from one of Goethe's poems: "It is blessed to be loved, but to have someone to love is even more blessed."

There are things here at the seminary that are not ideal. But the strange thing is that almost all our alumni have deep affection for the seminary. These feelings seem to grow much deeper after they leave school. Not long ago I ran into an alumnus while I was overseas. I had once criticized him wrongly while he was at seminary and I asked his forgiveness. He replied: "If there was unfair criticism, I've forgotten it.

What I remember is that when I left school, you walked with me to the gate and said you hoped I'd return soon." He said he saw his alma mater as a mother and wanted to come back regularly to see each flower and tree. So you see what, with the passage of time, is memorable about our school and what is forgotten. When I went to Fuzhou recently, a number of alumni took three- and four-hour bus trips to meet me, just to exchange a few words, take a few pictures. I was very moved and very grateful. Unhappy experiences quickly fade, while these sweet memories will never end. The seminary you have come to is special in this way. It is not easy to explain, it is something we can only thank God for.

David and Jonathan's friendship was a youthful friendship. They were patriotic young people. If you look at David's life, his love for God stands out. He wrote many psalms of praise for God as well as psalms of repentance. The thing that was most memorable for him in his later years was the building of the temple for Yahweh. It was an aspiration he had to pass to the next generation. The context of the Chinese Church today is the same. In the twenty-second chapter of 1 Chronicles, we read how David prepared for Solomon's building of the temple: "Now my son, the Lord be with you ... in building the house of the Lord your God ... With great pains I have provided for the house of the Lord one hundred thousand talents of gold, one million talents of silver, and bronze and iron beyond weighing, for there is so much of it; timber and stone too I have provided ... stonecutters, masons, carpenters, and all kinds of artisans without number, skilled in working gold, silver, bronze and iron. Now begin the work, and the Lord be with you."

We need not pose as a David or a Saul, but the message in this passage of the Bible cannot be denied. The new generation of believers among us cannot but hear the call of the older generation: "Young Chinese Christians, the Lord be with you, so that you may succeed in building the Chinese Church. We have prepared what is needed for the house of God; we have laid the foundation. Now begin the work, and the Lord be with you."

Our common goal is to build the house of God in the land of new China, so that all the people may see the light of the gospel. I am sure all of you are aware of the heavy responsibility we bear. Let us learn the lesson of love, so that our church may become a vessel worthy to be used by the Lord.

—Nanjing Seminary, Fall Semester,
September 4, 1983

&)

# THE BREADTH AND DEPTH OF
# THE LOVE OF GOD

In several lectures given here recently, I have spoken about God by speaking about women first. After several thousand years of patriarchal societies, we humans have become used to viewing God as male and to perceiving the loving heart of God through the role of the father. Human beings are not used to perceiving the loving heart of God through the female or mother love. The result is that our knowledge of God's love is incomplete and lacking in richness. Let me once again stress the special contribution women believers make to our view of God. I hope that women Christians have a sense of mission about the contribution they can make in this regard and that they will be bold to study the Bible and do theology independently, so that the church may gain a fuller and richer view of God.

Let us consider today the story found in 1 Kings 3:16–28. Two women who had just given birth appeared before Solomon. One baby was living; the other had been crushed when its mother lay on it. Only the two of them knew who was the mother of the living baby. Solomon was about to cut the living baby in two with a sword, half for each woman. The two mothers had completely different reactions to this. The woman whose own baby had been crushed by her was filled with envy; when she heard that the living baby was to be killed, she felt a rush of satisfaction. To her, there was nothing wrong with neither of them having a baby. She praised Solomon's decision. But the true mother of the living baby felt differently. She loved the baby and wanted it to live. This baby's life was so precious. As long as it lived, it had hope and a future. Whether the baby would return to her or not could be left for the future, but by no means could she let it die. Thinking that her baby would be cut in two, "compassion for her son burned within her," and she said, whatever happens, it must live, let her take it.

As we have seen, one of these mothers' hearts was filled with envy. Envy made her ruthless, made her hate life. In order that another woman not gain the joys of motherhood, she was even willing to allow an innocent baby to be chopped in half—perhaps the prospect even made her happy.

The other mother was so different and the difference between them lay deep in their hearts: this mother's heart was filled with love, love for the baby, love for life. She could endure insult because her love gave her hope and faith that sooner or later right would triumph over wrong, truth over falsehood and life over death.

I have not thought about this story for a long time. Recently we have been discussing the issue of Hong Kong's return to China. Hong Kong was Chinese territory, but was taken by England after the Opium War. Now the two governments have signed the Joint Declaration, Hong Kong will be returned and the two sides guarantee Hong Kong's prosperity and stability. The people of Hong Kong and their compatriots on the mainland are all very happy about this. But some people in the world and in the church do not want to see Hong Kong returned to the embrace of the motherland. These people want to apply so-called "tough measures" against China, and if they can, create chaos within Hong Kong—as long as no one gains, they balk at nothing. Doesn't this seem very like the envy of the bad mother?

Moving from Hong Kong to Nanjing and to our school, we find that the story has something to say to us, too. It asks us whether our common life permits mutual envy, hatred or tearing down—of course, it must not. Destroying others in order to get what we want is the worst thing we can do. What we want is mutual building up and mutual care. There must be genuine brother-sister relationships among all of us. Recently some students approached a group of teachers on behalf of a large number of their fellow students to express their concern for the atmosphere in the school. They were afraid that if our school did not deal strictly with certain bad things, many students would lose confidence in the school. This raised for us a very important and proper demand; it was also a great expression of support. We certainly cannot disappoint the students.

Let us turn back to the good mother in the Bible story. In her we have a blurry glimpse of the nature of God's love. This love embraces a care and protection for life. In order to allow human beings not to lose life but gain it, God is willing to sacrifice himself, become flesh, teach us, and give his very life. Our knowledge of this God is very small. I hope that through greater spiritual formation, more Bible reading and more theological reflection, more fellowship and, especially, through greater practice, we will all receive greater revelation, and in this way have a richer perception of the broad and deep love of God.

—Talk at Nanjing Seminary, 1986

# THE FRAGRANCE OF THE GOSPEL

Here in China, as well as overseas, in the church and in society, people are asking: Why are people in China turning to Christ? What is it that attracts them to the church?

Why does this question arise? Perhaps because people wonder why people still think about the things of God when the threats of aggression, war, hunger, exploitation and unemployment have receded considerably in China today. Perhaps it is because people wonder why someone would still become a Christian when being a Christian does not confer the rights and privileges it did in the past. Or it might be because Christians account for less than one per cent of China's population and Christianity is still viewed by many as superstition or a foreign religion—nothing special, hardly worth a second glance. Or perhaps the question arises because people wonder how long Chinese Christianity can last, when it is so small and weak and gets no donations or support from overseas? What is it then that makes some people want to sing the hymn "I Now Come to the Lord?" Different people, of course, have different answers to this question.

Some people attribute it to the influence of parents, family, friends, or Christian publications. There is such influence, no question about it, but such an answer skirts the original question, changing "why" into "how."

Others attribute it to the policy of freedom of religious belief: When there is freedom to believe, there will be people who believe in Christ. Of course, it is important that there is freedom of belief. However, would people believe simply because of the freedom of belief? Such an answer points up an important condition, but does not provide the most basic reason.

Another opinion says the numbers of religious believers have increased because there is a "crisis of faith" in China; i.e., people are not satisfied with socialism and have lost confidence in the government. This response ignores the facts somewhat. The masses of believers support socialism. They are actively involved in socialist construction and many have been selected as advanced producers and advanced workers. Before 1949, the people's complaints against the then government rose on all sides, they had no confidence in it at all. Why did the number of Christians not grow beyond a few hundred thousand during those years?

Still others give all the credit to Three-Self: When Chinese Christianity threw off its foreign image, people were willing to hear the gospel message. Three-Self was of course essential, but this response too turns an important condition into a basic reason.

There are those who claim that the church attracts people because of the good fellowship within the church—people are close, sympathetic, united, like brothers and sisters. Yes, this is how the church should be and many churches are just like this, but not all or not always. Interpersonal relationships in some churches leave a lot to be desired. Some people are disappointed, but still they do not leave the church—they say you have to keep your eyes on God, not on other people.

And finally, some give credit to miracles, faith healing and exorcism. But this is like the people who came to Jesus seeking healing or to be filled by eating the food, and left after a time (see John 6:66). How much less today can these things—healing and casting out of spirits, people raised to life through prayer, things that rely heavily on chance and not a little on cheating people—truly attract people to the Lord of Life? Paul did not detract from the gospel of Christ by treating it as some kind of healing trick. He tells us that Christ did not take away his physical weaknesses in spite of his prayers. Instead Christ told him: "My grace is sufficient for you, for power is made perfect in weakness" (2 Cor. 12:9). Is not the ability to recognize this a greater and more profound spiritual harvest?

None of the explanations given above will do. It seems that we must look for causes internal to the Christian gospel and not external ones, and we must first find the most fundamental of the internal causes.

The response given by Peter in the sixth chapter of John is to my mind the most satisfying: "Lord, to whom can we go? You have the words of eternal life."

Humans are made in the image of God. Only humans raise many ultimate questions and it is these questions the Christian message answers. Of course it will attract people to listen, and some people, having heard, will decide to turn to Christ. Questions about eternal life are ultimate questions.

People are not mineral, vegetable or beast, not the usual type of animal. People can think, but neither are they just thinking machines. Humans are much higher than all of these. Humans have the image of God; they are the soul of creation. Not long ago I toured a factory. One of the workshops was about the size of our campus, yet it took only four or five workers working six hours a day to run it—for the other eighteen hours, it was operated entirely by robots. Robots have accurate memories and their work is more precise than that of humans. They can respond appropriately to any changes that take place in their surroundings, assembling, testing and shipping the most complex electronic equipment without skipping a beat. Robots are clever, cleverer than Peter or you or me. But as clever as they are, questions about eternal life will never occur to them.

Psalm 8 verse 3 says: "When I look at your heavens, the work of your fingers, the moon and the stars that you have established; what are human beings that you are mindful of them, mortals that you care for them?" Why do only human beings ask such questions? The fifth verse answers: "Yet you have made them a little lower than the angels, and crowned them with glory and honor." This is the kind of animal human beings are, one that can raise ultimate questions.

For example, Why do we live? We continue to live because suicide is so painful, is that it? Or are we born simply to live and so we do? Or do we live simply for food, clothing and desire? How should we live? We are not dead—is that life? We breathe; our hearts beat—is that life? We get rich through exploitation; we claw our way to the top by stepping on the backs of others—is that a good way to live? Some people seek only inner peace. Is a life of inner peace the meaningful life?

There is something called goodness in the world. Everyone knows you should be good. Kant said, "Two things fill the mind with ever new and increasing wonder and awe, the more often and the more seriously reflection concentrates upon them: the starry heaven above me and the moral law within me." The moral law Kant speaks of as being within the human heart is continually urging, reminding, telling us to be good people and not to do bad things. The role played by this urge to self-perfection could not be greater. It is precisely the functioning of this moral law which makes the world a place where, on the whole, humanity is able to live. What chaos there would be in the world if people did not have such a conscience, if everyone were consummately evil and suffered no regrets. Where, then, does goodness come from? What is the source of goodness? The reason so many people believe in God, whether we call him Shangdi, Shen, or Tianzhu, the Creator, is because they have found there the source of goodness. Otherwise there would be no way to explain where goodness comes from. And not goodness only, but beauty, truth, and many lofty thoughts and feelings—for all these, the question of their source arises.

Beethoven's Ninth is a beautiful symphony. It would be an over-simplification to say that Beethoven gave us the Ninth Symphony. A more satisfying view would be that beauty exists in the universe and that Beethoven, among the most musically advanced of us humans, was attracted by this beauty and expressed it in the Ninth Symphony, just as in the beginning was the Word and this Word was expressed in Christ.

We can be charmed by a performance on the violin. If we were told that this music that so charms us is simply a product of catgut and tightly strung wire rubbing together, along with the finger movements of the violinist, we would hardly find it a satisfying explanation. But if we were told it was a bringing together of a kind of cosmic and ever-lasting beauty on one side, and the soul of persons of high sensitivity on the other, with musician as intermediary, touching the heartstrings of the latter by actualizing the former to the latter's enjoyment, I think you would all agree this is a more complete statement.

There are many other ultimate questions. Why is the world not a better place? Why is there not more good, more good people and good things happening? Why do bad people often have upper hand?

What is death? Does death end everything? Does death destroy everything—good and evil, beauty and ugliness, the true and the false, firm principles and selling one's soul? The final fate of all these things is the same, all written off at one stroke, changed into nothing-ness—is that the way it is? If we read the four gospels, we get the feel-ing that this cannot be Christ's view. Take the question of death—many people have felt their way pondering this question and some of them, in their searching, have come to Christ.

A question even closer to home: I know what I should do, but I do not do it. I know what I should not do, but that is what I do. What is going on here? The more conscience a person has, the more one requires of himself or herself, the more sensitive they are to this ques-tion. The reason many people come to Christ in spite of testing and oppression, the reason that they are unwilling to be separated from the cross, which is the sign of Christ's salvation, is because they have come to know that only by staying close to Christ can they shake off this cycle of evil.

There are other what we might call high-level questions about human life which will not be asked in this world unless human beings ask them.

Socialism is good; it is lifting our country out of "poverty and blankness." We support it as a matter of course. But the problems socialism must solve are raising socialist production and undertaking material, cultural and moral reconstruction. Responding to what I call the ultimate question is not part of the task of socialism.

To show our concern about the big issues in our nation, we should read the newspapers, but what the newspapers report are materials about politics, economics, society, culture, education, art and so on. Newspapers need not play up what we call ultimate questions. At least in order to guarantee the unity of the people, people should not be allowed to use the newspapers to explore them.

However, Christianity does indeed explore these questions and responds to them. I am not speaking here of that Christianity which advertises healing and casting out demons, nor that Christianity that concerns itself with the minutiae of everyday life, the kind that swallows camels and strains out gnats. The Christianity I am talking about is the treasure in the clay vessel, not the clay itself.

What Peter said—"Lord, to whom shall we go? You have the words of eternal life"—represents a very high evolutionary stage in humankind's quest for truth. If humanity can reach this level, then it is sublime.

Some people believe that human beings are nothing but machines capable of sin. In Nietzche's eyes, human beings were "a disease on the skin of the earth." Sometimes we hear talks in our churches, too, that denigrate humanity. Calvin said some good things about human beings, but he also said they were no more than "a worm five feet tall."

If this were true, people would never raise ultimate questions. Then whose questions would the gospel of Christ be responding to? As the old saying goes, it would be like playing the lute to a cow ... to a bug ... to a skin disease.

The Incarnation is an affirmation of people, an affirmation that the questions people raise are worthwhile questions, an affirmation that people are worthy to be taught, worthy of being redeemed. God will not destroy people who can raise such high level questions.

Justin Martyr, a theologian of the ancient church, observed that in every person born, no matter who, there is the seed of the Logos—the Word. We can envisage Christ as a full circle, and we human beings as arcs, long or short, that comprise it. There are points in common, there are connections, between the relative and the absolute.

Today, as always, there are people seeking Christ. As always some are unwilling to leave Christ. We need not look further for the fundamental reason why this should be so. It is because we humans sense that Christ addresses questions that we have been feeling toward in our hearts. Christ brings light, offers a message. And he has some grievances against us, some reproaches, as well as comfort and encouragement. This is deep calling to deep.

The most fundamental thing is that the truth of the gospel itself attracts people. Precisely because of its truth, the work of witness is important, Three-Self is important, freedom of religious belief is important, the purification of the church, that the church not be a stumbling block to people turning to Christ, but a lampstand drawing them to the Lord—this is important. Theological education must be done well and the question of what kind of theological students and teachers we should be is also important. All these things come from the gospel truth.

Let us entreat the Lord to order our thoughts, that we may know what is clay and what treasure, that our love may grow and grow, in knowledge and every sort of experience, that we may discern right from wrong and return all glory and praise to God.

And now let us pray in the words of St. Anselm, a theologian who lived at the turn of the 12th century. Some Christians are not used to using the prayers of ancient saints when they pray and this is their loss. When we speak to each other, we always try to use the most precise and beautiful language to express ourselves. When we speak with God, should we not all the more seek the best language and that most able to aid us in our own formation? Let us try to be in spiritual fellowship with St. Anselm and let him help us to pray:

Have you found, my soul, what you were seeking? You were seeking God, and you found Him to be that which is the highest of all, than which a better cannot be thought; you found Him to be life itself, light, wisdom, goodness, eternal blessedness and blessed eternity, and to exist everywhere and always.

You are wholly present everywhere and I do not see you. In you I move and in you I have my being, and I cannot come near to you. You are within me and around me, and I do not experience you with my senses.

I pray, O God, that I may know you and love you, so that I may rejoice in you.

And if I cannot do so fully in this life, may I progress everyday until all comes to fullness; let the knowledge of you grow in me here in this life, and there in heaven let it be complete; let your love grow in me here and reach fullness there, so that here my joy may be great in hope, and there be complete in reality. Amen.

—The Fragrance of the Gospel, 1985

ॐ

# JESUS BRINGS GOOD NEWS

People do not accept Christianity all that easily; it contains many things that are difficult to understand. The cross is one of these. Resurrection is another. There are many difficult passages in the Bible as well and dark chapters in the history of the church. The organized church grows apart from ordinary Christians, contradictions and divisions arise: All this can produce stumbling blocks to faith. In spite of this, people have not backed away, but have felt the attractive power of Christian faith. In many places around the world the number of Christians is growing. Why is this? Some think people turn to religion out of suffering, humiliation or hopelessness. But not all the facts bear this out. China is an exception. After more than a century of arduous missionary toil, by 1949 there were only 700,000 Protestant Christians in China. In the past thirty-six years, when people enjoyed a greater level of peace and dignity, the number of Christians, has not fallen, but has grown four or five times. This has been beyond the expectations of social scientists who thought that religion would gradually disappear in a socialist society. This phenomenon has helped us Christians to understand that the main causes of conversion to Christianity are not necessarily suffering and helplessness. We can attain a healthier soul by identifying with and joining in the people's liberation and humanitarian undertakings. In the first chapter of Luke, Zechariah prophesies that when we have been saved from our enemies and from the hand of all who hate us, we can serve God without fear in holiness and righteousness. We thought that socialist revolution could not accommodate religion, but reality impelled us to ponder this anew and to see revolution as an opportunity for religion to be cleansed and grow.

Religion does have its faults, yet there are so many willing to have faith. What is it that gives religion this power of attraction? Peter gives the most satisfying answer: "Lord, to whom can we go? You have the words of eternal life" (John 6:68).

Humanity stands at the apex of the animal world. We are the only living organisms that are able to raise the question of the meaning of life. The message of Christianity, that is, the Way of Life, is the answer to this question. This is why, no matter what sort of social system they live in, people are willing to hear the Christian message. Upon hearing, some people will be bound to discover that their questions have been answered in Christ and they will commit themselves to him and search no further.

Not long ago I toured a factory. One huge workshop there was run by only four or five workers working six hours a day—for the remaining eighteen hours, it was operated entirely by robots. Robots' memories are very accurate and their work more precise that that of humans. They are capable of monitoring the conditions in the workshop and respond appropriately to any changes. They can assemble, test and package the product and send it to the warehouse. Robots are really very clever. I would guess they are cleverer than most of us here. However, they will never ask questions about the meaning of life. Eternity has no significance for them.

Psalm 8 verse 3 says: "When I look at your heavens, the work of your fingers, the moon and the stars that you have established; what are human beings that you are mindful of them, mortals that you care for them?" Why do only human beings ask such questions? The fifth verse answers: "Yet you have made them a little lower than the angels, and crowned them with glory and honor." Human beings are the highest form of animal; high enough to raise ultimate questions. Why do we live? Is it only to die? Some people seek only inner peace. Inner peace—is that the highest good?

There is goodness in the world. Immanuel Kant said, "Two things fill the mind with ever new and increasing wonder and awe, the more often and the more seriously reflection concentrates upon them: the starry heaven above me and the moral law within me." This inner moral law compels us to eschew evil and do good. The functioning of this moral law is one extremely important factor in making the world a more livable place. If one day people were to lose this inner law, the world would immediately descend into chaos. It is worth noting that for those who are more aware of conscience, doing good is not limited to rule-keeping. Under the urgings of conscience. they strive harder, they buck trends and are careless of personal safety in order to engage in the fundamental transformation of social orders that enslave, suppress and oppress.

Where is the source of goodness? Many people turn toward God. For if God is not the source of goodness, how can we explain it?

Beethoven's Ninth is a beautiful symphony. But it is not enough to say that Beethoven is its source. A better explanation would be that beauty exists in the universe and Beethoven has touched this beauty and expressed it in his Ninth Symphony. There is something similar here to the way the Logos is expressed in Jesus Christ.

There are many more ultimate or penultimate questions. Why is the world not a better place? Why is there not more good? Why do bad people and bad things not only continue to exist, but flourish?

What is death? Is death the end of everything? Is everything—good and evil, beauty and ugliness, truth and falsehood—finally vanity? Is everything destroyed by death? If we read the gospels, we will feel that this cannot be Christ's understanding.

In our everyday lives we find that we do not do the good we should do, but do the wrong we should not do. The more people follow their conscience, the stricter the moral demands they will make of themselves and the more susceptible they will be to confusion. Why should this be? How can one break out of this evil cycle?

Throughout the ages, these sorts of questions have been posed only by humankind.

The socialist system is suitable for China. It helped our people out of extreme poverty and enabled more and more people to live more human lives. So, in China we support this system as a matter of course. But socialism is concerned with raising the level of production and with reconstruction of the material and the moral. The ultimate questions Christians have been considering are beyond the scope of the socialist system.

When Peter spoke, he spoke as a member of humankind: "Lord, to whom shall we go? You have the words of eternal life." This shows that humanity has reached a high stage in its quest for truth, a stage which becomes an expression of the sublime heights of humanity.

Some people think that human beings are mere machines. In Nietzsche's eyes, humans were "a disease on the skin of the earth." And Calvin, at least once, permitted himself to call human beings "worms five feet tall." I do not think that their accusations were in line with the mind of Christ. Let me quote Hamlet. "What a piece of work is a man! How noble in reason! How infinite in faculty! In form, in moving, how express and admirable! In action how like an angel! In apprehension how like a god! The beauty of the world! The paragon of animals!"

In the past thirty-six years, we have been in contact with many revolutionaries who, at the dictates of their consciences, have undertaken strict criticism and self-criticism. Like Christians who follow their consciences, they are strongly conscious of the fact that their actions have not attained the ideal and that at times they have acted against those noble ideals.

If humans were mere worms or disease, they would not raise ultimate questions and the gospel of Christ would be responding to questions of no concern to anyone, i.e., talking into the void. But we know this is not the case.

The Incarnation is an affirmation of humanity, an affirmation that their questions are worthwhile, that they are worthy to be taught and to be redeemed. God will not destroy a people capable of raising ultimate questions.

Justin Martyr, an early church theologian, made an important observation. He felt that the seed of the Logos is planted in every human heart. The experience of Chinese Christians in the last few decades draws us to such an understanding of humanity. If Christ is a full circle, we human beings are arcs, long or short, around his perimeter. We are all beings in process, unfinished. Links do exist between the relative and the absolute.

Whatever obstacles still exist today, people still turn to Christ in an endless stream. To those who in the depths of their hearts tremble with baffling ultimate questions, Jesus' coming brings light, good news, comfort and encouragement. It is the gospel that brings us to Christ. It is the gospel that exhorts human beings, from every age, every place and every sort of social system, to enter into his fullness and enjoy it together.

Now let us pray in the words of St. Anselm, who lived at the turn of the 12th century:

> Have you found, my soul, what you were seeking? You were seeking God, and you found him to be that which is the highest of all, than which a better cannot be thought; you found him to be life itself, light, wisdom, goodness, eternal blessedness and blessed eternity, and to exist everywhere and always.
>
> You are wholly present everywhere and I do not see you. In you I move and in you I have my being, and I cannot come near to you. You are within me and around me, and I do not experience you with my senses.

I pray, O God, that I may know you and love you, so that I may rejoice in you. And if I cannot do so fully in this life, may I progress everyday until all comes to fullness; let the knowledge of you grow in me here in this life, and there in heaven let it be complete; let your love grow in me here and reach fullness there, so that here my joy may be great in hope, and there be complete in reality. Amen.

—Talk at a Canadian Theological College,
March 1985

# HOW IS THE CHURCH TO LOVE CHRIST?

So when they had dined, Jesus said to Simon Peter, 'Simon, son of Jonas, lovest thou me more than these?' He said unto him, 'Yes, Lord, thou knowest that I love thee.' He saith unto him, 'Feed my sheep.' He saith unto him the second time, 'Simon, son of Jonas, lovest thou me?' He saith unto him, 'Yes, Lord, thou knowest that I love thee.' He saith unto him, 'Feed my sheep.' He saith unto him the third time, 'Simon, son of Jonas, lovest thou me?' And he said unto him, 'Lord, thou knowest that I love thee.' Jesus saith unto him, 'Feed my sheep.'" (John 21:15–17)

In an historic sanctuary such as this one, where saints all through the centuries have beheld the glory of God and gained strength for their witness by word and by deed in the world, as we together join them in offering to God the worship that is due to him, how deeply we become aware of his presence and nearness. John Huss and what he represented have long become a common heritage of humanity. And as we at this moment turn our thoughts to the sundry times and diverse manners in which God has spoken in the past unto the fathers by the prophets, we cannot but realize, with humility and yet with gratitude, the responsibility that falls upon us today to bear before history as their successors in the same procession.

The passage in St. John's Gospel reveals to us something of both Christ's expectation and of his anxiety for the church. Christ puts before the church the image of the shepherd—the protector, the encourager, the friend. This is what the church is expected to be. But, at the same time, Christ is worried that the church might lose its first love, fail to fulfill the function of the shepherd, leave the sheep uncared for and even give occasion to the wolf to molest the sheep. Out of his high expectation and his uncertainty, he asks repeatedly of Peter, "Lovest thou me?"

How is the church to love Christ? Let us gain some light by looking at Christ's love for the church.

"Christ loved the church and gave himself for it, that he might sanctify and cleanse it with the washing of water by the word, that he might present it to himself a glorious church, not having spot or wrinkle, or any such thing, but that it should be holy and without blemish." Here we are given to see that Christ's love for the church lies in his work of cleansing and sanctification.

The primary characteristic of the church cannot be its global coalition, no matter how imposing it may be to human eyes. The primary characteristic of the church must necessarily be its holiness.

The holiness of the church lies in its separation from the sins and evils of the world and the setting apart of itself for the service of love and justice and truth among men. Unity, if it comes of the Holy Spirit himself, promotes the true catholicity of the church and is, of course, to be prayed for and sought for. But a unity which tries to transcend or ignore the distinction between right and wrong, one which distorts or blurs the issues of good and evil, often becomes an inroad of all sorts of mistakes, dirt, degeneration and pain upon the life of the church. Thus, it is entirely thinkable that to separate can sometimes be just as much the principle for the church as to unite is at other times.

In Revelation the seven churches are criticized again and again for their sin of unholy associations, but not once is alignment exhorted.

As we assemble here in Prague these days to seek the cause of peace, it is required of us that we distinguish between right and wrong. "Follow peace with all men, and holiness." The search for holiness implies the giving up of moral nihilism.

Sometimes we hear the view expressed that it is not only futile but also a sign of human pride and self-righteousness to try to analyze facts or clarify issues because, it is said, everybody in the world is one of the unpeaceful ones and harbors within him an evil spirit of cold war. Sometimes, when the cause at the root of some tense situation in the world is about to be ascertained, a voice emerges to incriminate everybody in the "common guilt" and to call everybody indiscriminately to "repentance." Thus, before we are aware of the fact, use is made of our sound Christian teaching to the end that issues vital to the people are glossed over, responsibility for international lawlessness and tension is shifted from where it rightly rests and universally shared by all alike, and injustices to the masses of the people are allowed to stand as something not quite distinguishable from justice.

The unmerited reconciliation with God in Christ which is his free gift to us impels us to an irreconcilability with the sins and evils in the world and certainly does not exempt us from it. It has been rightly stated by Archbishop Nikodim in his speech that "the peace which Christ brought to earth presupposes not our being reconciled with evil and the forces of sin on earth but, on the contrary, our victory over evil and the liquidation of sin by means of unflagging struggle against them ... a bitter, obstinate fight."

When the wolf is attacking the sheep, the shepherd's responsibility is to take the side of the sheep and to protect them. What sort of a shepherd would he be if, in the name of fairness, he puts the wolf on a par with the sheep? In the same way, how dare we make ambiguous, equalized judgments between the victim and his victimizer?

Brethren, we have held this All-Christian Peace Assembly in the native land of the great John Huss. The Rev. Stephens has told us how our African brothers and sisters have been suffering yesterday and are still suffering today from the calamities of colonialism. The Rev. Fernandez Cebbalos has told us how Cuba has been invaded recently. We have heard the sound of the struggle for peace on the part of the peoples of all countries. All these inspire us today to make common cause, as Huss did in his days, with the large majority of the people everywhere in their fight against the forces of sin and aggression. This is a call of God to us today. To respond to it is our responsibility before history.

Today, in this Bethlehem Chapel, we are praying where once John Huss prayed, and we are praising God where once John Huss praised him. We cannot but recall how Huss, seeing painfully the corruption and degeneration of the church under the influence of foreign political power and the control of reactionary domestic autocrats, bravely unfurled the banner of holiness. It was not an empty, sterile, passive holiness which stood for nothing in the world of realities, but a holiness with content, a true concern for the suffering and the aspirations of the people, a search for their welfare and a resolute fight against sins and evils where they were. Our beloved Professor Hromadka told me that on the wall of the Czechoslovakian National Museum of Literature these words of John Huss have been inscribed: "Woe unto me if I remain silent. For it would be better for me to die than not to take a stand against great wickedness, as this would make me an accomplice to sin and hell." Even to this day the voice of John Huss has not lost its dynamic power in moving us in the depths of our heart.

Now, is this dividing of the right from the wrong, this taking of a side, contrary to our Christian faith? Far from it. This is exactly what is demanded of us by our faith. Is it a sign of the lack of love for Christ? By no means. A true love for Christ requires that. And is this self-righteousness? Certainly not. This is precisely what St. Paul prayed for before God when he said, "And this I pray, that your love may abound yet more and more in knowledge and in all judgment, that ye may approve things that are excellent, that ye be pure and blameless till the day of Christ."

Now the God of peace, that brought again from the dead our Lord Jesus, the great shepherd of the sheep, through the blood of the everlasting covenant, make you perfect in every good work to do his will, working in you that which is well pleasing in his sight, through Jesus Christ, to whom be glory forever and ever. Amen.

—Prague, 1961

# STRETCHING OUT OUR ARMS IN LOVE

If we look at the history of Sino-American relations of the last century or so, we are bound to be impressed by two things: First, in spite of some episodes of animosity which we can recall, friendly relations between our two peoples have always had the upper hand, and second, the Christians of our two countries have done much (and can now do more) in promoting mutual understanding and friendship. Thus, my fellow Christians in China are grateful to the American Christians for your prayers during the years when there was very little contact—even for some of your prayers that were misinformed. I've always felt God listens to many of our prayers with a grain of salt.

As soon as it was decided that I was to leave China to be in North America for a few weeks, not only to listen to and learn from North American Christians, as I eagerly wished, but also to speak to certain audiences, as I feared I would be obliged to, I began to realize what a tremendous lot of things have accumulated in the last thirty years to speak about within our Christian fellowship, and how hard it is to do the sorting out and to organize them in presentable forms. I found myself more or less in the position of your proverbial centipede, which has got so many legs as not to know which one to move first. This morning just let me share with you some insights on man and woman, i.e., on ourselves, which I have gained during my nearly thirty years' life as a Christian in new China.

I might as well begin by saying there is nothing strikingly new to tell you about human beings as sinners standing in need of Christ's salvation. During the past thirty years, I have seen ample evidence to confirm this conception of man. I have met and have been moved by many revolutionaries, men and women of high moral caliber, who have for thirty or forty or fifty years, forsaken everything in dedicating themselves to the cause of making China a more livable place for its people. I am deeply impressed by the grandeur of their fortitude and their self-sacrifice. In order to safeguard the cause of revolution, they are sensitive to their own shortcomings and inadequacies and are demanding in self-criticism and self-reform.

Yet, it is these admirable souls who would readily agree with Saint Paul that the good they want to do they somehow fall short of, and the evil they do not want to do they somehow do in spite of themselves. If people who set such high moral standards for themselves feel that way, then to us Christians it is clear there is no ground to suppose that the message of Christ's redemption and of the sanctification of the Holy Spirit has turned irrelevant or pointless. The failure of people to take the message of Christ to heart must be due to faults in the transmitter rather than in the message itself.

What is new to many of us Chinese Christians is the awareness that man is not only the sinner but also the sinned against, not only the violator of God's law but also the violated against, and the realization that the task of evangelism is not to convict man of sin but to stand alongside man, the sinned against of our society, to feel with him, to be for him. Just to convict man of sin is not evangelism proper. It does not necessarily move man to repentance and to acceptance of Christ as Savior. Jonah found pronouncing men and women as sinners a jolly, happy thing to do, as it fell very much in line with his chauvinism and snobbery. But there was no love and compassion in that pronouncement. It was a message of doom and not of salvation.

In the Gospels we often come across passages about Jesus having compassion on the people. Jesus' compassion was not just pity, not just almsgiving, not any condescending attitude to inferior beings, but fellow feeling and suffering together with the weak and poor and hungry, with those deeply hurt by an unjust system, with those non-persons who for generations have been alienated, dehumanized and marginalized, in short, ones who have been badly sinned against.

Merely to convict man of sin dispels. It was this compassion that propelled Jesus to identify himself with the people and, at the same time, drew the people to him. And it is only as we Chinese Christians shed our aloofness and get close to our own people that we come to know how much they have been sinned against and a Christian compassion grows in us. This compassion becomes our common language with them.

And as we return to the New Testament, bringing with us this understanding of the age-long plight of our people, we seem to understand Christ's sympathy with the sinned against better and are moved by his love more deeply. Bearing in mind what we get out of the New Testament, we listen to the Chinese revolutionaries who point out how our people have suffered under and are still bearing the consequences of the oppression of imperialism, bureaucratic capitalism and feudalism, commonly called in China "the three mountains." *There* is an area where Christians and the rest of the Chinese have come to see eye to eye.

This common good, with common language, as we say, is important to us because, standing upon this common ground, the evangelist can speak as one among the people and not as one speaking from abroad, or from above, or from outside. He speaks out of true love for the people and is free from the misanthropic Jonah mentality, with all its abhorrence of the people to whom he is sent.

It has been cleverly said that evangelism is for one beggar to tell another where to go for bread. Yes, but that is not evangelism in the full sense of the word. The beggars need to know that their hunger, their diseases, their sleeping on the sidewalks, their infant mortality, their unemployment, their begging, all of them, are not the will of God, but the result of the greed for power and money on the part of a few, and a result of their own passivity. We must help the beggar see that it is not the will of God for him to be so degraded, nor his lot to be begging, while a few at the top of society are running everything, enjoying all the good things of life and giving alms to beggars out of their wealth. It is only when men and women sinned against become our concern that God can put in our mouths his word of witness to Christ, the saver of sinners. Only then can we speak with authority so the common people will hear us gladly.

In other words, we have come to realize how lacking we really were in true love for our people. To love our people is not just to smile at them and be nice to them. It is to put ourselves in their position, to enter deeply into their feelings, to feel with them, to understand the justice of their cause, to be a united front with them, to be fellow fighters with them, and to see how all their revolutionary strivings and all their industrial, agricultural, educational, artistic undertakings can get a deeper grounding and bear greater fruit if they can be made consciously to relate them to the purpose of God and the spiritual resources at the base of the whole universe. Love does mean all of this.

"Yet forty days, and Nineveh shall be destroyed." That encouraging news overcame all Jonah's reluctance, because he had no concern for the people's liberation and the condemnation to destruction was precisely the kind of thing he enjoyed saying in places like Nineveh. But the evangelist who evangelizes in the spirit of Christ dares never pronounce a message of doom unless he is sure the message is of God and the pronouncement of it breaks his own heart. Where love exists, evangelism happens.

I should like to go a bit further. The sinned against of the world find themselves so helpless and loveless that they almost always tend to form themselves in groups, collectives, fellowships. I don't think the evils of fascist and semi-fascist groups should lead theologians to have an aversion to all human collectives. Human collectives, even those which do not bear the name Christian, can be vehicles of the grace of God.

To me, an incompletely Christianized Chinese intellectual who has got a sprinkling of our Confucianist heritage of putting oneself over and above the masses of the people, it was quite a pilgrimage in the course of these years to be really sold on the educative and spiritual potentialities of human social organization. Individuals are weak in one way or another. But there is an inspiration in human fellowship which enables comrades to rise to levels unreachable by the mere individual. It is the common purpose and common enthusiasm that inspires, transforms and uplifts.

A student friend of mine had a serious personal problem. He struggled with it alone at first and could not come out victorious. He shared it with his fellows and received help and strength from them. He began to look at things in a new light and as he emerged a happier and stronger man from his trials, he said, "Now I see in our new society today there are so many outstretched friendly arms upholding and supporting you. It is like the Salt Sea, in which you cannot sink." This throws some light on what the community of Christ ought to be like, and this, I understand, is what the Riverside Church aims to do.

We do not need to go to China for illustrations. Right here in the United States, a very well-known lady, a drug and alcohol addict, had to be sent to a hospital by her family because of the suffering her addiction was bringing to them. She did not like anything in the hospital, because she was received there as an ordinary patient, without special attention. She had to go to the group she was assigned to. She refused to talk there.

One day a fellow patient in the group was talking defiantly about the personal nature of addiction and its harmlessness to others. This lady knew from her own experience that the speaker was wrong and opened up with her own story of the suffering she had caused her loved ones. Instantly she became accepted by the group and began to be called by her first name. She was no longer just a diseased person, but also a part of the curative process in the hospital. And that helped, and soon she was liberated from her addiction entirely. Now, an unkind way of describing her is that she was brainwashed. But a more correct description is probably transformation or enlightenment or metanoia or taking a step forward, through the help of the group.

We recall that when the risen Christ was about to depart from the earth, the one thing he urged his friends was not to disperse, but to stick together in Jerusalem in prayer and expectation; and as we see now, that was the condition for the coming of the Holy Spirit. Thus, we cannot afford to take a negative attitude to the human collective. More and more Christians are realizing that the transcendent is encountered not so much "out there" as within the interpersonal relationships of finite beings. We really open ourselves to the holy and the sacred and to meeting God himself as we dive into the depths of human relations, no matter how secular they seem. God being love, it is only in love that we come into touch with the uttermost reality of the universe and get ourselves attuned to the character of God.

I understand that certain existentialist philosophers insist that human life, by virtue of its social character, is essentially alienating. They teach that human collectives are necessarily less moral than the individuals which compose them. They even say that human finiteness and sin are revealed with particular force in collective relationships and that the evil impulses in men and women may be compounded in collective actions until they reach diabolical proportions.

All these castigations of the collective simply do not tally with our experiences and with the Church's teaching on the indwelling of the Holy Spirit and his enabling grace. I wonder to what extent this misanthropy and aversion to the human collective is really a reflection of the growing individualism in secular culture and of the fear of those whose interest ultimately lies in keeping humanity fragmented. And maybe I am criticizing a theological phenomenon that has now phased out in this area. I should like to know.

So here I put before you some random thoughts from China, on human beings and on human collectives, which have grown on me and many of my fellow Christians in China these years. My intention is to be a listener and learner in North America, so that I will have a lot of things to take to my co-workers and fellow Christians back home.

—Riverside Church, New York City, 1979

∞

# BUILDING UP THE CHURCH

*"You have not passed this way before" (Joshua 3:4).*

The Church is the household of believers. Today in our household, we are celebrating a big event: the consecration of our beloved Sun Yanli and Shen Yifan as bishops in the Church of God. This is the first time bishops are consecrated since thirty-three years ago. This church was full long before the beginning of the service. Hundreds of late-comers are standing outside. This shows that Christians recognize this to be an event of their own.

In recent years Christians all over China are heartened and thankful over the fact that the call to "build up our church well" is growing louder and louder. The Church is not anything to be destroyed, but the Body of Christ, something to be built up, and built up well—this is a point that has gone deeper and deeper into our hearts and minds. In the '50s, '60s, and '70s, there were not a few persons both within and outside our church who assumed that the fate of church was extinction. Some thought it was a good thing; others thought it was bad. But they were agreed that the church did not have much of a chance to last in China and what was awaiting it was its demise. Today, many have given up this view; others are not talking about it even if they do not want to give it up. We are now talking about the building up of the life and work of our church. Even many of our friends outside the church are supportive of our efforts. We feel excited and encouraged.

To build up our church is not only a call or slogan. It shows itself in many actions:

In the last eight years, in Shanghai, Fuzhou and Nanjing, we printed and published nearly three million Chinese Bibles and New Testaments with Psalms. We now have the Amity Printing Press, a gift from many national Bible societies through the United Bible Societies, which gives first priority to fulfilling the orders of church bodies for printing and binding Bibles. In 1988 Amity is to produce 900,000 Bibles, including reference Bibles and Bibles in simplified characters.

We now have twelve theological schools with some 650 full-time students under training for church work.

There are now over 4,000 renovated and newly-built church buildings used for public worship. There are tens of thousands of groups of Christians meeting in homes, mostly providing them with good, normal church life.

The number of Protestant Christians has increased to several million.

We are publishing *Tian Feng* and other journals. In recent months the contents of our *Syllabus* have focused on rural readership. Several friends abroad have told us that our *Nanjing Theological Review* is probably the theological journal which enjoys the largest circulation in the world with 19,000 copies of each issue, including 4,000 copies in traditional characters for the benefit of readers overseas.

Thus, the church in China is building itself up. Christians welcome our work to govern ourselves well, to support ourselves well and to do the work of propagation well ourselves.

Yet, the work of building up our church is far from completion. There are in the church things that are not good, that should not have happened, that cause Christians sorrow. As long as such things exist, Christians do not feel at ease when worshipping. As is said in a hymn, "I often shed tears out of my love for the church." We need to see this state of affairs.

In some places relationships between colleagues are not good.

In some places relationships between religious believers and government cadres are not normal.

In some places there is poverty of spiritual ministration. In some places, if Christians of a particular denominational background are a minority, their special characteristics in faith and worship are not given respect or are not given sufficient respect. This is not conducive to unity.

In some places, the emphasis is not on evangelism and nurturing but on endeavors to seek fame and money.

In some places Christians are meeting out in the open air in summer and in winter, holding umbrellas in the rain or snow. Some feel sad upon hearing this. Others say, "They deserve it. Who asked them to meet anyway?" Here are two diametrically opposed attitudes to the people and to the church.

All these tell us the building up of our church involves a tremendous degree of dedication and a tremendous amount of work. It is understandable our Christian people worry and weep for the church in the face of difficulties.

In 1937, in Oxford, England, the conference on the Life and Work of the Church was held, from which came the cry; let the church be the church. This is the cry of the Christians throughout the ages. The church is not to be made into a bureaucracy, an office, a recreational center, an economic enterprise, a mouthpiece of anything not the church. First of all, the church has to be the church.

Today, our society in general takes a much more favorable attitude toward our church. More and more people think that Christianity and socialism are compatible. We welcome this point of view. Insofar as our faith permits, I like to see greater compatibility between our church and socialism. But, what the church does must first of all be compatible with God's loving purpose, with the teachings of the Bible, with the nature of the church as church, and with the rightful wishes of the masses of our Christians. Only then the church is the church.

The church in China is a part of the Universal Church. Which part of it? The part of it that is composed of the younger churches and that part of the younger churches, which is situated in a country with a civilization of thousands of years, now having entered the period of socialist reconstruction. Joshua's words "You have not passed this way before," are an apt description of our situation. We are poorly qualified to be explorers of the new path. But God has not asked what in our sight is a better qualified church to do this. Then, let us gladly explore. In bearing witness to Christ in this new situation, we want to be independent, but we also like to feel we are carrying on our work with the prayer and the blessing of the Universal Church.

The ordination of the two new bishops also needs to be looked at from the point of view of building up our church.

Some tried to understand the step we are taking as a restoration of denominationalism, particularly the restoration of the Anglican denomination. No, this is not the case. We practice the breaking of bread, but this is not the restoration of the Little Flock. We honor the Sabbath Day and practice the humility rite, but this is for implementing our principle of mutual respect in matters of faith and worship so as to insure our unity.

The episcopal system is followed not only by the Anglican Church, but also by Roman Catholicism, Orthodoxy, the Eastern Churches (actually churches in West Asia and North Africa), Lutheran churches in Scandinavia and North America, and the United Methodist Church.

What is more is that we, the church in China, are just *having* bishops and not adopting the episcopal system of church government. The church in New Testament days also had bishops.

By having bishops, the ministry of our church becomes complete, or more complete. It is an important step we are taking.

What are the roles of bishops in the church in China? It is hard to enumerate systematically. We will have to let the Holy Spirit lead us and enable us to see more clearly. Practice and see the whole meaning of our practice later on as we look back—this has been experienced many times. When Peter came down from the housetop and started for where Cornelius was, he also could not see clearly what was going to happen and could see still less clearly the whole repercussion of his action. Again, "You have not passed this way before."

This much is clear: We will have bishops, but we are not choosing the episcopal system of church government. Our bishops are not diocesan and not administrative: they have their authority, but their authority does not base itself on any written constitutional stipulation or on any executive position, but on their spiritual, moral, theological and pastoral ministration, on their service to others. Bishops are servants of servants. The better they serve, the greater their authority and the people's readiness to listen. The more democratic they are, the more powerful are their appeals.

I especially hope that our two new bishops can serve our church and our country in four respects:

(1) theological enrichment;

(2) renewal and improvement of the quality of our worship;

(3) upholding religious freedom and proper relations between church and state;

(4) strengthening the unity of our colleagues, including proper implementation of the principle of mutual respect in matters of faith and worship.

All our clergy and bishops are to depend on the power of love and of example, and not on the power of position.

In 1 Corinthians 11:1 Paul admonished the Christians: "Be imitators of me, as I am of Christ."

Paul dared to say this because he strived hard to imitate Christ. I do not dare to ask people to imitate me, because I know I lag behind in imitating Christ. Many of us feel pain when we realize how high is the demand this biblical passage puts on us and how far short of the demand we are. The distance between the demand and the reality is too great. But, since God has entrusted us with the task of building up the church in China, he cannot set the demand any lower.

Let us therefore ask the Holy Spirit to strengthen us, help us once again to resolve to imitate Christ, so that we also dare to say, "Be imitators of me."

We are on a new path, untrodden before. Let the Holy Spirit guide us. Let us support each other on the way as we build together the edifice which is the church in China.

—Sermon Preached at the Consecration of Two New Bishops, Shanghai, June 26, 1988

## OUR PILGRIMAGE

First of all I want to express on behalf of my wife and myself our heartfelt thanks to Victoria University for the honor you give us. Canada was the first country we came to from China, soon after World War II, to be with the Student Christian Movement of this country. The friendship formed in those days has proved to be especially lasting all through these years. I think it is not hard for you to visualize how, prior to the formation of the People's Republic of China in 1949, churches and many of their leaders too often did the job of legitimating unpopular regimes and how, after 1949, they had to change their course so as to legitimate themselves before the people. For the church in China to live down its Western image and to make the transition from its old, unenviable position to one which the Chinese people can somehow appreciate has been a gigantic task. I am glad to say that the stand taken by a number of Canadian Christians well known in China and by the Canadian churches as a whole has been very helpful to us in the process. We are also happy to see how the good relations between the churches of our two countries now continue to develop after the blackout of the years of the Cultural Revolution. I especially like to refer to Emmanuel College as the first college outside of China in forty years to help us in the training of our future theological teachers, now being followed by other colleges in several countries. This evening we are grateful to you beyond words for the symbolic way in which we two are brought to a closer bond with this university and, in doing so, you are also bringing our two countries closer together.

We have graduation exercises in China too. Speakers on such occasions often like to elaborate on an old Chinese proverb of eight characters which says that it takes ten years to grow a tree and one hundred years to grow a man or woman. The moral usually is that learning is a long process of growth and that to receive a diploma only marks the beginning of another stage of learning. You can see this is a proverb typical of an agricultural people.

The Bible has many ways of speaking of the relation between God and human persons. The pastoral background of the Israelites makes them feel especially at home when God is depicted as shepherd and the people as sheep. So we have "The Lord is my shepherd, I shall not want," and Christ himself is "the lamb of God who takest away the sins of the world." Christians elsewhere, through long exposure to this pastoral symbolism, have got used to it and have incorporated in into our spirituality. But there is another Biblical way of referring to the relation between God and human persons that people in agricultural countries can probably appreciate even more, and that is to speak of God as planter, as sower, as tiller of the land, and of human beings as plants, as trees, as wheat, as vines, as flowers. We read in the Gospels of the sower who goes out to sow, of the grain of wheat which falls into the earth, dies and bears much fruit, of the grain of mustard seed and the shrubs and the tree it becomes.

In the shepherd-sheep relation, the shepherd uses the rod and the staff a lot to prevent the sheep from going astray and resorts often to ordering and scolding and even whipping. What is expected of the sheep is that they should be docile, tractable and obedient. These are not the highest virtues human beings are capable of. In the agricultural symbolism, the planter uses no rod or staff but does what needs to be done and then waits for nature to take its own course. The plant receives nourishment from the soil, the air and the sun and grows. It takes years to grow a tree and much longer to grow a person and there can be no hastening. The planter figure is different from the shepherd figure in that the shepherd is busy directing and correcting the sheep all the time, while the planter knows the importance of waiting and not doing things when no doing is called for.

I am quite struck by the French linguist and historian Andre Haudricourt, who makes a contrast between what he calls the Eastern garden and the Mediterranean stable. He thinks the garden-like treatment of human beings is something taught by Chinese civilization, while the pastoral, shepherd-like treatment of human beings is Western and Judaeo-Christian. Animals are tamed with a stick and much shouting at. With plants, flowers and trees, we patiently wait because the only thing to do is to aid nature and not disturb it.

You may detect a small bit of Taoism in this approach. It is not any admonition to laziness, passivity or resignation. It shows that God in his love and patience and out of his respect for humanity holds his almightiness in abeyance in order not to impose his will on us. He plants, tends to the plant and waits for its growing into the fullness that is in Christ.

The aspect of human growth that concerns us Christians most has to do with the human search for transcendence, for surpassing what we can see and touch and taste and read in our daily newspapers. There is a universal dissatisfaction with staying where we are, a universal desire to transcend, to reach for something higher and deeper.

How do we account for the fact that, without missionary help from abroad and without any patronage from within China, the number of Protestant Christians in China has grown at least twice as fast as the population? There are still some doctrinaire theoreticians in China who make the opiate the definition of religion. They do not seem to be aware that their own logic is forcing them to conclude that there are causes in Chinese socialist society for more people to need to resort to opiates. An explanation closer to the facts is that the revolution has broken loose the age-old hold of feudal authority on the people's souls, and has unleashed the urge to question and depose the old status quo and to transcend it. There is a mental liberation which prompts the people to break the formidable barricade of conventional norms and values that have been accepted for thousands of years. One result of this mental liberation is that more people are now ready to look at Christianity as something worth looking at. A religion which holds up transcendence as divine nature and universal principle cannot but have its appeal to those ready to see changes.

We have some Christians who think it is important to play up God's immanence in history because it is supposed to accompany a progressive social outlook, while to dwell on God's transcendence seems to make Christians neglect their responsibilities here on earth. Many of us find it is not necessarily so. We have seen how fascist ideologies in East and West were full of the spirit of divine immanence, while the transcendent God disturbs people in their complacency, makes them thirst for a new quality of life, inspires them to look farther and up and gives them courage for reaching new heights. That is growth in the true sense.

We are witnessing here the graduation of a new class of theological students. We may not be certain these days of many things. But one thing certain is that human beings cannot be long in resting content in their day-to-day living, that there is an irrepressible human need to transcend, to break limits and barriers, to transform one-dimensional to multidimensional living. "God, you have put a restlessness in my heart, so that it can find no rest until it finds it in you." That is not only a prayer of St. Augustine, but also the yearning of men and women of all ages living within all sorts of social systems. It is this fact which makes theological students not superfluous but needed, for strengthening the Christian communities which bring people face to face with the transcendent God. We congratulate you for the completion of an important stage in your pursuits and wish you continued growth on the pilgrimage of scaling new heights.

—On the Occasion of Granting Honorary Doctorates to K. H. Ting and Siu-May Kuo Ting, Toronto, May 11, 1989

ॐ

# WHAT THE SPIRIT IS SAYING TO THE CHURCH IN CHINA

When the Christian Church first emerged, it had not yet become separated from Judaism. The first Christians were all Jews. Though they accepted Jesus Christ as Lord and were awaiting his return, they continued to practice circumcision and held to all the Jewish laws and customs, believing that only in this way could they please God. But a problem very soon arose. When non-Jewish Gentiles heard the gospel and received Christ as Lord, did they also have to become Jews at the same time and observe Jewish law and custom? At that time, some people thought that since Jesus was a Jew and Christians were a sect of Judaism, and since those who carried the gospel to the Gentiles were Jews, then of course when Gentiles became Christians, they should be circumcised and follow Jewish law and customs.

But Peter, Paul and Barnabas did not see it this way. They saw with their own eyes that Gentiles who did not keep the law also received the blessing of the Holy Spirit when they accepted Christ, so they did not favor imposing upon them the weight of all the Jewish demands. Paul proposed that a person should be counted righteous because of faith. In Romans 3, he says, "For we hold that a person is justified by faith apart from works of law." Any person who wants to be declared righteous before God does not use "the law of works," that is, depend on the law to gain merit, but rather "uses the law of believing in the Lord."

These were two entirely different propositions. The first would have the church continue to be limited to the confines of Judaism and the law. In this way, the church would be greatly restricted in what nourishment it could receive from Greek thought and would not have been able to develop universal teachings such as the Lord being the Word before creation, of the Word becoming flesh, of righteousness by faith, the teaching of the church, of the Holy Spirit, of three persons in one nature, and so forth. None of these would have been able to develop and grow. A Christianity dominated by a Jewish nationalism could not have spread to the whole world. According to the second view, which Paul held, the Christian gospel is proclaimed to people of every nation who all become righteous by faith. The gospel breaks out of the limited Jewish framework and is liberated from Jewish law and observances. Having undergone this breaking-out or liberation, the gospel is able to focus on the Lord and let people see that keeping the law is of no value, because only one who depends on the Lord in faith is able to emerge from death to life. This important focus of the gospel is not just a distraction, but is God's good news prepared for all the world's people. And the fact that China today has hundreds of thousands of believers is possible only because of this.

Acts 15 records that Peter, James, Paul and the other believers in Jerusalem held a meeting to consult on this matter. That meeting was very important in determining what kind of a church the church was to be, what kind of history humankind was to have in years to come. The Holy Spirit personally took part in this meeting, personally led and moved some people's hearts, opening their ears to God's own way of acting which Peter and Paul had seen when they were witnessing among the Gentiles. They then made the decision that when preaching to the Gentiles it is necessary to set aside the Jewish law. The meeting then issued a letter to Gentile believers in which they used the phrase "The Holy Spirit and us"—an uncommon expression—"For it has seemed good to the Holy Spirit and to us to impose on you no further burden ..." At that particular meeting, the believers and the Spirit worked together, made a decision together, so that the view of God which proclaimed righteousness by faith and called for liberation from Judaism achieved a great victory, and the Jewish faction suffered a great setback. As a consequence of this meeting, the embryo of the Christian Church was separated from Judaism and the Gentile believers of each region could order their own churches under the leadership of the Holy Spirit. They were no longer dependents of the Jerusalem church. From then on, whenever the church entered a new situation, it had to remove itself from the restraints of a previous group's traditions, the better to manifest the Lord's truth. We have seen that in the New Testament period churches emerged in a great many places, all cared for and guided by the Holy Spirit, each church with its own regional character, local color and distinct particularity. They were related to the Jerusalem church in mutual support but on an equal basis, without any one-way dependency or parent-child relationship.

Some say that the term "Three-Self" cannot be found in the Bible, and they are right. But is the Three-Self principle or theme not found there? I do not think we can say that it is not. What is treated in Acts 15 is exactly this principle, this theme. The demand of the Gentile churches, which Paul represents, is the "self" aspect of "Three-Self." To advocate justification by faith and to oppose meriting justification through law-keeping is to acknowledge that the Gentile church has cast off the so-called mother church's restrictions to follow its own path.

In the 2,000 years since then, wherever the gospel was preached, to whatever race or nation, this problem of going one's own way has gone with it. The problem is this: When the people of a place, race or nation, accept Christ as Lord, do they also accept the nation and culture of those who transmit the gospel as their own? Does believing in Christ mean cutting off one's relation to one's own people and becoming a person without a motherland—half-foreign?

There was a missionary to Africa who said that it was necessary for the African believer to become exactly like the white man except for the color of his skin. Is this a good guideline for mission? Today Africa has many independent churches with independent personnel, independent support and independent work. Is this wrong?

I would like to make two points. First, to extend the Lord's gospel, it is necessary to practice Three-Self. Second, to build up the Lord's body, it is necessary to practice Three-Self.

The person who believes in Christ is justified. This is certainly the gospel. But before a people can receive this gospel, there is a prerequisite, namely, they must first recognize that they need to be justified. This means they must recognize that they are not just; that they are sinners. Paul said he himself had the experience that the good he wanted to do he could not do, while what he did not want to do, he could not keep from doing. This is the effect of the rule of sin in the human body. If a person reflects humbly on this, he or she will recall having like experiences. But those who preach the gospel know that it is not easy to get a people to recognize that they are sinners. The natural person is not going to acknowledge this point because people always see themselves favorably. Sin is an alien concept. But this alien concept is integral to the gospel itself, is in fact internal to the gospel. We do not have the power to make it easy for people to receive the gospel, to cancel out this problem of sin, because, once it is done away with, a person is justified and no longer has need of justification, nor, by implication, of the gospel. A gospel that does not speak of sin turns out not to be the gospel. I have said all this in order to make clear that Christ makes one demand of those who carry the gospel: When they speak it they must emphasize sin, this alien concept which is integral to the gospel and cannot be avoided. They must exclude every other thing that is man-made, every factor added from elsewhere, and every obstruction outside the gospel. They must let go of every stumbling block that might make the gospel more difficult to accept, every con-nection of the gospel to colonialism, every entangling of the gospel with unequal agreements, everyone who speaks the gospel by saying one thing and doing another. Every such thing that can block the transmission of the gospel must be excluded.

Consider how in the last half of the 19th century and in the first half of the 20th century, China was the most important of all the for-eign mission fields for Western Christians, with the most missionaries, the most universities, high schools and hospitals founded. But the numbers of believers were few, no more than 700,000 at most, includ-ing the so-called rice Christians. Today, after thirty years without mis-sionaries, without subsidies from overseas, without founding schools and hospitals, when believers have had no opportunity to plan, the number who believe in the Lord has not grown fewer, but has increased, to even three or four times more. The causes for this are, of course, many, but the underlying cause which has had the most impact, is that the Chinese Church has experienced the Three-Self Movement. Through this movement, the church has largely sloughed off its Western church form, making more people willing to listen to what this Christian gospel might be. God actually made use of this Three-Self tool. Just think, today, when there is no Western oil, lighting or cloth in China, the continued presence of a Western church could cause severe harm to the spread of the gospel. The original 700,000 could not have increased to the present three million.

Three-Self, then, has been essential to the spread of the gospel. Beyond this, Three-Self has been necessary for another reason. In order to build up the Lord's universal church on earth, it is necessary for believers from every era, every ethnic group and every country—each coming from their own context—to know the Lord's immeasurable riches, to gather together, to share what they enjoy and to replenish the church's spiritual treasury, that the church's universal form may be truly recognized.

In Revelation, chapters 2 and 3, the Spirit writes letters to seven small churches in Asia Minor. Each of these churches had its own context, its own merits and shortcomings. Each had received Christ in its own way. The Spirit did not want to make all seven churches conform to a single pattern. The message to each church was not the same. But each of the seven letters ends with the same words, "Let anyone who has an ear listen to what the Spirit is saying to the churches." The Spirit was apparently willing for all the churches to share the guidance they received with each other and multiply the grace all the more through sharing. This is the reason why the Three-Self we teach in the Chinese Church does not include "self-sufficiency" or "self-isolation." For this reason, too, we are strengthening the relations among churches within China as well as developing and maintaining relations with the international church. We cannot *not* listen to "what the Spirit is saying to the churches."

In the twenty-first chapter of Revelation we see that Jerusalem will one day come down from heaven. This holy city is foursquare with three gates on the east side, three on the north, three on the south, and three on the west: twelve gates altogether. This tells us that in that time believers will come to the new Jerusalem from the four corners of the earth, forming rich and colorful processions representing the churches of every place and people. We hope that in that time,

China's church will form such a procession, entering the holy city from one of the eastern gates, offering ourselves to God. But if we do not build the Lord's own body in China according to the Three-Self spirit, we will be no more than a very small dot on the missionary map of the Western church.

I do not want to interpret the church's universal nature simply in geographical terms. The concept needs depth as well as breadth. Its depth is seen in the Lord's resurrection-day glory, reflected through the prism of every local church, the churches of every people, bringing even greater glory to Christ. This is what Paul spoke of: "For it is all for your sake, so that as grace extends to more and more people it may increase thanks-giving, to the glory of God."

Where is the universal church? Where shall we seek it? The universal church is not in New York or London, not in Rome or Geneva, but in concrete congregations. There is no universal church apart from local, concrete, particular churches, just as apart from you or I, Wang or Li, this man, that woman or this child, we do not find abstract people. The more the Chinese Church is able to progress in the Three-Self way, the more blessed it will be, and the greater the contribution it will be able to make to the spiritual wealth of the universal church.

This is the understanding of Three-Self, which I have received from the Bible. For the purpose of proclaiming the Lord's gospel and for the purpose of building up the Lord's body, Three-Self is a necessity.

Overseas there are people who say Three-Self came from the Communist Party. People who say this have not examined the scriptures; they have not even examined history. Long before the Communist Party appeared in China, there was in England in 1850 a certain Henry Venn who coined these three terms—self-government, self-support and self-propagation—saying that these were the true goal of church mission. He wanted to train missionaries like St. Paul, who did not plan to stay long in a place, but were expected, as soon as possible, to make themselves dispensable and leave. In the 16th century, the English church moved away from the control of Rome and established its own independent Anglican Church governed by the Archbishop of Canterbury. In the words of the present Archbishop, "That is also an instance of the Three-Self Movement."

Based on the Bible and on history, it could be said that wherever the gospel has been preached over the last 2,000 years, the Three-Self question has gone along, despite the fact that the term Three-Self was not necessarily used.

Some people have misgivings about Three-Self because they have been disappointed by the things some people have done under its banner. In responding to these people, we must communicate our desire to simply provide guidance, give help and pray for them, asking God to call them to recognize their error and correct it. But we do not want to judge people. Human weakness and hypocrisy are always with us. If this is our perspective, even the church will be offensive to us, for are not we all the same people? Are we so much stronger than they are? We must study the Bible to know the essence of Three-Self, hold tight to it and unite with other believers to work steadfastly to implement it.

I myself did not recognize or embrace Three-Self from the beginning. When Mr. Y. T. Wu and others from the first generation of church leaders began to advocate the Three-Self principle, I was still living in Switzerland. On my return home, though I did not oppose Three-Self, neither did I immediately support it. I wanted to wait and watch a little. My attitude was Gamaliel's: "If this plan or this undertaking is of men it will fail; but if it is of God, you will not be able to overthrow them. You might even be found opposing God!" (Acts 5:38–39). Later I saw more clearly. I recognized the New Testament church's strategy from my study of the Bible. I knew Three-Self was Paul's strategy; it came from the Lord himself. The resurrected Lord once revealed himself to his disciples and John quietly told Peter, "It is the Lord." It was as if I too heard those words: "It is the Lord." The hand of the Risen Lord was in control. So I took courage and embraced Three-Self.

Rev. Jia Yuming, one of our beloved and respected senior church leaders, testified that while he was still uncertain, he spent half a night waiting on the Lord and received the words, "The source is not polluted." He then resolved to embrace Three-Self. Later he was chosen to be vice-chairman of the national Three-Self Movement. From this we can see that rather than looking to people, we should look to the Bible, to the source. If we depend on people we may stumble; if we depend on the Bible, the source, we cannot be misled.

Let us place the path we have followed for thirty years before God's altar. Let us place there also the future path of the Chinese Church and let us seek the guidance of the Spirit. Let us pray for God's loving care:

> Where the church is corrupt Lord, cleanse it;
> Where it is in error, correct it;
> Where it is lacking, enrich it;
> Where there is division, grant it loving hearts;
> Where the power to witness fails, Lord bring it back
> and heal it;
> Where there is pride and complacency, instruct it;
> Where there is humility, goodness, unity and mutual
> love in the church.
> O Lord, bless and strengthen it.

> All this we ask in the name of Jesus Christ, the Head
> of the Church.

> Amen.

—Preached at the Thanksgiving Service for the 30th Anniversary of the Three-Self Patriotic Movement of Protestant Churches in China, 1984

# WHY THE THREE-SELF MOVEMENT?

**W**ithin certain circles the question of allowing Christianity to take local and national forms is never raised, for to raise such a question is to violate the so-called supranational nature of the church and to introduce a mundane political note into Christian faith in all its transcendence.

But the question was raised actually as early as there were Christians of the first generation. There was a growing number of Gentile converts to Christian faith. Should Gentiles in becoming Christians be expected to adopt Judaism too, just because Christianity was a sect within Judaism and because the evangelists to the Gentiles were themselves Jews? Were Gentiles to practice circumcision, for instance, in order for them to be Christians? The conference in Jerusalem, described in Acts 15, was held on this very subject. Its decision that Gentile Christians were to be free from observing Jewish laws and customs was truly momentous for the future history of Christianity and, consequently, for the future history of the world. The Pauline doctrine of justification by faith alone and not by works was liberating. It implied Christianity was not to remain a sect within Judaism but enjoy the freedom to maintain give-and-take relations with other cultures, with the potential of becoming a world religion. Frederick Engels in his study of early Christianity puts it this way:

"Gentile Christianity in rejecting all national religions and their ceremonies and addressing itself to all peoples without distinction became the first possible world religion."

This world religion is not to be a disembodied cosmopolitan faith. It is always local in that, in the course of its give-and-take it picks up local coloration wherever it is found. Alan Richardson in "An Introduction to the Theology of the New Testament" points out that the fact of "locality" is a very important aspect of the New Testament doctrine of the church. He says:

"The church is not like a school of Stoic or Epicurean philosophers, whose existence in a given place is quite accidental. The Catholic Church is always a local church, the church of some city or country; locality, nationality, and particularity are the essential marks of the Universal Church."

It is clear that, without the liberation of Christianity from its Judaistic captivity and its enjoyment of the freedom to express its faith in forms that would be intelligible to the Greek mind and later to the minds of other people, the theological creativity of Christianity would be severely circumscribed and its theological development retarded by its status within Judaism. Then, all Christian dogmas about Trinity, about Christ, about the Holy Spirit, about church and so on would remain at best in a very undeveloped state.

The question whether Gentile Christians be expected to be Jewish at the same time, reemerged in a different form in China four hundred years ago: Were Chinese in becoming Christians to be European or Western too because Christianity was a European religion and because their evangelizers came from Europe? Would a Chinese Christianity still be Christianity? Matteo Ricci showed a high respect for Chinese culture and worked for a Christianity that was a Chinese departure from European Christianity through its incorporation of certain native Chinese elements. In so doing he succeeded to make Christianity more communicable to the Chinese intellectuals of those days Kang Xi, the emperor in the early 18th century, actually became sufficiently sympathetic to Christian faith thus presented to have written a poem on the passion of Jesus Christ:

> With his task done on the cross,
> His blood forms itself into a streamlet.
> Grace flows from West Heaven in long patience:
> Trials in four courts,
> Long walks at midnight,
> Thrice denied by friend before the cock
> crew twice,
> His six-foot frame hanging at same height as
> two thieves.
> It is a suffering that moves the whole world
> and all ranks.
> Hearing his seven words makes all souls cry.

You will have seen that this poem, short of any appreciation of the resurrection, nevertheless reveals a very friendly understanding of Jesus Christ. It seems that conditions were ripe for the emergence of a religion that would be Christian and yet open to all that was true, good, and beautiful in Chinese national culture.

Unfortunately, under pressures from Rome, missionaries began to take an intransigent attitude as regards Chinese national culture and, in the name of guarding against syncretism, departed from Matteo Ricci's ways. Hence the ousting of missionaries at the order of the very same Kang Xi emperor.

It is worth nothing that Three-Self—self-government, self-support, and self-propagation—as an aim of church-building in any country to which missionaries are sent, was a long-accepted principle in enlightened missionary circles. Henry Venn, the chief executive of the Church Missionary Society of England, was probably the first person to put these three words together as the goal of missionary work. He did this in 1850 in a paper with the title "Native Church Organization" in which he also spoke of the "euthanasia of mission." The whole idea was that missionaries were to work in such a way as to make themselves dispensable. Roland Allen, a missionary in North China of the Society for the Propagation of the Gospel in the 1920s, was especially effective in showing that Paul's missionary way was to make churches independent and local, not holding to the apron-string of any "mother church."

China was a country of early nationalist awakening. The several waves of anti-Christian movements in the 19th and 20th centuries were not so much attacks or criticisms of the content of the Christian message itself as opposition to a Christianity actually or supposedly in the service of foreign penetration of China. This political issue was always made so much of that people with national self-respect would hardly want to hear what the message of Christianity was. As a result, that the church in China should be independent and that Christianity in China should be Chinese have been long-cherished ideals on the part of many Chinese Christians too. In the 19th century there was a Chinese convert who denied himself baptism until he traveled some one hundred miles by boat to receive it at the hand of the nearest Chinese minister. He started an independent Chinese congregation maintaining no relationship to any foreign mission. From the 1920s on, many independent churches emerged in China, advocating Chinese leadership and Chinese financial support. Some of them were even organized nationally. Thus, the Three-Self Movement or the movement of independence was not anything that came into being all of a sudden in 1950. Much groundwork had preceded it in churches in China and abroad. Quite a number of Western missionaries working in pre-Liberation China were supporters of the Three-Self ideal and worked hard in laying the foundation for the independence of the Chinese Church.

I think it is safe to say that, ever since 49 CE, the year of the conference in Jerusalem when the issue came to a head, all through the last 2,000 years, wherever the gospel reaches, whether it be a local area, or a tribe, or a nation, or a country, the issue of Three-Self inevitably arises, although the expression Three-Self is not always used. Haters of new China in Hong Kong try to tell us that it was the communists who imposed Three-Self on the Chinese Christians. They surely have studied neither New Testament documents nor history.

For the church in any country to have a selfhood of its own, a real and not a borrowed identity, is all-important; first, for evangelistic effectiveness in the country it is located in and, second, for the enrichment of the Church Universal in its understanding and worship of Christ. I will now dwell a bit on each of the two points.

Roland Allen wrote in 1902 in his *A Policy for North China* about what he called "the political difficulty":

> At present the Chinese commonly look upon the missionary as political agent, sent out to buy the hearts of the people, and so to prepare the way for a foreign dominion, and this suspicion has been greatly strengthened by the fact that Western nations have, as in the case of Kiaochow, used outrages upon missionaries as a pretext for territorial aggression.

Professor Varg, in his *Missionaries, Chinese, and Diplomats*, published in 1955, has this to say:

> So strong and continuous was the antagonism toward the missionary that he could never have attempted to Christianize the country had not the Western nations with their superior force upheld their right to be there.

The admixture of cross and flag gave a most ambiguous quality to the expansion of Christianity. You can easily visualize how frustrating it must be in that situation to convince listeners that the Christian gospel was something entirely separate from Western domination, and that, in spite of the Western packaging in which it came, there was in it the universal and absolute claim of the Lord Jesus Christ upon all men and women to which they must give heed. That explains our need for de-Westernization, not dissimilar to the need for de-Judaization for Paul and the early Gentile Christians.

Missionary leaders were not unaware of the danger to the cause of evangelism as long as the church in China was just an ecclesiastical protégé of an expatriate society. Celso Constantini, the first apostolic delegate of Rome to China, wrote on the ship taking him to China for the first time in 1922:

> "The political position of foreigners in China is based on a structure of privilege and sanction. By virtue of extraterritoriality, foreigners are not liable before Chinese courts. The judicial position of the church in China is itself tied to this structure, which offends the self-respect of the Chinese. Religion is tolerated by virtue of foreign treaties, the missionary is also considered a foreigner, suspected of connivance with foreign powers."

He also wrote:

> "The Apostles built Christian communities and placed at their head autonomous bishops. Among all the accusations against it, that of being a foreign religion is not found. If the Catholic religion appears to the Chinese as a foreign importation, tied to foreign political interests, is it the fault of the Chinese?"

His correct analysis, however, only remained on paper. In spite of what he said, by 1949, of the 140 Roman Catholic dioceses in China, only twenty were headed by Chinese bishops.

Those opposed to making legitimate accommodation to national culture and aspiration often elaborate on the danger of syncretism. Thus, this word has become associated with a certain triumphalism and intransigence typical of colonial empires.

It is worth recalling that Christianity, which originated in Palestine and Asia Minor, became a Western religion only because men and women took great risks in theology, in spirituality, and in art to express through the medium of Western cultural conditioning the wonderful works of God. The irony is that, as this Christianity with a selfhood all its own moves to the modern age and to the world scene, the cultural conditioning has been found to be a constriction to the capacity for the worship of a universal Christ and for the communication of the faith to those living in other cultures.

It was that situation which is mainly to account for the fact that, in spite of China being the mission field which received more missionaries and more mission funds than any other mission field, the number of converts was extraordinarily small. At the time of China's Liberation in 1949 the number of Protestants was not more than 700,000.

Today, thirty-five years after liberation and thirty-four years after the launching of Three-Self, the number of Protestant Christians has gone up to three million, according to a conservative estimate. People of course have become Christians out of many different circumstances, but the one underlying reason behind all these circumstances is that, today, the church in China has shed much of its Western image. Its Chineseness is not only apparent in the personnel of the leadership and in the source of its financial support, but also growing in ways of expressing the Christian faith in its thought, its worship, and its art and music.

Ours is not a church running educational, medical, and philanthropic institutions, nor one possessing sophisticated means of communication, but it is clearly an evangelistic and growing church. Christians are witnessing in places where they live and where they work. Now that the stigma of being a Western religion has pretty much been removed and people no longer say "one more Christian, one less Chinese," men and women in various walks of life are more willing to hear what Christianity is all about. The whole experience tells us that a church has to earn its right to be heard.

Three-Self is not generally anti-missionary. We are thankful to God for the gospel of Jesus Christ missionaries brought to China and for all the good they did in China. We make a distinction between Christian obedience to the Great Commission of Christ as given in Matthew 28 and the political, economic, and military expansion of Western colonialism. But while we do think there is time for Christians to go from one country to another to preach the gospel, we do think too there is a time for them not to go so that the church established there can come of age and be itself. Since the reopening of

China many old China missionaries have been back to visit and we are so glad to find them appreciating and endorsing the Three-Self principle and thanking God for it with us.

We have seen what Three-Self does for the evangelistic outreach of the church in China.

Three-Self is also important for the enrichment of the spiritual treasure of the Church Universal.

It can be said that any local or national church has two poles, its universality and its particularity. We need to conscientize ourselves to both. On two separate occasions in 1982 the Archbishop of Canterbury said:

> The Three-Self movement was known in the Anglican Church in the 16th century when the Reformers determined to have the Bible read and heard in English. They devised a liturgy in the language of the people and they established a church which, while not abandoning Catholic doctrine, had local autonomy and self-government.
>
> It is only if you cherish your identity and love your roots that you will have something to give to enrich the worldwide communion.

The fullness of the gospel of Jesus Christ is something only to be fathomed and made complete by Christians of all cultural backgrounds. The New Jerusalem when it comes down from heaven has three gates each in the north and the south, and the east, and the west, for Christians and churches to enter from all directions, to bring with them their peculiar treasures and insights into the richness of the Christ that is yet to be. The universality of the church only exists in all the particularities of the local church. The local church is the place where the meeting between Christian universalism and cultural particularities occurs to the maximum advantage. We Chinese Christians see ourselves to be a small procession entering New Jerusalem as the church of Jesus Christ in China with all its local colors, rather than a dot on the missionary map of other churches.

In Revelation, chapters 2 and 3, there are seven letters written by the Holy Spirit to the seven churches of Ephesus, Smyrna,

Pergamum, Thyatira, Sardis, Philadelphia, and Laodicea. These churches are situated in different cultural milieus, have their different strengths and weaknesses, and are faced with different problems. The Holy Spirit imposes no one pattern on all of them. So the messages are all different. Yet, at the end of each letter appears the same exhortation: "Let those who have an ear hear what the Holy Spirit says to the churches." So each of the messages is for the nourishment and enrichment of all the churches of Jesus Christ in the world.

So, when we in China say Three-Self, self-isolation is not one of them. We do want to be rooted in the Chinese soil, but we want at the same time to affirm our unity with Christians elsewhere and receive nourishment from the bosom of the one holy, catholic, and apostolic church which extends itself throughout the ages and exists in the particular churches living within all sorts of social systems and cultural environments. We cannot afford not to hear what the Holy Spirit says to other churches. We believe in interdependence of Christians across national boundaries, but we think we can enter into interdependence more truly if we first achieve more independence.

Catholicity in its breadth embraces the churches in all parts of the geographical world. Catholicity in its depth brings in the fruits of the encounters of Christian faith with all cultures. Catholicity in these two dimensions is still something in the process of realization. Three-Self is the way in which the Chinese Church makes its contribution to the realization of this catholicity. The Church Universal will be enriched in seeing what the gospel makes of the Chinese people as well as what the Chinese people make of the gospel.

The missionary vocation of any one group of Christians should not be in contradiction to that of the church in mission in its own country. Christians need to be on guard against any expansionism of their own selfhood which infringes on the sacred space that is the selfhood of another church. That has led us Christians of China to declare to the world that, in order to protect the emerging selfhood of our church from being trodden upon by international interventionism and to prevent the restoration of a foreign image to our church, the work of evangelism and church-building in China is the responsibility and task of us Chinese Christians ourselves, and that no group outside of China regardless of skin color should undertake any work of this nature in China without first consulting the China Christian Council. This should not be understood to be a refusal on our part to take our place in the Church Universal. It is a protective measure taken to secure a more favorable surrounding for the growth of Chinese self-hood and for evangelistic outreach, and a plea to international Christianity to take a sympathetic attitude, or at least a Gamaliel attitude to what Chinese Christians have been trying to do and to be. In old China our Customs were controlled by foreign interests and personnel. National industries were in ruin because there was no tariff to protect them in competition with foreign commodities which could sell at low prices in the Chinese market. As a protective tariff is all-important for the development of national industries, so today for the strengthening of the Chinese selfhood of our church, which in turn will be the edification of the Church Universal, the drawing of some protective line seems to us desirable.

You have noticed that the full name of the Three-Self Movement has the word "patriotic" in it. Because of what has transpired under the word "patriotism," there is a legitimate fear as to whether Three-Self is not a nationalistic or antiforeign movement. This fear, however, is not warranted because Three-Self only aspires to make the church in China Chinese, that is, just as Chinese as the church in England is English and the church in the USA is American.

As to patriotism and nationalism we need to make distinctions. There is the nationalism which gives its first loyalty to the nation or the state and upholds "my country, right or wrong." That is national chauvinism, under which criticism of wrong state policies is stifled and oppression and aggression justified. To call this patriotism is an abuse of the word which through the ages has acquired a content more noble and sublime. That Chinese Christians, especially their leaders, suffered so much during the Cultural Revolution for upholding their first loyalty to Jesus Christ and not to the political authorities testifies to the fact that when the word "patriotism" is used by Chinese Christians, it is not used in that chauvinist sense.

On the other hand, there is the nationalism that is born of the people's effort to resist foreign encroachment in defense of national territory, national culture, and national language which are being trodden upon by a dominant power. This must not be equated with the nationalism of the aggressor. There are moments when small cultures, cultures in which some great goodness and beauty reside, are being obliterated by the dominant force of a domestic autocracy or a transnational technological society, and when those who suffer from displacement and marginalization rise up in self-defense to make life livable. These occasions call Christians to choose to take the side of the people of their nation and be the supporters of a nationalism making for progress in history. Dr. Sun Yat-sen, a Christian, made a choice of this kind in his stand against Manchu despotism and foreign encroachment, and we are mindful of the support he got from friends in Japan.

Patriotism of this kind expresses itself in sorrow over national backwardness and humiliation, and in joy over the people's emancipation and achievements. We find examples for both in the Old Testament. Psalm 137 is an example of sorrow over national catastrophe:

> By the waters of Babylon,
>> there we sat down and wept,
>> when we remembered Zion.
> On the willows there
>> we hung up our lyres.
> For there our captors
>> required of us songs,
> and our tormentors, mirth, saying,
>> "Sing us one of the songs of Zion!"
> How shall we sing the Lord's song
>> in a foreign land?
> If I forget you, O Jerusalem,
>> let my right hand wither!
> Let my tongue cleave to the roof of my mouth,
>> if I do not remember you,
> if I do not set Jerusalem
>> above my highest joy!

Psalm 126 is an example of joy and thanksgiving over the people's achievements:

> When the Lord restored the fortunes of Zion,
>> we were like those who dream.
> Then our mouth was filled with laughter,

and our tongue with shouts of joy;
then they said among the nations,
"The Lord has done great things for them."
The Lord has done great things for us,
we are glad.
Restore our fortunes, O Lord,
like the watercourses in the Negeb!
May those who sow in tears
reap with shouts of joy!
He that goes forth weeping,
bearing the seed for sowing,
shall come home with shouts of joy,
bringing his sheaves with him.

From these two psalms and other biblical passages we know that a certain healthy love for the motherland is not foreign to the Scriptures and that, consequently, Christians should not adopt a nihilistic posture to it.

Patriotism in China today affirms the achievements made through the self-sacrifice on the part of millions of our fellow Chinese, and pledges that we will work for continuing the struggle against the evils that still linger in our society, for material and cultural elevation, and for greater justice and human dignity. That is a responsible love for nation. Christians need to care for the welfare of the people of the whole world in all their historical concreteness. It means for us caring for China, not exclusively but as our point of departure, the first stage in our love of mankind. This caring is not in opposition but extends itself naturally to internationalism.

We admire the words of Uchimura Kanzo:

"Jesus and Japan; my faith is not a circle with one center; it is an ellipse with two centers. My heart and mind revolve around the two dear names. And I know that one strengthens the other."

In the same sense as his, we like to say: our faith is like an ellipse with two centers, the two Cs; Christ and China.

One result of Three-Self in China is to land Chinese Protestantism in a postdenominational situation. Early in the '50s, with the war going on in Korea, there was the freezing of funds between the USA and China which completely paralyzed all the national and many of the provincial and diocesan denominational bodies as well as the National Christian Council of those days. They could hardly continue to give directions to their constituencies. Under those circumstances Christians became much more closely related locally across denominational lines. Because of the shortness of denominational history in China, denominational loyalty was not an impediment to the growth of the spirit of unity among Christians under the umbrella of Three-Self. Today, denominational structures no longer exist, but denominational characteristics in matters of faith and worship which Christians cherish are honored and preserved. The emphasis of the Three-Self Movement is on the development of the Chinese Christian's selfhood; while that of the China Christian Council is pastoral in the broad sense of the word, that is, the nurturing of the spirituality and intellectuality of our churches and groups. This includes the printing of Bibles, the publication of hymnbooks and journals and books, the running of seminaries and other theological training centers. These are all things which we find it possible for us to do together. We trust our present stage is transitional and will lead to the emergence of a truly Christian and truly Chinese Church of Jesus Christ rooted in the Bible and in the soil of China. But we have not been given to see clearly what, in God, the next step is.

Chinese Christians are faced with many other problems, such as the big age gap between our present church leaders and their successors still under training, the inadequacy in our work of pastoral nurturing, the existence of heretical teachings, and mistakes in ways the policy of religious freedom is implemented by cadres in some localities. But we are aware that churches have always moved forward in spite of all the problems they are plagued with. As we go forward on the path of Three-Self, supporting prayers on the part of Christians elsewhere mean a lot to us. We hope and pray that, through the visits Japanese and Chinese Christians are exchanging, a deeper sympathy, love, and relationship will emerge between the Christians of our two countries, to the strengthening of each other in the work of building up the Body of Christ.

—A Rationale for Three-Self, Doshisha University, 1984

# RUNNING THE CHURCH WELL

Today we celebrate the 45th anniversary of the Three-Self Patriotic Movement of Protestant Churches in China.

Under God's care, Three-Self has accomplished a tremendous amount, which I would like to enumerate as seven points:

(1) It has raised the patriotic consciousness of believers in general, so that they have an ardent love for their land and join in its socialist construction.

(2) Nationwide, it has basically accomplished the independence and self-government, self-support and self-propagation of the Chinese Church, so that following the Cultural Revolution, we have been able to progress to governing well, supporting well and propagating well; that is, to running the church well.

(3) It has improved the image of Christianity, so that more people in society are well disposed toward it, decreasing the obstacles to the implementation of the policy of religious freedom.

(4) It has promoted concord and harmony among denominations, preparing the way for the present postdenominational situation.

(5) It has offered a model of independence and self-government on a national scale for not a few Christians in Third World countries.

(6) It has exposed colonialist and imperialist use of evangelism in its invasion of China, and brought this to the attention of persons in church and historical circles worldwide.

(7) Chinese Christianity has its own special Chinese Christian characteristics, thus raising the status of the Chinese Church in the church international and gaining many friends.

The accomplishments of Three-Self are great. We must continue to support and develop the areas mentioned above.

However, all movements go through stages. Today, the Chinese Church has more or less realized self-government, self-support and self-propagation. As we celebrate the 45th anniversary of Three-Self, we must not rest on past accomplishments. History has already brought us to a new stage and given us new lessons to learn. Three-Self patriotism has rich new content: when we have attained self-government, we must govern well, self-support must mean well supported and self-propagation must become a situation in which propagation is done well.

The issue to be resolved in the first stage is, who is to run the Chinese Church? The answer is that it should be run by Chinese Christians ourselves. When this problem has been solved, we must unite with a greater number of people for the next step—genuinely and sincerely to run the church well.

In spite of the fact that the accomplishments of Three-Self are great, we cannot but admit that there are still many believers with whom we have not been able to unite. Many of them indeed are not opposed to self-government, self-support and self-propagation, even less are they opposed to patriotism, but their attitude to the Three-Self organization and to the China Christian Council is one of suspicion and lack of trust. They feel that these two organizations have no relation to whether or not the church is well run, have no interest in running the church well and expend no effort to do so. In order to accomplish the original intention of Three-Self and to improve its image, thereby strengthening our expanding unity, we must sincerely and wholeheartedly run the church well.

The great mass of believers loves the church fervently. The reason believers place their hopes on Three-Self, what they are seeking, is that the church be well run. They want the church to cast off whatever would cause the church not to be the church, whatever would thus distress believers, in order to make a better and stronger witness. At its inception, Three-Self promised and guaranteed these things repeatedly. If we do not recognize that the Three-Self Patriotic Movement has gone through stages, if we assume its circumstances haven't changed and therefore do not shift our thinking to running the church well, but allow a foul atmosphere to spread in the church, then no matter how lovely a picture we paint of Three-Self, we are just making empty promises to the believers, are we not? How can the mass of believes support us? Or welcome us? These days whoever exerts him or herself to run the church well will have the love and esteem of the believers. Whoever does nothing to run the church well, just muddling through, will not have the trust of the believers. The situation is just this simple and clear. Running the church well according to the Three-Self principle is a rather good slogan suited to the present stage. But it should not be a slogan on the lips only; it must be translated into action. At this late date, we, as those in authority in the Chinese Church, must realize that we find ourselves in the situation of competing for the masses with counter-revolutionary forces at home and abroad. Simply talking about Three-Self's past attainments is far from adequate. Today, Three-Self must take running the church well as its duty. Only in this way can it attract masses of believers to the Three-Self patriotic banner. Otherwise, the believers will say that we "do not love the church," that those of us who "lift up Three-Self," are in danger of being those the believers take offense at. Sadly, in some places, the erstwhile leaders of the Three-Self Patriotic Movement have become *persona non grata* to the believers.

The "well" in running the church well, has two levels of meaning for me. One is to gain the affection and support of the mass of believers; the second is to gain the recognition and sympathy of people in the broader society.

It has been said that to speak of running the church well is a diminution of Three-Self. Not at all, running the church well is a deepening of Three-Self. Only by striving to run the church well can we unite church workers and believers under the banner of Three-Self patriotism. To commit to running the church well is more formidable than a political declaration and is a much higher form of politics. Not to run the church well would be to drag down the prestige of Three-Self and would lose co-workers and Christians for the Three-Self cause. If we want to unite with believers today, we must strive to run the church well.

Now there are infiltrating forces from overseas that oppose us and want to harm us. They try to cause divisions among us. How shall we respond? By striving to run our church well and pleasing the believers. The more we do for the believers to like us and the less we do to make them dislike us, the more able we will be to unite with them. Then no matter how overseas forces strive to infiltrate us, they will fail.

Within the Three-Self Patriotic Movement there are differing points of view on matters of secondary importance. For example, the thinking of the new generation and that of the older generation is not entirely in accord. This is normal, but in general there can be mutual respect and seeking the common ground because on this point of running the church well, we have an adequate common language. Running the church well can unite us. By making running the church well our major direction, we can come together in unity.

If we want to run the church well, we must urge our colleagues to join us in paying attention to and studying many problems in our work; How can those who love the country and love the church do a good job of preaching, of leading worship, of improving the level of hymns and music in the church, of Bible study, of chairing church affairs meetings, of attracting believers to joining in the building up of the church? How, proceeding from faith, can we aid believers to love the country in addition to loving the church and to love the church in addition to loving the country? How can we interpret the Bible, construct a theology which is both of the spirit and of the world, harmonize the church with socialism, run theological education well, foster theological students to develop at the same time spiritually, morally, intellectually, physically and in community? And so on and so on. We must allow our co-workers and fellow believers to study these things together and put them into practice. By exploring these questions, we can mobilize and unite with many co-workers and fellow believers.

There are obstacles to running the church well: In particular, the very prominent cases of a minority in grassroots churches and at every level of the TSPM and CCC who act arbitrarily, wherever a minority or even a single individual has the final word and believers are not allowed to know of or be involved in the affairs of the church, where terms of office are not followed and finances are not made public. Other corrupt practices are born of such circumstances and believers are very dissatisfied.

If we have understood correctly, Christianity is not the same as some other religions. Adherents of some other religions can go into the temple, follow religious practices and be satisfied, but Christians cannot be satisfied with simply having a church to go to. A Christian is a limb of the church. Church affairs are one's own affairs and the Christian feels that how the church is run, well or poorly, is his or her own responsibility. A Christian cannot remain indifferent but must become involved.

Recently the Chinese People's Political Consultative Conference agreed that the CPPCC has three functions: political consultation, democratic supervision and political participation and discussion. I think that if we want to run the church well, we must also have these three functions. We should propose consultation, propose that believers have oversight over church affairs and that believers should be highly involved in the big decisions of the church.

Today, under the guidance of the theory of socialism with Chinese characteristics put forward by Comrade Deng Xiaoping, the whole country, people in all walks of life, are all striving to do their own work well. Doctors are striving to run their hospitals well; teachers are striving to run their schools well. Workers and farmers are doing the same in their factories and villages. Going all out like this to make the country strong is an expression of socialism. Since the Chinese Church is already part of the religious enterprise of the Chinese people themselves, our patriotic church workers should as a matter of course strive to run our church well. If people in all other fields and walks of life are striving to make things well run and only the church is poorly managed, how can we face the Chinese people and Chinese believers? If we are able to run the church well, believers nationwide will certainly thank us and we will be worthy of what our nation has entrusted to us.

The attainments of the Three-Self Movement founded by Y. T. Wu are great. I have enumerated seven, but there is an eighth, which I hope can be added on the occasion of the 50th anniversary of Three-Self. That is the fulfillment of the promise of running the church well, accompanied by the appearance in China of a church which measures up to the body of Christ and is patriotic as well as church-loving.

—45th Anniversary of the Three-Self Patriotic Movement of
Protestant Churches in China Shanghai, November 21, 1995

ಸಃ

# BUILDING THE CHURCH
# FOR THE FUTURE

When some time has passed, it is good to look back and see where we have come from.

In the 1950s and '60s, Chinese Christianity took three steps which attracted worldwide attention: 1) it upheld patriotism and achieved self-government, self-support and self-propagation; 2) it started Nanjing Union Theological Seminary to train new workers for the church; and 3) it broke out of its denominational fetters and achieved union.

One important thing we did after the Cultural Revolution was to create a Chinese Christian church affairs organ called the China Christian Council. Our main consideration was that in order to make the church well run, we must pay attention to church affairs. The Three-Self organization promoted patriotism and self-government, self-support and self-propagation, which were essential, but our church had a great deal of work to do in the area of handling church affairs also. Such work did not fall within the purview of the Three-Self organization as its nature was conceived and it would not have been able to do it well. The establishment of the CCC as separate from the TSPM was an announcement that we could not be content with simply running the church ourselves, we had to run it well. We must be not only self-governed, but well-governed; not only self-supported, but well-supported; and not only must we do propagation ourselves, we must do it well. Just as "red" becomes "expert" through practice, patriotism and Three-Self must be realized in running the church well. Running the church well is bound to attract more people to the work and this will increase the scope of our unity.

For Three-Self patriotism to be implemented in running the church well was a new step some ten years ago. Establishing the CCC was the organizational expression of this step. This was an important step; with this, leadership emerged in Chinese Christian church affairs and the work and ministry of running the church well began to develop.

Secondly, we adjusted our view of Christians overseas and rejected exclusivism. When you mentioned a missionary in the 1950s and '60s, you had to add "imperialist" before the name. We were really a bit self-satisfied then and had no international relationships to speak of. We did not use the term ecumenical nor did we say the Chinese Church was part of the church ecumenical. To say such things seemed questionable, as if the speaker was not firmly anti-imperialist. A sign of change in this aspect took place when the CCC became part of the World Council of Churches. This is not to say that imperialism did not invade China, nor that in its invasion of China it did not make use of religion and missionaries, but in judging events and people we must seek truth from facts and not go overboard.

Thirdly, theological thinking broadened. This was not very obvious, but there was a very important beginning. In general terms, sadly, there seems to be only one genuinely important doctrine in Chinese Christianity: If you believe in Christ, then you are justified in God's eyes; if you do not believe in Christ, then you are not justified in God's eyes. From a shallow insistence on this point have evolved many views contrary to common sense: So and so believes, so though he is counter revolutionary and a traitor, he will go to heaven. Imperialist aggression is bad, but the aggressors were Christians, justified in God's eyes, while the objects of their aggression were non-Christians, not justified in God's eyes, so the objects of aggression got what they deserved—its was God's punishment. There are not many people today who would actually say this, but the idea is still around. Notice to what extent emphasis on only one point of faith and no others can turn right and wrong upside down. According to this point of view, God is well aware that the majority of humankind is bound for the eternal flames of hell because they are unbelievers. Yet day and night without ceasing he keeps creating human beings. What kind of view of God is that? Where do we begin to talk about God's mercy?

We know that Paul spoke of justification by faith because the Pharisees attacked Christ and his disciples for not keeping the law. They stressed that in order to be saved, one had to observe each and every Jewish law—circumcision, keeping the Sabbath, all the dietary restrictions and so on. The doctrine of justification by faith arose to counter the Pharisee's reliance on observance of the law as the way to salvation. Justification by faith greatly enlarged the ranks of those who received the grace of salvation. Only in this way could those outside Judaism—the Gentiles—receive saving grace. Only then could Christianity evolve from a Jewish sect into a world religion.

Later Martin Luther too stressed justification by faith. This was because he opposed the Roman hierarchy and their methods of oppressing the masses, such as the selling of indulgences.

When we study a doctrine, we should ask what it stands in opposition to as well as what it says. There are many doctrines in Christianity besides justification by faith: the never-ending creation of God; the Incarnation, Christ's resurrection; the renewal of creation; the indwelling of the Holy Spirit which bestows wisdom; the Beatitudes; the greatest commandment, which is to love God and to love your neighbor as yourself; to do unto others as you would have them do unto you; not to be served, but to serve. Paul said that there are faith, hope and love, but the greatest of these is love—love is a higher virtue than faith. Why not stress these? If Chinese Christianity esteems only one doctrine, this doctrine could easily lead to the contradiction between belief and unbelief, which could lead to endless divisions, damaging the nation's stability. This cannot be God's will, can it?

The situation is changing and a theological renewal is underway. A growing number of co-workers no longer highlight belief/unbelief in their preaching, or speak only of heaven and hell, or of who is saved and who is not. Pastors who are responsible toward the people do not talk about countless upright people going to hell.

Today, a greater number of the messages being preached from

China's pulpits are ethical ones. Religion and ethics cannot be separated. A religion which says nothing about ethics is a very primitive and crude religion. Sadly, in Chinese Christianity even now, we still have people who, in order to highlight the contradiction between belief and unbelief, actually reject ethics and promote antinomianism. They make opposing camps of saving grace and ethics. On the excuse of raising high the grace of salvation, they stoop to saying that ethics is unimportant. Are they unaware of the great ethical content of the Bible? Six of the Ten Commandments have to do with regulating ethical behavior.

Theology has to do with faith and convictions held deep in human hearts. Adjustment is therefore slow; ethics, which enrich faith, develop only gradually. But theological changes are very fundamental changes and have already begun in Chinese Christianity. They are worth our attention.

Fourthly, along with changes in theological thinking, social concerns are being raised in Chinese Christianity. The Amity Foundation emerged as a response to the times ten years ago. More and more provincial and municipal churches are running dedicated social service organizations, taking it as their responsibility to alleviate the people's hardships. We do not hear much talk attacking the so-called social gospel any more. Recently we held a national meeting to exchange experiences in church social welfare work.

Fifthly, at present, we are changing our view of meeting points, or what are termed house churches, which are outside the Three-Self organization and adjusting our relationships with them. The majority of these meeting points are also self-governing, self-supporting and self-propagating. Those that identify with forces overseas operating behind a cloak of Christianity represent a minority. There are many reasons why these Christians and house churches remain outside the Three-Self organization; for example, (1) [the churches] are too far away and travel is inconvenient; (2) they are not used to what they perceive as different beliefs and rituals at the churches or to the sort of preaching that is done; (3) they feel there are not enough religious activities at the churches; (4) they have problems with the pastors at the church; (5) they were hurt by the leftist line and are afraid even now; (6) certain actions of Three-Self or the government have earned them the disaffection of the people and hurt their image. To this day some people look down on them and their defiance has grown; (7) discord sown by overseas influence.

Those who accept Jesus Christ as Lord are our brothers and sisters and we have no reason to exclude them. We should help them and serve them. In order to avoid forcing our views on others or forcing union, in order that one day we can consciously choose to be one and become one body, we have suggested to the Religious Affairs Bureau that permission to register churches and meetings points should not be contingent upon being part of the TSPM and CCC. They have agreed to this. Support of Three-Self is not one of the six requirements for registration. We do not make use of political pressure to force unity; we seek only that all churches and meeting points that carry on normal religious activities can enjoy a legal existence.

There are people in China who have very little or no sympathy for this step we are taking. Would-be infiltrators from overseas are also busy making up rumors, sowing discord and deepening divisions, and so this step is an arduous one. But it is in line with Jesus' prayer that we be one and with the desires of believers. We must then strive to undertake it.

In order to enlarge the extent of unity, I would like to mention here the work of so-called "private meeting points" in applying to the government for registration. Registration can be a way of bringing "underground" meetings points "above ground." It is not good for any nation to have religious believers who must believe and meet secretly. This is no demonstration of freedom of religious belief. "Above-ground," these believers are visible to others and to the government, who can then feel at ease with the situation. The believers can feel secure too. The regulations for registration announced by the Religious Affairs Bureau say that a church or meeting point need only fulfill six simple and easily met requirements in order to apply for and receive permission. This shows that the government is not using registration to reduce the number of churches and meeting points or to make trouble for them but that it wants to allow all normal religious activities to be public and legal.

To tell the truth, to divide normal religious activities into two—
those which have received permission and those which have not, or
into underground and aboveground, or public and private—this is the
old Soviet Union style, not that of socialism with Chinese characteristics. If we can do the work of registering religious venues well in
China, so that all religious activities can have public and legal status,
that will be achievement enough. This is religious work with Chinese
socialist characteristics. I am deeply hopeful we can achieve this.

Mr. Luo Guanzong and I requested a meeting with the Head of the
legal office of the State Council on the question of registration. This
Bureau Head said that registration was simply registration and should
be separate from regular work. The registration regulations did not set
out how regular work should be carried on. Such work might be very
good, but it should not be attached to the regulations. This would add
to what was subsumed under the work of registration. We should give
some thought to the intent and spirit of these remarks.

There are those who would take advantage of the opportunity presented by registration to have the qualifications of all clergy co-workers within their boundaries reviewed by the TSPM and CCC. This is
unacceptable. First of all, this extends the work of registration and
puts difficulties in its way. To insist that some of the "private" meeting
points that do not recognize the two bodies have their clergy reviewed
by them is simply coercion. Secondly, this is a huge job—where will
the two bodies find the strength to screen such a large number of
people unknown to them? Thirdly, since we have not yet succeeded
in enlarging the scope of unity, to set ourselves up as arbiters of other
people's qualifications would be to put ourselves in the position of
increasing the attacks on unity. The responsibility of the TSPM and
CCC in applying for government registration is to encourage and assist
churches and meeting points in the process. We should provide a
channel for communication by promptly reflecting to the government
problems and opinions on the church's side.

One can hardly believe that there are still those who oppose registration on grounds of being "citizens of heaven who obey only God
and not man (sic)." But these people did not refuse to be counted as
Chinese during the national census for the same reason. If they want

to have nothing to do with the government, does that mean they will not carry identity cards? The church is a spiritual organization, it is true, but on earth it is also a people's organization. I was recently shown an American publication exhorting Chinese Christians to resist registration in similar terms. If we adopt a closed-door approach to registration and throw difficulties in the way of the process, we will be doing just what these anti-China groups overseas want.

The five steps described above are patriotic and church-loving; they all make Christianity more compatible with socialism. They have been possible for two reasons; (1) because the government has restored order after the Cultural Revolution and undertaken a critique of the ultra-leftist line; and (2) because the time was ripe. Christians found them reasonable and acceptable and commended and supported them.

Looking at these five steps today, we find their common point in the rejection of the philosophy of struggle. They are about love, reconciliation and unity. They enlarge our unity and are pleasing to the believers.

In the Book of Revelation, the Holy Spirit instructs John to write letters to the seven churches, the first being to the church in Ephesus. The letter praises the church for its toil and patient endurance against evildoers, its hatred for the works of the Nicolaitans and its ability to discern false apostles. All of this is good. But the Spirit also accuses the church in Ephesus of having abandoned the love it had at first. When a church loses its love, it should remember from where it has fallen, repent and do the works it did at first. I think our Chinese Church can find great revelation from the Spirit's teaching to the church in Ephesus, hear the Spirit's demands and in love build up the body of Christ.

I would like to mention one other topic here, and that is "strengthen oversight in religious affairs." This wording has caused anxiety among many Christians, who feel that the policy has changed. Let me share with you how I see it.

(1) In principle, oversight is a good thing, not a bad one. Industry, agriculture, transportation, commerce, hospitals, schools and libraries all require oversight and religion is no different. An

order of service to be followed in worship is also a form of oversight. When we say run the church well, we could also be saying supervise the church well. We should not oppose oversight supervision of religious affairs.

(2) When we speak of strengthening the oversight or supervision of religious affairs, supervisors do not refer only to cadres in government religious affairs departments. Patriotic religious bodies of all religions, including Three-Self and church affairs groups from the national to the grassroots level, all have a supervisory duty; all are supervisors or overseers.

(3) The objects of this strengthening of supervision and oversight, in addition to the organizations at all levels from national to grassroots and venues for religious activities, also include government religious affairs departments at all levels.

(4) Supervisors must strengthen themselves. This goes for government religious affairs departments as well as for the TSPM and CCC of the Christian Church at all levels and for grassroots churches and meeting points. In recent years there has been an increase in contradictions within the church and we should propose that these be settled through consultation, allowing believers, patriotism and love for the church to be expressed in taking part in this supervisory work.

(5) Government supervision of religion is mainly concerned with politics and the law. It supervises activities that transgress the Constitution, laws and policies; it does not supervise church affairs. In church affairs, the government should respect the faith of the church and the good tradition and system of democratic supervision which the church has formed over time.

(6) Supervision should be done according to the law. There should not be criminal actions such as beatings and arrests, seizure of Bibles, hymnals or church property, or arbitrary collection of fees or imposition of fines.

(7) Church personnel should follow church regulations. Legal supervision of church affairs does not include decisions on church personnel being made outside the church. If the government has views on church personnel, the church should be

amenable and consider these and consult on them. Church
finances should also be handled this way. Regulation 145 of
the State Council says "The property and finances of a religious
venue shall be under the supervision and use of the supervisory group of that venue."

(8) The national TSPM and CCC, which have experience in
church affairs should play a greater role in leading and guiding
church affairs. This will be beneficial in strengthening supervision, but this is in no way to negate the principle of consultation.

(9) Regulation 145 of the State Council contains clear regulations
on the supervision of venues for religious activities. We should
study and respect it.

I would be happy to have your responses to the personal views I
have set out here.

—Speech to the Joint Standing Committee
of the TSPM and the CCC
Nanjing, April 24, 1995

ઈ૭

# THOUGHTS OF THE FUTURE UPON RETIREMENT

**B**ishop K. H. Ting has served as President of the China Christian
Council (CCC) and Chairperson of the Chinese Christian Three-Self
Patriotic Movement (TSPM) for three terms, altogether fifteen years.
*Tian Feng*, the magazine of the Chinese Church, interviewed him earlier this year on his retirement and posed some of the questions which
concern all Chinese Christians.

**TF:** Bishop Ting, has pressure been put on you from any quarter
to retire at this time?

**TING:** None at all. The principle put forward by the two national

Christian bodies (CCC and TSPM) of "not staying on over eighty" is a very good one. It is my hope that all colleagues over eighty should be able to retire and allow younger colleagues to shoulder greater responsibility. And I hope that after a few more years have passed, we can achieve a situation of "not staying on over seventy" and then "not staying on over sixty," so that older colleagues can all step down and allow younger colleagues to take over.

**TF:** You have been head of both the CCC and the TSPM for the past fifteen years, but now different colleagues will head each body. Does this indicate a split, or, will it lead to a split?

**TING:** No, in fact this illustrates the unity of our two national bodies. If there really were a threat of division, I certainly would not be retiring now.

**TF:** Mr. Guangzong Luo (Chairperson of the TSPM) and Dr. Wenzao Han (President of the China Christian Council) are both men of outstanding ability, but neither is an ordained minister. Do you think their election to these posts is appropriate?

**Ting:** Very much so. In their respective constitutions, neither the CCC nor the TSPM stipulates that either the President of the former or the Chairperson of the latter must be an ordained minister. Mr. Y. T. Wu (TSPM Chairperson in the 1950s and 1960s) was not an ordained minister. Many church organizations overseas have lay people in leadership positions. The important thing is that both men have been long-time supporters of Three-Self and of building up the church well, and that they stress unity and serve as good models for their Christian colleagues. Dr. Han's sermon at the closing worship of the Sixth National Christian Conference, for example, was generally felt to be deeply inspiring—three delegates went out of their way to commend it to me.

**TF:** Are you optimistic about the future of the church in China?

**TING:** A great many of us Christians have gone through the Cultural Revolution, and so it is difficult for us to be pessimistic these days. Now the policy on religious freedom of the Party and government has taken root in people's hearts, and although there are still shortcomings, we can be happy that channels for the exchange of views and consultation do exist. The church is at this moment in the process of putting younger people into positions of leadership, and the average age of delegates to the Sixth National Christian Conference was more than seven years lower than the previous one. It is understandable that the age of the highest leadership level cannot be brought down too quickly. The ratio of participation by women and lay people has also been raised, though we still cannot rest content in these areas. The response to these elections has been highly favorable among Christians here and abroad, including among overseas Chinese Churches, especially because Dr. Wenzao Han is no stranger to churches overseas. Chinese Christians are marked by their Bible reading, witness bearing, love for the church and love for the country; this too makes me optimistic.

**TF:** Several years ago you pointed out that Three-Self should be seen as scaffolding. Do you still see it that way?

**TING:** Yes I do. I said that the CCC and TSPM were both scaffolding for the construction of this great edifice of the Chinese Church. My vision was that one day a Chinese Church, one which was very well-governed, very well-supported and one in which the propagation of the gospel was going very well, would tower in all its beauty and splendor on the eastern horizon. The Chinese Church would by then have her own complete church order. When this resplendent edifice is completed, the scaffolding will be gone. I still believe this today, that is, CCC and TSPM are important and necessary, but they are not eternal. There is no basis in the Bible, and no theological justification, for making them perpetual entities, nor would it be acceptable to Chinese Christians. I think we have done enough if we have built our scaffolding well.

**TF:** There are a fair number of Christians in China still who do not belong to Three-Self. What is your view of this?

**TING:** Three-Self is a movement of the church as well as a principle for building up the church well. It has no membership structure, and so there is no question of belonging or not. When Y. T. Wu and others began Three-Self in the 1950s, there were many in the church both in China and abroad who opposed it due to a failure to understand what it was about. But today, there are very few who still oppose it because everyone knows Three-Self means self-administration, self-support and self-propagation, and this contributes to a common language between Christians and the general populace and facilitates our witness to Christ. Three-Self has accomplished a great deal of good. To take the Bible as an example, the TSPM and the CCC have already printed millions and millions of Bibles. Those Christians who "do not belong to" Three-Self, are also reading Bibles provided by the CCC and TSPM. The two bodies also do many other things which are beneficial to believers, so why should we want to oppose them? As for holding different views on certain things, or opposing the actions of certain persons, that is only natural. Such matters are open to discussion and improvement and we should not be excessively anxious about them. Certainly we should not lightly dismiss others as "anti-Three-Self." I feel that all those who respect the teachings of the Bible and acknowledge Jesus Christ as Lord are brothers and sisters in the Lord who should have mutual respect, conscientiously unite and consult with each other in everything.

**TF:** What do you plan to do when you retire?

**TING:** I am still Principal of Nanjing Union Theological Seminary, though I hope to retire from that position as well when it becomes possible. I would like to read all the books I have not had time to read, put in order the writings and papers I have done at home and abroad during years past, and take the time to pursue my mathematical pastimes.

**TF:** Many people have been concerned about you since your wife Siu-May passed away last year.

**TING:** Thank you for your concern. I live with one of my sons (an associate professor of English at Nanjing University) and his wife (a doctor) and my grandson (a senior middle school student), and they take good care of me.

**TF:** What are your hopes for Christianity in China?

**TING:** One is that unity be upheld, that genuine and complete mutual respect in matters of faith and worship be achieved, that at the same time all groups uphold unity by not making too much of their distinctive characteristics. Second, that the Bible's ethical message be developed hand in hand with the moral emphasis to be found in our Chinese culture, and that the influence of antinomianism within the church be eliminated.

**TF:** Are you satisfied with theological education at present?

**TING:** I cannot say that I am satisfied with it. Whether we speak of teachers and students in the learning process, of pastors preaching, or of those who engage in Christian literature work, I would like to see that beyond "satisfying believers," those involved should not forget that they must elevate the level of the believers, for, as St. Paul tells the believers in Philippi, he prays that "your love may overflow more and more with knowledge and full insight to help you to determine what is best, so that in the day of Christ you may be pure and blameless, having produced the harvest of righteousness that comes through Jesus Christ for the glory and praise of God" (Phil. 1:9–11).

**TF:** Is there anything else you would like to share with our readers?

**TING:** In the past fifteen years, I have become more and more aware of the fact that many Christians have been keeping me in their prayers and that there are a growing number of colleagues and fellow Christians overseas who also pray for me. These prayers stem not only from their love and concern for me personally, even more they represent a coalescence of everyone's care and concern for the Chinese Church and our Three-Self spirit. I personally have no special talent, but God has heard these prayers. They have upheld me, almost like a swimmer who cannot drown in the Salt Sea. And so I can say that those prayers have been transformed into material strength. I want to thank all those who have prayed for me, whether in China or overseas, whether known to me or not. I hope they will continue in the same way to support our new leaders with their prayers. I have also received a great many letters and Christmas cards, but I have answered hardly any of them. This is very impolite of me and I hope the senders will forgive me. I wish everyone health of body and spirit and progress in this New Year, 1997.

—January 1997

# QUESTIONS AND ANSWERS ON THE PRESENT-DAY CHURCH SITUATION

U nder the loving care and guidance of Jesus Christ its head, the church in China has gone through a decade of building itself up after a decade of catastrophe. All Christians concerned with the church's welfare must be thinking a lot about the path it has trodden in the last ten years. Before Christmas, 1989, a group of students of Nanjing Seminary had a visit with Bishop K. H. Ting, who is the principal of the school and currently heads up the two national church bodies. What follows is the content of the interview as compiled by a staff member of the *Nanjing Theological Review*, who conducted the interview, and Bishop Ting himself.

**Q.** *How do you evaluate the work of the church in China in the last ten years?*

**A.** During the previous decade the government has done much to implement the neglected policy of religious freedom, with the cooperation of people in different walks of life. At the same time, Christians in large numbers have thrown themselves into socialist reconstruction, service to the people and witness to Jesus Christ, all with remarkable results. The church is enjoying the goodwill of more and more people and a welcome increase in numbers. There are a growing number of non-church intellectuals who have shed their prejudices against Christianity and become willing to study it, to work with Christians and even to embrace the faith. Self-government, self-support and self-propagation have moved to a stage when greater emphasis is put on the need to govern ourselves well, to support ourselves well and to do the work of Christian propagation well. This is an appeal to doing a good job of building up the church, the Body of Christ that raises the spirits of our Christian people and will surely strengthen and extend our unity. In publication, theological education and the laying down of constitutions to make church government not haphazard, but systematic, much solid work has been going on. Bibles are no longer in severe short supply. The question of re-ordering the relationship between Three-Self organizations on the one hand, and churches and Christian councils on the other, has been placed on our agenda. The church in China, while adhering to the Three-Self principle, lives as a member of the Universal Church and enjoys the support of many other members.

But we are also faced with many problems. The age level of our colleagues nationwide shows little sign of coming down. Pastoral nurture and theological thinking are two weak links in our work and may even be said to have been neglected. The quality of Christians' spirituality is not high. There is also a lack of proper education on Three-Self. Certain problems in our post-denominational existence still linger and call for solution. In some places there is a lack of enthusiasm for implementing the principle of religious freedom. There are also places where Three-Self and the work of the church are not integrated and, as a result, Three-Self finds it hard to justify itself. I understand there is an ascendance of anti-China infiltration under religious garb from outside and of acts in violation of the law in some parts of China.

**Q.** *How do you see the place of evangelism?*

**A.** Christ instructed his disciples to preach the gospel to the ends of the earth. When a person finds in Christ his or her salvation, it is most natural for the person to want to tell others of Christ, and that is evangelism. On account of the large number of new converts, nobody can deny that the church in China is an evangelistic church. But I like to say at the same time that our church also has other tasks. Today, we also need to emphasize the importance of discipleship and spiritual nurture of those converted through worship, preaching and teaching, group experiences in Bible study and faith exploration and extension of Christian concerns. If we emphasize evangelism to the neglect of deepening and elevating, then the quality of Christians' faith will lack cultivation and discipline. They will become ill equipped in the face of wrong teachings or even succumb to them. Thus, the development of our church's evangelistic and pastoral educational capabilities needs to be simultaneous.

**Q.** *Some of us say that Three-Self has already completed its task, while others say this is not so. What would you say?*

**A.** I think it is much more worthwhile to see what the task is than to argue whether it has been completed or not. Any movement tends to form stages. The aim of Three-Self was to solve the question of the Chinese Church's self-determination. It asked that politically Chinese Christians be patriotic and in church matters be independent, that is, self-governing, self-supporting and self-propagating. The central question then was: Should the church in China continue to be governed by Western missionary societies and their agents, or by Chinese Christians ourselves? Today, so far as the influence of the Three-Self movement has reached, this question has generally been solved. If we continue to focus on this question, there is not much to dwell upon.

Today we have come to the stage for the deepening of our commitment to Three-Self. If the winning of the right of self-determination is the first part of an essay we are writing, our efforts to govern ourselves well, support ourselves well and do the work of Christian propagation well in accordance with the Three-Self principle is its second part. This is a task or mission that comes up by necessity after the church has achieved independence. Independence is not anything to boast about, but for the building up of the church. Only then can Three-Self enjoy a good image. For example, it was good to claim back foreign concessions and settlements in big cities but, after claiming them back, China needed to do a good job in municipal government; failing that, the people would again be disappointed. The task of building up the church is today on our shoulders. Our two church bodies and the thirteen theological schools all have the responsibility of studying and giving guidance as regards how to govern ourselves well, support ourselves well and do the work of Christian witness well. We like our theological students to be concerned with these questions, too.

**Q.** *What are the criteria for judging that the church has been built up well?*

**A.** Christians would not all agree on the criteria. This calls for us to study the question and to practice mutual respect. However, I do not think the differences are too big. All will agree that the building up of the church should follow the Three-Self principle and the principle of loving our motherland and our church, be true to New

Testament teachings and church traditions, give respect to the wishes of the members, stress and elevate the status of women in the church, be thrifty and not extravagant, encourage as much as possible lay participation, practice democracy in church life and decision-making and so on. I think many Christians will agree, too, if I say that our two criteria are satisfaction on the part of Christians and having the favor of the people around us.

**Q.** *Is building up the church well the same as re-ordering relationships?*

**A.** I think the building up of the church is a broader concept. In a well-built-up church of Jesus Christ, relationships do function well, but to build up the church is more than rationalizing relationships. The latter is only an ingredient or result of building up the church according to Christ's own mind.

**Q.** *What do you have in mind when you talk about re-ordering the relationship?*

**A.** What we are at present working on is the re-ordering of the relationship between Three-Self organizations on the one hand and churches and Christian councils on the other. According to the constitution of the National Three-Self Patriotic Movement Committee, its aim is: "Under the leadership of the Chinese Communist Party and the People's Government, to unite all Christians (meaning Protestants) to cherish our motherland and abide by the Constitution and laws of the state, to uphold the principle of self-government, self-support and self-propagation for the maintenance of independence of the church and to defend the fruits of the Three-Self Movement, to promote international friendship, to work for the construction of a strong, modern socialist China with a high degree of democracy and culture, to help realize the nation's unification and to contribute to the cause of world peace." I think this wording is good and necessary politically. It does not bestow upon Three-Self organizations the function of leading and administering the churches. In other words, Three-Self bodies are not bodies with ecclesiastical authority. They are not the substance of the church. So the wording is theologically acceptable. In those places where Three-Self organizations for historical reasons have somehow taken over the function of leading and administering the churches, the relationship is not in order and colleagues and

Christians feel it hard to reconcile that state of affairs with their faith in the Church of which the head is Jesus Christ himself. If Three-Self organizations will just divest themselves of this function and limit themselves to the tasks given them in the constitution so that the churches themselves and the Christian councils can look after their church affairs in a churchly manner, the relationship will be in order.

Q. *So the re-ordering of the relationship is not the same as the closing down of Three-Self organizations after all?*

A. The re-ordering of the relationship and the closing down of Three-Self organizations are two exclusive subjects. If Three-Self organizations are to be closed down, their relationships with other bodies would cease to exist and there will be no relationships to re-order. The premise for reordering a relationship is that the relationship must exist. So the continuation of Three-Self organizations is taken for granted.

Some persons have spread the wrong notion that the re-ordering of relationships and the closing down of Three-Self organizations or even the giving up of the Three-Self principle are one and the same thing. Hence the appearance for a time of an understandable but unwarranted agitation to come to the rescue of Three-Self. This shows us that the re-ordering of relationships is a sensitive subject for which much explanatory work needs to be done.

Q. *You said a moment ago that the work of pastoral care is poor and has even been neglected. Is that not an over-statement?*

A. If we take church conditions in China as a whole, I think our present state is just that. No doubt the majority of our pastors are working hard. But when the ratio between pastors and Christians is one to several thousand, can we say we are giving tolerably good pastoral attention to our flock? Can this situation have no effect on the quality and standard of our Christians' religious and spiritual commitment? What is fortunate is that we now have about two hundred graduates each year from our thirteen theological schools. It means 2,000 young colleagues in ten years. Then, there are those coming out of provincial and local training courses. So the situation will improve after the present most difficult period. Then we can begin to introduce specialized ministries of various kinds.

**Q.** *Would you say something more about inadequacy in theological upbuilding?*

**A.** It is good the church in China gives an important place to redemption in Christ, to the question of selfhood of the church and to mutual respect in matters of faith and worship in order to insure a high degree of unity. But so far our theological thinking is quite limited and uncreative and stands in need of opening up. We haven't dared to develop the themes of God's creation, of Christ as the cosmic Logos who loves and of the Holy Spirit's work of inspiration and sanctification in the world. Ecclesiology and ethical questions are very much beyond our perspective. We don't compare notes theologically both within China and internationally. Colleagues of the present generation have had to devote themselves almost completely to tasks calling for immediate attention and more and more of them have reached their exhaustion point. I attach my hope for the church's theological flowering to colleagues of the new generation. Then, let us not forget the contributions of those non-church intellectuals who have discarded their prejudices and have turned sympathetic and appreciative as regards the church. They have written books on church history and on the Bible and have translated a good number of important theological writings into Chinese. There are a dozen or more of them on my desk. Some of them can very well be used as reference books in our theological classes.

**Q.** *How do you assess the problems and shortcomings in our church?*

**A.** Socialism is a new advance in human history and we can't expect its birth and consolidation to be all smooth and easy. To build up socialism in such a big, old and populous country as China is an even harder task. And to build up the church in this society is again something new in church history. Thus, it is only to be expected that many problems will come to light.

I wish our students to keep all their life, their youthful idealism, vitality and principledness and yet to know their need for humility and the art of gaining stability and unity through seeking common ground and allowing differences. It is important to be concerned with and able to analyze our problems and shortcomings, but let us remember that for 2,000 years now the church, under God, has endured in spite of and through all its problems and shortcomings to become what it is today. I myself feel sorrowful and concerned over the pathological phenomena in our church I hear about from time to time but, at the same time, I am relatively calm because things are in God's hand after we have done what we can to remedy them.

Some of our graduates go to their church assignments with "righteous indignation" and, after arrival, go on the offensive right and left as if they were Don Quixote. They soon land themselves in an impossible situation. We have heavy responsibilities and ours is a long pilgrimage. If, after reaching our posts, we are not first of all humble and don't try to understand the total situation as it is so as to get ourselves firmly established there, anything else is of little consequence. We must be good at achieving cooperative relations with Christians and other people of as many sorts as possible. We mustn't let problems throw us off our balance. We need to both take problems seriously and realize that they are ultimately insignificant.

—Questions and Answers, 1990

# ON SCHOOLS OF THEOLOGY

**W**ithin as well as outside the Christian church, there are people who look down on theology, or are even hostile to it. Some in our church publicly declare that "being spiritual" is enough, that theology is secular knowledge and that to study theology is to attack faith. Guided by such thinking, one seminary chose another name for itself rather than be termed a theological seminary. Some people in society still believe that religion is reactionary and theology even more so, that religion is a fraud and theology an even bigger one, that religion is an opiate and theology an even stronger narcotic. Under the influence of such thinking, some people lump all religions together without regard for their inner content: the religion of the reactionaries is religion, the religion of the progressives is likewise religion and both are opiates and frauds. In such a view, there is no need to differentiate among the different gradations within Christianity.

Theology is the church in the act of thinking. If religion and the church exist, then this church will certainly think. It will ponder many questions about the Bible, about the church, the society and the nation, and questions of values. There are of course differences and discrepancies between this and that type of thinking. For example, the Bible: Do we grasp it word by word or do we let the whole Bible speak? These are two different paths to understanding and interpreting the Bible. There are great differences among preachers—what they emphasize and what they downplay in the Bible, their ways of preaching—which are dictated by a preacher's theology. I believe that in general within the church those who have studied theology have more enlightened views, because a theologian must bring his or her faith in its entirety into line with reason, and so he or she has many views which must perforce be more enlightened. A religion without theology is rudimentary and primitive, it is a religion which does not think about issues, a religion which is incompatible with reason. Now there are many co-workers who argue for historical progress by striving to deal with real issues biblically and theologically. There are also some using the Bible to prevent human progress. I think it is extremely unjust to say that they are all dealing in opium. This is not a scientific attitude, nor one of seeking truth from facts. It does not help to develop theology and culture in a good direction.

Other people say, let religion remain reactionary and do not prettify it with patriotism and socialism. If you do, you will be committing an even greater fraud. I do not think in this way. We are not in the business of cheating people; we want to bring the principles of the Bible into play. If they say it is a greater fraud for Christians to talk about patriotism and moreover, to speak in a rational and convincing way so that believers will in good conscience love their country, then I think that Premier Zhou Enlai, rather than urging Christians to learn patriotism and undertake the Three-Self Patriotic Movement as he did, should have allowed Christians to be backward, the more backward the better. Then, the road we have followed in the last thirty-nine years has been completely wrong, and the Cultural Revolution approach to religion correct.

My topic for this meeting is a theological question that churches worldwide face and it has engendered a great deal of discussion. How shall we deal with culture, religion, science, art, philosophy, history and people's movements outside Christianity; that is, how shall we approach all truth, beauty and goodness outside Christianity?

Why has this issue become so prominent? For us in China, of course, it is because after Liberation we came into contact with many people and things that we had never encountered before: communism, the people, revolutionaries, liberation movements and people's power. All these were outside Christianity. In the past we Christians closed our doors and busied ourselves being Christians. Now our doors are open, and how we shall deal with these things theologically has become an issue for us.

Churches in Western countries, and in many Third World countries as well, are concerned with this issue for a variety of reasons. One is that they have discovered Eastern religions. The existence of these religions was not unknown to them in the past, but in the past they believed that truth lay in the West. They saw other religions as absurd, primitive and not worth bothering about. In recent decades, they have discovered these religions right next door. There are many Hindus, Muslims and Sikhs in British cities. In Birmingham, for example, there are Sikh and Hindu temples. Once Christians have had direct contact with other religions, they discover the adherents of these religions are not as ignorant as they once thought. They discover that the prayers of others have much in common with our Christian prayers. Other religions have not made degenerates of people. Hinduism produced such great persons as Tagore and Gandhi. Thus how Christians should look at other religions has become a new theological issue.

Another reason is that Christians have discovered that many of those who make great contributions in science and the arts are not Christians. For example, Arab medicine had a great influence in the history of Western medicine. Chinese acupuncture is growing popular in the West today Neither Arab nor Chinese medicine arose within a

Christian context. So many things from outside Christianity have contributed to the course of human progress. This has caused many Christians to question how we should look at these things theologically.

Still another reason is that we find many non-Christian people of excellent character, with high moral standards and a great spirit of self-sacrifice—people like Norman Bethune and Lei Feng, for example. People may be non-Christians and still have high moral character. And after all we Christians are not all of sufficiently high moral character. True, there are few people in our world today of particularly high moral character, but even this small number is enough to pose a theological problem.

There is yet another reason, one which makes people even more inclined to question how we should understand theologically all truth, beauty and goodness outside Christianity. This is because more and more Christians are discovering that Christianity and Christian theology seem to have their share of faults. The forces of colonialism have often used Christian theology, for example, and it was used to oppose and kill the Jews.

Because these questions have arisen in the last few decades, when we peruse Western theological publications, we find that many of the essays deal with them in some way. I will deal with the various responses by categorizing them into five types that I will discuss further below.

Since we are making a study, I do not think we should casually assign things to this or that "school" or "grouping" and consider our study done. To say that someone is of a certain school or faction is to label that person or that view. We can hang an identity on them, but this does not really solve the problem. I feel that no matter what this person has published, we must believe that he or she has made an effort to speak reasonably of Christianity and is making an effort to speak in its defense. The main trend in the world today is opposition or indifference to Christianity. The majority of people simply have no interest in it. In such circumstances, I think that if a person is able to speak on behalf of Christianity, he or she deserves our respect. We should acknowledge that we have something in common with that person. We may think that the view that person puts forth is not so great, but let us not reject it or say the person is not spiritual or not orthodox. We should ask what question the person is trying to deal with. Is it only in trying to solve this problem that he or she puts forward such an idea? If that person's solution to the problem does not satisfy you, what solution would you propose in its place? What is he or she saying? And to what extent? What did he or she not say? We must get things clear first. We must not misinterpret others. There are few theological debates in China at present. Some small controversy will always give rise to a situation in which the opposing view is distorted beyond recognition and then brought down. It is easy to defeat an idea if you twist it first. Like a straw man, it cannot fight back. We may in this way lose ideas which would have a lot to contribute or reveal to us. Thus, we must be clear about what a person is saying and what he or she is not saying. Criticism should not be exaggerated. This is the approach of seeking truth from facts and feeling after the truth.

The first of the five approaches I want to discuss is ignoring the problem and refusing even to consider the issue, as if we were not aware of its existence. In spite of the fact there are so many viewpoints outside Christianity waiting for us Christians properly to understand and deal with, there are some Christians, theologians included, who do not admit the existence of such questions, and therefore, simply do not consider them. Persons with this view account for a rather large proportion of Christians.

From the 4th century on, Christianity became identified with the ruling powers of Europe. This state of affairs prevailed on the whole for a dozen or more centuries. Overseas this is referred to as the Constantinian Era. Christianity occupied a position of power and this situation was an accepted truth, an unalterable principle. If someone was discovered to have a different view, the church authorities or the Inquisition would deal with them. The church was joined to all power and authority. Because it had power, the church's thinking was closed. It maintained its power within a specific world and knew and asked nothing about the world outside. This long period of self-centered self-aggrandizement, ignorant and uninterested in what lay outside, has been difficult to eradicate, even to the present. When Christianity was carried to Third World nations, this attitude went with it and was taken over by not a few believers in the Third World, where it persists over a wide area. In China, for example, even though there never was any Constantinian era, the European attitude of turning a blind eye to non-Christian culture which marked that era continues to a certain extent. Believers and co-workers influenced by it feel that theology only means how this part of the Bible relates to or is connected to that part of the Bible. Dealing with culture, belief, concepts, or movements outside the church is no business of theology. Such an attitude is basically unstable, for when the wind blows the grass sways. This attitude easily turns into the second type.

The second attitude or approach we can, for the moment, term the "theology of two opposing armies" or "the angels of light theory." This is the attitude that if there is any small good outside the gospel or the church, this is the work of Satan in the garb of angels of light sent to deceive or entrap us. This is a theological view characterized by the belief that Christianity is sharply opposed and sharply at odds to all that is non-Christian. Under the slogan of "none but Christ," this view feels anything outside Christ is corrupted, evil and of Satan. Christ is not only opposed to sin, Christ is also opposed to good, because human good is worthless and is in essence a false angel of light sent by Satan. Tertullian asked: "What has Athens to do with Jerusalem?" Jerusalem represented the church for him, while Athens meant worldly knowledge and philosophy. He felt the two had nothing in common.

A very large part of the missionary movement of the Western churches in the 18th and 19th centuries was basically undertaken with this kind of thinking. Missionaries came to the Third World to evangelize, consciously or unconsciously negating everything about the people of the place. The ethnic religion and culture they saw as devoid of merit. Progressive or not, good or bad, it all had to be denied. A missionary to Africa once said: "Except for the color of their skins, we want to make Africans into Europeans."

Some Western theologians representative of this view stress Jesus Christ as Lord, which is right. In their writings however, this means that, because Jesus Christ is Lord, anything or anyone that does not know Jesus Christ as Lord is without value. When the international missionary movement met in Madras in 1938, a book by Hendrik Kraemer, who stressed the discontinuity between Christ and everything outside Christ, was very influential. The feeling was that Christian missionaries had to negate anything and everything that fell outside Christianity. Kraemer felt that all Asian religious phenomena were expressions of human pride and foolhardiness. This of course functions to negate all folk religion and people's movements.

In 1957, a West German theologian who spoke at Nanjing Union Theological Seminary illustrated his talk on the blackboard. He drew a flight of stairs on one side with steps coming down from the left to the right, from top to bottom. Across from it was another flight of stairs coming from right to left. In the middle, where the two met, a cross stood. The steps represented human culture—the more elevated the culture, the further it was from the cross; the more primitive the culture, the closer it drew to the cross. Culture and the cross were at odds. To spread the gospel of the cross, we must negate local culture. The influence of this sort of missionary theology—a theology negating Third World culture—upon the missionary movement was great and lasted long. These days critiques of this theological viewpoint frequently appear in Western churches, where it is termed triumphalism, the mindset of the (self-proclaimed) victor. In the early days of Liberation in China, this second attitude, that everything outside Jesus Christ is worthless and should be denied, was very much on the rise in the church. Some clung to the verse "the whole world lies under the power of the evil one" (1 John 5:19). Ignoring the rest of the Bible, these people taught that Christians had to be hostile to the world, human life, culture and historical progress.

The third approach is the exact opposite of the second. It affirms that all truth, goodness and beauty outside Christianity are part of God's creation. Though these things are outside Christianity, they are not outside God and also contain God's revelation. Their leaders or promoters are also servants of God. They represent humanity's search for God, the discovery, knowledge and service of God. In my opinion this view could be termed the theory of parallel revelation, the belief that revelation does not come only from Jesus Christ.

This view does not lack a certain basis within the Old and New Testaments. For example, Israel could accept blessings from another country. Abraham accepted a blessing from Melchizedek. Cyrus was King of Persia and also respected the will of God, rebuilding the holy temple in the holy city. Nebuchadnezzar did God's work and so God gave him Egypt. In Isaiah 19, Egypt is called "my people" and Assyria, "the work of my hands." In the Old Testament, there are many affirmations of the Gentiles, for example, Abel, Enoch, Noah, the Queen of Sheba, Pharaoh's daughter, the father-in-law of Moses, Rahab, Ruth and so on.

Jesus' parable of the Good Samaritan also seems to illustrate this view. Many New Testament passages tell us that the apostles certainly did not reject absolutely the things of this world. For example: in 1 Corinthians, chapter 10 verse 26, "For the earth and its fullness are the Lord's;" 1 Timothy 4:4: "For everything created by God is good, and nothing is to be rejected, provided it is received with thanksgiving;" James 1:17: "Every generous act of giving with every perfect gift, is from above, coming down from the Father of lights;" 1 John 2:29: "If you know that he is righteous, you may be sure that every one who does right has been born of him."

Clement, a father of the ancient church, explained this by saying that the river of truth is one, but from this side and from that side, many streams flow into the river. And Thomas Aquinas said that all truth, no matter who speaks it, comes from the Spirit. Calvin represents orthodoxy for many of us, but he said that when we come across a writer from outside the church, we should learn the light of truth from what he has written. Though the human mind is degenerate and corrupted, yet it has the high abilities that God has given it. If we believe that the Spirit of God is the source of all truth, we should not deny or belittle truth itself, no matter where it appears, or we will insult the Spirit of God.

Modern foreign theologians have also spoken to this subject. American theologian Robert MacAffee Brown noted that students sometimes find his praise of Albert Camus, an existentialist and atheist, astonishing. He tells them that there is a part of him that can really relate to Camus; there is a part of him willing to say a fervent Amen to what Camus is saying; there is a part of him that does not want to refute Camus but rather to take up arms with him to oppose the enemies both despise, though they take their orders from different places. And though we humans cannot enjoy final peace in this world, MacAffee Brown is not willing to denounce the world or despise it.

A former Archbishop of Canterbury, Archbishop Coggan, said in one of his books that we must have an appropriate view of the Spirit of God. In the expanded creation of God, the Holy Spirit is the carrier of all truth, goodness and beauty. Wherever theology, philosophy, art, or science enters into darkness, ignorance or error, there the Spirit of Truth must do its work. Wherever the forces of sickness or death are vanquished, there the Spirit of Life is acting. Wherever the abhorrent is deterred, there God's Spirit of beauty and goodness is doing its work of creation and re-creation. God is not some Super-Leader who only gets interested in the affairs of the church. He is behind every discovery, invention and scholarship; he is the source of all truth, the source of all beauty. Thus, in the laboratory, in the study, in the atelier, in the tenement, if anyone becomes a vessel of God's ministry, that person is the servant of the Most High, though he or she may not be aware of it, and though because of this, his or her truth, goodness or beauty may lack a certain richness.

An Indian theologian once said that if we put a negative film of Jesus into the developing bath of Indian philosophy, the photograph will show a special color unknown in the past to humankind, which may shape the gospel for the present age.

I quote so many sources because I want to illustrate that many Christian intellectuals today are drawn to the theory of parallel revelation, and also, that it has a definite biblical basis.

It is worth noting that the theological views I just described do not all stop at parallel revelation. For example, Archbishop Coggan also has a strong Christology. But in introducing parallel revelation, I felt that his statement here could serve very well as representative. We have many in Chinese Christianity who are happy to accept such a view and see frequent examples in the pages of the church monthly *Tian Feng.*

I am not at all against this viewpoint. Hearing it, we Christians are satisfied in one way, yet dissatisfied in another. Why should this be? Because this view leads to a question: What status is left for Christ Jesus? If all have revelation, then what is the special role of Christ Jesus? The Gospel of Christ then becomes just one revelation among many, does it not? So we must move on to the fourth and fifth views.

The fourth approach believes that Jesus Christ is Fulfiller. Yes, every religion, every people's movement, all artistic creations can perhaps show forth something of God's revelation, but these are unfinished. They await fulfillment and Jesus Christ is their fulfiller. Clement, quoted above, also said that philosophy was a preparation for the New Testament. It is the teacher of the Greeks just as the Old Testament was the teacher of the Jews. To say philosophy is God's revelation does not make it inferior to the Old Testament. Plato is no more than the Moses hidden behind the Greek language. By this he means that the Israelites have the Old Testament as their preparation for receiving Christ. The Greeks are not Israelites, but have their own Old Testament, that is, Greek philosophy. He felt that as God's revelation, Greek philosophy was not inferior to the Old Testament, and even that Plato was Moses speaking Greek.

This view has received a lot of attention in history. There is a Latin saying with a long history in Christianity, *Praeparatio Evangelica*, or preparation for evangelism. This means that many things in the world which are not the gospel, which are outside it, yet function as a preparation for people's acceptance of the gospel. Outside Christ there are many things which are awaiting their moment. These are like fingers pointing to Christ, pointing in the direction of Christ, so that people may see Christ. In the words of another former Archbishop of Canterbury, William Temple, all these many things find their completion, what he called their correction and coronation, a lifting up, a fulfillment, in Christ. Greek philosophy, Chinese philosophy, thought and art outside the church can reach a high level, but only in Christ can they reach their peak.

You may have heard of the Norwegian theologian Karl Reichelt who came to China and set up a center, now in Hong Kong, for the purpose of introducing Christianity to Buddhists. Many monks came there to dialogue and study. Reichelt was also of the view of Christ

Jesus as Fulfiller. He used the analogy of a mountain where there was a silver mine. If you dug in certain places on the mountain, you might strike silver, but this would be silver mixed with stones, other metals, mud and so on, very impure. But if you followed the vein of silver, you would find very pure silver. Most religions or the truth of other religions is very mixed and impure, but Christ Jesus is the heart of the lode and there you can find pure silver. Another analogy says that when we look out the window when it snows, there will be snow all around the edges of the window panes, but the center of the pane will be clear and we will be able to see through it to the scene outside. This means that other religions can let some light get through, though it looks dim and unclear, while Christ Jesus is like the center pane unclouded by snow. Through him we can see the greater truth of God. I think this view is corroborated by the first two verses of the first chapter of Hebrews: "Long ago God spoke to our ancestors in many and various ways by the prophets; but in these last days he has spoken to us by a Son."

The fifth approach recognizes the cosmic nature of Christ Jesus in addition to his human and divine natures. This is a vast topic which human wisdom cannot begin to fathom. But we cannot set it aside either, and I feel it is worth exploring. It is a recognition of Christ Jesus' pre-existence, of the fact that he was with God before the creation of the universe, that he is one member of the Trinity, and that all things were created through him. He is the Word become Flesh. He looks after the entire universe.

Let me read six passages from the Bible so that the words of Scripture may help me explore the cosmic nature of Christ:

(1) John 1:1–4. "In the beginning was the Word, and the Word was with God, and the Word was God, He was in the beginning with God. All things came into being through him and without him not one thing came into being. What has come into being in him was life, and the life was the light of all people."

(2) John 1:9: "The true light, which enlightens everyone, was coming into the world."

(3) John 1:14: "And the Word became flesh and lived among us,

and we have seen his glory, the glory as of a father's only son, full of grace and truth."

(4) Philippians 2:6–11: "Who, though he was in the form of God, did not regard equality with God as something to be exploited, but emptied himself, taking the form of a slave, being born in human likeness. And being found in human form, he humbled himself and became obedient to the point of death—even death on a cross. Therefore God also highly exalted him and gave him the name that is above every name, so that at the name of Jesus every knee should bend, in heaven and on earth and under the earth, and every tongue should confess that Jesus Christ is Lord, to the glory of God the Father."

(5) Colossians 1:15–20: "He is the image of the invisible God, the firstborn of all creation; for in him all things in heaven and on earth were created, things visible and invisible, whether thrones or dominions or rulers or powers—all things have been created through him and for him. He himself is before all things, and in him all things hold together. He is the head of the body, the church, he is the beginning, the firstborn from the dead, so that he might come to have first place in every-thing. For in him all the fullness of God was pleased to dwell, and through him God was pleased to reconcile to himself all things, whether on earth or in heaven, by making peace through the blood of his cross."

(6) Hebrews 1:2–3: "A Son, whom he appointed heir of all things, through whom he also created the worlds. He is the reflection of God's glory and the exact imprint of God's very being, and he sustains all things by his powerful word."

The cosmic Christ is a vast subject. What the Bible says of it is not said very directly and so many people do not pay it much attention or do not dare to engage it. But an increasing number of theologians are paying attention to it. Teilhard de Chardin, for example, says that Jesus not only has a human nature and a divine nature, but a cosmic nature and that the whole of creation is within the scope of Christ as Lord.

The theory of the ancient church fathers, like Origen and Clement, was expressed as *logos spermaticos. Logos* means Word. This theory held that due to the fact that Christ was the pre-existent cosmic Christ, there was a tiny seed of the Word in each person.

The Indian theologian Mathias Zecharias said that in the past our view was to see the church going out, bringing the people of every nation and place into the embrace of the church (meaning the missionary movement). Today, the vision that moves so many Christians is different. We see Christ leading the whole created world and all humankind toward the goal of being with him. This work of creation makes use of all human movements that are progressive, liberating and humanizing. ("Humanizing" is a word we seldom use in China. It means that in our present society there are many places where people are not treated as human, where they are made to be non-human, so the proposal is humanization, that is, to give these non-persons back the human dignity they should have.) The church is not God's only vessel, but the church still has a central place, where people know him, make him known and worship him. But the saving work of Christ is not limited to the church; this work involves the whole cosmos. We are to see the cosmic nature of salvific grace. Just as Vatican II said, outside the axis of the church, can be found many factors related to truth and holiness. Those people who are willing to act according to the dictates of their consciences will find the help of salvation is all around. The Second (Vatican) Council, held in the 1960s, led to a great reform in Catholicism, including a reform in theology. One especially important point in this was that Vatican II recognized that what lay outside the church was not simply sunk in depravity or marked for annihilation.

The whole direction of thought which developed from Vatican II spurred the German Catholic theologian Karl Rahner to propose that certain people should be termed "anonymous Christians." He meant that many outside the church who do not call themselves Christians, may never have come into contact with Christianity, or may never even have heard the word "Christianity," are very good in character and actions and perhaps had received much worthwhile revelation from other religions. These people could be recognized as Christians in all but name. Many Christians welcomed Rahner's idea, but it also met with opposition. The opposition felt that if we say this and Christians still consider themselves to be in the right, then Buddhists can also see certain people as Buddhists in all but name. How would we like that?

Rahner's view has some basis in church tradition; he did not make it up out of thin air. Augustine once said that every religion contains some of the truth and the truth each contains is in fact the truth of Christ, though the name of Christ is not mentioned. Augustine felt that before Christ came into the world, the church was already in existence. From Abel on, all righteous people belonged to Christ and to the church. Another church father said that we believe that whoever strives to do good, has a share with God. According to our faith, through the grace of God, such people will have a place in God's house. We believe that this principle applies to all. In the Word of God, Christ, all humankind has a place; those who act according to what their conscience tells them, are all Christians, even though others may say that they are without God. His examples are Socrates and Heraclites, who he says are in fact in Christ.

I cannot say that this view is wrong. It reflects a very high Christology. In Matthew 25 when it comes to the Lord Jesus' teaching about the judgement on the last day, God does not ask whether you exalted Christ, but whether you gave a cup of water to a thirsty person. "Truly, I tell you, just as you did it to one of the least of these who are members of my family, you did it to me." We cannot but treat very seriously this teaching of our Lord Jesus; we cannot act as if he had not said it.

Among these five approaches, the Cosmic Christ seems to embrace many aspects of the issue set out at the beginning: It enables us on the one hand to affirm the Christ of the New Testament and to affirm the very high Christology of John and Paul, while taking an enlightened and open approach to the truth, beauty and goodness of this world.

We can imagine that some friends outside the church might take great exception to numbers three, four and five, and ask how we could gather all the attainments of humankind in this world into God and Christ. My response is that since we allow people to believe in Christianity, we must allow them to work out questions in terms of

Christian theology. If they can make sense of issues in this way, then they will be able to involve themselves more in historically progressive enterprises. Otherwise they might fall prey to seeing all that is true, good and beautiful in this world as being of Satan and become susceptible to hostile forces. Believers seek a theology that will be of more use in resisting the type of theology that tends toward the reactionary. This seeking should be encouraged.

—Shanghai, 1997

# UNCHANGING FAITH, EVOLVING THEOLOGY

The reconstruction of Chinese theological thinking has become a central issue for China's Protestant Christians. Yet, since embarking on this great venture three years ago, success has so far been limited. This is only natural, as the renewal of theological thinking touches upon people's personal thoughts, and the rectification of thoughts cannot be achieved overnight. We can say that, over the past two or three years, the problem of reconstructing theological thinking has created divisions among China's Christian intellectuals. Some observers think that the existence of such differences indicates chaos. I do not agree. Since launching the idea of the reconstruction of Chinese theological thinking, theological discussion in China has livened up, and lively and chaotic are two very different things. Through lively discussions we will reach a more sophisticated level of theological understanding and will ultimately achieve a higher level of unity, which is what the Chinese church needs.

When we talk of reconstructing theological thinking, we first need to clarify the difference between theological thinking and basic faith. Our basic faith was codified centuries ago in the "Apostle's Creed" and the "Nicene Creed." In our efforts to renew our theological thinking, we respect the basic faith condensed within these two creeds. However, the world has changed over the centuries and so have people's ideas. In order to interpret these two creeds in ways suited to our times, we need to rectify our theological thinking. Otherwise, we would have to change our basic faith, which should remain untouched.

Reconstructing theological thinking is nothing new, we find numerous examples of it in the Bible. Over the past two millennia, the Christian church has continually reconstructed its theological thinking. We even find instances of this in the Old Testament. For example, one of the biggest transformations in theological thinking was the change from polytheism to monotheism. Descriptions of such groundbreaking changes in history deserve our attention. They highlight the fact that basic faith does not change but the understanding and practice of that faith does change over time.

Similarly, instances of the reconstruction of theological thinking can be found in the New Testament. Jesus Christ himself is an important example of the rectification of theological thinking. Through his understanding of the Jewish Sabbath, Jesus helped free his followers from the overly rule-oriented interpretation prevalent among some of his Jewish contemporaries. Liberation from rules was developed even further by Paul in his discussion of justification by faith. This thinking made an important contribution by changing Christianity from a small group within the Jewish religion to a faith open to everybody. This development was further promoted by the church council which took place in the year 49 and where it was decided to open Christianity to non-Jewish believers.

Without this latter council and its theological breakthrough, there would be no Chinese Christians today, and we would not be discussing faith matters today either. Therefore, the church council of the year 49 represents an important correction in theological thinking.

In fact, we find similar instances not only in the Bible but also in church history. Martin Luther is a case in point. His condemnation of church practices, like the selling of papal indulgences, marked an important departure from the theological thinking of his times. Luther was followed by other reformers and reform movements, each of which illustrates the rectification and also the diversification of theological thinking.

From the above we can see that, throughout the past 2,000 years, new theological ideas have continually appeared, and reconstructing theological thought is not some recent Chinese invention. In that sense, our current efforts to renew our theological thinking are in complete accordance with church tradition and history.

The missionaries who brought Christianity to China can be divided into two groups: The first group comprises those who came to China offering services like schools, hospitals and universities. In general, they were not too concerned with evangelizing among those they sought to help. In contrast, the second group is made up of those who came explicitly as missionaries with the aim of increasing the number of believers in China. For them, the annual number of converts was the measure of their success. In order to attract potential believers, these missionaries resorted to two measures. One important way of making Christianity attractive was through the material advantages it could bring to the potential convert. For example, children of Christian parents would gain access to Christian schools, scholarships for studies abroad and so on. The second tool used by missionaries was their descriptions of heaven and hell. For China's simple-minded ordinary people, the threat of hell and the prospect of heaven were very strong incentives to accept Christian faith. In fact even today, many Chinese become Christians primarily in order to ascend to heaven.

This leads us back to the question of justification by faith. The notion of justification by faith has played an important role in liberating believers—first, when Paul fought the "legalism" among Jewish believers and a second time when Martin Luther voiced the idea in order to oppose the pope. However, in many developed countries today, the idea of justification by faith has been watered down because it easily creates conflicts between believers and non-believers. In this context, it is worth noting that, in the modern Chinese Bible translation of 1979, the expression "justification by faith" does not appear a single time. Instead, the expression "to have a harmonious relationship with God through faith" is used instead.

Today, as we meet here at Nanjing seminary, the staff and students here are polarized. A great number of students work hard to partici-pate in the reconstruction of Chinese theological thinking—they re-read the Bible, write papers, discuss and reflect. I think they will be the future pillars of the Chinese church. But there are also a number of indifferent students who exert a bad influence on their fellow stu-dents. Just as Nanjing seminary is polarized at this point in time, so our whole church is divided into different groups. This diversification does not mean chaos but rather reflects a diversity of theological reflection and will help us to renew and deepen our theological think-ing.

I hope that, after a lengthy period of time, a new form of Chinese Christian faith will emerge, a rational Christianity which, at the same time, has a strong sense of right and wrong; a Christian faith that emphasizes Christ, morality and a loving God. Such a Christianity would bring an important message to the whole world.

—March 11, 12, 2001,
a summary of a speech made by Bishop K. H. Ting to a postgraduate
class of pastors at Nanjing Union Theological Seminary in September
this year. The full text of the speech appeared in October's issue of
*Tian Feng*, the magazine of the China Christian Council.

એ

# THEOLOGY ADAPTING
# TO A CHANGING CULTURE

Recently there has been much talk in Chinese Christianity about theological reconstruction. Theological reconstruction does not attack or change basic Christian faith, but safeguards it. Through theological reconstruction, our basic faith will be expressed in terms that are more accessible and more reasonable, and this will aid believers in their understanding and will strengthen basic faith. And non-believers, our friends outside the church, will be more willing to hear the good news the church has for them. We should not fear theological reconstruction then, but welcome it as a good and important development. Christianity has been in existence 2,000 years, and during this time, theological reconstruction has been constant, and the process has resulted in better theology. If we do not want to call this reconstruction, we may term it development, adjustment or improvement.

I would like to discuss a number of examples to show how, though our basic faith does not change, it is usual for theological thinking to undergo adjustments large and small.

Before the slaves were freed in the U.S., they were treated as little better than animals on the southern plantations. The church then believed that black people did not have souls, but had been born simply to labor for the whites. Some black people even believed this themselves. This view provided a theological basis for the oppression of black slaves and their maltreatment by the slave owners. Capitalism had begun to develop in the northern part of the nation, and Lincoln led the north in a civil war against the south under the banner of freeing the slaves. After the war, many pastors and theologians began to affirm the humanity of the African Americans—they were also children of God and could be baptized into the churches. Later African Americans started their own churches and seminaries. This is a modern example of how the church can, and must, adjust its theological thinking. This particular change was vast and came about quite quickly. It also brought about the demise of the southern slavery-based economy, an Illustration of the way in which developments in theology and capitalist society are interrelated.

Birth control, which the church historically opposed, is another example. The church's opposition was based on the biblical exhortation to "be fruitful and multiply," seen as a blessing from God. As a result many believers had large families, which impoverished them and kept their educational level low. Today, the situation is greatly changed and one- and two-child families are the norm in Europe and North America. The new theological thinking is that it is not God's intention that people be poor and downtrodden. It pleases God more for parents to put their energies into raising one or two children well. As for China, the church no longer advocates large families, nor do many believers want to raise six or seven children. This also marks a big theological adjustment.

Other attitudes that were once supported with biblical evidence and have now been supplanted by new theological thinking include polygamy and the church's opposition to divorce.

Do we find examples of adjustment in theological thinking in the Bible? Many. Take Acts, chapters 10–15, for example. Peter's theology was quite simple in the beginning: He took everything over from Judaism—that the Israelites were God's chosen people, observance of the Sabbath, circumcision, etc. On accepting Jesus as Lord, he added the belief that Jesus was the awaited Messiah. Under the gradual guiding and revelation of the Holy Spirit, that brought him down from the rooftop to meet the gentile Cornelius, he came gradually to the realization that Jesus was not only redeemer of the Jews, but of the gentiles as well. Together with Paul, Barnabas and others, Peter held the meeting in Jerusalem where the decision was taken to break out of the bonds of Judaism and allow the good news to be preached to the Romans and Greeks. To do this, the Christians had to abandon the Jewish customs such as keeping Sabbath and circumcision. These changes allowed Christianity to evolve into the world religion it is today. That meeting in Jerusalem, which took place about 49 C.E. and is recorded in Acts 15, was crucial in the history of the church. This one example is sufficient to show that there is historical evidence in the Bible of theological thinking in the church being adjusted with the guidance of the Holy Spirit.

There are people in the Chinese church who like to point to the contradictions between so-called modernists and so-called fundamentalists, putting theological reconstruction in the so-called modernist camp and saying that the so-called fundamentalist theology needs no adjustment. They insist that theological reconstruction is factional infighting. They are mistaken. Were Peter, Paul and James modernists? In 49 CE there was neither modernist nor fundamentalist. For 2000 years, the Holy Spirit has been guiding constant adjustment of theological thinking without regard to camps or factions.

A couple of months ago, I was looking through the most important publication of American fundamentalism, or we might say evangelicalism, *Christianity Today*, and saw a report about a conference
among pastors and theological educators on the topic of the fate of
non-Christians after death. Some felt that as non-believers they
would go straight to hell, where they would suffer the fires of eternal
damnation. Some felt this would be too merciless an action on God's
part and proposed the idea that after death both the flesh and spirit of
non-believers would be destroyed, something they felt to be more
humanitarian. And there was a third view: because of God's grace,
non-believers too would share in eternal life. Such a conference
shows that within fundamentalism or evangelicalism people also feel
the need for adjustment of theological thinking, and that things are in
process.

These examples tell us that changes are always taking place in theological thinking in the church. Theology in this way differs from the
church's basic faith, whose tenets, such as belief in the Trinity, Christ's
incarnation, death on the cross for all and resurrection after three
days, are firm and unwavering. Precisely because these tenets of basic
faith do not change, it is imperative for theological thinking to change
with the times and make necessary adjustments. Change takes place
in theological thinking in order to protect and safeguard our unchanging basic faith. We firmly believe that the cross brought to completion
the work of bringing God and humanity together, but how this came
about, we cannot say for sure, and this gives rise to numerous theological views. We need not fight over these, but can adopt an attitude
of mutual respect. Changes in theological thinking take place in order
to safeguard the immutability of basic faith.

The appropriate distinction between basic faith and theological
thinking was an important development achieved through theological
study in the Chinese Church by the TSPM in the decade from 1940 to
1950. This development enabled Chinese Christianity to guarantee
maintenance of a pure basic faith while having a lively thinking and
witness, and was beneficial to bringing about unity among Christians
on the basis of their common basic faith. We cannot but recognize that

making the appropriate distinction between basic faith and theological thinking is not something humans could invent on their own; it is
the Holy Spirit leading the church. We recall that the letter to the gentiles from the Jerusalem meeting said, "The Holy Spirit ... and us."
Today the experience of the church in China is even more marked by
the presence of the Holy Spirit working with us.

Jiang Zemin, chairman of the Communist Party of China, called
for an active adaptation of religions in China with socialism. There is
no reason at all to oppose this. Suppose we do not adapt to socialist
society. Shall we then adapt to capitalism, imperialism or feudalism?
For the good of our nation, as well as for the survival and witness of
the church itself, we should naturally adapt to socialist society. This is
the natural choice of every responsible citizen and every responsible
believer. We cannot be satisfied with a mere politic expression.
Genuine adaptation must have an intellectual foundation. For
Christians, genuine adaptation must include theological adaptation.
Our pastors should not content themselves with preaching a word
from fifty or one hundred years ago. Adjustment must take on vitality of expression and be marked by Jesus' promise, before he left us,
that he would send the Spirit among us to lead us into all truth.

Friends, the 21st century is upon us, a century in which educational levels will continue to rise. Even now, many intellectuals come
to the churches full of expectation, willing to listen to our message.
They arrive full of expectation, but leave full of disappointment. Why
should this be? The church is growing, but our message does not
attract people with a modern mindset. Let us welcome theological
reconstruction with open arms, so that the church will no longer fall
behind, but be a lively community that keeps up with changing times.

Recently, the TSPM/CCC set up a "Theological Reconstruction
Promotion Team" whose function is to 1) heighten awareness of the
importance of theological reconstruction among our co-workers and
fellow Christians, especially clergy; and 2) assist church offices closely
involved in theological thinking (seminaries, publications departments, etc.) to thoroughly implement the spirit of theological reconstruction. Our goal is to gradually raise the theological level of
Chinese Christianity and foster understanding of theology in world

Christianity so that we would be able to participate in theological exchanges with Christians all over the world. This is truly a great responsibility and I hope all our colleagues and fellow Christians will support it. I am retired from my positions in the TSPM/CCC, but I will do my utmost to support this endeavor which is so important for the future of our church.

—Based on a summary in *Amity News Service* 2000.3/4.2.

૭૦

# MAN: AN INCOMPLETE CREATION

**Question**: Please explain what you mean by "semi-finished products."

**Bishop Ting:**

I would like to respond to this question on the basis of light gained from Bible reading.

Our God is the Creator. Creation is a long process, not something God finished in six days and has been resting from ever since. The first chapter of Genesis tells us that God was pleased with what he created in these six days. But how primitive this world would be and how immature our knowledge of God if we were to think that God's creation is limited to these six days and after this he stopped creating. God said of those first six days that it was good, but from then on, God's creation had to deal with human sin, it had to resolve the question of human sinfulness. Creation was not as simple and easy as in those first six days. But God is the Lord of creation, yesterday, today and tomorrow. God never quits half way. Creation is continually in process. And this creation will certainly be carried to completion. The created world is a semi-finished part of God's overall creation. It is a work-in-progress. It is being transformed, but still needs work. The term "semi-finished product" is not found in the Bible, neither is "electric light" or "television." But "semi-finished product" may be an effective term from people in modern industrial societies.

As for us, in addition to statements about humans being in sin without any merit, the Bible also says, "What are human beings that you are mindful of them, mortals that you care for them? Yet you have made them a little lower than God, and crowned them with glory and honor" (Ps. 8:4–5). These different views of the Bible are not contradictory. The meaning is simply that in the process of being created, people experience reversal, difference, before and after states. Works-in-progress are those that are not yet finished, not seconds or rejects. To be semi-finished products in God's hand is honor and glory, but we must be humble, know our own shortcomings, and not imagine that we are already complete.

On the evidence of many passages in the New Testament, it seems quite appropriate to say that we are "semi-finished." For example:

"When I was a child, I spoke like a child, I thought like a child, I reasoned like a child; when I became an adult, I put an end to childish ways. For now we see in a mirror, dimly, but then we will see face to face. Now I know only in part; then I will know fully, even as I have been fully known" (1 Cor. 13:11–12).

"Not that I have already obtained this or have already reached the goal; but I press on to make it my own, because Christ Jesus has made me his own. Beloved, I do not consider that I have made it my own; but this one thing I do: forgetting what lies behind and straining forward to what lies ahead, I press on toward the goal for the prize of the heavenly call of God in Christ Jesus" (Phil. 3:12–14).

Even the Incarnate Christ, while living as a human in the world, underwent a process of growth: "And Jesus increased in wisdom and in years, and in divine and human favor" (Luke 2:52).

Biblical theology is a comprehensive field of study. It would be erroneous to say that the Bible's assessment of humankind is based on only one passage. Personally, my view is that if we see everyone— Adam and Eve, the elder son and the younger son in the story of the Prodigal Son, Peter and John, Rahab who helped bring the Israelites into the land of Canaan, and Mary Magdalene, as well as Priscilla and Aquila, teachers of theology and theological students, scientists and producers—all as works-in-progress in God's great enterprise of creation, we can avoid raising humankind too high, but also avoid scoffing at it. This would be a more moderate approach. Do you favor replacing religion with morality?

I cannot speak for other religions, but as for Christianity, I do believe that Christianity should lift up ethics and morality. But this is in no way to suggest that Christianity is concerned only with ethics and morality and even less to suggest that Christian faith be replaced with either.

Both Christianity and its forerunner, Judaism, have a tradition of placing great emphasis on ethics and morality. Six of the Ten Commandments both profess are matters of ethics and morality, such as honoring one's father and mother, not stealing, avoiding sexual sin and so on. The Bible is a book with a great deal to say about ethics and morality. The Old Testament prophets extended the scope of ethics and morality from matters of individual behavior into the social and political arenas.

In spite of this, ethics and morality are not equivalent to Christianity and cannot supplant it. The core of Christianity is faith and doctrine. Christian faith and doctrine are contained in the Apostles Creed and the Nicene Creed, both ancient creeds. Ethical and moral concepts change slowly, moving with the times. Neither is theology the same as faith and doctrine, rather both ethics and theology explain faith and doctrine, and inevitably change according to people, time and place. There is only one Christianity, but there are many and various theological views within Christianity. Even within the one Bible, there are many theological viewpoints, as well as different ethical and moral concepts.

Any advanced religion values ethics and morality. Einstein once said, "A giant leap in the historical evolution of human religion takes place when religions of fear turn into religions of morality," and I agree.

An essay published in Hong Kong recently stated that any Christian who emphasized ethics and morality was denying the uniqueness of Christ. This writer even went so far as to say that Christians on the mainland spoke of ethics and morality in order to curry favor with the Communist Party. Does this writer not know that for thousands of years before there was a Communist Party on earth, countless ancient sages like Confucius, Mencius, Mo Tzu, Socrates, and Paul, along with nearly every writer included in the Bible, held ethics and morality in high esteem? All this about currying favor with the Communists only goes to show that the focus for this author lies in opposition to the Communist Party, and that failure to oppose it is tantamount to favoring it.

**Question:** You made the courage and spirit of sacrifice of the People's Liberation Army in fighting the floods widely known, and praised the soldiers highly, pointing to their actions as an expression of love. But we Christians know that compared to the holy love of God, this love is hardly worth mentioning. Christians should glorify God and spread God's holy love, they should not praise humans. What is your reaction to this?

**Bishop Ting:**
I have thought of such questions often since the floods. Let me explain my views further.

I understand why some Christians feel that only God's love is true and holy love. Perhaps because they have seen or been deceived by people who use love as a cloak for their actions in order to achieve their own selfish ends. Simple souls have suffered at the hands of such people, and the experience has left them bitterly disappointed, feeling that all human love is false and unreliable. They feel that God's holy love is the only thing they have to rely on.

I sympathize with those who have been deceived, but as a Christian I firmly believe that behind the whole cosmos and the created world, there exists God the Father, the Lord of creation. Love is the impetus for all his movements and work, it is his most basic attribute. God is the invisible Lover in the cosmos. His justice emerges from his love, rather than being opposed to it. God is even now in the process of creating. I believe the three persons of God are one, for this process of creation includes the Son's moving example and redemption, and the Holy Spirit's revelation and sanctification. This three-in-one God is now in the process of gradually transforming the obstacles to his work of love and his work of the kingdom into helpers and co-workers worthy of him. In this long process one can imagine that there are some works-in-progress coming to completion, while others turn their backs on God, choosing destruction instead.

Years ago at Nanjing Union Theological Seminary, I spent half a day each week for several weeks introducing liberation theology, the theology of Teilhard de Chardin and process theology. Theologians in these three areas, along with theologians in many other fields, all praise God's love. They see it as God's most basic attribute and believe that this is the pinnacle of revelation in the Bible. Some religions, especially less developed ones, view justice and discipline as God's highest attributes, seeing God as one who rewards good and punishes evil, the judge and avenger who holds life and death in his hand. People easily see such a god as one who would destroy for revenge and punish the innocent with the guilty. This tendency stands out in some parts of the Old Testament, in spite of the fact that in some passages very beautiful language is used in describing the love of God (for example in Hosea where he uses his personal experience to speak of God's bands of love). But in the New Testament, we meet the Incarnate Son in the Four Gospels, in whose person God is pleased to show forth his love, or a loving God. Paul's justification by faith also points to that Christ who, prompted by love, was raised up on the cross, thus liberating humanity from the bonds of the law. Later in 1 John 4:8, the New Testament language is very direct: "God is love."

In more and more countries today, beatings, revenge and punishment are no longer the principles for dealing with crime. Rather the guiding principles are education, persuasion and reform. Some countries have even abolished the death penalty. Yet among us Christians, some are still hostile to others (non-Christians), threatening them with the day of judgment when they will be punished and Christians vindicated. We should give much thought to how this relates to our Christian concept of God.

During television coverage of the floods, we saw a five or six year old child clinging to a branch, about to be swept away. Without a thought for his own safety, a PLA soldier guided his small boat over, grabbed the child and took her to safety. This act, braving death to save another, is love. I cannot believe such love to be very small, hardly worth mentioning. I believe this is a great and holy love, and that the creator of this love is God. Seeing love like this, God is most certainly pleased, and we Christians, too, should be thankful for it and should not demean it. Can it be that we as Christians should criticize and demean even the good actions of others? Is this normal? Can our Christianity have no common language with the rest of our people? John 3:16 tells us "For God so loved the world. ..." May we know the will of God and see the world with loving hearts.

—*Nanjing Theological Review*, No. 2 (1999), p. 50.

## ℵℷ

# THE BIBLE: A SOURCE OF TRUTH FOR CHRISTIAN AND NON-CHRISTIAN

Not only is the Bible an authoritative religious classic that guides the faith and behavior of Christians, it is also an important artifact and crystallization of human culture and continues to influence that culture. The Bible has been translated into over 1,000 languages. Just as one cannot have a profound understanding of Chinese culture without studying Buddhism, without a study of the Christian Bible one cannot have a profound understanding of Western languages, history, philosophy, literature, music and art. In his own investigations, Engels placed great emphasis on the study of the Bible. He wrote three important dissertations on the historical facts of early Christianity based on biblical materials. In his *Peasant War in Germany*, he described the divisions taking place in the church in a time of upheaval and studied the way in which radical theologians represented by Thomas Muenzer exegeted the Bible to accompany mass struggle.

The Bible took shape in Palestine, a crossroads of the three continents of Asia, Africa and Europe. It is a great contribution to the world from the Hebrew people. Not a single book, but a collection of sixty-six books from different periods, its earliest materials were gathered together around 1000 B.C.E. The latest part comes from the 1st and 2nd centuries C.E. In addition to the stories about the creation of the world and humankind's beginnings, its contents include history, law, folk songs, psalms, legends, political commentary, letters, proverbs, and impassioned accounts of words and actions that join religious zeal to patriotism. Throughout the Bible, we see described the suffering, urgency, penitence and pleas to God for redemption of the Hebrews. These are often expressed in their special language and symbols.

For a long time, the word "opiate" has been spoken of as Marx's definition of religion, as if it was adequate to show the essence of religion. Thus, dealing with any issues which involved religion or religious believers centered on the word opiate; to ignore this would have been unorthodox and disloyal. During that time, all study of religious phenomena and collection of materials was dominated by this definition. Hegel said in *Discourses on Philosophy* that there was nothing easier in the world than to pull together some materials by arbitrarily relying on some principle. If this is true, there is no need even to open the Bible in order to declare it filled with opium. As for the important position of the Bible in human culture, there is no need to mention it. In this way it has nearly become a banned book. One result of this has been to deprive several generations of Chinese intellectuals of their right to come into contact with this important historical treasure.

Today the situation is changing. More and more scholars are publishing essays which recognize that even if religion does function as an opiate for certain people under certain circumstances, its narcotic function is only one of its functions, not its whole function, and not its main function for all people under all circumstances. Thus the opiate is not an adequate definition of religion. Everyone knows that religion has played other roles in history and continues to have other functions in today's world. For example, it often serves as a tie to bind the masses together, and has moved the masses to rise up against oppressors and aggressors. When a people has gained new life, it unites believers to participate in construction. Opiates can do none of this. Today people treat religion in a more levelheaded way and in a spirit of seeking truth from facts.

The image of the Bible has been warped, but today there are signs that it has recovered its true demeanor.

I heartily welcome the publication of *New Thoughts on the Bible* by the three young authors Yang Huilin, Fang Ming and Geng Youzhuang. Whether I agree with all the views expressed in all of the essays gathered here is unimportant. The important thing is that in their approach to religion and the Bible, these authors are able to cast off the trappings of simplification and an anti-religious tradition. They appreciate a religion that is cultural, ethical and service-oriented and which responds to ultimate human concerns. They are symbolic of a new generation of intellectuals who are appearing on the horizon. It is a particular pleasure for me to be able to cooperate with this group of young scholars who are making a contribution to raising the cultural standards of the Chinese people.

Let me quote Qu Yuan: "Long, long had been my road and far, far was the journey; I would go up and down to seek my heart's desire." This book is a record of that search and will attract many more people to share the journey.

—Preface to *New Thoughts on the Bible*, 1989

# THE TRUTH REPRESENTED BY
# THE RESURRECTION

That one who has died should live again goes against common sense. People have difficulty believing it. Christ's resurrection is a stumbling stone embodied in the very fabric of Christianity.

But consider for a moment—today a quarter of the world's people believe that Christ rose from the dead. This fact is not so easily brushed off. People are not too clear about the facts of Christ's resurrection, but millions of people believe that the truth represented by the resurrection is profound and this non-commonsensical faith has endured for 2,000 years. Though no one can explain it clearly, it cannot be written off.

To put it in everyday Chinese terms, the truth of the resurrection has a mass base. If we were to say that death is all in all, the end of everything—good and evil, beauty and ugliness, truth and falsehood—all brought to an end by death, people could not accept it. It is also unacceptable to say that annihilation is the ultimate fate of humanity, because there is no righteousness in the assertion, no reasonableness, no justice, no sense of right and wrong, and no love. That a life like that of Jesus should end in death—that is not how the universe should be. On this point, many people are of one mind.

We can find ideas similar to that of resurrection outside Christianity. "Some People," a poem by Zang Kejia begins: "Some people live, though they are dead; some people are dead, but still they live."

You know that I admire Wen Yiduo very much. On the anniversary of his assassination by the KMT, Guo Moro wrote:

"Soon it will be dawn in China, and all around the country there will be countless

Wen Yiduo's—of gold, of stone, of cement.

You are a good seed and with the dawn in China, with the rays of the sun, all around and on for uncounted years, there will be countless Wen Yiduo's.

From one come many. Like your name, like you yourself, they represent truth.

It is not your death I remember today, it is rather your life I celebrate."

The Ming poet Tang Xianzu writes in *The Peony Pavilion* that, solely on the basis of human intellect, it is difficult to imagine a return to life from death, but on the basis of human affections, that is, deep and profound feeling and intuition, life from death is a "certain" truth.

To use the language of faith, God is Master, Ruler. He is Master of the cosmos, of nature, history and the world. Not that everything that happens in society and history is the will of God, but through everything that happens—right or wrong, good or evil, beautiful or ugly, sorrowful or happy—God's love is at work, guiding all, accepting all, transforming all, making everything into an offering from Jesus to

God. Gaining life through death, gaining joy through pain, gaining strength through weakness—this is an experience not only of the Risen Christ, but more and more becomes our personal experience. As a nation, as a church, as citizens, as believers, in the midst of black clouds and suffering, we hear a voice calling us to set our minds at ease and believe: "It is the Lord" (John 21:7). Behind all phenomena, behind what lies at the back of things and even beyond that, at its most fundamental, "It is the Lord," the Lord's hand, the Lord's love, the Lord's will. This is the source of our Christian comfort, peace, faith and hope.

—Resurrection: Reaching Toward Faith, Nanjing Seminary, 1984

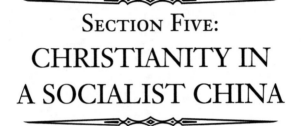

SECTION FIVE:
# CHRISTIANITY IN A SOCIALIST CHINA

# A Wide Door for Effective Work Has Opened, and There Are Many Adversaries

The Student Christian Movement (SCM) and the World Student Christian Federation (WSCF), as you know, have played an important role as a training ground for generations of the leaders of the ecumenical movement. My association with the SCM and the WSCF taught me a lot about the necessity of entering into the diversity of the riches of Christ as gathered together in the Church Universal. What we see as an individual, or as a church, or a country or race or culture or gender as ultimate truth is at best a provisional unity of truths, like an arc of a circle to be completed in the full circle of Jesus Christ in whom the whole truth abides, as we will discover when we cease to see things dimly as in a mirror. This view has had a long-lasting effect on my thinking all these years since my return to China.

What made me and my wife decide to return to China, i.e., the People's Republic of China? We just felt that, since we were Chinese and since it was in China that we had received the major part of our formal education, it was in China where we could serve the people and the church best. We didn't know much about the communists. Our assumption was that, as fellow Chinese, we had enough in common to be able to discuss matters together, although perhaps not always with ease. This I found to be on the whole true during a larger part of my forty years in China. But the assumption was completely naive and unwarranted during the ten years of the ultra-leftist Cultural Revolution.

When we reached home in the early 1950s, the Three-Self Movement was already in full swing. I became supportive of the movement because I wanted the church in China to be Chinese by becoming self-governing, self-supporting and self-propagating. Only a church with a Chinese selfhood could expect to gain its right to be heard by our fellow Chinese. The Three-Self Movement was not an invention of the Chinese Christians. It was Henry Venn, a Church of England priest and the executive secretary of the Church Missionary Society, who in 1850 put these three objects together as the aim of missionary work in Africa. I think Rufus Anderson in America did the same thing more or less at the same time. All through history, the church has always wanted to identify itself in some degree with local situations. When the Christian gospel was first presented to the non-Jewish world, the question arose as to whether the evangelists were to take with them Jewish customs and practices and were to make converts into Jews of sorts. De-Judaization was the decision of the conference specially called in Jerusalem to face that situation. Later, when the gospel reached Europe, people with foresight took risks in theology, spirituality and art so as to make it a religion that could speak to the minds and hearts of Europe. When cultural conditioning has become constrictive for a church in approaching a new area or a new epoch, changes are called for.

As we look back at the Three-Self Movement, we realize we should not be preoccupied with our selfhood for too long a time. The selfhood of any particular church cannot stand all by itself but must be related to the Church Universal in all its geographical and historical expanse, from which it receives its nourishment and to which it brings its partial grasp of the richness of Christ. Hence, we cherish our relation with the World Council of Churches and our ties and our give and take with the world's Christian communities.

There are in China two groups of people with whom I have contacts and about whom I will now say a few words: (1) the Chinese intellectuals and (2) the Chinese atheists and communists.

In recent years, Chinese intellectuals are more open and friendly to Christianity than probably any time since the arrival of Christianity in China in the 7th century in its Nestorian form, and the work of the Jesuits in the 16th and 17th centuries. The intellectuals took an attitude of superiority and suspicion toward the missionaries who, for the sake of survival, had to try their best to show that Christianity was not too different from Buddhism and Confucianism. Missionaries tried to justify their presence by taking with them astronomy, geometry and science. They took over from Buddhism and Confucian classics terminologies and from Chinese scholars their dress and manners. After the formation of the People's Republic of China in 1949, with the vogue of materialism and especially with the ascendancy of ultra-leftism, the rejection of Christianity has been marked by equating it to the opiate.

A new epoch began with the nationwide criticism of ultra-leftism following the downfall of the Gang of Four who controlled the Cultural Revolution. The intellectual climate for Christianity has entered a new stage of "basing judgments on facts." In the last fourteen years or so, many scholars have turned to saying that the opiate is only one of the roles religion plays and not a good definition of religion. Under certain circumstances, such as those described by Frederick Engels in his *Peasant War in Germany*, religion plays a progressive role. Under the influence of more open-minded Marxists, a distinction is made between religion and superstition. They affirm religion as a part of human culture and as contributory to its development. There has arisen an appreciation of Christianity and the Bible. Christian theology is valued as a branch of Western philosophy and for that reason Chinese intellectuals have translated a great many Western theologians into Chinese, including Tillich, Niebuhr, Hans Kung, Rahner and Moltmann. This may not be exciting to Christians and theologians in the West, but is epoch-making in China after all the devaluation of religion.

We of Nanjing Theological Seminary are especially aware of the changed intellectual climate around us. In the '50s our seminary was just a dot on the map of Nanjing, a center of superstition not worth paying attention to and, hence, ignored by the teachers and students of the universities in the city. Today, we are, at the same time, the Center of Religious Studies of Nanjing University where our teachers share in its educational programs. *Religion*, a semi-annual publication of our center, goes to all universities and many social science institutes, and is a good means of communication and dialogue with the non-Christian scholars of religion in China.

I especially like to refer to the "culture Christians" who are the opposite of the European "cultured despisers of Christianity." They have embraced Christian faith except that they do not believe in sacraments and in going to church. They are bridges or half-way houses between the church and the intellectual world and, therefore, our important allies.

Now, about the communists and atheists.

The Marxist Chinese Communist Party stands for atheism and does not have any love for religion. But atheists are not all of a piece. While there are those who still cannot think of religion apart from the opiate, there are now those in growing number who subscribe to "the five natures of religion in China," an analysis coming from the leading circles of the Communist Party which elaborates on (1) the rootedness of religion in the masses of the people, (2) its affinity to ethnic minority races, (3) its international connections, (4) the long life it has before it, and (5) its complexity. This pragmatic understanding of religion gives important support to a fairer treatment of religion and a more liberal and careful implementation of the principle of religious freedom.

I am inclined to think the Chinese Communist Party is not the same as the Party in the former Soviet Union in that it puts a strong emphasis on the United Front. The prosperity of the country is given first place in its program, rather than the propagation of an ideology. The Party understands that it needs to unite all elements in the population that aspire for national prosperity. In order for this unity to be possible, ideological differences must be relegated and minority characteristics such as religious faiths respected. That is the very practical basis for the Party leadership's readiness to give allowances to religious freedom. Unlike the former Soviet Union, there has not existed in China any anti-religious organization or much direct anti-God propaganda.

I am not terribly upset by the advocacy of atheism because the fact that God was, is and will be forever is not changed by any human denial of his existence. In our overwhelmingly secular society, even the very attempt to deny God is sometimes helpful by calling people's attention to the question of God. It at least leads some people to consider God as an option. In 19th-century Europe, Nietzsche, in putting forward the thesis on the death of God, actually enlivened people's interest in the question of God.

After all, who are the gods whose existence the atheists deny? They are often the tyrannical Jupiter who chains Prometheus to a cliff because he does good for humanity, and the ruthless underworld King Yen in Chinese popular religion who sends out emissaries to fetch people to be thrown into hell fire as punishment for their misdeeds. Atheistic humanism may be looked upon as one form of human seeking after God. We can join forces with humanitarians of many sorts to oppose the idolatry in those views of God that diminish human dignity and block human liberation. Some of my friends are surprised that I sometimes speak as highly as I do of certain atheists and communists. There is a part of me which utters a hearty "Amen" to what they advocate and exemplify, a part of me that refuses to rebuke them, but rather warms to them and wants to work with them against forces we both want to combat, even though we get our orders from different chains of command.

Some persons in the West think that Chinese Christians should be anti-communist and should demonstrate a spirit of combat in dealing with the government. Their assumption is that since communists are atheists, they are destroying religion and, hence, the mandate for the Christians is one of confrontation and martyrdom. We have not easily called for martyrdom. It is not good for the welfare of the church and of the nation. As long as there is common ground between communists and Christians as Chinese citizens, as long as there is space for us to maintain Christian worship and witness and church life, and as long as ways are open for useful dialogue on the implementation of the principle of religious freedom, we see no justification for thinking that atheists are our enemies and that belligerency is called for.

How do we approach these two groups of persons in dialogue and Christian witness?

There are two approaches which have been found to be fruitless. First, to present Chinese intellectuals and atheists with a set of antirational, fundamentalist Christianity which we have so much of in the Chinese Church, with its demand that all biblical narratives be taken as literal history, a demand highly unacceptable to Chinese intellectuals and atheists. To me, if they can appreciate the Bible as containing symbolic truths, it is good enough. Second, to challenge them with a so-called Asian theology which is largely an adaptation of liberation theology calling for a basic revolutionary change in society by a transfer of power. This sounds irrelevant, if not outrageous, to those who think of China as in a post-liberation period of history and of themselves as having had much to do with the bringing about of that liberation which they do not want to see uprooted.

From my limited experience, the approach to our Chinese intellectual and atheist friends has to focus on the personality of Jesus as a great lover. Jesus tells us about the father who has trust in the prodigal son and waits for his return, about the shepherd who has his ninety-nine sheep in the fold and yet cannot bear to lose one that is missing. We see a Jesus who weeps with those who weep and rejoices with those who rejoice, a Jesus who protects a person who has erred and asks her not to err again, a Jesus who has loved his friends and loves them to the end, who washed his friends' feet on the eve of his departure from them, one who told his friends, "Do not let your hearts be troubled, believe in God, believe also in me." This Jesus introduces a new scale of value in which Sabbath rules are subordinated to human needs. The picture we get of him in the New Testament is fragmented but touches the chord in all that is best in human nature: the lonely man, homeless and self-forgetful, with his out-pouring of love and sympathy, his suffering and agony, his victory over ruthless power. On the basis of their understanding of the universe and history as a creative process, I would then try to help them see somehow that, at the back of this process and guiding it, is the very love as exemplified in Jesus. Instead of bringing in the question of the divinity of Jesus, I would like them to see the Christ-likeness of this love with a capital "L" which we call God.

The philosophy of struggle has been made the ruling philosophy in China for decades. It culminated in the Cultural Revolution when people were taught not to love men and women, but to suspect them as enemies and to engage in class struggle which should be looked for everywhere. It is love that China needs. The reality of love as shown in Jesus and as the very essence of the whole creative process in the universe has a freshness and vibrancy that is nothing short of a gospel. God is the Cosmic Lover, not the cosmic tyrant. Love is God's supreme attribute, over and above all his other attributes and subordinating them all. Love is the force directing God's ever-continuing work of creation, redemption and transfiguration.

Even when he is not recognized under a conventional name—even when he is not named at all—he is the inescapable energy of love which moves through all things and which works in all things for the creation of the richest possible good. In this process the whole world and all humanity are half-made products finding their fulfillment in being co-workers or co-creators with God.

Some may wonder if the faith I try to introduce is not simplistic, in that nothing is said about the human predicament or a fuller Christology. But what I am trying to find is a point of entry. We do not require a package deal in people's acceptance of the Christian religion, i.e., press them to subscribe at one go to the whole course of the Christian creed. To see in Jesus the great lover and the great revealer and exemplifier of the love that runs the universe is already accepting a lot of the Christian revelation.

We Christians are fewer than one percent of the Chinese population. We are at a disadvantage in many ways. We literally started from square one at the end of the Cultural Revolution, which had deprived us of all our churches and ministers. We are faced with many opportunities as well as difficulties. Paul says near the end of 1 Corinthians: "A wide door for effective work has opened to me, and there are many adversaries." It is interesting that the conjunction used is "and," not "but." This conveys the idea that opportunities and difficulties are often companions. We like to think that, in our small way, we are doing an experiment on behalf of the Church Worldwide. As a Union alumnus and as the recipient of the Union medal tonight, I like to think that we are doing this with the blessing of Union Seminary.

—Union Theological Seminary, New York City, October, 1994

# DEVELOPMENT
# OF CHURCH STRUCTURE

During this meeting we must study an issue which has been a deep concern and a topic of frequent discussion among co-workers and fellow Christians: how to re-order the internal relationships of the church, and first of all, the relationship between the Three-Self organization and the church.

I would first like to present the background of this issue as far as I understand it.

The contribution and achievements of the Three-Self Patriotic Movement initiated by Mr. Y. T. Wu have been immense. It has brought about significant changes in Chinese Christianity and in world Christianity:

(1) It has raised the banner of patriotism in the church in new China, uniting the masses of Christians to love their country and to participate in the building of socialism.

(2) Through the practice of Three-Self and patriotism, Christianity has changed its image among the people. It has lessened the difficulties in the implementation of the religious freedom policy. It has provided a better environment for Christian activities. It enabled the church to hold its own through devastation such as that wrought by the Cultural Revolution.

(3) The behests of the former generation of church leaders to be independent, self-governing, self-supporting and self-propagating have been actualized throughout China. They paved the way for our present goal: to govern well, to support well and to propagate well.

(4) It promoted unity and harmony among various traditions, and provided favorable conditions for a postdenominational church.

(5) It has presented one model for selfhood and independence among Third World churches.

(6) Its exposure of the damage done to the missionary movement by colonialism and imperialism has drawn the attention

of historians, church leaders and Christians in general world-wide. To a degree this has encouraged a rethinking of mission in its theory and practice.

(7) In the Church worldwide we have won the friendship of many leaders and fellow Christians. At the same time they have been helped to see the hope in the Church and this has strengthened their faith.

Like any other human movement and organization, the Three-Self Movement led by the Three-Self organization is not without shortcomings and mistakes. But its accomplishments are great and clearly recognized by all. We cannot deny that the Three-Self Movement has been a tool in the hand of God.

As we know, the goals of the Three-Self Movement are only to promote patriotism and to promote self-government, self-support and self-propagation within the church. Its aims are quite limited; it is not within the boundaries of its goals and responsibilities to manage or direct the church. No version of the constitution of the Three-Self organization ever stated that its task is to run the church.

From the beginning of this movement this has been an important emphasis, and made clear to co-workers and believers that the Three-Self Movement was not to lead or supervise the church. It is only to call Chinese Christians to love their country, and at the same time to insist that the church in China should not be dominated by churches of other countries.

The reason a vast number of Christians supported Three-Self in the early days (within three years, more than half of the Christians in China signed their names to the Manifesto), was that they realized that only when the church practiced Three-Self could there be a future for the church. They wanted to manage the church well, to witness well. In the Three-Self Patriotic Movement they found the hope and channel for doing so. Three-Self does not interfere with faith, and does not run the church. It only promotes selfhood and independence, to open up a future for the church. Therefore Christians could rest assured.

Yet as time went on there have been changes in the functions of the Three-Self organization. These are understandable changes. The Korean War led to the freezing of church funds between China and abroad. Financial assistance from mission boards stopped. Many denominations found their leadership and management paralyzed. Three-Self organizations found it necessary to begin shouldering the responsibilities of various functions of church leadership and management. Then, with repeated political campaigns, the centralization of leadership was increasingly stressed in China and this affected the church also. In many places the actual power of leadership for church work unavoidably became centered in Three-Self organizations. In many places the Three-Self moved from a Christian movement and mass organization, which was originally meant to lift high the banner of patriotism, to promote self-government, self-support and self-propagation, to a position side by side with, or even above the church. It became a management department, like a church and yet not really a church; like a government yet not really a government. Many co-workers and fellow Christians did not understand and could not explain these tendencies. In carrying out the work there have been conflicts and contradictions. These have made our unity difficult. In other words, the relationship between Three-Self as an organization and the church is not in order. This has posed the issue of re-ordering the relationship.

Our work in the church needs to have an adequate basis in faith and theology. The church is a social organization. But from the perspective of a Christian's faith, thinking and frame of mind, the church is different from social organizations such as the Women's Federation and the Red Cross. It is not like any other organization. It has its sacred dimension. The church is not only a spiritual fellowship of believers, it is the household of God, the temple of the Holy Spirit. It is the body of Christ with Christ as its head. As our hymn says, the church is "made by holy water and holy word, a new creation of the Lord." Also, "the church is the golden lampstand." In the Apostle's Creed and in the Nicene Creed, after expressing our faith in God the Father, the Son and Holy Spirit, the fourth stanza goes on to say that we believe in the church. We can see that Christians throughout the ages have accepted the church as part of the Christian mystery, and part of the Christian faith.

Precisely because of the place of the Church in Christian doctrine,

Christians find it uncomfortable and out of order to have any other organization set above the church. They would feel uneasy if the position of Christ as head of the church were taken away. Therefore, the idea that "Three-Self leads the church," or "the church is to be a religious organization administratively run by the Religious Affairs Bureau" grates on the ears of Christians. This is not to say that Christians do not love their country, or do not support their government, nor is it caused by the anti-new-China feelings of Christians abroad. It is a matter of faith. For those who are not Christians and who do not understand Christianity or comprehend the thinking and feelings of Christians, this phenomenon is difficult to grasp.

In the fifth chapter of the Letter to the Ephesians Paul spoke of Christ's love for the church, of his giving himself, cleansing the church with water and word, so that the church can be sanctified, and presented before him in splendor, without spot or wrinkle, holy without blemish. In the early days of Three-Self we frequently used this passage of scripture to speak about the sanctification of the church. It is worth mentioning now that, after the washing it should be the purified church, and not the water that remains. The Reformation Movement initiated by Martin Luther successfully completed its task after many decades. The result was a reformed church, not the maintenance of the movement itself. The church will remain always, while movements and their organizations are to serve the church. The essence of Christianity is the church and not any movement. From time to time it is necessary to adjust the functions of a movement.

With these considerations, many co-workers and fellow Christians feel that, since the Three-Self Movement has accomplished its basic task and reached its important goals, a time of adjustment has arrived. The nurture and preservation of the church (Ephesians 5) must be carried out by the church in the church's own way. No other organization can take its place.

Co-workers, fellow Christians, I often think of John the Baptist who was so important, yet so humble. At the time of his birth his father Zachariah prophesied: "And you, child, will be called the prophet of the Most High, for you will go before the Lord to prepare his way." This shows us the position of John the Baptist in God's history of salvation. When John met Jesus face to face thirty years later he proclaimed: "I am not the Christ, but the one sent before him." He even said, "He must increase and I must decrease." It seems that John was saying that when a movement to prepare the way loses sight of the fact that its task is a preparatory one, that it is not to supplant Christ, then it will inevitably retrogress, and rather than a stimulant, it will become an obstruction.

Some of our co-workers may question whether our self-governing, self-supporting and self-propagating continue to face problems. There are centrifugal forces. With the opening of China there is infiltration from abroad. In addition, there are people engaged in illegal activities. Is this an appropriate time to speak of re-ordering the relationship? Here we need to make clear that the goals of the Three-Self Patriotic Movement are limited to promoting love of our country and the Three-Self principle. If it goes beyond these, it will take over the rightful functions of the church and lead to many problems. We need to manage the church well, to govern it well, support it well, propagate well, and promote unity and stability among co-workers and all Christians who come from various traditions and backgrounds. We need to pay attention to building up theology and theological education. We need to nurture and teach Christians so that they can resist infiltration from abroad, and discern misinterpretation of the Bible and truth and recognize all false teachings, to witness for Christ and to propagate the Gospel. All these are endless tasks. They can be carried out within the church rightfully and effectively under the auspices of the church and the Christian councils. It is for the sake of carrying out these tasks that we need to deal with the relationship question. Reality has shown that while the relationship has not been re-ordered, our work has been jeopardized. "Expanding our unity" has often been an empty phrase. Reactionary infiltration from overseas and illegal activities are banned by law. This is a task of the appropriate government departments, and has never been a function of Three-Self organizations.

Some colleagues may ask: If the functions of Three-Self are so limited, why did we wait until now to raise the question, rather than raise it earlier? I think one of the reasons is the "leftist" line which began to assume prominence in the 1950s and eventually became the dominant line. The work of the church was severely disrupted and damaged. Under the circumstances we could not put this issue on our agenda. The second reason is that since the end of the Cultural Revolution our churches have been busily negotiating for the return of properties, reopening and building churches, setting up home meeting points, publishing the Bible and Christian literature, and establishing theological schools. Therefore this issue has not been a priority. The third reason is that we need substantial experience before we can locate where the problem is and have the wherewithal to solve it. The establishment of the China Christian Council in 1980 to work on governing well, supporting well and propagating well can be considered an important step toward this re-ordering of the relationship.

Are we to eliminate Three-Self? Absolutely not. Three-Self is our principle and guiding direction. No matter what change takes place in the function of Three-Self organizations, this will not mean that we give up Three-Self as a principle and guideline. We should realize that to lift up and promote Three-Self is the ongoing work of the church in China and all its members. It is far more effective to demonstrate the validity of self-government, self-support and self-propagation when the church and the China Christian Council can govern well, support well and propagate well.

No matter how we re-order our relationships, our principle of mutual respect for various faith traditions, liturgies and their unique characteristics will not only remain unchanged, but will also be implemented better so that no single tradition will feel slighted. We especially urge those who are in the majority to be more loving and understanding to those who are in the minority. As we set rules and regulations we must consider the uniquenesses of the minorities. We also hope that those in the minority would consider the good of the whole, and not exaggerate the differences in faith and liturgy and ignore the oneness given by Christ in our basic faith or take action that is harmful to our unity.

The leadership provided by church affairs bodies to their subordinates and to the grassroots congregations should be churchly and pastoral, and not administrative control with abuse of power. It should provide direction and assistance on theological bases and principles.

The hope placed on us by the masses of Christians is to conscientiously attend to the work of running the church well. Only when the church is well managed can it become the center of unity for all those who claim Jesus Christ as Lord in our land. Therefore the placement of personnel within the Christian community must reflect the demand for a well managed church. Instead of sticking to one pattern, we should be open to all avenues to place in important positions all who are willing to serve Christ and the church. We must learn from all co-workers and fellow Christians who can make a contribution in running the church well, especially those who have gained the trust and respect of Christians in the nurture of the spiritual life and those who can safeguard the rights of the church. Whether they are old or young, we should not detest or exclude them. If there has been estrangement in the past, let us forgive one another in the Lord and seek reconciliation. Then there will be a new great unity for Chinese Christianity. We urge all pastors, evangelists and workers to rekindle the fire we had when we were first called to serve, to rededicate ourselves, to free ourselves from secondary matters, to concentrate and hold fast, so that we can become shepherds of great spiritual resources, the treasure and riches of the church in China.

At the same time we also realize that managing the church well is a gigantic task. We need talents of all kinds. No matter how we re-structure or re-order, we cannot afford to lose any colleague who wishes to continue to labor for the church. We need to arrange staffing carefully so that each can develop his or her potential and be properly placed to work together with the same mind for the work of the church. We should also take care of their material benefits.

In all we do we should consider how we can benefit the upbuilding of the Church of Christ and unite Christians under the banner of "love-country, love-church." Therefore all that is improper for the church and displeasing in the sight of Christians should be firmly rejected, no matter who has initiated it. At least we should not hasten to do it without consulting with the national church council and the national Three-Self organization. Some of our friends do not believe in religion. They do not know what religion is all about and have no love for the church or understanding of the thoughts and feelings of

Christians. They may make suggestions out of good intentions, but these will not be acceptable to Christians. We should explain patiently and clearly why these suggestions cannot be accepted.

For a long time, the government Religious Affairs Bureaus have been giving us tremendous help. But many co-workers have wondered, as we find it necessary today to re-order the relationships within our church, how far we can go toward solving the problem if we do not also re-order the relationship with the government? Yes, this is an important issue. Yet we should know that the leadership in the Party and the government is already aware of the situation. The essence of the Thirteenth Party Congress includes a readjustment of the functions of government Religious Affairs Bureaus. It is considering seriously the rectification of its relationship with various religious groups. I believe that we can anticipate the principle of church-state separation being put into greater effect. The government and the religions should co-exist on a long term basis in a relationship of mutual monitoring and of equality. The relationship of the government and the China Christian Council and Three-Self should not be along the lines of "strengthening government control." Resolute non-interference should be the stance toward the numerous normal religious organizations and activities. For the small number of counter-revolutionary, illegal activities coordinated with infiltration from abroad there should be tightened control, not the opposite.

The government has made great efforts in the implementation of the policy of religious freedom. It has given help politically, provided services and given suggestions to the religious sector according to the policy and guiding principles of the Party and government laws and regulations. These we have appreciated. But when it comes to the work of the church in the areas of personnel, property, finance, organization, administration and church affairs, the government should give respect, instead of interference, so that the church can be managed well in its own way. We have reason to believe that this spirit will be reaffirmed and implemented on all levels including the grassroots. We religious people, as admonishing friends of the Party, also have the responsibility to hasten this spirit to becoming a fuller reality. To read-just the relationships both within the church and between church and state is vital to our doing our work well and to the greater unity of Christians. If not, our country will suffer and so will the church.

Some people think that our deliberations and searching would cause attacks from anti-China forces in Hong Kong and abroad, on the grounds that we are admitting that Three-Self was a mistake and that it is time to quit and so on. No matter what we do, whether we make adjustments or not, there will not be any good word from them. But when we build God's Church so that Christians are more satisfied, drawn closer together and achieve greater unity, then God will be more glorified. Some people overseas are so eager to be anti-Communist that they even create false documents and fabricate the seal of the Communist Party. How can we expect from them any proper response to our thinking, our hopes and aspiration to love our church and manage it well?

Of course it seems abrupt to some church leaders who have little contact with the grassroots churches to bring out the issue of re-ordering our relationships at this time. Yet co-workers and fellow Christians everywhere have been aware of the existence of this problem and have long been discussing it. Recently we brought a number of co-workers together for discussion on this issue and I was happy to see how enthusiastic the discussions were. Everyone is concerned about the larger picture without any selfish territorialism. We should be grateful.

Should there be any change? What is to be changed? How can change come about? We need not draw hasty conclusions. I hope all our co-workers and fellow Christians will participate in the discussion, express your ideas and say all that is in your mind without reservation, with only one goal: to build the church in our country so that it really becomes a church of beauty for Christ.

—Speech to the Joint Standing Committees of the
TSPM and the CCC Shanghai,
December 1988

# MR. Y. T. WU:
# A LASTING INFLUENCE FOR MARXISM
# AND CHRISTIANITY, PART I

**M**r. Y. T. Wu was my teacher and good friend. I feel deeply that his life was one of ongoing renewal in his thinking.

Many people maintain the type of thinking they inherited from the previous generation all through their lives and never undergo any kind of renewal in their thinking. But Y. T. Wu was not like that.

In 1917, Y. T. Wu came to know Christ as "a great and sublime personality," and became a Christian. From what I know this was a significant step on Mr. Wu's path of renewing his thinking. He wrote of it in 1947:

"One spring night thirty years ago, I was in the home of an American friend. I read the Sermon on the Mount in Matthew's Gospel for the first time. Like lightning, those three chapters woke me up from my slumbers. I opened my eyes and saw a vision. I saw a great, noble personality, awesome and gentle, deep and penetrating—He took hold of my soul. He almost stopped me from breathing. When I returned home, I cried out for joy. I was moved to tears. I could not help confessing to this vision, Lord, you are my Savior" (from "Christianity and Materialism" in *Daxue Yuekan*, July 1947).

One of the mottoes of the YM and YWCAs is "Not to be served, but to serve." Another is "Know the truth and the truth will set you free." Influenced by the social reform ideals of the YMCA, Y. T. Wu determined to give up his high-paying job in the Customs and work for the YMCA, in charge of publication and national student work. Through this work, Mr. Wu came into contact with the larger movement of progressive youth, was deeply influenced by them and made his own contribution to helping these young people.

Y. T. Wu was furious over the Marco Polo Bridge Incident (1937). He opposed Japanese aggression in China and was disgusted by the KMT's policy of non-resistance and their attempt to annihilate the Communist Party. Mr. Wu then posed a question to Chinese Christian students which was discussed in many universities and at almost every Summer, Fall, Winter and Spring Camp: Is it enough for Christians to be concerned only with personal salvation, or should Christians be concerned about social reform? That was a greatly enlightening question. Personal salvation meant the Christian's solitary pursuit of goodness through spiritual cultivation, prayer, Bible reading, repentance, worship and leading others to Christ. It meant achieving self-excellence and the belief that this was the only and fundamental path to national salvation. The rest was all high-minded and worthless sloganeering. And social reform meant recognizing the semi-colonial nature of Chinese society, recognizing the strength and path to saving China in its time of crisis, recognizing personal responsibility in the national salvation movement, recognition that only solving the problems facing the nation would solve the problem of personal reform. I was greatly helped by him in this discussion. I was then a student in St. John's University in Shanghai, unconcerned with social reform. I was basically a member of the personal salvation camp, yet I did not want to be a traitor to my country. I was disgusted when I heard some students fiercely debating which country China should submit to. As to how China could be saved, I was at a loss. When I heard Y. T. Wu introduce Jesus Christ as a patriot who love his people and as a hero who sacrificed himself to save them, it was like a breath of fresh air. I gained some political insight and from then on I was convinced that reforming China was the top priority. My preconceptions about Y. T. Wu vanished, and I formed a good opinion of him.

Some people in the Chinese Church are biased against Y. T. Wu as a "social gospeller." From the passages below, however, we see that he advocated uniting the social gospel with personal salvation.

"The Risen Christ not only wants to be Master of our personal life, in today's dark and chaotic world, he should also be the strength and compass of our social life" ("The Dawn after the Darkness," *Tian Feng*, no. 5, April 1947).

"The world is on fire; the social struggle grows ever fiercer and social antagonisms grow ever sharper. The hardships faced by Christian students will be ever greater. What path should we take then? How can we bring the whole Gospel of Jesus—the personal gospel and the social gospel, the gospel of peace and the gospel of revolution—fully into play in this great age?" ("The Chinese Christian Student Movement: Retrospect and Prospect," *News*, No. 25, January 1948).

After the First World War, a group of Western Christian intellectuals had a deep sense of the injustice of the war on both sides and felt deep guilt for having supported it. Under the influence of Gandhi's non-violence and non-cooperation movement, they advocated reconciliation and opposed all wars. They felt that oppression and aggression should be opposed, but their methods were limited to the political, economic, cultural, religious and people's movements. There could be no recourse to military weapons. Mr. Wu was deeply influenced by pacifism and became the leader of the Chinese Fellowship for Reconciliation.

After the Marco Polo Bridge Incident, Mr. Wu criticized the KMT policy of non-resistance while advocating reconciliation. He discovered that the number of like-minded people grew increasingly smaller, and he, too, began to speak less of reconciliation. But his final rejection of reconciliation and his advocacy of military resistance came after he saw with his own eyes the havoc wreaked by Japanese planes on Shanghai. To my knowledge, this was the second significant leap in the formation of Y. T. Wu's thinking, to be a Christian and reject reconciliation with Japanese enemies.

For the sake of historical accuracy, I should point out that objectively, reconciliation can be the ally to non-resistance and capitulationism. But, Y. T. Wu was a patriot, opposed to Japanese imperialism, who supported the boycott of Japanese goods and non-cooperation with the Japanese, as well as international calls for political and economic sanctions against Japan. He was only opposed the use of military force. It would be unjust to equate his idealism with KMT non-resistance.

After his rejection of reconciliation, Y. T. Wu threw himself into the resistance movement without reservation. As the war continued, the resistance movement became divided and some went over to the Japanese side publicly. This led to something new in Y. T. Wu's thinking and faith: He began to urge unity and oppose friction; he advocated democracy and opposed tyranny. Among Chinese Christian leaders at the time, the mainstream favored Chiang Kai-shek. There were some who aided the Eighth Route Army and the people of the liberated areas, but they were few and were not vocal about it. It was truly commendable for a Chinese Christian like Y. T. Wu to wave the banner of democracy, cooperation with the Communists and resistance to the end.

Under Y. T. Wu's protection, many progressive young people joined the YW and YMCA, taking up responsibilities in all areas during both the war against Japan and the war for liberation. In the occupied areas and the KMT-controlled areas, the Y's in many cities helped guide young people toward progressive social organizations.

Y. T. Wu had never related himself to the KMT nor had any good opinion of it. But for a fairly long period, he still placed his hopes on the KMT, hoping it would respect the wishes of the people and run the country well. But in the latter part of the War, he began to lose all his illusions about the KMT.

At the same time the Communist Party and liberated areas began to assume a more important place in his consciousness. In his eyes, the Communist Party had been raised from being an object for cooperation and union to being the leading force in the Chinese revolution and the hope of the Chinese people. Y. T. Wu was by then no longer an ordinary patriot, resister or democrat he had become a friend of the Chinese Communist Party. He was filled with confidence for the coming of new China. He offered this guidance to young Christians of the day:

"The end of an era is both dark and light; it is chaotic, yet there is also the beginning of order; there is death, but also the beginnings of new life ...

"We need not mourn the end of the old era, but should be joyful at the coming of the new. This is our vision, this is our faith; this vision and this faith can make us strong and patient. It can help us feel no nostalgia for the old corrupted husk, but rather like a prophet or a warrior, give all our strength for the seedlings of new life" ("The End of an Era," *Tian Feng*, No. 21, September 1946).

In May 1949, on the eve of the founding of the People's Republic of China, Y. T. Wu went to Prague as a delegate to the World Peace Conference and I traveled from Geneva to meet him. We talked non-stop for hours. Y. T. Wu was filled with pride that the Chinese people, under the leadership of the Communist Party, had liberated the nation and were establishing new China. He was completely involved in this great enterprise. I asked him whether he would still support the Communist Party if it oppressed religion. His answer was that he would, because China is so vast and religion is only a very small part of it. He went on to speak of many principles and facts to show why the Communist Party would inevitably administer the policy of religious freedom. He felt there would always be deviations, but that these could be corrected. He warned me to be careful of propaganda from anti-China groups overseas.

Let me turn now to the next breakthrough in Y. T. Wu's thinking. Friends outside the church may have some difficulty understanding its significance and arduousness for him.

Mr. Wu of course worshipped Christ deeply. But before Liberation, though he did belong to a church, he was not optimistic about the leadership of the organized church. He kept out of it as much as possible, speaking more about the "Christian movement," a less concrete, harder to define concept. This "Christian movement" was separate from the leadership of the organized church. It would not sully itself by association. On the church's side, some considered him as a rather arrogant, if forward thinking, intellectual, some derided him as of the "youth party," and some accused him of being "without faith." Around Liberation, Mr. Wu joined the Chinese People's Political Consultative Conference, becoming the representative of all Chinese Christianity. The trend of events in China and abroad put Mr. Wu into this position of leadership. Without a doubt, no one more suitable could have been chosen. However, in this way he was immediately faced with the problem of how to represent all of Chinese Christianity and how to unite and lead well all the people in the Chinese Church. This was another milestone for Mr. Wu in the process of renewing his thinking. It would be like having to unite the whole Chinese Church, including denominational leaders who have not had much to say to each other in many years. It may be difficult for those outside to understand the inevitable adjustments he had to make in his thinking and the huge demands this placed on him. It should be noted that Zhou Enlai met with Y. T. Wu and other Christian leaders a number of times in 1950 for earnest discussions during which he warmly praised the Three-Self principle Christians had raised in the past. This, along with Zhou's friendly concern for his work over the years, was quite influential in Mr. Wu's switch from youth and literature work to working for the whole church, which meant he became increasingly identified with the church and with the masses.

As a fully ecclesial leader, Mr. Wu initiated the Three-Self Patriotic Movement, uniting the whole church on the foundation of patriotism and enabling the Chinese Church to achieve self-government, self-support and self-propagation, becoming the first Third World church to be entirely independent and a self-governed church of national scope. The church gained the praise and esteem of Christians worldwide and created the conditions for the next step, that of governing well, supporting well and doing the work of propagation well. In order to create the possibility for Christians of all denominations to unite on the foundation of Three-Self patriotism, Mr. Wu advocated mutual respect in faith and liturgy, rather than forced unity. This principle is even now being implemented in all our Christian work. As the leader of all denominations, but never the leader of a single denomination, Mr. Wu did a great deal for all denominations in the implementation of the policy of religious freedom.

There was a time in Y. T. Wu's life when he found it hard to "renew" his thinking—during the Cultural Revolution era. From what I heard in Nanjing, Y. T. Wu professed himself "at a loss to understand" the Cultural Revolution. He spent most of it behind closed doors at home. He died in 1979, after the Third Plenum of the Eleventh Party Congress. He saw that Party policies were being re-implemented, and he derived a great deal of comfort from this.

Following his death, the Three-Self Patriotic Movement of Protestant Churches in China and the China Christian Council continue to raise high the principles of self-government, self-support and self propagation initiated by Mr. Y. T. Wu and the work we inherited from him to run the church well, making the church well governed, well supported and one in which the work of propagation is done well. Running the church well is the aspiration of all Christians; it illustrates through praxis the inevitability and correctness of Three-Self and is the thing most capable of uniting Christians under its banner. At the same time, running the church well is a demand and a contribution Christians should make to the nation, one of the ways they can express their patriotism. This is to say that building up the church well is one of the proper meanings of loving the church and one of the proper meanings of patriotism. This will be a true realization of Y. T. Wu's vision for Three-Self.

We have seen that some people's thinking never changes throughout their lives. Some can only hold on to what was considered revolutionary at one stage, after that they are mediocre and incompetent. For the rest of their lives they accomplish nothing or even obstruct the revolution. For several decades, Y. T. Wu was able, time and again, to accept new thinking, to break out of old patterns again and again. Throughout his life he accepted advice readily and maintained his revolutionary freshness. For me he truly was a fine teacher and a good friend.

—Speech at the Meeting to mark Y. T. Wu's 100th Birthday, Beijing, September 1989

$$\wp$$

# MR. Y. T. WU, PART 2

Y. T. Wu's passing away was a big loss to Chinese Christianity as well as to China. Articles are written in his memory not just to express personal feelings of loss, but to enable more people to know of Y. T.'s contributions to Church, to society, to China and to the world so that they, with some familiarity with the struggles their predecessors went through, may know better how to make their choices in new circumstances.

Chinese Christian theological thinkers down to Y. T.'s time were on the whole a prejudiced generation. It was hard for them to shed the shackles acquired from their exposure to Western capitalist culture. When historical development was such that the question of basic structural change in society presented itself with full force, when the cause of the Chinese people's liberation under the leadership of the Communist Party was advancing might and main and Liberated Areas were long in existence, embracing tens of millions of the people, consolidating and enlarging themselves day and night, and demanding every Chinese person to make up his or her mind about them, these theological thinkers were found to be disappointingly poorly informed, one-sided and narrow-minded. A leaf before one's eyes is enough to prevent them seeing Mount Tai, as we say. These intellectuals gave themselves the right to assume that the West represented the mainstream of human history, that Western ideas only were high-class, axiomatic and full of vitality, and that the rule of the Kuomintang and its government was right and proper, capable of giving leadership to national salvation, especially if polished with a veneer of Christianity. If we will only look into their writings we will see that the objective facts of the Chinese people's liberation movement and of the Liberated Areas were non-existent in their consciousness. Or, if there was any awareness at all, they were treated as a temporary aberration of no consequence, certainly not something worth making any study of. Most claimed to take God as the object of their studies, extolled their own objectivity and transcendence of politics, felt themselves to be over and above the mundane world. As a matter of fact, however, their background and upbringing certainly conditioned them in all their more important judgments without their knowing it. What they wrote and said had many political implications, usually echoing the views of Western powers and the KMT. Among them, whole-hearted supporters of the KMT were few and far between, but the attitude of most amounted to little more than voicing grievances in small matters but giving way on main issues. Thus, to the people, theirs were voices of deception, bringing the people to passive acceptance of their state of bondage. Then there was the small group which was more blatant and violent, putting forward all sorts of vilification of Communist and progressive forces to give vent to pent-up hatred.

But Y. T. was out of the common. He gave importance to history, to the people and to the people's movements. He looked at things in historical terms. As early as the beginning of the 1930s, he saw the great significance of the people's liberation movement in China, began to attach hope to it and adopt theological views helpful to overcoming his alienation from it and to relating himself to it in good will. He brought many Christian youths into sympathy with it and, at the same time, absorbed from it insights for his own theological nourishment and growth. To understand Y. T., it is important to see that Y. T. was always aware that, before God and before humanity, the theologian has to face the question of political accountability. He had to shout from the housetop, calling the Church back to the standpoint of the prophets and Jesus Christ, to be on the side of the people and of justice without counting the cost. As a result, he was like John the Baptist and had to face the opposition of church authorities and of the KMT. In reality, however, it was precisely Y. T. who gave Chinese Christianity some new ingredients, or restored some old ingredients to it, enabling it to take on a fresh image before the Chinese people.

My contacts with Y. T. began in the mid-1930s, a crucial time of national crisis caused by the aggression of the Japanese militarists and their occupation of the provinces of the Northeast. At that time Y. T. was in his last stage as a pacifist. In answering questions before an audience, he would still refer to his opposition under all circumstances to taking up arms, but he had already ceased to want to propagate non-violence. What he dwelt on most was the question of national salvation. He said, if we Christians merely did our devotion behind closed doors, or just sought personal salvation and a place in heaven after death, that was still self-centeredness and showed that we still were not saved from our captivity by selfishness. Christians needed to realize there was the question of the social system. Only after the social system in China underwent a basic change, objective conditions would emerge to make personal transformation possible. And the first task of the moment was that of national independence and liberation. China needed a political restructuring so as to be streamlined to the requirements of the national struggle for liberation. He spoke out loudly for a united front of all patriots, particularly between the KMT and the

Communist Parties, for an all-out mobilization to resist the aggression of the Japanese militarists.

Y. T., in his speeches, presented a Jesus who stood with the masses of the suffering people, ready to go through the torture of the cross and to shed his blood for their liberation. This quality on the part of Jesus was presented as in harmony with the very constitution of the universe, i.e., benevolence, and was therefore of eternal value. Y. T. said that he himself took this Jesus to be his Christ, the center of his life, from whom he received abundant life and learned that the supreme meaning for life was to enable the masses of our people to share in life abundantly.

Even while listening respectfully to Y. T., I had in one pocket my lexicon on New Testament Greek and in another my textbook on the Thirty-Nine Articles of the Church of England. The education I was receiving led me to absorb myself in questions of Christ's two natures and of his place and role in human redemption. A Christology such as Y. T.'s which put Jesus back in to his contemporary history as well as right within the realities of our own national conflicts struck a fresh, compelling note in my ears. It opened up before me a whole area I had not known to exist and hence had never entered, but which now summoned me. At that time, on the one hand, I felt myself to be above politics and indeed above the world but, on the other hand, I was quite dissatisfied with Chiang Kai-shek's non-resistance policy vis-à-vis Japanese aggression, which had resulted in the loss of the entire Northeast, and was disgusted with many of my schoolmates leading a life given to wine and nonsense, some so imbued with the comprador mentality and lack of patriotism as to be discussing which was the best world power for China to become a colony of. When I saw how closely Y. T.'s love for Christ and his concern for the well-being of the people were harmonized and how his loyalty to Christ generated in him a great passion for truth, for life's ideals and for the people, I as a young man seeking something meaningful in life felt inspired and sensed that a direction for my seeking had been pointed out to me.

Today, I still think that, on the view of God, Y. T., in criticizing the prevailing tendency to dwell on divine transcendence alone and in his eagerness for us to see the immanence of the transcendent God in nature, in history and in people's movements, was not only being conversant with classical Chinese notions and therefore evangelistically important, but also playing, both theologically and politically, an enlightening and liberating role. He opened up a sluice-gate for many Chinese Christians to take their place in the movement for national salvation with their faith intact, as well as for intellectuals mindful of the national fate to take their place among Christians. He saved a portion of Chinese Christianity from just being a tranquilizer and painkiller for people in humiliation and suffering.

To this day I am not one who understands and embraces Marxism in its entirety. But the change in my attitude to Marx from blind animosity to respect was also due to Y. T. I had never read directly any of the writing of Marx or Engels and all that I knew of them I had got from the writings and hearsay of Western and pro-KMT Chinese intellectuals. Marxism was a monster, not worth a look-in, ascertained by one scholar after another to be nothing but trash ... But Y. T. assumed an open-minded attitude toward Marxism. In one of his speeches to us he used this quotation from a certain Marxist author:

"Labor produces miracles for the rich, and yet sheer poverty of the workers. Labor creates the palaces, but at the same time slums for the workers. Labor creates beauty, but at the same time makes the workers deformed. Labor produces machines to take the place of manual work, but sends some workers back to barbaric labor, and turns the other workers into machines. Labor creates wisdom, but makes fools and idiots of the workers."

I felt moved by this quotation because it so aptly described the polarization in Chinese society. The simple language also impressed me with its poignancy. And it came from a Marxist. This not only made me more sympathetic with the victims of exploitation and oppression in our society, but also shocked me out of my unwarranted contempt for Marxism. From this we know that all the worthless slander and noise enemies of Marxism make against it will in the long run only defeat their own purposes and cannot really retard its spread.

Not slighting but giving importance to history, picking history up from the dust, looking at it from the people's standpoint, finding in it the mission of Christians and our partners in the fulfillment of the mission—these were what made Y. T.'s approach different in theory and in practice from that of the other theological thinkers of those days. Compared with the liberation theology of Latin America today, Y. T.'s Christology and hermeneutics were not so well thought out and hence failed to reach such heights. But, as far as the pointing out of the direction is concerned, he was in a true sense a forerunner in the evolution of a theology that relates itself positively with the aspiration and struggle of the Third World peoples in their fight against colonialism, feudalism and reaction, for independence and democracy.

After my contacts with Y. T. during the few years prior to and following the outbreak of the War of Resistance against Japan, it was not until May 1949, with the People's Liberation Army taking over Nanjing and Shanghai and Y. T. in Prague for a meeting of the Word Peace Council, that I had another chance to talk with him at great length. I was then in Western Europe on a visit to Czechoslovakia. We spent a lot of time together, on the eve of the establishment of the People's Republic of China.

On that occasion Y. T. told me what he saw of the new life of the people in the Liberated Areas, particularly the spirit and interpersonal relationships that had emerged as a result of the people's new position as masters of their own destiny. He referred to Matthew 25 and said that the communists denied Jesus Christ but put love into practice, while many Christians never ceased to profess Christ and love verbally but could not bring themselves really to present him to the world owing to the lack of love for the masses.

I asked Y. T. a question which disappointed him. New China is indeed admirable, but if the government tries to do away with religion, are you still going to support new China? Y. T. reproved me gently for giving grounds too easily to rumors in the Western press about the persecution of religion in China, but said among other things, "Even in the eventuality that religion will be harassed, I will still love this motherland." (I hope this will not be quoted out of context.) He said he was sure that in new China problems and grievances of all sorts could be settled through a democratic process of consultation. He spoke of the important place of the United Front in the national life of new China, and on the theoretical and political basis of the policy of religious freedom to which the Communist Party had adhered in the Liberated Areas and the national People's Government soon to be established would adhere. Y. T. was certain that the implementation of the policy of religious freedom would not be a question if we took the situation as a whole, but he was not oblivious of the many local problems that would arise. These could not be finally eliminated without extensive and intensive education on the religious policy, not only for adherents of various religions, but also for the general public and the cadres on all levels.

At that time Y. T., like many other Chinese church leaders, seemed to be only counting on the implementation of the policy of religious freedom by the government, without any strong realization yet that Chinese Christianity had no right to feel complacent by depending for its survival on that policy, and that Christians needed to work hard to make the Chinese Church self-governing, self-supporting and self-propagating, if we were to have a footing for carrying on conversation with our fellow-citizens, not to say bearing the Christian witness to them.

On that occasion Y. T. said that the coming of the Kingdom of God was a hope beyond history and that he would not equate new China with the Kingdom or think of her as reaching directly to the Kingdom. However, Y. T. stressed even more strongly that this hope on the part of Christians was not to lead us into disregarding our tasks within history. The fulfillment of historical tasks and the realization of the super-historical hope were not unrelated entities. To clarify how they were related was to Y. T. a theological assignment the times had given to us. Y. T.'s point, in my understanding, was comparable to the thinking in terms of the ultimate and the penultimate which I was encountering in Europe in those theologians who wished to be true to the faith and at the same time get involved in the world. In those remarks of Y. T.'s there were already germinal the thoughts which Chinese Christians later summarized with four characters: *ai guo ai jiao*—love our motherland and love Christianity.

ఴ

My wife and I did not come back to China until two and half years after the visit with Y. T. in Prague.

If before the liberation Y. T. in theological thinking devoted himself more to his conceptions of God and of Christ and to politico-ethical questions, after the liberation he paid greater attention to ecclesiology.

That Christianity in any country should be self-governing, self-supporting and self-propagating and thereby become a religion with a national character of its own is a vision any church in a Third World country needs to give priority to in its ecclesiology. This is a platitude now. Since the middle of the 19th century missionaries and national church leaders with foresight have been giving voice to this task. What is regrettable is that for so long it has been only a voice. Few churches have actually achieved complete Three-Self. Only Y. T. made use of the whole trend toward independence in newly-liberated China and led the Chinese Christians to take the Three-Self path on a national scale. It was a mass movement and it occurred under special historical circumstances and, consequently, not all things developed in accordance with the intentions of its leaders. But, in thirty years, the Three-Self Movement can at least claim the following three achievements:

(1) Christians are no longer behind others in their love for the motherland. "One more Christian, one less Chinese" has become past history. Christians are rendering their contributions in many fields to national construction.

(2) Chinese Christianity is autonomous not only in personnel but also organizationally, financially and politically. There is now a foundation upon which to build up for the Chinese people as well as for Christians elsewhere a Christian Church rich with Chinese characteristics.

(3) As a result of these two achievements people in China are coming to take a more enlightened view of Christianity. They no longer look at it as a foreign religion. The relationship with the Chinese people is becoming normalized. The number of Christians is increasing and not decreasing.

All these changes are important to the Christian cause in China as much as they are important to the stability and unity of our country. While we are thankful to God for his love and gracefulness in making these changes possible, we cannot but recall also the faith, courage and resourcefulness which Y. T. demonstrated all these years.

Three-Self aims at making Christianity Chinese. In any country it is only if Christianity can achieve independence from the influence of foreign political powers and the bounds of foreign historical traditions that the radiance of Christ can beam through the prism of national culture and come out with a brilliance all its own. The people will only feel at home in the presence of this brilliance, and Christians the world over will be enriched by it in their knowledge of the riches that are in Christ. It is only thus that we can speak of the "contribution" of a local church to other churches. If the churches in various countries are not first of all independent and do not take their own paths, then interdependence and give-and-take within the Church Universal will remain as words only.

The Three-Self task of Chinese Christianity is by no means completed today. The question of cultural transformation and upbuilding is harder than that of political belonging. When we think of the captivity and hesitation on our theological front, when we note how much old and Western stuff our life of worship and devotion still exhibits in disharmony with the Three-Self ideal, we are aware that we are not fulfilling the original wishes of Y. T. and other forerunners. We hope that the next thirty years of the Three-Self Movement will witness its in-depth cultural development. In this stage Chinese Christians ought to dare to be ourselves and to blaze a new trail by giving due attention to the accumulation and development of our insights, and to the solution of our problems in our own ways, thus to enter more deeply into Christ and to explore and appropriate in a bigger way the rich treasure of truth that is in him.

80

The middle of the 1950s to the middle of the 1960s was a period during which I had many contacts with Y. T. Aside from consultations on work, we found ourselves often together discussing questions which came to be called between the two of us those of "theological line" or "theological reconstruction." Those were occasions for personal sharing between two Christians which I associate to this day with taking together the breakfast of Cantonese raw fish rice porridge in the Wu household.

For one thing those chats unfolded Y. T.'s high evaluation of the role of Paul. Y. T. was not prejudiced against Paul, although in post-Liberation China there were those who capitalized upon his teaching on the justification by faith so as to sow discord between believers and non-believers and to show contempt for the unbelieving revolutionaries. Y. T. thought highly of Paul for his work in extending the wisdom and worship of Judaism to the whole world. We owe it to Paul that the Christian gospel broke loose from its Jewish shell and became the treasure of all humanity. This breakthrough was of inestimable significance in the making of human history. Paul was a rebel with great courage and resoluteness. Justification by faith was put forth not in order to create cleavage between those with faith and those without. It actually played down greatly the contradiction between the circumcised and the uncircumcised. Justification by faith meant that circumcision was no means to justification. It went a long way in overcoming Jewish religious and nationalist chauvinism and in broadening the Jews' perspective by propagating the equality of all human beings before God. Therein lay the liberating effect of the doctrine. For the transformation of Christianity from a sect within Judaism to a world religion, Paul played a decisive role. Early in the 1950s there was a gust of wind within Chinese Christianity caused by some who preached that Christians should regard all nonbelievers in Jesus Christ as evil, and regard all crimes committed by Christians as having been covered up by the blood of Jesus, basing all of this antinomianism on the Pauline justification by faith. We know that this was not only politically reactionary, but theologically, biblically and historically distorted.

I think we may say that Y. T. in starting the Three-Self Movement was doing something comparable to the historical role that Paul played in that they both caused the Christian religion to rid itself of certain deformities and narrowness and ushered it into a new stage of history.

Y. T. often spoke of the poverty and misery of a religion which revolved around the belief-unbelief axis. In such a religion Christ is only for my use and to my advantage. He gives me salvation and peace of mind as a payback to my belief. It is still self-centeredness and is a negation of Paulinism. If we do not try to hold to what entered into our mind first, or to seek in the Bible what we prefer in order to strengthen our prejudices, but listen to the Bible in its sum total and pay attention the highest point Biblical revelation reaches, we shall see that the realm of God's concern extends itself much farther than the circle of those who recognize him. In Y. T.'s later life he liked to go to Hebrews to affirm Christ as the heir to the whole universe and the whole universe as being sustained by his word of power, and to Colossians where it is said that all things are held together in him. Y. T. felt strongly that, to us who live in new China where the people have gained the political power which had been denied them for thousands of years, the New Testament references to Christ as the sustainer of the whole cosmos cannot but carry a special meaning and sense of reality that is pivotal to our further theological exploration.

Y. T. did not approve of the theological line implicit in certain circles which presented a Redeemer not quite at one with the Creator, in a small way a repetition of the old Gnostic and Marcionite heresy. Y. T. spoke with passion on behalf of the unity of God's work of creation, redemption and sanctification. To him the significance of Nicaea did not lie in stressing the division or the equality of the three Persons and even less on their taking the center of the stage one after another in three successive historical periods, but rather in upholding the truth that the three reflect the several aspects of the permanent character of the one God. Y. T. gave a big place to the Holy Spirit's work of sanctification, recognizing the Holy Spirit as the bestower of all values and virtues in humanity, opposing the delimitation of his work of sanctification and renewal to the church and to established ecclesiastical orthodoxy or orthopraxis.

We often went into the question of nature and grace as one of the ways the politico-theological line was drawn in Chinese Christianity in the early '50s. He was naturally adverse to pitting the one against the other. If nature is indeed so fallen and rotten, the enemy of grace, then the dichotomy between the Creator and the Redeemer would set in again. To Y. T., to make grace a negation of every particle of truth, goodness and beauty in nature and history would be to deny anything in common between the Christ and humanity, and to make of him a one hundred percent alien to the human world into which he came. That amounts to a virtual denial of true Incarnation. I can still see as in a movie how human and childlike Y. T. was in his joy when he was given the quotation from Thomas Aquinas: *Gratia non tollit sed perficit Naturan* ("Grace does not supplant but perfects nature").

Some may question: While there may be biblical grounds for making the whole creation and not just redemption the subject of theology, the whole humanity and not just the church the object of his concern and the whole cosmos and not just religion the domain of Christ's lordship and the Holy Spirit's work of sanctification, were Y. T. and his friends not pushing themselves into the tip of the ox horn, i.e. e., asserting a lot of irrelevancies?

I do think these theological questions had or have great practical relevancy to Christians. Y. T. was helpful to Christians theologically in broadening their perspective, turning them from a contempt for the world and history to seeing their importance, from alienation from human beings and lack of concern for their welfare to loving them and caring for their welfare, and in finding in the world, aside from the opposition of faith and unfaith, also that of goodness and evil, justice and injustice, progress in historical terms and reaction. All of this plays a liberating role in the thinking of those who want to keep to the Christian faith and yet move toward realities and toward love of the motherland.

Y. T. readily agreed to the assertion that religion often plays the role of opium. But to use the opium formula as the approach to all religious phenomena was to him a dangerous over-simplification. Under different circumstances different theological points of view play quite different roles, some narcotic, others expanding the Christians' awareness, some defending the rule of reaction, others raising critical and conscientizing voices. For instance, it would not be fair to lump together the theological voices that go to defend the Three-Self Movement and those which sang the praise of the KMT, all under the word opium. Narcotism is one of the roles religion sometimes plays, but not its only role, and not its main role under all circumstances.

I have set down here a few glimpses into Y. T.'s personal theological excursions to show that as he got advanced in age, he remained mentally as keen as ever. He was making efforts to bring his subjective knowledge in line with objective facts as long as he lived.

Y. T. and I had no direct contact almost all through the years of Cultural Revolution. When we met again in Beijing in 1975, the first question we got into after the long separation was whether from now on Chinese Christianity could do without church buildings and clerical professionalism. Y. T. was still the idealist he had always been. Throughout that conversation and in our subsequent conversations we never had time or interest to go into our personal experiences of the years of the Cultural Revolution.

&#8365;

A person such as Y. T. could not but have some enemies and could not help being misunderstood. As early as the 1930s he was labeled "heretic," "unbeliever," "atheist," "Communist." The world does contain individuals who make themselves known as being "spiritual," seemingly transcending all material quests and not yearning for anything from the world and, yet, in their dealings with others, they can sometimes go to extremes of unfairness and unscrupulousness. Because Y. T. supported the cause of the people, he got slandered and vilified on all sorts of things by such people. I can recall one who, on the basis of the title of one of Y. T.'s books, *No One Has Ever Seen God*, attacked him for propagating atheism, knowing well that Y. T. was only quoting part of a verse in John 1, to bring out in the book what follows: "The only Son, who is in the bosom of the Father, has made him known." Y. T. in that book and, in fact, in his life, was trying to show that the character of this God whom no one has seen has been revealed in Jesus Christ, and calling people to come to behold and adore, and then to go to put into practice what we have seen.

In truth, Y. T.'s faith in Christ was of the most stable sort. I do not know where to find another Christian in China who not only kept his own religious faith steadily but also carried on so persistently and carefully conversations with atheist revolutionary comrades on the truth embodied in Christ. Several cadres in leadership positions in party and government have spoken respectfully of Y. T.'s quiet conversations with them on his religious convictions. Some of them testified that their interest in reading the Bible was due to Y. T.'s influence. Should not such slanderers feel ashamed?

Many Christians are in search for spirituality but most of them do not seem to go into the biblical meaning of the world. They become credulous, catch at shadows and are sometimes fooled. If by spirituality is meant belonging to or siding with the Holy Spirit, if we in accordance to Christ's teaching judge a person by the fruit he or she bears, and if holiness, integrity, justice, love, faith, hope are fruits of the Spirit, then we have to acknowledge that Y. T. at the depth of his personality was a most spiritual Christian. He hated darkness so much as to work hard for its demise; he yearned for the brightness and joy of the New Heaven and the New Earth so much as to strive for the approximation of earth to it. Were these sentiments due not to the educative enlightenment and guidance of the Holy Spirit, but to the personal fantasy of an individual human being?

Y. T. used to tell his audiences that Christian prayer was not any attempt to make God change his good and holy will, or to influence God to do for us what was in violation of his nature, but was to open up the windows of our souls so as to allow the light of God to shine into our inner darkness, to melt away our stubbornness and prejudices so that our thoughts, feelings, words and deeds may be brought to be one with the nature of God. If a person had not gone through real, deep experiences in personal cultivation and devotional life and absorbing study of the Bible, could he or she have produced this lofty conception of prayer out of thin air?

∽

Y. T. was our good teacher and beloved friend, a pride of the Chinese people and of Chinese Christians. God could have molded such a thinker and doer only through the struggles of our Chinese history and our Chinese Church. The value of the work of all other theologians in China before Liberation could not be high as a result of their stand against and fear of the people, the most important factor in human history, and also as a result of their blindness and prejudice, at that time impossible to overcome, as regards the Chinese people's liberation movement, the one greatest reality in contemporary Chinese history, which remained outside their field of theological vision. Hence we feel their contributions were not comparable to Y. T.'s, even though there are still those abroad who look at their writings as precious gems while relegating Y. T. more or less to the rank of the alien.

I think neither our traditional Chinese "good death at the end of a long life" nor the traditional Western "eternal rest in peace" can adequately mark the conclusion of the kind of life and witness exemplified by Y. T. More and more Christians in China and in other Third World countries are taking up the same views as his and are augmenting and amplifying them, even though many do not necessarily know of him. So the cause Y. T. gave himself to is flourishing. I like to think that, today, in a place much closer to the presence of God, Y. T. is continuing in his search for truth and in his practice of truth as he sees it, continuing in his life of adoration and dedication, and continuing to be our co-worker, strengthening our endeavors on earth.

—Mr Y. T. Wu, Part 2, 1981

ℰℐ

# MR. Y. T. WU,
# PART 3

Y. T. Wu was an outstanding person in the Chinese Church. He distinguished himself by consistently carrying on a dialogue with his times: He always advanced with the times. He let himself be challenged and educated by each new period and, in turn, left his imprint on the period in which he lived. He differed from most other Chinese theologians in that he did not worship foreign books, nor did he lightly accept the official KMT propaganda. His own theological ideas developed through his dialogue with his times, especially through his dialogue with the young people who represented progressive trends. To use a term popular among Christians in the world today, Y. T.'s theology was quite contextual. The opposite of the contextual approach is departure from and disregard of reality, that is, saying only those things that are unrelated to any period of time, forgetting one's social responsibilities and disregarding the social consequences of one's viewpoint.

Before Liberation, Y. T. groped for the direction toward which his epoch was advancing and went forward accordingly. That did not at all mean throwing aside his faith in Christ, or carrying it like a burden. On the contrary, he deepened his faith in Christ in such a way that faith became the motive force of all his actions. Moreover, he helped a countless number of young Christians who had a sense of justice and who were eager to save China, to turn all kinds of corners to go forward with him in the same direction, and to throw themselves into the tide of the nation's advance, carrying with them their faith in Christ. At the same time, Y. T. also attracted a portion of youth outside the Christian Church and brought them into the national salvation movement. Y. T.'s main work was not that of a preacher speaking from a pulpit. But no one can deny that, by taking the particular posture he did, he witnessed to Christ in a unique way and changed people's prejudices toward the Christian religion into positive feelings. Can we say this is not preaching? Of course not. This is very effective preaching indeed. At that time, there were many preachers and pastoral workers, but not many were able, as Y. T. was, to spread the Gospel among the fine young people who were so impelled by a sense of urgency to save the country. Due to the fact Y. T. Wu was progressive on many issues, there emerged a progressive wing in the church, and the reputation of the church rose. Thus, Y. T. paved the way for others to preach. I wish to ask those who like to find fault with Y. T., if it weren't for what Y. T. advocated from that time till after Liberation, what would people's impressions of the Christian Church be? Would there be many people willing to speak up for the Christian Church, to help it enjoy its freedom and maintain its legitimate rights? How much religious freedom would you be enjoying?

We are at the end of the 1980s. Times have changed. Our situation is no longer the same. The question arises as to what it means today to learn from Y. T. Wu. I would like to share with you some ideas on this question.

(1) Like Y. T., we must value Christian spirituality and communion with God, constantly recollecting ourselves in God's presence, waiting, listening, and deepening our awareness of the Spirit so that spiritual growth may take place day in and day out.

Y. T. never publicized his spiritual life; he seldom spoke of it. But he believed and attached great importance to prayer. I will quote three things he said:

> Reading the Bible and praying are the main methods for Christian self-cultivation ... The self-cultivation of a Christian consists in maintaining throughout his or her life, the attitude of dwelling in silence in the presence of God. What prayer means above all is not so much petition as coming to a personal awareness of truth in silence. The purpose of prayer is not to make objective facts fall in line with subjective wishes, asking God to grant everything we ask ... On the contrary, prayer brings us to a state of awareness of truth and shows us the road we must follow ... Prayer puts all our subjective wishes and desires before God so that the light of truth will help us discern the black from the white, the right from the wrong, and the degree of respective importance and urgency of these wishes. We can then make decisions as to our attitudes and our actions ... Prayer lifts our life and puts it on a higher level.

> Prayer is basically an attitude of longing for God, or longing for truth ... When a religious person prays, he or she can feel consoled and encouraged in a special way because faith tells us that the truth revealed by God is the way and the life, wisdom and power, and that we share in all these when we offer ourselves to truth, that is, to God.

> Prayer integrates and harmonizes everything in life under the will of God. The greatest prayer is not asking for this or that either for oneself or for others, but asking to know the truth, to know the will of God in order that it may be accomplished. The incessant prayer of one who knows how to pray ought to be "May thy will be done."

Here we see Y. T.'s sublime understanding of prayer, an understanding which is in harmony with the prayer Christ himself taught his
disciples (the Lord's prayer), and with Christ's own prayer in the
Garden of Gethsemane. This is a spirituality of the most exalted kind
which does not center around one's own self. It does not use prayer to
make God do what we want. On the contrary, through prayer, we
readjust our relationship with God, abandoning our own selfishness
and seeking harmony with God's truth. In this way, we consecrate to
God the potentiality within our own being so that it may flourish and
be brought to a higher level and that, invigorated, we may be made
partakers in God's work of creation, redemption and sanctification.

Today, our church is weak. An important reason is the fact that our
colleagues are busy attending all kinds of meetings, and attending to
hundreds of small affairs. We have neglected to some degree, or even
totally neglected, the need of spending time before God in listening
and in waiting. And the result has been a loss of strength. That lesson
is not important only for any particular period of time or any set of circumstances, it is something for all times and under all circumstances.

(2) We must pay special attention to contextualization and restore
the place of ethics and morals in our theological reflection. In our
work, we must strengthen service programs.

Two or three decades before people began to talk about "contextualization," Y. T. had actually practiced it. His own reflections in
Christian theology kept abreast of the work of liberation of the Chinese
people in an organic, not in an awkward way. What he taught was in
fact liberation theology, although he did not use that term. Regrettably,
that line of contextualized theological thinking has discontinued in
China and remains on the fringes only. Our theological thinking lacks
an intention to dialogue with our times and actual realities. It talks a
great deal about that which is close to heaven; it says little about what
is close to us.

Yes, what the gospel gives to humankind is eternal truth. What we
want to propagate is precisely this truth. But eternal truth chose the
form of Incarnation to enter into our world. This should have tremendous mind-opening implications for us.

Our country was liberated in 1949. "The Chinese people have stood up." This was tremendous. This was liberation in one sense of the word. Our country is still at the first stage of socialism today and, up to now, quite a few people still suffer from ignorance and poverty in varying degrees. A further liberation from the bondage of natural and man-made disasters is needed. Liberation in this sense is bound to be a long historical process. Understanding liberation in this sense, it does not seem correct to say liberation theology is irrelevant for Christians in new China.

A cursory reading of books on liberation theology by Latin American Christians would tell us that, there, the acceptance of Christ as the Incarnate Son of God and as the Savior on the Cross who redeems human beings from sin is beyond any doubt. Those writers only re-read the Bible, teach and witness to the Gospel in relation to the questions of socio-political and economic liberation which are of general concern to the people of Latin America. In so doing, they enable Christians to start from the great love of Christ and his salvation to an awareness of their own responsibility in the task of liberation of humankind.

Taking a look at the situation of the church in our own country today, we do see many Christians are good citizens of new China, participating in the four socialist modernizations, many giving unstintingly of themselves in the process. However, in their theological thinking, too many have kept elements that are not at all suitable to the context, elements of which the main theme is detachment from the real world. They communicate these elements and consolidate them in such a way that Christians are led to hold in contempt the real world and everything in it, whether good or bad. There is the dichotomy between theology and its context. That is to say, their acts are not supported by their theological understanding, or their acts lack theological undergirding. The effects of such unsuitable viewpoints in theology may not be felt for the time being, but in particular climates, they may play a decisive role, and unfortunate consequences will then follow.

Bonhoeffer, the theologian who was executed by Hitler because he joined an anti-Nazi organization during World War II, emphasized the this-worldly nature of Christ's Gospel. He pointed out:

"He who runs away from the earth does not find God, but only another world, his own world. He never finds the word of God which comes in this world. He who runs away from the world to find God only finds himself."

A few hours before his execution, he wrote the following words in his prison cell:

"The Christian has no last line of escape available from earthly tasks and difficulties into the eternal, but, like Christ himself ... he must drink the earthly cup to the dregs, and only in his doing so is the crucified and risen Lord with him. This world must not be prematurely written off, in this the Old and New Testaments are at one."

These words happen to coincide with many of Y. T. Wu's sayings.

To contextualize theological thought and to bring theology into dialogue with its context—this was what Y. T. did in his lifetime. I believe this is what he would like to see us do today, not just one or two at a time, but so many that a trend takes shape.

Y. T. Wu's greatest concern was the suffering of the people. It was out of his concern for humanity and his pressing desire to rescue people from untold sufferings that he launched into the movement to save China, got involved in the democratic movement and the war of liberation, and supported the Chinese Communist Party and the socialist system.

Today, the lives of the Chinese people have improved markedly. This is not a simple matter in a country with one billion people. But there is still a long way to go before reaching the level of people's aspirations. Phenomena such as the shortage of medicine and doctors, helplessness before natural disasters, the low level of culture, the lack of civilized behavior, the numbers of handicapped, deaf and blind are not uncommon. Christians ought not to remain untouched by all these. These things ought to stir up compassion and humanitarian sentiments in Christians.

In some places in the Chinese Church, those who promote service are called "unspiritual" and scoffed at as "social gospel people." To juxtapose the rendering of service and being spiritual as two opposites is to polarize the spiritual and the societal. Then, the more spiritual one is, the less he or she will be willing to render services or to be concerned with society. That person will then be the most selfish person, "refusing to lift a finger even if by so doing, the world may benefit." Can we distort the meaning of the spiritual in this way?

Yes, Jesus Christ is the center of Christian faith. People need to know him. It is our church's primary duty to help people to know him. But it was precisely the same Christ who said, "The Son of Man has come, not to be served, but to serve and to give his life, for the redemption of many." This last phrase has often been used to negate the spirit of service, that is, to set Christ's giving of his life to redeem humankind at odds with service to one's neighbor. In reality, judging by this saying, "to give his life" and "for the redemption of many" both bear upon the meaning of "to serve" and constitute the supreme example of "serving the neighbor." How can it be used to negate the high place service ought to have in the Christian Church?

Today, there are too many things to be done in China. They cannot all be done by the state. The government wishes that the people would take the initiative and engage in various works for the service of society. I think to serve is in keeping with the teachings of Christ. This is also what Y. T. Wu would wish to see. Some people have already brought up this point: What TSPM advocates, that is love country, love church, must not remain in the realm of theory and slogan, but be made visible in deeds of service to society and to the church. These words are worth pondering.

There are many kinds of service programs. The promotion of literacy; cleanliness and hygiene; good family relations; equality between men and women; thrift in weddings, funerals and other ceremonies; care for the handicapped, the sick and the poor, the fight against the buying and selling of brides; works undertaken for the common good and to protect the environment: All are worth our effort. All these programs can be ways and means for Christians to serve their neighbors and to witness to Christ.

For the church to emphasize service in her works, our theology ought to hold high ethics and morals, allowing them to occupy their rightful place in our theological construction, akin to the place they have in the Bible. Given the state of the church in our country, the starting point for contextualization seems to be the restoration of the ethical and moral content of Christianity.

Christianity is a religion that emphasizes ethics and morals. A very large portion of the Bible is on loving one's neighbor and on social justice. A church that despises ethics and morals cannot be a Christian Church.

In the church today, there sometimes arises a current that opposes ethics and morals. Whoever discusses ethics is thought of as belittling the gospel. Some even distort the doctrine of "justification by faith" to say that, provided one has "faith," one is insured and all one's actions—whether good or bad—are covered by the blood of Christ and the person need take no responsibility for them. As to a person "without faith," no matter what good he or she does, no matter how great a contribution he or she makes, all actions performed by such a person are necessarily against God and therefore worthless. Can such doctrines be derived from the gospel of Christ? That is going too far and has become antinomianism, the negation of law with faith.

In China, where Confucianism has had a deep impact, the question of ethics is particularly important from a missiological point of view. Many have been brought to Christ because they were first attracted by the ethical content of the gospel. When the young Y. T. Wu first came into contact with Christianity, it was precisely the most sublime and selfless ethical standard of the Sermon on the Mount that moved his heart. He said:

> One spring night thirty years ago, I was in the home of an American friend. I read the Sermon on the Mount in Matthew's Gospel for the first time. Like lightning, those three chapters woke me up from my slumbers. I opened my eyes and saw a vision. I saw a great, noble personality, awesome and gentle, deep and penetrating—He took hold of my soul. He almost stopped me from breathing. When I returned home, I cried out for joy. I was moved to tears. I could not help confessing to this vision, "Lord, you are my Savior."

Today, many people are searching for goodness, lantern in hand. They are looking for a good way of being in the world. They have come to the church to look. But if our church slights morals, does not elevate the Sermon on the Mount, and scarcely speaks of it or of morals, is this not tragic?

To pay more attention to service goes hand in hand with putting emphasis on contextualization and on ethics in our theological work. It is integrating faith and works, knowledge and action. This is something that Christian faith implies; it is also what the church in the context of our country needs in order to renew itself and to witness to Christ.

(3) The church and all its organizations ought to be a school for the democratic spirit. The church and works related to it are to be governed well by cultivating democratic habits.

During the KMT period, Y. T. Wu held high the banner of democracy to oppose dictatorship. The rule of the KMT has long since disappeared on the mainland. Today, under the leadership of the Chinese Communist Party, China has a socialist system. Democracy has assumed a new content. In this new era, the full realization of socialist democracy still awaits broad democratic education. The church must not exclude herself from this task.

The Christian Church confesses God as the Creator of the whole human race. Christ's redemption is extended to all men and women. The Holy Spirit inspires wisdom in all people. One finds here the seed of the democratic idea. Protestantism that emerged out of the Reformation is itself a precursor as well as a product of the democratic revolution.

Today, we are saying that the church should not only be self-governing, self-supporting, and self-propagating, but she should also be well-governed, well-supported, and well-propagated. Good government requires first of all the development of the democratic spirit and a democratic style of work. To run the church well implies the idea of people's participation in management. It is with the democratic spirit that we can run the church well. At present, the church in various places is facing a number of problems, many of which are connected with a lack of democratic spirit. To run the church really well, any one person or any group of people cannot be allowed to lay down the law. The democratic spirit ought to permeate all church organizations on different levels.

Due to age-long conditions in China, it is still quite common to encounter patriarchal ways of running the church, whereby one person alone has the say. This is contrary to the tradition of the New Testament church and alien to the spirit of socialist democracy.

Before Liberation, when Y. T. Wu lived in Shanghai, he joined a particular congregation there. I wondered at the time what that church could offer to an intellectual with progressive political ideas and good theological grounding such as Y. T. I asked him that question and he answered me by saying that the congregation being Cantonese speaking, it suited him and his wife. Moreover, that was a democratic church relatively speaking, he pointed out. Representatives of the congregation were members of various organizations looking after the affairs of the church. It was not a church where one or two people laid down the law. There words impressed me deeply.

If we wish to avoid conflict and make our church a fellowship of love, we must let the democratic spirit penetrate into all our relationships—those among colleagues, between the pastor and the flock, between the preacher and the faithful, between the pastor and church groups, among members of each church group, among the faithful, between the Three-Self Patriotic structures and the churches, between believers and non-believers, etc. That is a necessary pre-condition. The democratic spirit consists not only of majority rule in voting, but also of respect for other people's opinion and giving them due authority if they are given their office; as well, it consists of keeping in touch and keeping informed. On major issues, we must seek consensus in charity and in a spirit of fellowship, after full consultation and discussion, having taken into serious consideration the desires and aspirations of others. We must avoid coercing others and pay attention to our unity and cooperation. We must not readily believe hearsay, and we must guard against the sowing of discord, whether done wittingly or unwittingly.

Recently we have been discussing the re-ordering of relationships, that is, re-ordering the relationship between the TSPM and the churches. In the final analysis, this too is an issue of democracy. Things cannot be well done without centralization and the exercise of leadership. At the same time, we cannot afford not to let the people be masters in their own house. How to correctly understand centralization and decentralization, leadership and democracy, how to combine and unite those factors well, I think this is the assignment given us by Chairman Mao. Even in the smallest unit that is a grassroots church or meeting point, we must do our homework well.

To build our church well is not only a demand of the broad masses of believers, it is also one made upon the church by socialist new China. For it cannot be good for the country if all goes well in every other area except in the church. This is why to run our church well is an act of love for both church and country. It is a point of convergence of loving our country and loving our church. Reading through Y. T. Wu's writings after he launched the Three-Self Patriotic Movement, we find that he did not found the movement for the sake of founding it. His aim was the building up of the church in China. Today, we are to build the church. There is much we need to learn from our predecessors, each one of whom has left us with things from which we can draw good lessons. In my limited view, as we commemorate Y. T. Wu today, the three points mentioned above are what we must learn from him above all else. My view is probably biased, and I hope my colleagues in the church and friends outside the church will be kind enough to share their views with me.

—Speech at the Memorial Meeting on the 10th Anniversary of the Death of Y. T. Wu, Shanghai, 1989

ঙ্গ

# Is Religion an Opiate?

In China, religion is primarily a united front matter and is not treated as a life-or-death ideological problem. This view embodies a consistent teaching of Chairman Mao, Premier Zhou and the Central Party Committee: In religion, the central task lies not in "struggling against religion," leading to its weakening and destruction, nor in making atheists of theists, but rather in seeking the common ground while respecting differences and strengthening political unity with the masses who are believers, while placing differences in matters of belief among the people within the scope of mutual respect. As Premier Zhou said in 1957: "Everyone can support socialism, atheist or theist alike ... people's ideas are multifarious. So long as their activities do not hinder political life or economic production, we should not interfere in their affairs." This view, which holds high the united front in religious work, must be linked to a deep understanding among the people of (1) the rootedness of religion in the masses of the people; (2) religion's affinity to ethnic minority peoples; (3) its international ramifications; (4) its continued existence over the long-term; and (5) its complexity.

Clearly, some who call themselves Marxist-Leninists do not have such an understanding. They treat religion mainly as an alien ideology, and unnecessarily exaggerate its alien character, equating it with political reaction. They exaggerate the role of propagating atheism. They assume this as a matter of course and make up crude atheist and anti-religion propaganda. They deal with the people's requests to hold religious activities by use of administrative measures. All these things offend the religious sentiments of the masses. These people think setting limits on and weakening religion is a "good thing," when actually it only serves to create an uneasy relationship between cadres and the masses, causes the Party and government to lose the good opinion of the people and, damages the interests of the united front and the Party.

As regards China, following the restoration of order after the Cultural Revolution, the critique of "leftist" errors and the study of Central Party Document 19 (1982), the number of those who maintained the latter view and methods has been greatly reduced. We now see the appearance of a new kind of relationship between the cadres and the masses. A new common language which cadres in religious work and believers have found through their goals of improving economic production, enriching the nation and revitalizing China, has replaced the former antagonism between those who wanted to bring about the demise of religion and those who were against them. People have found that believers are the same as everyone else, with the addition of faith and some religious activities. Believers are also concerned about economic production and making a living, about the prosperity of the nation, about the development of young people. Thus, as long as suitable care is shown for the special characteristics of believers, and there is cooperation in production, the common language will be greatly increased and clashes can be completely avoided.

It should be mentioned here that citizens who are religious believers are also normal citizens. Some scholars of religion inappropriately term all believers "religionists." People who make an 'ideology' of religion, who narrowly reject common sense and science, who understand and deal with everything in terms of religion, are actually very small in number. In terms of ideology, the vast majority of China's religious believers are patriots at the very least. This is more in line with the facts and in line with the Central Committee's assessment (as in Document 19).

In order to further reduce the number of those who hold the inappropriate viewpoint and apply the erroneous methods mentioned above, I would like to offer some views on a statement by Marx.

The importance of this statement has been exaggerated to an inappropriate level by some. I refer to the statement "religion is an opiate of the people." Some people have taken this statement out of the context of the surrounding text as well as isolating it from the whole body of writings by Marx, Engels and Lenin on religion. They speak of it as Marx's definition of religion, as pointing to the very nature of religion, as an idea original to Marx, as the nucleus or marrow of the Marxist view of religion, and so on. They think it is a formula for understanding and dealing with any religious question. Actually, Marx speaks of religion as opiate only once, almost glancing over it, and that was in his youth, when he spoke grandly of alienation.

The idea that religion is an opiate of the people is by no means original to Marx. In Germany alone, several decades before Marx mentioned it, those intellectuals I will mention below, and there may be others, published similar views. Some even used similar wording.

1) P.T. von Holbach in his *Le Christianisme devoile* (1761): "Religion is the art of making men drunk with enthusiasm, in order to hinder them from attending to the evils with which those who rule them overwhelm them here below. With the help of the invisible powers with which one threatens them, one compels them to bear the misery in silence with which the powerful

afflict them, one makes them hope that, if they consent to be unhappy in this word, they will be more happy in another."

2) Goethe criticized the German revivalist F.W. Krummacher's volume of sermons, *Blick ins Reich der Gnade* (1828), calling them "narcotic sermons."

3) Hegel (1770–1831) in his *Religionsphilosophie* compared Indian religion to a man "decayed in body and spirit, who finds his existence grown dull and insufferable" and is therefore at pains to create for himself with opium "a dreaming world and crazy happiness."

4) Feuerbach, in the notes to the first edition of his *Pierre Bayle* in 1838, wrote that "the man therefore who charms with enticing and flattering words of eternal joys and threatens separation from himself with the intimidating words of eternal hell, used methods of compulsion ... he administers opium to him to extract from him his word of honor in a condition where the passions of fear or hope have clouded his vision."

5) In his *The Nature of Christianity* (1841), Feuerbach again spoke of the "narcotic influences" of Christian language and also of the "halo of sanctity" with which Christianity surrounds marriage in order to cloud the reason.

6) Heinrich Heine, in the fourth book of his discussion with Ludwig Borne (1840): "As the individual opens his arteries in despair, and seeks in death a refuge from the tyranny of the Caesars, so the great mass plunged into asceticism, into the doctrines of mortification ... of the Nazarene religion. In order once and for all to thrust from itself the misery of life at that time ... in order to number their aching heads with organ-tones and the tolling of bells." "For men for whom earth has nothing more to offer, heaven is invented. ... Hail to this invention! Hail to a religion which poured for a suffering race of men some sweet narcotic drops into their bitter cup, spiritual opium, a few drops of love and hope and faith." Ten years later he said: "When a little grey dust is poured into my fearful burning wounds, and then the pain at once ceases, shall not one say that this is the same calming power which shows its effective-

ness in religion? There is more relationship between opium and religion than most men dream."

7) In 1841, when he was still a theology professor in Berlin, Bruno Bauer wrote in his essay *Der Christliche Staat und unsere Zeit*: "The theological organization in the most Christian State was able to 'carry matters so far through its opium-like influence' that it finds no more trace of resistance and all the instincts of free humanity ... are lulled to sleep."

8) The next year he wrote that: "Religion in its opium haze speaks of a new condition hereafter."

9) Edgar Bauer, the younger brother of Bruno, in his short story *Freedom and Myself* (1842) wrote: "Others drug themselves with religion, they would wish to enter the seventh heaven, and in so doing forget the earth."

10) Moses Hess in *Einundzwanzig Bogen aus der Schweiz*, written in 1843, ranks intoxicants, opium, religion and brandy side by side and says: "Religion is well able ... to make tolerable the unhappy consciousness of servitude ... just as opium does good service in painful illnesses, faith in the reality of unreality and in the unreality of reality can indeed give the sufferer a passive happiness."

Clearly, Marx did no more than to quote a phrase often used by enlightened people in intellectual and religious circles of the day. To say that this phrase is an innovation of Marx is hard to accept. To say that it is the nucleus of Marxist views on religion not only seems to theorists a kind of unfortunate error in common sense, but lowers the Marxist religious view to a level long achieved by bourgeois intellectuals and enlightened religious thinkers.

Marx and Engels lived in a class society. Let us first discuss religion in a society made up of antagonistic classes. Religion is a complex social phenomenon that plays many roles. Its role as an opiate in society, its narcotic role, the role it has played to obliterate the spirit of rebellion among the toiling masses, is, of course, a fact. But this is only one of the roles it plays, certainly not its only role—and by no means its main role under all circumstances.

Opium causes people to sink into a stupor. In Western countries today, among certain reactionaries (for example, those high up in Christian fundamentalist bodies in the U.S. who call themselves the "moral majority"), religion is manipulated through preaching that fans the fervor of the believers and draws them toward the extreme right, so that they become supporters of the political forces of reaction and tools to attack the masses. This role of religion plainly surpasses by far its role as opiate.

Religion often provides the ideology for peasant movements, functioning to connect and motivate the masses. In *The Peasant War in Germany*, Engels commended Muenzer for "spreading revolution, having political religious thinking." "Muenzer's political doctrine followed his revolutionary religious conceptions very closely, and as his theology reached far beyond the current conceptions of his time, so his political doctrine went beyond existing social and political conditions. ... His program, less a compilation of the demands of the then existing plebeians than a genius's anticipation of the conditions for the emancipation proletarian element that had just begun to develop among the plebeians, demanded the immediate establishment of the kingdom of God, of the prophesied millennium on earth." Engels believed that the plebian clergy of the German churches in the middle ages "gave the movement its theorists and ideologists, and many of them, representatives of the plebeians and peasants, died on the scaffold." There are many other examples like this—the Taiping Rebellion is one—but it is not necessary to mention them all here. The role played by religion in peasant movements is much greater than what is suggested by the term "opiate."

In some European bourgeois democratic revolutions and even in certain workers' struggles, religion played a similar role. Engels felt that "the Calvinist Reformation served as a banner for the republicans in Geneva, in Holland, and in Scotland, freed Holland from Spain and from the German Empire, and provided the ideological costume for the second act of the bourgeois revolution, which was taking place in England." Marx pointed out that in England, "Cromwell and the English people had borrowed from the Old Testament the speech, passions, and illusions for their bourgeois revolution." Lenin did not propose to view all religion as a monolith. He stressed the internal divisions in the Russian church, "the sectarian movements in Russian Orthodoxy, in many of their aspects, are one of the democratic trends in Russia." He proposed "absorbing them into the democratic socialist party." He said: "We socialists ought to support such movements as this, that the demands of the upright and honest among the clergy be thoroughly realized." Lenin also pointed out that "the struggles of the democratic and proletarian elements sometimes take the form of the struggle of one religious idea against another." Obviously, under certain conditions, the role played by religion is far different from that played by an opiate.

Today, quite a number of religious believers and persons in religious circles support, are involved in, and even serve as leaders of people's democratic movements in the Third World. In South Korea, many Christians are involved in demonstrations, strikes and protests to oppose fascism. In Latin America and the Philippines, under the banner of liberation theology, quite a few priests (and some bishops) have lost their lives because of their involvement in mass movements and armed struggle.

It would be forced and implausible when considering class societies with these and many other types of religious phenomena, to explain religion solely in terms of being an opiate.

Thus a more realistic and objective view would be to admit that in class society, opiate is not a sufficient definition of religion, but rather a role religion may play, and moreover just one of its roles and not by any means its only role.

During the rectification campaign in Yenan, Chairman Mao said: "Up to now, there are still quite a few people who see isolated words and phrases from the works of Marx and Lenin as ready-made cure-alls, as if having these one can cure any disease without lifting a finger." This is a statement that still has value today.

Lenin has this to say about making definitions: "What is meant by giving a 'definition?' It means essentially to bring a given concept within a more comprehensive concept. For example, when I give the definition 'an ass is an animal,' I am bringing the concept 'ass' within a more comprehensive concept." In the same way, if we want to define religion, we ought first to put it into a broader conception. But opium is simply one of the roles of religion. To make opium the definition of religion is to cover up the comprehensive with the partial and embrace all aspects of religion. Hence the difficulty and bewilderment in trying to use opium as the one explanation of all religious phenomena. In attempting to do so, people find this approach explains very little. At times, they are only fooling themselves as well as others and they treat the many other religious phenomena as if they are hardly worth a glance.

Marx certainly did not call for attacks on and destruction of religion because religion played the role of an opiate in certain circumstances. He felt that the transformation of this world was the only path to eliminating the religious tendency. In the same essay, Marx exhorted people to turn "criticism of the Kingdom of God" into "criticism of the mundane world," and "criticism of theology" into "political criticism." At almost the same time as Marx was writing this (1843), he wrote in another essay that religion was "narrow-mindedness," saying that religion "is not the cause of secular narrow-mindedness, but its manifestation." He disapproved of regarding the overcoming of human religious narrow-mindedness as the path to secular liberation. He said that religious narrow-mindedness could only be overcome by ending secular captivity. Thus, he had no illusions about being able to do away with religious faith, instead he put forth "political liberation" as the prerequisite for human liberation from all fetters, including spiritual ones.

It is the belief of Marxism that as long as humankind is blind to the alienating power of nature and society, it will have no way to grasp its own fate and the emergence and existence of religion is inevitable. In this sense, human religiosity is a normal phenomenon. As long as the natural and social sources for the existence of religion continue to exist, even if atheism is very well propagated (this is extremely difficult), there will not be many people who will accept it and turn away from religion. If it is poorly propagated, it will stimulate the religious sentiments of the believers and provoke people's outrage on their behalf, as well as giving rise to sympathy for and interest in religion. Would this not function indirectly to help propagate religion? We religious believers do not necessarily agree with these views, but we do rather appreciate them.

If the narcotic function of religion is one of the roles it plays in class society, then it cannot be a sufficient description of religion's roles in a classless society. In class society, it mainly fulfills the need of the reactionary ruling class to numb and control the masses. When the historical stage of socialism arrives and the exploiting class no longer exists as a class using the narcotic function of religion for its own ends, how shall we see our way to continuing to define religion as opiate?

What transformations will take place in religion in a socialist society is a new question, one that cannot be answered with recourse to the writings of Marx, Engels and Lenin. The religion of which Marx, Engels and Lenin spoke was the religion of class society. The religion with which Marx and Engels were familiar was primarily that of western European class society, while Lenin knew mainly the religion of Imperial Russia. They did no study of religion in a socialist society.

After liberation in China, each religious group put a great deal of effort into uniting their respective adherents. On the one hand they eliminated reactionary forces and illegal activities within their religion and undertook religious reformation; on the other hand they led their adherents on the path of socialism, contributing to the realization of the four modernizations in China and to enlarging the united front internationally. Each of China's religions has undergone a partial qualitative change and has turned onto a course that is healthier and more in harmony with socialist new China.

If we were to say that religion is an opiate of the people in socialist society, just as it is in class society, then those who would say this must speak up—which class is it that needs religion to anesthetize the people? If this is not the case, it functions at most as a kind of self-numbing, not its best use, but no more harmful than banishing melancholy with wine, not something that needs to be opposed or something that we must strive to destroy. Making a political problem of it in order to destroy it might seem a clever plan, but actually will only succeed in losing the sympathy of the people.

We ought to make a distinction between religion as narcotic for self-numbing today and religion as narcotic as it was used in the past by the reactionary ruling classes to control the people. We should recognize that the seriousness of the problem has been greatly reduced. If we lump the two together, this is, to say the least, a slapdash way of theorizing and research, and politically it is still the old business of "class struggle as the key link" in dealing with today's religious questions; this can lead to great harm.

Today, we should pay greater attention to religion's role in exhorting people to do good. This aspect of religion can be beneficial for unity and stability and economic production in socialist society. If the standard for the united front is not communism but patriotism, people can appreciate that believers' "good behavior" is good for the nation and need not scoff at it simply because they do not begin from a Marxist standpoint. As long as what believers do is acceptable, religion will be more compatible with socialism and we should allow different paths to the same goal.

The Bible says "There is no authority but by act of God" (Rom. 13:1), and in the past the KMT used this to control the people, attempting to make them bow down to their rulers. But now, when Christians say this under the people's government, they can no longer be considered reactionary. Rather, it is beneficial to unity and stability. Plainly, religion does not at all function as an opiate in all circumstances. It can play many roles and is not necessarily antagonistic to socialism.

In the Central Committee Document 19 of 1982, the word "opiate" no longer appears, and the Party has cast off dogmatism and a doctrinaire approach, beginning instead with the reality of religious phenomena in China's historical stage of socialism. This gives full expression to the fine tradition of seeking truth from facts.

Actually the discussion of religion by proletarian revolutionary leaders like Marx and Engels is very rich. In China, as early as 1950 during the meeting of the CPPCC, Premier Zhou pointed out that with the victory of the revolution, it was not necessary always to emphasize religion as opiate; the important issue in religion now was to isolate and reform the small number of political counter-revolutionaries.

When Marx and others spoke of an opiate, they meant a narcotic, but in China we have had a tragic history in which imperialism imposed opium and the Opium War on our people. Our people harbor a particular hatred of opium. The equating of religion to the opiate (which some writers have changed to opium) confers on it a criminal nature and relegates religious believers among the people to the status of opium addicts and turns religious leaders into opium dealers. Thus, this equation serves the promotion of ultra-leftism in religious work.

There are still a lot of people who, though they are not religious believers but atheists, express in their thinking and work the subjective deviation of idealism. Furthermore the results of this kind of deviation are frequently more serious than the results of belief in religion. Not long ago, a scholar of religion once again claimed that the four modernizations could not be realized unless religion was abolished. Some cadres in religious work did not seek to unite believers under the banner of socialism, but took the prohibition and destruction of religion as their task—these are the inevitable results of a one-sided emphasis on religion as opiate and opium. Philosophically this is subjectivist idealist thinking, the result of which is to incite hatred of religion. It is not conducive to national unity and stability.

Speaking of opiates, is religion in fact the only one? There are many things that can become opiates of the people. Politics, too, can bewitch people and function as an opiate. Some rebel factions during the Cultural Revolution blindly acted on the slogan "always three steps to the left" and "as regards Chairman Mao's teachings, carry out what you understand; carry out what you don't understand too." A famous writer described his mental state during his time in detention in the so-called "cow shed" this way: "I actually made 'ignorance' the goal of my transformation, I admitted that I had done not one good thing my whole life, I admitted everything I had written was 'poison', I really thought that only the few 'model operas' were art. Settling for irrelevancies, I was completely taken in by the logic of the rebel factions, and the more I thought about it, the more I thought that the rebel factions were right—I was a criminal." Many religious believers would be glad they had not succumbed to a narcotic to that extent. In saying this, I am not trying to smear politics; I just want to point out that when we call something an opiate, we have not exhausted the possibilities of that thing. An individual is always subject to human weakness; it is difficult to avoid subjective errors.

The Central Party Committee has done a meticulous study of the basic understanding and policy on religious questions during China's socialist period, summing up the experiences and lessons of thirty years since 1949, making a complete re-study in theory and policy and further, pointing out that whether this question can be adequately dealt with is of vital significance for national stability and ethnic unity, for the development of international exchanges and resistance to infiltration by hostile forces overseas. This Document has been of great help to me and I am still studying it. Today the most I can do is raise a few questions for us to study and resolve together.

—On Religion as Opiate, A Talk with Friends
Outside the Church, 1985

# RELIGION AND SOCIALISM: CAN THEY CO-EXIST?

Since the Third Plenum of the Eleventh Communist Party Central Committee (December 1978), social scientific thinking in China, including research on the study of religion, has become extremely dynamic. New thinking and new viewpoints have emerged, and the discussion has been unusually animated. In the new climate of reform and openness, there have been increasing breakthroughs in the study of religion. Religion as an ideology is far removed from the economic base; but if we speak of the social impact of religion, we find that religion is very close to real life and to socialist reconstruction in China. Tens of millions of religious believers from all walks of life live among us and in all walks of life participate in the socialist construction of the spiritual and material aspects of our culture. Theoretical breakthroughs in the study of religion in recent years are helpful for a realistic approach to understanding and dealing with religious issues during China's socialist period and are thus useful in summoning the will and the strength of the believing masses to the magnificent enterprise of constructing a strong socialist nation in China.

## (1) REPLACE DOGMATISM WITH A "SEEK TRUTH FROM FACTS" APPROACH IN RESEARCH.

Dogmatism has had long-standing influence in social scientific circles in China, going back to "leftist" Soviet impact on scholarly circles. In the study of religion, "leftist" dogmatism has been worse than in other areas. Even after the Third Plenum of the Eleventh Central Committee, a minority of authoritative voices concerned with the study of religion continued to uphold Marx's dictum, aimed at the Germany of his own day: "religion as opiate." These people made this into a universal truth, eternal and unchanging, and simplified the study of religion as no more than "the criticism of theology." Their so-called research was in fact the type which is totally isolated from reality, moving from concept to concept but never beyond the covers of a book, and which knows nothing of the actual religious situation. They basically ignored national cultural differences, differences of historical setting and the different roles religion may play in different eras or even at different times within the same era. Such people are not acquainted with even one religious believer, let alone count one as a friend, nor have they ever tried to enter into and understand a believer's thoughts and emotions. They have done no investigation or research into the role and contribution of religious believers in the economic, cultural or political life of society. They have a kind of inborn prejudice and abhorrence toward religion, and have allowed emotion to supplant Marxist methods.

As early as 1984, the well-known Chinese scholar Luo Zhufeng, in a paper entitled "Towards a Specifically Chinese Theory of the Study of Religion," observed:

> Marx's discussion of religion was entirely "Germany-centered," and did not represent generalizations or all-inclusive statements … Marxist theory on religion teaches us that comprehensive and correct understanding cannot be a matter of wish-fulfillment in which everyone gets what he wants. Even Lenin, in his

discussion of religious issues, began with the actual
Russian situation of his day. His approach was "Russia-
centered." ... Our approach today should be "China-
centered," because China has its own national
conditions and character which differ from those of
Germany or the Soviet Union ... The study of Marxist
theory on religion must begin with the actual situation
of China, and must establish a theory which is specifically Chinese. We cannot mechanically copy others. If
we do not proceed in this fashion, we will never be
more than scholarly dwarfs.

*Religion under Socialism in China* is a product of precisely this type of
"China-centered" approach. It begins from the actual Chinese situation, relating theory to practice, seeking truth from facts, testing out
truth in practice and developing truth as a line of thought. For this
work, the Institute for Religious Studies of the Shanghai Academy of
Social Sciences sent some ten teams of comrades away from their
books and into cities and villages in thirteen provinces and municipal-
ities to undertake broad-based social scientific investigation. Altogether
over one hundred samples of material were collected and dozens of
reports on their findings written. The investigations were carried out
without preconceptions, proceeding from actual situations and were
broadly based, unfolding new lines of inquiry. The findings were ana-
lyzed, after which they were subjected to incisive comparative investigations. The people at the Institute for Religious Studies were able to
produce this epoch-making and highly influential book on the study of
religion in China because of the correctness of their ideological and
research methods, and because dogmatism had been utterly cast off.

## (2) RELIGION IS A MULTIPLEX, MANY-LAYERED SOCIAL ENTITY. SCHOLARSHIP SHOULD NOT LIMIT ITSELF TO THE PHILOSOPHICAL AND DOCTRINAL ASPECTS OF RELIGION

Religion incorporates philosophical viewpoints and doctrinal thinking,
but it is not only these. Religious believers believe in theism, they
believe in various doctrines, and they conduct themselves according to
the doctrines they follow. But a religious believer is certainly not a narrow philosopher, even less a "fideist" as some would have it.

In the philosophical realm it is necessary to draw clear lines between idealism and materialism, theism and atheism. But genuine historical materialists have never extended this philosophical line to distinguish the politically backward from the politically progressive, nor the revolutionary from the counter-revolutionary. Historically, we find many examples of people who have maintained a philosophical idealism or even theism, who have yet been quite progressive politically. The liberation theologians of Latin America today and the Black South African religious leader Archbishop Desmond Tutu, are contemporary examples. This is because religion is not simply an ideology, but is also an extremely complex social phenomenon. In *The Economic and Philosophical Manuscripts of 1849*, Marx stated:

> If for me religious philosophy were the only genuine religious existence, then I could only be truly religious by being a religious philosopher, and if that were the case I would deny real religious belief and believers.

But real religious belief and actual believers can accommodate and accept many new ideas and phenomena.

Religious believers have been caricatured in China as "fideists" and "simple-minded," "with eyes unwilling to see earthly beauties and ears unwilling to hear its sounds," as people who feel that "anything not found in Scripture is not fit for thought," as freaks who see "all reasonable requests to improve the material life as the root of all spiritual evil." Such portrayals, based entirely on subjective imagination, are profoundly insulting and deeply repellent to religious believers. Such portrayals fit Lenin's taunt: "(they) attribute the most blatantly ignorant views to the opponent and then attack them. This is the habitual practice of people who are not very intelligent." In fact, the negative effect of religious doctrine on a person is extremely limited. The majority of those who promoted the Enlightenment and rationalism were the monks and theologians of the day. During the more than three hundred years from the publication of Thomas Moore's *Utopia* in 1516 to the peak of utopian socialism in the 19th century, the great majority of utopian socialists all bore some Christian coloration. If we look at scientists throughout history, we will see that many have been religious believers. Religious faith has not been a hindrance to them, and we cannot discount their scientific discoveries and achievements because of it. In the article on Xu Guangqi in the Chinese Encyclopedic Dictionary introducing his role as a Ming-dynasty scientist and his contributions to social productivity, there is no mention of the fact that Xu was a pious Catholic. Keeping such "closely guarded secrets" shows either misgivings that religion will defile science, or anxiety that science will elevate religion. Actually, history is replete with examples of science and religion joined in one person. Tolstoy was a staunch believer in God and Christ, a writer who even bordered on the fanatic in religious matters; yet Lenin affirmed him as "an artistic genius," saying he "mercilessly critiques capitalist oppression … a clear-headed realist who has discarded all masks," and "has created masterpieces of world literature." Lenin did not discount Tolstoy's literary merits or his contributions to the social struggle wholesale simply because he was staunchly religious, nor did he let the latter's artistic genius obscure the fact that he believed in God.

In his essay "On religious systems," Chen Yaoting attempts to use systematic philosophy to understand religion. In his view:

> The systematic approach understands religion, or any religious system, as a social entity composed of religious believers, organization and thought, as one branch of the spiritual systems of human society. It both reflects the hardship brought upon humankind by the natural world and sustains religious believers' protests and laments against real hardship along with their hopes and quest for the ideal life. … Of the three components of the religious system, it is only the believers who play a key role in the system's development under normal social conditions. … The reason religious believers are dynamic people with an intimate relationship to the natural world and to the political, economic and other elements of society lies in the fact that the religious system is an open one. … And what makes the believers the most dynamic part of the system is the fact that they reflect the most up-to-the-minute demands of social, material and spiritual production. To see religious believers as not sharing in this world, as "alienated" individuals who take no part in human life, does not

accord with the facts; to depict them as "superhumans" who have no care and concern for mortal nations, politics or social economy but only for "paradise," is also out of line with the objective realities of religious systems. There is not one historical record relating to religious "alienated" individuals and "superhumans" which is not a distorted reflection of the social problems of the day. (*Religion*, No. 1, 1986).

To refrain from concentrating on philosophical and doctrinal issues, to study religion as a multiplex, many-layered social entity, to employ systematic philosophy and not simply mechanistic materialism in the study of religious systems: these are the basics of a correct understanding of religion.

### (3) HAVE AN APPROPRIATE UNDERSTANDING AND EVALUATION OF THE IDEA OF RELIGION AS THE OPIATE OF THE PEOPLE

Some authors, familiar with a few Marxist phrases, but with no grasp of the spirit of Marxism, slide easily into equating religion with opiate in any consideration of religious issues. They feel that as long as that formula or label is kept in view, any issue impinging on religion can be readily explained. They take the assessment of religion as the opiate of the people to be original to Marx, as the quintessence of the Marxist view on religion, as a penetrating insight which lays bare the true nature of religion.

In fact, more than ten German philosophers, social thinkers and men of letters before Marx made the same or similar pronouncements on religion. Marx was simply repeating what others had said before him: he was not making an original observation. Furthermore, in those days, opium was used medicinally as a painkiller, it had not yet been put to use as an addictive drug. In considering whether "religion as opiate" can serve as a definition for religion, Luo Zhufeng has observed:

How can we say that Marx simply took "religion as opiate" as a definitive statement? Hadn't he linked it to "protest" and "lament" right before that? How can we quote out of context, seeing only "opiate" and "nothing else?"

There has been a negative side to the role of religion in history. It has functioned socially as a self-induced anesthetic of the people as well as having been manipulated to anesthetize them. But this has not been the only historical role religion has played, and is certainly not its primary one, under whatever circumstances. Religion has functioned to mobilize and unify the people to throw themselves into the revolutionary struggle. Engels affirmed this in his the *Peasant War in Germany*. Some writers on religion have invented the so-called "cloak theory," whereby religion is seen as no more than "a cloak covering the people's eyes and ears" in peasant revolutionary wars, ever dooming them to defeat. This is a distortion and simplification of history; in fact, Engels referred to religion not only as "a cloak," but also used terms such as the peasant revolution's "standard" and "armor." Let us ask, if religion is solely an opiate, how-could it also be the standard and armor of peasant uprisings? As for the defeat of peasant uprisings, that requires scientific analysis; to turn "throwing on the cloak of religion" into the major factor in this defeat is, to say the least, overly hasty.

The Archbishop of Recife, Brazil, Dom Helder Camara, has said to Christians there: "When I give bread to the poor, people call me a saint, but when I ask why the poor have no bread to eat, then I am called a Communist." A sermon such as this plays a tremendous role in exposing the dark side of society and in arousing the conscience of the people. Isn't this role of conscientization the exact opposite of the befuddling opiate role mentioned above? In Camara's religion, to make "reasonable calls for the improvement of material life" is far from "occasions of sin for the spirit." Can a religion which raises such questions as: "Why don't the poor have bread to eat? What sort of party is the Communist Party? Why should the people oppose the Communist Party?" be equated with religion which calls upon the people to submit meekly to oppression and exploitation?

Document 19 of the Central Committee of the Communist Party of China (1982) makes no mention of the religion as opiate thesis. Only in its discussion of pre-Liberation exploitation and class control of the masses in China does it mention that religion was at that time used as a spiritual device to tranquilize the masses. Similarly, the volume *Religion under Socialism in China* does not allow the "opiate theory" to dominate its inquiry and research. The editor does not deal with the opiate issue until the Afterword. There, he raises three points:

A. "Opiate" is a picturesque term used to describe the negative role religion is made to play in class society.

B. Historically, the role of religion differs in different eras and social conditions. These differences cannot all be subsumed under the term "opiate."

C. It is even less possible to explain the role of religion in socialist society by the term "opiate."

These three points represent an important breakthrough with regard to the "opiate theory." The debate which has raged in religious studies over the "opiate theory" since the Third Plenum of the Eleventh Central Committee, has been dubbed the "Third Opium War." From the looks of it, this "Third Opium War" has basically ended, for there are now very few scholars studying religion who continue to expound its "opiate nature."

## (4) RELIGION HAS ITS ETHICAL DIMENSIONS AND THESE PLAY A POSITIVE AND SUPPLEMENTARY ROLE IN SOCIALIST SOCIETY

The view of religion most widespread among people is that "religion encourages goodness." Many officials at the grassroots report that in areas where there is a high number of religious believers, there are few criminal activities. Religion exerts a guiding and restricting influence upon the behavior of adherents. But there was a time when certain scholars of religion, under the influence of "leftism," inflexibly advocated a division between religious creeds and ethics in order to discredit religion. They said that the ethical dimensions of religion were reflections of the relationships of production and not directly dependent upon religion; that religion governed only the relationship between the believers and God while social relationships lay outside its purview. It has even been said that since the last six of the Ten Commandments on the Old Testament dealt with behavioral ethics, they were not an integral part of religion. It would therefore be interfering with ethics for religion to speak of the matters contained in the last six commandments.

In this regard, Yan Beiming's essay "On Religious Ethics During the Socialist Period," points out that:

> Each religion not only promotes its own sense of moral-
> ity, but also emphasizes moral cultivation, and an entire
> set of creeds and practices which uphold and protect
> moral integrity, far surpassing non-religious ethical
> schools ... The strength of the strictures of religious
> ethics is, quite simply, second to none. One wouldn't
> know where to begin in trying to prove a statement to
> the effect that religion has no ethics ... And it is thanks
> to the great force of these strictures of religious morality
> that it produces such strikingly concrete results in the
> adherents of each religion. There is factual evidence of
> this. In China, and especially in the minority areas, a
> noteworthy phenomenon has been discovered through
> actual social investigation: the majority of believers, of
> whatever religion or sect, were found to be law-abiding,
> enthusiastic in helping others, and unlikely to do
> wrong... According to what a comrade who studies
> juvenile delinquents told me: "Among young hoodlum
> elements who are repeat offenders, it is very difficult to
> find any from the churches, temples or mosques, which
> shows that the bonds of religious morality are a power-
> ful influence and play a not insignificant role, not only
> among the middle-aged and elderly believers, but
> among young people as well. (*Investigation of Religious
> Issues*, Shanghai: Shanghai Academy of Social Sciences
> Religious Studies Center, 1984).

Another opinion has it that though religion includes ethics, in essence this is morality in service to the counter-revolutionary ruling class; therefore, religion and socialist society by contrast, are as incompatible as fire and water. As Luo Weihong points out in "The Social Function of and Changes in Religious Morality During the Socialist Period":

> Religious morality is a moral concept based on the reli-
> gious world view and closely linked to religious teach-
> ings. It is a system of standards and rules of behavior, a
> special realm within social ideology, which draws
> together the different ideologies of religion and morality.

It is both a type of morality and a part of religion. ... Historically, many ruling classes have used the will of God as a means of coercing the people into acquiescence to their counter-revolutionary rule. Religious ethical teachings thus became the spiritual implement for maintaining their counter-revolutionary rule and played a negative role. In socialist society, this mistaken theoretical system of religious morality cannot change, but it no longer attaches itself to a counter-revolutionary ruling class nor does it continue to pursue moral expositions on behalf of that ruling class; its negative political role has disappeared as well. ... During the socialist era, religion still encourages people to do good and religious circles are active in doing good for society. This present goodness, both in essence and in content, has undergone a change from that in class society. ... Socialist morality is a completely new stage in human moral development, different in essence from morality of past historical eras. However, it is not at all divorced from, or without links to the morality of past historical eras. Quite the opposite, it must critique those quintessential elements of the heritage of historical moralities. Socialist morality must naturally incorporate moral principles and standards universal to all human social life, which have been shaped over the long period of human development and are embraced by various classes. Although it belongs to a lower order, such social morality provides a minimal level of morality which can maintain the social order and is therefore indispensable. Religious morality which mirrors these principles and standards, can therefore be adapted to socialist morality and is one with socialist spiritual civilization. (Ibid.)

## (5) RELIGION CAN BE COMPATIBLE WITH SOCIALISM

Theoretical research into religion in every socialist country since the October revolution (1917) has held that religion and socialism are irreconcilable opposites. Marxists who speak of the compatibility of religion and socialism might be seen as "right deviationists" or be considered as having lost their way. A religious believer who does so, might be seen as an opportunist or as harboring ulterior motives.

But the facts of the matter are that in the thirty-odd years since Liberation in China, the majority of religious leaders have supported socialism. As for the laity, the vast majority are daily engaged in socialist production. To our knowledge, in many areas, the proportion of Christians who have been chosen by their colleagues as advanced or model workers is greater than that among non-Christians. The various religions in China have undertaken considerable reforms. In contrast with the past, these have resulted in great strides toward adjusting to the socialist trend. The facts are there for all to see. This is considering the matter from a religious viewpoint. On the national level, though the leading party of China stands for atheism and confesses no religion, it recognizes the reasonableness of religion and its legal status, and opposes any actions aimed at destroying or discriminating against religion. Only illegal and counter-revolutionary activities disguised as religious which, along with superstitions, are not part of religion, and which threaten national interests and the lives and property of the people, are opposed. However, normal and proper religion is firmly protected by law. The preceding two points are the foundation for the compatibility of religion and socialism in China.

The first to allude to the compatibility of religion and socialism was Hu Qiaomu. In October 1982, while drawing up the sixth Five-Year Plan, he mentioned in his report that study of religious topics should include research into the bases for the occurrence and continued existence of religious phenomena in China, and how it could become compatible with Chinese socialist society, and how it might play its proper role. ("Explorations into the Religious Issue" 1983).

Xiao Zhitian of the Shanghai Academy of Social Sciences says in his 1985 paper "A Tentative Enquiry into the Problem of the Compatibility between Religion and Socialist Society in China":

> ... compatibility is based on patriotism and socialism, under the guidelines of the Chinese Constitution, and not on the criterion of materialism, nor with the purpose of "wiping out" religion. In a country like ours, with a population of one billion, it is inevitable that there will be different levels of ideological thinking. In order to achieve our unprecedented and gigantic task of socialist construction, a latitudinarian policy must be

adopted, for it is impossible to impose uniformity in ideas and beliefs. To launch debates on issues between theism and atheism is also harmful. Only by insisting on the four basic principles and by implementing the policy of religious freedom can a positive response be aroused in religious circles.

Some people stress the assumed antagonism between religion and socialism, holding that believers in their role as laborers can take part in socialist construction, but that the religion they believe in can only play an obstructive and disruptive role in socialist endeavors. This is contrary to fact and to truth. One's actions are always governed by one's thinking. The participation of religious believers in the modernization program is due in a way to their acceptance of patriotic education and socialist policies, but they are also bound to interpret their deeds in terms of their religious teachings. Some believers who take a negative and pessimistic attitude and stand aloof from reality have been influenced by their religious beliefs; but other believers who are devoted to the motherland and are law-abiding, positive, and enterprising, have also been motivated by their religious convictions." (*Religion*, No. 1, 1985).

Xiao Zhitian believes that the positive role of religion which is beneficial to society is manifested in the following respects:

(1) Workers, peasants and intellectuals who believe in religion are engaged in developing industrial and agricultural production, raising scientific and technological levels and doing their utmost to open up new prospects for China's socialist modernization program; (2) By calling on patriotism, certain ideas and beliefs promoted in religious circles can mobilize believers to take an active part in the current modernization program; (3) Certain religious moral teachings can guide believers to reject evil and do good, and this is conducive to the stability and unity of society; (4) The religious tradition of service for public welfare can contribute to the building of socialist spiritual civilization. (Ibid.)

Of course, there are both compatible and incompatible aspects of the relationship between socialism and religion. In order to promote the four modernizations, we must continually strive to overcome the incompatibilities. From the religious point of view, this means that each religion, within the bounds of acceptability dictated by its beliefs, is called to move ahead in eliminating whatever is not in accord with socialism, and to develop that which is. At the same time, non-religious circles are called to resolutely cast off leftist influences, to rid themselves of the type of thinking which encourages the destruction of religion, to implement policy, and to create conditions for each religion to carry out its work successfully.

When mutual compatibility replaces mutual destruction, there is a new spirit abroad in the world which represents a vast breakthrough in research into religious issues in China during the socialist period.

### (6) RELIGION SHOULD BE SEEN AS AN INTRINSIC PART
### OF THE SOCIALIST CULTURAL LEGACY

In speaking of the socialist critique of the historical cultural heritage, some people always treat religious culture as the dregs of historical culture, as a part which may not be accepted as part of the inheritance but must be cast off. This is superficial and reveals an ignorant attitude toward historical culture.

Zhao Fusan observes in his address "Religion, Spiritual Culture and National Unity," given at the Third Session of the Sixth Chinese People's Political Consultative Conference:

> ... the literature, poetry, art, music, dance, sculpture and architecture of every nation, and consequently its philosophy, its morals, its social customs and the history of how its way of life has developed, have all in varying degrees been influenced by religion ... If we were to suppose that a culture with a religious pattern brought about through the impetus of religious thought and feeling simply belongs to the mere refuse of that people's civilization and is to be rejected, does it imply that so far as China is concerned, the greater part of the artistic treasures of Dunhuang, the carvings and sculptures of Datong, Longmen, Maijishan and Dazu ... are they all to be rejected?... When we deal with European

culture, are we to reject Dante's *Divine Comedy*, da Vinci's *Last Supper*, Raphael's *Madonna*, the complete range of Michaelangelo's frescoes in the Sistine Chapel in the Vatican, Milton's *Paradise Lost* and *Paradise Regained* ... the many musical works of Bach, Hande, Mozart and Beethoven, and the whole range of European medieval philosophical thought? It is quite evident that were we to do so, we would be very foolish.

Zhao Puchu, president of the Chinese Buddhist Association, in an article entitled "The Influence of Buddhism on Chinese Culture Should Be Studied," points out:

It is inevitable that every people, in the process of the development of its culture, will meet with the question of how to treat the relationship between religion and culture. Buddhism has had a tremendous influence upon and role in Chinese culture, and it has left a resplendent heritage of Buddhist culture in Chinese history ... This being the case, does Buddhism still have a role to play in the developmental process of the new people's culture under socialism? Human cultural development is a continuous, unbroken process, traditional and modern culture cannot be completely severed. We must absorb all that is of value in the essence of traditional culture and bring it to enrich the development of the new socialist people's culture. Traditional Chinese culture incorporates Buddhist culture ... thus, in formulating a strategy of cultural development today, we should earnestly raise the issue of the study of the quintessence of Buddhist culture." (*Fayin*, No. 2, 1986)

In "Our National Culture: Modern and Traditional," Wang Meng, China's Minister of Culture, has stated:

The phenomenon of religion is in no way a simple cosmological view which exists in human life. It is in fact a cultural phenomenon, embracing morality, art, psychology, philosophy and even science and social custom, along with a coalescence of national sentiment ... Marxist teaching has no way to sympathize with or assent to religion as a cosmological view, but Marxism must treat religion scientifically as a cultural phenomenon.

To link religion with historical culture, to see the religious phenomenon as a cultural one, to affirm that there are in religious culture
those things which can be accepted, is beneficial to the building up of
a new socialist people's culture in China. This may be an even greater
breakthrough in the study of religion. This is why one prominent conclusion in the essay "Are socialism and religion mutually compatible?"
is:

> We must not make religion into an antagonistic element
> which socialism cannot accept. We must not only see
> the negative aspects of religion, but make it an intrinsic
> part of the historical cultural heritage of socialism, and
> do all in our power to enhance the positive role of reli-
> gion in socialist construction. (*Theory & Information*, No.
> 148, 1988)

### (7) THE LEADERSHIP AND ADMINISTRATION OF RELIGIOUS AFFAIRS WORK MUST BE REFORMED

There has long been an over-concentration of power in China's system
of religious affairs leadership and administration, resulting in serious
abuses in the system's taking on for itself things which should be left
to religious groups. Following the publication of Document 19, Ru
Wen stated in his address "What I Have Gained from Studying this
Document":

> The separation of government from enterprises is now
> being implemented throughout China. Yet, as we look
> at the relation between government and religion, the
> fact of their non-separation is, in some places, causing
> serious problems. This is not conducive to strengthening
> the bridge-building role of religious groups between the
> Party and the masses, and thus extremely deleterious to
> rallying the masses of religious adherents around the
> Party. Document No. 19 stresses that cadres must take
> seriously the role of patriotic religious organizations at
> all levels and must do a good job of leadership in order
> to avoid monopolizing the tasks involved. Religious
> organizations must be permitted their work and rights,
> and must be enabled to form close links with religious
> believers ... Presently there are some areas in which

conditions are entirely at variance with this, where everything, including the internal affairs of the religions themselves, hinges on government cadres. These cadres have no understanding of religion, do not appreciate the thoughts and sentiments of religious believers, do not respect religious traditions; yet those in religious circles do not dare speak up. The harm caused to religious believers by this state of affairs has resulted in their being driven into the arms of bad elements and enemies, and patriotic religious groups have lost many people in the process. (*Religion*, No. 2, 1984)

In his address to the National People's Political Consultative Conference following the Thirteenth Party Congress, Zhao Puchu went further and raised the issue of reform of the leadership and administrative systems in religious affairs or, in other words, the issue of separation of religion and the state. He said:

For a long time the administrative and leadership systems relating to religious affairs have suffered from the abuses of over-centralization of power and a monopoly of religious work by these organizations; this is entirely unsuitable in the current situation of openness and reform, and obstructs the development of religious work. We must undertake reforms in a sound and positive way. The key issue in these reforms is based on the spirit of the principles raised in Zhao Ziyang's report at the Thirteenth Party Congress on the separation of Party and government, of state and management, reform of the cadre system, rationalization of Party and administrative organs relating to people's organizations, and the implementation of the separation of religion and the state.

Separation of religion and the state refers to the fact that the functions of responsible government departments and religious organizations, temples, mosques, and churches are separate ... the key to resolving this issue lies in the rationalization of the leadership of administrative departments and the right of religious organizations, to govern themselves according to their own characteristics. Religious believers themselves should have control of religious venues and this control should be institutionalized. Responsible government departments carry out the leadership of the state administrative organs toward religion, implement the policy of religious freedom, safeguard and monitor the constitution and related laws, regulations and policy, and coordinate the interaction of religion and other sectors of society. We must reform the mechanistic practices of the administrative and leadership system and its methods in working with religious organizations. Religious organizations must become true people's organizations which carry on their work independently and according to their special characteristics, enjoying the right to administer their own personnel, property and affairs under the leadership of Party and government and within the scope of the Constitution, laws and policies of the nation.

At present, some comrades engaged in the study of religion are giving thought and attention to the issue of reform of the system of religious affairs leadership and administration. They are pondering the following question: in a socialist country, what should be the relationship between the political authorities and religious organizations? Some feel that such formulations as "administrative leadership," or "strengthening administration" are not as desirable as a simplified formula such as "leadership in politics; self-government it religion." This would mean that the function of Party and government departments is to carry out the policy of religious freedom, to resolve problems and contradictions in the implementation of policy, and to assist religious organizations in terms of guiding policy. However, their function is not to interfere in normal religious affairs and activities, while curbing illegal religious activities. Other comrades object to what has been promoted as the "three designates": designated place of worship, designated leadership, designated jurisdiction system. They feel that religious organizations have not been consulted with regard to these methods and that they represent a departure from the policy of religious freedom. It is as if a teacher receiving an invitation to lecture in another part of the country or a student wishing to attend a lecture somewhere had first to get approval from the Ministry of Education!

There are also those who feel that what has been termed "strengthening administration" in religious affairs does not sufficiently distinguish between the legitimate and the illegal, and at times verges on a guiding ideology which would set limits to and suppress religion. Indeed, the realities as we understand them, are as follows: in a small number of areas, the spirit with which this "strengthening of administration" has been applied has meant that religious activities should be acceptably short, not long; acceptably small, not large in scale; rituals should be acceptably simple, not complicated; and held with appropriate frequency, not too often. Even worse, in some areas, a kind of "permitted to leave, but not to join" pact has been forced upon religious organizations, with all sorts of regulations limiting outsiders entering churches, some even advocating that "members of the church may drop their membership." All these are done in the name of "strengthening administration," but are in fact putting into practice a line of church destruction, one which fundamentally contravenes the spirit of the freedom of religion stipulated into the Constitution.

The result is that religious activities are driven underground where they become fair game for bad elements. Is it any wonder then that some believers are saying: The policy in every area is now reform and openness, but tight control is unique to religion?

The issue of reform in the system of administration and leadership in religious affairs represents a new breakthrough in theory and research on religion following the enlivened spirit of reform since the Thirteenth Party Central. It is our hope that the responsible departments will give serious consideration to the views of the theoreticians and give ear to the voices of religious circles. This will help to arouse a positive response among religious believers, to bring religious activities out from underground and into the open, to bring believers who have drifted away back into religious organizations, and to establish the international reputation of the Chinese government for its conscientious implementation of the policy of religious freedom.

—Recent Developments in the Study of Religion, 1989.
Co-authored with Wang Weifan.

℘

# THE CHURCH AND CHINA'S
# NEW CONSTITUTION

Following a nationwide critique of the extreme leftist line that dominated our country during the Cultural Revolution, order was restored. Our people care about socialist democracy and law. Together with legal experts, they have taken part in two years of painstaking effort, including four months of nationwide discussion and consultation. Now at long last the Chinese people have a new and appropriate Constitution.

Because I am on the Commission for Constitutional Revision of the National People's Congress (NPC), I took part in the entire process of drafting this new Constitution. I would like to report to my co-workers and fellow Christians on the formulation of the article dealing with religion (the Thirty-sixth Article).

Long before the Commission was formed, we Christian delegates to the NPC and the Chinese People's Political Consultative Conference (CPPCC), in concert with leaders of other religions, had already made a formal representation to the NPC and CPPCC. This representation advocated the deletion from the 1978 Constitution of the "leftist" wording of the article on religion. In effect, we were opposed to the statement in this article of "freedom to propagate atheism," without a corresponding statement of the freedom to propagate theism. We felt it unnecessary to state that there was "freedom not to believe in religion," because the concept of "religious freedom" includes the freedom not to believe. "Freedom of speech" does not require a statement of "freedom not to speak," nor does the "freedom to send letters" require a statement of "freedom not to do so." We felt that the wording of the Eighty-eighth Article of the 1954 Constitution, "Citizens shall have the freedom of religious belief," a model of simplicity and clarity, should be restored.

These proposals seemed extremely fair and reasonable to us.

However, because of the long-standing influence of "leftist" thinking, our proposals met with some opposition, and some of those who opposed us were people of considerable status and influence. They advocated retaining the wording of the article on religion found in the 1978 Constitution.

Happily, religious circles and believers across the country commended our proposal. It also garnered the support of intellectual, political and legal circles, as well as government cadres concerned about socialist democracy and law. The Religious Affairs Bureau under the State Council (RAB) had given their opinion to the Commission in writing, supporting our proposals. This fact in itself is enough to illustrate that the RAB's concern was to implement the policy of religious freedom and protect the legal rights and interests of each religion. People overseas attacked them by saying that their aim was the destruction of religion. This is too superficial and ignorant.

We know that since the Third Plenum of the Eleventh Party Congress, the Central Committee has resolutely restored order and implemented each policy. Vis à vis religion, it has resolutely overcome subjectivism and dogmatism and implemented the policy of religious freedom. This situation prevails throughout the nation. The Commission has also been resolved to restore order and eradicate "leftist" views and formulations in religion, and adopt all fair and reasonable views put forward by religious circles. My co-workers and fellow Christians will certainly have noted that the draft constitution given to the people for discussion restores the wording of the 1954 Constitution with regard to religion. Adherents of all religions in China experience this as the lifting of a heavy burden and a surge of heartfelt joy.

During the more than two years of constitutional revision, we leaders of the China Christian Council and of the Three-Self Patriotic Movement of Protestant Churches in China put forward many views that were given due consideration by the Commission. We can say that those views related to the religious policy were all adopted. Our Christian compatriots in Hong Kong and Macau also held a forum and expressed their valuable views on the draft constitution.

In the very first version of the draft, wording appeared to the effect that religion should not be involved in politics, education or marriage.

People who are not adherents of any religion frequently lack sensitivity in this area, and have no perception how this phrase "should not be involved in" grates on the ears of religious believers. We in religious circles had a responsibility to reflect this situation to the Commission and we did so. The Commission valued our opinions, and after studying the issue, avoided this type of wording. Incidents such as this show us the spirit of democratic consultation as it is expressed in our national political life. At the same time, we see that you cannot have consultation by looking at only one side of an issue. Thus we should actively take the initiative to express our views, so that consultation can take place. If we did not make our views known, the final version of the Constitution might have retained some unsuitable wordings.

Another example: My co-workers and fellow Christians might recall that the draft constitution sent out for a four-month period of discussion by all the people contained a statement to the effect that no one had the right to use religion to undertake counter-revolutionary activities. This is of course correct. However, religion is not the only means to counter-revolutionaries' hands—they can also turn speech and publications to their own ends. Today the vast majority of believers in all our religions are patriotic. Why should counter-revolutionaries only be mentioned in connection with religion? Our Buddhist friends raised this issue and persons in other religions also felt it had merit. We appealed to the Commission to delete this phrase. They duly considered our view and, with the agreement of the majority of Commission members, it was decided to delete this phrase. This is yet another expression of the spirit of democratic consultation.

The present Constitution stipulates that religious bodies and religious affairs shall not be under foreign domination. This is powerful support by our nation's people for the realization of independence by Chinese Catholicism and for the realization of self-government, self-support and self-propagation by Chinese Protestantism, an expression of care for our newly born self-run churches. It cannot be made any clearer. What is being opposed here is "domination" from outside; it in no way affects us in normal exchanges on a basis of equality with international religious circles. We believe that only an independent and self-governing Chinese Church can truly benefit the international church, and in like manner, only such a church can benefit from the international church. Some people overseas have made groundless statements that this sentence in the Constitution is meant to prohibit Chinese churches from international contacts. Perhaps they do not understand the meaning of "domination"?

I have taken part in the whole process of constitutional revision and I deeply feel that the highest leadership of our nation is resolved to implement the policy of religious freedom, to enable the believers of each religion to contribute to the nation with easy minds and hearts. Because China is a vast and populous country, because of the confusion "leftist" things have caused in people's thinking in former years, thorough implementation of the spirit of religious freedom at every level, in every department and corner, cannot be done without obstacles. However, since the central leadership is so resolved, we can be optimistic, knowing that our efforts at implementing policy and striving for socialist democracy and rule of law, are not in vain. This Constitution represents the interests and views of the people of the whole nation. We must respect it, cherish it and protect it, and oppose anyone and anything that would offend against it.

—The Church and China's New Constitution, 1983

# THE STRENGTH
# OF DEMOCRATIC SOCIALISM

I have been a committee member of the CPPCC for about three-quarters of those forty years. I have not been very active during that rather long period, and I have frequently been absent. Some things only seem precious to you after they are gone. It was during the years of the Cultural Revolution that I frequently thought of the CPPCC and often missed it. There was one particular time when I went to Shanghai and someone told me that on the wall around the Shanghai

PPCC six big character posters had appeared which said "How can politics be subjected to consultation?" I did not dare to go see them, but I wondered then whether there would be a CPPCC afterwards. If one day there was a CPPCC again, I should be a more conscientious delegate.

A political consultative conference is not an administrative department of the nation, nor is it one of the legislative organs. Its nature is consultative, with people from all sectors consulting about the important issues of the country, drawing on collective wisdom, enabling everyone's understanding to be increased and unified, and then to bring along an even broader group of delegates so that the business of the country can be done well. This is truly added democracy. It is not as simple as the minority following the majority. It is much more complex than the raising of a hand or the casting of a ballot, because a great many facts must be laid out, a great many principles discussed. Sometimes things have to wait, and therefore progress may be slower. But it allows everyone to think things through clearly, and enables strength to be gathered together rather than diminished, pooling the wisdom and efforts of all. I feel that this is the point where democratic socialism is superior to Western democracy.

The CPPCC is an important embodiment of the united front guiding policy of the Chinese Communist Party. To my knowledge, although revolutionary and social movements can proceed without uniting people to strive together, the Chinese Communist Party, of all parties in power worldwide, stresses this point particularly. In the 1920s, Chairman Mao asked, "Who are our enemies, who are our friends?" in an analysis of the political attitude of people at all levels of society. The United Front has become a science. The Chinese Communist Party has developed the theory of the United Front to a high degree, setting up United Front departments at every level within its own organization, basing its dealing with issues affecting intellectuals, the ethnic bourgeoisie, ethnic groups, religion, overseas Chinese, Hong Kong, Macau, Taiwan and its striving to unite with people all around the world, on the United Front principle and promulgating a whole range of policy on it.

Forty years of history tell us that when policy has been carried out according to these principles, the hearts of the people turn to the Party and the country is united and stable. Whenever it has gone against these principles, the nation has been unstable and the people have suffered. The central leadership group set up by the Fourth Plenum proclaimed that the line and policies in force since the Third Plenum of the Eleventh Party Congress would not change. This proclamation was widely welcomed for the very reasons given above.

Those of you here may know that some of us Christians began something called The Amity Foundation, a people's organization whose aim is to serve society. Philip Wickeri, an American and its Overseas Coordinator, has written a study of the United Front in China—this was his Ph.D. dissertation—which was recently published. The four Chinese words on the cover—*qiu tong cun yi*—(seek the common ground while reserving differences) were written by Mr. Zhao Puchu, head of the Chinese Buddhist Association. The author studied the United Front, the CPPCC and religious policy and has much that is profound to say on the topic. I am very happy to have this book, which deepens the understanding of us overseas. People overseas are familiar only with the three branches of power—legislature, judiciary and administration. The United Front and the consultative conference are very unfamiliar overseas and must be introduced. I have in the past spoken on the united front and the consultative conference several times overseas and my listeners found this very new and fresh. I often tell people overseas that the Communist Party is only a leading party and that they should not call China "Communist China." It would be better to say "United Front China."

Of course there are failings in the work of the CPPCC. One may be that we do not consult enough, another that our supervisory role is inadequate. Supervision is extremely important. People are only human after all and when they hold power, they often find it easy to ignore democracy and even go so far as to use power for their own ends. Thus, where there is power there should also be supervision. It is not enough to depend solely on intuition and the individual conscience. Problems will still occur with supervision, but these can be much more promptly corrected—one need not wait to act until the problem is very serious. I hope, and I believe, that in the years to come, consultation and supervision will be strengthened and democratic socialism in our country will be greatly developed.

—40th Anniversary of the Chinese People's Political
Consultative Conference, 1989

∞

# RELIGIOUS LIBERTY IN CHINA: MY PERSPECTIVE

It was with joy and thanksgiving that I received the invitation to this International Conference on Religious Liberty.

Religious liberty is not only a legitimate right of religious believers the world over, but also an index of the degree of liberty in general enjoyed by the people of any given society. Hence it is of great concern to all who bear in their hearts the cause of people's rights and histori-cal progress. The International Religious Liberty Association regards religious liberty as an integral part of the struggle for human dignity and is rendering invaluable service to ensure it. This receives the hearty support of the Chinese people.

What I propose to do is first to dwell a bit on the question of reli-gious liberty in China and then to make a few observations out of the Chinese experience.

A unique point about the Chinese nation for thousands of years is that ours has been a people rather lacking in religious spirituality and fanaticism. The Chinese mythology as regards the origin of the uni-verse is different from those of many other ancient cultures in that it does not ascribe the origin to divine creation but plays up the role of Ban Gu, a mortal, who used tools to work on primordial materials already in existence. Thus, the Chinese story has a strong naturalist and humanist streak in it. Later, sections of heaven were found to be falling apart, but no divine intervention was evoked; it was Nü Wo, another mortal, who mended the heavens. As to the origin of human civilization there is no story in China corresponding to Prometheus going to heaven to steal fire from the gods. Our story instead tells of great persons who taught people to get fire by drilling wood, to build nests with wood as human dwellings, to invent tools for farming, to taste all kinds of herbs to find medicines for curing diseases.

China is the homeland of Confucius. Influenced by his rather agnostic teaching, China makes much of ethics in human relationships and not much of religion. He asks, "Not being able to serve human beings, how can we serve ghosts?" "Not knowing about life, how can we know about death?" He teaches us to "respect gods and ghosts but keep them at a distance."

Thus, the Chinese nation has achieved little in religion. Only Taoism is native to China; the other main religions are imports. We see little religious fanaticism in China, and no religious wars have ever occurred. Religion has not been an important factor for communal strife. An emperor in medieval Europe was made to walk barefoot through the night to seek the forgiveness of the Pope—such a thing could never have happened in Chinese history, for religion in China never stood on a par with state power, much less over and above it. There were surely theism-atheism debates, but no scholar suffered demotion or the loss of a job because of advocacy of atheism. The well-known atheistic writing *The Demise of Gods* by Fan Chun was preserved for posterity by his Buddhist opponents. All of this tells us that religion is no big thing in China and that, in matters of religious faith, the Chinese have on the whole adhered to the principle of "live and let live."

However, it does not follow that the fate of religion has been smooth and uneventful. It has not been so in the thirty-seven years since the founding of the People's Republic of China either.

About religion the first National Constitution of the People's Republic of China said simply that: "All citizens are free to believe in religion." That was good enough. 1966 marked the beginning of the Cultural Revolution, which was nothing less that an attempt to liquidate culture itself. The government, the Communist Party and all other democratic parties had their power wrested from them. A new

National Constitution, promulgated at the instigation of the Gang of Four, laid down that citizens have "the freedom to believe in religion and the freedom not to believe in religion and to propagate atheism."

That Constitution was imposed on the Chinese people by the ultra-leftists. It mentioned the freedom to propagate atheism, but said nothing about the freedom to propagate theism or religion. As a matter of fact, during the Cultural Revolution, not only the freedom of propagating religion, but also that of religious worship was denied. According to one outspoken leader of the Cultural Revolution in Shanghai, the freedom of religion was nothing more than the freedom for people to have a god in their mind. During those years churches and temples were entirely closed down in large areas of China.

After the Cultural Revolution, the work of the National People's Congress became normalized. Its Commission on the Revision of the National Constitution mobilized personages in all walks of life both within the party and the various religions and outside them, to work together to produce a new draft. This new draft was presented to the people in a nationwide referendum. For four months it was discussed and changes proposed. Eventually a new National Constitution was adopted by the National People's Congress. Here is what the present Constitution says about religion in China:

All citizens of the People's Republic of China are to enjoy the freedom of religious belief.

No state organ, social organization or individual has the right to force a citizen to believe in religion or not to believe in religion, or to discriminate against a citizen on grounds of the citizen's religious belief or the lack of it.

The state is to protect all normal religious activities. Nobody should make use of religion to carry on activities which jeopardize order in society, human physical health or the educational system of the state.

Religious organizations and affairs are not to be directed by foreign bodies.

This article on religion is obviously longer, more detailed, and consonant with the universal principle of human religious freedom.

The freedom to propagate atheism has been deleted as has the freedom not to believe in religion. Of course, these deletions entail no deprivations. It goes without saying that the freedom of religions belief implies the freedom not to believe and also the freedom to propagate atheism. The point is that those two freedoms do not need to be mentioned. Today, the whole Chinese people need to unite as one so as to work together for national prosperity. Religious believers are included too. The state must do nothing to offend the feelings of the religious believers.

The article lays down definitely that there should be no discrimination on religious grounds. This is new as compared with past Constitutions. The point here is that before the law and state believers and non-believers stand as equal and believers of different religions are also equal. There is no state or official religion in China and no religion is to enjoy any special privilege or to suffer from any special disadvantage.

The article stipulates that religion in China are to be administered by Chinese adherents and not directed from abroad. This is based on lessons learned since the 19$^{th}$ century and supports the movement on the part of Chinese Christians for independence and for self-government, self-support and self-propagation. But let us note that what is said here speaks to the directing of religious work from abroad. We should not understand it to mean the banning of normal international relations. Religious groups in China are maintaining many international contacts and activities all based on equality and none involving the question of "direction."

Aside from the National Constitution, Article 147 of the Criminal Code stipulates that any member of a state organ is liable to imprisonment for up to two years if this person deprives citizens of religious freedom and violates the customs and mores of minority nationalities. The incorporation of this article in the Criminal Code stifles those who would deal with religion according to their own will.

Apart from the Constitution and the Criminal Code there are written instructions and directives of the Central Committee of the Communist Party of China to its membership. These emphasize that questions of religion should primarily be approached from the standpoint of the United Front, i.e., of uniting religious believers in the task of nation-building. Believers and non-believers are equal citizens of the country. Religious beliefs do not make a person an enemy of the nation. One statement says: "In implementing the policy of freedom of religious belief, and in dealing with all religious questions, the fundamental ground or starting point is to unite all believers and non-believers so that the will and strength of all can be put to the common goal of building up a strong socialist nation." A well-received statement from the Central Committee of the Communist Party of China is this: "The differences in thinking and belief on the part of believers and nonbelievers are differences of a minor importance." Let us note that the word used here is "differences," not "contradictions," and they are "differences of a minor importance." I do not think our preachers would make such a declaration, but the Communist Party of China has actually done so.

Under the guidance of the Constitution, the Law and the directives of the Party, China in recent years has been working hard to reverse the ultra-leftist political line rampant during the years of the Cultural Revolution. Many churches and temples have been restored or built. Since 1979 over 4,000 church buildings have been restored or newly built by the Protestant Christians. Churches are increasing for the Protestants at the rate of no fewer than one per day. At the same time tens of thousands of Christian groups worship in other meeting points, including homes. There are ten Protestant theological training centers with some five hundred students training for future pastoral ministries. Protestants are publishing books and several periodicals. Since 1981, over two million Chinese Bibles have been printed and published in three cities of China.

In China, atheism is a topic of discussion mainly among social scientists, particularly philosophers and historians. There is no journal or organization specially to oppose religion or propagate atheism. The situation between believers and non-believers as well as between believers of various religions is basically one of live and let live.

Of course, in our vast land, there is an unevenness in the implementation of the policy of religious freedom and, therefore, much work yet to be done. But, taking the nation as a whole, and excepting the Cultural Revolution, it is only right for us to say that religion enjoys a good amount of freedom. This is so not because the Communist Party has a high opinion of religious doctrines, but because it seeks foremost to unite the whole people in the cause of nation-building. In order to make this unity possible, minority characteristics, including religious ones, need to be respected. Ours is a developing country, still backward in many respects, and our people understand that we cannot afford the luxury of communal conflicts kindled by religion.

The masses of the Chinese Christians love their country, support the people's government, actively engage themselves in working for modernization and do not support divisiveness. However, this does not imply that their first allegiance is not to Christ but rather to the state, or that they relinquish the principle of independence from the state in its faith, life, work and administration. We in China strictly adhere to the principle of the separation of state and religion. In matters of religion the main job of the government is to implement correctly the policy of religious freedom and to protect the legitimate rights and interests of the various religions. Matters related to the church itself are decided upon by the proper authorities of the church without interference by the government. If the government does try to interfere, I am sure the church will object. Thus, to say that the church in China is an official church or government-run church simply because Chinese Christians support socialist new China is, to say the least, a misrepresentation of the true situation and can only bring confusion rather than understanding.

An old, time-tested principle to ensure Chinese unity is that of seeking or emphasizing our similarities and maintaining or respecting our differences. People dwell on this as an everyday principle, apply it to all sorts of human situations, between religions, between nationalities (of which we have fifty-six in China), between believers and non-believers and, in fact, in all walks of life. We find in it the key to preserving peace and making progress.

Besides Protestantism there are in China Buddhism, with possibly 100 million adherents; Islam, which is the main or only religion of ten minority nationalities; Taoism, which is native to China; and Roman Catholicism which, like Protestantism, came from the West. Religious freedom is enjoyed by these religions exactly as it is enjoyed by Protestantism.

On the basis of our Chinese experience, I now comment on four matters which may be of importance to the consideration of religious liberty as a global issue in connection with peace and communal unity.

(1) Religious liberty is a legal matter but not just a legal matter; it is a question of human rights but not just a question of human rights. In defending religious liberty, we need to ask also: what are the leaders of the religion for which liberty is sought going to do with the liberty once they have it? What are the social consequences of their ways of using that liberty? In the long run, the amount of liberty a religious group enjoys in a given society depends on the image that group presents before the public, and that image depends in the long run upon the actual performance of that religious group, that is, upon what use is made of liberty in the name of religion.

For instance, during China's war of resistance against Japanese aggression, there were Protestants in China who preached from the pulpit that the aggression was ordained of God: The Chinese had sinned and God sent Japanese troops to punish them. That incurred the resentment of many who asked, "Have the Japanese people not sinned? Why has not God sent Chinese troops to occupy Japan?" During the war of liberation quite a number of foreign and Chinese church leaders were entirely without sympathy for the people's liberation struggle. When the People's Liberation Army approached the Yangtze River in its drive southward, some preachers asked Christians from the pulpit to pray that God would drown the army in the river. What a cruel and inhumane prayer that was. Some of these same persons continued to adopt a hostile attitude to the new people's state and the Communist Party. All of this only led people to recall that Christianity was imposed on China with the help of unequal treaties and extraterritoriality and was called "foreign religion." In fact, it was common in those days for people to say: "One more Christian gained, one more Chinese lost." This being the situation, do we have the right to expect our people in China, in their new-won liberation, in considering religious liberty, to refrain from pondering what it might mean to the nation as a whole for a Christianity of that sort to enjoy full freedom of religion in the proper sense of the word? And if international public opinion is mobilized to bring pressure to bear on a nation of self-respecting people to force their retreat before a Christianity of that sort, is it hard to understand that this people resent such imposition from outside and recall the means of the imperialists, only taking this time the form not of gunboats but of organized "public opinion"? This bombardment makes the people even more skeptical as regards the justice of giving liberty to a Christianity hostile to China.

During past years there were people abroad who would never consider the kind of "Christianity" that Roman Catholic clergymen were required to advocate, nor whether the Chinese people could tolerate a "Christianity" which split not only the Chinese Catholics but also the Chinese people, and dealt with the question of their loss of freedom only in terms of abstract human rights. We think it important to see that they were not simply Roman Catholic bishops and priests. They were also executors of a whole series of instructions to work against the state power of China from a Vatican which could not tolerate the success of a people's revolutionary movement, especially one led by a communist party. According to these instructions Chinese Roman Catholics were not allowed even to read the *People's Daily* and their children not allowed to wear red scarves. Only those Roman Catholics who listened to these directives to the extent of standing against the new revolutionary state were considered good Christians. The clergy used their prestige to lead many a Chinese to depart from love for the motherland and to take to the blind alley of working against it. In this way, they offended the masses of the Chinese people and lost their freedom in testing the strength of people's power. They were victims of the anti-China political line of the Vatican of that time. Some still assume that anybody with a church position should be given the privilege of exemption from penalties for criminal offences, and given unlimited freedom to do what they like, with the state and the law deprived of their authority over him or her. This is not our view of religious liberty or national sovereignty. People do not seem to expect many other countries to grant this sort of liberty to citizens.

Thus, the question of religious freedom in the concrete is not exclusively a question of religious freedom. It may actually undermine other people's freedom to enjoy the very new life they have entered into. No state would assume that, because someone or something is related to religion, the situation is only a religious one, or just one of human rights, shorn of political implications and consequences.

Today, the church in China is self-governing, self-supporting and self-propagating. Existing apart from any Western political, military, or economic interest and domination, it depends only on the truth of its message as witnessed to by Christians through words and deeds, and on the good will of the people around it. We bear witness to Christ not against our people, nor under their curse and ill-feeling. The sympathy and goodwill of the rest of our people is an asset to the work of evangelization. To put Christ above all requires that. It is a far cry from putting the state above Christ. Three-Self has gone a long way in winning people's goodwill for Christianity and earning for the church its right to be heard. It is surely an important factor for the growth of the Chinese Protestant community in the last thirty-seven years from 700,000 to three or four million.

(2) It is not necessarily a deprivation of religious liberty for a religious body to give up or lose certain privileges it enjoyed owing to the favor of secular powers in former days.

The 20th century has seen rapid changes in history and society. In these changes certain groups have gained power and certain other groups have lost it. In a number of countries religions find themselves in an entirely new environment. It is only natural that, while maintaining the integrity of their respective faith commitments, religions choose to open themselves to new spiritual insights and to make certain changes called for by the times in order to perpetuate themselves and to bear an effective witness in society.

During the Land Reform in China, large tracts of land owned by Buddhist temples had to be dealt with in the same way as those owned by landlords—in accordance with the Land Reform law—whereby the amount of land over and above a certain limit had to go to the landless peasants. Protestants in China did not own much land but extraterritorial rights, protected by unequal treaties, meant that foreign missionaries in earlier years, and even Chinese converts to a certain extent, were beyond the jurisdiction of Chinese law courts. With our dependence on the political and economic superiority of Western powers, we belittled other religions and would go so far as to go to preach Jesus Christ in Buddhist temples on their festival days and attack the tenets of Buddhism.

Now, if the loss of these privileges amounts to the loss of religious freedom, then religious freedom becomes a tool for protecting the special privileges of a small number of people and, after such a denigration, we can hardly speak of the sacredness of religious freedom any more. In fact, relinquishment of special privileges can only result in raising the moral quality and prestige of the religious groups concerned and thus win for themselves appreciation and goodwill on the part of the public.

In the thirty-seven years since liberation, Chinese Christians have come to see more clearly the truth that the church shows strength when it is weak and gains power when it falls into powerlessness, in the same way as Christ's risen life emerged from death and the tomb only after much suffering. It was not when we had thousands of Western missionaries with us, many universities, schools and hospitals that we could put religious liberty to good use and lead many to turn to Christ. Religious liberty becomes a property the Chinese Christians can use well to enlarge our witness and to build up the Body of Jesus Christ only since Liberation, when none of these missionaries and institutions remain. In the words of an Old Testament prophet: "not by might, nor by power, but by my spirit, says the Lord of hosts" (Zech. 4:6).

(3) We have come to see that whether those in authority believe in this religion or in that and, indeed, whether they believe in religion at all, is not a deciding factor when we come to the question of whether religious beliefs are respected.

In the last thirty-seven years we have met in China many atheists who do all they can to implement the policy of religious freedom. Their starting point is to serve the people, and this may include enabling religious believers to enjoy a good religious life so as better to unite religious believers behind the motherland. At the same time, there are religious believers who have no respect for other people's religious faiths, trying only to uphold their own religion or denomination and intent only on liquidating other religious groups.

There are some persons abroad whose interest is to fan anti-

Communist hysteria and they never cease to belabor the fact that communists do not believe in God. It is true that, today, God does not seem to have provided us a way in which to bear a good witness for Christ to the Communists. This to me is a mystery and a call to wait. But, in the life of the nation, to be theistic or not is a matter of personal conviction and hence a private matter, while the implementation of the policy of religious freedom concerns the welfare of great multitudes of people and is hence a political duty. State officials obviously must work in accordance with the Constitution, the laws and state policies, and not act from their personal attitudes toward religion. For almost 2,000 years the Christian Church has co-existed with all sorts of non-Christians and atheists and found common ground with them. There is no cause for alarm and panic.

Political states and those in governing positions should not be expected to heap special kindnesses upon religion. If they can show respect for religious liberty and conscience, refrain from repressing religion, treat all religions with equality, look after the legitimate rights and interests of all religions, this is good enough. On the other hand, when those in governing positions begin to harp on their own religiosity, advertise their having been born again, and boast about their benevolence to things spiritual, let us be wary of their patronization.

(4) Religious liberty is not a benefit given in generosity by some persons to some other persons. Its realization and development are based on vigilance and practice, including those of religious believers themselves. The involvement of religious believers in the process is important because it is the religious believers who can best perceive when respect for religious feelings has been trespassed upon. In China believers of various religions took an active part in the process of revising the article on religion in the National Constitution, and they have been rewarded with very satisfactory language.

But, in order fully to realize the rights guaranteed by the Constitution, our various religious bodies and those state organs having to do with religion still have much to do.

One of the things we have found is that to help our social scientists in their study of religion to take into consideration more aspects of the

Chinese religious situation so that their conclusions can be better rooted in actual facts as they exist in China today, is of great importance to the making and the understanding of the policy of religious freedom. Social scientists in China are emphasizing that Marxism must not be dogmatic or just a collection of quotations from classical authors. It only offers the standpoint, the point-of-view and the methodology. Their understanding of truth needs to be based on facts and practice. They are to be creative and to develop human knowledge so that the conclusions and policies reached are relevant to the objective situation here and now. This, we think, is also a call to us religionists to do our part. For instance, in the study of religion, only very few social scientists in China are limiting their horizon to the concept of religion as opiate. On the basis of facts and practice, they affirm that religious believers on the whole are not behind others in their patriotic service to China's modernization, that religious ethics can motivate and guide believers to a moral life, to contributing to social stability and unity in the interests of socialist reconstruction. They find, for instance, a good proportion of Christians have been elected to be model or advanced workers. They are thus taking a new look at religion as it is. Many social scientists in China are saying that "opiate" must not be taken as a definition of religion. It is a role religion plays under certain circumstances, but not its only role and by no means always its main role. We appreciate and welcome all these and other results of unbiased research, a research based on facts and not just on any classical definition. More and more Christian intellectuals have come to see their responsibilities and opportunities in the field of the study of religion as a social science and have begun to participate in it. Thus, religious believers are sharing in the whole process of researching and of the making and implementing of the policy of religious freedom.

These observations based on our Chinese experience are, I hope, of relevance to the global struggle for religious liberty.

My last word is one of gratitude. Thank you for listening and thanks to the Association for giving me the opportunity to make friends and to increase knowledge.

—New Delhi, 1987

🔊

# THE CHURCH AND STATE

The Basic Standpoint and Policy on Religious Questions in China's Socialist Period," Document 19, adopted by the Party Central Committee in 1982, is an important document. To see why, compare it to documents and essays on religion from the Soviet Union, or with those China has produced in the past. Comparisons such as these show that this document is in a different vein, and its views are fresh and incisive. A very special characteristic of this document is that it does not proceed from concepts and definitions, but from the reality of China, from the present situation of society and religion in China. In its approach, it adopts the invaluable style of seeking truth from facts.

The most evident expression of this approach of beginning with present reality lies in its title: "The Basic Standpoint and Policy on Religious Questions in China's Socialist Period." This tells us that the document is not dealing with religious questions in the abstract, but about religious questions in China, and not with religious questions in China in general terms, but religious questions in China during the socialist period. Religious questions in China are specific; religious questions in China during the socialist period are even more so. Chairman Mao promoted the method of paying attention to specifics in doing research, rather than being content with generalities. With regard to the study of war, Chairman Mao believed that while the general laws of war should certainly be studied, it was even more necessary to study the laws of revolutionary wars, and that it was absolutely vital to study the laws of the Chinese people's revolution.

Marx and Engels studied religion in general but primarily understood religion in Western Europe. Lenin was primarily familiar with religion in Russia. They had little understanding of religion in China, which has its own special characteristics. For example, the role of religion in China has always been much smaller that its role in Europe. In Chinese history, divine right has never overridden the rights of rulers as it did in Europe. There was an emperor in Europe who, because he offended the Pope, had to walk a long distance bare-foot and at night, to beg the Pope's forgiveness. We cannot imagine anything like this in Chinese history. Among Han Chinese, religion has always been subordinate to politics. In Europe, church laws have also been political precepts, and the study of law was long under the dominion of theology. This prompted Marx to say, "The criticism of religion is the premise of all criticism." But in China, religion has never occupied such a commanding position. In China, the feudal code of ethics and the patriarchal clan system have held the place taken by religion in Europe. The slogans of the May Fourth Movement were "Down with the feudal system" and "Down with Confucius." Criticism of feudalism or the patriarchal clan system was "the premise of all criticism" in China. It would be inappropriate to copy Europe in China.

Marx and Engels did not speak of the historical stages of socialism, nor did Lenin have time to study religious questions in the socialist period. What changes took place in the status and function of religion after the people took political power? How should religious questions be dealt with in the socialist period? These were extremely novel sub-jects. To copy from Europe, from the old ways, or from the period of reactionary rule, would not do. As Lenin said, for example, "The pres-ent source of religion is the dread of the unchecked forces of capital-ism. These forces truly are unchecked, because the masses cannot foresee them, and because the proletariat and small landholders might meet them anytime, anywhere in the course of their lives. This is what happens when they meet 'sudden,' 'unexpected,' 'happenstance,' bankruptcy and destruction that turns them into beggars, paupers, and prostitutes, even forcing them to starvation."

These words were very much in line with the situation in Russia at the time, and are quite appropriate to capitalist countries and Third World countries where the people have not yet become their own mas-ters, but they are not appropriate for socialist new China. If we simply go by the book, how will we be able to explain present religious questions in China? Can the continued presence of religious believers be attributed to blind bourgeois forces that will suddenly turn people into beggars and prostitutes? Lenin said: "All the oppressor classes must play two social roles in order to maintain control; one is the executioner and the other is the priest. The executioner suppresses the protests and uprisings of the oppressed. The priest comforts the oppressed, painting for them a far-off vista of reduced suffering and sacrifice if they maintain the conditions of class rule ... and this weakens their revolutionary resolve."

If we quote this with reference to present-day China, we are defeating our own purpose. Can the machinery of a country with the people in charge function to chop off the people's hands? Would our country really want to use religion as a "tool of the spirit" to break the people's revolutionary resolve? And as the young Marx said: "*Religious* distress is at the same time the *expression* of real distress and also the *protest* against real distress. Religion is the sigh of the oppressed creature, the heart of a heartless world, just as it is the spirit of spiritless conditions. It is the *opium* of the people." To apply this quotation mechanically to socialist China will cause problems. Are the Chinese people still "oppressed creatures?" The first paragraph of Document 19 says: "The exploiting classes needed to use religion as their spiritual means to anesthetize and control the masses." But China today is not under the rule of exploiting classes, and the Communist Party and the people's government certainly do not want to anesthetize the people. If we still emphasize that religion is an opiate, then we must come out and say it—which class is it today that wants to use religion to anesthetize the people?

Since the reactionary ruling class that used religion to numb the people and the conditions that made people accept exploitation and oppression no longer exist, then if religion functions as an opiate, it is only in the sense that wine may be used to banish melancholy. Not its best use perhaps, but entirely permissible. If no distinction is made between the present and the past when we speak of the ruling classes' manipulation of religion to anesthetize the people, then, our attempts are, at the very least, theoretically sloppy. In politics, we will be bound to continue "taking class struggle as the key link" in dealing with religion and it will be difficult to keep from falling into all kind of "leftist" methods in our work.

We have new Christians now, who have turned to Christian faith, in their own words, "because religion makes us do good."

Christianity speaks of love, industriousness, sincerity, reconciliation, endurance, self-denial and doing good to others. In the old society religions might have been susceptible to manipulation by the reactionary ruling classes, so those classes welcomed their propagation, the better to use them to drug the people. Today, however, there has been a fundamental change in the situation—political power is firmly in the hands of the people. The political and social function of these Christian persuasions is no longer the same. They can be aids rather than obstacles to strengthening stability and unity and to increasing production. People who wanted to practice these Christian virtues were never very willing to participate in "rebel" groups during the Cultural Revolution.

There is a passage in the Bible to the effect that authority is instituted by God, and people should submit to it. The KMT used this to tranquilize the people, to make them docile and obedient. But when Christians say this today under the political authority of the people, they cannot be judged reactionary. For some Christians, this idea strengthens the relationship between believers and the government. This Christian code of conduct is good for social stability and is conducive to people living and working in peace and contentment. Such Christians are more in harmony with socialism, and they are much better than people who smash and grab or pursue selfish interests. Many Christians in the countryside want nothing more than to be able to gather together once a week. They participate actively in production and their record in meeting their quota of grain for the state is very good. Pastors encourage this. Furthermore, the believers are very cooperative and local cadres are well disposed toward them. Plainly, religion does not simply play the role of opiate. It may have many roles, depending on the time and conditions; it is not necessarily antagonistic to socialism.

In sum, religious questions during China's socialist period are special. What was done in foreign countries and class societies cannot simply be copied. What is special about this document is first and fore-most that it does not simply go by the book, but proceeds from real-ity. Today the Chinese people have entered a historical period where class struggle is no longer the key link. We should have knowledge of religious questions appropriate to this period.

We note that the word "opium" does not appear in Document 19, not even once. Only when the rule of the exploiting class in former days is mentioned is the word "tranquilize" used: "The exploiting classes needed to use religion as their main spiritual means to tranquil-ize and control the masses." In this the Document is very different from many documents dealing with religious questions found in the Soviet Union and in China in the past. In the past some people thought that it was unmarxist to speak of religion without calling it an opiate. I do not think it is entirely by chance that this document does not men-tion the word. It has thrown off dogmatism and bookishness, and does not begin with concepts and definitions. It is an expression of the fine Party tradition of beginning with reality. Explaining all religious ques-tions by the opiate theory has always been inadequate; it is even less viable as an explanation of religion during the socialist period. Why insist on it then? There is a reluctance among some people to go and study actual conditions; they would rather latch on to one or two well-known phrases in dealing with things. They think "opiate" is part of the nature of religion and that the theory of religion as opiate is a uni-versal or eternal truth. They go so far as to say that it is original to Marx. Actually, some decades prior to Marx, the phrase was already on the lips of enlightened bourgeois scholars in Germany, including those in religious circles. To claim it as an idea originating with Marx, is degrading, not exalting, to Marx.

Actually, the writings and teachings of Marx, Engels, Lenin and Chairman Mao on religion are extremely rich, comprehensive and pro-found. But "religion is opium," is the only phrase that comes to some people's minds and they rely on it in all questions touching on religion. The result is that they can hardly avoid being simplistic. It was Zhou Enlai who took exception to continuing to trumpet the opium theory when we were already in the socialist period. In 1950, during the CPPCC, Premier Zhou told the people: "Do not think that slogans used during the revolution should be used even more fervidly after victory. Quite the opposite. During the revolutionary period it was necessary to make the principles clear. Now that we have political power, there are times when it is not necessary to emphasize that 'religion is an opiate.' The issue is that we must be good at isolating the minority of stubborn reactionaries." These words deserve our attention. The first special characteristic of Document 19 is its elimination of outmoded language; it begins its study of religious issues from the present reality of China and puts forward a brand-new viewpoint.

Secondly, it makes an appropriate assessment of religion and religious circles in China's socialist period.

In the debate over guiding thought for religious work, there has been the dispute between the five natures and the two natures of religion. The five natures are (1) the rootedness of religion in the masses of the people, (2) its affinity to ethnic minority peoples, (3) its international connections, (4) its continued existence over the long-term, and (5) its complexity. This theory of the five natures is an important development and a great contribution to Marxism by the Chinese revolutionary movement. The Document does not use the term "five natures," but the spirit of the whole undeniably affirms them. In the latter half of the second paragraph, the five natures are mentioned one by one in detail.

The so-called "two natures" of religion assert its reactionary nature and its deceptive nature. This document in no way advocates or plays up religion in China's socialist period as reactionary or deceptive.

Reaction is a political concept. The most that could be said of religion would be that it is mistaken or erroneous knowledge. And there are a great many people with this or that kind of error in knowledge. The idealism of subjectivism is even more prevalent. People with errors in understanding may be politically reactionary, but they may also be revolutionary, progressive and patriotic. The equation of religious faith with political reaction is a method used during the Cultural Revolution.

The Document makes the following assessment of religion and religious circles in China today: "After Liberation there has been a thorough transformation of the socio-economic system and a major reform of the religious system, and so the status of religion in China has already undergone a fundamental change. The contradictions of the religious question now belong primarily to the category of internal contradictions among the people." "We did away with imperialist forces within the churches and promoted the correct policy of independent, self-governed and autonomous churches, as well as the 'Three-Self Movement' (self-propagation, self-administration and self-support). The Catholic and Protestant Churches ceased to be tools of the imperialist aggressors and became independent and autonomous religious enterprises of Chinese believers. We abolished the special privileges and oppressive exploitative system of feudal religion, attacked and exposed those reactionaries and bad elements who hid behind the cloak of religion." "By far the majority of [religious professionals] are patriotic, law-abiding and support the socialist system. Only a very small minority opposes the Constitution and socialism to the extent of colluding with foreign anti-revolutionaries and other bad elements." We note that the Document's approach to religion is scientific, coolheaded and seeking truth from facts; it does not shy away from its subject. It has a very high assessment of religious circles thirty years after Liberation. This is in line with Comrade Deng Xiaoping's statement a few years ago that "Religious circles have made great progress."

As for having a deceptive nature, Engels and Lenin both pointed out that to see religion as the product of a meeting between a fool and a trickster is a bourgeois view. This is not to say that nothing deceptive ever happens in religion, but that the sources of religion are much deeper. It is a great over-simplification to say that religion is no more than a trick and would not exist if not for tricksters.

One-sided emphasis on the reactionary and deceptive natures of religion will inevitably lead to a struggle with religion, to a line in work that attempts to destroy religious faith. We have suffered enough distress from such a line.

Thirdly, the Document makes very clear why the Party is involved in work in the area of religion and what kind of work it should do, what the fundamental starting point and aim is, what the basic task is and is not.

There is a hypothesis which says that since Marxism is atheist then the intent and goal of the Party's work in religion must be, by whatever means, to place all sorts of obstacles in the way of religious belief, to make nonbelievers of believers, to employ all sorts of methods in the struggle with religion in order to limit and reduce it. This is the line that reached its full expression during the Cultural Revolution period.

The Document deals with extreme clarity with the true intentions of the Party toward religion. "The basic starting point and firm foundation for our handling of the religious question and for the implementation of our policy and freedom of religious belief lies in our desire to unite the mass of believers and nonbelievers and enable them to center all their will and strength on the common goal of building a modernized, powerful socialist country." The basic task of the Party and government in religious work is "to firmly implement and carry out its policy of freedom of religious belief; to consolidate and to expand the patriotic and political alliance in each ethnic or religious group; to strengthen education in patriotism and socialism among them, and to bring into play positive elements among them in order to build a modern and powerful socialist state and complete the great task of unifying the country; and to oppose hegemonism and strive together to protect and preserve world peace." It is worth noting that in speaking of the starting point, foundation and basic task of the Party's religious work, the Document says nothing of reducing the number of religious believers, struggling against religion, or limiting or destroying religion.

But there are those who pass over this aspect of the document without really seeing it and persist in thinking that religious freedom is just a phrase and the true intent of the Party remains to do away with religion by all possible means. In this case, dealing roughly with religious questions among the people, creating tension between the Party and the masses are all feasible. To justify themselves, they exaggerate the few instances of chaotic and abnormal phenomena in religious matters as if they were emblematic of the whole situation. This differs greatly from the assessment of the situation given in the Document.

As for the so-called "unchecked flood" of religion, we should not exaggerate this. It is certainly not a result of the implementation of the religious policy; rather it can often be attributed to failure to implement religious policy and other policies. Some people are frightened out of their wits at tales of a "religious flood" and become ambivalent about implementing the religious policy, shouting about "religion being out of control," "propagating atheism," and so on. This gives the green light to creating confusion at the grassroots and suppressing the people. This is just asking for trouble. Religious fanaticism cannot be maintained for long. What should be done is to allow the policy to be carried out. The masses will turn to the Party and bad elements (if there are any) will be isolated, exposed and dealt with.

Talk of a "religious flood" is an undiscriminating assault on religion, an all-out attack. Such a characterization makes no distinctions, does not allow for differentiation in the treatment of things and does nothing to enlarge unity. It leads easily to enlarging the scope of attack. Two years ago in one locale in Hubei province, there was an increase in the number of Christians and the sweeping statement was made that this was a "religious flood." But investigation promptly showed that there were at least two sets of circumstances that had to be distinguished: (1) one person had been pushing faith healing and driving away evil spirits, claiming the end of the world was near, in order to cheat people of money. (2) Two miners had got together a group of Christians, but they were against healing and driving away evil spirits and refused to accept gifts. They taught that people had to achieve the "three satisfies"—satisfy the Party, satisfy God and satisfy others. This latter example was not unpatriotic, represented a relatively healthy type of religion and should not have been lumped together with the first example, as if both were part of the "flood." China makes distinctions in treatment even among imperialist countries. How much more then should it do so among religious believers.

Among believers we find that the large part of religious activities are normal ones. Beyond this, the Document mentions three other things, which it does not include among normal religious activities. "The resolute protection of all normal religious activities suggests, at the same time, a determined crackdown on all criminal and anti-revolutionary activities which hide behind the facade of religion, which includes all superstitious practices which fall outside the scope of religion and are injurious to the national welfare as well as to the life and property of the people." These are two distinct "resolves."

The Document does not hold that religion will exist permanently. However, it is not going to disappear during our present stage, and even less can the cadres of our religious affairs departments be expected to take responsibility to struggle with religion in order to achieve its destruction. For cadres of religious affairs departments to desire to both unite the masses of religious believers and abolish their religious faith would be an irreconcilable contradiction. They could not, in this case, do their work well. The Party Central has responded to this in Document 19: "We must further understand that at the present historical stage the difference that exists between the mass of believers and nonbelievers in matters of ideology and belief is relatively secondary." Belief and nonbelief are not described as a contradiction, but as a difference, and a minor difference at that. I think this statement is to serve to sober up those distracted by the opiate theory, and those promoting the reactionary and deceptive nature of religion and those bent on sweeping away, attacking and limiting religion.

The task of the religious affairs departments is to implement policy and unite believers. They are not charged with opposing religion, propagating atheism to believers or making nonbelievers of believers. For this point to be made clear and communicated publicly to those related to religion will be very good for the correction of "leftism." For many years, too much was heard of "the reactionary nature of religion," "struggling against religion," "hurrying the demise of religion," "establishing no-religion areas," and "talk about religious freedom is just for the benefit of foreigners." Unless we clearly negate all this now, it will be difficult to rectify "leftism" and difficult to change the image of government religious affairs departments among the believing masses as anti-religion departments, difficult to dispel the misgivings of the believing masses, difficult to establish true friendship with the believing masses, difficult to unite them.

I believe the central spirit of Document 19 lies in showing exactly what the intentions and desires of the Party are in its religious work.

Fourthly, the Document asks for improvement in the relationship between the government and religion in some areas. The country is presently engaged in putting into practice separation of state and commerce. Turning to religion, the failure to separate religion and state is quite serious in some areas. The problem is that this failure is in no way conducive to mobilizing the patriotic strength of religious circles as a bridge between Party and masses. And so it is not conducive to uniting the broad mass of religious believers around the Party.

There are three passages in the Document which emphasize that cadres should stress the role of patriotic religious bodies at all levels. If the cadres are good at leading, if they avoid taking over and allow the religious bodies to play their role, then they can be in close contact with the believing masses.

(1) "The basic task of these patriotic religious organizations is to assist the Party and the government to implement the policy of freedom of religious belief, to help the broad mass of religious believers and persons in religious circles to continually raise their patriotic and socialist consciousness, to represent the lawful rights and interests of religious circles, to organize normal religious activities and to manage religious affairs well."

(2) "We must strengthen the government organs responsible for religious affairs, to enable all cadres who give themselves to this particular work to study the Marxist theory of religion in a systematic way, to thoroughly understand the Party's fundamental viewpoint and policy on the religious question, to maintain close relationships with the mass of religious believers, and to consult on equal terms with persons in religious circles in order to cooperate and work together."

(3) "All patriotic religious organizations should follow the Party's and government's leadership. Party and government cadres in turn should become adept in supporting and helping religious organizations to solve their own problems. They should not monopolize or do things these organizations should do themselves. Only in this way can we fully develop the positive

characteristics of these organizations and allow them to play their proper role and enable them, within constitutional and lawful limits, to voluntarily perform useful work. Thus they can truly become religious groups with a positive influence, and can act as bridges for the Party's and government's work or winning over, uniting with and educating persons in religious circles."

At present there are still individual locales where these conditions are not met. Everything (including those things that are properly the affairs of religion itself) is under the control of the cadres. These cadres do not understand religion, do not understand the thoughts and feelings of religious believers and do not respect religious traditions. People in religious circles dare say nothing and so these cadres act in many ways which are injurious to religious believers and force them into the arms of bad elements and enemies, causing patriotic religious groups to lose many of the masses.

For example, in some places "patriotic pledges," "Eight Not-Alloweds," or "Ten Not-Alloweds," are perpetrated under false use of the name of religious groups. This is extremely unfavorable to uniting believers around patriotic religious bodies. Forcing such things that lack a mass base upon patriotic religious bodies can only cause believing masses to look down upon persons in patriotic religious circles. A quick end should be made of these practices. Of course, if these pledges contain no anti-religious content or language, if believers have been consulted and are happy to accept them, that is, if they have a mass base, then that is another story.

China's enemies overseas says that our religions are officially run and some ultra-leftist persons within China think that is the way it should be. They claim that people in religious circles should not be allowed to be in charge of their religion, for only then can the Party lead. This is the legacy the Cultural Revolution. The leadership of the Party consists in communicating the Party's correct line and policies to the masses; it is leadership with a mass base which is thoroughly implemented by reserving to the masses their duties and rights.

Some "leaders" in religious circles do not try to represent the legal rights and interests of those circles. They know how to curry favor, they seem to act on whatever is said and are very willing to accept bad leadership, Then, they cannot act as bridges. Rather they increase the estrangement from the Party and cause the cadres to be isolated. If cadres want to unite the believers, they should not despise religious leaders who love religion, nor should they blindly welcome and depend on religious leaders who do not love religion, because it is their love of religion that gives these leaders their mass base. For cadres to rely on leaders who do not love religion and distance themselves from religion-loving leaders in order to make their work easier can, in the end, only do damage to the work. There is a great need today to help church leaders not to distance themselves from the masses and to have more of a mass character.

Comrade Deng Xiaoping has said: "All levels of our leadership organs are engaged in supervising things they should have no part in; they handle them poorly or not at all. These things simply need definite regulations and can then be delegated to commercial, business or social units, allowing them to deal with such things themselves according to democratic centralism. These things could be handled very well, but bring them all to Party organs, to Central departments, and they become very difficult to handle. No one has magical power to handle such onerous and unaccustomed things. It can be said that this is one of root causes of the bureaucratism peculiar to ourselves these days." This seems appropriate to our government's reforming religious work.

Finally, I would like to say that this Document is an expression of the Party's strong resolve to implement the religious policy, but it is not the only expression.

In the recent Constitutional revision, the revisions of the article on religion are a good expression of the spirit of the Party Central Committee. As a delegate of the National People's Congress, I was also a member of the Commission on Constitutional Revision. Looking over the large amount of materials from the two years of meetings of the Commission, I find that there were many on the Commission who supported the proposal to retain the wording of the 1978 Constitution on religion ("freedom to propagate atheism"), and some of these were important cadres or well-known scholars. But the Party Central supported returning things to normal, so that as the drafts of the revised Constitution appeared, the 1978 wording on religion had been removed. The Religious Affairs Bureau under the State Council wrote to the Commission expressing support for the draft put forward by religious circles. This was in line with the spirit of the Central Committee. It is especially worth noting that a certain tone which can easily lead people to feel that religion is being discriminated against—religion may not be involved in this, religion may not be involved in that—has been eliminated. The whole process reflected the resolve of the Party to uphold truth, return things to normal, implement policy and unite with believers.

I should also point out that the Party Twelfth Plenum deleted the clause in the draft Party Constitution forbidding Party members to believe in religion. This deletion of course does not imply that the Party is in favor of Party members believing in religion, but it reflects once again the trouble the Party Central has taken to unite with the believing masses and avoid offending believers' feelings by accepting the views of religious circles.

These facts attest that, with regard to religious questions, the Party Central opposes and has overcome the errors in thinking left over from the Cultural Revolution. Many cadres in every department and district are striving to understand this spirit and to put it into practice, thereby doing well their work of uniting with the believing masses. This makes us optimistic and full of hope. It can be affirmed that Document 19, a theoretical document, will, after testing in practice, play a greater and greater role.

I look forward to your views and corrections or comments on what I have said here today.

—The Church and State, 1984

# Daring to Love
# the Church and Country

The friendship between myself and my co-worker, Huang Peiyong, began during the War of Resistance against Japan when we were both involved in Christian student work in the Shanghai Student Christian Union (a union of the YMCAs, YWCAs and other organizations of Christian students in the more than thirty secondary and tertiary educational institutions in the city). We got along very well, frequently walking home together from our Shanghai Union headquarters (then in the YWCA Student Division at 999 Bubbling Well Road). He was studying at Shanghai University and I had graduated from St. John's not long before and was serving as a Student Secretary in the YMCA. Later he went to the interior.

We were next together in Shanghai a few years after Liberation. He was working then in the Student Division of the National YMCAs, where he was assistant to the Director, Mr. Jiang Wenhan. I worked first at the Shanghai Christian Literature Society and later at Nanjing Theological Seminary. Peiyong and I kept in close touch all along.

I think Peiyong's greatest contribution to Chinese Christianity was in the area of theological construction. In the early 1950s, there were two extreme and opposing trends in Chinese Christianity. One believed that God had already retreated from (or been pushed out of) the world he created, that the world now belonged to Satan and that all that was good in the world was merely an illusion created by Satan to tempt people. Christ's sacrifice on the cross was meant only to save the few who believed in him, to enable them to escape the eternal flames of hell. Christians and non-Christians formed two opposing camps with nothing in common and no common language. The other believed that the 1949 Liberation and the founding of the People's Republic of China meant the realization of the gospel of Christ in China and the coming of the Kingdom. Christ was the revolutionary proletariat and the apostolic church was communism in embryo. The aim of the church on earth lay in moving people to live by the Sermon on the Mount and sacrificing themselves for others. In this way the Kingdom of Heaven would spread across the earth. These two trends in thinking were opposed to each other, but were united in leading many Christians to become disappointed in the church, leaving it and finding their way elsewhere.

Starting from his concern for the truth of the Bible and his zeal for the nation, Peiyong could find no way to commend the first trend. As for the second, he felt deeply that it was a politicization of Christian faith which should not be and which was not in line with the Bible. It was not something a believer could accept. In that period, many co-workers feared both the left and the right and frequently lamented "the difficulties of self-propagation," and did not dare to raise much biblically-based criticism of these two trends. Faced with these two errors, Peiyong, starting from biblical teaching, raised persuasive views through preaching, lecturing and writing, safeguarding Christian faith theologically, so that it would not become distorted. He helped the mass of believers both to dare to love the church and to dare to love the country. When he found misinterpretation of scripture, he corrected it, bringing relief to many Christians who felt as if they had laid down a heavy load and could join in the Three-Self Patriotic Movement with easy hearts.

At that time, some people only highlighted politics and ignored the necessity of theological construction, even to the point of saying that Chinese Christianity did not need theology. Peiyong had a pertinent argument which is not out of date even today: Theological exploration cannot take the place of political thinking, but theological exploration can return distorted faith to its correct way and ensure that new things and new ideas not become obstacles to Christians. The role this played cannot be easily ignored.

Just when there was plenty of scope in the church for Peiyong's talents, he left this world. We cannot understand why this happened. Luckily, the number of those in our church has not been falling, but growing with the vitality of new life. In this, Peiyong can find comfort.

—On the 30th Anniversary of the Death of Huang Peiyong,
September, 1992

☙

# LET US WORK FOR THE REUNIFICATION OF CHINA

A s all the people of China, including those of Taiwan, were enjoying the Spring Festival, Jiang Zemin, Secretary General of the Chinese Communist Party and President of China, contributed to the people's happiness when he issued an important statement on a question of concern to everyone, that of the reunification of the motherland across the Taiwan straits.

In order to develop relations across the straits, and promote the course of peaceful unification of the motherland, this important statement by Jiang Zemin further expounded the basic guiding principle of "peaceful unification; one country two systems" put forward by Comrade Deng Xiaoping. In reaffirming the prerequisite of one China, he put forward a whole series of new policies on several important issues, making a special point of showing care and consideration for the Taiwan authorities and people of every sector in Taiwan, with a complete lack of condescension and with extreme tolerance and magnanimity. His forbearance in dealing with such profound contradictions is an example to the whole world.

My attention was especially drawn to the fact that Secretary General Jiang proposed first of all to formally conclude the hostilities between the two sides, undertake negotiations and come to an agreement. This is an attitude of seeking truth from facts, a step which Chinese at home and abroad and peace-loving people the world over would warmly support. Let there be no intention of using military means to break the stalemate between the two sides. We want the two sides to negotiate from positions of equality, put down their arms, and improve relations. People of good will cannot fail to perceive the sincerity in this. With such sincerity, no difficulty is insurmountable.

Taking this step creates an atmosphere for negotiations for peaceful reunification. Negotiations for peaceful reunification are by no means a case of the large oppressing the small or the strong the weak. The important thing is to speak frankly and sincerely, so that there can be a common effort to arrive at solutions acceptable to both sides. Of course, this is a situation that has to develop over many years and I dare not imagine that it will be easy for the two sides to come to a common understanding. But speaking with one another is always better than not speaking.

Jiang Zemin also welcomed all political parties and people from all sectors in Taiwan to exchange views with us on relations across the straits and peaceful reunification. This means that both the parties to and the scope of discussion have been enlarged. As a member of the religious sector, I feel I can say that those of us in religious circles are in agreement with Secretary General Jiang's statement. We support the proposal and we welcome those in religious circles on both sides of the straits to have more frequent and broader exchanges.

Secretary General Jiang made a special point of expressing his opposition to Taiwan independence. As a Chinese Christian, I particularly want to say something about this.

Every Chinese knows, from kindergarten or Primary One on, that Taiwan is Chinese territory and that it is an unalterable principle that Taiwan return to the motherland. Taiwan independence is an unwarranted proposition. Taiwan Christians, including some very influential church leaders and clergy, frequently express their hope for early peaceful reunification of the motherland. These are the sentiments of our own flesh and blood compatriots, who are also our brothers and sisters in Christ. But there are also today forces among Taiwan Christians promoting Taiwan independence, who are even now working for entry to the United Nations under the name "the nation of Taiwan." A certain American denomination supports them, even saying, "Taiwan was an independent country in the 19th century." We Chinese Christians, whether on the mainland or in Taiwan, must be on guard against the plan to split the nation into "one China, one Taiwan." We oppose Taiwan independence. Informed persons in international Christian circles sympathize with the position of the China Christian Council on the Taiwan issue, and for this we are deeply grateful.

There is a story of how a rich man in ancient Israel divided his land between his sons as he was dying, giving the eastern fields to one and the western fields to the other. At harvest time, the elder son, thinking of the needs of his younger brother's family, and the younger son, thinking of the needs of the elder brother's family, set out separately on the same evening to walk in the direction of the other's place, each carrying a great deal of grain. They collided in the darkness, spilling their grain upon the ground and embracing each other. When people later heard this story, they said, "How beautiful it is when brothers live together in harmony." This remark can still be found in the Bible today. According to legend, the place where the two brothers embraced was where later generations built the Holy City of Jerusalem. The "salem" in the name Jerusalem means peace. It is my fondest hope that all the problems across the straits can be readily solved and that those on either side can, as in the legend, embrace one another.

—Statement at the Meeting of Religious Leaders to Study Secretary General Jiang Zemin's Speech on Peaceful Reunification of China Beijing, March 7, 1995

## ହେ

# THE INFLUENCE OF JAPANESE AGGRESSION ON CHURCH AND STATE

On August 15, 1945, the Japanese Empire surrendered and the Chinese war of resistance ended in victory. Chinese soldiers fought heroically through the war against the massacres inflicted by the Japanese Imperial Army. This extreme tragedy for the Chinese people was unparalleled in human history. In terms of our own history, the eight-year war of resistance against Japan was like a big school for us Chinese, waking us up and transforming us.

Before the war broke out, I attended middle school and university in a church-run university in the International Settlement in Shanghai. It is difficult to believe it today, but there was actually discussion among some of my classmates about the relative merits of China being taken over by various countries. Some preferred the United States, others England, and a few said it might as well be Japan. Hitler had taken power by then and some said Germany would be best. Then the war with Japan broke out and the political atmosphere in the school rapidly underwent a huge change. Not a few classmates moved to Yenan, many joined the New Fourth Army in northern Jiangsu or the Huainan area and got involved in resistance work. This transformed them utterly and many joined the Party.

Lenin said, "Revolution is necessary because there is no other way to overthrow the ruling classes, but also because the class which overthrows the ruling class can only purge itself in the midst of revolution and only then build a new foundation for society." Applying this to our own history, I think we can say that the war of resistance against Japan was necessary not only because there was no other way to overthrow the rule of the Japanese imperialism, but also because the strength to overthrow Japanese imperialism had to be cleansed of impurities in the midst of the war in order to prepare itself to establish a new China.

Within Christianity, as in other social groups, there were some progressive people who joined the revolution and some backward people and reactionaries, who became traitors. During the eight years of the war, Bishop T.K. Shen in Xian and Bishop Zheng Hepu in Kaifeng provided safe houses for Communists and others traveling there. Bishop Shen received and protected group after group of young students on their way to Yenan. Under the influence of these two bishops, the Anglican Bishop of Hong Kong, R.O. Hall, came to sympathize with the resistance, assisting guerillas in Guangdong. It was a pastor who accompanied the journalist Edgar Snow from Shanghai to Yenan. I know at least one foreign missionary who was in China during the war of resistance against the Japanese and during the War of Liberation, who used her legal status to transport medicine to the Eighth Route Army. And I have personally seen a letter signed by Comrade Dong Biwu inviting the Anglican Church of China [Chung Hua Sheng Kong Hui] to open up work in the liberated areas. In many cities in occupied areas and areas under KMT rule, the YMCAs, YWCAs and churches made activities possible and provided legal cover for progressive mass organizations and individuals. I should also mention the YMCAs' service work to soldiers and the Youth Singing Movement for National Salvation initiated by Mr. Liu Liangmo. True, these things were not universal and most were undercover, but today they should serve as the legacy of a fine Christian tradition, which we should admire and study.

From these facts we can see that political alliance while reserving differences in matters of faith was already a principle of the Communist Party and liberated areas during the war of resistance. We can also see how well and how successfully this United Front principle was carried out. Bishops Shen and Zheng were unwavering Anglicans in matters of faith and they supported the war of resistance, opposed the dictatorship of Chiang Kai-shek and the KMT, and supported the united government proposed by the Communist Party and democratic unity. At the time, the Christian with the most foresight, unafraid of violence, who led the masses of youth on the path of democracy and national salvation was Mr. Y. T. Wu. Mr. Wu later founded the Christian Three-Self Patriotic Movement. All these facts illustrate that religious faith does not necessarily oppose the revolutionaries' principles. All of are in gradual process of acquiring a more adequate worldview.

Goethe said, "The tree of life is ever green." This seeking the common ground while reserving differences—the principle of the United Front—has been maintained today and is an extremely precious tradition. It is the evergreen tree of life. Recently the CPPCC promulgated three points: political consultation, democratic supervision and political participation and discussion, and these, too, are heirs of this precious tradition of seeking the common ground while reserving differences.

Today we commemorate the 50th anniversary of victory in the war of resistance against Japan. We know that the United Front is one of the three magic weapons that made this victory possible. We must stress our historical experience, and clearly recognize who our friends are in this great socialist enterprise. We need to do more propaganda for the united front, for ethnic unity, for political unity, for mutual respect in matters of faith and for seeking the common ground while reserving differences. We must apply this principle fully in religious work as in all work, thoroughly root out oppression and bias against religion and unenlightened phenomena among religious believers. All this will benefit our socialist enterprise. We must cherish this seeking the common ground while reserving differences tradition of the united front, safeguard it and let its light spread so that people everywhere will know that this is socialist democracy, a higher form of democracy.

Today, as we commemorate the 50th anniversary of the world war against fascism and of the Chinese people's war of resistance against Japan, I cannot help but mention a strange phenomenon in world history, an inglorious and disgraceful state of affairs. Japanese imperialism is still distorting history today to make themselves look good by unscrupulously claiming that the Japanese were not aggressors in China and Asia. In their hands, history can be made up as one goes along to suit one's own desires. Executioners who slaughtered innocent people can be dressed up as lovely girls. They rely on might, believing that whatever they dare to say is the truth. In a recent issue of an American magazine, I read that the annual Japanese military budget is greater by far than ours in China. This tells us that in order for our grandchildren and their grandchildren to be able to live in peace, we cannot do otherwise than to oppose and prevent the resurrection of Japanese militarism. We must safeguard our peaceful lives so that they will never again be threatened by the forces of aggression.

—50th Anniversary of Victory over Japan, Beijing,
August 15, 1995

# APPENDIX

# ‰

# OPENING ADDRESS

Today, August 5, 1984, we remember the 30<sup>th</sup> anniversary of the founding of the Three-Self Patriotic Movement Committee of Protestant Churches in China. We are very happy that leading cadres from the Central United Front Department, the National People's Political Consultative Conference, the Religious Affairs Bureau of the State Council, the Association for Friendship with Peoples Overseas, the Beijing Municipal United Front Department, the Beijing Religious Affairs Office, and administrative offices of the State Council are able to join with us in these activities. Although the founder of the Three-Self Patriotic Movement, Mr. Y. T. Wu, as well as many leaders of the Movement in its early days and during this thirty-year period—for example, Bishop Robin Chen, Rev. Chen Chonggui, Dr. Du Yuqing, Rev. Xie Yongqin, President Ding Yuzhang, Dr. T. C. Chao, Rev. Cui Xianxiang, Bishop Jiang Changchuan, Rev. Jia Yuming, Rev. Tso Guishen, Rev. Wang Zhen and others—are no longer with us, we are still happy, because many of the other founders and early Three-Self leaders are with us here today.

At this morning's service of thanksgiving, I said that since the 1<sup>st</sup> century, for 2,000 years, wherever Christianity has spread to, the Three-Self issue has gone with it, even if the term "Three-Self" has not been used. Today in Africa, for example, there are many independent churches, as well as others struggling for independence, struggling to throw off the control of the "mother church." Plainly, Three-Self follows the principles of divine justice; it is a lesson history has set for the believers of every nation. Long before there was a Communist Party in China, there were people in China and overseas proposing self-government, self-support and self-propagation. Anti-China groups abroad claim that Three-Self was forced on Chinese Christians by the Communist Party. These people have studied neither the Bible nor history.

For thirty years, Three-Self has indeed received the support and encouragement of our Party, government, the media, persons in all walks of life and the broad masses of the people. Today especially, we cannot help but think of our beloved Premier Zhou Enlai, our close friends Department Head Zhang Zhiyi, Bureau Head He Chengxiang, Bureau Head Xiao Xianfa, Bureau Head Qiao Liansheng, and Deputy Bureau Head Gao Shan, all of whom put forth so much effort on behalf of our work and in implementing religious policy. The Constitution stipulates that: "Religious bodies shall not be under foreign domination." This is a capsule expression of the support and encouragement Chinese Christians have received from the whole nation, top to bottom, in realizing Three-Self.

The number of Christians in China has grown, not diminished. Though there have been many twists and turns in the Three-Self path, though its work has not always been what it might or should be, it has improved. Many people who had all sorts of reservations about Three-Self now praise it, and so Three-Self has grown strong and has not weakened. The number of Christian churches and individuals internationally who commend Three-Self is growing, not diminishing.

Chinese Christianity today is not only self-governing, self-supporting and self-propagating, it is trying to be well run, well supported and to do the work of propagation well. Thus we now have the China Christian Council, which does a great deal of the work of church affairs. The task before us is enormous. We must do an even better job of being guided by the Holy Spirit, of being vessels worthy to be used by the Holy Spirit. We must do an even better job of respecting the special characteristics in matters of faith of Christians of all backgrounds. These things are necessary in order to make Chinese Christianity rich and varied, to consolidate our unity and enlarge it and to move the broad masses of believers to get involved in building the four modernizations in China, while at the same time building up the body of Christ. We must continue to bear our responsibility to do well the work of nation-building on the national and local levels, and to improve the image of Chinese Christianity before humankind.

—30th Anniversary Celebration for the Three-Self Patriotic Movement
of Protestant Churches in China Beijing, 1984

# Ꙇ

# Speech at the Memorial Service for Ms. Wu Yifang

*"The word became flesh, and lived among us" (John 1:14).*

W
e gather here today as co-workers, brothers and sisters in Christ, students and friends, to remember Dr. Wu Yifang.

Why do I mention the first chapter of John's Gospel? Over some thirty years ago, foreign newspapers carried varying reports of Dr. Wu: It was said that she was not in her right mind, or that she had lost her freedom, or had committed suicide. A few years ago, they reported that she had abandoned her faith and renounced Christ. I once made a special point of asking her whether she had renounced her faith in Christ. Her reply was that having seen all manner of Christianity, in China and overseas, she felt that there were many forms of Christianity she could not accept. "I feel further and further from all these forms," she said. "You could say I have abandoned them, but I believe in the Christ of the first chapter of the Gospel of John, I am growing closer to that Christ and my Christianity is the Christianity of the first chapter of John."

I think that many Christians in China have had a similar experience in the last thirty-odd years. We have become separated from certain forms of Christianity, from some of the externals of Christianity and we do not place great importance on the non-essential things. And thereby, Jesus Christ himself has been made manifest, and has become close and real to us. The gospel of Christ is a treasure and this treasure is hidden in a vessel of clay. Gradually we have come to know that we must discern what is the treasure and what is only the clay, in order not to mistake the one for the other.

If a person can accept the Christ talked about in the first chapter of the Gospel of John, then we should say that person's faith has not diminished or shrunk; certainly it has not been abandoned. Rather, it has become greater and more profound. From the first three Gospels to John's Gospel is not a journey away from truth, but a more profound entering into truth.

In the first chapter of John, we do not see Jesus the healer of the sick, but rather the pre-existent Christ, the Word who was with the Father in the beginning, and this Word is God. This pre-existent Christ was not created but begotten and all creation was made through him. He is the origin of all truth, all goodness and all beauty. He became flesh and dwelt among us, full of grace and truth. This Christ is the heir of all things, he is the reflection of God's glory, the exact imprint of God's very being and he sustains all things by his powerful word. In order to have the ability to believe in this Christ who sustains all things, a person's view of the cosmos, of history, of life, of what it means to be human, must be greatly changed, and changed to be closer and closer to Christ. Many Christians in China have gone through such an experience over the last thirty years and have reached the heights of the Christology of John's Gospel. Wu Yifang was one of these. Of this Christ, we all in our own ways say with Peter, "Lord, to whom can we go? You have the words of eternal life" (John 6:68).

Dr. Wu and I have both been in Nanjing for the past thirty years and saw each other frequently. She was the President of Jinling Women's University and later served as Head of the Jiangsu Provincial Education Department, as Deputy-Governor of Jiangsu Province, as a delegate to the National People's Congress (NPC) and to the Chinese People's Political Consultative Conference (CPPCC), as Deputy-Chair of the National Association for the Promotion of Democracy and as Deputy-Chair of the Jiangsu PPCC. Because she had served in these capacities, anti-China people overseas vilified her and vilified new China. This is how I came to know and understand Wu Yifang. The pre-existent Word she was deeply convinced of created in her an upright heart and opened her mind. She was always engaged in the search for truth, was always pushing beyond herself, seeking, embracing and embodying unlimited truth, beauty and goodness. In all her positions, she served as a person of conscience, as a patriot and as one who demanded of herself at all times and in all situations that what she did benefit the people. At the same time, as a follower of this Christ, she strove always to overcome the gap between Christ and the people through her own actions, so to enable more people to change their views of Christ and approach Christ. She did not speak a lot about Christ, but her concrete words and actions tore down the walls separating the people from Christ, gave the people a better impression of Christ and shortened the distance between Christ and the people. Isn't this too spreading the gospel? Isn't this witnessing?

Let me give an example. When the Gang of Four was in power, the wording of the clause in the Constitution on religion was very unfair. On the positive side, it said that citizens had freedom of religion; on the negative side, it not only said there was freedom not to believe in religion, but postulated the freedom to propagate atheism. Our Ms. Wu was extremely angry with those people who remained unwilling to change this wording after the fall of the Gang of Four. She felt that in the country as a whole, there was plenty of freedom to propagate atheism, so there was no need for the Constitution to mention it. She also felt that freedom of religion naturally implied freedom not to believe in religion; to express the opposite was unnecessary and to do so would only serve to make religious believers unhappy. There is no need to belabor the point. Ms. Wu's arguments were always fair and reasonable, interesting and convincing on a popular level. When she heard that the Head of the Religious Affairs Bureau under the State Council, Qiao Liansheng, had written to the NPC Committee on Constitutional Revision expressing his support of its proposal that "the freedom not to believe in religion and the freedom to propagate atheism" be deleted, she was extremely happy. Later when the NPC formally adopted this Constitution, Ms. Wu was especially satisfied with the wording of the Thirty-sixth Article on religion, saying that it was better than she had expected.

Looking back at Wu Yifang's life, this episode seems to be both an expression of her patriotism and of her love for the church. She exerted herself on behalf of democracy and the rule of law in China, and worked to create conditions for the witness of the church.

We should not limit our view of witness to a narrow understanding, as if only preaching about Jesus as the Lord of salvation to non-believers qualified. Keeping silent when we should open our mouths is bad, but silent witness is also witness and is also pleasing to God. Fighting for a good Constitution, working for just causes in our nation, improving the image of the church and making it pleasing to the people, causing people to be more willing to hear the gospel the church is preaching—all this is in the nature of evangelism, because all this prepares the way of the Lord. This is a great revelation we can get from the example of Wu Yifang.

Dr. Wu was ninety-three when she died. She worked her whole life and never retired. She had to spend her last two years in the hospital, but she did not stop working. Many people came to her hospital room to consult with her and she often asked to be temporarily discharged from hospital in order to attend meetings.

After Wu Yifang died, a memorial meeting was held in Nanjing and it was packed. The eulogy mentioned that she was a Christian, a leader of the Three-Self Movement, and messages of condolence from the Three-Self Patriotic Movement Committee of Protestant Churches in China, the China Christian Council and church groups overseas were read. The newspapers also reported that she was a Christian. Is this not a good thing? This is witness. That a person of high character can be called a Christian—such a person has already done excellent work in preparing the way of the Lord. Preparing the way of the Lord and spreading God's word are both excellent forms of witness.

Wu Yifang spread love among the people her whole life. She had no immediate family members, but I was deeply touched to find so many people in tears at her memorial service. Many of them had been her students. She was a very well loved person. Many of those who cried did not know the Christ of the first chapter of John's Gospel as she did, but this Christ had an impact on them through Wu Yifang. We need to be aware of this. Revelation 14 says that those who die in the Lord rest from their labors and their deeds follow them. Wu Yifang's deeds followed her around the world and all of us can find the effects of what she did in ourselves. We must thank God for the work of Dr. Wu Yifang.

A few years ago I wrote an essay memorializing Mr. Y. T. Wu. I would like to use my closing words from that essay to close my talk today:

Neither the traditional Chinese idea of "a good death at the end of a long life," nor the Western "rest in peace" can adequately mark the conclusion of the kind of life and witness exemplified by Dr. Wu Yifang. I would rather say that today, in a light that is much closer to God, Dr. Wu continues her quest for truth, continues the practice of truth, continues her prayer, service and worship and continues to be our co-worker, helping us in our efforts.

—Memorial Service, Shanghai, January 19, 1986

## THE TREE OF LIFE IS EVER GREEN

Today we gather before God to remember our beloved colleague, Bishop Zheng Jianye. The Scripture verse I have chosen is one which is frequently used at funerals or memorial services, and I think it is especially appropriate to read it today. Bishop Zheng's life was indeed a life of labor and his labors will continue to bear fruit.

I met Zheng Jianye in 1937, fifty-four years ago. I also knew his father, Bishop Zheng Hepu, and many of his brothers and sisters. During these fifty-four years, there were periods when I saw Jianye daily and others when I did not see him for years at a time. But no matter whether I saw him or not, he knew my thoughts and I his. When we were together, we never stopped talking. In 1949, he and his wife were in Canada while I was there, and I went to see them. We talked together for several days. At times we had different views, but we understood each other extremely well.

In the early days of our friendship, he was a student at Soochow University, a very well-read young man with a wealth of ideas, and in this respect he never changed. He would gather information, gain an understanding of the circumstances, think through the problems and explore the issues to form his opinions. This was his consistent pattern, whether in the Shanghai Christian Students Union and the Student

Fellowship we organized in the Shanghai Community Church in 1942, or when studying abroad, in the Henan Anglican Church or the Anglican Church of China, in the National Committee of the Three-Self Patriotic Movement of the Protestant Churches in China or in the China Christian Council. He was extremely good at cutting through the mass of routine and raising issues to the theoretical level. This enabled him to get twice the result with half the effort.

One of Zheng Jianye's special talents was his ability to start from practical facts and concrete situations and arrive at a universal. This is seeking truth from facts. He most disliked glib slogans delivered in a loud voice. Marx once said, "The traditions of our dead forefathers entangle the minds of the living like a nightmare." If I look at the lives of my friends, Zheng Jianye was able to cast off the fetters of tradition and gain freedom of thought. He was familiar with ecclesiology and also with the hearts and minds of the masses of Christians. He was never one to force things or people. Several years ago, one of the leaders from the Central Committee once said to me, "You people in the church leadership must never do things which the ordinary Christians do not like." What warm concern such sincere advice shows for our church. It is an apt description of Bishop Zheng. I cannot think of a single time he ever advocated anything in the work of the church which Christians would be displeased with or oppose. Because of this, he captured people's hearts and there was much good feeling toward him among his colleagues and fellow Christians. He always began with practicalities and proposed appropriate measures. He never made high-sounding suggestions which would have a deleterious effect.

There is one important principle behind our Chinese Christian unity: In matters of faith and worship, Christians from various backgrounds all respect one another. We call this "mutual respect." Zheng Jianye was tireless in thinking of ways to enlarge this unity to its fullest extent to achieve mutual respect. I remember one meeting of the National Chinese Christian Conference in the 1950s when, in order to unite with one or another denomination, after arguing and pleading, he even began to cry during the session. Later someone asked him, "What were the feelings which caused you to do this?" Quite clearly they were love for country and love for church, because unity was one of our nation's hopes for us, as well as the prayer of Christ. Not long before Jianye was taken ill, he proposed seven principles of Christian unity which are still frequently mentioned today.

During the past ten years, we have been consistent in stressing that the church should be well managed, self-run and well run, self-propagated and well propagated. It is worth my mentioning here that Zheng Jianye was one of the earliest to commit himself to making the church well run. He spoke of it with me when he returned to the Henan Diocese of the Anglican Church of China. It was clear to me that he had come forward with the aspiration of achieving the difficult task of making the Henan Anglican Church well run. He helped Bishop Robin Chen to go to each and every diocese, to organize study groups, to reorganize diocese, to consecrate Bishops and to get the Anglican Church back on the right course.

Zheng Jianye was not only a student of theology, but of social science. Let me give an example. Marx, speaking of German thinkers, once made a remark the gist of which is that criticism of religion is the prerequisite for all criticism. There are people in China who think that then of course we should do likewise, that in China there should be criticism of religion on a grand scale. Jianye wrote an extremely persuasive essay in which he brought much evidence to bear in order to illustrate that things from Germany could not be taken wholesale into China, because China is not Germany. In China, it is not religion which functions as religion does in Germany, but rather several thousand years of feudal thinking and the patriarchal clan system. This alone is the "nightmare that entangles the minds of the living." So in China the prerequisite of all other criticism is criticism of this system. Another example: A few years ago, together with colleagues from social scientific circles, Bishop Zheng co-edited the volume *A Dictionary of Religion*. He maintained a seeking truth from facts approach throughout, opposing the argument that religion is opium. Following Jianye's reasoned approach, we find in the introduction and entries in that volume no mention of opium as the nature of religion. For the times, this was truly an impressive feat.

I should not speak too long. But I want to say this: For fifty-four years, Zheng Jianye was my true friend and mentor; even more, he was my teacher. I believe many of his co-workers, fellow Christians, and friends share my feelings.

When we were young, we never thought of death; we knew only the joy of life which filled our hearts. It's different now. Our loved ones, those in the same generation, are dying one by one. Where do we find consolation? All that God has made is good, especially people. As Shakespeare said, "What a piece of work is man." God is love, therefore, it cannot be that it is the fate of all these good things and good people to be obliterated. As on that day when Christ took up several loaves of bread and a few fish, so he will accept them, bless them, give thanks to his father in heaven and break them. And in his hands they will be changed, they will multiply and will be offered up to God.

In the Communion liturgy of the Anglican Church there is the following prayer: "And we also bless thy holy Name for all thy servants departed this life in thy faith and fear; beseeching thee to give us grace so to follow their good examples, that with them we may be partakers of thy heavenly kingdom."

Death is change in life, not its end. Within the realm ruled by God's love, positively no good thing or person can be lost or destroyed. It is as Goethe said, "Dear friends, the golden tree of actual life springs ever green." Death is but the transition from one stage of life to another. In our prayers, especially in the Blessed Sacrament which our Lord Jesus established, we are in communion with each other. And this is where our comfort lies.

Let us pray: We ask the Lord's mercy, to go before us and lead us, to support us from behind, to encourage us through the example of the saints who walk before us. May our prayers hold us up. Accept the work of our weak hands, correct our errors. May they become a pleasing offering, in the name of Jesus Christ our Lord. Amen.

—Eulogy for Bishop Zheng Jianye, 1991

# IN MEMORY
# OF REV. EDWARD HEWLETT JOHNSON

It was with a heavy heart that I received the news of Rev. Ted Johnson's death via a telegram from a friend in Canada. The news occasioned many days of sorrowful reminiscences for me. His death was an irreparable loss for my family and me, for the Canadian Church, for the Chinese Church and for Canadian-Chinese friendship. The gospel of Christ is a great bridge whose span is the relationship between humankind and God and between persons. But even for Christians, with their profound belief in eternal life, death remains a chasm, an unsolvable mystery. Even the links of friendship and affection cannot join this shore with that one. I cannot help exclaiming with David: "How the mighty have fallen!" (2 Sam. 1:19).

Rev. Johnson and I were friends for over thirty years. After the Second World War, the Canadian Student Christian Movement, on the urging of Rev. Johnson and others, decided to invite a young Chinese pastor to serve as a secretary. After being introduced to them by some colleagues here, my wife and I left to take up the post in 1946. And so our friendship with Rev. Johnson began.

Ted Johnson studied mathematics and theology in his university days. During the 1930s, he had been a missionary in northeast China, and on returning to Canada, worked with the Presbyterian Church in Canada. Later he went to the United States to do Christian student work. My work as a secretary with the World Student Christian Federation frequently took me to the U.S. During that time Ted and I often worked together and frequently ate together. In 1950 my wife and I, with our son, went to live in Geneva and he came to visit. Later, we returned to China and after that we didn't hear from him. In 1956, we went to London. He happened to be there, too, and we were able to have a heart-to-heart discussion. Afterwards, there was another long period without contact, during which he served a term as Moderator of the General Assembly of the Presbyterian Church in Canada. He also visited China five times, making a trip to see us in Nanjing each time.

On the first visit in 1972, his wife Kitty came with him. On another visit he brought his children, who had been born in China, and I was happy to be able to accompany them traveling the Yangtze River from Wuhan to Nanjing.

The changes in Ted's attitude toward new China over time were all quite sensible and rational. He once told me that for a very long period of time, he was influenced by the anti-China propaganda appearing in foreign newspapers and periodicals, especially essays with pretensions to scholarship—he took them all for the truth. This propaganda led him to believe that the Chinese Communist Party was like a great unreasoning scourge and that new China was a prison without a single redeeming feature. The China he loved was the ancient China, now past history. It was with such an attitude that he suddenly discovered in 1956 in London, that my wife and I were still alive and, after talking with us, that our life and work went on as normal. This really "shook" him, he felt he "had had the wool pulled over my eyes," and he decided that he would undertake to read the book on the new China by his uncle, Hewlitt Johnson, the Dean of Canterbury. That was the first I knew of their being uncle and nephew. Thus, his concern for China was rekindled and he began to study it anew, making a conscious effort to throw off many of his former biases and developing goodwill and friendship for it.

When a Canadian journalist assigned to Beijing wrote an untrue article about China, Ted Johnson, based on what he had heard and seen on his several visits, wrote a refutation contrasting China new and old. In order to introduce the new China to Christians in North America and promote friendship between the peoples, he joined with several other Canadian church leaders to establish the Canada China Program of the Canadian Council of Churches. It was this organization which, with the support of Ted Johnson, Bill Smaley and others friendly to China, published literature and organized all sorts of meetings, particularly the large-scale international gathering of Protestants and Catholics held in Montreal in October last year, called "A New Beginning." To show our support, Chinese Protestants and Catholics sent a ten-person delegation to the meeting. This meeting was much more ecumenical and representative than similar meetings held in recent years, with many church leaders from the Third World present. It was a meeting where the people and churches of new China gained the sincere support of friends and discovered from them how we might do better. It was a precious time of sharing in the Lord and the fruit of many years of work on Rev. Johnson's part. It was most appropriate that he delivered the welcoming remarks at the meeting.

The change in Ted Johnson tells us that anti-China propaganda is not to be feared. Like other forms of misinformation, it is a paper tiger that will not stand the test of facts. China has many problems; we have never claimed that it is perfect. But some people, whatever their motives, under the guise of "concern" for China or on the pretense of helping people to "pray" for China, take the slightest fact and blow it out of proportion, painting new China as completely beyond the pale. Though this might seem to "succeed" for a time, twisting of facts cannot produce truth, and the end result is simply to do harm to one's own position.

Ted Johnson's turnabout also tells us something about missionaries. Any missionary who came to China with the purpose of benefiting the Chinese people, has come away from a visit to the new China feeling there is no cause for antipathy. They may misunderstand the new China for a time, but when they contrast the new and old China and see the progress that has been made—the elimination or alleviation of people's sufferings—their attitudes change. Seeing the facts, such people will be happy for the people of China and will thank God. Their wish for new China will be that its people quickly cast off backwardness and continue to advance. There are other former China missionaries like Ted Johnson who dare to change and we very much welcome their friendship.

In 1972, during the Cultural Revolution, when Rev. Johnson and his wife accepted the invitation of the Association for Friendship with People Overseas and made that trip to China, they asked to visit us in Nanjing. We were together for two days. I introduced what I knew about the situation of Christianity in China at the time—no churches, no seminaries, no pastors, no baptism, no feast days, a lack of facilities able to accommodate larger numbers for worship. Just we Christians, primarily family members, meeting in small groups in our homes to pray, read the Bible, encourage one another, pastor and support one another. Because Ted had been under the impression that Christianity had been completely eradicated from the soil of China, his joy on hearing what I had to say was beyond my expectations. He quoted the words of Jesus: "For where two or three are gathered in my name, I am there among them."

On later visits, after the fall of the Gang of Four, he was happy to see the policy of religious freedom reinstated, more and more churches opening and church activities being carried on openly, rather than underground. He listened carefully to the lofty aspirations of Chinese Christians to build up the church under the guidance of the Holy Spirit, and it made him very happy. He felt that since liberation had brought new life to the Chinese people, the church should break out of its rut, reflect on new theology, experiment with new models, open new paths: These were necessary for the growth of the gospel in China and represented a contribution Chinese Christians could make to the spiritual riches of the churches of the Third World, and to all the churches of the world. At the same time, only an independent, self-governed Chinese Church would know how best to benefit from other churches. Ted Johnson was one of the fiercest opponents of those overseas who disregard the independence of the Chinese people and the stand of the Chinese Church, pretending to be concerned about the gospel in China while serving their own ends.

I was aware for some time that Ted had heart trouble. On his last visit to Nanjing, we had him try Chinese heart medicine. At the Montreal meeting, he already seemed quite feeble, though he was as relaxed and happy as ever. As the Chinese delegation prepared to return to China, his deep affection led him to make a special trip from Toronto in eastern Canada to Vancouver in the west, where we spent two happy days together, at the end of which he bid us farewell one by one. I did not understand it well enough at the time, but looking back now I see that this trip was a wonderful urging of the Holy Spirit, telling us that our unity in the Lord with Ted Johnson was eternal. It was also a prayer for eternal unity between the Chinese and Canadian people and Chinese and Canadian Christians, that they might go forward together.

Let me close this memorial with the words John heard from heaven:

And I heard a voice from heaven saying, "Write this: Blessed are the dead who from now on die in the Lord." "Yes," says the Spirit, "they will rest from their labors, for their deeds will follow them."

—In Memory of Rev. Edward Hewlett Johnson, 1980

# A FRIEND REMEMBERED

One calls many people "friends" in life, but true, close friends are rare. It is difficult to say how my close friendship with Luo Zhufeng came about, but in general it grew through sharing the same intellectual pursuits, through discussing work and research.

In the early 1950s, when several of our seminaries joined to form Nanjing Union Theological College, the Chinese Christian Three-Self Reform Movement (later the Three-Self Patriotic Movement) Committee (with Mr. Y. T. Wu as Chairperson) sent me to work in that Seminary. Mr. Luo was then Bureau Head of the East China Religious Affairs Bureau and was very concerned about the work at the Seminary. He was particularly interested in the impact of politics on theology and the role theology played in believers' political attitudes. We had a great deal to discuss. He came to Nanjing and stayed in the Seminary many times, and we would drink coffee together in the evenings, talking late into the night. I gained a great deal from our discussions.

In those days there was a Three-Self Reform Movement Committee on campus which had been set up in the old Nanjing Seminary days and which arrogated all power to itself, taking over leadership in everything—the principal, the dean and so on, were purely nominal. It resembled a political power or a party or a church, though it was none of these and those in charge had little understanding of theology. The people were very critical of it, but no one dared to speak openly. Seeing this state of affairs, Comrade Luo suggested a reordering of relationships. He felt that Three-Self was a mass organization and should return to its original role. The affairs of the Seminary should by rights be dealt with by the principal and the school affairs committee. We made these adjustments and things ran much more smoothly. It became possible for the staff to realize its potential. With the restoration of order after the Cultural Revolution, we Christians in China stressed running the church well and organized the China Christian Council, separate from the TSPM. In 1988, we also proposed a reordering of that relationship, following the same spirit we had in the Seminary earlier.

One thing which set Comrade Luo apart from most of the cadres involved in the government's religious work was his ability to take theology seriously. Some had a very slapdash approach, seeing all religion as reactionary, as opiate, so the more reactionary it was, the more narcotic its nature and all that could be done was to let it self-destruct. Theology could not be taken seriously and did not merit study. Luo Zhufeng never subsumed all religion and theology under the heading of "reactionary" or "opiate." This was because he sought truth from facts. He saw many, like Y. T. Wu and Rev. Huang Peiyong, whose theology helped believers to cast off whatever obstacles their faith created and enabled them to embark on the patriotic and socialist path. He also saw that others' theology caused believers to oppose Communism and new China. How could both be called "opiate"? At Comrade Luo's urging, I began to study the fundamentalist theology that dominates Chinese Christianity, while continuing to keep up with international theological trends.

Premier Zhou Enlai once met with the leading comrades of the Religious Affairs Bureau to discuss the necessity for careful study of religion. He noted that it was especially important to read the Christian Bible and to understand the special characteristics of all denominations. I, too, attended that meeting. I feel deeply that Luo Zhufeng's approach to religious work is that advocated by Premier Zhou.

During the Cultural Revolution, the rebel factions scrutinized the theological essays I had published in the *Nanjing Theological Review* and labeled me "anti-atheist." They went to Luo Zhufeng for corroboration.

He told them that the principal of a Party school would naturally write essays promulgating Marxism, so why did they expect the principal of a Christian seminary to write essays promulgating atheism? They could not answer him. At that time he was seriously attacked himself and set up his bed in a cramped stairwell. This became his home. When I heard this, I was very moved. Here was a person in the midst of troubles who would risk his own neck in order to uphold the Party's religious policy and protect a friend of the Party—compare that to someone who, in order to protect him or herself, or to gain favor and advancement, would throw stones at a fallen comrade. How great the one and how insignificant the other.

Luo Zhufeng and I lived far apart and saw each other only rarely, sometimes not for months at a time. But whenever we spoke, it was as if we were continuing yesterday's conversation—we could truly speak what was in our hearts. His death leaves an irreparable gap in my life.

—In Memory of Luo Zhufeng, 1997

# PREFACE TO THE *DICTIONARY OF BIBLICAL LITERATURE*

The Christian Bible is an extremely influential book. It has been translated, entirely or in part, into over 1,000 languages. In China in the last decade, the Amity Printing Press in Nanjing has printed over ten million Chinese Bibles. In addition to this they have printed Bibles in numerous ethnic minority languages. Just as one cannot have a deep knowledge of Chinese culture without studying Buddhism, one cannot understand Western philosophy, history, literature, language and art without studying the Bible. Engels greatly appreciated the study of the Bible. Based on his analysis of the research of 19th-century Christian scholars and materials in the New Testament, he wrote three important essays on the revolutionary nature of early Christianity. In his Peasant

War in Germany, describing the church splitting up in the turmoil of the late Middle Ages, he expressed special appreciation for the biblical exegesis of Anabaptist theologians such as Muenzer, who called for and motivated the grassroots masses to become involved in the struggle against feudalism. Since this is so, we cannot simplify the essence of religion and the Bible by use of the term "opiate."

The Bible is not a single book. It contains sixty-six books of varying lengths, the earliest written over 1,000 years ago B.C.E., the latest over a hundred years after Christ. It contains the stories of the Hebrew people about the origin of the world and the beginnings of humankind, including history, law, psalms, folk songs, legends, political commentaries, proverbs, letters to churches, and impassioned accounts in which religion is closely linked to patriotism.

Some people think that the Bible contains a lot of material that is not in line with current scientific views, and therefore is not worth our attention. This is a harmful view. The Bible's value does not lie in science, If we are interested in science, we can read modern scientific works; we need not go looking for scientific truths in the Bible. We would not ask of any other ancient volume that it be in line with the scientific theories of today. The Bible is not valuable for its science. But who can deny the Bible's high literary, ethical, philosophical and spiritual value? Value in these areas is not diminished by its primitive scientific views. This is the way we would approach any ancient book.

In intellectual circles in China today, an increasing number of people have cast off their repugnance toward Christianity and the Bible and become well disposed toward it. They would like to know what message the Bible has for people. But because of historical and cultural differences, reading the Bible is not as easy as reading some literary work. The *Dictionary of Biblical Literature* can help us overcome these obstacles and I welcome the publication of this Chinese edition, particularly since it is the crystallization of friendly cooperation between Chinese and American scholars.

—Preface to the *Dictionary of Biblical Literature*, 1997

ॐ

# A REVIEW OF
## *RELIGION UNDER SOCIALISM IN CHINA*

In recent years there has been a brisk growth in social science research, including research on religion. With the objective of seeking truth from facts, new ideas and viewpoints have arisen on all sides, along with very animated discussion, much livelier than our own theological discussions. Fortunately, we Christians have also been a part of this.

We should not regard the research on religion in the social sciences to be as unyielding as a piece of iron. Because of lively thinking, a healthy variety of ideas at various levels has appeared. For example, there clearly are two different approaches among those doing research on religion. One is only willing to see the generalities of religious phenomena, always drawing a line between religion and non-religion, and taking religion as nothing but religion, like a piece of iron: it is singular, unitary, with little or nothing in common with non-religion. This approach, makes no careful distinctions, saying that "all religions are opiates," and thus prevents the discussion from going any deeper.

Other researchers have discovered that one cannot treat different religious phenomena in the same way; although all of them are religious phenomena, their social, historical, and political functions are quite different, so these researchers will not jump to conclusions about religion, feeling that specific analysis of concrete religious phenomena is essential.

Some writers ignore the differences between national cultures throughout historical periods, as well as the unique characteristics of each religion; they talk about religion in a general and abstract way, as if their theories can be the standard for understanding religion in any nation and any period of time. The present book edited by the well-known scholar Luo Zhufeng does not approach religion in this way. The title of the book is worthy of our attention. It does not discuss religion in a general way: rather, it approaches the subject of religion in China.

Nor does it discuss the topic of religious issues in China in a general way; it deals with religious issues in the socialist period in China. This book follows the best Marxist traditions, approaching religion not from a definition or concept, but from the real situation of religion in China today. Therefore, religious leaders will not feel as if the book is "scratching the boot while the foot continues to itch," nor will they feel wronged or misunderstood. This book gives a clear, theoretical presentation of the origin and purpose of the religious policy of the Chinese Communist Party in a very convincing way, a policy that is scientific rather than expedient.

Chairman Mao was strongly opposed to dogmatism, but as far as research on religion is concerned it seems extremely difficult to get rid of dogmatism. The reason may be that many religious researchers do not know even one religious believer, to say nothing of having friends among them, so how can they be sensitive to their thoughts and feelings? They build the cart behind a closed door, making contact only with books instead of religion. Since they have been told since childhood that religion is opium, and since they are quite familiar with China's disastrous experience with the Opium War, they find religion so abhorrent that they unconsciously substitute emotion for science. Another reason is that "leftists" in religious work have not been systematically criticized since rectification was begun. Even so, since the Third Plenum of the Eleventh Party Congress in 1978, the situation has changed. Many thought-provoking articles in the field of social science research have been published, most of them in scholarly journals devoted to philosophy and the social sciences published by colleges and universities. This book is a significant contribution to this research.

The book makes the following points:

(1) IT APPROACHES RELIGION AS A SOCIAL ENTITY WITH VARIOUS ELEMENTS AT DIFFERENT LEVELS, INSTEAD OF LIMITING IT TO RELIGIOUS DOGMAS ONLY
Religious doctrines are important for believers, since no church or member can speak or behave contrary to those doctrines. But this does not mean that religious believers can only do what is stipulated in those doctrines and are prohibited from doing anything not stipulated. There are many new ideas and new things in the world that religious

believers can accept and support without violating religious doctrines. This shows that there is a breadth of freedom for religious believers; but some religious researchers take it for granted that God and religion are completely authoritarian, and that religious believers can only do what religious doctrines say; so, thinking that believers are oppressed by these doctrines, they are determined to liberate them from the prison of religious dogma. They regard themselves as critics of religious dogma. For them, religious research means research and criticism of religious dogma and propagation of atheism in order to "liberate" religious believers. This is a great misunderstanding.

Several years ago someone wrote an article expressing the opinion that a religious believer will become an "idealist," therefore religious belief will make one become an "eccentric." Such a person, he said, becomes muddleheaded, taking the "physical body as the grave of the soul," and regarding the "improving of one's reasonable, material needs as the source of sin for the soul," even to the point of "closing the eyes to the colors of the world" and "closing the ears the sounds of the world," and "if it is not written in the scriptures one should not think about it," and so on. They describe believers in these simplistic terms in order to spread a fear of the dangers of religion, with the result that religious believers feel wronged and upset. The reason for this is that religious research scholars have no acquaintances among religious believers. This reminds me of what Lenin said: "It is the usual practice of a not very bright person to impose obviously foolish ideas on his enemies and then criticize them."

So let us put aside the issue of religious doctrines and ask this question: Even if there are errors in religious doctrine, would that cause believers to be always in error, looking ridiculous, accomplishing nothing, and, whatever they do, ending up in trouble? I believe Lenin would say no. Lenin knew that Leo Tolstoy was a devoted Christian and a landlord; despite his rather fanatical religious beliefs, Lenin regarded him as a "talented artist," noting that he "thoroughly criticized capitalist exploitation," "was a most sober-minded realist" who "tore off the masks of hypocrisy," and "created literary works in the top rank of world literature." Although Lenin did not believe in God, he shared a good deal of common language with the theist

Tolstoy. He did not ignore Tolstoy's contributions to literature and social struggle, or the fact that he was a talented artist, because he was a committed religious believer. This kind of broad-mindedness is praiseworthy. Religious policies based on the principles of the united front contain the same idea: A religious believer can at the same time be a patriotic socialist and member of the united front, and his religious beliefs should be respected and protected. This kind of broad-mindedness is also admirable.

The influence of religious doctrines on people's minds and behavior is after all, limited. Many scientists in ancient and modern times have been religious believers. Their religious beliefs did not prevent them from accomplishing scientific achievements; in fact, some scientists relate their scientific achievements to religious inspiration.

*Religion under Socialism in China* does not ignore the differences between the teachings of various religions, nor does it ignore the specific positions of religious doctrine in each religion, but the writers of this book do not get mired down in religious doctrine. They treat each religion as a social entity, with its doctrines, believers, sects, administrative system, principles and regulations, literature and arts, theology and history, ethics, subgroups and organizations, and opinions on contemporary social issues—and the ways in which it either contributes to or harms society. Scientific research on religion should take all these into consideration with equal emphasis.

## (2) THIS BOOK GIVES A BALANCED CRITIQUE OF THE APHORISM THAT RELIGION IS THE OPIATE OF THE PEOPLE

Some writers who only know some of the sayings of Marx but do not understand the spirit of Marxism are very likely to approach religious issues by identifying religion with opium, believing that as long as they stick to this formula all religious questions can be easily explained. They take this saying as originating with Marx, as the marrow of the Marxist viewpoint on religion, and as the succinct expression of the essential nature of religion. It seems strange, if opium is to Marx the essence of religion, how he could mention this so lightly, with no amplification. How could Marx's creative writings on religious issues consist only of this single phrase, one which was used by others both inside and outside the church before his time? Does this raise or lower Marx? Fortunately, among the social scientists doing research on religion, few are still using the theme of "religion as an opiate."

Regrettably, we cannot say that religion never functions as an opiate. As Christians, we should ask ourselves whether or not we allow religion to function as an opiate in ourselves. We remember that when some compassionate persons offered Jesus wine mixed with gall to numb his feeling of pain while he suffered on the cross, he refused it after tasting it.

Religion functions in many ways in society; religion can even mobilize and unify people for revolutionary struggle. This was confirmed by Engels. Only one of the functions of religion is that of an opiate or anesthetic; that is not the only function, nor is it the main function under all circumstances. Therefore, it is quite inadequate to define religion as an opiate.

Dom Helder Camera, the retired Catholic Archbishop of Recife, Brazil, once said, "When I give bread to the poor, I am called a saint; but when I ask why can't the poor have bread, I am called a Communist." Such preaching is very effective in exposing the darkness of society and awakening people's conscience. Is not this function, which arouses people, the opposite of opium, which puts them to sleep? His words, which "raise a reasonable demand for improving the material life of people," certainly do not "create the reasonable need to improve material life as the source of sin for the soul." Can the religion that raises serious questions, as Camera's does, such as, "Why can't the poor have bread?" and "What kind of party is the Communist Party?" and "Why do people oppose the Communist Party?" be identified with a religion that functions as an opiate, demanding that the people submit to oppression and willingly accept the blows and kicks of their enemies?

Our people's liberation movement, socialist construction movement, and Protestant Three-Self Movement, and the work of Dom Helder Camera all have the same goal, which is human justice. We should oppose the narcotic function of religion and educate religious believers to be clear-minded.

As for the concept that religion is an opiate, I do not think it is a significant theoretical breakthrough, though somewhat suggestive;

which is to say, it does not provide a breakthrough for resolving theoretical questions. One can say that it is also "a flower which bears no fruit."

*Religion under Socialism in China* does not bog down in a discussion of religion as an opiate. The editors raise three points on this question in the closing chapter of the book: 1. "Opium" is a metaphor for the negative function of religion in the particular context of a class society; 2. The historical function of religion differs in different times and social contexts, and cannot be indiscriminately defined as "opium"; 3. Even less can the function of religion under socialism be described as "opium."

I think that these three points are scientific, fair, and quite acceptable to us Christians.

### (3) THIS BOOK ACKNOWLEDGES THE ETHICAL CONTENT OF RELIGION AND HAS A POSITIVE ATTITUDE, AFFIRMING THE FUNCTION OF RELIGIOUS ETHICS FOR THE MAJORITY OF RELIGIOUS BELIEVERS UNDER SOCIALISM

All religions "admonish people to be good"—this is the most universal view of religion. It is reported by many local officials today that there is little crime in places with numerous religious believers. Religion has the function of guiding and disciplining people's behavior. But there was a time, under the negative influence of leftism, when some research scholars of religion divorced religious ethics from religious dogma in order to defame religion, claiming that religious ethics are a reflection of the people's customary behavior norms, and have nothing to do with religion; religion is only concerned with the divine-human relationship, they said, but not human relationships. One person even claims that the last six of the [Judeo-] Christian Ten Commandments deal only with ethics, and thus do not belong to religion as such. By including these six commandments, he says, religion is intruding upon ethics. Fortunately, religious teachings are not determined by this scholar, otherwise we would be left with only four commandments. It is worth reminding this writer: Is it not true that, according to historical materialism, religion itself is also the product of social productive relations?

*Religion under Socialism in China* contains absolutely no quixotic attacks like this. It maintains that different roads can lead to the same destination: "Both religious doctrine and religious ethics admonish religious believers to be good instead of bad. If they work for the good of the nation and the people, whoever they are and whatever their motivation, the results benefit socialist modernization. Religion can be in harmony with socialist society when seen from this viewpoint."

This is also an important reminder for us Christians. Christianity is a religion which lays emphasis on ethics. The Bible distinguishes between right and wrong, goodness and evil, and good and bad behavior, much of it is about how society and political life should be. But some Christians only pay attention to salvation of the individual, accusing the Christians who are also concerned with ethical behavior of having impure faith, and also saying that whose who do not distinguish between right and wrong and who do not believe in Christ in a certain way are bad. I would like to point out to them that, as Christians, they have gone to be part and parcel of those outside the church who hold leftist views.

## (4) THIS BOOK DEALS THEORETICALLY WITH THE SUBJECT OF HARMONIZING RELATIONSHIPS BETWEEN SOCIALISM AND RELIGION

During the time of leftist domination, any Marxist who spoke of harmonizing socialism with religion would have been considered guilty of [political] apostasy, while religious believers who did the same thing would have been called opportunists.

It has been more than thirty years since Liberation, and leaders of all religions in China are supporters of socialism. As for religious believers, the majority of them are working every day in socialist production. We have been informed that the proportion of Christians selected as model workers in many places is higher than those in the general population. All the religions in China have undergone many reforms, and, compared with the past, they have made great progress toward socialism; this is obvious to everyone. This is from the side of religion.

From the side of the nation, although the ruling party advocates atheism and openly expresses its nonbelief in religion, it acknowledges the rationality and legality of religion and its right to exist, and opposes any act to destroy or discriminate against religion: it only attacks counter-revolutionary sabotage and criminal activities which hide under the guise of religion, as well as all superstitious activities that do not fall within the parameters of religion and are harmful to the interests of the nation and the lives and property of the people.

How should we deal with this, since it is not a matter of who extirpates whom? We can only ask that both sides work together so that some kind of mutual accommodation can be achieved.

To put forward this task of mutual accommodation requires, on the one hand, that all religions, insofar as their own beliefs permit, step up their efforts to eliminate those things which are not compatible with socialism and to carry forward those things that are compatible with socialism; on the other hand, it requires that nonbelievers resolutely get rid of leftist influences, clean out remnant old ideas of wiping out religion, and enforce the policy to provide the essentials needed for all religions to carry on their religious affairs better.

In recent years, Protestant Christians have emphasized the Three-Self principle in order to run our churches well. We have given first priority to seeing to the spiritual needs of our members, providing what they love and giving support to our church; at the same time we have run the church in a way that is compatible with socialism so that the people [masses] will have affection for it. We know that if we only emphasize accommodation to socialism, the church will gradually give up its particularity as a church, and will be in danger of losing unity with the believers. But if it has only one goal, to run the church well, while ignoring the Three-Self patriotic principle and the need for compatibility with socialism, the church will inevitably be spurned by the people, and perceptive church members will stay away as well.

There is a new spirit abroad in the world—to replace mutual extirpation with mutual accommodation. This offers great potential for theological students to devote themselves to running the affairs of the church well, and this is a very welcome development.

(5) THIS BOOK DOES NOT EXCLUDE RELIGIOUS BELIEVERS, BUT WELCOMES THEM TO JOIN IN RESEARCH ON RELIGION AND EXPRESSES APPRECIATION FOR

## THE CONTRIBUTIONS OF RELIGIOUS BELIEVERS TO THIS RESEARCH

I mentioned earlier that some scholars who carry on research in religion do not know even one religious believer. Worse than that, some people think that research on religion can only be carried out in the absence of religious belief; they are opposed to religious believers taking part in research on religion.

Lenin said that Marxism is able to "win universal historical significance because it does not throw away the most valuable achievements of the bourgeois period; on the contrary, it absorbs all things of value accumulated throughout the development of human ideas and culture for over 2,000 years."

Before and after Marx, religious believers among natural and social scientists, as well as religious scholars, have made great contributions in the sciences. At present, those doing serious-minded research in the sciences need every valuable legacy from the past. To cut off cooperation with religious believers because of their religious faith can only be called sectarianism. We say that the kind of religious research that rejects the results of research by non-Marxist scholars, while allowing self-proclaimed Marxists to "set up a new shop," will inevitably bear no fruit. And the three essays by Engels on the early history of Christianity are sounder because of the use they make of the results of research by German Christian scholars.

As a matter of fact, when I read the works of our Marxist scholars on religion, I find that they quote the works of many scholars from both East and West; some are recognized authorities; moveover, often they are religious believers. As a result, these Marxist scholars put themselves in a ridiculous position: Religious researchers can cooperate with religious believers abroad, but not those in China!

Most of the contributors to this book are non-believers, but some are persons with religious faith who use scientific methods of research, treating religion as a social and historical phenomenon; they neither advocate nor oppose religion. From the perspective of Christian faith, we feel that this book is inadequate, especially in dealing with the reasons for the persistence of religion over time. But we have no reason to expect this to be a book for the church. Compared to other works of research on religion [published in contemporary China], I think this book is the least dogmatic, the most perceptive in its explanation of the party's policy on religion, and the most convincing in its arguments. I would like our students to know that this book deserves our serious attention.

—Foreword to *Religion Under Socialism in China,* 1988

[1] *Religion under Socialism in China,* Luo Zhufeng, ed., translated by Donald E. MacInnis and Zheng Xi'an, M. E. Sharpe, 1991.

శ్రీ

# FAREWELL REMARKS ON A VISIT TO INDIA

As our two-week visit draws to a close, we would first of all like to express our most sincere thanks to the leaders and members of the churches in India. Every moment of our visit was filled with friendship and fellowship in the Lord and hymns of praise to God rose at every place we went.

I felt deeply on this visit the greatness and high aspirations of the Indian people. Though it suffered a long period of rule from an alien country, India remains India. India dares to believe in, to love, to respect and to maintain the cultural tradition it is justly proud of. Everywhere one sees Indian women wearing the sari, a garment of dignity, beauty and long history, walking with calm confidence. This tells us that the Indian people cannot be subjugated, nor their civilization destroyed. India had a highly developed civilization in ancient times. It constructed so many grand edifices and produced many thinkers. With this as their heritage, the Indian people will not be subjugated. The retreat of international adventurers from India was a judgment of history, as was their retreat from China.

My faith in God is one with my faith in the people. My theism is utterly incompatible with hostility to the people.

We came to learn from the church in India. Compared to India, the situation in China is much simpler. China has never had a caste system. We do not have over a dozen languages separating us—dialects of

Chinese are commonly spoken by ninety-five per cent of our population. We have many religions, but no doubt due to the influence of Confucianism, there is little fanaticism; the religions coexist harmoniously and we have had no religious wars in recorded history. Several years ago, the demise of the landlord and capitalist classes was officially announced—former members of these classes now work honorably for their living. On this trip, we have seen that the churches of India exist in a much more complex environment that we do in China, and we admire you and pray for you. Even more, we can learn from you. You have established the Church of North India and the Church of South India. This is an experience we can learn much from. Theologically, you have explored the question of revelation of truth vis à vis other religions and the truth, goodness and beauty outside Christianity. This is just what we are dealing with in theology and we can benefit by knowing what you have learned.

Like many Indian church leaders, I believe that those who have been pushed to the margins of society will one day wake up and struggle for the human dignity which is rightfully theirs as sons and daughters of God. Until these people gain their freedom, their situation remains a wound on the body of the churches in India, the church ecumenical and humanity itself. May the whole church—not just a minority within it—become their prophets, advocates and protectors, their encouragers, their servants, their mothers, weeping when they weep, rejoicing when they rejoice. Then, when that day comes, they will see the church not as something alien to them, but as a friend that shared in their suffering.

It is with a deep faith, hope and love for the churches of India and for the Indian people that I bid you farewell. Wherever you are, may God bless you and bring us to meet again before long. Let us encourage one another with the words of Paul: "For we now live, if you continue to stand firm in the Lord" (1 Thess. 3:8).

—Farewell Remarks, Visit to Churches in India, 1985

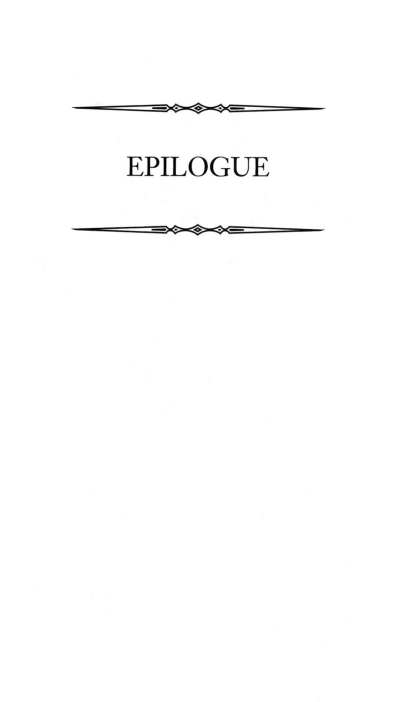

# EPILOGUE

# ❧

# Twelve Questions for Bishop Ting

*In the Summer of 2004, Bishop Ting was asked to respond to some of the questions most commonly asked by Christians outside China.*

1. **Q**. Every time I visit China, I see new churches, churches full of young people. Why are so many people interested in Christianity today?

   **A**. All over the world people are eager to find out if religion has something important to say to them. We regret that too often what is given to them by our churches is found to be disappointing. Hence the growth of many salvation formulas offered in the market. Since the Culture Revolution, the government has been improving its understanding of religions. The policy of Religious Freedom is implemented more and more thoroughly. Besides, Chinese Christians are bearing witnesses for Christ in their daily life. They are spreading the spirit of Christianity through their deeds.

2. **Q**. Christians in China underwent severe persecution, especially during the Cultural Revolution. What can you tell us about the situation today?

   **A**. The Chinese people see today that the Cultural Revolution was actually a movement to adulterate culture and China before the world. Fortunately, it has been successfully brought to an end. Its chief leaders have been brought to trial under the law. A nationwide re-education in opposition to ultra-leftist political thinking has been going on since the end of Cultural Revolution. Religions and their leaders are now enjoying their respected position in society. Newspapers publish long theoretical and theological articles on religion by sociologists and religion scholars. Condemnation and ridicule of religion is no

longer respectable. This is a very different atmosphere from the
years of the Cultural Revolution.

There was a time when Bibles were scarce in China that
people copied them by hand but in the past decade millions
have been printed.

3. **Q.** Can you comment on what has happened to change the situation and what impact these many Bible have on the church
culture?

**A.** With the generous help of the United Bible Societies, a good
up-to-date Bible printing press is now in existence in Nanjing.
Since its establishment it has produced nearly 40 million complete Chinese Bibles and a smaller number of Bibles in the languages of Chinese minority nationalities. What is more, more
and more universities are offering courses on religions as compared with the days of Cultural Revolution. No one can deny
that life is very much more relaxed.

4. **Q.** We in the West hear that there are Christians in China who
are still afraid to worship openly. Do you know of such
Christians? Why are they afraid? What would you response be
to their fears?

**A.** I personally don't know such Christians. At present there are
about 50,000 churches and meeting points that are packed with
people on Sundays. They are encouraged to worship in the registered churches, but if the meeting point is not registered, it is
not necessary to feel afraid either, as far as they are not doing
anything that is illegal or anti-governmental. Registration of
churches and meeting points is required by the government,
which is for the convenience of management.

Fear is an emotion that tends to be lingering. But it weakens
in association with fellow Christians who maintain strong faith.
Thus my response is to encourage Christians to be in fellowship
of mutual trust and love.

5. **Q.** "Questions of Basic Christianity" published by the CCC/TSPM
affirms the Apostles' Creed, the Nicean Creed and other historic
Christian doctrines. Does the TSPM/CCC and, more specifically,
you yourself, still affirm the historic Christian doctrines and

what does it mean to apply them in a Chinese context?

**A.** I do affirm my faith with all Christians as formulated in the Apostles' Creed and Nicean Creed, although I admit my inadequacy to explain the creeds well. I recognize them as two good ways to summarize the essential content of the Christian faith. To apply them in a Chinese context is a real challenge for us. This is also one of the tasks for our Reconstruction of Chinese Theological Thinking. We are trying to use modern Chinese language to explain these two ancient creeds, presenting to our people who Jesus Christ is and why we have faith in him. We hope through our effort, Christianity can be of help to the social stability and construction and thus it can be understood and accepted by more and more Chinese people. To recite a creed together is also a way to affirm our oneness with Christians elsewhere in their faith and confession.

6. **Q.** "Theological Reconstruction" and the "Theology of Love" are unfamiliar terms in the West that may be easily misunderstood. You have been accused of creating a "Salvation through Love" theology. What do you mean by these terms?

**A.** Theological Reconstruction aims for the church in China to hold to a theology that is true to biblical teaching and relevant to present-day thinking in China. I have never used the expression "theology of love." I do not think I want to criticize it until I can be sure of what it means by anyone who uses the expression. Justification by love is a poor and misleading imitation of justification by faith. I have never approved of its usage. It can cause a lot of confusion and is not conducive to clear definition of terms.

7. **Q.** The political leadership of China is generally understood to be atheistic in their beliefs, yet Christianity in China by all accounts is growing and prospering. How do you explain this and what do you say to Christians in the West who believe the church can only prosper in a capitalist democracy?

**A.** I think people in the West have many misunderstandings about Chinese communists who claim to be atheists. Ever since 1949 when the present government was established, the policy of religious freedom has been repeatedly promulgated. After the Cultural Revolution, the policy was re-implemented. The growth of the number of Christians and other religious believers has proved that the government is serious with this policy. Communists may be atheists themselves but they respect others who have religious faith. Two or three years ago, the government admitted publicly that religious people can be positive strength in Chinese socialist construction. Party leaders require communist officials to respect and understand the religious people and to unite them. They have realized the good effect religion may bring to society. If they can do their job of uniting people of various kinds of faith well, society and country can be stable and in peace. As to those who believe that Christianity can only prosper in "democratic West," I think they might lack knowledge and strong faith in the amazing work of God and the Holy Spirit.

8. **Q.** Some Chinese Christians have called you a Marxist/Communist. What is your response to them?
**A.** I feel sorry for them for the time and energy wasted. The spirit of scientific research requires us to go further than labeling and name-calling.

9. **Q.** For the past fifty years, Christians in the West and specifically in the U.S., are decreasingly attending denominational churches while increasing in independent churches. China also no longer has any denominations but it has moved to a unified church. Can you compare and contrast these historic changes? How does the CCC handle what were formerly denominational distinctives?
**A.** Before the Liberation, China was full of various kinds of denominations that came from western countries. It was an historic event that Chinese churches were gathered together in order to survive after being cut off with their Western mother churches. Three-Self Patriotic Movement Committee was established in 1950, calling Chinese Christians to leave aside the denominational differences but to be united under the Apostles' Creed and Nicean Creed. With the principle of mutual respect

and understanding, Christians of different denominations worship together in the same church. We have a common liturgy and hymnal book all over China. The new generation who becomes Christians after the Cultural Revolution has little idea of denominations.

We respect the Christians who stick to their denominational distinctives. At the same time we are trying to equip our members, especially young and new members, with biblical teachings without denominational distinctives. We need to be aware of the strength and weakness of each denomination so that we can have our own theology that is rooted in our culture instead of the denominational distinctives.

10. **Q.** I have heard you say that advanced training and professionalism is one of the greatest challenges facing the church in China today. Could you comment further?

**A.** Christianity developed well and fast in the past twenty years in China. We severely lack well-trained church workers, lay leaders and volunteers. Christian education is a whole life education that churches need to put emphasis on. On the other hand, as more and more universities offer courses on the study of Christianity, we are having many more well-educated believers in the church, who need advanced explanations on Christian faith. Theologians coming from churches need to be able to communicate and dialogue with scholars in academy or universities. Chinese churches have their own special experience on this land, and we need good theologians to construct the Chinese theology so that we can offer our contribution to the ecumenical world.

11. **Q.** In the past few years I have visited more than ten seminaries throughout China ... many of them in new facilities. Can you tell us what is happening in higher theological education in China?

**A.** Because the number of Christians in China grows so fast every province feels the pressure of lacking trained church workers. Theological education has long been the main task for Chinese churches. In many Chinese cities, every year one

Sunday is called Theological Sunday. All the offering of this Sunday is designated for theological education. Many provinces use this fund to support the seminary or Bible school in that area. Christians in China are eager to offer their help to this project. It is for this reason that you find many seminaries with new facilities. Actually, there are many training classes at different levels all over China, which has helped training many lay leaders and volunteers. Partner churches outside China also offer their help to our theological education, to which we are very grateful.

12. **Q.** The China church owes much to the faithful leadership of older Christian leaders. What can you tell us of the leadership of the future?

**A.** The young generation is in a golden season for the growth of Christianity in China. They are facing different challenges and trying to take advantage of the present opportunities. I am sure they are going to do their work well.

—Summer 2004